KD

D1594989

"The Patriot, Hezekiah Whitt"

BY:

Colonel Charles Dahnmon Whitt

ISBN 978-1-931672-62-7

Jesse Stuart Foundation
Ashland, Kentucky
2010

First Edition June 2010

Published By:
Jesse Stuart Foundation
1645 Winchester Avenue Ashland, KY. 41101
606 326 1667. JSFBOOKS.com
dahnmonwhittfamily.com

THE PATRIOT, HEZEKIAH WHITT

The Building Of America Series

Preface

This is a story about a great man, A Patriot to the Free State of Virginia; Hezekiah Whitt lived from 1761 to 1846.

This Narrative is based on the life of Hezekiah Whitt, his Indian wife Rachel Cornstalk Skaggs, and many more people. We will go to many places and have many adventures.

Hezekiah Whitt will find a beautiful land while scouting for Indians. This place is in present day Tazewell County, Virginia on the "Waters of the Clinch." It would become his beloved home for many years.

I will be as accurate as possible, but I will use my thoughts to fill in the missing links. This will be historic, as well as fictional. I will try to keep names, places, and dates as accurate as possible.

Hezekiah was a rebel to the King of England, but a Patriot to his home country, the Free State of Virginia and the new United States of America. Will you travel with Hezekiah as he goes on campaigns against the Indians, Tories, and spies out the Indians and defends his liberties against the King of England?

You will meet Hezekiah's family and be with the Whitts as they make a life on the "Waters of the Clinch."

Indian stories abound as Hezekiah becomes a prominent man in the new County of Tazewell.

Indiana, Illinois, Ohio, Kentucky, Tennessee, Missouri, Virginia, what is now West Virginia and Canada are all mentioned in this collection.

This Narrative is a Preamble to the book, "Legacy, The Days of David Crockett Whitt.". These two books are a series on "The Building of America." Go to http://dahnmonwhittfamily.com for more information on "Legacy, The Days Of David Crockett Whitt"

This narrative, "The Patriot, Hezekiah Whitt," is based on the life of Hezekiah Whitt, his Indian wife Rachel Cornstalk Skaggs Whitt.

COLONEL CHARLES DAHNMON WHITT

THE PATRIOT, HEZEKIAH WHITT

Chapters

COLONEL CHARLES DAHNMON WHITT

THE PATRIOT, HEZEKIAH WHITT

THE PATRIOT, HEZEKIAH WHITT

THE PATRIOT, HEZEKIAH WHITT

Dedicated To:

My late Father Marvin B. Whitt, who always had faith in my abilities, and instilled in me the need to follow the Lord Jesus Christ.

My Wife, Sharon Cogan Whitt, for her support of my efforts to be an Author. For editing and leaving my little pieces of paper alone.

My big Brother, Larry Paxton Whitt, who advised, encouraged, and also edited for me.

My Big Brother Jerry B. Whitt for believing in his little brother.

The Rebels that have been proven right and now we call them Patriots.

Memorial Bench dedicated to Marvin B. Whitt and all Coal Miners. Located in Richlands, Virginia.

THE PATRIOT, HEZEKIAH WHITT

Chapter 1

The First Whitts In America

This story will have to start with John Witt. He is the first Whitt I know of coming to this new land called America. John Witt, Whitt, or Whytt was his name, according to whoever wrote it down. Mostly you see it as Witt. I don't have much real recorded history on John, but I will reveal all that I have gleaned from published records.

During this time in history the protestant faith began, as Bibles were translated into several tongues. The common people began to read and understand God's word. Many of the higher ups in the established church did not like this because the common people discovered that knowledge is power. The common people had their blinders off and realized that they could seek God's will without paying money to a church official. They had been kept blind so the church could extort money, even from the poorest peasants.

This action brought on many problems and conflicts. The established church had a breaking away from within as people learned about grace, faith, and how to serve Jesus Christ. John Witt was one of these new Protestants; he was an outcast for practicing this new way of serving Jesus Christ. John started out in the established Church, which was a forerunner of the modern Catholic Church.

I have a record of a baptism in 1645, of an infant one Jon Whytt in Sterling, Kilseth near Edinburg, and a port in Scotland. He was listed as an altar boy in 1653 also in Sterling, Kilseth. John immigrated to the English Colony, now Virginia in 1659. Before this John lived and worshiped in France as a French Huguenot. (French Protestant)

His father Robert Whytt may have been born in Ireland. The angry Irish Catholics ran out many of the new Protestants, about this time. They fled to England, Scotland, and even to France. John met his wife Ann Daux, the daughter of a business man, Walter Daux. Walter and his wife Mary Plaine Daux resided and had a business in London for a time. It appears that the Dauxs were also break-a-ways from the established church. A lot of this was going on at this time because of new knowledge and persecution. I am not for sure if John met the Dauxs in England, France, or in America. I have their wedding in about 1669, in Albemarle County Virginia. This may be a fact, or not, at any rate John Witt married Ann Daux and they had at least 5 children, all sons. It is thought that John and Ann may have had daughters, but I have no records of this.

The first born according to my knowledge was William Guillaune Witt. He was born in 1675, in Charles City County, Colony of Virginia. He was married to Mary Mildred Daux in 1710 in Virginia.

William died June 13, 1754 in Saint Ann Parish, Albermarle County, Virginia. He is buried in Saint Ammish Church Yard.

THE PATRIOT, HEZEKIAH WHITT

The next son was John Witt II, born in 1676, in Charles City County, Virginia. John II died about 1751 in Goochland County, Virginia. John married Ann Lavina Rogers.

The third son was Edward Witt, born about 1682, in Bristol Parish, Virginia. Edward died about 1752 in Halifax County, Virginia. Edward Witt married Mary Elizabeth Pettipoole.

The fourth son was Charles Witt. Charles was born about 1685. The fifth son Richard Olney Witt was born about 1690 in Charles City, Virginia. Richard died about 1769 in Butte County, North Carolina. Richard Olney Witt was married three times. He first married Elizabeth Liptrot about 1720. His second married Regina Witt in 1736, in Halifax County, Virginia. He thirdly married Mary Kimbrough after 1752.

Richard Olney and Elizabeth Liptrot had seven sons, not sure about daughters.

The first born was Jesse Whitt born about 1723.

The second son was Richard P. Whitt whom would become a Baptist Minister later in life, and would add the prefix Reverend to his name. He was born about 1725 either in North Carolina or Virginia. The Reverend Richard P. Whitt died April 25, 1812, in Montgomery County, Virginia. He is buried in Dunkard's Bottom, Montgomery County Virginia, on the old home place. The cemetery is southwest of Childress on State route 693. The Whitt's cabin was located about 200 feet west of the road on the south bank of Meadow Creek. The cabin was moved in 1931 to the Radford Collage campus for use as a museum. It was moved again in 1953 to become a private dwelling near New River's Claytor Lake. I will revisit Reverend Richard P. Whitt a little later.

The third son William Whitt was born about 1728.
The fourth son was John Whitt, born about 1729.
The fifth son was Joshua Whitt, born about 1731.
The sixth son was Edmund Witt, born about 1733. He died before 1790 in Surry County North Carolina. (Now Stokes)

The seventh son is Hezekiah Witt, born about 1735. He died about 1790, in Rutherford County, North Carolina. This Hezekiah is the namesake of my Hezekiah!

Notice that some of the sons kept Witt, while some went with Whitt. Today many Witts and Whitts are blood relatives!

This is a good time to mention the wildness of this country during these early years. Just a few miles from the settled coast, virgin timber covered much of the land. The lands were teaming with wild animals, and the streams were full of all kinds of fish.

Also lurking in the shadows of the great forest, were the Indian Braves, ready to protect their lands. The Native Americans had made the mistake of trusting the pale faced people from across the waters. Now the greedy land hungry whites encroached even further, crossing the Blue Ridge.

Now let's get back to Reverent Richard P. Whitt, son of Richard Olney Witt.

THE PATRIOT, HEZEKIAH WHITT

It seems that the Whitts liked the frontier lands west and south of Charles City County Virginia where the patriarch John Witt settled. The Lands were free in many cases. I have a record that the Reverend Richard Whitt was in South Carolina for a time. His son Hezekiah was reported as being born there. Next we see that the Reverend lived in Surry County North Carolina. (Now Stokes County)

Next, according to records, The Reverend Richard Whitt lived for a time in Henry County, Virginia.

Finally in 1769 Reverend Richard moved to Fincastle County, Virginia. (Now Montgomery County) There he settled with his wife Susannah Skaggs Whitt and growing family. They settled on Meadow Creek of the New River. This is where James and Rachel Skaggs, the parents of Susannah lived. This area was known as "Skaggs Old Ferry."

It would have been very interesting to see the frontier Whitts traveling along in single file. Some of the children were pushing the livestock; the older boys were carrying the Brown Betsy muskets. Most likely Susannah rode a saddle horse or mule with a baby at her breast. Richard leading the way with his eyes peeled, and a prayer on his breath! An older son would be the follow up as rear guard.

The Reverend Richard was a skilled carpenter, as well as a preacher. There is enough in the records to attest of the "Whitt Mill," which was run by the family for sawing logs to make lumber for the settlers. This would explain how the later Whitts became house builders and mill rights.

The Reverend was also outspoken on the division of Church and State. These early Baptist were persecuted somewhat for these beliefs. The Reverent Richard said, "The government has no business in family records and marriages!"

Reverend Richard was prepared to fight for his land. He was mentioned as a Captain in the local militia before the revolt against the King of England. Indians were mostly at peace with the whites, during this time, but you had to be careful not to get your hair lifted.

Now when Reverend Richard Whitt and Susannah moved to their new home on the New River they brought with them six children.

Their first born was Robert Whitt, born in South Carolina in 1755.
The second child was Abijah Whitt, born in South Carolina in 1757.
The third child was Rachel Whitt, born in South Carolina in 1759.
The fourth child was Hezekiah Whitt, (whom this writing is about) born 1761 in South Carolina.

The fifth child was Elizabeth Whitt, born in South Carolina in 1765.
The sixth child was Edmund Price Whitt, born in South Carolina, 23 March 1767.
The rest of the children were born in Fincastle County, Va. (Now Montgomery)

THE PATRIOT, HEZEKIAH WHITT

The seventh child, but first child born in Montgomery County was Richard Thomas Whitt, in 1769. He would grow up to be a medical doctor.

The eighth child would be Archibald Whitt, born about 1770.
The ninth child was Ruth Whitt, born June 17, 1772.
The tenth and last I know of was Susannah Whitt, born 1774.
Shortly after Susannah was born the Indians were alarmed at the increase of encroachment into their lands. They sent many small bands of angry braves into the sparse settled areas of the white man. They looked for isolated cabins or even small burgs to administer their mischief. The raiding parties of painted Indians were ruthless in their manner. They meant to set an example to the whites, so they would think twice before moving into their lands. They killed children as well as men and women. Sometimes they would carry off a child or woman to adopt into their tribes. Those left dead and mangled were also scalped.

Don't get me wrong, the whites were just as ruthless as they stole the red man's land.

Mostly it was the Shawnee out of the Ohio towns or the Cherokee from the frontier area of Tennessee that came into southwest Virginia. The Ottawas and Shawnees were hitting the settlers in western Pennsylvania.

The settlers in the frontier areas pled for help from the Governor of Virginia. The Governor was the Earl of Dunmore, appointed by the King. Dunmore had appropriated lands for settlement in western Virginia and Pennsylvania. This infuriated the red men. The Governor decided to defeat the Indians once and for all. This would be settled at the battle of Point Pleasant Virginia. (Now West Virginia) This happened at the confluence of the Kanawha and Ohio rivers, on October 10, 1774.

Andrew Lewis had a party of militia heading up the Kanawha and camped at the mouth on the Ohio River. Chief Cornstalk led his braves and planned an ambush on that morning. The surprise was lost as two of the Virginians rose early wanting to go into the woods after a fat Tom Turkey. What they saw were hundreds of painted Indians, hiding in the undergrowth!

It was an awful hand to hand battle that lasted many hours. Finally Cornstalk pulled his warriors back, for fear of another white army thought to be approaching. The battle might have even been won by the Indians, but since Cornstalk pulled out, the whites claimed the day. This would cause Cornstalk to sign a treaty and cede new lands to the land hungry whites. I don't have a record of any of my Whitts participating in this fight.

In March of 1774 the "Intolerable Acts." was passed on the Colonist, by England. This was in reprisal of the "Boston Tea Party."

In June 1774, a new quartering act was authorized, which required the colonist to allow British troops to move into their homes.

THE PATRIOT, HEZEKIAH WHITT

The seeds of liberty were being planted. In September and October of 1774 the first Continental Congress was held in Philadelphia. Twelve of the colonies had attended. Georgia is the only one absent.

So you see the Whitts of Fincastle County were right in the middle of all of this. Liberty was not just a thought anymore, but actions were taken!

Pipe Tomahawk, top for peace and bottom for war!

Chapter 2

The Whitts Arrive on Meadow Creek

The Richard Whitt family came to their new home in May 1769. The Whitt family meandered in single file, to the land of James and Rachel Skaggs late in the afternoon. James and Rachel came running out to meet them.

"You are a site for sore eyes!" exclaimed Rachel Skaggs.

"Where have you fellers been?" asked James Skaggs, "we been looking for y'all for two weeks."

Susannah answered, "We have been trying to get here, but first one thing then another been a holding us up."

Richard went over and took the baby Richard Thomas, so that Susannah could get down. All the children ran to hug their Grandparents.

"Richard, y'all put your stock over in the pasture and get back, so's you can get a bite of supper," said James Skaggs.

"Thanks James I think we could eat, been traveling since breakfast," answered Richard.

Robert, Abijah, and little Hezekiah drove the animals into the split rail fenced pasture. The Rev. Richard went with the boy and unloaded the pack animals placing their goods and tools over in a good dry corner of the barn.

"Boys be sure to water and feed the horses and mules," said Reverend Richard Whitt as he headed to the Skaggs house.

"We will," hollered the 14 year old Robert Whitt.

The girls and Richard followed the Skaggs into their spacious log house. The hugs and happy greeting were still going on when the boys got in. Susannah and daughter, ten year old Rachel helped Grand Maw Rachel Skaggs rustle up some supper.

The children's ages in 1769 was Robert 14, Abijah 12, Rachel 10, Hezekiah 8, Elizabeth 4, Edmund Price 2, and little Richard Thomas had not yet had his first birthday.

The Whitts had traveled from Henry County Virginia, on the border with Surry County, North Carolina. The trip took about a month because of the young children, and moving livestock. Also they had to be vigilant on the trail for the perils of Indians or outlaws.

I have been saying they were heading to Fincastle County, but that is just partly true. The Counties were sub-dividing and adding new names regularly at this time. In 1769 Meadow Creek was in Augusta County. In 1770 the name would be Botetourt County,

THE PATRIOT, HEZEKIAH WHITT

and in 1772 it became Fincastle County which stretched all the way to the Mississippi River. It was then divided into Montgomery, Washington, and Kentucky County. Kentucky County is now the Commonwealth of Kentucky.

The family had a hurried meal set before them and James asked Reverend Richard P. Whitt to ask a blessing.

All heads were bowed and every eye was closed, except for maybe two year old Edmund Price Whitt. Baby Richard Thomas was resting easy in an old cradle.

"Our dear Lord, we humbly come before your throne of grace. We thank You for Your loving kindness. We think You for your great protection. We think You for your bounty that You graciously provide. Almighty God we pray for Your wise counsel and good health on this family. We ask for Your great strength as we are lifted like on eagle's wings. We pray that You bless this land and ask that the differences between King George and the colonies be settled without the letting of blood. I ask this in the name of Jesus the Christ. Amen," prayed by Richard.

The Whitts ate like starved rabbits. On the table was set fresh baked wheat bread, butter, sweet potatoes, and onions and lettuce from the early garden. And James Skaggs carved on a nice Virginia ham and dibbed it out to each hungry person. Buttermilk and tea were the beverages, along with cold well water.

After the meal the children went out to explore their new land. They also went to the barn to prepare sleeping arrangements in the hay loft. This will be their abode during the summer nights while Reverend Richard and the boys built a new log house.

The Reverend and James had a little corn liquor after their meal and fired up their pipes. The ladies and younger children settled in the sitting room to talk and reminisce. James and Reverend Richard discussed the building of a log house and also the need of a saw mill. This was one thing James had in the back of his mind for a long time. He knew that his son-in-law had the ability and know-how to build a saw mill. This little community needed one badly. They also discussed the place to build the new family cabin. James explained that he would help him purchase the land in time. James had just cut off tracts and sold them to James Skaggs Jr. and Henry Skaggs, two of his sons. He also told about selling land to his friend Thomas Mastin, a white man, but raised by the Indians. All of this talk about a saw mill had been mentioned before. It was this thought that prompted Rev. Richard to move here. Also the sheep had no shepherd! He wanted to build a church and spread the Baptist faith wherever he could. Of course Susannah Skaggs Whitt had no objection to moving close to her parents.

It was starting to get dark; Rachel and Hezekiah frolicked in the yard chasing fireflies! Richard and James sat on the porch watching the twilight envelop the New River Valley. A whippoorwill could be heard in the distance. Reverend Richard Whitt smiled as he took in the setting. "This is good ground," he whispered. James nodded in agreement.

THE PATRIOT, HEZEKIAH WHITT

All the chores were done and the four oldest children went to the barn followed by their Paw.

"Sleeping in the hay is much better than sleeping on the trail," Richard said.

All the good nights were said and Richard quoted his night time saying, "To bed, to bed, said sleepyhead! Oh No, said Slow! Put on the pot said Greedy Gut, and we will eat before we go!"

The four children laughed even though they had heard it about every night.

After they all settled into their beds of straw their Paw prayed the night prayer.

Morning came quickly this new day in New River Valley. Richard and the children that had slept in the barn' were up and about. Hezekiah had already been to Meadow Creek and looked it over.

"Paw I have been to the creek and seen a place to build your mill," sounded Hezekiah.

"We will get a good look after breakfast," answered Richard.

When Richard and the children came in the Skaggs house, Susannah was explaining why it took them an extra day or two to get here.

"Richard spied some Indian sign along the trail, so he had us backtrack about two miles for safety," she said.

"What happened next?" asked mother Rachel?

"Paw went scouting to make sure them red niggers was gone," replied fourteen year old Robert Whitt.

Susannah turned quickly and sent him daggers from her fierce eyes for butting in and using that language.

"Sorry Maw, I forgot myself," replied Robert sheepishly.
Sixty year old James Skaggs smiled at the Reverend. Richard smiled back.
"Well what happened next?" ask Mother Rachel.
"After several hours had past Richard came back and told us it would be safe to travel on," answered Susannah.

"How much time did you loose there?" ask James Skaggs.
"Altogether bout two days," Susannah answered.
   "Tell them about the storm and flash flood we had, just after getting started," sounded Richard.
"That's right we had just been on the trail a day when that cloud bust hit us early in the morning" answered Susannah Whitt.

"The sky was dark as night and we was jest breaking camp when we heard this boom of thunder," inserted Richard.

THE PATRIOT, HEZEKIAH WHITT

"That's right we got our stuff and all the young-uns and got back in our lean-to as quick as we could, I never saw it rain so much in all my born days," Susannah said widening her big brown eyes.

"Tell them about the creek we were camping beside," said Richard.

"Yep, that little creek was only about a jump across but when we started to load up to leave it turned into a big muddy wave. We had to grab and run again, this time up the hill to get out of its way!" Susannah explained while waving her arms.

"Only by the grace of God was we spared," inserted Richard.
"The God of all creation really demonstrated his mighty power that day," added Susannah.
How long was it fore y'all got out of there?" asked James?
"Not as long as you would think, that creek went down in only a few hours, by the time the sun was high we were traveling again," replied Richard.

"We didn't get to fer that day cause of the mud and late start," reiterated Susannah.

"Did you all meet anybody on the trail?" ask James.

"We did meet a couple of fellers coming from out east; they said that there is a storm a brewing between us and the Mother Country. They keep pressing us, and we ain't gonna stand for much more," they said.

They also said, "The British are inciting the heathens against the whites!"
"Who was these fellers?" ask James.
"One was an Elswick the other was a Fleming the best I can recollect," answered Richard.
"They were heading south toward Surry County, North Carolina," the Fleming feller said.
"We told them that we had lived on Stewart's Creek for awhile," inserted Susannah.
"They said they had never been there, but was aiming to warn the folks about the savages having an uprising," continued Richard.

"Were they walking or on horseback?" asked James.

"They were on horseback and traveling light," answered Richard.

"We told them about finding some sign that a party of Creeks or Cherokee had been through the north part of Henry County," Richard added.

"What did they say to that?" asked James.

"Not much, cept that they would be a looking out for them," answered Richard.

"I sure don't like the sound of all of this, I thought the Indians were getting all settled down," James exclaimed.

The Whitts and Skaggs finished breakfast and got started on the new day. James took Richard out in the upper section of his property. This was the edge of his property and

THE PATRIOT, HEZEKIAH WHITT

was heavily wooded with tall poplar and some hardwoods. It was on a little rise overlooking the Skaggs farm. It also had a nice spring of good clear water.

"This is where you can build your cabin, what do you think Richard?" asked James Skaggs.

"I think it is a wonderful place for our cabin!" answered Richard enthusiastically.

"Paw are we going to be in the woods," ask Hezekiah?

"Well I guess we might, course we are cutting down enough trees to build with," answered Richard.

"My land is getting smaller all the time, since I have been selling it off," said James.

"Me and Rachel decided to start cutting it down some since we are getting older, you know I am already sixty years old," stated James.

"No sir, you hold your age real well," answered Richard.

You got neighbors all around you, but not too close, over there is Thomas Mastin's place, then back over there is "Little" James Skaggs's place, and to the far end is Henry Skaggs farm," explained James.

"It has been along time since I seen "Little" James and Henry, how have they been?" ask Richard.

"Just fine, James Jr. is a farmer and very stable, but Henry is the adventurer and has itchy feet," said James.

"Henry has always loved the woods and adventure," agreed Richard.

"Yes he does, he traveled with the Long Hunters deep into Cain tuck back in 1764, he is quiet prominent as explorers go," bragged James.

"Did he have any troubles out in the wilderness?" asked James.

"He brushed into the Indians a few times, but mostly stayed away from them, he came back with enough pelts to buy a farm," explained James.

"Indians don't travel much in the winter, they call January the hunger month, so that is when you do your trapping," added James.

Hezekiah was close by and taking in every word. The unexplored wilderness, trapping, and the thought of matching his wits with the Redman held quiet an attraction to the eight year old Hezekiah.

As Richard, James, and Hezekiah walked the area purposed for the new cabin, Richard asks how long James had lived along Meadow Creek.

"Well I have been around here since before 1749," answered James.
"Over twenty years, it is a might tamer now ain't it James?" asked Richard.

THE PATRIOT, HEZEKIAH WHITT

"A might, back then a lot of Indians came through, mostly just ignored me," James exclaimed.

"What kind was they Grand Paw?" Hezekiah asked.

"Mostly Cherokee I reckon, but Shawnee came around sometimes, mostly just hunters," James explained.

"What about that mister Mastin that was raised by the Indians?" asked the inquisitive Hezekiah?

"Well, from what he has told me the Shawnee killed his folks, and adopted him into their tribe. After he was purty well grown he ran off to Caintuck, and saw how the white folks live," stated James Skaggs.

"Tom took a hankering to come back towards the east and make a new start as a white feller," explained James.

"He told me that he knows the great Chief Cornstalk, even played and hunted with his sons," added James.

Hezekiah stood there big eyed taking it all in.

"Well let's get some tools and lay out our new cabin," said Richard.

"Can I help you Paw?" ask Hezekiah.

"Yes, I want you to help and you can go fetch Robert and Abijah also," said Richard, "Get your hatchets too!"

As Richard and James walked back toward the Skaggs's house, Richard ask, "Sir does the folks round here know I aim to start a church here abouts?"

"Sure do, I have been telling them you were coming, they are most pleased with the idea," answered James.

"Wonderful, wonderful, God is so good!" exclaimed the Reverend Richard Whitt.

Richard and the boys took ax and hatchet to the trees in the proposed spot for the new Reverend Richard P. Whitt family home. The chop, chop of the axes rang through the valley. It wasn't long before Thomas Mastin, Henry Skaggs, and Young James Skaggs showed up carrying axes.

Richard stopped the work long enough for proper greetings. All three of the men shook hands with Richard, Robert, Abijah and Hezekiah Whitt. Hezekiah was especially thrilled with meeting Thomas Mastin and Henry Skaggs because of their extensive experiences with the Red Men. Henry was just back from a long hunt on the waters of the Clinch near modern day Baptist Valley in Tazewell County. Story goes that Henry and a Knox fellow had accumulated over 1500 skins during the winter. They came into camp after checking their traps to find they had been plundered. They found out later that a half breed by the name of Will Emery cleaned them out. Henry had not been back to Meadow Creek for very long. Of course Hezekiah was glad to meet Uncle James Skaggs also.

THE PATRIOT, HEZEKIAH WHITT

The senior James Skaggs and Rachel had two other sons out and about, Charles and Richard Skaggs.

After Richard explained the plan of building his cabin and where he wanted it; four experienced men wielding their axes began to fall timber. Hezekiah was amused at the music the axes made with their constant chop, chop, chop! Before long a nice cleared out section on a little rise revealed itself among the trees. Robert, Abijah, and Hezekiah followed the men and began chopping off the smaller branches and dragging them out into the meadow where they could be cut into firewood or burned.

Richard was thrilled at the progress because of the help of his benevolent new friends. Also, he whispered a little prayer to God with thanksgiving.

Ding, ding, sounded the dinner bell way across the meadow from the James Skaggs house.

Susannah screamed out loudly to carry her voice across the vast meadow, "All of you come and get it!"

Richard waved his hand over his head in acknowledgement.

"Well fellers we better get on over and have some dinner or the women folks will get in a tizzy," Richard said.

Henry and James grinned at the word tizzy.

Thomas Mastin said, "I can go over an get a bite at my place."

"No Thomas, I am sure Maw wants us all to come and eat, I'm sure they cooked up a big mess for us," said Henry Skaggs.

The four men sank their axes into a log, then Robert, Abijah, and Hezekiah followed suit and stuck their hatchets into the same log.

Henry Skaggs turned to Richard and smiled at the site of the boys as they all walked toward the James Skaggs home.

When the men got to the house Susannah poured water from a fine pitcher into a matching bowl.

Grand Maw Rachel spoke out, "Wash your paws and take a seat!"

The men smiled and follow her orders. After a fine country dinner the men headed back out to resume their work. Hezekiah could not help, but ask Uncle Henry Skaggs about the long hunts and he also asked Thomas Mastin about living with the Indians. They told him a few stories and began swinging their axes again. Richard gave him a look as if to say, don't bother the men while they are at work. Hezekiah went back to hacking off the smaller branches and piling them up.

THE PATRIOT, HEZEKIAH WHITT

Rachel Whitt the oldest daughter of Richard brought a bucket of cold water and a dipper to the men. Richard thanked her for her efforts and told her all they needed was a dipper. Richard pointed to the nice spring about twenty yards away.

"Shucks you mean I wagged this ol bucket of water all this way for nothing," sounded Rachel.
"Well honey you didn't know about our spring, you were trying to help," replied Richard.
"We needed a dipper any how," replied Robert in her defense.
The men took a water break and some lit pipes while others took a chew. They stood around for a few minutes discussing the cabin plans until Hezekiah brought up the Indians again.

The men worked until supper time and called it a day. They were all tired and Richard picked up Hezekiah and let him ride piggyback across the big meadow to the James Skaggs's house.

After supper and the chores done, Richard joined the senior James Skaggs on the porch for a smoke and conversation. They mostly talked about the progress on the new Whitt House. Richard bragged on the Skaggs men and Thomas Mastin for their great help. He talked about his plans for the next day or so. He wanted to gather up foundation stones and even put in a puncheon floor. Also he needed to get some glass from the east to put in a couple of small windows. James told him that he may have to put in some greased skins until the panes arrive. He explained that was all they had for years out in the frontier. Richard agreed and understood.

"Those ol greased skins let in a lot of light if they are stretched out real good!" exclaimed Richard.

"Sorry I didn't get out to help you fellers today, I did some gardening and it looked like an old man might just be in the way," said James.

"You would never be in the way, but we had plenty of good help today!" exclaimed Richard.
"I may need your advice on a few things as we build," added Richard.
"I will help if I can, I know you are a fine builder," answered James.

THE PATRIOT, HEZEKIAH WHITT

Chapter 3

Living On Meadow Creek

Richard took a day here and there to plow and get out the corn. He also planted beans, pumpkins and various other vegetables. This was the middle of May and crops had to be planted. Robert, Abijah and Hezekiah were a great help. Other days they would gather stone for foundations and chimneys. The boys gathered many from the creek. They would load a sleigh and have the mule pull it to the location. Hezekiah even handled the mule when the older boys allowed it.

Reverend Richard Whitt sent out the word to all the neighbors within riding distance that he was holding church meetings on the Sabbath of each week. He was going to put God first, then family, and country. He figured if he did the duty of ministering to the people, God would take care of the rest.

There was a nice little knoll not far from the new cabin site. Richard and some of the neighbors gathered and had a work day. They set up boards in a semicircle and even made him a crude pulpit. This would be the first Baptist church in the area.

The first Lord's Day came and God blessed the little outdoor church with a large attendance. They had a great time in the Lord that day. They sang many hymns and the Reverend preached for two hours. Then the folks brought out their baskets of food and set them together. It was blessed and given out in share and share a like fashion.

The reverend had a chance to offer the principles of the Primitive Baptist, was The Blessed Hope and a strong statement of separation of Church and State. He spoke strongly against the state keeping records and marrying people. Births, death records, and such were the responsibility of the church.

The Blessed Hope meant what it said even these early Baptist weren't sure they were saved. They put their hope in Jesus Christ and hoped for the best. Well, anyway that is how they thought. They lived Godly lives, but the use of tobacco and spirits were allowed. They thought all things given by God was clean and put here for a purpose. It was alright to use it. Everything in moderation!

Henry, young James Skaggs and Thomas Mastin helped get the new Whitt House roughed in and under roof. Richard would have time to finish the home before cold weather came to the New River Valley. He laid up the chimneys front and back. The kitchen had a large cooking fireplace and even an oven. The other end had a fireplace in the sitting room and one on the second floor. The second floor was just a high roofed attic for bedding areas. Richard took his time and built a strong warm log house for the family. By late fall 1769 the house was finished enough for the family to move into and the crops yielded a bounty. All was going good for the Richard Whitt family in their new home.

THE PATRIOT, HEZEKIAH WHITT

Hezekiah was almost nine years old and a good help to his mother and father. He helped his brothers Abijah and Robert saw and split the wood needed to keep the family warm in the winter of 1769. The winter came and went fast. Richard, Robert, Abijah and Hezekiah did a lot of hunting and kept wild meat on the table. Hezekiah was becoming a good marksman with his .32 caliber squirrel musket. It wasn't really his, but he laid claim to it. It was a smaller bore than the Brown Betsy, but weighed almost as much. He had trouble holding up the long heavy barrel. Richard taught him to rest it on a limb or against a tree. Richard taught all the boys the principles of shooting, aim small and hit small.

Richard also said, "Hold your breath and squeeze the trigger."

Hezekiah went on a few hunts with Uncle Henry Skaggs and even once with Thomas Mastin. Both were stealth in their manner of hunting. They had learned this type of hunting from the Indians. They taught Hezekiah to be invisible and noiseless in the woods. He was making good progress learning not to step on twigs and always keeping cover in front of you, he also learned to approach from the downwind side.

It was crowded but during the winter the little Baptist church met every Sabbath in the Whitt House. Some days when the weather was bad some of the flock couldn't attend services, but they were remembered in the prayers. They enjoyed lifting their hymns to the Lord. These early Baptist had their own way of singing. The song leader would word or recite a verse and then all would join in and sing in a slow deliberate manner. Then the routine was followed through for each verse.

It was now a new year 1770 and reports of Indians doing mischief was heard from time to time. No one close was killed or carried off by the meandering redskins.

The Colony of Virginia was once again changing its counties and borders as the whites moved deeper into the wilderness. The Whitt House on Meadow Creek in the New River Valley was in Augusta, but now it is in the new County of Botetourt. This county was named for the popular governor Lord Botetourt. The Governor died suddenly while in service of the Colony of Virginia.

Another thing that would happen in 1770 was the fine new Court House for James City County would be built in Williamsburg the capital of the Virginia Colony.

Susannah Whitt, the wife of Reverend Richard Whitt was great with child. The little brother of Hezekiah Whitt would be born in the new County of Botetourt in the year of 1770.

On March 29th 1770 (date not confirmed) Hezekiah was nine years old. He was straight and tall for a boy of his age. Children grew up fast in the frontier hills of Virginia.

Baby Archibald came and Susannah had no great problems. She was tended to by Mother Rachel Skaggs and the oldest daughter Rachel helped some. Hezekiah was not too impressed with the little red, squirming baby that seemed to cry all the time. Of

THE PATRIOT, HEZEKIAH WHITT

course Hezekiah would learn to love his little brother in time. Archibald was named after his cousin Archibald Skaggs, Uncle Charles Skaggs's son.

Susannah would enjoy a week's bed rest as was the custom. It was an old wife's saying that it took a full week for everything to get back in place after giving birth. That is about all the rest frontier Moms ever got!

It had been a fairly dry winter, but the spring of 1771 brought an enormous amount of rain. It rained for days and the farm work was suffering. Not only that, every creek became a river and every river became a lake. The water did not get into the Whitt House or the neighbors homes nearby, but many folks did get flooded out. Farm animals had to be rescued and some were even lost. It was such a great flood that there is still a flood marker in Henrico County. (Now modern day Richmond.) It is listed in the National Historic Register to attest to the flooding in 1771. The flooding finally cleared and things began to get back to normal. Crops would be late and most likely sparse this year.

Hezekiah followed after Henry Skaggs and Thomas Mastin as much as possible. He could not get enough of the stories of Indians and untamed lands. He was especially interested in the land on the waters of the Clinch River. Henry Skaggs painted a beautiful picture of it with his descriptive stories. Hezekiah could not imagine two men trapping out 1500 skins in one winter. That was a fortune in that day and time.

After a nice family Christmas, January 1, 1772 rolled in on a Wednesday. The weather was cold and it was snowing those little feathery flakes. The trees all looked like they had been painted with diamonds. "What beauty the Lord has given us to start a new year," stated the Reverend Richard Whitt.

"No man could capture this with brush and paint," replied Susannah as she looked out of the new window pane.

"I wonder what this year will yield, well what ever comes I know that our sweet Jesus will be with us," replied Richard.

"We just wouldn't worry about the future right now we have a good warm house, food, and good health to be thankful for!" exclaimed Susannah.

"Did you know that this is leap year?" ask Richard.

"What does that mean Paw?" ask Hezekiah.

"Well, that means the gals can chase the boys this year," inserted Susannah.
Richard stood there listening with a big smile on his face.
"Gals always chase after the boys, only in a sneaky way," replied Abijah.
After a good laugh, Richard explained that every fourth year they add a day to February.

THE PATRIOT, HEZEKIAH WHITT

"That is because a year has 365 ¼ days and it is hard to live out a ¼ day. This year February will have 29 days," he explained.

"Some busy days fly by and seem like a ¼ day," exclaimed Susannah.

"I like the other way, about gals chasing the boys!" replied daughter Rachel. Everyone laughed.

A young man destined to be great got married this day, January 1st 1772. Thomas Jefferson a Virginia lawyer and planter married Miss Martha Epps Wayles Skeleton.

Also in 1772 Meadow Creek was in a different county. They changed names and boundaries again. The new county was Fincastle. It was a great big county and ran all the way to the Mississippi River. Later it would be divided into three counties, Washington, Montgomery and Kentucky. Yes Kentucky was a county in Virginia at one time.

The Colony of Virginia was under the Governorship of John Murray the 4th Earl of Dunmore. He was born in Scotland in 1732. King George II first appointed him Governor of the Province of New York. But after Governor Botetourt died suddenly, Dunmore was placed in the Governorship of the British Colony of Virginia. Governor Dunmore would be busy in the next few years dealing with the Indians and dissatisfied citizens.

A little bit of future history, Governor Dunmore would be displaced in 1776 by Patrick Henry, but King George would not recognize the Free State of Virginia and continued to pay Dunmore until the end of the Revolutionary War in 1783.

Almost like clockwork, another baby came to Susannah and Richard. On June 17th 1772 baby Ruth was born. She was a healthy little girl that would grow up to have a family of her own way down the road. Susannah did well once again, but they were going to have to find out what caused these new babies every other year! Susannah was now forty two, and she could not keep up this pace.

The Reverend Richard Whitt was proud of this new little Whitt girl and named her after Ruth in the Bible. He was proud of all his children, none were lazy.

Hezekiah Whitt was a tall straight eleven year old now. He had become quite the hunter and farmhand. He was always ready for a hunt or fishing trip. He had picked the brain of Henry Skaggs and Thomas Mastin and heard most every story they had about the wilderness. They enjoyed telling the tales about as much as Hezekiah did hearing them.

The American Colonies were becoming more dissatisfied with the way the British imposed laws and taxes on them with out any representation. In 1765 they had imposed a stamp act which really was unpopular. The folks in America had to buy stamps and place them on almost all of their paper work. The stamps were placed on documents, licenses, playing cards, and even newspapers. The Skaggs and Whitts were not bothered quite as much out in the frontier, but if they had exchanged land or bought a

THE PATRIOT, HEZEKIAH WHITT

newspaper they had to pay for the stupid stamps as some called them. What made the American Englishmen mad was that these taxes were imposed without their consent. There had been the sugar act and even a tax on molasses.

The British was trying to raise funds to pay for their war they had just won against the French. They called it the French and Indian War, here in America. The British kept a lot of troops in the colonies because of the Indians and other powers that may want to move in and take land.

Most all of the King's subjects in America enjoyed their tea just like they did in England. This newest act of 1773, The Tea Tax, would bring one more strain on the people in the colonies. This act would allow a drawback of the duties of customs on the exportation of tea to any of his Majesty's colonies or plantations in America.

Even Richard Whitt and others that were far from the costal cities enjoyed their tea. Now that greedy King even taxed their tea. This was over the top to tax their favorite beverage. There would be much unrest because of the Tea Tax. Late in 1773 men from Boston dressed as Indians went aboard the ships in the port that were laden with tea. They broke open the containers and threw all the tea into the sea. This infuriated King George.

Some other things that happened in 1773 were the first insane asylum opened in Virginia. Some of the folks joked that the King was driving them all crazy and they would need the asylum.

Also in 1773 Benjamin Franklin penned a new saying, "There never was a good war or bad peace." Ben was a thinking man and he sensed that a real struggle was developing between Great Britain and the American Colonies.

There were other gentlemen that began to speak out about the unjust taxes and a loss of simple liberties. Patrick Henry, Thomas Jefferson and Richard Henry Lee were outspoken about all of this. One thing they did in 1773 was to persuade the House of Burgesses to appoint a committee of correspondence for Virginia. The same thing was going on in the other colonies. This was set up to share news, mobilize public opinion, and coordinate actions against Great Britain. This would be the catalyst that would unite the colonies. This would lead to something big one day, "The United States of America."

Out in the frontier, stories kept coming in about Indian attacks. One such attack occurred October 10th 1773 in the Powell Valley now Lee County Virginia. Here in eastern Fincastle County the Skaggs and Whitts became more vigilant even though they were not in the deep frontier of Virginia.

THE PATRIOT, HEZEKIAH WHITT

They were building America and would become rebels against the king!

Chapter 4

The Preamble To War

This massacre on the Powell River sent waves of panic through out frontier Virginia. Hezekiah was very alert and wanted to know every detail about the attack on the Boone and Russell men. James had met Daniel Boone and had heard of Captain William Russell. Thom Mastin had few words to say about it, but he was clearly alarmed.

The butcher of Daniel Boone and Captain William Russell's sons occurred on October 10th 1773. The party was a second group bringing supplies and cattle for the trip to Kentucky County. The main party was ahead and was going to wait for every one to catch up so that there would be a large group of armed men to travel through the dangerous portions of the trail.

The attack happened at the head waters of Wallen's Creek in today's Lee County. There is a marker on the highway near Cumberland Gap, but this is wrong by several miles.

This little party left Russell's place in Castlewood and followed the trail laid out by Indians and the Long Hunters years before. They crossed the Clinch River at Hunter's Ford, now Dungannon. They went through Hunter's Valley, Rye Cove, and crossed Powell Mountain at Kanes Gap on to the head of Wallens Creek.

About three miles passed Wallens Creek the main party set up camp to wait for the others. The others were 17 year old Henry Russell, James Boone, two Negroes named Charles and Adam, Isaac Crabtree, two Mendenhall Brothers and another youth called Drake. This little party was driving some cattle and leading pack animals laden with flour, supplies and farm implements. The Young men were pressing the party along trying to meet up with Daniel Boone's party that was waiting ahead. On October 9th 1773 darkness was coming on strong and the little party had to make camp. They camped right on the warrior's path about three miles from the Daniel Boone party. Spirits were high and the excitement of adventure was with them. They had no idea of any danger about.

There was a band of Indians on their trail. The Indians probably knew about the larger party ahead and was afraid to attack them. But these young men and Negroes laden with supplies would be easy to surprise and defeat. There was supposed to be a peace between the Indians and frontiersmen, but who would know about an attack way out here in the wilderness.

The little party camped right out in the open and had a big fire burning. The sounds of wolfs howling frightened the Mendenhalls because they were more or less greenhorns compared to the rest. They were visibly afraid. Crabtree was an experienced woodsman and he had a little fun with the frightened Mendenhalls. He laughed and jeered them saying that they would hear buffaloes bellowing in the tree tops once they got to Caintuck.

THE PATRIOT, HEZEKIAH WHITT

All the party went to sleep without placing a guard. They felt no danger and slept like babies. The Indians crept close to the camp during the night and as dawn broke they fired their muskets and arrows at the slumbering pilgrims. Some were killed outright while most of the others were wounded. Henry Russell and James Boone were both shot through the hips and rendered defenseless. The Indians tormented the youths with their knives, and the young men grabbed at the sharp blades. Their hands were sliced mercilessly!

James Boone recognized Big Jim a Shawnee warrior among the marauders. James called him to help because the Boones had befriended him in the past. Big Jim was as blood thirsty as the rest. The other braves took this calling out to Big Jim as weakness and decided to make an example of young Boone. The Indians pulled out toe nails and finger nails as he pleaded to Big Jim to end his life. Henry Russell went through the same thing. James Boone remarked to Henry Russell that most likely all their folks had been killed. The two young men had many stabs and cuts all over their bodies as they gave up the ghost. The two Mendenhall brothers and young Drake lay dead. One other ran off but was not heard of again until a John Thorp moved there years later. He found bones in a crevice and it is presumed to be one of the parties.

Adam the colored man ran off and hid in a woodpile along the creek. He witnessed the whole gory affair. Crabtree ran off wounded and was the first to reach the Daniel Boone party. Adam finally got away, but got lost. It took him eleven days to get back to the frontier inhabitants. The other colored man Charles was taken prisoner and carried off with the horses and other plunder. The Indians had traveled about forty miles and a dispute arose as to who Charles belonged to. The chief of the party put an end to the quarrel by tomahawking poor Charles.

When word reached the Daniel Boone party, shock hit the camp. Daniel sent his brother Squire and a small party back to bury the bodies and gather what might have been left behind. Squire was to scout out the camp and evaluate how many Indians were in the party. Daniel stayed behind and organized a defense in case of an attack from a large war party.

When the Squire party got to the sight of the massacre Captain Russell and Captain Gass had arrived on the scene. They were horrified at the sight they found. The bodies were a bloody mess of cuts and wounds. Many arrows were sticking out of the young men. Several painted hatchets and war clubs were lying by the bodies as a declaration of war.

Rebecca Bryan Boone the wife of Daniel and mother of young James sent sheets with Squire to use as burial shrouds. Squire and Captain Russell carefully wrapped the two young men together and buried them together. All the others were buried decently. The bodies, all of them had been ripped open, but no scalps were taken. The Indians did not want to be caught with white scalps in a time of so called peace.

THE PATRIOT, HEZEKIAH WHITT

After the graves were cared for the cattle were rounded up and they drove them to the fortified camp of Daniel Boone. The next day they held a meeting and voted as to what they would do. Daniel wanted to push on into Kentucky and settle on the Kentucky River. Most, however, voted to head back east as they had lost their spirit of adventure.

Most of the party headed back to their former homes, but Daniel took his family back to Castlewood. He borrowed a cabin and a slave from Captain Gass for the winter. Daniel suffered more shock than he showed. He had nightmares that wild animals dug up young James and ate him. That winter Boone quietly retraced his tracks back to the awful sight of the massacre. Daniel reverently dug into the grave and found that young James and Henry had not been bothered since they were buried. Daniel covered them up with great tears streaming down his face. After he got the graves back in tact he gathered stones and placed them on top to protect them from being dug up. Daniel quietly went back to his family in the borrowed cabin along the Clinch River.

He stayed there until 1775, then went back to establish a settlement on the Kentucky River. They named the place Boonsboro!

The news of the massacre reverberated throughout the frontier. The folks along the New and Holston Rivers became much more vigilant. The Skaggs and Whitts talked much about this. Hezekiah took all of this in and became well aware of the dangers in the woods. He also realized that a life could be snapped out in an instant.

January 1774 has now rolled around. The Whitts and Skaggs all had a nice Christmas and are now looking forward to the spring of 1774. Only thing there is trouble in the air. No one knows how big or how soon, but the British intend to punish the colonies over their insubordination. Right now the Indians are the threat. Lord Dunmore has tried to help protect the frontier and will launch an assault on the Indians by using the Virginia Militia later this year 1774.

The Reverend and Susannah Whitt are in a family way again. Mother Rachel has laid down the law to Reverend Richard.

"No more babies," she said.
"We just can't help it!" replied Richard.
"You better help it if you want to have a wife!" She said.
"I understand what you mean," Richard said humbly.
Baby Susannah the last of the Richard Whitt clan was born on a cold morning in January 1774. Little Susannah came through it fine, but Mother Susannah had a hard time. She hemorrhaged some, but with many prayers and reading the blood verse in Ezekiel 16:6, the scarlet flow subsided. Hezekiah killed the older rooster and sister Rachel prepared a big pot of chicken soup. After Susannah rallied and consumed a bowl of rich chicken soup and drink several cups of water and tea she wanted to get up. Mother Rachel, daughter Rachel and Reverend Richard insisted on her laying still. Susannah gave in to her family. She had a great tiredness and fell into restful sleep.

THE PATRIOT, HEZEKIAH WHITT

Susannah would be a bed patient for at least a week and maybe longer because of the complications.

March 29, 1774 came in on a snow shower. Hezekiah had his 13th birthday on a blustery day.

"I thought it was going to be spring," Hezekiah said.

"That was wishful thinking," replied mother Susannah.

"I have a dread for warm weather to come this year, the Savages will be worse this summer I am afraid," exclaimed Reverend Richard.

"Paw, if them infidel redskins come round here, we will send them right back to where they came from," stated the young Hezekiah.

"I pray it don't come to that, but it is happening already up in the waters of the Ohio," answered Reverend Richard.

"Governor Dunmore will have his hands full this summer I am afraid," continued Richard.

By the 25th day of April 1774 Governor Dunmore took action.

WHEREAS I have Reason to apprehend that the Government of Pennsylvania, in Prosecution of their Claim to Pittsburgh and its Dependencies, will endeavor to obstruct his Majesty's Government thereof under my Administration, by illegal and unwarrantable Commitments of the Officers I have appointed for that Purpose, and that that Settlement is in some Danger of Annoyance from the Indians also, and it being necessary to support the Dignity of his Majesty's Name, and protect his Subjects in the quiet and peaceable Enjoyment of their Rights; I have therefore thought proper, by and with the Consent and Advice of his Majesty's council, by this Proclamation, in his Majesty's Name, to order and require the Officers of the Militia in the District to embody a sufficient Number of Men to repel any Insult whatever; and all his Majesty's liege Subjects within this Colony are hereby strictly required to be aiding and assisting therein, as they shall answer the contrary at their Peril. And I do farther enjoin and require the several inhabitants of the Territory aforesaid to pay his Majesty's Quitrents, and all public Dues, to such Officers as are or shall be appointed to collect the same within this Dominion, until his Majesty's Pleasure therein shall be known.

GIVEN under my Hand, and seal of the Colony, at Williamsburg, this 25th Day of April, 1774, in the 14th Year of his Majesty's Reign.

Dunmore,   God Save The King

As you can see by this proclamation Governor Dunmore means to hold on to the lands claimed by the Colony of Virginia and also put down any annoyances made by the Indians.

The folks out in the frontier were always anxious for news. Somehow news came to them very quickly. The year of 1774 was a busy year and a lot of uneasiness came along

THE PATRIOT, HEZEKIAH WHITT

with it. The King was upset with his children across the sea in America. He thought they were ungrateful for his protection and help. The Colonies were tired of taxation without representation. The Indians were mad because of the white encroachment over the mountains and into their hunting lands.

Hezekiah was almost grown, or so he thought. He was mostly interested in running through the woodland hunting or fishing in Meadow Creek or up and down New River. He did see the need to study the three R's. Reverend Richard and Susannah took time mostly through the winter to teach the children penmanship, the three R's and about business and how to be polite. The main thing Richard taught was reading the Bible. He would read to the smaller children and the older one's would read some every day in God's Holy Word.

Hezekiah was very curious about everything, he never ran out of questions. He sensed the apprehension he saw in his parents and in the Skaggs family. He knew that trouble was coming to the costal towns and would creep across the mountains eventually.

On June 2, 1774 Britain enacted the Quartering Act. This was another thorn trust into the side of the colonies. The new law demanded that the people open their homes to the King's Soldiers. The soldiers just moved in and took over many family homes.

The northern port colonies had become indignant of the slave trade. Rhode Island on the 13th of June 1774 was the first Colony to prohibit importation of slaves.

Way out in western Fincastle County, (Now Kentucky State) James Harrod had started the first settlement. June 16, 1774. Harrodsburg was established as the first town in Kentucky County. If the Daniel Boone party had gone on back in 1773, Boone would have established the first settlement.

On, September 5, 1774 the first Continental Congress met in Philadelphia, Pennsylvania. It was attended by 56 members from twelve of the thirteen colonies. Only the Colony of Georgia did not attend. The outspoken Patrick Henry represented Virginia, and urged vigorous collective measures against the Mother Country. He became more outspoken each year and defended liberty and the rights of Virginia.

Meanwhile back in the Indian country along the waters of the Ohio, the younger Indians had had enough of the whites; they wanted to drive the Long knives back across the mountains. But the older more mature chiefs were not in a hurry to pursue such a great challenge.

On Thursday October 6, 1774, Cornstalk, the great and principal chief of the Shawnees had become overruled.

Cornstalk had not become chief because he was not brave or because he ran from trouble. He had been in many fights and always fought bravely. He was using his good sense and judgment when he stood before the tribesman.

THE PATRIOT, HEZEKIAH WHITT

He used logic in explaining the situation. He stated that the Shawnee had but 800 warriors, 1000 if they count the Mingo, Delaware, and Wyandot. The Shemanese (Whites) have three men to our one. They have better and newer guns then we have.

"I ask you once again to think of our race," stated the great Cornstalk.

This plea fell on deaf ears; the expressive braves were itching for a fight. If Cornstalk would not lead then Pucksinwah and Blacksnake the second in command, would lead them against the devil whites. Reluctantly Cornstalk agreed to lead the bloodthirsty hoard against the Shemanese. (Whites)

"But let us hear what the spies have to say, they have been watching two large armies of the Shemanese (whites) coming this way as we speak," Cornstalk exclaimed.

Dunmore the Shemanese leader had the most men and he was way up river by Wheeling and it would take much time to come down the river with his clumsy army. Another smaller army of about 800 men was closer. The chief Lewis of the Virginia fighters was almost at the mouth of the great Kanawha know as Point Pleasant. (Point Pleasant Virginia, now West Virginia) Behind Lewis about a day were 300 more Shemanese herding cattle and bring supplies for the main army.

Cornstalk listened intently to his spies and calculated out a plan to strike the smaller Lewis Army before reinforcements could arrive.

"If we beat the Shemanese there, we can ambush the smaller army. Then we will have a chance against the larger army of Dunmore," Cornstalk explained.

Cornstalk stood before the anxious army of braves and stated, "We will attack the Lewis army as soon as possible. There will be no turning back once we undertake this fight, the seed of war is in the ground, will it sprout or be cut down I don't know."

In a short time Cornstalk was leading his army on horse back toward the mouth of the Kanawha on the great waters of the Ohio. The Indians were all in one accord, two notable young warriors that had never been in a fight rode excitedly. They were Chiksika the older brother of Tecumseh and the other was a white man turned Indian that would rise to be the warrior chief of the Shawnee years down the road.

The Indians were carrying canoes between two horses, one on the left and one on the right. They would head to a little creek about a mile above the Point and Cornstalk would give his orders there.

Back in Fincastle County many men had left their homes and were either with the Commander Lewis or were up near Fort Pitt with Governor Dunmore. Captain James Skaggs and some of the militia stayed at home to protect the area because small bands of Indians were about, but many of the local men were in the Lewis army or with Dunmore. Henry Skaggs was a sergeant and was detached with 12 men. Several other Skaggs were in the service of Virginia. Hezekiah was too young to be in this fight and

THE PATRIOT, HEZEKIAH WHITT

the Reverend Richard held prayer meetings with the families round about Meadow Creek. The prayers were lifted for the safety of the men of the Virginia Militia.

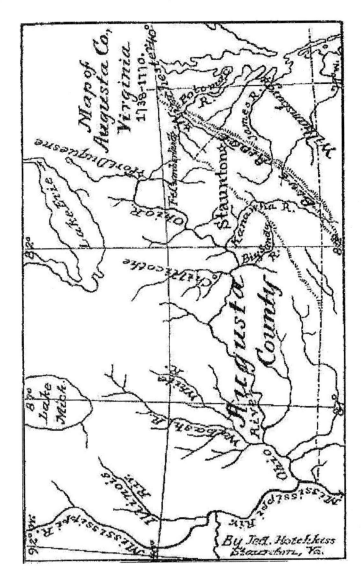

Augusta was one big County in Virginia as it took in all the land to the Mississippi River. It really belonged to the Indians at this time.

Chapter 5

The Long Years of War Has Come

On the evening of Sunday, October 9, 1774 an army of Indians accumulated on the north shore of the Ohio River just across from Point Pleasant. This was a natural point, the land between the Kanawha and the waters of the Great Ohio. Chief Cornstalk held a conference with his sub-chiefs and determined the only way to attack Lewis and his Long Knifes was from the rear. Lewis had water all around him except from his rear. Some of the chiefs that helped with a decision were Black Snake, Silverheels, Pucksinwah the father of Tecumseh, Red Eagle, and Cornstalk's son Elinipsico.

The Indians decided to move upstream about a mile to a little creek, here they could cross over in several trips, without giving up their surprise. Cornstalk gave hard orders for the braves to keep quiet and move stealthily back down the south bank of the Ohio and come in behind Lewis's Militia. It was imperative that Cornstalk's warriors surprise the Shemanese, and attack at first light on Monday, October 10, 1774.

That evening the militia had settled on the point and had no idea there was an Indian around let alone one thousand of them. The men visited with each other as they cooked, ate, and talked about their families, and how they were going to put down the Indian problem once and for all. Colonel Lewis had given them this day to rest. He walked all around the camp and talked with the men. He knew he had a good army and they would do well under fire. Militarism was not too important in the militia, with the exception of following orders when in combat. Nobody cared if you marched in step, and no uniforms were worn so a button buttoned, or not did not matter. The men were also in one accord, they meant to teach the Indians a lesson or two.

Earlier today Colonel Lewis had held a church service and talked on the Twenty Forth Psalm. He was not a preacher, but it seemed to be left to him to officiate.

After walking through the camp he held a quick meeting with his company commanders and bid them a good night. The camp was completely relaxed. Tomorrow the three hundred other soldiers driving the cattle and bringing supplies would arrive in camp. Then the order to move would be given.

Up the river about a mile hundreds of warriors were crossing the Ohio in their trusty birch bark canoes. The canoes made several trips carrying about ten horrid painted warriors each. So far Cornstalk's plan was working perfectly. In the wee hours of the night the Indians moved in. The warriors formed a semi circle around the point, cutting off any escape the Shemanese might try. Cornstalk had them right where he wanted them. His brave warriors would surprise and kill every Long Knife in the un-suspecting camp.

Just so happened two buddies in the militia had decided to get up early and go after some turkey they had heard last evening. It was just barley gray daylight when the two rolled out, grabbed their muskets and headed south toward the woods. As the two come up on the Indians they brought up their muskets and fired a round dropping two braves. About a dozen shots rang out from the Indian side. One of the two militiamen fell dead; the other somehow ran back into the camp without a hair missing. He screamed as he ran straight to Colonel Lewis's tent.

"Indians Sir, the woods are full of hundreds of Indians," shouted the distraught militiaman.

The camp came alive with eight hundred militiamen getting behind cover with their trusty Brown Betsy muskets in hand. The surprise was now null and void. The whites had a fight on their hands but were all experienced woodsmen.

Colonel Lewis sent for his company commanders, James Fleming and Charles Lewis the Colonel's younger brother. As Fleming and Lewis ran up to Colonel Lewis was cool and calm. He directed the commanders, Charles Lewis to form a battle line from the Kanawha one third ways across the point. He told James Fleming to start at the Ohio side and form a battle line a third way across the point.

"Most likely I am kin to James Fleming, as Fleming is my mother's maiden name. I will uncover that link someday with a lot of work and luck," Dahnmon

"I will take the rest of the men and cover the middle, soon as we are ready we will advance on them Red Devils," he commanded.

All of this went on while under a fierce fire from the one thousand Indians shooting from behind cover in a dusky light.

Some folks will differ with me, but I say the American Revolution started in the dawn of Monday, October 10, 1774. Most folks will say the war started on April 19, 1775 in Concord, Massachusetts as the Patriots faced the red coated British in the battle of old North Bridge. No one knows who actually fired that first shot, but a new cliché was coined at that battle. It was called, "The shot heard around the world!"

The battle of Point Pleasant was a furious battle mostly hand to hand. At first many shots rang out as the militia moved into the woods. Before long the sun was rising but the visibility got worse as the black powder smoke hung on the ground. The Long Knifes and the Painted warriors were now in close proximity. Some of the Indians threw down their muskets after a shot or two and waded in with war clubs or tomahawks. The brave frontiersmen fired as long as they could and then faced the dreadful looking Indians swinging their muskets like clubs. Blood and sweat mingled on the warring factions. An enormous amount of energy was spent in this five hour struggle.

Charles Lewis fell dead as a ball tore through his head, about the same time James Fleming went down as a ball tore through his body just below the ribs. He was not dead, but out of commission.

THE PATRIOT, HEZEKIAH WHITT

Both sides fought as hard as possible. Hand to hand went on for about five long hours. Around noon the sides separated and took pot shots at each other until around 5:00 PM. An Indian came to Chief Cornstalk and informed him that the other three hundred Long knifes were coming up the Kanawha and would arrive in about three hours.

Chief Cornstalk gave the word to get the dead and wounded and fall back into the woods. As Colonel Lewis watched the Indians melt into the woodland, he felt relief and did not pursue. This would be counted as a great victory for the Virginian's because the Indians fell back first. There was no big win even though the Indians left. Colonel Lewis lost half of his commissioned officers and fifty two of the militia, a total of seventy five dead. There were about ninety wounded and unable to continue the fight. The losers (Indians) had only twenty two killed and eighteen wounded. If Cornstalk had stayed the course history would have been different that day.

This would be the saddest day in the life of Chief Cornstalk because of what it would mean to the Shawnee Nation. Now the proud Shawnee Nation would have to yield to Dunmore.

On Tuesday October 11, 1774 Cornstalk pushed his weary army toward the Scioto Towns. He was angered by what he heard as some of the Indians talked. They were not talking of another battle, but of signing a treaty. Cornstalk was further angered as his allies the Delaware, Mingo, and Wyandotte rode off toward their respective villages as soon as they got across the great Ohio River. They rode off with their heads bent low as they passed Chief Cornstalk. Just a few days ago this horde of warriors stated that they were ready to die in battle.

As soon as Cornstalk got back to the village he called for a council. This meeting was humble and nothing like the expressive one held before the battle. Cornstalk stood and commended his brave warriors for a strong fight. He then ask if it was all for nothing? He explained that he heard many talking to sign a peace treaty with the Shemanese.

"My ears are filled with shame as I heard these words," said Cornstalk.

"I warned you and wanted to sue for peace from a strong position, all of you wanted to fight," continued the great Chief Cornstalk.

The Chief was very emotional as he addressed the council. He explained that the Shemanese was coming toward them by two ways.

"Do we kill our women and children and face the Shemanese in battle until we are no more?" asked Cornstalk.

The Indians could not answer! The angry Chief held up his bloody tomahawk for all to see, and then he savagely thrust it into the ground.

"Since you are not willing to fight, then we will meet the Shemanese and make peace," exclaimed the somber Cornstalk.

THE PATRIOT, HEZEKIAH WHITT

The warriors roared with approval. Chief Cornstalk sent out his fleet young runners to Governor Dunmore with his peace proposal. A temporary peace was made and the Shawnee ceded the lands south of the great Ohio River to the whites for a promise of peace. I said temporary peace because things were happening between the British and American Colonies that would affect the peace with the Indians.

As the smoke settled and the militiamen returned home jubilantly another year was upon them. The new year of 1775 would be a busy and uneasy year for the Reverend Richard Whitt family and Hezekiah would be fifteen on March 29, 1775.

"Wars and rumors of War," declared Reverend Richard Whitt, "This could be the beginning of the End Time!"

He was right about one thing; there were many rumors of war. Every paper, letter or person coming from the east told the stories of the British bearing down and the Colonies offering stiff opposition. Those papers, documents and such, no longer carried the official British Stamps on them. People were openly protesting in many ways. The colonies were growing closer in unity as the need presented itself. The Thirteen United Colonies were about to form the United States.

On February 9, 1775 the British Parliament declared that the Colony of Massachusetts is in rebellion. At first the folks out in the frontier were not taking sides. As things progressed the frontier folks began to lean toward the new plan for each colony to become a free state. Right now the Indians were stinging by the defeat at Point Pleasant, but in a matter of a short time, things can change.

The Whitts and Skaggs were living day by day pretty much as usual. Planting in spring went on just as before. Hezekiah was a tall strong lad of fifteen and could do a man's job on the farm. He had gray eyes, dark brown hair, and a crease in his chin. This crease in the chin of many Whitt's is sometimes called the "Whitt Chin." He did what he was told, but had a hankering to head deep into the wilderness. He dreamed about a beautiful valley know as the Clinch. Someday Hezekiah would live that dream. He was taught about duty to God and to family. He would have a duty to his new country, the Free State of Virginia. Hezekiah was trying to balance want, and duty. He always did his duty and would put his wants off until a new season would come.

Hezekiah spent every hour he could out in the woods hunting and sometimes fishing. When he had time Hezekiah would venture several miles from home and explore new grounds. One day when he was several miles out he heard a musket fire. It sounded different than the normal musket fire. It sounded weaker revealing that the powder charge was smaller than normal. Henry Skaggs had told Hezekiah that Indians always put in less powder while loading their muskets. They did not always have access to gunpowder so they loaded conservatively. Hezekiah moved swiftly toward the sound of the shot while keeping quiet as possible. He crept over the crest of a small ridge to see four Indians retrieving a buck deer. Hezekiah kept low and stayed concealed behind cover. He took a second to scan the whole area to see if there were more Indians. He saw none so he concentrated on the four. They had no paint on so he concluded that they were just hunting. He watched as they field dressed the buck. He watched out of curiosity. Hezekiah had never observed real live wild Indians in the woodland before. He was amazed as he watched the presumed shooter of the deer, cut out the heart and hold it high and made some kind of gesture. The Indian took a big bite of the warm bloody heart. Then he passed it around for the other three to share. This made Hezekiah a little squeamish in the stomach. He would have to ask Uncle Henry or Thomas Mastin what this meant. Hezekiah stayed in cover until the Indians cut the deer in four pieces loaded it on their backs and headed off in a trot toward the west.

As soon as Hezekiah got back home he went straight to Uncle Henry and told him about his experience. He told him that he saw them eat the warm bloody heart and that they had blood all over their faces.

"They do that to get the strength of the dear," Henry explained, "I have heard of them even eating a man's heart if he was considered a challenging enemy."

"Do they think this will make them strong or is it just a jester of their superiority?" ask Hezekiah.

"They think that if they kill an enemy or even game and eat the heart they capture the great strength of their quarry," explained Henry.

Hezekiah told his story time after time, even to the little brothers and sisters.

"Don't tell that story to the babies, they will have nightmares," scolded mother Susannah.

Some other topics to talk about during this progressive year were the building conflict between the thirteen United Colonies and the overbearing King George III. The subject of Indians was talked about a lot. A notable Virginian was now known across Virginia and all the colonies, and that was Patrick Henry. He was an outspoken force for freedom and States Rights. At the second Continental Congress on March 23, 1775, he coined the phrase, "Give me Liberty or give me Death!" Little five year old Archibald Whitt went about saying it over and over, "Give me Liberty or give me Death!"

"That baby shouldn't be a saying such as that'" stated mother Susannah.

"Well, that is what they hear now days, we can't expect much else," said Reverend Richard.

The older children Abijah, Rachel and Hezekiah thought it was funny the way little Archibald said it.

As the summer came on, the frontiersmen got word that they were in a new nation. On June the 7, 1775 the United Colonies became the new United States of America. Much was said about this, mostly approval, some Tories (Those loyal to the King.) were not too happy.

THE PATRIOT, HEZEKIAH WHITT

On June 14, 1775 the United States Army was formed. The new Commander-in-Chief of the army was appointed June 15, 1775; they chose Colonel George Washington of the Free State of Virginia. July 3rd General George Washington took charge of the army at Cambridge, Massachusetts.

More news, the new United States has its own currency, three million dollars was minted on June 22nd. The new U.S. Coins were silver and of the size and weight of the Spanish Dollars.

Another service would have to be replaced since the King was not in charge of the new United States. July 26th Benjamin Franklin became the first Post Master General to organize the important service.

"Postal service has to be better than it was," grumbled the declining James Skaggs.

Age was catching up with James and he was referring to the poor postal service here in the frontier areas.

Finally King George III caught on. On August 22nd the king proclaimed that the colonies are in open rebellion.

So many people were alarmed of all that was going on. Reverend Richard Whitt prayed long fervent prayers for the new nation and for the leadership. He also preached many sermons on liberty. The actions of this new little nation brought on many conversations.

This new nation knew that Great Britain had a huge and powerful navy. On Oct 12, 1775 the Continental Congress formed a United States Navy and ordered that a fleet be built.

The Virginia militia in eastern Virginia was called up during this year and marched under Patrick Henry to Williamsburg. Lord Dunmore had seized gunpowder and guns, Colonel Patrick Henry and his men took it back. Lord Dunmore was pretty much through as acting Governor. Looking ahead we will see the spirited Virginian Patrick Henry become the first Governor of the Free State of Virginia.

Dunmore needs help, bad, he on November 7, 1775 made a plea to all Negro slaves. He offered to free any slave that would join the British Army.

The Continental Congress realized that the British Navy carried Marines on all of their fighting ships. On November 10, 1775 Congress formed the United States Marine Corps.

With so much going on, folks had plenty to discuss and digest. There were the Indian problem and land hungry whites rushing into the western end of Fincastle County which in time would be known as the Commonwealth of Kentucky. The new government tried to keep peace with the Indians by asking folks not to migrate into the Kentucky lands.

It was like an endless flotilla coming down the Ohio River. If an Indian showed himself on the banks of their own land, they would promptly be fired upon. Many Indians were killed and this brought outrage especially among the young hotheaded braves. They

COLONEL CHARLES DAHNMON WHITT   38

THE PATRIOT, HEZEKIAH WHITT

explained that the Shemanese were destroying the herds of buffalo and elk that fed the Shawnee. What was Chief Cornstalk to do? He gave his word to the white chief Dunmore not to war against them anymore. Yet the whites were not doing their part. "We will defend ourselves and our land if they cross the waters of the Ohio," stated Cornstalk.

The white men were discouraged to migrate west, but folks like Daniel Boone had it in their blood to explore the western end of Fincastle County. During the spring of 1775 Boone with about 30 other men made a trace through the Cumberland Gap to central Kentucky. They were supposed to build a road, but it was not much more that a horse trail. They took their axes and cleared brush from the Warriors Path. This was not a new route; it had been used by the Indians for years. It was new to the white people. Boone was a risky kind of guy; he took his family and other settlers into Kentucky and settled on the Kentucky River in the fall of 1775. It was risky because this fine land was claimed by the Shawnee and other factions of Indians for their hunting grounds. There had been several Indian attacks on the waters of the Clinch, Holston and Powell Rivers in 1773 and 1774. One was mentioned earlier that took the life of Daniel Boone's son James on the Powell River in present day Lee County, Virginia.

So much was going on during this time and the family of Reverend Richard Whitt had much to talk about. The new year of 1776 was coming on and it would be a dreadful year for the white settlers west of the Blue Ridge. They would consider 1775 as a peaceful year compared to 1776. Hezekiah was just about a man and he now joined in on all of these talks with the family and others he came in contact with. He especially loved to talk with his friend Thomas Mastin and his uncle Henry Skaggs.

Hezekiah's Grandfather James Skaggs was declining in his health and would have to resign being Captain in the Virginia Militia. James had been a pioneer in the early years crossing the Blue Ridge and settling on the New River, near present day Radford, Virginia. James could tell a lot of stories about the old days as he called them. Indian stories, hunting and fishing trips were always a delight to hear about. Hezekiah really loved to hear James Skaggs' stories.

This new year of 1776 would bring on more caution and fortitude. Any one going into the woodland had better be aware and stay vigilant or they could very well lose their hair. Hezekiah had been taught by the best and he could disappear into the woodland and blend into the foliage. He really loved these skills that Henry Skaggs and Thomas Mastin had taught him. Not only were they beneficial for hunting, but they could keep you safe from any of the two legged foes that may lay in wait. Occasionally Hezekiah would see an Indian party pass by or a frontier bandit. Hezekiah used his wisdom and savvy and avoided confrontation.

The militiamen met often and prepared for war. They marched, held target practice, and learned together about the enemy abroad and here at home. Abijah, Hezekiah, along with Reverend Richard Whitt were participants and even little Edmund tagged along. James Skaggs was the Captain, but feeling that his age and health would be a hindrance resigned and Thomas Ingles was appointed by the Fincastle County Committee of Safety. Hezekiah hated that his famous Grandfather James Skaggs would no longer be the Captain. James took Hezekiah for a walk along Meadow Creek and explained that the rigors of leadership and war would be too much for him in his declining years. He explained to Hezekiah that the young men like him would be called to be patriots of this new country.

"You young men will stand strong and secure the peace and inherit the liberties you deserve," James Skaggs explained.

"Grand Paw, I am ready to fight for my home and family," answered the sixteen year old Hezekiah.

"I know you are!" answered the patriarch James Skaggs.

"I have been learning from Uncle Henry, Thomas Mastin, and of course you and Paw," said Hezekiah.

"Yes, I have heard really good reports on your progress and I know about your militia practice," James said, "also I have seen and eaten the fine game you have brought home."

Hezekiah only smiled, as his Grandfather boasted about him.

A lot was going on in the east with the British having a troop buildup. They were even bringing in mercenaries from Germany called Hessians. In the west the Indians were on the warpath. They took up the hatchet on the promises by the British. The British promised them the moon. They told the Indians that after the war the whites would only live east of the mountains. They told them that the red brothers could win their land back if they help the King defeat the land hungry whites that came across the mountains to kill the Indian's elk and buffalo.

The area along this part of the New River was not being molested too much because of the stronger numbers of militia. The frontiersmen along the New River kept up a spy system and at a minutes notice the militia could come together. To the west and not too far away, on the Clinch, Holston, and Powell Rivers and the creeks that feed them the many bands of warriors roamed. The war parties looked for weak and unprotected cabins or even little villages to attack. They would swoop in and surprise the whites. They would kill, plunder, burn down the cabins, kill the stock and carry off women and children to adopt into their tribes. Sometimes if they had time they would take a man captive just to delight themselves by torture once they got to a safe area. During this year the Cherokees were the worst even though the Shawnees were on the move again.

Not only did the British give the Indians big promises, but they gave them gifts of new muskets, ball and powder and knives and hatchets. They brought food, blankets, iron pots, and beads for the women. One other gift that the red men craved was given by the British. This was whiskey, sometimes called firewater by both sides. The British were good buddies to their red brothers, or so the Indians thought. The British were so lowdown that they paid a bounty for the white scalps the Indians brought in.

Another action taken by the Virginia Government was to do away with Fincastle County

THE PATRIOT, HEZEKIAH WHITT

that had been named for a Brit. They took the County that ran plumb to the Mississippi and divided it into three parts. Montgomery, Washington and Kentucky Counties were formed in 1776 and would be more organized by 1777. Meadow Creek, (Now Radford), would be a part of Montgomery County. This was a year that so many things happened it was hard to keep up. New government, new leaders, and new enemies were apparent.

To the east the British were trying to defeat the small armies of the Continental Congress led by George Washington. To the west, north, and south, the different Indian factions were on the prowl collecting scalps. Many deep into the frontier had moved into forts. These little forts were small and people were thrown into crowded conditions. They had to deal with new problems. Crops could not be planted nor harvested. The only food they had was what they carried in or what daring hunters like Daniel Boone, Simon Kenton or Henry Skaggs could bring in.

The battle of Long Island Flats, (Near modern day Kingsport, Tenn.) fought on July 20, 1776, and the whole Cherokee Campaign under Colonel William Christian in the fall brought some relief.

In that battle the Cherokee had a force of three to four hundred warriors. The frontier spies came in a rush yelling that the Indians were right behind them. Several frontiersmen ran out to meet them and several Indians were brought down with hot lead. According to a settler near there, James Anderson, the whites were out numbered three to one.

After the Indians moved on, the men and boys went out and scalped the dead Indians. The report was that the whites only lost three men. They must have been fortified and behind good cover while the Indians were out in the open. The Shelby Fort (in present day Bristol) held as many as 100 families at a time. The fort was built to house about ten families.

After this battle the Indians divided into many small war parties and traveled into many places hoping that they may find scalps and plunder. The whole frontier from Montgomery to the far side of Kentucky County was a target to the red men.

Back in the east the Continental Congress came to the truth that free blacks should be in their Army. The British took any black they could get for their army. They promised any slave freedom after the war.

The Continental Army shelled the British in Boston and on March 17th the British evacuated to Nova Scotia. By May 2, 1776 the French and Spanish agreed to aid the American rebels with weapons. On June 12, 1776 Virginia adopted a Declaration of Rights. June 23, 1776 a final draft of the Declaration of Independence was submitted to the United States Congress.

June 29, 1776 Virginia adopted the state constitution and Patrick Henry was made the first Governor of the Free State of Virginia.

COLONEL CHARLES DAHNMON WHITT

THE PATRIOT, HEZEKIAH WHITT

This next statement is really important!

The Continental Congress resolves that, "these United Colonies are & of right ought to be Free & Independent States!" This is where the individual states stand that they are their own country. The State comes first then the United States. This thinking was part of what would lead to the War Between the States in the next century. It also presented a present problem for the Commander-in-Chief George Washington; he couldn't order any one state to send money and manpower for the war effort. General George Washington had to learn diplomacy and politics to get what he needed. Sometimes he just about begged.

The 4th of July 1776 the Declaration of Independence was signed and the connection to Great Britain was severed. Now there was no turning back and no holds barred. The rebels of King George III would take on a new name. They would become Patriots to their new state and to the United States.

Many people died on both sides, in the year of 1776. The British had an upper hand, but on Christmas day 1776 General George Washington crossed the Delaware River with his Army and surprises and defeats Hessian troops. The 26th Washington wins at Trenton. The new little country of the United States had a long way to go, but a win now and then really helped. The Frontiersmen to the west were kept busy by the Indian factions most of the year of 1776.

Patrick Henry the out spoken Virginian was elected the first Governor of the free and independent State of Virginia on July 5, 1776.

Governor Patrick Henry

THE PATRIOT, HEZEKIAH WHITT

Chapter 6

Hezekiah Becomes A Patriot

With the news of the county being renamed much discussion arose.

"Wonder why they named it Montgomery?" asked Hezekiah.

"Didn't you hear about General Richard Montgomery being killed at Quebec last year?" answered Reverend Richard Whitt.

"He was over the Continental Army up in Canada and got himself killed," continued the Reverend.

"Yes, Paw I do remember something bout that, wasn't he a good leader back in the French and Indian War?" ask Hezekiah.

"Reckon he is an American hero, we sure could use some more like him." explained the Reverend.

"Paw don't you worry, General Washington will pull us through and win us the prize of liberty, we just have to hang in and wear down the Indians and the Redcoats," stated Hezekiah.

"You make it sound so simple and you speak wisely for such a young man," said the Reverend.

"Paw, I learned from you and Grand Paw Skaggs, you all are the wise ones," replied Hezekiah.

"Thanks son, what wisdom I have come from God, He is the keeper of all wisdom, always ask Him for wisdom when you talk to Him," exclaimed The Reverend.

"Yes Sir, I will try to remember that, it sure makes sense, since He is the maker of everything," answered Hezekiah.

"Like I said son, you speak wisely for a young man," resounded the Reverend.

"Paw what was the first way into this area?" ask Hezekiah.

"Son you ask a lot of questions, I reckon the first folks come in here by Catawba Valley. (Named for a branch of the Cherokee) They crossed over the mountain that divides the water. Our water runs toward the west and over yonder the water runs back towards the sea," explained the Reverend, "They used to call it the resting place once they clum bout a thousand feet outa the valley!"

"Paw, you sure do know bout a lot of stuff," answered Hezekiah.

"Since we are in a new county where will the seat be put, Paw?" ask Hezekiah without taking another breath.

THE PATRIOT, HEZEKIAH WHITT

"I hear they will have it at Fort Chiswell, it is a good place cause it is at a cross roads," answered the Reverend with a grin on his face.

"What is it Paw, why are you ah grinning like that?" ask Hezekiah.

"Shucks son, you changed directions without even backing up," exclaimed the Reverend.

"Sorry Paw, I just want to know stuff," exclaimed Hezekiah.

"I know son, reckon you are learning, by asking all them questions," answered the Reverend.
"Paw, how did it get its name?" ask Hezekiah.

"How did what get its name?" asked Richard, "You just jump around, my mind can't keep up with you!"

"Sorry Paw, how did Fort Chiswell get there?" ask Hezekiah.

"Oh! They build it during the French and Indian War to put troop's way out here for the protection of the settlers and be a buffer between the Indians and the settlers," replied Reverend Richard.

"Paw, Abijah is a regular militiaman, ain't he?"

"Yes he is," Answered Richard.

"Paw I been ah thinking, I think I would rather be a spy rather than a regular soldier," stated Hezekiah.

"I think you would do a good job at that when you get old enough," answered Richard.

"I will be seventeen in March and you know I can stalk and shoot good as ary full grown man," exclaimed Hezekiah.

"I know, but you are so young, and I don't want nothing to happen to ya!" replied Richard.

"Paw, there's fellers younger than me in the militia," stated Hezekiah.

"They ain't Indian spies, do you know what that requires son?" ask an earnest Richard.

"Purty much, I reckon," replied Hezekiah.

THE PATRIOT, HEZEKIAH WHITT

"Son you have to spend weeks out in the wilderness with out fire or even shooting your musket, you will be cold and lonely. You will have to run many miles to warn folks when you know the Indians are a coming!" exclaimed a solemn Richard.

"Paw, I can set snares, trap, and catch fish in silence, I don't mind being out by myself, I even feel closer to the Lord when I am out in his wild lands," answered Hezekiah trying to make his case.

"If and when the time comes we will see," answered Richard, "I do understand about being close to God out on the mountains."

"Paw, I think the time is a coming soon, ever day we hear reports about the war in the east, and about the Indian attacks north, west and south of us, yip it's a coming soon," replied Hezekiah.

"Enough of that talk for today, better go get your chores done, your Maw will be wanting to set supper," answered Richard.

"I'll git-er-done Paw, be done fore you can skin a cat," answered Hezekiah.

The Reverend Richard grinned at Hezekiah and went in the house.

Richard was very proud of his family, especially the skills that Hezekiah possessed. Richard had a dread in his heart that he and his older sons would have to step forward to protect his family and the Free State of Virginia. He put it out of his mind when Susannah took him into her arms.

"What are you dwelling on, Richard?" asked Susannah.

"Just the times I reckon, what is that wonderful smell coming out of the kitchen?" he asked trying to chance the subject.

Robert Whitt the oldest son disappeared during this time. He left early one morning on a mild day in January 1777 on a routine hunt and never returned. Many hunters would stay out until night or even the next day, Robert never came back even on the third day.

The Reverend gathered all of the best scouts to form a search, had a prayer and the scouts went in different directions. Abijah, Hezekiah, Edmund and even Archibald joined in the search. Hezekiah followed Roberts's tracks for about a mile, but lost them on the rocky bank of New River. They even had a tracking dog on the trail, but it was too cold.

Reverend Richard followed Hezekiah and the dog, but it was as if Robert vanished from the earth. They never found any sign of foul play or any other sign to figure out the mystery. All the trackers eventually came to the place where Robert's tracks ended. They all looked for some sign, a broken twig, a partial track, a pushed over weed, they even looked for Indian sign. Robert Whitt was gone.

THE PATRIOT, HEZEKIAH WHITT

The Reverend Whitt was in tears as he called everyone around him out in the woodland where Robert's tracks ended. The reverend had everyone kneel down and he led in prayer for the return of Robert and for his safekeeping.

"Lord, if you have called Robert home please let us have some sign," prayed Reverend Richard Whitt.

A warm feeling came over the little group of trackers and family. They felt the wonderful Holy Spirit as the Comforter calmed their spirits. The Reverend broke down in great lamentations even though he knew Robert was in the Lord's hands.

After returning home the Reverend gathered his Susannah, the other children, the Skaggs and neighbors to tell them of the happenings and to have a memorial service for Robert. There was much lamentation when everyone heard the news. After much praying and many talked of the good virtues of Robert calmness fell over the group.

These people were quite resilient and knew that life could be very short, west of the Blue Ridge.

Many people speculated that the heathen Indians carried Robert off. Some said he fell into New River and was washed away, but there was no sign of any of this. No one knew if Robert would ever be heard of again. Life must go on was the mindset, when a loved one was snatched from their midst. At least a mangled and butchered body was not found.

In the early spring of 1777 it was time to show which side you were on. The Reverend Richard Whitt, Abijah Whitt, Hezekiah Whitt, and Edmund Whitt signed the Patriots Oath. They signed and took Montgomery County's oath of Allegiance to Virginia as a Free and Independent State. If the new nation failed, they would all be hanged for treason!

The Reverend was already a veteran of the French and Indian War serving out of North Carolina.

Hezekiah would join the spies under Major Thomas Mastin of the Virginia Militia. Over the next few years he would have many duties and march with the militia. Right now he was doing what he felt called to do, and that was to travel west to the headwaters of the Clinch River and be an early warning messenger if the Indians came that way to attack and plunder. This was a dream choice of duty for the seventeen year old Hezekiah Whitt and his leader Major Thomas Mastin had all the confidence in the world that Hezekiah would perform his duties to the fullest.

For now Edmund and Abijah Whitt would serve with the Captain Thomas Ingles of the Montgomery County Militia in the southwest on the Holston River. They would deal with Tories and the Cherokee Indians. Hezekiah would be looking for Shawnee, Mingo, Wyandotte and a few other tribes that would travel southeast to do their mischief.

THE PATRIOT, HEZEKIAH WHITT

Major Thomas Mastin knew what to expect on their mission for the entire summer and way up into the fall. He was not sure that his spies did, so he called a meeting to prepare them for this undertaking. He knew that they were all good woodsmen and loyal to the Free Independent State of Virginia. Yet to live in the woods all summer and way up in the fall, in complete silence without campfires and being constantly diligent would test the metal of any man.

Joseph Oney, Archibald Prator, Hezekiah Whitt and Lazarus Damron, would be together starting out, then they would divide and eventually spy as lone scouts.

Major Thomas Mastin called a meeting of his spies just after Hezekiah's seventeenth birthday on March 29, 1777. The Major gathered the spies together to inform them of departure, and get them ready for the rigors ahead.

The Major informed the men that there were six forts on the waters of the Clinch. They were established during the Dunmore war. There may be some settlers there about or they may have fled by now. I will tell you where these forts are and you are to go there as you scout. You are to warn the people you find to head back east until this threat is passed. He mentioned Elk Garden Fort, Witten's Crab Orchard Fort, Maiden Springs Station, Moor's Fort, Blackmore's Fort, and Glade Hollow Fort. He explained the location and stated that some were on the head waters and some were further south on what he called middle Clinch River.

Major Thomas Mastin told the men that they were to report at first light on April 1st. Some of the men laughed at the date.

The Major stopped and ask, "What are you laughing about?"

"It's April Fool's Day sir that might be fitting for this bunch" replied the militiaman.

"Nonsense, there ain't a fool in this bunch, I picked every last one of ya!" exclaimed the Major.
The men got quiet and he went on explaining the mission.

"Now men we will march out on the morning of April 1st and when we get out into the wilderness we will divide up into fours. After we get close to the Clinch River we will divide again into twos. Once we get to the spying grounds we will divide again and you will be on your on as a single scout in your designated area. We will have a meeting place set up and meet every two days with your partner. I will roam about and meet up with you occasionally," Major Thomas Mastin explained.

"The main thing you are to leave as little a sign as possible, I don't want one of them savages following you around," he added.

"Thomas, what do you want us to bring?" asked Hezekiah.

THE PATRIOT, HEZEKIAH WHITT

"Private Hezekiah you will address me as Major or Sir when we are on duty," the Major said, "you are to bring your musket, powder and lead, a bed roll, a knife, a tomahawk, rawhide strands, fishing line and hooks, grease and about a pint of meal and plenty of jerky and parched corn.

"Sorry Sir," said Hezekiah.

Thomas nodded his head and went back to talking.
"The best thing you can take is your skills and good old commonsense," exclaimed the Major.

"Now I will take questions," stated the Major.
"Sir, if we can't have a fire, how do we cook?" asked Archibald Prator.
"Damn, damn, you light a fire and you are dead understood?" asked the Major.

"You will eat bugs, worms, snakes and raw meat along with your meal, jerky and corn," he exclaimed.

"Sir, what are our orders if we spot Indians?" ask another man.

"You will stay ahead of them if possible, let your partner know if possible and do not take them on by yourself," the Major said, "you are to warn any and all settlers in the warriors path, that is our mission."

"What if the Indians find us out?" ask another spy.

"You are to do your duty the best you can and stay out of shooting range, get to your partner or head for the first settlers cabin or fort," explained Major Thomas Mastin.

"Everybody have an understanding of our mission now; I have picked you because of your hunting skills and of your loyalty to Virginia, any more questions?" ask Major Thomas Mastin.

"Hearing none I ask Hezekiah Whitt to pray!" stated the Major.

Hezekiah was shocked somewhat, but nodded in response.

Dear Heavenly Father, I beseech you to put your hand on your humble servants. Lord we praise you and pray in Thanksgiving. Lord go with us out into the wilderness and protect us from the heathen. Help us to keep your commandants as we spy and as we fight the enemy if it comes to that. Lord I ask that you help us with our spying and help us shoot straight and fast if we are called upon. Lord help our brothers to the east as they fight the Red Coates and Tories. Lord we are the Free and Independent State of Virginia please let us win so that name will stick. Lord, I think I said bout everything, so forgive us for a sinning and doing wrong! One more thing Lord, please watch over our folks here at home and bring us back safely. If you require our lives rush us off to

THE PATRIOT, HEZEKIAH WHITT

Heaven fore the devil knows we are dead. I ask all of this in the name of your beloved Son, Jesus Christ. Amen.

Amen, Amen sounded the entire lot of spies.

The major addressed the men one more time.

"Gentlemen, we have a very important job, we are the first line of defense for the settlers and forts, I will assign your spying ground as we travel west, some of you may go as far as the Louisa River, (Levisa fork of Big Sandy) some will go to the Powell and yet some will go to the Tug. All of you will see the beautiful Clinch. I will see you on Fool's Day he said with a grin. Dismissed." said their leader, Major Thomas Mastin.

The Indian spies went home to get ready. This was Monday, March 31st. The men were fired up and ready to go mentally, they talked on the way back home about their upcoming adventure. They knew this was not just an adventure but that some of them may not come back. Hezekiah left with his friend Thomas Mastin and walked about a quarter of a mile back to the Whitt House. He told everyone that he was ordered to meet at Thomas Mastin's home at first light tomorrow Tuesday, April 1st and start their mission.

Susannah welled up in tears as she heard the news.

"I knew this was coming, but not so soon," Susannah said in a sob.

"Maw, it will be alright, the Lord will keep me safe, and I know a thing or two bout surviving in the woods," stated Hezekiah.

"You are so young, I just can't stand for you to go out in the dangerous wilderness, I know Abijah, Edmund, and even your Paw will be sent out afore long!" exclaimed Susannah.

Wanting to change the subject Hezekiah spoke up, "Paw, guess who Thomas called on to pray at the meeting?"

"Prayed at the meeting," injected Susannah, "Lord even Thomas is worried!"

"Now Susannah, Thomas always has someone pray at militia meetings, he probably picked Hezekiah cause he's my son and he knows Hezekiah is a Christian Man," stated Reverend Richard.

"That's right Paw, I was a little surprised, but Thomas did ask me to pray," said Hezekiah.

"Tomorrow is Fool's Day, hope that don't mean anything," stated little sister Elizabeth Whitt.

This brought smiles and a chuckle or two and lightened up the serious atmosphere.

THE PATRIOT, HEZEKIAH WHITT

"Well son ya better get your gear together," Richard said, "Do you need any help?"
"No Paw, I know bout where ever thing is, I will round up my things," stated Hezekiah.

"Hey Hez, you want to borrow my heaver sack, it is bigger than that little one of yours?" asked Abijah.

"I think it might be better brother, thanks for the offer," answered Hezekiah.

It was a somber time at the Whitt House the rest of the day. Hezekiah went over and spent some time with James and Rachel Skaggs, his grandparents. James Skaggs was proud as punch of his grandson. Yet he had a fear of what could happen when Hezekiah ventured into harms way.

After little sleep, Hezekiah arose on Tuesday April 1, 1777 and got ready for the spying mission. Susannah had biscuits baking and brown gravy bubbling in her iron pot. The whole family was up and moving around, none wanted to miss giving Hezekiah a grand farewell. After Hezekiah choked down his gravy, he was ready to head out the door. He had on his dark almost black buckskins, coonskin hat, heaver sack, and on his wide leather belt he had a big skinning knife and tomahawk. Also he had a bed roll crossing his other shoulder and tied at his waist. He also had his powder horn, patch, and ball bag on the heaver sack side. On his feet he wore moccasins as was the rule for going scouting or hunting in Indian country. White men's boots were a sure give away.

Hezekiah stood there as if on inspection while each sibling came in a line to hug their brother. The littlest was three year old Susannah Whitt (sister). Hezekiah picked her up and kissed her and gently sat her down to greet the next. Little five year old Ruth was next, then little eight year old Richard Thomas. Next was Edmund, and then out of sequence was Archibald. Then his other sisters Rachel and Elizabeth were next. Then Abijah walked up and patted Hezekiah on the shoulder saying, "You will do just fine little brother."

Next Richard and Susannah came and hugged their son, Susannah was holding back tears. As Richard held his son he lifted a prayer that all could hear. He prayed mostly for the safe return of Hezekiah and that all would be well.

Hezekiah was trying to get out the door without showing a tear. Edmund spoke up, "hey big brother ain't you going to take your Brown Betz?"

Everyone laughed at the look on Hezekiah's face as he picked up his musket. Hezekiah was now on his way cross the big meadow to Major Thomas Mastin's cabin.

As Hezekiah got to the Mastin cabin most of the other Indian Scouts were there. They were greeting each other and talking about the mission when Major Thomas Mastin came out with his pipe stuck far back into the right side of his mouth, smoke was rising as a pleasant little cloud.

THE PATRIOT, HEZEKIAH WHITT

"Fall in men," the Major said loud enough for all to hear. The men rambled around and found themselves in two lines of eight each. The lines were not too straight, but that was not a problem for a spy unit.

Major Thomas Mastin addressed his spies and greeted them. He gave them a quick overall as to what they would be doing and gave them the orders of, "Left Face, Forward March," and the little company headed toward the Skaggs' Ferry owned by James Skaggs Jr. They would ferry across the New River and march toward the southwest toward the County Seat, Fort Chiswell.

Rendition of a Militiaman.

THE PATRIOT, HEZEKIAH WHITT

A rendition of an Indian Spy.

Chapter 7

What Beauty, The Waters Of The Clinch

After the militia spies got to Fort Chiswell in the evening and stopped for a rest while the Major checked in with the Montgomery County Officials. The Spies would stay the night with town's people. They would sleep in the dry barns and enjoy their last cooked meal for sometime. The spies mingled with the folks and enjoyed the last of any settlement of this size.

Colonel William Preston, the County Lieutenant, was in Fort Chiswell that day on business. He was appointed by Patrick Henry and had almost complete authority over all Montgomery County Business. When he heard that Major Thomas Mastin and his company of Indian Spies were there he hastened to meet them. Colonel Preston applauded the men and told them how thankful he was of their service. He told them that they were the early warning service that all the remote cabins and forts needed. He explained that he understood the sacrifice and danger they were facing. After he finished the little spy company cheered for the Colonel.

Colonel Preston explained that he had to leave so that he would get home in the morning; he told them that it was safer for him to travel at night. He had a good steed and could outrun most trouble. He told them that he lived on the family plantation in Draper' Meadow. (Now Blacksburg)

Early the next morning after a cooked breakfast, thanks to the people in Fort Chiswell, The company of spies marched out. After they reached the deep woods the Major stopped the men for a rest. He sent one man forward for a mile or so to check for trouble. Then he had the men find a big pile of leafs and undress. He told them to waller all of their clothes and even things in their sacks and pouches in the leafs. He reminded them not to loose any of their gear in the leafs.

The Major said, "If you find animal droppings smear your moccasin's soles in it, but don't get shit all over you."

Hezekiah grinned at the Major at this, and he grinned back.
One spy whispered to another, "Has the Major lost his mind?"

"Nope, the Major is a smart man, he wants us to get all the white-man smell offen us," said the spy.

Then all the men understood the exercise. They looked funny there naked as jay birds, dancing around and rubbing every garment with leafs. They even took off their moccasins and rubbed leaves inside them. Gradually the men put all of their clothes

THE PATRIOT, HEZEKIAH WHITT

back on, some had leafs sticking out of their buckskin sleeves and their buckskin britches.

The Major had them form up in columns of two again. He addressed them and explained that from now on there would be no talking, no smoking and no unnecessary noises. As they were about to march out the scout that had been sent on ahead returned. The Major talked with him a minute and the scout headed for a pile of leafs. The Major told him to do as the others had and for him to catch up as quickly as possible.

They reached the area where the Major had decided to split the unit. This would be the meeting place on the way back home also. He would take eight of the men and head north through Rocky Gap towards the upper waters of the Clinch. The other eight would travel southwest toward present day Rural Retreat. An earlier name was Mount Airy, but there was no name at this time. One reason they changed the name from Mount Airy to Rural Retreat was the confusion with Mount Airy, North Carolina.

This group would head for the waters of middle Clinch River from Castles Woods, to the scouting grounds of the Swords Creek area.

The Major told the sections of eight to divide into fours after another day, then on the next day to divide into twos. He had a rendezvous area picked out for the four to meet, and likewise for the twos to meet and then go back and scout some more. The scouts were to stay in the scouting grounds until told to pull out or have to go and give the alarm of savages on the warpath. The Major would travel the entire upper and middle waters of the Clinch. Everyone knew of the described locations of landmarks, cabins, and frontier forts. If Indians or even their sign was discovered the scout was to move swiftly to their partner if possible; if not go at top speed but quietly to the cabins or forts that may be attacked by the Indians.

The lower party would have to cross the upper Holston River before reaching the Clinch. The upper party would cover the scouting grounds of present day Tazewell down to present day Swords Creek. The Major quietly explained his orders.

"From this point on there will be no fires, no smoking, no firing of muskets except to save life, no noise, don't break twigs or step on branches on the ground, nor anything that may alert a party of Indians," explained Major Thomas Mastin.

When you relieve yourselves, you dig a hole and bury it, that means pissing too, the Indians have better noses than a good hunting dog," continued the Major.

"Men I don't want you to talk, only a whisper if necessary to save life, you may use an "owl hoot" or a "wolf howl" to communicate when trying to rendezvous," the Major said, "make damn sure you ain't hooting to a dab-burn Indian."

This is a dream come true to the young Hezekiah. He would get to see the lands and waters of the Clinch and maybe more. He would be able to match wits with the wild Indians from the Ohio towns. He knew if he was not vigilant he could very well loose his life. Yet Hezekiah loved the challenge and wanted to prove himself to Major

THE PATRIOT, HEZEKIAH WHITT

Thomas Mastin, the other spies and to the folks around Meadow Creek. (Now Radford, VA.)

Morning came with a heavy overcast, as the men awaken and got their gear ready for travel. It was a quiet awaking as the men only whispered when a need arose. Major Thomas Mastin waved his arm overhead in a circle as a sign to circle around. The men came close to hear what the Major had to say. He reminded them of their orders and wished them good scouting.

As the men stood there in that little circle, the major nodded and signed for Hezekiah to pray quietly! Hezekiah prayed real low, some could hardly hear. He mostly thanked God for the blessings, and then he prayed for the safe return of each scout. After a quiet Amen, the men looked up and the Major gave them a signal to split up, and move out! Nine men moved toward Rocky Gap and the upper waters of the Clinch, eight went southwest toward Rural Retreat and the middle waters of the Clinch.

Hezekiah was appointed as forward scout this day. He was to stay about a quarter of a mile ahead of the other eight following toward Rocky Gap. He felt thrilled that Major Mastin had that much confidence in him.

Hezekiah moved out in a swift but quiet walk to put some ground between him and the others. After he got a good distance ahead he slowed to a scouting walk and began to scan everything in a panoramic view. He looked close and far ahead for anything that did not belong, but everything was in its place and there was nothing to cause him to be alarmed. He settled down and began to enjoy the view and all of God's creation.

As Hezekiah moved along being very vigilant, he thought about many things. He thought about the folks back on Meadow Creek, and what may lie ahead. He was pleased that he was heading to the waters of the Clinch and would be able to see this grand land with his own eyes.

Hezekiah saw and heard elk, some woods buffalo, deer, and a multitude of small game and birds. He saw thickets of mountain laurel that covered the north sides of the mountains and filled the hollows. He thought about how many Indians could be hiding there; the whole Shawnee Nation and the Cherokee's included could be concealed by the mountain greenery.

Hezekiah munched on some parched corn and chewed some jerky as he traveled along. There would be no stopping and cooking on this trip. As he traveled up the steep grade he began to heat up and get thirsty. Not far ahead he saw a nice limestone spring.

"Thank you Lord," Hezekiah said in his head.

As he got close to the spring Hezekiah gave the whole area a look. He did not want to be caught unawares while bending down to fill his water container. Hezekiah saw nothing out of the ordinary so he approached the spring cautiously.

THE PATRIOT, HEZEKIAH WHITT

Something was moving in the weeds around the spring. On further inspection Hezekiah discovered a big black snake in the process of eating a copperhead snake. Good boy, Hezekiah thought.

Hezekiah moved in and got his cool water and did not bother the black snake. Hezekiah thought it was early in the year for snakes to be out, but the weather had been unusually warm lately and the snakes might have hibernated close together near the spring.

After he was refreshed he again moved up the grade being very stealth. He paid close attention to his surroundings and listened with all of his capacity while holding in a breath every few feet when he stopped just for that. The Lord was giving him a safe scouting and very enjoyable too.

Hezekiah thought back to the spring. Hezekiah prayed a thankful, but silent prayer for putting the black snake there to eat the dreadful copperhead that could have bitten him. Lord you are so good to me, thought Hezekiah.

The evening shadows became long and Hezekiah knew that darkness came early in the woodland, so he saw a good place off the trail that would serve as a camp. He stopped for the day to wait for the rest of his party. About a half an hour passed and he got a glimpse of the Major and the others ambling up the grade.

Hezekiah got up and gave a wave of his hand over his head to attract the company of scouts. The Major was ahead so he saw his young friend waving. He stopped after waving a sign of recognition and turned to the other seven men following. He pointed up the trail to Hezekiah. Hezekiah waved again to the onlookers. The little group of spies continued their walk toward Hezekiah. When the spies were out in spying ground they did not march in step as this caused too much noise.

As the group came to Hezekiah all shook hands with a greeting, but there was only limited whispering. All the men had stopped at the spring and filled their canteens. Major Thomas Mastin made sign language signifying that he saw the snakes. Hezekiah smiled that he understood.

The men found themselves a place in the area and settled in for a rest as the darkness closed in around them. The Major posted a man on watch, then assigned two more to relieve him in sequence.

The men would split up again in the morning, all basically traveling southwest toward the head waters of the Clinch. The country was beautiful and teemed with herds of elk and deer. There were small herds of bison and plenty of bears in these woods, also wolf packs and panthers were about. The creeks were full of fish and the beavers had worked diligently to build many ponds. Otters played by sliding down the slick banks into the beaver ponds. Hezekiah was excited and filled with the joy of Gods creation.

Since Hezekiah was one of the younger men Major Thomas Mastin assigned him to upper Clinch River. He would travel from the headwater to below what is now Cedar Bluff and follow up all the creeks as he reached them. He was to move slowly and observe all things. He was looking for the most discerning Indian sign that would give warning that warriors were on the move. The other seven scouts would travel down the Clinch to an assigned scouting ground. The Major would leave Hezekiah and start a travel all the way down the Clinch to an area, now Saint Paul and Castlewood.

Hezekiah was to check on Crab Orchard Fort and give warning if he discovered any Indian sign. He found the fort, but it was empty. There was not a dab of food and it didn't look like it had been garrisoned for sometime.

The other eight spies were to do the same in the middle Clinch. They were to scout from Saint Paul up river to where Little River joins the main fork of the river. Some of the scouts were to travel up the Little River fork to the beginning called Maiden Springs. Little River literally comes out of a cave as cold clear water at Maiden Springs.

The spies were given orders to scout for a month and meeting their buddy every few days at designated points. After that, if no sign of Indians was found, move back to the other side of Rocky Gap where they first divided.

Hezekiah reached the mouth of Indian Creek and followed it up for a few days. He had not found any new Indian sign so he looked over the area at leisure and fell completely in love with this new land. He actually took his tomahawk and chopped out on marker trees laying himself out a track of land of about one hundred acres. Part of the track was covered with virgin Cedar trees of great size. He was not suppose to build anything on this scouting, but he built himself a lean-to in the lower part of Baptist Valley across a hill from Indian Creek on the waters of the Clinch. (Where he would some day build his cabin) Hezekiah vowed to return here some day and build his home.

Hezekiah scouted round about up hill and down, he even went to the top of Clinch Mountain and Paint Lick Mountain. He discovered old warrior paths and on Paint Lick Mountain he came up on Indian paintings on the cliffs. They were not new but seemed to be a sign marking directions to the many passing Indians over the years. Hezekiah studied the paintings way up on the mountain above a great salt lick at the base of the mountain. One of the pictures looked to be a great fire bird or thunder bird. He could not but guess to their true meanings. He also saw the great herds that came to the salt lick in the valley below to get their cravings satisfied.

Hezekiah was truly hungry but did not break the order to fire his musket or build a fire even though he was tempted. He did catch some fish and crawdads and ate them raw. Crawdad tails are quiet good and digestible raw. He gathered some new greens and eats some of them as he found them. He mixed his cornmeal with water and made dough like substance and ate it to keep up his strength. He was tired of jerky and parched corn and would be ready for a nice cooked elk steak or even a fried groundhog. Even a possum sounded good when his stomach gnawed with hunger. There is no fruits or berries to be found in southwest Virginia in the spring only a few nuts that were left from the fall and most not eatable. If you could find a ground squirrel's den and dig it up, there may be some good nuts still inside.

THE PATRIOT, HEZEKIAH WHITT

It was all worth it to Hezekiah, to see the beautiful waters of the Clinch and the mountains that bounded it. He never found any sign of the Indians on his scouting, the Shawnees from the Ohio Towns were halfway keeping the treaty of Point Pleasant. During this time it was the Cherokees doing mischief way down in the Tennessee country on the lower Clinch and Holston Rivers.

Hezekiah talked to God everyday out in this beautiful wilderness. It seemed that he was the only man on earth and God was the only one to talk to. He told God that he was thankful for this beautiful place and for the protection God afforded him. He prayed for the folks back home and for the protection of the other Indian spies. He also prayed that Virginia would keep it's independence that she had declared. He also ask God to give him a piece of this rich land right here where he staked his claim.

Just to be sure the last couple of days or so Hezekiah scouted on down the Clinch to the wide valley with the rich soil. (Now called Richlands) He followed the river on down to the area between Red Root Ridge and Road Ridge to (the way to Louisa River now called Levisa Fork of the Big Sandy River) where the little town of Raven is today. He went about a quarter mile more and went up a creek to a water falls. (Now Mill Creek)

Hezekiah found some moccasin foot prints in the sandy bank by Mill Creek and became alarmed. He looked all around and listened carefully. After a good scout he decided it was most likely the tracks from one of the scouts. Hezekiah had a good scout and was ready to turn northeast up the Clinch and slowly make his way toward home and the meeting place.

When Hezekiah got back up to Indian Creek he had to go up it one more time to see his most coveted ground. After he looked it all over and spent the night in his lean-to he headed across a ridge to (what is now called Green Mountain) the Clinch River again. Time passed fast and it was May, time to start back to the rendezvous on the other side of Rocky Gap.

Hezekiah journeyed toward Rocky Gap in a scouting mode. He knew that it was very possible to come up on a war party of painted warriors at any given time or day. He gradually met up with the others spies. He met his partner, then two others, then two more and the other two as they passed through the gap. They met each other with sign language and jesters as they were still in the scouting grounds.

They spent the night on the south side of Rocky Gap in a laurel thicket, eating some of their last portions of jerky and parched corn. They did stop at the good limestone spring and get a supply of the water. There was no sign of the black snake. Next morning was a wet dreary day for May. After a scout went back up the hill for a last look they all began to descend the grade to their main rendezvous.

About noon the eight spices came up on the camp of Major Thomas Mastin and the other spies. The Major spoke out and greeted them all out loud. Everyone looked amazed at hearing the human voice again after a month in the wilderness.

THE PATRIOT, HEZEKIAH WHITT

Hezekiah said, "Hello, howdy, how are you?" just to hear his own voice. It sounded so strange to hear his own voice.

Everyone laughed, until the middle Clinch spies began giving their reports. Seriousness changed the expression on all the spies' faces. The spies reported that on their way back that they had witnessed what the savages had left behind in their onslaught. Several cabins had been burned and ravaged bodies were left by the un-Godly Red Devils. The Island Creek Fort on the lower New River was in danger of falling if it was not shored up with more militia.

Major Thomas Mastin took immediate action and ordered Hezekiah Whitt to run ahead at his most progressive speed to Fort Chiswell and report to Colonel William Preston that Island Creek Fort was in Jeopardy.

Hezekiah took off at full speed and left the spies behind. He ran as fast as possible. He was surprised how he had this much steam, but knew his strength came from his Lord. He reached the Colonel late in the evening and gave the report.

Colonel William Preston took action by summoning three young militiamen to ride with his orders to gather the militia and for them to meet about twenty miles down river from Meadow Creek as quick as possible. The three riders left with haste and were soon out of sight.

Hezekiah was fed a great supper of meaty stew, cornbread, and fresh milk. He even enjoyed a big slice of apple cobbler for desert. He slept like a log and was awaken early to begin a march with the spies, Colonel Preston, and other militia that was raised in the night in and around Fort Chiswell. This group was heading to the rendezvous about twenty miles below Meadow Creek at Hiawassee on the New River. From there the companies would join together and march south to Washington County to Island Creek Fort. (Now Carroll County Virginia bordering North Carolina)

THE PATRIOT, HEZEKIAH WHITT

Chapter 8

Marching With Lieutenant Israel Lorton

Hezekiah marches over to Hiwassee on the New River with the Commandant, Colonel William Preston, where he would join up with another local militia under Lieutenant Israel Lorton. This was nothing like the spy mission he just came off of. The men marched noisy and meandered to the south in formation like a slow giant snake. If there were any Indians about and you could count on it that there was, the army was to scare them with their coming. Hezekiah was a little excited, a little afraid, and yet proud to be marching to defend the Island Creek Fort.

Every now and then Colonel Preston would ride his grand steed back down the line of marching men. He would give encouragement and try to hurry them along.

"Forward, forward, men we must get to Island Creek before the savages attack, the fort is not garrisoned with a strong army," Colonel Preston said, "We must hurry to their salvation!"

The men would hurry for awhile and then slow down again as they became weary. Again and again Colonel Preston would ride back with encouragement.

Also in the long line of militiamen was Hezekiah's father, Reverend Richard Whitt, his two brothers Abijah Whitt, and Edmund Whitt serving under Captain Thomas Ingles. Hezekiah was allowed to go back down the line and march with his local militia and visit his family for a spell, but he had to return to the front to Lieutenant Israel Lorton because he was under his draft. Hezekiah learned that all was well at Meadow Creek and the crops were out. He also heard that as soon as things calm down the Reverend and the rest of the family were planning on building that sawmill they had put off for years for one reason or another.

Way out front was Major Thomas Mastin and two other spies scouting to insure the Preston army would not be ambushed. Hezekiah wished in a way that he was out in front doing the scouting with his friend Major Thomas Mastin.

From time to time one of the spies ran back and gave a report to Colonel Preston from Major Mastin. The way was clear, but much sign had been discovered.

The forward spies were to shoot Indians on sight if they thought it prudent. Their main mission was to keep the main militia army from being ambushed.

The army stopped for the night, posted guards, and cooked supper. After evening muster Hezekiah headed over to visit with his Paw and brothers. They had a long talk and good visit before Hezekiah went back to his unit. Hezekiah elaborated on the beauty of the lands and waters of the Clinch River. His story telling made all of them

# THE PATRIOT, HEZEKIAH WHITT

want to see this beautiful land that teemed with wildlife and virgin trees. Hezekiah even mentioned giant cedars on the tract he was claiming.

"Son, if you build a cabin out of cedar logs it will last hundreds of years with little upkeep," Reverend Richard exclaimed.

"I know Paw, that is one reason I am so covetous of that wonderful place," answered Hezekiah.

Colonel Preston strolled throughout the entire camp and gave encouragement to all the men. He had a meeting with his company commanders. The men talked up until darkness and the order was given to retire. Hezekiah went back to his company and went to bed on his bedroll he had used for the past two and a half months.

Hezekiah rolled up in his bed roll and talked to his God. He gave thanks, ask for forgiveness for every sin by thought, act, or deed, he asked God to go ahead of the army and protect them from the heathen Indians. He prayed for General Washington, his Governor Patrick Henry, and Colonel Preston. Hezekiah was really worn and tired; before he knew it morning had come.

Lieutenant Israel Lorton addressed his unit after the men had their speedy breakfast, gave them their marching orders, and had a prayer. He reminded the men that Indians were about and to be vigilant against ambush.

Major Thomas Mastin had come in during the night and gave a report to Colonel Preston and was out scouting ahead before daylight. The little army was being watched by the Indians, but they were only spying for the Indians and not strong enough to attack.

Colonel Preston had the men assembled in marching formation and he addressed them.

"Good morning Patriots, I beseech you to put forth your best effort today to get to the fort as quickly as possible. Your countrymen are in harms way and we must get to them before the savages attack. Talk little and be very alert of the eyes in the woods," said Colonel Preston.

Colonel Preston nodded to his company commanders to have the men move out.

Right face, right face, right face, could be heard down the long line. Forward march command was given and the men moved out at a slightly faster pace than yesterday. All the men realized the seriousness of getting to Island Creek Fort.

The men marched twenty two miles that day and were getting close to the fort. Major Thomas Mastin came back and joined Colonel Preston to give a quick report. He informed the Colonel that the fort was surrounded by hundreds of painted Indians. He suggested that the Colonel have the men make a lot of noise and march right to the fort. Colonel Preston had the musicians come to the front and play loud as possible and the men to sing. There was a bagpiper, two fiddlers, a bugler, a fife and one drummer. They all played Yankee Doodle and the men roared the course over and over. Indians had never herd bagpipe or fiddle music! With this combination and the singing it confused the Indians and they moved away from the front of the fort as the army marched right in.

"Damn, I ain't never seen nutten like that," said Captain Thomas Ingles as the strong gates of the fort were closed behind them.

Colonel Preston was greeted by the forts commander, Captain Henry Patton. He gave the Colonel a big hand salute and a big smile.

"So glad to see you sir, that was a grand entrance if I ever saw one, Sir," exclaimed Captain Henry Patton.

"Well it worked, Major Mastin should get the credit for it he thought it up, I thought we may have to fight our way in," answered Colonel Preston in a more somber tone.

After a few days the Indians had to do something, their pride was hurt because they had just sat back and let the white devils walk right in to the fort without firing a shot. The Indians launched an attack with flaming arrows. Some struck the roofs and the settlers merrily knocked the wood slabs off from inside. These roofs were designed in this fashion for such times as these. Some of the fiery arrows struck the palisade walls and were quickly quenched by pouring water down on them.

The Indians saw that this was not working so they gathered together in mass at the front of the fort just out of shooting range. The Indian fighters gathered on the wall and at gun ports mostly on the front side. The Indians come screaming at the fort, many were carrying brush and a couple was carrying torches. A lot of shooting went on and many Indians fell. One of the braves that were carrying a torch fell on top of a couple carrying brush. The three became human torches, and cheers went up inside the gate.

It was the first time Hezekiah lined up his sights on a man. He felt a little sad, but knew that the screaming Indians would not hesitate to kill him. Hezekiah aimed at one of the Indians carrying a torch. He gently squeezed the trigger and the Indians head flew back with such force that it lifted him off his feet. Hezekiah was shocked, thrilled, and bewildered at the sight.

"Hurry and reload, them Injuns are still a coming, Son! "Said an old militiaman crouched beside him.

Hezekiah did not linger on what just occurred, he threw powder down the barrel of his Brown Betz, dropped in a ball and rammed it home. Next he hurriedly primed the pan and was aiming at another charging Indian. Hezekiah let go and the Indian fell. Hezekiah did not reflect on this, but went back to loading in robot fashion and let go again. Another Indian fell as the noise was deafening from all the shots. The fort was engulfed in black powder smoke from all the shooting.

The chiefs from the edge of the woods signaled to the braves. The Chiefs realized that not even the proud Indians could survive such a withering fire. None of the warriors reached the fort, so the chiefs called back the warriors before more would be lost. As the Indians begin to disappear into the woodland, the men in the fort cheered.

Without warning several men ran out of the fort as Colonel Preston screamed for them to return.

"It could be a trap!" he exclaimed.

The Indian fighters had their dandruff up and could not hear anything as they went for the scattered dead and wounded. A few of the fallen Indians were still alive, but not for long. The Indian haters jumped from body to body taking scalps and weapons from the fallen braves. The bodies were hacked, kicked and beaten. Even some of the Indians lost an ear to the horrid mob.

A few shots rang out from the woods; luckily the shots never killed anyone.

Finally an officer ran out and restored order and had the men run back into the gates of the fort.

Hezekiah and the other Whitts did not take part in this desecration. Some of the crazed white-men ask why the Whitts and others did not go out and get their trophies.

"We only stoop to the level of the heathen when we do such horrendous things," stated the Reverend Richard Whitt.

"We are civilized and Christians, not savages," exclaimed Major Thomas Mastin.

As the shameful men came back into the gate Colonel Preston greeted them with stern orders to fall in. He gave them a stern talking to.

"We are not savages, and we are not a mob, he scolded, did you not hear my orders to stay in the fort?" he asked.

The ranks were silent and did not try an answer.

Colonel Preston explained that the Indians often played a trick like this to draw folks out of the fort where they could be dealt with.

The guilty ones had a forlorn look on their faces as a child that just got a spanking. After the bashing of words, the men knew that they were in the wrong, and could have run into an ambush.

Hezekiah took a few minutes to breathe and reflect. He knew that he had done something this day that would change him and stay with him all the days of his life.

The Indians saw what they were up against and divided into small war parties. They moved out into different areas and burned empty cabins, barns, and killed any livestock they could find. After awhile there were only a few Indians about to watch the fort.

Colonel Preston sent out a few spies at night under darkness to see what the Indians were doing. Hezekiah was one that went out into the darkness the second night. He would not come back into the fort until at least an hour after dark. Most every fort had a

THE PATRIOT, HEZEKIAH WHITT

sally port for such an entrance or exit. Hezekiah was scared, but he never showed it. He bolstered his bravery by taking his Lord Jesus Christ with him.

About an hour after dark Hezekiah crept close to the sally port gave an owl's hoot and waited for an answer. About a hundred yards behind him answered another hoot. Finally a hoot came from the sally port and Hezekiah moved slowly and quietly in. The little door of the sally port was closed quietly and Hezekiah was greeted quietly. He immediately went to Colonel Preston and Captain Patton to give his report.

Hezekiah saluted his superiors when he approached.

"Welcome back scout, what is going on out there?" asked Captain Patton.

"Not much Sir, I know of only three Indians spying on us, I could have snuck up on everyone of them," reported Hezekiah.

"Did they see you?" ask Colonel Preston.
"No Sir, but they knowed someone was about," answered Hezekiah.

"What do you think Captain?" ask Colonel Preston.

"Sir, I think in a day or two we will be safe, and maybe Ya-all should head home and see about your family and crops," stated Captain Patton.

Hezekiah was dismissed to go and eat and get some rest.
As he was leaving, Colonel Preston said, "Good job, Whitt!"

"Thank you Sir, just doing my duty," answered the young Hezekiah Whitt.

Colonel Preston had learned Hezekiah Whitt's name because of being around him all the way from Fort Chiswell. Hezekiah had scouted ahead of the militia on the way to Hiawassee also.

Back up in the Ohio Shawnee Towns the younger more spirited Shawnee warriors were becoming more and more agitated. With the British inciting them to war with the Americans, the frontiersmen shooting at every Indian they saw, and not being able to hunt in their old hunting grounds, the young braves were hard to hold back.

Chief Cornstalk was an honorable man and meant to keep his word to the white-man after the battle of Point Pleasant. Even though Cornstalk had given his word to Governor Dunmore and now Dunmore was siding with the British against the Americans, there was a principal. He told his people not to get in the middle of the white-man war.

The British working out of Detroit were sending agents among the Indians and promising them their land back if they would run out the land hungry Americans. They also brought many gifts to their Red Children such as new muskets, powder and ball, combination pipe-hatchet tomahawks, iron pots, looking glasses, beads, blankets and white-mans fire water. The British even promised to go into Cain-tuc-kee and to the great Ridge, (Blue Ridge) with their Indian friends to drive the land hungry Americans back across the mountains. They even promised to take some of the great guns, (cannon) to knock down the American forts.

So you see the deck was stacked against Chief Cornstalk and keeping the peace. For now Cornstalk pleaded with his people to stay out of the white man's war. Already some white scalps were being taken and sold to the British for bounty. The British would buy prisoners, or scalps. The Indians would even take the scalps from babies, children, and women. At first this mischief was hidden from the Great Cornstalk, but as the year of 1777 went along things got worse. The Cherokee brothers from the south were already on the warpath against the Americans. Chief Cornstalk knew in his heart that he was losing control of the younger hotheads, and would have to make a decision soon as to what to do.

Back at Island Creek Fort a few days after the victory, Colonel Preston ordered all the militia that had come to the aid of the fort to march down the river toward home.

Hezekiah asked Lieutenant Israel Lorton if he could go and march home with his Paw and brothers under Captain Thomas Ingles.

"Permission granted, tell the captain I have transferred you over to him and he can discharge you with the rest of his company when he lets them go home," stated Lieutenant Lorton.

Hezekiah gave him a big salute and said, "Thank you sir."

"Thank you Hezekiah Whitt, I know what you did here in defense of the fort," stated Lieutenant Lorton.

Hezekiah smiled and went straight to Captain Thomas Ingles. The Captain was glad to have Hezekiah march back to Meadow Creek with his company.

"Go back and march with your Paw and brothers. I will be calling on you to scout ahead later on," stated Captain Ingles.

"Thanks Sir, I will be ready when you need me," answered Hezekiah as he saluted his captain.

Hezekiah was marching with his Paw and brothers Abijah and Edmund within minutes.

"We herd what you did, little brother, and are mighty proud of you," stated Abijah.

The Reverend Richard and Edmund signaled with a smile. Hezekiah blushed and smiled back.

THE PATRIOT, HEZEKIAH WHITT

Once back to Meadow Creek Captain Ingles discharged his company and walked about shaking every man's hand. He told them to go home and check on their family, catch up with the farm work and be ready for another call up.

"Gentlemen, it is far from over, I have been informed that the Shawnee are crossing over the Ohio River in war parties again, just be ready!" exclaimed Captain Thomas Ingles.

The men shook hands and went to their respective farms.

The Reverend Richard Whitt sighed in prayer, "I pray that our God will be with us in whatever the enemy brings, Amen."

"Amen," sounded Abijah, Hezekiah, and Edmund in unison.

The Tomahawk was a favorite weapon of both the red and the white.

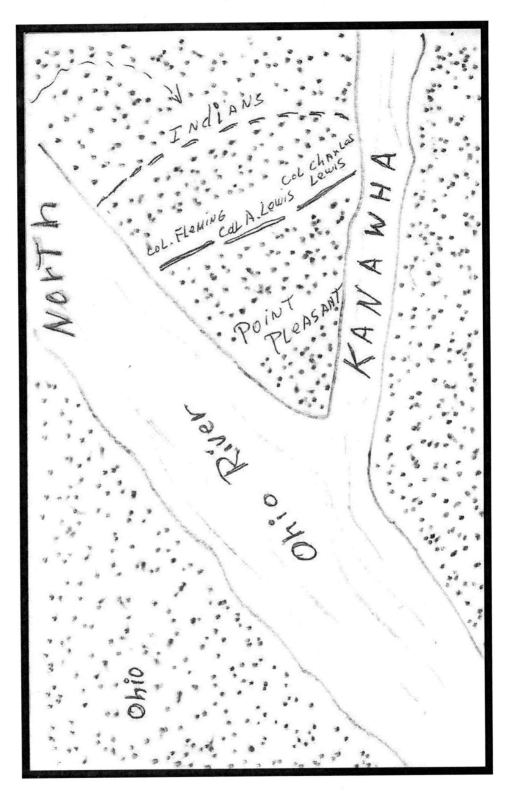

Chapter 9

Murder At The Point

Chief Cornstalk, the principal Chief of the Shawnee, has toiled within himself as to what course to take. Hamilton, the red coat British leader working out of Detroit, was doing a good job of inciting all the Indian factions from New York to Illinois. The Shawnee and Delaware has held back, but with the Wyandot, Mingo, Miami, Ottawa, and Illinois already taking up the hatchet, plus the Cherokee and Creeks from the south, what choice is left for Cornstalk.

Chief Cornstalk talked to every person that he respected great and small, male and female, to gain advice. Cornstalk saw it a lose, lose situation. If he stayed neutral he may even have to fight the British and his red brothers of the other tribes. The British brought many gifts even into the Shawnee towns. The other tribes belittled some of the Shawnee braves, because they were not for another war. Some even called the great Chief Cornstalk a little squaw.

Chief Cornstalk was as brave as any person walking upon the earth. He was also as wise as any person, yet he was caught in a trap between the many factions of the time.

At last he decided to fight with his red brothers if it came to that, but being an honorable man he must go to Fort Randolph at Point Pleasant. He would go to the very spot where the battle was fought three years earlier. The Shemanese (whites) had built a fort on the Virginia (Now West Virginia) side of the Ohio River to keep the Indians on their side of the river. Only thing the Shemanese had crossed over to the Indian side many times and shot at every Indian they saw.

Cornstalk would go and talk to the white chief Captain Arbuckle in the fort. He would explain his stance and give warning that war was coming. Cornstalk was honorable and if he talked to the Captain, surely he would be honorable also. Since the treaty had been broken many times during the past three years in smaller ways, and war was imminent, Cornstalk would give warning to the Shemanese man to man.

Chief Cornstalk conversed with his friend Red Hawk the Chief of a smaller tribe called the Delaware. Red Hawk was a good ally and friend and had respected the decision of the great Chief Cornstalk. Cornstalk asks Red Hawk to travel with him to the fort of the Shemanese. He did not want to take a large force with him to alarm the Shemanese and maybe start an unplanned war.

So on Tuesday, October 7, 1777, Chief Cornstalk, Chief Red Hawk and an unnamed trusted Shawnee brave crossed the waters of the great Ohio River from what is now Gallipolis, Ohio.

THE PATRIOT, HEZEKIAH WHITT

They paddled the single bark-canoe through the cool flat waters on that October day, to the ugly walled wooden fort that marked the spot where so much blood was poured out three years earlier.

The hills were beautiful with the colors of fall. The hues of red, yellow, brown and green painted a picture that no man could duplicate. We can only imagine what thoughts were going through the Chief's head. Was it on the beauty of the day, the past battle and the many slain tribesmen, or more on choosing words to tell the Shemanese Chief, Captain Arbuckle?

Within minutes of the canoe sliding its nose on the Virginia shore, loud voices could be heard.

"Injuns, Injuns, coming up the bank of the Ohio," shouted guards at their posts on the Palisade wall.

"How many?" screamed another voice from deep inside the fort?
"Three, I only see three," shouted the sentry on the wall.
In a minute more a detail of ten armed men ran to meet the two chiefs and the brave. Cornstalk stood straight and brave to greet the whites. He held up his arm as a sign of peace.

"Cornstalk come, talk to white Chief!" Cornstalk said in a grunting broken English dialect.

The armed detail kept their muskets at ready as one of them spoke, "Come on Injuns, I will take you to the Captain."

Chief Cornstalk frowned at the Shemanese and walked stately toward the open gate with Red Hawk and the brave close on his heels.

Chief Cornstalk turned to Red Hawk and spoke lowly in Shawnee, "the Shemanese fear even three brave Indians!"

Red Hawk nodded and smiled in agreement.

Captain Arbuckle stepped out of a large room within the log structure. He put his arm up in a sign of peace to the approaching Indians. As they got close Captain Arbuckle spoke up sarcastically, "What can I do for you gentlemen today?"

Chief Cornstalk answered, "Come talk, White Chief!"

Captain Arbuckle commanded the armed guard to show the Indians into his office and put down their muskets. As the muskets were lowered Chief Cornstalk nodded to Captain Arbuckle in approval.

Captain Arbuckle led the Indians to his office which was a spacious log structure back against the outer wall. Next Captain Arbuckle sat down behind his crude desk. The two chiefs approached with the brave behind them. They stood in front of the desk and were not asked to have a seat.

COLONEL CHARLES DAHNMON WHITT

THE PATRIOT, HEZEKIAH WHITT

"I am Cornstalk," said the chief.
"This Red Hawk," he continued.

"Why did you come here?" Asked Captain Arbuckle?

"Honor, I come talk honor, hard time coming," answered the Chief.

"What do you mean, hard times are coming?" ask Captain Arbuckle.

"Three years go by since talk at camp Charlotte, I gave word to keep peace, stay on our side of Ohio, and not fight Shemanese," stated the great Chief.

"Much water flow since and we have talk treaty, never sign paper, but try to keep treaty, since this you Shemanese have war between you," exclaimed Chief Cornstalk.

"Yes Chief, the Red Coats have bared down on us Americans, we must throw them off so we can be our own nation," explained Captain Arbuckle.

"I come today, Shemanese break treaty too many times; we can not hold back, young braves talk to Red Coats, get much gifts. I no longer want hold them back! We have suffered much from Shemanese, and there is no more treaty, I come to you in honor to tell this you!" stated the great Chief.

Captain Arbuckle rose up and ordered the soldiers to take the three Indians into custody.

"We are at war with the Shawnee again, you three will be my hostages against attack," stated Captain Arbuckle.

The three Indians were surprised but did not try to fight back. Chief Cornstalk thought if he came in honor he would be treated in honor. The Indians looked at each other in amazement and followed the soldiers to a holding cell just on the other side of the office wall. This was a guardhouse for law breakers of the army. The guards released a soldier from the cell and shoved the Indians into the room.

"Shemanese have no honor!" stated Red Hawk.

Chief Cornstalk grunted in agreement.
Captain Arbuckle figured that if he had the big chief, the Indians would not attack Fort Randolph. He ordered that the Indians be treated good and well fed while they were prisoners.

Next day another canoe is paddled across the great Ohio by a single Indian. Since Cornstalk and the others did not return across the river, Elinipsico, the son of Cornstalk came to see about his father.

Elinipsico went through the same drill as the other Indians had the day before. He stood in front of Captain Arbuckle's desk and asks about his father.

THE PATRIOT, HEZEKIAH WHITT

"I come to find my father, since he did not return across the Ohio, I saw his canoe on the bank, where is Chief Cornstalk and Red Hawk?" ask Elinipsico.

"Oh! They are just fine, they are visiting us for a few days," stated Captain Arbuckle.

The guards displayed an evil grin at his words.
"Will you take me to my father?" asked Elinipsico

.

"Sure will, you boys take this fellow back to visit his daddy," stated the Captain.

The soldiers escorted Elinipsico to the guardhouse, opened the door and shoved him in.
"My son, why did you come here?" asked Chief Cornstalk.

"You didn't come back across the Great River, so I came to see about you," answered Elinipsico.

"You should not have come, these dogs have no honor and are holding us hostage!" exclaimed Red Hawk.

"Who can figure out a white man, they make no sense and lie so easily," stated Elinipsico.

"Why do they hold us?" asked Elinipsico without taking a breath.

"Sit down here on this floor and we will reason together," said Chief Cornstalk as he lowered his hand toward the puncheon floor.

As they sat down Elinipsico noticed that the room was very dark. The only light came in from the back wall where two gun ports were located, and they had only one candle burning.

"Do they think we are badgers or groundhogs?" asked Elinipsico.

Cornstalk took out his pipe and filled it with kinnikinnick, took the candle that was handed to him, and lit the aromatic blend. The others waited patiently for their chief to finish.

"Well son we are not ground animals, these white dogs think that our warriors will not attack if they hold us, we must be patient and see what the Great Spirit has in store for us," Chief Cornstalk calmly said.

"Do you know what day this is?" asked Chief Red Hawk.

"Yes brother, I know this day has meaning, three years ago we and the Shemanese struggled here. I think back, if we did this, or if I did that could we have defeated the Shemanese? Would we even be sitting here in the darkness wondering if we will see the sun again, if not for that thing or this thing? The Great Spirit has blessed his red children, and now he may take us to his bosom before we leave here," explained the Great Chief.

COLONEL CHARLES DAHNMON WHITT

THE PATRIOT, HEZEKIAH WHITT

The chief passed around the pipe and each took it and inhaled the soothing smoke. After a few minutes of silence the unnamed, but trusted brave that accompanied the Chiefs spoke up.

"Matchemenetoo, Matchemenetoo, (evil spirit, the devil) Shemanese is full of Matchemenetoo!" stated the brave.

Chief Cornstalk reached over and touched the brave on his knee as he was sitting cross-legged in front of him.

"Be brave, all of you, if the Great Spirit calls us we shall go bravely, are we not Indians?" asked the Great Chief.

The other three nodded their heads in the dim light. Smoked the pipe and took turns telling stories of the good old days, before the Shemanese damaged Mother Earth. Cornstalk told about the days when food was plentiful.

"We hardly done any work at all, we spent much time making new little Indians," laughed Chief Cornstalk.

The other three Indians laughed out loud. The guards outside the door wondered what on earth the Indians could be laughing about in their circumstances.

Chief Cornstalk was doing this to take his brothers minds off their plight. He knew deep down that they may never ride freely on in the grasslands, enjoy a sunset, or even see the sun again.

The cracks of gun shots could be heard across the Kanawha River. The four Indians became silent as they listened intently.

A soldier from the fort just paddled across the Kanawha River and came running to the fort. The gate was opened to receive him. He was one of two men that had gone out early to do some deer hunting. He and his companion were ambushed about a mile from the fort.

"Them Red Devils jumped us just down the river bout a mile, they fired at us and we turned to find cover, John was hit bad, so I took off to get away. After I was a piece off I stopped and looked back. They were hacking on poor John. I took a real good aim and let loose on the one that looked like a chief. The shot knocked him plumb off the ground. They looked at me and here they come. I high-tailed it to the canoe and paddled fast as I could," stated the soldier.

Captain Arbuckle stepped up and ordered a patrol of a dozen soldiers to go out and bring John back and destroy the enemy if possible.

After about two hours passed the men could be heard returning to the fort. They had John's body what was left of it. The whole fort was in an uproar. A mob was formed by the returning soldiers and the other men joined in.

THE PATRIOT, HEZEKIAH WHITT

"Revenge, Revenge," yelled the men as they broke into the part of the fort where the guard house was located.

"Stand and be brave brothers, today we will be with the Great Spirit," exclaimed Chief Cornstalk.

"My son you were sent here to die with your father, rise up and stand bravely," continued Cornstalk.

All four of the Indians rose up and stood bravely as the noise came toward the door. The guards that were outside the door stepped aside as the mob appeared. The door was thrown open and the mob was taken aback for an instant as they witnessed the bravery of the four Shawnee Indians.

Finally the leader of the mob broke the silence by saying, "By Gawd, it is that devil Cornstalk!"

He fired his musket and all the others followed suite, and all four defenseless brave Indians slumped to the floor. Chief Cornstalk had no less than eight lead balls pass through his body. It was simply murder. An honorable man and his tribesmen were killed trying to do an honorable thing and give warning to the whites at Fort Randolph.

As Chief Cornstalk lay with his life's blood pouring out he said in Shawnee: "I was the border man's friend. Many times I have saved him and his people from harm. I never warred with you, but only to protect our wigwams and lands. I refused to join your paleface enemies with the red coats. I came to the fort as your friend and you murdered me. You have murdered by my side, my young son...For this, may the curse of the Great Spirit rest upon this land. May it be blighted by nature. May it even be blighted in its hopes. May the strength of its peoples be paralyzed by the stain of our blood."

Cornstalk spoke his last and gave up the ghost.

By now Captain Arbuckle arrived on the scene, looked around and said, "Damn, Damn, we will have hell to pay now!"

Captain Arbuckle gave orders for the mob to clean up the mess and take the Indians out and bury them. They took Cornstalk and buried him in front of the fort facing both the Ohio and Kanawha Rivers, but they carried Red Hawk, Elinipsico, and the brave to the bank of the Kanawha River and rolled them into the water never to be seen again in this age. Elinipsico left four orphans; most of Red Hawk's and Cornstalk's children were grown.

The Governor, Patrick Henry, had a fit when he heard what had happened. In a moment of vengeance the Shawnee Nation was changed from neutral to a fierce enemy. He ordered an investigation and for the murderers to be punished. He wanted to send a formal apology to the Shawnee nation but didn't think it would help anything.

Point Pleasant, Virginia was many miles from Williamsburg, Virginia and the investigation effort turned out futile, no soldier was ever convicted of the murder of the

THE PATRIOT, HEZEKIAH WHITT

great Chief Cornstalk. Captain Arbuckle was right in his first assessment; the frontier would be aflame for years as the Indians would try to avenge the deaths of Chief Cornstalk, Red Hawk, and Elinipsico! Some folks even say Cornstalk cursed Point Pleasant!

Word traveled fast through the frontier about the murdered Cornstalk. Some of the far distant forts in Kentucky County and northwest Virginia will have to evacuate and head back east. The Virginia Militia will be very busy and the Indian spies will not get much time off as the year with three sevens comes to an end. (1777)

This picture depicts what Cornstalk is thought to look like.

He is my GGGG Grandfather.

COLONEL CHARLES DAHNMON WHITT 75

THE PATRIOT, HEZEKIAH WHITT

Chapter 10

The Shawnees Take up The Hatchet

Thomas Mastin was in shock and ashamed after he heard about the pointless murder of the respected Chief Cornstalk.

"Chief Cornstalk was respected by both Indians and white folks, he was a gifted leader in war and peace, we all could learn from this great man," stated Major Thomas Mastin.

Hezekiah hated the news too. It was pointless and it meant that many people would die. He respected the great chief also, just because of the stories his friend Thomas Mastin had told him.

It was winter in early 1778, and a dread clouded over the frontier as they all knew what the spring would bring.

Up in a place called Valley Forge Pennsylvania, General George Washington has his ragtag Army in winter quarters. They are lacking in materials and especially shoes, but they are not lacking in resolve. Old Ben Franklin found a good Major in France and sent him to Washington under pretence that he is a General. It didn't matter because the Major was a great soldier and teacher. He gathered a few men from each company and gave them intense military training. As these men learned the tactics of the then, modern warfare, they returned to their company and began to teach the rest of the men. The Army gained both training and a new confidence that they would take to the upcoming battles! It was like George had a new United States Army.

Hezekiah Whitt along with most of the frontiersmen was doing what ever farm work they could in this late winter. Hezekiah and his brothers caught a dry spell and plowed up a lot of ground for spring planting. While they were waiting for the actions of spring, they planted potatoes, as they knew they would be busy later on. They decided to do this early, but they took great pains to build up a big hill of each planted potato to guard against freezing. They also did a lot of hunting and wood chopping. This was good therapy as well as being beneficial to the families.

Word reached the frontier that on February 5, 1778 South Carolina was the first State to ratify the "Articles of Confederation." This was a forerunner of the Constitution. It joined the various free and independent States as one Nation to fight off the British. Each state still had its own power to govern and became volunteers in supplying men and money for the war effort. From the very beginning the States wanted the right to be their own country, but saw the need to join for more power in wartime!

On February 6, 1778 England declared war on France and on the same day France recognized the United States as a free and independent Country, and they signed a treaty of aid with this new independent country. This was the very first treaty the United

THE PATRIOT, HEZEKIAH WHITT

States signed. This was really good news for this new struggling country. Not only was it good for the United States, but it was good for France since they were at war with the British.

It seemed like William Skaggs, son of James Skaggs Jr. grew up over night and had mastered the art of wood lore. Hezekiah had taken him hunting and fishing in the pre-war years and noticed that William was very adept at hunting and very stealth at moving through the woods. Actually William was a couple of years older than Hezekiah, but Hezekiah reached his wood lore maturity early. This spring William Skaggs would become an Indian spy with the Virginia Militia. They would need every one that was capable to be the early warning for the frontier farms and forts.

Major Thomas Mastin held weekly meeting with his spies during the winter and early spring of 1778. They would head out toward the west just as soon as the first signs of spring appeared.

Out in western Virginia, Kentucky County, Colonel John Bowman returned with 100 cavalrymen for the defense of the forts. Daniel Boone thought it a good time to take the men from the fort at Boonsboro to Blue Licks to make salt. The Indians should not venture across the Ohio for another month or so, Boone thought. Boone got himself and twenty-seven other men captured, when none other than Chief Blue Jacket (White man turned Indian) and a large party of Shawnee Braves showed up. They caught Boone out by himself leading his horse loaded down with buffalo meat killed for the salt makers. Daniel was somewhat surprised to see a whole army of Indians on this snowy day. Daniel merrily addressed the Indians as they closed in around him on their horses.

"Hello, I'm Daniel Boone, "he announced.

I think Daniel was relying on his reputation to save his life. There is a long story about this, but I will just hit the highlights. Daniel Boone found out that Blue Jacket was taking his Shawnee Braves to Boonsboro to attack. Daniel Boone decided to gamble because he knew the fort would fall to the Indians with most of the men gone. Most of the defense was out here making salt. Daniel Boone struck up a deal with Blue Jacket. Boone told him he would give him twenty-seven men with out loosing one brave, if they would be treated kindly and not be killed or tortured. He made Blue Jacket promise not to make the men run the gauntlet when they reached the Ohio Towns. Blue Jacket agreed. Blue Jacket was elated! He would have 27 prisoners and even Daniel Boone, without firing a shot.

The Indians followed Boone to the Blue Licks where he walked in and told the men not to resist. The Indians came in and took all twenty-seven of the men captive. First thing Blue Jacket did was set up a gauntlet line to make the men run through. Boone "Raised Cane," with Blue Jacket; Blue Jacket laughed and said, "I promised not to make them run the gauntlet when we get to our Ohio towns!"

THE PATRIOT, HEZEKIAH WHITT

The fort at Boonsboro was spared because of Daniel Boone's actions. So you see the Shawnee were not waiting for fair weather, they captured the salt makers with snow on the ground.

George Rogers Clark, a Major in the Virginia Militia, went to Patrick Henry with a bold plan to strike the British holdings in Illinois on the Mississippi River at Kaskaskia. If Clark could strike, surprise and defeat them it would give the United States the west. Clark wanted no less then three hundred and fifty men. Governor Henry liked the plan, but could not furnish any men. He gave Clark the authority to raise an army from the Watauga settlements in Tennessee and the frontier counties of Virginia.

He would gather men at Fort Pitt, go down the Ohio to the Falls at Corn Island and that would be a meeting point. (The Falls of the Ohio is modern day Louisville, Kentucky.) Clark had sent messengers into Kentucky County to spread the word about the need for volunteers. Major Clark and his little Army of a hundred seventy-five (A total of all he raised) would have victories this year. (These men were the cream of the crop) Another hope for Clark was to relieve the pressure of Indian attack in the western counties of Virginia.

As the Dogwoods bloomed, war parties were coming up the Big Sandy River and its tributaries. Some would follow the Tug, some the Louisa, (Levisa fork) while others would come up the Kentucky River. They would cross at different gaps, some used Pound Gap, and some used Cumberland Gap. Some of the Indians used the warriors path that later became the Kentucky Turn Pike that followed Road Ridge to the Clinch Valley at Raven, Virginia. They would infiltrate the Powell valley, the waters of the Clinch and the waters of the Holston. They were all out for revenge to kill, capture, and take scalps. Their red coat friend, General Henry Hamilton, Governor of the British Western Lands in Detroit paid a good price for scalps, and a lot more for live prisoners, plus he gave out many gifts to his red children the Shawnee. The main goal of the Indians was to rid their hunting grounds of the land hungry Shemanese. (White men) The main goal of the British was to defeat their rebellious brothers and reclaim America.

Hezekiah and the other frontiersmen enjoyed the home life, and being with the family. Hezekiah was getting on towards marrying age, but had not met the right girl as yet. He enjoyed being around the fair sex, but had no desire to get hitched to any as yet. Just about every girl he knew was of some kin to him. But in that day it was not uncommon to marry a cousin.

It was time for Hezekiah Whitt and the other Indian spies to head for the west into the waters of the Holston, Clinch, Powell, Levisa and Tug forks of the Big Sandy rivers. Hezekiah was anxious to see his Clinch River and the area later to be called, Baptist Valley. He called his dream farm, "Cedar Grove."

THE PATRIOT, HEZEKIAH WHITT

He did have some dread of the painted Shawnee warriors, but being a Christian he was ready to go if the Lord called him home. Mother Susannah Skaggs Whitt cried every time Hezekiah or his brothers marched off to spy or fight the Indians.

It was the first week of March 1778 that the Indian spies marched west toward the waters of the Holston and Clinch Rivers. It was more or less the same scenario they followed the year before. The new spies learned from the experienced spies. Only thing different was that they may stay out in the wilderness until cold weather showed again. They were set up the same way as before, you spied by yourself, but met your partner every two or three days at a designated place and time. Their main goal was to protect the farms and forts to the east of the Clinch River.

They simply moved about hunting for Indian sign. If they found where Indians had passed or saw any Indians they were to warn the folks to the east. They were not to take on the Indians by themselves, unless cornered. They were to have cold camps and no fires for any reason. The goal of the spies was not to let the Indians know that white men were in the woods.

As the spies moved into the scouting grounds they divided up into smaller groups and subdivided until each spy was by himself. They would meet up with their buddy every two or three days. They were to serve this way until the end of October unless things changed.

William Skaggs was assigned to serve with his spying buddy, Thomas Ray. Hezekiah and others were paired off the same. Most of Major Mastins spies were assigned scouting grounds at the head waters of the Clinch and down river to about Castlewood. William Skaggs and Thomas Ray had the area that extended to the "Big Cane Break" on Big Sandy River. This may have been the "Tug Fork." It was about 30 miles from the head of the Clinch and that would be the Tug Fork. (Present day West Virginia.) They had a rendezvous set up about a mile below the cane break. William and Thomas were set up to meet two other spies and exchange reports. As they traveled toward the rendezvous William saw fresh moccasin tracks in some soft ground. A war party of about 12 Indians were heading toward the east toward the settled areas. They were headed up a buffalo trace that followed a creek that fed the Tug Fork.

William and Thomas Ray changed course and took a route that would bypass the Indians. They would try to reach the cabins and forts before the Indians. Hezekiah was scouting near by and heard the two men running east and went to investigate. Two men running make a different noise than any other critter in the woods. Hezekiah didn't know if it was Indian or white. He got ahead of them and saw it was William Skaggs and Thomas Ray. They gave a quick report to Hezekiah and he ran on ahead as they were about winded after running some ten miles.

It was important that the spies beat the Indians so a defense could be set up. When Hezekiah reached the little settlement about an hour ahead of William and Thomas, he found out that the Indians had struck an isolated cabin or two, but had not done much damage. The Indians had caught one man out about a quarter of a mile from his cabin and gave chase. The man had his musket as was the rule, so he ran toward home, stopped and fired at the Indians killing the one in the lead. The Indians paused for an instant and ran after him again. The Indians fired several shots but none found their target. The man would stop and aim his empty gun at his pursuers and they would instinctively jump and dart off the trail and seek cover. The man gained a little ground each time. The man made it to the cabin where his oldest son held open the door for him and held a loaded Brown Betz. The man took the musket and took aim at the scrambling redskins and let loose. Another Indian fell.

Most likely the Indian's shots missed because of their shooting habits. They always loaded light to save powder, and they didn't squeeze the trigger, they jerked the trigger. Most Indians never became marksmen the caliber of the frontiersmen because of this. Some frontiersmen learned to load on the run; Lewis Wetzel, Simon Kenton and Daniel Boone are the only ones I know about. Think about it, pouring powder down the four feet plus barrel, dropping a ball, pulling the ram rod and ramming the ball home, and then you had to prime the flash pan, cock, and aim. They did all this while running, except the aiming part. Far as I know no Indian mastered this. It would not surprise me to learn that some of the Indian spies with the militia developed this skill.

The settlers gathered in the little fort at Elk Garden, near modern day Lebanon, Virginia. The Indians moved on to easier pickings!

In the spring of 1778 this happened many times. The spies gave an important service as an early warning, but did not detect every war party. Almost all the tribes in the Ohio country had warriors on the prowl. Many people were killed and a lot of women and kids were carried off to be adopted. When an Indian was killed the family would seek to replace them with a captive. Many young whites adapted to this way of life after being adopted. The white boys learned to love the Indian ways! Indian boys had a free spirit and did the hunting and fishing. The Indian women did ninety percent of the work.

After things died down around Elk Garden, Hezekiah Whitt, William Skaggs and Thomas Ray headed back toward their scouting grounds. After a day or two they were almost back to their scouting grounds. Hezekiah Whitt's scouting partner, Paul Shaver, was undoubtedly wondering what in the world happened to Hezekiah. All he could do was show up at the rendezvous.

Hezekiah decided to cross the Clinch and scout up his beloved Indian Creek as it was part of his assigned scouting grounds. He had not had a chance to check on his Cedar Grove since he left Meadow Creek. Hezekiah did not walk the Indian paths as part of his training. He was walking through the woods on the ridge above Indian Creek so he could observe the trail and have a wider margin of view.

Hezekiah moved slowly and stopped to look and listen every little bit. Hezekiah heard something slightly behind him down on the trail. He froze and turned only his head enough to see the trail slightly behind him. There on the trail was three Indians heading up Indian Creek. They were moving fast but very cautiously. They seemed to be on the way back toward the Tug Fork, most likely to the waters of the Ohio. Hezekiah did not move and the three Indians soon were out of sight.

It was standing orders not to take on the Indians by your self, only to observe. Hezekiah noticed that they were not wearing the devilish paint of war and the last Indian in line walked with a limp. The Indians stopped every now and then and looked all around, mostly behind to see if they may have pursuers on their trail. One looked right at Hezekiah, but he was not able to pick him out from the surroundings. Being perfectly still and wearing the flat black colored buckskins was like camouflage. Hezekiah could take a breath again. He sat down to watch. There may be more warriors coming from the east or those three could double back. Hezekiah waited until almost dark and found himself a rock house, (over hanging cliff that made a good place to sleep and rest in.) to spend the night in. He carefully raked the leaves about to uncover any varmints or snakes.

Hezekiah had a restless night after seeing the Indians so close by. A little fear is good for an Indian spy, because it makes him cautious and more in tune with his surroundings.

Hezekiah was to scout his beloved tract of land that he hoped to own some day, and then the evening of the next day, he was to rendezvous with William Skaggs, Thomas Ray, and Paul Shaver across the ridges near the "Big Cane Break." It was the same rendezvous as the last. Hezekiah would have to move a little quicker today and tomorrow to make the twenty or so miles.

Hezekiah moved around the ridges overlooking his dream farm. He took in the beauty as he slowly moved his head about creating a panoramic view. He could see the old lean-to that he had built from cedar branches a year earlier. It didn't seem to have been disturbed. Hezekiah slowly made his way off the ridge and headed to the good limestone spring in the little valley. Hezekiah looked round about one more time before getting down to get his water. He filled his canteen again after drinking his fill.

Hezekiah headed up a hollow that is now the road to Bandy, Virginia and began crossing the ridges towards the Tug Fork. Hezekiah traveled about fourteen miles this day and would meet his friends tomorrow evening, God willing. He watched closely for signs, but moved faster than usual on a mission. He followed the tracks of the three Indians for a way, hoping that the other spies were not discovered. The Indians thought that white men could not be as savvy in the woods as they.

After a better night of sleep under another rock cliff, Hezekiah headed to the rendezvous. That evening around 6 PM the four men converged to the little clearing and greeted each other with a firm handshake. They patted each others shoulders while displaying big smiles. They got close so that the whispering could be heard; they dared not speak out loud this deep in the scouting grounds.

THE PATRIOT, HEZEKIAH WHITT

Paul Shaver was especially happy to see his friends because they all had disappeared from the area. They explained about the Indians. Paul also saw the three Indians heading toward the Tug Fork, he revealed.

The four set up another time and place to meet in four days. This time they would meet at the mouth of Indian Creek. (Now, modern day Cedar Bluff, VA.)

On the fourth day they converged on the Clinch at the mouth of Indian Creek and Major Thomas Mastin was with Hezekiah Whitt.

The spies were lean and in need of some good hot nourishing food, so the Major ordered them back toward Rocky Gap and on home to Meadow Creek for a rest. The Major would send another group of spies out to the edge of the scouting ground, while his best spies went home for a month of rest with their families.

Hezekiah was famished and ready to eat when he arrived at the Reverend Richard Whitt log house. Mother Susannah saw him coming and ran out to embrace him. She cried great tears of joy as the rest of the family made their way to meet Hezekiah.

"You are skinny as a whippoorwill," stated mother Susannah as she gave him a big smile.

The Reverend was praying a prayer of thanksgiving as he reached his son. The whole family had a group hugging session and poor Hezekiah could not get into the house.

"I love all of you too, but let me in the house and feed me some vittles," said Hezekiah.

Mother Susannah joyously led her son into the big log house, and had him sit at the table while everyone hovered around him. The house was filled with love as shown by the smiles and clatter of the family.

It had not been too long since the family ate dinner, so Susannah had leftovers warming. The whole family gathered around Hezekiah as he enjoyed his cooked and warm meal of meat, potatoes, and early vegetables from the garden. In between bites Hezekiah told of his spying adventure and the Whitts told him of the news from the east about the war. Mother Susannah sat beside him and kept patting him to make sure he was really home. It was a grand homecoming, but everyone knew that it would be short lived.

All the frontier families had to take extra precautions just to work the fields and be out anywhere. They carried their muskets wherever they went. They kept them near by while working the fields or even going to get water or wood. They were the forerunners of the Boy Scout Motto, "Be Prepared."

During this time every family tried to keep a normal routine, but it was very hard. Some families spent the entire summer closed up in one of the little frontier forts. When outside work was being done someone was charged with being on watch with a loaded musket.

The Reverend Richard Whitt continued holding worship services, but everyone carried a musket or pistol to and from church. Many prayers went up in these services, not only

THE PATRIOT, HEZEKIAH WHITT

for thanksgiving and for salvation, but for the free and independent State of Virginia. They prayed for the fighting men trying to beat back the British and Indians. They prayed for protection and kept the blessed hope, just in case they were called home.

The spies of Major Thomas Mastin enjoyed their time at home with family and friends, but were on call. They were basically minute men, ready to run out with a musket and short time provisions in a minutes notice. All through the frontier these men ran out many times to combat the Indians that went about committing atrocities.

A lot of the men from the Meadow Creek area, including Abijah and Edmund Whitt had served off and on down the New River and even southwest on the Holston. Hezekiah didn't have to go deep into the scouting grounds the rest of the year. He went out several times for a short scout and brought home some elk or deer meat.

Finally the worst times of 1778 came to an end around the last of October. The Whitt family had worked together and had a bountiful crop. The girls had been a factor; they really pitched in during these trying times. It was not uncommon to see the bonnets and long sleeved dresses moving about in the fields. Mostly they did the hoeing and gathering, but many women mastered the hard work of plowing behind a team of oxen or mules. The ladies of that day did not want to have a tanned skin; that is why they wore long dresses with long sleeves. They also wore the big bonnets to shade their pale faces. Only part that got tanned was their hands and some wore gloves. They were actually cooler dressed this way as their clothes were light in color.

After November and the cold winds of winter came, the Indian threat subsided. The folks in the frontier could breathe a little easier, but they still kept up their guard! The winter months would give them time to make repairs and plan another farming season in the spring. Also the families could socialize with each other. They could have some corn shuckings, quilting parties, and the men would help each other work the tobacco. Sometimes a few fellows would get together to make a little moonshine and do a little sampling.

All the Indian Spies would also make repairs on their muskets and gear for another season in the wilderness. Many of the frontiersmen were fine gunsmiths.

Something had to be done about the Cherokee and Creeks from the south; they were reaching further into the settled areas of the "Old Dominion," which had become the nickname of Virginia. The following spring would bring the same trouble and fears to the frontier. The Spies would be out in the spring of 1779 in the spying grounds both west and south.

With the French on our side and a better trained army, General George Washington will give the British fits, and on the frontier the settlers will take the war to the Indians for a change.

Chapter 11

Hezekiah's Heart Is Captured

The spring was coming and giving hope in this new year of 1779.

The Indian spies would head to the head waters of the Clinch again, if all was well they would start south on that river and meet up with many other militiamen. Colonel Shelby under the authority of Colonel Preston had planned an offensive action on the Indians on the south side of the Tennessee River.

Major Mastin with many men this time, would meet up with other groups of militia on the way down the river. This time William Skaggs was budded up with Hezekiah and after a quick scout into the scouting grounds they would head down the river. After they met up with other militia they would ride the river on rafts being built by Colonel Shelby's militia. The Clinch would be deeper and better navigated that far south.

Hezekiah had been at the edge of the Tennessee country two years ago when they went to the relief of the Island Creek Fort. William Skaggs had not been that far south yet, so it would be an adventure for both young men. Hezekiah could not but think of the three Indian warriors he laid to rest on that mission. William Skaggs knew about it though, through the stories told around the militia campfires.

Hezekiah confided in him about the experience, after much prodding from William. He told William that it was nothing to brag about, that it was sad that he had to end the life of three human beings, even in war.

"Do you think I will have to kill an Indian?" asked William Skaggs.

"Well the odds are we will be in a scrap with them, after all that is why the Colonel has ordered us to go down there," replied Hezekiah.

"What's it like to be in battle?" asked William.

"It's scary, thrilling, and not fun, you know that you are putting your life on the line when the Indians come screaming at you, you just have to do your duty," explained Hezekiah

"You will be alright, you just fight with the rest of your friends, keep your head down, and remember that you are a better shot than most of the red skins," stated Hezekiah trying to ease William Skaggs mind.

Down near present day Saint Paul on the Clinch, Major Thomas Mastin's little army met up with more Militia. They had several log rafts prepared for the journey. Their next rendezvous would be with Colonel Campbell's militia. They came over from the Holston with his army. Edmund and Abijah Whitt were with them under Captain Thomas Ingles. This was a mighty force of crack-shot militiamen assembled to take the war to the Cherokee Indians at their village called "Chickemaugy." This was a principal village of the Cherokee Indians just south of the Little Tennessee River.

THE PATRIOT, HEZEKIAH WHITT

The militia was well organized on this mission. They were to keep down noise and move as swiftly as possible. They were going to try and surprise the village, even though they knew some Indians would escape because of their spy system.

Everything worked for the militia; the Indians were just starting to move out when the militia encircled "Chickemaugy." The Indians broke through the east side and headed for the mountains. (Great Smokey Mountains)

The Indians were trying to escape to the south, west, and north also but the militia had those avenues of escape closed. The only way out for the Cherokee was to the east and they had to fight through a thin line of militiamen to do that. Many Indians were killed or captured.

The militiamen even rescued some whites that had been held by the Indians. The rescued whites were very afraid of the militiamen at first.

As soon as the shooting slowed down the militia set fire to the lodges, gathered all the horses, and tore down anything standing. They gathered all the captured Indians into a group and made them sit together with guards all around them.

Details went out into the corn fields and cut down the corn and destroyed all the crops. They thrashed through the squash and pumpkin vines. They piled up the cornstalks and tried to burn them, but the stalks were too green. Militiamen drug the downed corn shocks to the river and threw them in. The idea was to get rid of all the food so that the Indians would either starve or spend all their time food hunting instead of attacking the settlements.

A Captain Bean proposed that a party of militia go after the retreating Indians. Some thirty men, including William Skaggs, joined Bean and they took off with haste toward the eastern mountains. They followed the Indians east for awhile and turned north following the many tracks that the Indians left. The Bean party crossed some of the Cumberland Mountains and surprised them at an encampment. They attacked with all the fierceness thirty men could muster. The Indians scattered again after many fell to the well aimed shots of the militiamen.

More Indians were captured, including three boys and one girl, and a beautiful Indian maiden. William Skaggs captured them all together where they were trying to hide. He took charge of them and they were his trophy to take back. The three Indian boys were full of spunk and tried to fight William, but he subdued them and calmed them down with some food he gave them. William made sure the captives knew he meant them no harm.

Back at the main village the white hostages that had been adopted by the Indians were interviewed by the officers to find out whom they were and how long the Indians had held them. Many of the adopted were now Indians, at least in their minds.

One of the men looked really familiar to Abijah Whitt, so he went and got Edmund Whitt to come and look at him.

THE PATRIOT, HEZEKIAH WHITT

The man looked back at the Whitt brothers intently for a long minute.

The man that looked more Indian than white spoke in perfect English saying, "Hello brothers Abijah and Edmund!"

"Damnation, Robert is that you?" blurted Abijah.

"How is Maw and Paw, and the rest of the family?" Robert asked.
Abijah and Edmund ran and embraced their long lost brother. All three of the men wept with joy.
"We have a bunch of catching up to do, Maw and Paw are just fine, brother Hezekiah is here somewhere, he will just die when he sees you," answered Abijah.

Major Thomas Mastin had Hezekiah out scouting the grounds to the south and west of the Cherokee Town. And he had not seen Robert as yet.

"What took you so long to come after me?" asked Robert.

"We thought you fell in the river and drown, we searched for days, but could not find you! It just about broke Maw and Paw's hearts. We had a funeral and everything," stated Abijah.

"The Creeks (Indians) took me and paddled swiftly down the New River, and then they traded me to the Cherokee for a horse," stated Robert Whitt. Robert was the oldest son of the Reverend Richard Whitt Family.

"You would think I would be worth more than a bay mare!" said Robert.

Abijah and Edmund smiled.

Robert Whitt spoke in a somber tone as another tear rolled down his tanned cheek. He looked to be in good health, but all Indian. He wore a breach cloth and buckskin chaps and sleeveless shirt. They were decorated with beads as was his moccasins. His face and arms were tan and with his long hair, Robert looked every bit an Indian.

Back across the Cumberland Mountains, Captain Bean marched his militia and the prisoners toward the northwest to a creek that flowed into the Powell River. They set up camp here to wait for the main army to return from the south. Bean posted guards, sent out spies to scout out the area, and sent hunters to get meat.

They had brought back about a dozen hostages, all squaws and children counting the three boys, one girl and the Indian Maiden that William Skaggs captured. Many of the men eyed the beautiful Indian Maiden, but dared not brother her.

Back at "Chickemaugy", the army had broke camp, and were heading back with the freed whites, the Indian prisoners, and what plunder they had captured.

Hezekiah Whitt had got back last evening and spent many hours with his long lost brother Robert Whitt and of course Abijah and Edmund Whitt.

THE PATRIOT, HEZEKIAH WHITT

The Reverend Richard and Susannah will be so happy to see Robert, but they had never given up that Robert was alive. It was a feeling, that faith and praying for Robert, had given them. Every night they both prayed earnestly for Robert.

Robert Whitt would make a splendid Indian spy, but would not be given a chance for now. The militia did not fully trust the rescued whites, at least until they got back further north. Some of the whites had lived as Indians for many years and who knew what they might do.

Finally, the main army reached Captain Bean's camp and was pleased to see the other hostages and plunder they had captured. Captain Bean gave a report to Colonel Preston and the other officers at a meeting.

Colonel Preston was pleased with the mission and accomplishments. Colonels Campbell and Severe had done a fine job getting their militia in place at the onset. Captain James Campbell's Militia played a big part as well. They were out of Washington County, Virginia.

"Gentlemen, we have given the heathen a black eye and they should be quiet for a time," stated Colonel Preston.

"With all the reports in, stating our scarcity of provisions I am going to order disbandment of the main army, I will rely on each officer to get his men and prisoners back to their respective homes. The militiamen will get their discharge from their commanding officer. The rescued whites will go with which ever militia that is close to their homes. The captives will be the property of whoever captured them. We may need some for a prisoner exchange someday. You have permission to adopt some, if you think it prudent, but do it legally at the courthouse.

So the next morning, Major Thomas Mastin took charge of the Meadow Creek Militia with Captain Ingles second in command. After marching northeast for a day they crossed the Clinch and continued on toward the Holston. A few spies were sent ahead and back, but no fresh Indian sign was found.

At night much visiting took place around the campfires. The hunters had good luck so the men ate pretty well on elk, venison, and small game. They just didn't have many vegetables other than wild greens that some of the men picked.

Hezekiah, Abijah, Edmund, and Robert Whitt visited every chance they got. Sometimes cousin William Skaggs and even Major Thomas Mastin would sit around the campfire with the Whitts. The four children and lovely Indian maiden would be wherever William Skaggs was.

The Indian maiden had captured Hezekiah's attention. She had a great smile for Hezekiah when she looked his way. He never felt this way about a woman before. This woman was the enemy, what was he thinking? It didn't matter he was twitter-patted any time they were close, but he never let on.

THE PATRIOT, HEZEKIAH WHITT

Thomas Mastin was able to carry on a conversation in the Shawnee and Cherokee tongue. One evening he was flabbergasted to find out that the Indian maiden was the daughter of Chief Cornstalk and the four children were the orphans of Ellinipisco, Chief Cornstalk's murdered son.

"What are your names?" ask Thomas Mastin.

Each child answered by saying their name "Outhowwa Shokka," "Low Hawk," "Mountain Raven," and "Thomas."

The beautiful Indian maiden spoke next, "I am Rachel."

Hezekiah Whitt made note of this, but said nothing.

"How on earth did you all end up down here in the Tennessee county?" asked Major Thomas Mastin.

"After my father, the great Chief Cornstalk, was murdered at the point, my sister Greenbrier took me and my brother's children in for a while. She lives on the rising sun side of the Ohio River with her husband Reuben Kinnison. With all of the fighting, Greenbrier sent me and the children to the south for our safety. A party of Shawnee was going to visit our brothers the Cherokee and agreed to take us. We did not expect the Shemanese to attack Chickemaugy Town," stated Rachel.

"It was a bad thing that happened at Point Pleasant, you probably don't remember me living with your people, but I was treated good after I proved myself by running the gauntlet. Your father treated me good and I found him to be an honorable man. I was saddened greatly by the news of the senseless act of the soldiers." stated Major Thomas Mastin.

"What will become of me and the children?" asked Rachel.

"I am not sure, you all will either be adopted by some families or be used in a prisoner exchange," said The Major.

"It is a sad thing that our peoples can not live in peace!" exclaimed Rachel in good English.

Those sitting around the fire were greatly surprised by her good English, but none said anything.

"Yes it is, I am so sorry about your father and brother, I am inclined to adopt you and the children, if William Skaggs does not, but for now we will just have to wait and see," explained Major Mastin.

"I am not sure about anything right now," inserted William Skaggs.

THE PATRIOT, HEZEKIAH WHITT

Abijah asked Robert to tell about his time with the Indians. All became quiet as Robert moved about on the log he was sitting on to become more comfortable. Abijah and the others filled their pipes and lit up as they relaxed to listen to Robert.

"Well, as I said I was out by the river (New River) aiming to do a little fishing when I was surprised by four Creek Indians that had been way up the river out of their usual southlands. I first thought they were Shawnee, but they were different in dress and looks. They all had long hair and no part of their head was shaved as the Shawnee often do. They were pretty rough with me so I submitted as I was so overwhelmed. They took me down river about a quarter mile and put me in the long canoe. It was late in the afternoon and they really paddled hard to get out of the area.

In a few days we were at the Chickemaugy Town. The Cherokee came and greeted the Creeks and eyed me closely. They talked for awhile and one of the Cherokee brought out a bay mare for the Creeks to inspect. They came to an agreement and I was shoved to the ground in front of the Cherokee.

The Cherokee Chief gave a command and a long gauntlet was formed by every Indian that was big enough to swing a switch or club. They formed two lines shoulder to shoulder with just enough room for me to run through. I was to run through and if I made it to the end of the line I would not have to run again. There was much excitement and noise as they got ready. I was stripped down naked and without warning I was shoved down to the ground in front of the first few club wielding Indians. I thought they were going to kill me before I could get up and make my run. I prayed for Jesus to help me to the end, and I took off. After awhile I was numb and the beating clubs and switches lost their sting. Somehow, I guess with God's help I made it to the end of the line. I was black and blue and mighty red. I had little streams of blood oozing out all over me. The squaws used my privates as their number one target. They laughed so hard when they hit the bull's eye. I wondered if I would still be a man after this.

The Indians young and old cheered for me when I made it all the way to the end. They counted me as brave, heck I was just glad to make it. I was taken to a lodge and cared for by three squaws. They made some kind of green paste and rubbed me all over. It sure took away the pain. I must have passed the test to be adopted. After a couple of weeks my scabs came off and I was taken to the river with a number of Squaws and stripped. They took me out in the river, (Little Tennessee River) and rubbed me with sand until I was red as a redbird. They laughed and chattered and finally let me out of the river. They gave me a loin cloth and laughed in merriment as I put the thing on.

One of the squaws said that I was Indian now; I had all my white skin washed off. As time went on I became trusted and was allowed to go on hunts and fishing trips. They brought me out a musket and we had a shooting match. I beat every one of them and I thought I might be in trouble again, but they honored me for my shooting ability. I was afraid that I would have to go on a raid against my people, but that never happened. I figured that in time I would have to go to war against my people, thank God you come and got me. All in all I was treated well after the onset, and was accepted as an Indian.

COLONEL CHARLES DAHNMON WHITT

THE PATRIOT, HEZEKIAH WHITT

They named me "Metequa," it means musket; I reckon it meant I was good with a musket. I felt honored to have that name. I kept my faith in God and lived each day that God gave me, hoping for a chance to escape," explained Robert Whitt.

The twenty four year old Robert Whitt would need time and a lot of love to get back in the groove as a white man. He would never be the same, but the experience was not all bad. He did not tell everything about his Indian life. We don't know if he took a wife or ever fired upon the white man. Some things are better not to be known.

After Robert talked those closest to him reached out and gave him a pat.

"After talking with you I am forming a trust of you. After you get settled in at Meadow Creek I will talk to you about becoming an Indian Spy," said Major Thomas Mastin.

"I would like that; I could make up lost time as a defender for my country, the free and independent State of Virginia," stated Robert Whitt.

"How did you know about that?" asked Hezekiah.

"Oh you would be surprised what the Indians know, you know they get regular visits from the red coats don't you?" answered Robert, "They call each state a fire, so they are fighting the thirteen fires."

After Robert's discussion, Hezekiah changed the subject by addressing Rachel directly for the first time. He looked at Rachel and had trouble speaking.

"Rachel, how did you learn to speak English so good?" asked Hezekiah.

Rachel turned and looked into Hezekiah's soft gray eyes. Her beautiful black eyes danced with a sparkle of excitement demonstrating a whole-other language that only a young woman can do.

Hezekiah melted down as Rachel spoke directly to him.

"I have heard the English tongue all my life as well as Shawnee, also being around my sister Greenbrier that married a white man. My people, the Shawnee have had many Shemanese visitors, and have adopted many as their own. As I grew up I played with white children and we learned from each other," explained Rachel.

Chapter 12

New Friends, A reunion, Securing Religious Freedom

To start this chapter I thought I would like to emphasize the importance of Christian Religion in these early days by including a bill written in 1779 and later introduced to the Virginia General Assemble by Thomas Jefferson. It became law on January 16, 1786. It is puzzlement to me why it took so long to become law.

Section I

Well aware that the opinions and belief of men depend not on their own will, but follow involuntarily the evidence proposed to their minds; that Almighty God hath created the mind free, and manifested his supreme will that free it shall remain by making it altogether insusceptible of restraint; that all attempts to influence it by temporal punishments, or burthens, or by civil incapacitations, tend only to beget habits of hypocrisy and meanness, and are a departure of the plan of the holy author of our religion, who being lord both of body and mind, yet chose not *to propagate it* by *coercions on either, as was in his Almighty power to do, but to extend it by its influence on reason alone; that* the impious presumption of legislators and rulers, civil as well as *ecclesiastical, who, bring themselves but fallible and uninspired men, have assumed dominion over the faith of others, setting up their opinions and modes of thinking* as *the only true and infallible, and as such endeavoring to impose them on others, hath established and maintained false religions over the greatest part of the world and through all time: That to compel a man to furnish contributions of money for the propagation of opinions which he disbelieves and abhors, is sinful and tyrannical; that even the forcing him to support this or that teacher of his own religious persuasion, is depriving him of the comfortable liberty* of giving his contributions to particular pastor whose morals he *would make his pattern, and whose powers he feels most persuasive to righteousness; and is withdrawing from the ministry those temporary rewards, which proceeding from an approbation of their personal conduct, are an additional incitement to earnest and unremitting labors for the instruction of mankind; that our civil rights have no dependence on our religious opinions, any more than our opinions in physics or geometry; that therefore the proscribing any citizen as unworthy the public confidence by laying upon him an incapacity of being called to offices of trust and emolument, unless he profess or renounce this or that religious opinion, is depriving him injuriously of those privileges and advantages to which, in common with his fellow citizens, he has a natural right; that it tends also to corrupt the principles of that very religion* it *is meant to encourage, by bribing, with a monopoly of worldly* honors and emoluments, those who will externally profess and *conform to it; that through indeed these are criminal who do not withstand such temptation, yet neither are those innocent who lay* the bait in their way; *that the opinions of men are not the object of civil government, nor under its jurisdiction; that to suffer the civil magistrate to intrude his powers into the field of opinion and to restrain the profession or propagation of principals on supposition of their ill tendency is a dangerous fallacy, which at once destroys all religious liberty, because he being of course judge of that tendency will make his opinions the rule of judgment, and approve or condemn the sentiments of others only as they shall acquire with or differ from his own; that it is time enough for the rightful purpose of civil government for its officers to interfere when principals break out into overt acts peace and good order; and finally, that truth is great and will prevail if left to herself; that she is the proper and sufficient antagonist to error, and has nothing to fear from the conflict unless by human interposition disarmed of her natural weapons, free to argument and debate; errors ceasing to be dangerous when it is permitted freely to contradict them.*

Section II

We the General Assembly of Virginia do enact that no man shall be compelled to frequent or support any religious worship, place, or ministry whatsoever, nor shall otherwise suffer, on account of his religious opinions or belief; but that all men shall be free to profess, and by argument to maintain, their opinions in matters of religion, and that the same shall in no wise diminish, enlarge, or affect their civil capacities.

Section III

And though we well know that this Assembly, elected by the people for the ordinary purposes of legislation only, have no power to restrain the acts of succeeding Assemblies, constituted with powers equal to our own, and that therefore to declare this act irrevocable would be of no effect in law; yet we are free to declare, and do declare, that the rights hereby asserted are of the natural rights of mankind, and that if any act shall be hereafter passed to repeal the present or to narrow its operation, such act will be an infringement of natural right.

Thomas Jefferson was really proud of this bill that became law in the free and independent State of Virginia. Jefferson had many accomplishments to be proud of, like being the third President of the United States, The Louisiana Purchase, The Lewis and Clark expedition, the National Road and many other things, but writing this bill was his most cherished accomplishment, even above the Decoration of American Independence he authored. He was so proud of this because it was for the people and that was the conscience of the common people of Virginia. Many people came to America for this purpose, the right to worship as they believed and they believed in Christ.

As the little company of militiamen under Major Thomas Mastin journeyed toward Meadow Creek they took time each night to have a brief worship service with prayer and scripture reading. This was an awakening for the Indian captives and even for Robert Whitt. Rachel, the beautiful Indian Princess, was especially interested in the Christian Faith when she heard that Jesus rose from the dead and promised that all who accepted Him as Savior would likewise be resurrected.

Next day as Rachel walked along, Hezekiah just happened to be walking close by.

THE PATRIOT, HEZEKIAH WHITT

"Hea-Kiah, do you think that Jesus was not plumb dead, He may have just been hurt bad and come too," stated Rachel right out of the blue.

"Hezekiah, He-ze-kiah, that is how you say my name, and no Jesus was not just hurt bad, He was dead, He really rose from the dead just like Lazarus," stated Hezekiah.

"He-ze-kiah," said Rachel with a wide smile showing her beautiful white teeth.
"That's it you got it right!" exclaimed Hezekiah smiling back at Rachel.
"How do you know Jesus was plumb dead and who is Lazus?" asked Rachel.
"That's Laz-ar-us, he was a friend of Jesus and he had been buried for three days and Jesus raised him up to life," explained Hezekiah.

"How you know bout all this?" ask Rachel innocently.

"It is in the Bible and it is also by faith, I will show you in the Bible tonight if you like," said Hezekiah.

As they continued walking up the New River Valley, Rachel practiced saying, "He-ze-kiah and La-ar-us."

"That's right, you are pronouncing it right now," said Hezekiah.

That night after supper Rachel sat beside Hezekiah and said, "Read to me from the By-bul."

"Bible," said Hezekiah as he got out his Bible and opened it.

William Skaggs and the four Indian children sat with anxious ears to hear the reading, as did Brother Robert Whitt. Abijah and Edmund sat back as Hezekiah witnessed with the word of God.

First Hezekiah turned to Luke 19 and read starting at verse 31.

31. Then he took unto him the twelve and said unto them, Behold, we go up to Jerusalem, and all things that are written will be accomplished.

32. *For he shall be delivered unto the Gentiles, and shall be mocked. And spitefully entreated, and spited on:*
33. *And they shall scourge him, and put him to death: and the third day he shall rise again.*

Hezekiah closed the Bible and looked at Rachel. She looked back with expectant eyes.

"Who was he talking to, what does it mean the twelve?" asked Rachel.

"He was talking to his chosen students called disciples, they was twelve of them," answered Hezekiah.

Hezekiah took a stick and made 12 marks in the dirt. Rachel nodded in understanding.

THE PATRIOT, HEZEKIAH WHITT

"Who are the Gen-tulls that got Jesus?" asked Rachel.

"That would be us, all peoples that are not Jews like Jesus was Gentiles," explained Hezekiah.

"Why would we mock and spit on Jesus?" asked Rachel.

"Because he said so and if we were there we would not believe on him then," explained Hezekiah.

"What is scourge?" asked Rachel.

"That is whipping kinda, like the gauntlet only you are tied so you can't run, they just about beat you to death with skin-rope (leather) holding iron at the ends to tear the meat," explained Hezekiah.

With tears in her big round brown doe-eyes, Rachel asked, "Why did we do him like that?"

"Jesus loved us so much he gave Himself as a sacrifice for our sin so we could come back from death and live with him in Heaven," explained Hezekiah.

"You said they would put Him to death and He would rise the third day, did this happen?" ask Rachel.

"Sure did, many people saw him on the cross and also saw his limp body after they took Him down from the cross, and yes He was plumb dead Rachel," said Hezekiah.

"What is this cross he was on?" asked Rachel.

"It was a cut tree with a short tree fastened crossways. They stretched Jesus arms out and drove iron spikes through each hand and in his feet. He hung there about three hours before he died, then they stuck a spear in His side to make sure He was plumb dead!" exclaimed Hezekiah.

"If he was God why didn't he just kill all the Gen-talls?" asked Rachel.

"If He done that we could not rise again and we could not go to live with Him, He stayed on the cross because He loves us that much." explained Hezekiah.

The children, Rachel, William Skaggs, and others were moved with the Holy Spirit. William Skaggs was feeling the spirit as he heard that still small voice, but he was not ready to surrender. He got up and walked away.

"What must I do to get to rise again?" asked Rachel in a somber tone.

"Do you believe that Jesus rose again, and do you believe he hears you when you speak to Him in prayer?" asked Hezekiah.

COLONEL CHARLES DAHNMON WHITT

THE PATRIOT, HEZEKIAH WHITT

"I do, what must I do to be saved?" asked Rachel speaking for the little group.

"You have done the first part by believing, the second part is to accept Jesus as your Savior and let Him move into your heart, then you will rise again," said Hezekiah.

"I want this," said Rachel.

"Me too!" exclaimed two of the children.

Robert recommitted himself to Christ in a silent prayer.

"Well just bow your head and talk to Jesus, ask Him to forgive your sin and come into your heart and live with you. Tell Him that you believe in Him, and you will be saved," said Hezekiah in a soft voice.

The little church meeting brought four souls to Jesus that night as they prayed and surrendered to Jesus. Many happy tears flowed and the whole camp came around as they found out what was happening. Robert Whitt had been saved from the Indians and now he was saved from sin, all in about a week. Rachel did a little Indian dance and chanted I love Jesus Christ in Shawnee. All four of the children followed suit and danced with Rachel their aunt.

It had been a wonderful night and everyone was so happy. They would all be slow going to sleep and slow to get up the next morning. Major Thomas Mastin was as happy as the rest and the camp they didn't get on the move until about the ninth hour.

In a few days, about an hour behind the forward scout, the Meadow Creek Militia ambled into the settlement. The scout informed them that the little army would be here soon and word spread quickly. All the families began to gather to greet their loved ones. Susannah Whitt was out in front because she had three sons to welcome home. She didn't know about the fourth.

The scout told the people that they were bringing back an Indian maiden and four Indian children. He also told Susannah that her sons were safe and had a surprise for her.

Finally the militia came into view about a quarter of a mile away. They were marching in columns of two as Major Mastin brought them closer. He halted the men about fifty yards from the gathered families. He had them do a left face and dismissed them.

The militiamen ran to their awaiting families. Abijah, Hezekiah, and Edmund ran close together shielding Robert from sight. He had been given some white-mans clothes and did not look as much Indian now.

The three sons reached Susannah and had a group hug. About that time they spread out and Robert Whitt was standing face to face with mother Susannah.

THE PATRIOT, HEZEKIAH WHITT

"My Lord and my God you have answered my prayers, Robert was dead now he lives," shouted Susannah as she fell on Robert with great tears of joy. Roberts father Reverend Richard heard the commotion and ran to the sons and saw Robert.

"Thank you Jesus," said the Reverend as he moved in to hug Robert.

All the sisters, smaller brothers and the Skaggs family all rejoiced as they had the great reunion.

William Skaggs, Rachel and the four Indian children stood and took it all in. Some of the folks had mixed feelings as they saw the five Indians standing there. The white families never felt threatened by Rachel and the four children, but could not but resent the sight of an Indian.

Thomas Mastin stood there also enjoying the sight of the reunion. He was now just a neighbor, not a military leader.

After all the hugs, Hezekiah introduced Rachel and the other four Indians to all the folks that had gathered for the greeting.

"These Indians are not heathen, but born again Christians," stated Hezekiah.

The group smiled as they felt some relief by not having to fear or distrust the children and Rachel. The ladies moved in and greeted the red children and the beautiful maiden Rachel. It was wonderful and a bit surprising for the two cultures to accept each other this way.

William Skaggs, wanting to get the credit, spoke up saying, "I captured them!"

"Well what are you going to do with them?" asked Thomas Mastin sounding more like the Major.

"Me and my wife Mary will keep um for a spell, till we can figure out what to do with um," answered William.

"If you are agreeable I and Agnes will adopt the children, being as I know Elinipsico and Chief Cornstalk," stated Thomas Mastin. (Agnes was an Indian)

"You mean to adopt them as your own children?" ask William Skaggs.

"Sure do, me and the misses ain't got no children and looks like this would be our only chance," replied Thomas Mastin.

"Well about Rachel, reckon me and Mary can keep her for a spell," replied William Skaggs.

Mary Skaggs the young wife of William walked up to Rachel and took her hand. Rachel looked at her and smiled.

"Well that settles it for now, the four children will come with me and Rachel can stay with the Skaggs," said Thomas Mastin.

THE PATRIOT, HEZEKIAH WHITT

"Skaggs, that will be my name," spoke the beautiful Indian maiden.

"I feel honored," said the senior Rachel Skaggs wife of James and mother of William. "Oh, I didn't know there was another Rachel Skaggs," said Rachel the Indian. "That's all right honey, reckon this world is plenty big enough for two of us," said the senior Rachel smiling broadly.

The folks all laughed at the announcement.

Susannah and Richard took Robert by the arms and headed to the house. Abijah, Rachel Whitt, Hezekiah, Elizabeth, Edmund, Archibald, Ruth, and Susannah Whitt followed. Reverend Richard Whitt had baby Richard Thomas in his right arm and Robert by his left.

Thomas Mastin and the four Indian children headed across the meadow to his log house to meet his wife Agnes. William Skaggs and wife Mary Simpson Skaggs headed to their cabin with Mary holding the arm of their new friend, Rachel Skaggs.

There would be much merriment this evening on Meadow Creek. There would also be much thanksgiving for the returning men and for now a little peace from the war.

Hezekiah knows where the beautiful Indian maiden, Rachel Skaggs lives and will ponder on this thing for awhile.

The days of peace will not last, but for now the war is not in their face. The Indian spies will continue to go out and watch for intrusions from the Indians.

To the west in Ohio country the British were working up all the Indians for a large scale attack on Kentucky County. The British Army Captain Henry Byrd had come to address a gathering of Indian Chiefs. He wore his bright red uniform and even brought a cannon to demonstrate to the Indians. The tribes represented there were Shawnee, Wyandots, Hurons, Ottawas, Tawas, Tuscarawas, Chippewas, Delawars, Miamis and Potawatomies. The Girty brothers Simon, James, and George along with the British Indian agent Alexander McKee were there and constantly reminding the tribes of the murder of Chief Cornstalk, Black Fish, Red Hawk and other Indian leaders. These men had sided with the British and were well know to the Indians. Kentucky was more isolated than the settlements on New River, so this would be a good chance to run out the frontiersmen and claim the entire west for the British.

For now there was some peace especially to the east on Meadow Creek. 1780 will be another year for blood to spill in Virginia, especially the western parts.

There would be a good harvest on Meadow Creek and maybe some merriment in the form of corn shuckings, and other gatherings. People would get to know the new Indian friends that lived among them; the three Indian boys, the little girl, and of course Rachel Skaggs the Indian maiden.

THE PATRIOT, HEZEKIAH WHITT

Robert Whitt would have to get adjusted to his new way of life back with his family. He had acquired hunting skills and a new love for the woods and streams while with the Cherokee. Robert would spend much time in the woods and do some scouting in the region. Sometime later he would earn the trust of the settlers and go out on the far frontier with other Indian spies. At some point Robert traveled all the way to Jackson County, Ohio. Of course it wasn't called Jackson County until March 1816. The area was best known in the early years for the Indian salt works on Salt Creek.

Thomas Jefferson was elected the second Governor of Virginia on June 1, 1779.

The dreaded Tomahawk!

Chapter 13

Hezekiah Claims His Land

After a peaceful winter with family and friends, Hezekiah heads out with the Indian spies to the waters of the Clinch. He had enjoyed this winter and had admired Rachel Skaggs, the beautiful Indian maiden, but kept his distance. They both had good chemistry toward each other, but neither advanced their feelings.

This spring Hezekiah rode his horse Johnny and took more supplies including an ax, rope, and a few tools. Hezekiah decided it was time to lay claim to his dream farm on Indian Creek. Thomas Mastin had tried to discourage him, saying it was too early, even though he was thinking the same thing. Hezekiah had confirmed that he would use the utmost caution. The Reverend Richard Whitt and Grand Paw James Skaggs told Hezekiah he would be getting land around Meadow Creek after the war came to an end. Hezekiah had this dream of owning the land on Indian Creek close to the Clinch River and was not going to let it go.

All of the other spies rode horses this time also. They left on a cold windy morning about the middle of March, 1780.

The spies separated as usual and Hezekiah headed to Indian Creek just as soon as he could after scouting a large area around what is now Tazewell County, Virginia. Once he felt secure that no warriors were around or had been around, Hezekiah moved into the old lean-to he had build two years before. He had to cut more cedar branches and repair it somewhat. He scouted about for a few hours each morning then he went to work building his cabin.

Hezekiah decided on a spot about twenty yards from his limestone spring right in the Cedar Grove. It was on a fairly level ground. First thing Hezekiah did was gather some good stones to use for foundation. He used his horse Johnny to pull the stones to the site and he laid out the foundation. It was going to be about 16 feet by 16 feet.

He picked out the biggest Cedars and downed them for the walls. Cedar is known for durability and if kept off the ground could last for 200 years. Even though he was using good materials he was rushing the job because of time and danger. He built his chimney of smaller logs and coated them with clay mud. He and Johnny worked furiously building the cabin. He did however go out for two or three hours a day to scout and forage for some food.

Hezekiah's friend and kin, John Hankins, also laid claim to land close to Hezekiah Whitt's Claim. They both would petition the State of Virginia by right of settlement and pay a fee of ten shillings silver into the treasure of the State of Virginia. Hezekiah's claim was for eighty-four acres.

THE PATRIOT, HEZEKIAH WHITT

At night when things were quiet except for the stirring of night creatures and maybe the eddy in the creek doing a little bubbling, Hezekiah thought of home and the war. He hated this war, but knew they must pursue it to the end to win the prize of freedom. Another thought kept jumping into his head even though he tried to push it away. It was that beautiful woman with the big round brown eyes. He hated to admit it, but he was in love with Rachel Skaggs and wanted to bring her here to this Heaven on earth.

Things in the east were heating up for another summer of fighting. In April the newspaper, the Virginia Gazette moved from Williamsburg to Richmond, and also Governor Thomas Jefferson was pushing to move the state capitol there also. So on May 1, 1780 the Capitol of Virginia was officially in Richmond. The move come about to make it harder for the British to attack it. Richmond has been the capitol since and is still today. (During the civil war years the Yankees claimed it was in Wheeling.)

A strange thing happened on May 19, 1780 in the New England area. Many folks thought it was the end of time; others took it as a sign for this or that. About midday almost total darkness fell on New England. To this day it has never been explained. (I think it was a sign for the British to pull out.)

May 12, 1780 the British defeated the American Patriots in Charleston and then occupied Charleston South Carolina. General Cornwallis wanted to make short work of South Carolina and move to North Carolina eventually driving on Virginia.

Hezekiah was back in Meadow Creek by the middle of May with good reports from his spying expedition. The Indians were not concentrating on middle Virginia. The Indians were concentrating on Kentucky County, and would be led by 100 red coats and about 70 green coated Canadian Rangers. Many tribes would send warriors to kill or drive out the white intruders that had settled their prime hunting grounds. This summer would be hell for Kentucky County, Virginia.

The militia men around Meadow Creek got out their crops and gardens while they could. They all knew that they could be called up at any time. The British were having their way against Patriot General Gates and would be moving north. Virginia was asked and agreed to send militia into the Carolinas.

In the early summer Hezekiah, Abijah, Edmund, Robert, and Reverend Richard Whitt along with the other militiamen were called up by Colonel Preston to go to South Carolina to join General Gates. The lead mines in Montgomery County were picked as the rendezvous for the troops. Here Colonel Cloyd took command. He marched with the main body of the army into North Carolina. Colonel Cloyd recognized the value of the lead mines as a target to the British and Tories. He left a strong guard behind under Colonel Saunders. Hezekiah was part of this unit they stayed for about a month.

With the cat away the mice will play. So the Tories and deserters knowing that most of the militia was gone south began to do mischief among the settlers. Stealing, raping and all un-Godly things were being done. Colonel Preston ordered out the militia that was available to serve under Captain Daniel Trigg. Hezekiah along with his comrades put

THE PATRIOT, HEZEKIAH WHITT

down the uprising. Hezekiah and Reverend Richard Whitt served with Captain Trigg in Virginia for about a month. Tories were raising cane in both Virginia and North Carolina.

The Patriots were shocked when one of their Generals turned traitor. On September 25, 1780 Benedict Arnold left the fight for freedom and joined the British. What a mistake this was!

On October 7, 1780 the militia known as "Over the Mountain Men," defeated the British at Kings Mountain. These men were from Virginia, North Carolina, and Tennessee. They fought the larger British with Indian tactics, shooting from behind trees and cover. The British drove them back several times with bayonet charges. The militia had no bayonets, but with determination they kept coming back and won the day. It was considered a turning point in the Revolutionary War. These men had learned their fighting tactics by fighting Indians.

After hearing of the victory at King's Mountain, Colonel Cloyd took his troops to North Carolina to put down the large number of Tories that were creating outrageous acts against the settlers. In a lot of way it was out and out civil war between the citizens. I think the Tories would have sided with the patriots if they thought they had a chance to win. On October 14, 1780 Colonel Cloyd's army caught up with a larger number of Tories at the Yadkin River and attacked with his little army of about 350 militiamen. He was up against as many as 600 Tories. The Loyalist leader Colonel Samuel Bryan was killed early on and the Tories became unorganized without a leader. The Patriots gained the upper hand and the Tories were put down. This battle also gave the Patriot's cause a shot in the arm. When the Congress heard these reports it was a great encouragement to them. The new United States knew that they were winning the war. Citizen soldiers were winning the liberty.

The winter was coming on and the folks around Meadow Creek could relax a little. They could harvest their crops and get ready for winter.   Hezekiah talked to his father and mother about his feelings toward Rachel Skaggs. They said that they would support him if he wanted to marry her. The Reverend told Hezekiah that some folks would talk and try to cause some trouble, but if you and Rachel love each other things will work out.

"This is a new country, and new things will come about." said Susannah Whitt. "Rachel is a sweet Christian girl and being Indian should not make a difference," stated Reverend Richard Whitt.

Hezekiah along with the permission of William Skaggs began to court the Indian Maiden Rachel Skaggs. They spent a lot of time together and Hezekiah told her about the cabin he built on the waters of the Clinch. He described the area in detail and she began to love it all so. She told him that her people had come to it many times with great hunting success.

THE PATRIOT, HEZEKIAH WHITT

"The Shawnee name for the Clinch is Pellissippi," added Rachel.
"Well that sounds funny after calling it the Clinch for so long," answered Hezekiah.
Rachel laughed!

"There is plenty of game in the area, a man will not starve there," stated Hezekiah.

"What about a woman?" asked Rachel?
"A woman neither," said Hezekiah slightly blushing.

Finally, the Reverend Richard began to get supplies and materials together to build the long awaited Whitt Saw Mill. He dug out his old drawings and started to do the planning for the Whitt Saw Mill. Everyone was glad since it had been put off for so long because of the war with the Indians and British.

The Reverend would have plenty of help if the militia got to stay home for awhile. He had all of his family plus many of the Skaggs family. Reverend Richard Whitt hoped to be sawing wood by the summer of 1781. This was a fairly new concept this far passed the Blue Ridge. Most folks have heard of grist mills and many have seen one, but a water powered saw, that would be great.

Back in the Ohio country in the month of August the Indians were on the receiving end. The men from Kentucky County were joined together under Colonel George Rogers Clark and were on the offensive against the Indians. There were 1000 frontiersmen on their way to confront the Indians and put an end to the atrocities the Indians were so good at. I will just give you the official report from Colonel George Rogers Clark to Governor Thomas Jefferson. (Direct quote)

Fort Jefferson at Louisville
Kentucky, County
August 22, 1780

To *His Excellency*
Thomas Jefferson
Governor of Virginia

Sir:

By every possible exertion, and the aid of Colonel Slaughter's corps, we completed the number of 1000, with which we crossed the river at the mouth of Licking on the first day of August and began our march on the 2nd, having a road to cut for the artillery to pass, for 70 miles, it was the 6th, before we reached the first town, which we found vacated, and the greatest part of their effects carried off. The general conduct of the Indians on our march, and many other corroborating circumstances, proved their design of leading us to their own ground and time of action. After destroying the crops and buildings of Chillecauthy we began to march for the

COLONEL CHARLES DAHNMON WHITT

THE PATRIOT, HEZEKIAH WHITT

Picaway settlements, on the waters of the Big Miami, the Indians keeping runners constantly before our advanced guards. At half past two in the evening of the 8th, we arrived in sight of the town and forts, a plain of half a mile in width lying between us. I had an opportunity of viewing the situation and motion of the enemy near their works.

I had scarcely time to make those dispositions necessary, before the action commenced on our left wing, and in a few minutes became almost general, with a savage fierceness on both sides. The confidence of the enemy had of their own strength and certain victory, or the want of generalship, occasioned several neglects, by which those advantages were taken that proved the ruin of their army, being flanked two or three different times, drove from hill to hill in a circuitous direction, for upwards of a mile and a half; at last took shelter in their strongholds and woods adjacent when the firing ceased for about half an hour, until necessary preparations were made for dislodging them. A heavy firing again commenced, and continued severe until dark; by which time the enemy was totally routed .The cannon playing too briskly on their works they could afford them no shelter. Our loss was about 14 killed and 13 wounded; theirs at least triple that number. They carried their dead during the night, except 12 or 14 that lay too near our lines for them to venture. This would have been a decisive stroke to the Indians, unfortunately the right wing of our army had not been rendered useless for some time by an uncommon chain of rocks that they could not pass, by which means part of the enemy escaped through the ground they were ordered to occupy.

By a French prisoner we got the next morning we learn that the Indians had been preparing for our reception, moving their family and effects: that the morning before our arrival, they were 300 warriors, Shawnees, Mingoes, Wyandotte and Delawares. Several reinforcements coming that day, he did not know their numbers; that they were sure of destroying the whole of us; that the greatest part of prisoners taken by Byrd, were carried to Detroit, where there were only 200 regulars, having no provisions except green corn and vegetables. Our whole store at first setting out being only 300 bushels of corn and 1500 of flour; having done the Shawnees all the mischief in our power, and after destroying the Picaway settlements, I returned to the post, having marched in the whole 480 miles in 31 days. We destroyed upwards of 800 acres of corn, besides great quantities of vegetables, a considerable portion of witch appear to have been cultivated by white men, I suppose for the purpose of supporting war parties from Detroit. I could wish to have had a small store of provisions to enable us to lay waste part of the Delaware settlements, and falling in at Pittsburg, but the excessive heat, and weak diet, shew the impropriety of such a step. Nothing could excel the few regulars and Kentuckyans that compose this little army, in bravery and implicit obedience to orders; each company vying with the other who should be the most subordinate.

I am sir, your most humble
And obedient servant, George Rogers Clark

COLONEL CHARLES DAHNMON WHITT

THE PATRIOT, HEZEKIAH WHITT

Now the Virginians were taking the war to the British, Indians and Tories not just to the south, but to the west and north. General Washington was doing well in the east and the patriots had higher hopes of winning their liberty much sooner.

Things around Meadow Creek were calm with most of the men back home from the Carolinas and other parts of action in this country wide war.

Abraham Henderson had proposed to Rachel Whitt and she gladly accepted. The wedding was preformed by her father Reverend Richard Whitt. The chivalree brought some much needed fun.

Hezekiah and Rachel spent time together when possible and Hezekiah was sure in his heart that he wanted to marry this beautiful Indian Princess. Rachel was fitting in well in the white world and learned all she could about how to serve her new master, Jesus Christ. She too wanted to spend her life with Hezekiah Whitt.

Thomas Mastin officially renamed two of the Indian boys while one boy did not want to change his name at this time. Thomas named the youngest boy "Low Hawk," to Hezekiah N. Whitt, and the other he named Thomas Bailey Christian. He was named for (Thomas) Mastin; Bailey was one of his mother's names, (Bailey) Standing Deer. Christian was just a good name for those that follow the Lord, of course. Hezekiah N. Whitt was named in honor of the friend of Thomas Mastin, Hezekiah Whitt. The little girl, "Mountain Raven" he named Sarah Mastin.

The third boy, Outhowwa, would go back and live with his people in the Carolinas in time. Thomas Mastin would take him when the fighting was through. Sarah Mastin would go also for a visit. In years to come Sarah would meet her husband Bear Adkins from North Carolina.

Rachel Skaggs name become official as did the children at the courthouse in Montgomery County and Hezekiah signed as a witness for Thomas Mastin. Hezekiah Whitt was honored that Thomas Mastin named one of his Indian children for him.

Old Brown Betz.

THE PATRIOT, HEZEKIAH WHITT

Chapter14

The British Yield

1781 will be a year for America to remember. 1781 is a year that will bring better times to the people of Virginia. 1781 will be a year of new beginnings if the folks can get through it and they will. These Americans have a will to survive and beat back overwhelming odds. To me 1781 will be a year that the scales are tipped and America will get her just rewards of freedom.

On a cold snowy day in January 1781, the Whitts sat around the log house talking as they mended equipment and did whatever work they could. These times are good for family bonding and the children usually get some good teaching in the three "R's".

The men ventured out only to feed the stock, bring in wood and water, and shovel paths to the important places like the barn, well, and of course the family privy. Not much chance of an attack from the Indians, they don't do much in January which they call the hunger month.

Thomas Mastin's new children and Rachel Skaggs are eager to learn the English in reading and writing. They all prove to be excellent students because of their desire to learn.

Hezekiah has spent some time with Rachel and taught her to read the Holy Bible. She has so many questions about God and the twelve tribes of Israel. Hezekiah has had to include the Reverend Richard in some of their discussions. Once Rachel improves her penmanship she will be as literate as or more than most folks along the New River.

Well anyway, on this cold snowy day the Whitts discuss the sawmill building and they had big hopes it can be done this year. They also talk about the war and happenings from the east.

That devil turncoat, Benedict Arnold, led an expedition up the James River and burned Richmond, the new capital on January 5th, 1781. The Virginia government was scattered and would be attacked again later.

"He (Benedict Arnold) will have hell to pay, if the Patriots get hold of him," said Hezekiah.

"You don't have to use that word," said mother Susannah.

Hezekiah acknowledged her with a nod of his head and a smile on his face. Hezekiah went back to his chore of rubbing oil into his leather skins; this kept them pliable and waterproof.

"Paw do you have bout everything ready to finish the sawmill?" ask Robert?

THE PATRIOT, HEZEKIAH WHITT

"Most everything, I got to get some stones cut for the grist mill part. It will serve two purposes, we can grind corn and we can saw lumber," stated Reverend Richard Whitt.

"How does the saw work, Paw?" asked Edmund.

"When the water turns the wheel it sends power to the flywheel which in turn pushes a leaver up and down. The lever is hooked to the big straight saw blade. As you know when a saw blade is moved through wood it cuts it," explained Reverend Whitt.

"You mean the saw blade sticks up and goes up and down, Paw?" ask Edmund.

"That is exactly right, son, the saw blade is held upright and supported so it can reciprocate," answered the Reverend Richard.

"What is reciprocate?" ask Archibald as he sat back listening to the older folks talking.

"It means up and down, back and forth, like you boys do on a regular crosscut saw. One is pulling, the other is pushing, understand son?" asked the Reverend Richard.

"Yes sir it is hard work, the mill will do the hard work for us wouldn't it Paw? Asked Archibald?

"Somewhat, yet there will be a plenty to do, the main thing is it cuts nice boards and plenty of them," stated the Reverend Richard.

"What about the grinder, what makes it work Paw?" asked little sister Ruth?

"Honey it works about the same, I have to pull a leaver or two to send the power to the grinding stone instead of the saw. The grinding stone sets on top of the set stone and we just add grain and it grinds it," explained the Reverend Richard Whitt.

Ruth acted like she understood every aspect of it and the older brothers all grinned.

Much of the work was done and Richard hoped to be sawing lumber in the spring of 1782.

The Articles of Confederation are ratified by the last state, Maryland, on January 30, 1781. On March 1, 1781 the Continental Congress adopted the Articles of Confederation. This gave General George Washington more power to acquire men, money, and materials from the thirteen Independent States, to support his army.

On March 15, 1781 the Patriots gave the British a good lick at Guilford Court House in North Carolina. The British suffer a heavy loss. Slowly but surely the Americans are gaining ground against the biggest and most powerful army in the world.

Benjamin Franklin's work and time in France has paid off. The French will send thousands of troops and many ships to aid the Americans.

Jack Jouet rides on June 3, 1781 to warn Governor Thomas Jefferson that the British are coming to Richmond again. The government is scattered again. Thomas Jefferson's term, as Governor, ran out during this action and William Fleming the same officer that helped win the victory at Point Pleasant, became the third Governor of Virginia. His term was short lived as he only served from June 3, 1781 to June 12, 1781. The Virginia Legislature met again and on June 12, 1781 elected another temporary Governor. Thomas Nelson Jr. served from June 12, 1781 until November 22, 1781. Yet one more temporary Governor, David Jameson served from November 22, 1781 until December 1, 1781. Then a regular Governor was elected for three years, this was the sixth Governor, Benjamin Harrison V, was his name.

Back to the month of April on Meadow Creek, Hezekiah and the other Indian spies prepare to head west to the waters of the Clinch and further. Hezekiah went over to William Skaggs to visit his sweet-heart, Rachel Skaggs. It is a fair early spring evening and he takes her for a stroll along the banks of New River. (Present day Radford, VA.) Hezekiah had decided to tell Rachel how he feels and ask her to marry him. He would give her plenty of time, but did not want to come home to find her wed to another. Hezekiah walked her into the woods so he could talk to her. He took her hand and looked upon her beautiful face. She anxiously looked back with her big brown eyes.

"Sweetheart, as you know I have feelings for you and I am leaving tomorrow for the scouting grounds," whispered Hezekiah.

"I love you Hezekiah, are you ever going to ask me to marry you?" asked Rachel with anticipation.

"That is what we are here for, will you marry me?" asked a blushing Hezekiah.

"Yes, Hezekiah I will marry you, we need to wait for a little while until the dangers are over, even though I want you now," stated Rachel Skaggs.

"I want you too, but you are right about waiting, I want you to promise yourself to me because I love you very much," explained Hezekiah.

"What will you do when someone calls me your red nigger squaw?" asked Rachel.

"I better never hear such talk from any man, I may send him to his maker before he is ready to go," said Hezekiah in an explicit tone.

"I hope you never sin against Christ or any man because I am an Indian," said Rachel.

"I just need to know that you will wait for me and not wed another while I am out in the wilderness," stated Hezekiah.

Rachel took Hezekiah into her arms and gave him a long passionate kiss and let her feelings do the talking. Hezekiah looked into her eyes and passionately said, "I love you and will cling to you in my memories while I am out in the wilderness."

"Have no fear husband to be, I will wait on you and not wed another while you are away," promised Rachel.

Hezekiah walked Rachel back to her white father and mother, William & Mary Skaggs. He went into the cabin to talk to William.

THE PATRIOT, HEZEKIAH WHITT

William I need to talk to you for a minute, would you allow me a minute?" asked Hezekiah.

"Well it's about time, yes Rachel may marry you, but please wait for awhile till we can end the dangers of this war," stated William Skaggs.

Hezekiah was a taken back by surprise, but momentarily regained his composure.

"Well son wern't that what you wanted to know, could you and Rachel get hitched?" asked William.

"Yes, I was fixing to ask you that vary thing, but wasn't ready for so quick an answer," Hezekiah said, as he continued to explain that the wedding was not to take place soon.

"You thought she might not wait if you didn't purpose now and get my permission didn't you?" asked William.

"I had to know that Rachel would wait for me and I could hold on to that while I was out in the spying grounds," explained Hezekiah.

"We understand," answered William and Mary.

"Father William, I am so glad you approve, I do love Hezekiah with all my heart," responded Rachel Skaggs. (Rachel called William, father, even though he was not many years her senior.)

Early in the month of April Hezekiah rode out on Johnny and gathered with the other spies. Major Thomas Mastin was in charge again. All the spies were mounted for this expedition. They took more food and supplies then usual; they would be allowed small fires to cook and warm by. It is unlikely that the Indians will be on the war path. They will be out foraging for food, but will still be very dangerous if encountered. Colonel George Rogers Clark and his Kentuckians had taken away their food by firing the fields of corn and vegetables in the Ohio country.

The spies will dismount and do the real spying on foot once they are deep into the scouting grounds. Hezekiah was to travel across the Clinch to the headwaters of the Tug Fork and go down those waters for two or three days. If he saw any sign he was to pursue the trail to determine the purpose of the Indians. If the Indians were hunting, or on the warpath the spies were to take appropriate action and get word to the nearest fort or settlement.

After arriving on Indian Creek, Hezekiah looked over the area and went in to check out his cabin he built last year. Everything was pretty much as he left it, but grown up somewhat. Hezekiah put Johnny in a corral that he built over the little branch that flowed from the limestone spring. He had plenty of grass and water to do him for several days and the fence would help protect him from predators.

After everything was satisfactory to Hezekiah, he left on foot to explore the Tug Valley. He crossed through the area that is today, Bandy, Virginia. He stayed off the warriors' path directly, but traveled adjacent to it. He came close every now and then to check for

THE PATRIOT, HEZEKIAH WHITT

Indian sign, but only found old moccasin tracks that were well faded. The tracks could have been months old and were left in soft ground heading in the direction of the Ohio River. This was good news because they were heading away from the settlements and were not fresh sign anyway.

Hezekiah took a little chance by downing some game with a shot from his musket. When he did this he would sit for about thirty minutes after a shot to see if it drew Indians to him. He would fix a small fire and cook his meat and keep the fire during the night for comfort. He would build his fire in an area that helped shield the light from long distances. He would build it in a gully or in a rock house. He was always careful not to let it get too big.

After things got quiet Hezekiah would let his mind wonder back to that Indian Princess he loved so dearly. He remembered her touch and of course the passionate kiss she gave him the night before he left. He always returned to the dream of them living in bliss on his new farm on Indian Creek.

Hezekiah did his job well; he traveled way down the Tug as far as present day Williamson, West Virginia. After Hezekiah was satisfied that the settlements were safe from the bloodthirsty Indians he worked his way back to Indian Creek. Hezekiah stayed cautious, but felt at peace with the beautiful lands and streams that God had created here on the waters of the Clinch. He was amazed at the plentiful amount of elk, deer, beaver, bear, and predators like wolfs and panthers in this new land. One evening Hezekiah sat back and counted over a hundred elk as they passed. He also saw a few woods buffalo. Passenger Pigeons were so thick they shut out the sun when a flock passed. This would be like the Garden of Eden, if Rachel Skaggs was here to enjoy it with me, thought Hezekiah.

Hezekiah brought corn seed with him on this trip. He fashioned a homemade wooden plow and had Johnny pull it to plow up about a third of an acre. He planted the corn as part of the requirements of securing his farm by right of settlement. After making a few more improvements on the farm Hezekiah was ready to get back with the spies and head home to Meadow Creek. The first thing he did was to search for John Hankins that had been making improvements on his land not too far away.

John Hankins was an uncle to Hezekiah as his wife Elizabeth Skaggs Hankins was a sister to Hezekiah's mother Rachel Skaggs Whitt.

Occasionally John and Hezekiah spent an evening together at one or the others land. They were still keeping an eye out for marauding Indians. They talked about the future and about the war. Hezekiah would have to mention his wife to be, Rachel Skaggs. John was glad that Hezekiah had found a mate.

"A woman is a good thing to have," stated John Hankins.

"Well the Lord made them for our mates," replied Hezekiah.

THE PATRIOT, HEZEKIAH WHITT

The spies got back to Meadow Creek and reported the good news; there was no new sign of Indians on the warpath. After a good reunion with family and friends, thoughts were on the happenings in the east once again.

It was about the middle of the summer 1781. The little country called the United States had held off the powerful mother country for six years. The American army was still struggling somewhat even though they had improved and had some success. The British were occupying New York City. General Cornwallis had finally emerged from the Carolinas. He had captured Charleston, Richmond, and was headed to Chesapeake Bay, Virginia. General Washington was holding on by a thread waiting for the promised help of the French.

The French landed 6000 troops in Rhode Island. The French Fleet had gathered in the Caribbean to get ready for battle. The French General Comte de Rochambeau met with General George Washington to form a plan to rid America of the Redcoats.

Washington wanted to attack the British in New York City. Rochambeau was fearful of attacking a well fortified army. He was still not sold on the abilities of the Continental Army; he recommended marching south and confront Cornwallis in Virginia.

General Washington finally agreed and the two armies marched from White Plains, New York toward the tidewater of Virginia. They arrived there in early September 1781 with about 9000 American and 7000 French troops. About the same time the French Fleet arrived in the Chesapeake Bay and attacked the British Fleet. The British fleet retreated to New York; this left Cornwallis and his army stuck in Yorktown.

After five days of cannoning the British, the French and American Army attacked the fortified position. The two armies overwhelmed the British the night of October 14, 1781. Cornwallis had no choice but to surrender and on October 19, 1781 at 2:00 PM he did just that. Some say Cornwallis sent a subordinate officer to do the duty. Some say he offered his sword to the French General and he refused it. The French General told Cornwallis that he should give it to General Washington as his was the Army that bested him. The British had to yield to the new little nation and at the treaty of Paris in September of 1783 they signed the document that granted the United States their Independence. But for now the fall of 1781 the war for all intents and purposes was over. There would be some scattered fighting, especially in the western parts of Virginia.

The news of the great victory spread like wildfire even into the Indian towns' way out into Ohio country. The Indians had a name for the thirteen states; they called them the Thirteen Fires. The Indians hopes of pushing the Shemanese (Whites) back across the mountains was all but lost. The frontiersmen were so happy with the victory. There were little community celebrations all over the new United States.

John Hanson was elected by the Congress in 1781 to be President of the Congress to serve a full term of one year. Actually there were two before him. Many say he was the first President of the United States. This is false, he was President of the Congress, the

THE PATRIOT, HEZEKIAH WHITT

United States would not have a President as we know it until the father of our country, George Washington, was elected. Hanson was elected and no one would even run against him. George Washington was for him.

The Reverend Richard Whitt has just finished his mill; he built it with the help from his family and neighbors. So much work had been put into building a dam, digging a water trace and putting together a clocklike mechanism to saw wood and grind grain. People from all around came to see the mill come alive when the sluice gate was opened and the power of Meadow Creek turned the great water wheel. It was so exciting to see the wheel turn. The crowd roared with exuberance.

The builders had dug a water trace off of Meadow Creek and built an under-shot mill. Under-shot means that the water runs against the bottom of the water wheel instead of dropping on it from the top. They had a few problems at first because of it being a dual mill. It was primarily a saw mill, but also had two smaller than normal grinding stones for grinding grain. The Reverend had to make little adjustments here and there. He had set up a platform to handle the logs; Hezekiah and Abijah rolled a 12" log over on the platform and pushed it into the upright reciprocating blade and the chips flew as the log was cut. The Reverend Richard Whitt praised God and declared the mill was a great success. Hezekiah and all the brothers got a lot of building experience and a sense of value for providing a much needed service to the community. It seems that most Whitt men have a God given talent to build things and be handy with their hands.

Hezekiah and Rachel Skaggs set the date for their wedding to Friday, January 11, 1882. Now to the planning of the wedding, Mary Skaggs (Rachel's white mother) and Susannah Whitt (Hezekiah's mother) would do most of the planning with some input from Grandmother Rachel Skaggs. Of course they would include the Indian Princess, Rachel Skaggs. To Rachel this was an awful lot of nonsense, all this planning was new to her, but she went along with all of it.

When the four women were taking a tea break, Rachel opened up to them about how it would happen in the Indian world. Rachel explained that the available Indian maidens would dance on a warm summer night. They would sway and move about in a large circle, dancing to the rhythm of drums and flutes. As the maidens danced the available braves would come out and pick the maiden they had previously flirted with. If the woman and man were in the same heart they would dance breast to breast yet letting their arms dangle to their sides. Sometimes the dance would excite them so much that the maidens would become so moist that little streams would run down their legs. Some children would think the maiden had an accident. The couple would go to the lodge of the brave and their marriage would be consummated.

Susannah and the others were blushing as Rachel finished this description of the Shawnee marriage.

"We do it different, we include the Lord and take vows in His presence," said Susannah.

"What is this vows?" asked Rachel?

THE PATRIOT, HEZEKIAH WHITT

"It is a promise the bride and groom make to each other in the presence of the Lord and witnesses. In your case you would promise to Hezekiah and Hezekiah would promise to you to always love each other and never lay with (be intimate) another," explained Susannah.

"I love Hezekiah and would have no reason to find another," stated Rachel.

"You can do that dance thing with Hezekiah after you are wed," said Grandmother Skaggs with a big grin.

"Mother!" exclaimed Susannah!

They all laughed with glee.

A rendition that may look like Rachel, but I think Rachel was more beautiful.

Rendition of
Princess Rachel Cornstalk Skaggs Whitt

Chapter 15
Hezekiah Marries Princess Rachel

The Indians are still causing problems in western Virginia. Indians were striking the area of Wheeling all the way down the Ohio River to the Missouri lands. Most of the trouble is still being caused by the defeated British. The British were not openly doing this but secretly invoking the Indians against the Border States. They had caused many of the chiefs and braves to become alcoholics. They continued to give "Firewater" to the Indians.

The drunken Indians sometimes became a problem even to the British. One example of this was Chief Logan of the Mingo tribe; he was denied whiskey one day because he was drunk and disorderly. Logan threatened the British by saying he would go to the Americans and get his whiskey. The British could not allow any of the Indians to turn against them, so they had some men follow him back to his cabin where they murdered him by hacking him in the head with a tomahawk.

There were fewer war parties now on the waters of the Clinch, but occasionally the whites and red men would collide. Fewer Indians ventured close to Meadow Creek, but the frontiersmen stayed cautious. Attacks by Indians on secluded farms and traveling whites would go on for years to come. The last known reported Indian raid in Virginia was carried out in 1794 by "Chief Benge" the half breed Cherokee. He was killed by Lee County militia near Big Stone Gap, Virginia. So you see the dangers were still very real in the seventeen-eighties.

The Whitts and Skaggs enjoyed a real nice Christmas in 1781. This was the first Christmas that Indian Princess Rachel Skaggs celebrated the birth of her Lord, Jesus Christ. She especially enjoyed the holiday spirit and the exchanging of gifts. Hezekiah gave her a big kiss under the mistletoe which was a new custom she learned about.

The date was set for January 11, 1782 for the wedding of Hezekiah Whitt and Rachel Skaggs. William Skaggs and Mary, (Her white mother & father.) were glad to see Rachel so happy. Hezekiah was also looking forward to the wedding. Plans were being made and the whole community had heard about the betrothal.

Some negative talk was spreading around mostly in taverns and shadowy places. How could this white man that had killed the enemy Indians marry a squaw? Hezekiah even heard that his brother Robert Whitt that had been held hostage for so long by the Indians was showing displeasure of this upcoming union. It was reported that Robert Whitt had called Rachel Skaggs, "Hezekiah's little red nigger whore!" Hezekiah was not concerned with some of the scoundrels in the county, but for Brother Robert, to cut him and Rachel down was hard to take. Hezekiah prayed that neither Rachel nor her white father, William Skaggs, would ever get word of it.

Hezekiah went to his father, Reverend Richard Whitt and confided in him and ask for advice. The Reverend called a family meeting and Robert was to be there. Richard was

THE PATRIOT, HEZEKIAH WHITT

quiet angry, but kept his composure. He set the meeting for Sunday afternoon as he thought after preaching he would be better able to conduct a serious family meeting without raising his voice or losing control.

About 4 PM the Whitt family finished Sunday dinner and was having another cup of tea. Susannah had the younger girls; Ruth & Susannah clear the table and take the baby, Richard Thomas, into the sitting room to play by the fireplace. Robert was sitting in the hot seat beside his father. He was quite jittery and pale.

Richard whispered a prayer and started the dialogue about the problem.

"Hezekiah and Rachel are going to be wed and this family is with them in this decision. I know that Rachel is an Indian, but she is also a lovely young lady that has decided to follow the Lord Jesus Christ," stated Richard Whitt.

"I have heard that someone is calling Rachel dirty names just because some of her people have hurt some of our people, Rachel is innocent and is in-love with my son Hezekiah," Susannah spoke up startling some of the family.

The Reverend Richard nodded at his wife with approval. Robert first thought that they were taking sides with a heathen Indian over their own son, but began to see both sides of the coin.

"Paw this meeting is about me, I would like to say a few words if that is alright!" exclaimed Robert.

"I did say some unsavory things about Hezekiah and Rachel getting married, but I had been drinking too much. I was with some fellows that were pretty much Indian haters and I fell in among them. I knew I should not let anyone talk about my brother, let alone say bad stuff myself. I am glad you had this meeting and I feel very bad about sinning against God and Hezekiah, I am so ashamed!" stated Robert Whitt.

Susannah Whitt put her arms around Robert showing approval. Next Robert stood and faced Hezekiah.

"Hezekiah, will you please forgive me for this wrong I have wrought you?" asked Robert?

Now it was time for Hezekiah to do the right thing even though he was quite hurt by Robert.

Hezekiah stood and looked Robert in the eye and said, "Brother, I do forgive you, and if Rachel gets word of this you will apologize to her!"

"I am truly sorry brother and I will be glad to ask her for forgiveness if you would have me do that," stated Robert.

"Thank God that He (God) has bound this family back together," stated the Reverend Richard Whitt.

THE PATRIOT, HEZEKIAH WHITT

The pressure was off and the family began to hug each other. The three youngest, Rachel, Elizabeth, and Richard Thomas came back into the room and got in on the action. Robert held on to Hezekiah for a long time and continued to say, "Forgive me brother!"

"I do, now turn me a loose, I can't get my breath," said Hezekiah with much humor.

Now there was peace in the Whitt family again. William, Mary and Rachel Skaggs did not get any direct reports of foul talk. It is a good thing that William had not heard some of the talk, there could be a funeral as well as a wedding.

Rachel came over to do some planning with the Whitt family. Hezekiah and Rachel had already asked Reverend Richard Whitt to perform the wedding and that was lovingly agreed too.

They would have the wedding on Friday, January 11, 1782 at the Baptist Church. They decided to keep it a small wedding, mostly family and close friends because of the words that has already been said. Rachel and Hezekiah were in a jovial mood and looking forward to the wedding day.

Hezekiah had acquired a small cabin on the banks of New River and had been getting it ready. Rachel would stay with William or with the Whitts if Hezekiah was called up to go on a spying mission. Hezekiah wanted to head right out to his cabin in Baptist Valley on Indian Creek, but recognized the folly of taking his bride further into the frontier. Rachel was also anxious to go to the new home Hezekiah had made on the waters of the Clinch.

Hezekiah, along with Robert, Abijah and little sister Ruth went to the cabin and set up some furniture and fixtures in preparation for the move after the wedding. Ruth, being observant and inquisitive noticed that Hezekiah had only one bed set up.

"Hezekiah, ain't you going to get another bed?" asked Ruth?

"No honey we only need one bed," answered Hezekiah.

"Well, where is Rachel going to sleep?" asked Ruth?

Hezekiah turned red as the others burst into loud laughter.
This brought an opportunity to explain to Ruth.

Hezekiah explained, "When grown-ups get married they can sleep together just like your Maw and Paw do."

"Are you and Rachel going to be a Maw and Paw?" asked Ruth?
Robert and Abijah were grinning and enjoying watching Hezekiah squirm.
"Well some day, I reckon," said Hezekiah slightly blushing.

THE PATRIOT, HEZEKIAH WHITT

"That brave militiaman can go out and fights Indians, but little sister scares him to death," said Abijah.

"Let's get back to work and quit the foolishness," said Hezekiah.

They all went back to setting up and moving things in, but they all had a smile on their face.

Finally Friday the eleventh of January rolled around. The little Baptist church was filling up as friends and family gathered to witness the wedding of Hezekiah Whitt and Rachel Skaggs.

Thomas Mastin and his wife Agnes (Indian maiden) was there with the four Indian children which were Rachel's nephews and niece. Of course William and Mary Skaggs were there to give away the bride. The Reverend Richard Whitt was there to perform the ceremony and support Hezekiah. Susannah Whitt (Hezekiah's mother) was there along with Robert, Abijah, Rachel and Abraham, Elizabeth, Edmund, Archibald, Ruth, Susannah, and little Richard Thomas Whitt.

Grandfather, Captain James Skaggs, Rachel, and others in the Skaggs family were there to see Hezekiah and Rachel tie the knot. This wedding would bring a much needed break from the stress of the war.

Of course Hezekiah was there dressed in his best clothes. He had his long hair pulled back tight in a tail. His face was shaved except for a well trimmed mustache. Hezekiah was a stunningly handsome young man, tall and straight.

Rachel Skaggs, the Indian Princess, was beautifully dressed in a long light blue dress. The ladies had prepared the dress and Rachel had added some beads and designs that really enhanced the wedding dress. Her long black hair was parted in the middle and tied with blue ribbons on either side. Rachel had a beautiful face and her red skin glowed, making her light blue dress look even better. They used very little make-up during that day, but Rachel never needed any. Rachel was slightly tall compared to most of the ladies of the day, and carried herself as a fine southern lady. She had learned so much since she entered the white world.

The church was decorated with a nice finished wooden cross, and Hezekiah had hung his flag on the wall. A few bouquets made from dried flowers were placed at the end of the pews. The flag was the Betsy Ross style with 13 white stars in a circle on a blue background. It had 13 red and white strips like the United States Flag of today. The flag had been given to Hezekiah on one of his missions with the militia.

The Reverend Richard Whitt was at the front of the church holding his worn Bible. On his left was the groom, Hezekiah Whitt. To his left was Brother Robert Whitt, the best man. Robert was proud to stand up for Hezekiah after his past misguided actions. To the right stood Hezekiah's sisters Rachel, Elizabeth, Ruth, and little Susannah. The sisters served as bridesmaids, and were thrilled to be part of the wedding.

THE PATRIOT, HEZEKIAH WHITT

At precisely 6:30 PM, the Reverend motioned for the bride to come forward. They chose this time because it was good luck to get married when the hands of the clock was coming up.

It was cold that day, but not as cold as it was a few days before. People had come and built a big fire in the fireplace to knock down the chill, yet many wore coats and cloaks.

They had no music but Rachel swayed down the aisle escorted by William Skaggs, her white father. The people in the church all stood in reverence. When they reached the front of the church they stopped.

"Who givith this woman to be wed?" asked Reverend Richard Whitt?
"Her Mother and I do," stated William Skaggs as he turned to take a seat by Mary.

Rachel stepped up beside Hezekiah Whitt, her husband to be.

Bride and Groom face each other and join hands," commanded the authority figure, Reverend Richard Whitt.

The Reverend went through the vows with both the bride and the groom and they both answered appropriately. He had them kneel while holding hands. Next he opened his old worn Bible and begin to read from Ephesians 5:21.

21 Submitting yourselves one to another in the fear of God.

22 Wives, submit yourselves unto your husbands, as unto the Lord.

23 For the husband is the head of the wife, even as Christ is the head of the church: and he is the savior of the body.

24 Therefore as the church is subject unto Christ, so let the wives be to their own husbands in every thing.

25 Husbands, love your wives, even as Christ also loved the church, and gave himself for it;

26 That he might sanctify and cleanse it with the washing of water by the word,

27 That he might present it to himself a glorious church, not having spot, or wrinkle, or any such thing; but that it should be holy and without blemish.

28 So ought men to love their wives as their own bodies. He that loveth his wife loveth himself.

29 For no man ever yet hated his own flesh; but nourish and cherisheth it, even as the Lord the church:

30 For we are members of his body, of his flesh, and of his bones.

31 For this cause shall a man leave his father and mother, and shall be joined unto his wife, and they shall be one flesh.

THE PATRIOT, HEZEKIAH WHITT

32 This is a great mystery: but I speak concerning Christ and the church.

33 Nethertheless let every one of you in particular so love his wife even as himself; and the wife see that she reverence her husband.

"Rise up children, with authority of the church I pronounce you husband and wife," stated the Reverend Richard Whitt.

"Husband you may kiss the bride!" added the Reverend.

Hezekiah took Rachel into his arms and gave her a long passionate kiss.

After the kiss was concluded the Reverend stepped between the husband and wife and presented them to the people.

"Friends and relatives, I now present you with Mr. and Mrs. Hezekiah Whitt," stated the proud Reverend Richard Whitt.

The folks cheered and begin to form a line to the front of the church to shake the hands of the newlyweds. Robert was the first to shake hands with Hezekiah and hug Princess Rachel Skaggs Whitt.

Susannah stepped up and made an announcement that all were welcome to come to the Whitt House, for cake and a celebration for the marriage of Hezekiah and Rachel.

Grand paw James Skaggs' fine buggy and white horse was hitched out front for the couple to ride in. After a reception at the Whitt House, the couple would ride the buggy to their new home on the banks of New River.

Robert, Abijah, Edmund and sister Rachel had planned a chivalree after the couple was alone in their cabin. It was cold, but folks were use to being outdoors all year round, and a little cold air would not stop the merriment.

After having cake and tea, the Reverend Richard Whitt had the homemade wine brought out from the cellar, and toasts were in order. The fine smooth wine was passed around to each waiting glass. One toast and another was presented. Here, Here, could be heard again and again as different folks presented a toast to the newlyweds.

There was not a lot of room, but the sitting room was cleared for dancing and the Reverend let loose on his fiddle. Hezekiah and Rachel took the floor to be the first dancers. Both of them were new to dancing, but they created a nice waltz type dance as they circled the floor.

Soon others joined them on the crowded floor. A good time was had by all and the time begin to slip away. Finally, the time came for Rachel to throw her bouquet to the prospective brides and leave with Hezekiah in the borrowed buggy.

Now Hezekiah was not the first in the family to get married, Rachel Whitt and Abraham Henderson were wed in 1780. Rachel remembered vividly the chivalree the family and friends gave her and Abraham and now it was payback time.

THE PATRIOT, HEZEKIAH WHITT

Everyone cheered as Hezekiah and Rachel drove off in the buggy. Rachel snuggled close to Hezekiah against the cold January air.

"I love you Rachel, we will be at our home in a short time," said the excited Hezekiah.

"I *Dah-quel-e-mah* (love) you!" I can hardly believe this day is here and you are my *Wahsiu* (husband,)" said Rachel excitedly in Shawnee.

"It is and you are and the same to ya!" answered Hezekiah not really sure what she said.

"I hope the fire is still burning in our cabin, but you can warm me regardless," stated Rachel seductively.

Hezekiah had his arm around Rachel and squeezed her shoulder lovingly.

"There's the cabin, I see that smoke is still coming out of the chimney," said Hezekiah as he guided the white horse to the cabin.

"You go and throw some wood on the fire and I will tend the horse," said Hezekiah.

Hezekiah walked Rachel to the door, picked her up and carried her into the cabin. He sat her down and she gave him a big bear hug, then he went back out to tend the horse.

While Hezekiah unhitched the horse and put him in the corral and put out some feed, Rachel got the fire built up and turned down the bed. Hezekiah finished up with the horse and grabbed an arm load of firewood and hurried into the cabin. Rachel had the fire burning and it gave off a dancing light. She had her coat off and was wrapped in a blanket.

Hezekiah took off his coat and walked to his bride. When Hezekiah got close she opened her blanket to him. Rachel had nothing on under the blanket and her most secret treasures were revealed to Hezekiah. She wrapped the blanket around her husband and began to dance slowly while holding Hezekiah close.

Hezekiah's keen ears heard something moving around outside. With years of watching and listening for danger, Hezekiah took action. He grabbed his musket off the pegs over the fire place and cracked open the door. Poor Rachel was left standing there holding her blanket.

Cowbells, horns, and any other number of noise makers came to life. Many voices could be heard shouting and cheering.

"Come here Rachel, don't be scared, it's a chivalree," said Hezekiah.

"Look at them, we sure surprised them," said Abijah.

Hezekiah's sister Rachel and her husband Abraham Henderson truly enjoy the chivalree, as they remembered theirs from two years ago.

"All right folks, you got us, now go home and get out of the cold," stated Hezekiah loudly.

THE PATRIOT, HEZEKIAH WHITT

"God bless you," said the familiar voice of Paw, Reverend Richard Whitt after the noise died down.

"Thank you," said Rachel and Hezekiah as the crowd begin to move away.

The noise makers kept making the noise as they begin to head back home. They were very merry and having a great time as they traveled down the road. Some were feeling the spirits and some were just happy for Hezekiah and Rachel.

Again all was quiet except the crackling of the wood fire. Hezekiah hurriedly dropped his clothes and joined Rachel in her blanket again and they resumed their wedding dance. With this the excitement grew rapidly and Hezekiah took his bride to bed and consummated their marriage that would last some sixty four years.

THE PATRIOT, HEZEKIAH WHITT

Chapter 16

Hezekiah Takes Rachel To The Clinch, 1782

When Mr. and Mrs. Hezekiah Whitt awoke on their first morning of marriage they snuggled. After more loving, Hezekiah got up and built up the fire to warm up the cabin. Rachel began their first breakfast. They had food in the house, thanks to Mary Skaggs and Susannah Whitt. They had cornbread, milk, honey, butter, and other leftovers that were brought to the cabin yesterday. Susannah and Mary had gathered food and provisions from their own family's cupboards as well as gifts from others. They had cornmeal, salt, pepper, yeast, potatoes, sweet potatoes, all kinds of dried foods including beans and lentils, a slab of bacon, and a cured ham. There was even a container of tobacco and a little brown jug of corn squeezens for medicinal purposes.

It was a custom to help newlyweds this way and the name, "House Warming," started this way. Hezekiah will be doing some hunting as the need arises.

This year would see a rise of people moving to Kentucky and other western parts of Virginia. Some of the folks from the Meadow Creek and other areas would be migrating with their families to the western waters. The folks that had seen the Clinch Valley were in love with it and hastened to move there even with the great threat the Indians posed.

Thomas Mastin, Joseph Ray, Henry Harman, Robert Moffett, the Ingles brothers, James Burke, Thomas Maxwell, Joseph Perry, James Perry and some of the Skaggs brothers would be going west this year or next. Some of these folks would pay a big price for their dreamland, but not in money. Hezekiah burned to go also, so with much pondering and talking to Rachel, they decided to go to his Cedar Grove on Indian Creek, now part of Washington County. This valley was already being called "Baptist Valley," because the first settlers Hankins, Skaggs and Whitts were firm Baptist. These honest upright people believed that they only needed the one true government and that was God's Laws. They supported the government of Virginia because it was based on Christian beliefs and freedom.

Sorrowful reports would come in from the western waters as some frontier folks met their fate. The British may have given up organized battles, but underneath they were keeping the Indians fired up. The Indians loved their hunting grounds in Kentucky and on the Clinch and were not about to give it up without a fight.

Hezekiah Whitt, Thomas Mastin and others decided to leave Meadow Creek and go to Baptist Valley together as a group. They decided that the best time to leave would be about the middle of April 1782. The men in the group the better, as strength is in numbers. It is less likely that the Indians would attack a sizeable group.

Hezekiah and Rachel consummated their marriage regularly, guess what? Rachel will be a Maw in October and the baby will be born at Hezekiah's Cedar Grove, in

THE PATRIOT, HEZEKIAH WHITT

Washington County (Now Tazewell County.) on Indian Creek. Rachel will be with-child as they travel through the mountains to the waters of the Clinch.

Hezekiah and Rachel look forward to going to their new home on Indian Creek. They talk about it every day as they plan out the trip. Hezekiah has acquired a good strong mule to carry Rachel and to use as his work mule on the new farm. They would have to travel light because there was not a road that could handle a wagon. A few cooking pans and kitchen stuff would have to go as well as salt and cornmeal. Seeds for corn, beans, squash, lentil, flax, and others including tobacco seed would be in the packed items. What ever they could carry, they brought.

There would be at least two books on the trip. The Holy Bible and "Pilgrim's Progress" it was by the Englishman John Bunyan. This book was very popular with the early Americans because it illustrated the Christian Life in day to day dealings with temptation and living right with God.

After supper was over every night Hezekiah and Rachel would light up their pipes and relax while reading from either the Bible or Pilgrim's Progress.

Hezekiah went over all of his gear from his musket to his bridles and such. He acquired another Brown Betz and taught Rachel to load and shoot. She was a natural with the exception of holding up the long heavy barrel. Rachel found out that if she could rest it against a tree or across something she could really improve her accuracy.

"Rachel, remember to aim little, hit little. Hold your breath and squeeze the trigger," instructed Hezekiah.

The first signs of spring came to the New River Valley and the men and their families were just about ready to head west to the waters of the Clinch. The men had a meeting about the first week in April and decided to leave on the 15th of April 1782.

Susannah had tears a few times fearing for the safety of Hezekiah and Rachel, but she always cried when any of her family would go in harms way. On April 14th the Reverend Richard Whitt family gathered for a little get together and have a good visit before so many would venture off into the wilderness. After eating and having a good visit the Reverend prayed a long prayer asking God to go with the Pilgrims to the Clinch Valley. The family hugged and Susannah gave Rachel an old broach that was handed down to her through the Skaggs family.

"It will give you good luck as it has my family," said Susannah Whitt.

"Thank you so much, Mother Susannah," said Rachel in a most approving voice.

Next morning with the dawn the pilgrims gathered at Major Thomas Mastin's farm to travel together. Thomas Mastin and Agnes his Indian wife and the four adopted Indian children took the lead. Hezekiah in his almost black buck skins and Rachel in her light tan doe skin dress were second in line, but this position would change many times as they traveled through the old scouting grounds. Different men would take the point and

THE PATRIOT, HEZEKIAH WHITT

the rear guard from day to day. A watch would be on duty every night, with all the men taking turns.

There was also a large crowd of family and friends gathered around to see them off. The hugs and kisses were going on and Thomas Mastin was thinking about time.

"Alright folks are we going to hug all day?" asked Thomas.

"Daylights fleeting, we got to get a going." said someone from the group.

The Pilgrims were ready to leave, but wanted to get one more hug from a loved one. Finally the caravan of about thirty rode out two by two.

Hezekiah was riding his big gray horse, Johnny and Rachel was on her sure footed mule. They were carrying everything they owned packed and tied all around and behind the saddle. Of course Hezekiah had his trusty musket laid across his saddle in a convenient posture, as did the other men.

Major Thomas Mastin led the pilgrims southwest toward Fort Chiswell. This little county seat of Montgomery County would be the last settlement of any size the Pilgrims would see. In about eight years (1790) the County of Wythe would be formed and the town of Wytheville would be built about eight miles to the west of Fort Chiswell. But now only a few cabins were scattered about. The party should make it to Fort Chiswell this day as it is about twenty miles. Riding the horses is much faster than just walking plus much more gear can be carried. Because women and children are in the party twenty miles is a really good day of travel. As the party goes deeper into the wilderness eight to ten miles may be all they travel in a day.

Then after a few breaks through the day the pilgrims arrived in Fort Chiswell about an hour before sunset. There is not enough lodging in the little town to accommodate all the folks, so they set up a camp at the edge of the burg. Some folks went to the mercantile to get a few little extra things like tobacco, jerky, and a treat of stick candy for the children. It was mostly just a place of amusement, as they would be leaving the last mercantile on their journey.

There were a few officers of the court in town on county business. Colonel Preston was in town and when he heard that Major Mastin was leading a group to the west, he made a point to come and visit them. He kept emphasizing the point of being safe as the Indians would be quite disturbed that they were moving in on the Indian's hunting grounds. His words did not dishearten the anxious travelers. They were ready to go to their dreamland on the waters of the Clinch.

After a night's rest the folks began to roll out of their blankets. Most had set up a lean-to to keep the night's dew or rain off.

Hezekiah rolled over to Rachel and said, "don't take long to stay all night here does it honey?"

Rachel laughed and replied, "You crazy, white man!"

THE PATRIOT, HEZEKIAH WHITT

Rachel suffered a little each morning because of her morning sickness, but she did not let it hold her back from her duties.

They all got up, had breakfast, gathered the hobbled horses, and packed for another days travel.

Thomas Mastin called for a quick meeting and discussed the days travel. He asked Hezekiah to lead in prayer and they all mounted up to leave Fort Chiswell. Thomas Mastin had explained that it was about twenty miles to Big Walker Mountain and he hoped to reach the base of the 3,400 feet mountain in this days travel.

Major Mastin also set up a roster for an advance spy to travel ahead a mile or so for the safety of the pilgrims. Hezekiah would draw this duty every few days. Robert Moffett rode off to get ahead of the others and to start looking for Indian sign. Finally, everyone had their gear tied on their animals and were mounted up for the adventure that lay ahead.

After about ten miles the party stopped for a break, this was about two miles northwest of present day Wytheville. The virgin timbers lorded over the trail and the leaves were grown to about half the size of full summer growth. Rachel looked about and smiled at Hezekiah. She began to feel the freedom of the wilderness. She loved the whites she had met, but a wonderful feeling came on her as she remembered her childhood in the wilderness. Even though she grew up in the Indian towns, she was in the great woods much of the time. Hezekiah understood thoroughly as he also loved the sights, smells and freedom of nature all around.

They did not linger too long on their break, just enough time to stretch and go behind some bushes to take care of business. The ladies went on one side of the trail and the men went to the other side. One of the men stood guard so that they would not be surprised by an Indian attack. The animals were watered at each stream or spring. Once again the pilgrims were on the move. They had the goal of reaching the foot of Big Walker Mountain before retiring for the night. Rachel was doing pretty good considering that she was with child. The baby was not due until October so she was only about three months along.

They had a good afternoon and were coming up on Big Walker Mountain about 6:00 PM. Robert Moffett came riding back and met with the Major. He had not seen any new Indian sign, but he had found a good spot to set up camp; a nice limestone spring was near by. He reported it to be about a half mile ahead. The word was passed back rider to rider and all were happy to be stopping for the night. From here on some days the pilgrims may only get six to twelve miles a day because of terrain and security against attack.

The party of frontiersmen and women arrived at the camp Robert Moffett had picked out. It was a nice level ground with new grass for the animals and it appeared to be a good place for defense. One end of the mountain meadow was big rocks that could be used in defense. They would set up their camp here with the open meadow exposed so that any intruders could be easily spotted. The spring would supply all the water they needed.

The folks took all of their gear off the horses and began setting up camp. The lean-tos were set up and fire wood gathered. Robert Moffett stood guard while all of this was going on. Hezekiah would be the forward spy the next day.

As Hezekiah looked around at the camp sight he said, "The elk and deer have created this mountain meadow by grazing here for a number of years."

"There is much meadows like this in the Ohio country, buffalo graze there," replied Rachel.

"I would love to see that someday, but I love the mountains around our farm," Hezekiah said.

"One mountain to the southwest close to Elk Garden Fort has two great rocks on top; they resemble a house and a barn," explained Hezekiah.

"You have told me of these beautiful mountains, valleys, streams, and the great cedar grove, I can picture them in my head," said Rachel.

"Did your people that explored the Pellissippi (Clinch River) ever describe the beauty they saw?" asked Hezekiah.

Rachel looked up approvingly at Hezekiah for using a Shawnee word.

"Yes but not as much as the bounty of elk, deer, beaver, and bear," answered Rachel letting her big brown eyes shine.

After supper and after the evening chores done the folks sat about the campfires smoking or chewing tobacco. Hezekiah and Rachel read from the Bible the passages pertaining about the "Promised Land"; this gave them hope as they reflected on their pilgrimage to their new land on Indian Creek. Of course they knew about God's promise was also about Heaven and the resurrection.

After everyone turned in and things got quiet, Hezekiah loved his bride quietly. Before they knew it the sun was creating little diamonds of light on the heavy dew in the mountain meadow; the last watch build up the fires and went about awakening the folks. A big bull elk and some of his wives were eating on the spring grass on the far side of the meadow.

Hezekiah, remembering his assignment of forward scout, hurriedly prepared so he could get to it. He ate some corncakes and molasses, saddled Johnny, checked the prime on his musket and rode off to the north.

This will be a hard day for the pilgrims as they will travel uphill most of the day. They had to cross Big Walker Mountain at a slight gap on top. It would be a bright day as the sun was at their backs and shining into the woods and lighting the path. The other side of the mountain would be cooler and much darker. The mountain laurel would be thick

THE PATRIOT, HEZEKIAH WHITT

and could hide hundreds of Indians. Hezekiah would be doing his best scouting to detect any dangers.

About a quarter of a mile from camp, Hezekiah dismounted and led Johnny up the mountain trail. It was the last part of April and early spring was here. The brush and trees already had leaves abounding. This shut out the visibility into the deep woods. Hezekiah continued to scan the area with his keen eyes and occasionally stopped to listen. He could hear a Tom Turkey gobbling for a mate and a crow called out to his black friends. A rat-tat-tat could be heard in the distance as a big Redheaded Woodpecker did his thing on a dead tree. Way up ahead a squirrel crossed the trail. These critters were all a good sign that the two legged kind were not about. Much can be discerned by watching the act ivies in the woods.

Today's journey was hard because it was all uphill. The pilgrims would have to walk the horses and mules most of the day to keep them fresh in case of trouble. If trouble came the animals were the best chance of escape.

The pilgrims were all in a jovial mood as they climbed up the mountain, because each step brought them closer to their new home on the waters of the Clinch. They were allowed to talk as they traveled so that listening ears in the woods would discern that they had many men and many muskets.

Hezekiah topped Big Walker Mountain through a gap and stopped to look and listen. He could see the valley before him and it was a wonderful sight. There was no sign of another human being in the whole valley. Today the town of Bland is located there in the valley. As Hezekiah took it all in he had to lift up a prayer to thank his Maker for allowing him to be apart of this great scene. Hezekiah praised God and thanked Him for His loving-kindness. He forgot and spoke out loud to Johnny and it kinda startled him to hear his own voice. Johnny turned his head and rolled his big brown eyes to see what Hezekiah was up to. Hezekiah smiled and patted his loyal horse.

Hezekiah was on the move again scouting for trouble. He figured the party of frontiersmen would try to make it into the valley before stopping for the day. There would be plush grass and cool clear water down in the valley. The walking was better on the downhill side of the journey. The leaves were not as thick, but the Mountain Laurel made up for it. Even in the afternoon there was not much light on this north side. Still no sign of Indians had been found, but Hezekiah stayed alert. Way down the trail Hezekiah saw a mother bear crossing the trail with her little twins on her heels. This could be trouble if he did not keep a good distance from the she-bear. He would give her time to get on to where ever she was taking her babies. By the time the party got to this point she should be gone, thought Hezekiah.

Hezekiah made it down into the valley and over to a creek. There was a nice meadow with all the requirements for the pilgrim's camp. Hezekiah saw a nice buck down by the creek and decided to take it for food. He gently raised his trusty musket and let go, the ball found its mark just behind the shoulder and the deer dropped. Hezekiah reloaded

COLONEL CHARLES DAHNMON WHITT   126

and sat for about ten minutes for the deer's life to pass and to see if the shot may have attracted any Indians. He went to the deer and field dressed it and hung it from a limb. It was not long before he saw his friends coming out of the deep woods on the edge of the meadow.

Major Thomas Mastin lifted his arm high to signal the parties approach. Hezekiah waved his hand high in recognition. Rachel now saw Hezekiah and bubbled with excitement. The newlyweds missed each other in the days of separation.

Agnes, Thomas Mastin's wife, noticed this and said, "You better get use to it honey, a country man doesn't stay home all the time."

Rachel gave her a quick glance and turned her eyes back to her husband. Hezekiah walked proudly to his bride, trying not to attract attention. He helped her down from her mule and gave her a casual hug. Frontier people did not openly court or flirt even to a wife.

Hezekiah took her to a nice place to set up their lean-to and helped with the unloading, and then he went over to Major Thomas Mastin and gave him the good report of no Indian sign. Thomas thanked him and ask if the area around camp had been gone over. Hezekiah told him he had circled about ten polls around the meadow after killing the deer and again, no Indian sign was found.

"Good job Hezekiah, I can always count on you to be thorough in your spying," said Major Thomas Mastin.

"Thank you Thomas," answered Hezekiah.

"Now go and be with your wife and get you some rest, I want you to be the rear guard tomorrow," said Thomas Mastin.

"That will be fine, if we have a good day, we will be nigh on to Rocky Gap tomorrow night," said Hezekiah optimistically.

After a good nights rest, the morning brought different weather. It was cold and the sky was gray. The wind whistled through the trees and made an eerie sound as the pilgrims prepared for another day's journey.

"My goodness, if it weren't bout May I would swear it was going to snow," said Hezekiah as he dug out a heavier jacket.

Rachel smiled at Hezekiah as she took a heavy jacket that Hezekiah produced for her.

"Blackberry winter," said Rachel.

"Well it is some kind of winter," answered Hezekiah as he pulled his coat tight around his neck.

"Look over there, see all the blackberries blooming," said Rachel as she pointed.

THE PATRIOT, HEZEKIAH WHITT

"Guess you are right, it shouldn't last long, May is just about here," Hezekiah said.

The forward scout had already ridden off and the pilgrims mounted up. Rachel decided to ride at the back of the formation to be with Hezekiah. One of the Indian children, twelve year old Thomas Bailey Christian, also went to the back to ride with Aunt Rachel. He would be with Rachel while Hezekiah took his little rides to the rear about every half an hour to make sure trouble was not coming up on them from the rear.

The cold wind whistled down the valley causing the pilgrims to pull their collars tight around their necks and add another layer of clothing. Some of the ladies wrapped themselves and a smaller child in a blanket. The weather was the big topic that day. Some commented that the wind was like a February wind. It was a noisy day also as the wind sing through the trees and rustled the leaves on the forest floor. The horses were nervous and special care had to be taken not to let them become spooked and maybe try to run off.

Hezekiah turned back and retraced their tracks every now and then just as a precaution. He never discovered anything that gave him any alarm. Hezekiah went back and forth all day until he caught up with Rachel and her nephew, Thomas Bailey Christian, in the evening just before they ended the days travel.

The forward scout had found a camping ground with a creek and big hill on the back side and a good days feeding of new grass for the animals. He had been thinking about the wind as well as a place of good defense when he picked this spot. The pilgrims could camp around some boulders and there were some rock houses along the hill that would give shelter from the wind. If an attack was to come the Indians would have to cross the little meadow in the open. Major Thomas Mastin thanked the forward scout for a job well done.

As the ladies cooked the wind subsided as it often does in the evening hours. The air was still cool for the end of April, but after the wind died down the topics of talk went back to the Clinch Valley, and the happiness they expected to have there.

Hezekiah had the first watch after supper and would be able to get some sleep around midnight. Nothing out of the ordinary took place on Hezekiah's watch so he was relieved by another man. Hezekiah found Rachel and hurriedly got into her bed roll and she pulled him closer to warm him up. After a little loving the couple drifted off into a good sleep.

The dawn brought a new and better day weather wise. It was cool but the wind had lain down and this made everyone have a better disposition. Hezekiah had no extra duties today so he could spend the entire day riding and talking with Rachel. They were about five miles from Rocky Gap and the travel would be a little easier until they started up the mountain to Rocky Gap. Rachel was pleased to have her man riding beside her again.

THE PATRIOT, HEZEKIAH WHITT

The day was going good and the pilgrims stopped for a dinner break at around noon. The forward scout and an unidentified rider came riding up and headed over to Major Thomas Mastin. The two riders dismounted and stood to talk to the Major. They talked for a full twenty minutes and everyone was looking on expectantly. Finally the rider mounted up, turned and waved to the onlookers and rode off toward Fort Chiswell. The pilgrims all gathered around Thomas Mastin and the forward scout.

"Well folks we will have to have a meeting, I guess now is as good a time as any," said Thomas Mastin.

"What's it all about Major Mastin," asked one of the group.

"Let's all go over there where you can sit down against that little knoll, that way all of you can see and hear," suggested Thomas Mastin.

After everyone had sat down and became quiet Thomas began to speak.

"That feller that just come gave me a very bad report, it seems that some militia under the command of Colonel David Williamson done a very bad thing that may affect every white person west of the Blue Ridge," said Thomas Mastin.

"Major Mastin, what happened?" asked Hezekiah?

"They dun went and massacred 97 defenseless Christian Indians, ain't none of the Indians in the Ohio country gonna be happy bout it," exclaimed Thomas Mastin.

"Good God, what on earth were they thinking?" asked a man in the back before he thought.

"Well let me tell you all the whole story and we can discuss our problem once I'm done," said the Major.

Major Thomas Mastin reported, everyone got quiet and the Major began to tell the people the whole report.

This past winter (1781) the Delaware's and Mohawks have severely harassed the settlers in western Pennsylvania. General Daniel Brodhead decided to teach the Indians a lesson. He let his hotheaded Colonel David Williamson have a hundred militiamen and gave him a free hand. He even told Williamson to do a thorough job and teach the Indians a good lesson.

Let me back up a little and tell you about these particular Indians, They are Christians called Moravians cause some Moravian missionaries came to them and preached the Gospel of Jesus Christ to um. They moved out mostly two themselves because they no longer wanted to fight their white brothers.

Anyway the Moravians had a really bad winter and their Chief Abraham took back to their summer camps to try and gather some food from their catches, and even glean corn left in the fields. He divided his people up and sent them to three different summer camps. Abraham had an even 150 people counting women and boys so he sent 50 to

Salem, 50 to Gnadenhutten, and 50 to Schoenbrun. Abraham and his 50 folks were lucky to find good corn still in the field after the winter had worked it over. They were gathering the corn when Colonel David Williamson's bunch spied um. He took fifteen men and made a make-shift boat and crossed the Tuscarawas river and came up on Abraham and his people in a friendly manner.

The main part of the militia went on to Gnadenhutten with out being seen by the Indians. The militia found only one brave and his wife there and promptly tomahawked them and hid their bodies.

Back with Abraham there was braves, women, and boys working the field and most had a weapon of some sort. There were more Indians there then Williamson had thought, so he took the friendly approach. As he and the fifteen militiamen came close they waved in a friendly manner. Abraham and his people waved back and smiled at their white brothers.

Williamson, being the snake that he was started off with a big lie. He told them that he and his men had come to take them close to Fort Pitt where they could come under their protection and have good food and good shelter. He told them just to quit working and come with them and they would feed them.

Abraham smiled widely with this grand news because his people were almost destitute. Abraham called his people over to meet the Colonel and share the good news. Next Colonel Williamson ask Abraham to gather all of their weapons as a gesture of good faith.

The Indians placed themselves into the hands of the whites for the promise of food and shelter. This was such grand news Abraham asked about his people at Salem camp. The Colonel said sure they will be welcome also, send two runners and have them meet us at Gnadenhutten. Abraham sent two fleet footed boys to share the news and for them to head to Gnadenhutten.

The 48 Moravian Indians and the 15 militiamen all crossed the Tuscarawas River in the boat two or three at a time. They used a vine rope to pull the boat back and forth. Finally the Indians got to Gnadenhutten to find them selves surrounded by 100 militiamen all pointing muskets at them. Chief Abraham stepped up to the Colonel and asked him what was going on. Old Colonel Williamson ignored Abraham and ordered that all the Indian's hands be tied behind them with rawhide thongs.

There was a good sized mission building and a big meeting lodge, close by. The Colonel had the men and boys herded into one of the buildings and the women into the other. Once in the buildings the Indians were forced to the ground and their ankles were bound like their hands.

About two hours later the 52 Indians arrived from Salem. They walked into the little village joyously fully expecting to be fed and cared for.

THE PATRIOT, HEZEKIAH WHITT

Colonel Williamson once again came out friendly to greet the 52 Indians. He informed them that Abraham and their brothers were waiting for them in the buildings. He also told them that Abraham left orders for them to put their weapons in a pile and not bring them in for their worship service. They piled up their weapons and went toward the buildings like sheep led to slaughter. They were tied just like the others. Chief Abraham was saddened that he had caused them to come there.

A total of 98 Indian men, women and boys sat tied in the two buildings. Outside was a strong ring of armed guards and there would be no escape. There was no food, water or toilet privileges the rest of the day and the whole night. The Indians suffered greatly, especially the women and boys.

Colonel Williamson called a meeting the next morning. He asked them if they should march the Indians on a troublesome trip to Fort Pitt or should they go ahead and execute them right here and save everyone a problem. He reminded the militia how the Indians had killed and plundered and how it affected every family. He told them that General Brodhead had given him strict orders to teach them a good lesson.

He then gave a forcible talk about he thought they just as well take care of the problem right here and now. He said it in a way that if any disagreed were Indian lovers. He took a vote by having those in favor of marching them to Fort Pitt take a step forward. 15 of the 100 militia had enough starch to step forward, the rest sided with Williamson.

Colonel Williamson went to Chief Abraham and gave him the verdict of his court. He told him that all the Indians would be put to death.

Abraham was so shocked he had a problem starting his speech. Abraham told the Colonel that he gave God as his witness that every Indian there was innocent of any crime. Abraham explained that they were all Christians and lived to serve the Lord, but were ready to die in Christ if it comes to that. Then Abraham asked for another night that every Indian would have time to pray and prepare to die.

Colonel Williamson agreed to it, but thought to himself, God better have mercy on them because he sure wasn't going to.

During the night the militia cast lots to see who would do the executing. Captain Builderback and 24 other men won the unlucky chore. Builderback entered the building with the 24 men carrying a big hammer. He had all the Indians to rise to their feet and turn to face the wall. With out warning the burley Builderback came up behind Chief Abraham and gave him a vicious blow, crushing his skull. The Chief fell to the floor flopping and jerking. Builderback took his knife and scalped the innocent Chief Abraham. He continued to the right killing the next 13 Indians in the same fashion. Each blow made an eerie devilish sound and blood spattered all about.

Next Builderback handed the hammer to Private George Bellar and told him to go on down the line. Builderback complained that his arm was tired. As the private went about doing his sinful task, Builderback took his knife again and scalped the other 13 Indians that he sent on to Jesus.

The Indians were very brave, they did not make a sound, cry, plea, or beg for mercy.

A Private Otho Johnson could not take it any longer; he abruptly vomited and ran out the door. The door did not close completely and two Indian boys noticed it. The two boys had worked on their leather thongs all night and were successful in getting them off. This morning they put the thongs on loosely to fool the Shemanese. The two teenage boy Indians bolted out the door and ran around the corner. Their fleet feet carried them faster than they had ever ran before, in a minute they entered the woods without even a shot being fired their way. The militiamen knew if the boys made it to the woods they would never be caught, they were jest boys anyhow.

The boys ran the seven miles to Schoenbrum in record time; you might say they ran like scared rabbits. The boys gave the alarm to the other 50 Moravian Indians that were there gathering food. The Whites were alarmed that the Indians were there and had been missed. They rushed there only to find an empty village.

Colonel David Williamson surely taught the Indians a lesson on March 8, 1782. He killed 35 men, 27 women and, 34 boys, all innocent blood.

The Indians in the Ohio Country now had 96 more reasons for revenge. The rider you saw talking to me was taking the alarm to the east, because the Indians are not one bit happy about this blatant massacre. They will be out for blood even more now.

Thomas Mastin stood there silent for a full minute looking at the faces of his friends. No one said anything from the group.

"Friends, we must decide today whether to go on to the Clinch or turn around and go back to our old homes," stated Thomas Mastin.

The folks talked amongst themselves for about ten minutes and a hush fell over them.

"What say you," asked Thomas Mastin?

"Go to the Clinch," sounded the majority.

"All right folks, lets hurry up and get a bite to eat and get back on the trail, we should get to the foot of the mountain leading up to Rocky Gap today," exclaimed Thomas Mastin.

The families went back to their camp area and had a quick dinner. By 1:00 PM the pilgrims were on the trail traveling toward Rocky Gap. The Major told the people to take extra precautions, "we sure don't want to be caught off guard by a war party," he said.

"I hope we made the right decision sweetheart," Hezekiah said to Rachel.

THE PATRIOT, HEZEKIAH WHITT

"Don't fret, we will be just fine, we are a large group and we have that Whitten's Crab Orchard Fort to fall back to once we get to the Pellissippi, I mean the Clinch," stated Rachel.

"Yes and the most important thing is the Lord will be with us," answered Hezekiah.

John and Elizabeth Skaggs Hankins rode with Hezekiah and Rachel and they talk about the happening in the Ohio country with the murders. They also talk about the increased dangers now present because this evil man committed such atrocities.

They arrived at the foot of the mountain that leads up to Rocky Gap and set up camp. Two spies went out to cover the ground that surrounds the camp. From now on two men would stand watch together, one on one side and one on the other. This will require much more from each man, but a chance cannot be taken.

Around the campfires this evening much solemn talk took place. No one was really scared but a good respect of the danger was about. Talk of Colonel Williamson came up very often. How could someone hate Indians so much that they would kill so many Christian Indians? The lesson he taught was not the lesson meant by the General. Now the frontier will have to pay. When bedtime came Hezekiah was asked to read some scripture and then offer up a prayer. After the prayer everyone felt more secure and could sleep in peace.

Hezekiah did not serve as a camp watch this night, but he would be the forward spy today. The gap at the top of the mountain would be a likely spot for an ambush so the Major wanted his best spy to check it out.

Hezekiah hurriedly helped Rachel get packed, ate a quick breakfast, saddled Johnny, checked his prime in the flash pan and rode off toward Rocky Gap. The climb was hard so after about a quarter of a mile he got down and led his horse. This way he could study the ground and surroundings better. By around 10:30 AM he reached his limestone spring that he always loved to stop at. He looked the area over really good before getting down filling his canteen. Neither snakes this time nor Indians about, so he filled his canteen, brought Johnny over to let him drink. The water was so cool, clear, and had a wonder taste. After Johnny drink, Hezekiah took a stick and cleaned back the little banks of the pool so that his friends could drink when they got there.

Hezekiah started his scouting again taking pains to observe everything and listen to the woods. The birds and critters were out and about which he knew to be a good sign.

By 1:00 PM Hezekiah was at the gap. He went into it slowly as he guided Johnny around so many ground rocks. He tied Johnny to a bush and walked and listened. He made a circle of about fifty yards all around the gap and was satisfied that no painted Indians were about. He left a sign on the trail by the use of sticks and stones that all was well. He next untied Johnny and they continued through the gap and down the other side.

THE PATRIOT, HEZEKIAH WHITT

Major Mastin's Party was already at the spring and all got a cool, clear drink, including the horses and mules. There were no cattle, sheep, or hogs on this trip. In another year all the families hoped to go back east and get animals to start themselves a herd.

Hezekiah was now half way down the mountain. He had taken his time to really do a good job of spying, after all he had a wife to think of now, besides his friends. He thought of her often and worried about her traveling with-child.

Hezekiah scouted out the first meadow and picked a camp near a creek. Once again they could camp among some boulders and have a good place for defense. He and Johnny went all around the area and checked for any sign of trouble, but felt good that he found none. He saw a young elk and took it for food. The pilgrims would eat well tonight and have good protein for the rigors of travel.

Just as Hezekiah finished field dressing the elk he turned to see the pilgrims emerging from the mountain.

When Rachel saw Hezekiah she was excited and the baby within her quickened. Oh what joy this brought her, she could hardly wait to tell Hezekiah and let him feel the baby kicking around.

Hezekiah emerged from the edge of the woods where the elk still lay and walked to meet his wife and friends. Major Thomas Mastin rode ahead to greet Hezekiah and get a scouting report. Hezekiah gave him the report of "no Indians" and about killing the elk for the party.

"Go and hug your wife and then get back on watch till we can set up camp," instructed the Major.

Hezekiah smiled broadly at the Major and turned to meet Rachel. He led her horse over among some boulders where he planned to hang their lean-to. He helped Rachel down and she grabbed him and held him tightly for a good minute.

"My dear husband, our baby is having a hissy-fit in my belly, he loves to kick," exclaimed Rachel.

Rachel took Hezekiah's hand and placed it on her belly so he could experience the movement of their baby.

"My goodness is he alright?" asked Hezekiah as the baby gave another kick.

"Yes, he is just fine, well we are calling the baby a he, he might be a little girl," said Rachel.

"Could be, but no matter long as he is fine," said Hezekiah with a grin.

"Well honey you better go and stand watch so's we wouldn't be surprised by attackers,' Rachel said as she pushed Hezekiah gently toward his duty.

THE PATRIOT, HEZEKIAH WHITT

Hezekiah mounted Johnny and rode to a little rise in the meadow where he could see in all directions. The pilgrims went about unpacking their animals and took them to the creek for water and then hobbled them in the meadow where they could feast on the new lush grass.

Burk was assigned the first watch and relieved Hezekiah of his duty. Hezekiah went to Rachel and helped her finish setting up their camp, gathered firewood and proceeded to take care of Johnny and Becky, the mule.

Rachel was so proficient at building a fire and cooking out doors. When Hezekiah got back to her she had hoecakes frying in a pan and in a big cast iron skillet she had one great big elk steak cooking. Hezekiah brought a bucket of water from the creek and sat it near by.

"Well woman, you sure are good at what you do," said Hezekiah.
Rachel smiled and said, "I will show you tonight!"

Hezekiah turned a little pink and gave her a sneaky little grin.

Next morning the pilgrims packed up and rode in a new direction. They turned southwest toward their destination. The forward guard had been gone for at least twenty minutes as they formed up two by two. Today they would reach the Bluestone River, and follow it to its source. This next camp would be near modern day Gratton. This was on the headwaters of the south fork of the Clinch River. The pilgrims had another good day of travel and were thrilled to be on the waters of the Clinch. Those souls that had never saw it before marveled at the beauty and also were much impressed at the abundance of game. Even the veteran Indian spies admired it as if it was the first time that they laid eyes to it. Rachel also was impressed and called it Pellissippi one more time.

That evening the pilgrims enjoyed the water right out of the small stream they called the Clinch. Agnes, the wife of Thomas Mastin was also esthetic as she also said aloud, "Pellissippi."

"Dear wife, let's start calling it the Clinch," said Thomas Mastin.

"I just wanted to say it out loud one more time, I will try to speak the American way from now on," replied Agnes.

Next day they traveled to modern day Pisgah, about two miles from modern day Tazewell. They headed there because that was where the Witten Fort, also know as Crab Orchard Fort was built. They intended to make that the headquarters for a few days. They traveled down the Clinch to that location. The pilgrims were now up-beat again with no sign of the Indians. Also the beauty of the Clinch River Valley laying between majestic mountains would lift anyone's spirits.

THE PATRIOT, HEZEKIAH WHITT

They arrived at Witten's Fort to find it empty. The fort was small but built very strong. It looked like it was designed for about a dozen soldiers, but thirty settlers could fit for a few days if they had to. The fort was on a knoll right in the middle of a grown up meadow. It looks like the builders of the fort cut down the trees so no painted Indians could sneak up on them. The meadow had been used by a few elk and deer, but for some reason it was not heavily grazed.

The weather was mostly fair now in the first half of May 1782. The settlers (I can call them settlers now.) set up their lean-tos here and there, but mostly in the edge of the woods. After camp was made Major Thomas Mastin called a meeting for all the men. He told them that he thought, for safety sake, they should all stay close to the fort for a few days. He also wanted to send out eight spies to check for Indian sign. He told them that a days ride out and a return trip should be sufficient to detect any bad news. He also told them after the scouts return and if they give positive reports we can all go to our homesteads.

Of course Hezekiah was one of the eight men chosen to spy. He was to ride northwest and check out Middle Creek, Greasy Creek and the head waters of the Tug Fork of Big Sandy. Major Mastin gave him this area because that was one of the main Warrior's Paths.

Next morning the spies all rode out at about 7:00 AM. The men kissed their wives and children if they had any and were soon out of sight. The evening of the second day the scouts started to arrive. Hezekiah didn't get back until just before dark. The lightning bugs were already rising from the grass and twinkling to attract a mate. The Major had heard seven reports already and hoped a good report would be given from his friend, Hezekiah Whitt. Hezekiah trotted Johnny into the big meadow where all the settlers were camped. The major had been watching for Hezekiah and as soon as someone said here he comes, the Major went out to meet him.

"Hello Hezekiah Whitt, what have you got to report?" asked the Major.
Hezekiah pulled Johnny up right in front of the Major and stepped down.
"Thomas, I have good news, I found no new Indian sign," said the Indian spy.

"Great, we will have a meeting in the morning and then I will let everybody loose to go to their new homes," stated the Major.

"I am about famished, hope Rachel has something cooked up for me," stated Hezekiah as he turned toward Rachel. Hezekiah led Johnny right up to their lean-to and dropped the rein. He ran over to his awaiting bride. She greeted Hezekiah with a hug and a kiss.

"Sit down here husband, I will fix you a big bowl of elk stew, and while you eat and rest I will tend to Johnny," she instructed.

"Johnny can wait for a few minutes, I can tend him soon as I eat," answered Hezekiah.

THE PATRIOT, HEZEKIAH WHITT

Rachel gave Hezekiah a big bowl of elk stew, a cornpone, and a cup of cold water. Hezekiah sat down on a log by the smoldering campfire and began to inhale the meaty dish. Rachel slipped away and took Johnny to water. She brought him back to the meadow and hobbled him for the night. She also took an old piece of dried deer skin and rubbed him down to make sure he was dry. She returned to find Hezekiah sitting there smoking his pipe so she filled her pipe and joined him. The baby gave a little kick as soon as she sit down.

"Well the baby knows his paw is home," said Rachel.

THE PATRIOT, HEZEKIAH WHITT

A rendition of Hezekiah's Cedar Grove and cabin around 1782. Notice the little corn field to the left and the fine limestone spring meandering through the front.

Chapter 17

Look Rachel, There It Is

Next morning the Major called a meeting after everyone had breakfast and began to pack up once again. The people all gathered in front of the fort. The Major addressed the settlers.

"Good morning every one, I just wanted to say a few words before we embark to our new homes. I appreciate each and every one of you for the way you traveled together and were so diligent to safety. As you all know the spies all gave good reports and I recommend that you go to your land and start enjoying this grand country. If any of you see, hear, or even smell the foe from the Ohio waters, send out the alarm to your closest neighbor and head for this fort. Be very careful to take every precaution to guard against an ambush. Always keep your musket close by while you work and carry a knife of tomahawk on your person. Now I have bent your ears enough with words you already know. I think we should have a prayer before we head out. Hezekiah, would you mind to lift a prayer?" spoke Major Thomas Mastin.

"Let us pray, Almighty God, we lift praise to you this morning for your loving-kindness, your protection and watch-care of your humble people. Lord you have brought us through your majestic mountains and over rivers to this wonderful land. Thank you for giving us this most wonderful land here on the waters of the Clinch. Now Lord we ask for your continued love, direction, and your strong arm of protection. Lord please forgive us for our sinful deeds that we have done, spoke, or thought. We ask this in the name of Jesus Christ, Amen," prayed Hezekiah Whitt.

Everyone said, "Amen!"

The folks shook hands, hugged and spoke kind words of farewell as they headed to their horses and began to embark on the trip to their new home. Some of the folks did not have a cabin and could use some help from friends as soon as they could get settled.

Most of the folks in the party were heading down the Clinch River to settle in Baptist Valley, or along Indian Creek. Not many settled right on the Clinch River because it was so open to the dreaded painted Indians that would surely show up. Most traveled together and came to the mouth of Indian Creek, which they called Indian. (Now, modern day Cedar Bluff.)

Thomas Mastin and his family stopped off at his homestead, up a little hollow from Indian Creek, the John Hankins family stopped off in the edge of Baptist valley where he had his cabin prepared. Hezekiah was feeling very anxious as he turned up what is now Green Mountain Road and stopped at the base of a great Cedar Grove. He nudged Johnny to go a little further so that a trail into the cedars could be seen. Hezekiah led Rachel up the short trail and stopped.

THE PATRIOT, HEZEKIAH WHITT

"Look Rachel, there it is," Hezekiah said while pointing to a cleared ground with the little cabin standing stately against the back-drop of virgin cedar trees.

While sitting on Betsy the mule, Rachel reached over and squeezed Hezekiah's arm affectionately.

"What do you think Mrs. Whitt?" asked Hezekiah.

"I have not the words to describe my thought, except how beautiful it is, praise God for giving us this paradise," said Rachel.

"Well said, lets get on over there and start our lives together in this wonderful land, I want to show you our fine limestone spring first," said Hezekiah.

Hezekiah directed Johnny to the spring and Betsy, carrying Rachel and the unborn little Whitt followed. The little corral was still standing so Hezekiah helped Rachel down and put the animals into the corral. The spring's stream flowed through the corral so they could drink. Rachel headed on over to the little pool that came right out of the ground from under a big limestone rock. She knelt down and filled a container with the cool, clear, refreshing water and drank.

"It is as you said husband, truly God has shined his blessings on us," said Rachel.

"Let's go and see the cabin, sweetheart," said Hezekiah.

They walked to the cabin and Hezekiah opened the door cautiously not knowing what may have moved in since last summer. The sun shined into the cabin and lit the interior of the little 16' X 16' cedar cabin. Rachel saw the fireplace and that was about all there was to comment on.

"I love my fireplace," said Rachel approvingly.

"Well it is temporary, I want to cut limestone blocks and lay it up to stand the test of time and also it will be safer," explained Hezekiah.

"What else do you have planned to build?" asked Rachel.

"We have a bunch of stuff to do, get out a crop, build a good bed, put on a better roof of removable slats, make some furniture, build a barn," said Hezekiah.

Rachel stopped him in mid sentence.

"Slow down Hezekiah, you are wearing me out, we ain't gonna get it all done today," exclaimed Rachel.

"I know sweetheart, one important thing I meant to add was, get everything ready for our baby," added Hezekiah.

"Mister Whitt, you are so special, I am glad that our God sent us together, said Rachel in a loving tone.

"Me to," said Hezekiah.

THE PATRIOT, HEZEKIAH WHITT

"Well you go and get the horse and mule and bring them up here and I will start putting our stuff in the cabin, it looks like we could get a rain," said Rachel.

Hezekiah brought the animals close to the cabin and started unpacking them. Rachel began to move in to her new home.

"I was so glad to see our cabin, I was concerned that the Indians may have burned it to the ground," stated Hezekiah as he helped Rachel get their things into the cabin.

"Well don't be a fretting, our Lord has protected it for us," replied Rachel.

Well honey, you look around every time you come out and make sure there are no hidden dangers about, either two or four legged," instructed Hezekiah.

The Whitts enjoyed their first night in their cabin. It got dark early because of the sun blocking majestic cedars. It also took some time to get light in the morning. The little cornfield got more light than the cabin because of location and of course the trees were gone.

As time goes on Hezekiah will expand his fields for crops, but for now their farm was mostly hidden from the Indians that traveled the warrior's path, up and down Indian Creek.

This new day would keep the couple busy working around on their little farm. The corn stalks were still mostly standing and some corn ears were still in fair shape. The weather and critters had done some damage. This would be the first harvest from a year ago. Hezekiah planted the corn and had to leave it. Hezekiah would gather the corn and save the best to make cornmeal; the rest along with the fodder would be given to Johnny and Betsy.

After the field was cleared, Betsy would pull a plow to prepare for this years crop. Hezekiah and Rachel brought seed with them to plant. It was the first week in May and the tenth of May was traditionally corn planting day. They would be planting squash, corn, beans, lintels, flax, onion seeds, and they had about 30 Potatoes. They would carefully peel the potatoes and leave a little chunk at each eye. The eyes with the little chunks would be planted. This way they could be both eaten and planted. (Nothing was wasted by the early Virginians.) Also Hezekiah would have a little area for their tobacco. They also had about a dozen apple seeds which they hoped would one day be an orchard.

After breakfast was over, Hezekiah went right to work. He got down his old wooden plow that had hung in the cabin since last year. He then went to the field and cut all the corn stalks and pulled the ears. He made a fodder shock over close to the corral. He then sorted the corn, picking the best for Rachel to use and the rest would be fed to the animals. After the field was cleared the best he could get it, Hezekiah hooked Betsy to the plow. The ground was really rich and plowed better than he thought. There were still roots to contend with and as he made the plowed area larger it got tough. New ground is always tough, but mostly rich.

COLONEL CHARLES DAHNMON WHITT   141

THE PATRIOT, HEZEKIAH WHITT

Rachel had sorted their items from the packs and placed around in the cabin. While Hezekiah plowed she went around the edge of the Cedar Grove and gathered limbs from the hardwood forest for firewood. Hezekiah was alarmed when he saw her that far away from the cabin. He immediately stopped plowing and ran to fetch her and help get the firewood back to the cabin.

"What is the matter?" asked Rachel.

"I don't want you this far from the cabin without me on guard, don't you realize the danger?" asked Hezekiah.

"I am sorry, I just want to be of good help husband," replied Rachel.

"I don't know what I would do if I lost you, please let me know when you need wood or even water," answered Hezekiah seriously.

He hugged her tightly and gathered all the wood he could drag and headed for the cabin. Once he was sure Rachel was safe, he went back to plowing. He would have to plow another day and then he would have to make a harrow to smooth the ground and break up the clods. After that was done he could earnestly plant their field.

Rachel was a good worker and she knew a lot about farming. She had learned it from childhood as a Indian maiden. The Shawnee women are experts in growing crops. She has already told Hezekiah she needed many little fishes. She wanted to stick a fish in the ground beside of each hill of corn and even the other plants. Hezekiah was working on a plan to catch some fish out of Indian a little later once the corn plants popped out of the ground.

Hezekiah was concerned about Rachel having help when the baby came. He was concerned about her doing so much work also. Rachel told Hezekiah that Aunt Elizabeth Hankins and Agnes Mastin had both talked to her about helping with the baby when he came. They were both great midwifes even though they were from very different cultures. Also she told him that women have been having babies since this world started, Eve never had anybody but Adam. Hezekiah was pleased that an experienced midwife would be with Rachel when the time comes.

"I see that you are still calling the baby, he," said Hezekiah.

"It just seems right, I think the Lord will send us a man-child," said Rachel.

"I will not argue on that, if the baby is a boy, I would like to name him James after Grand Paw Skaggs," said Hezekiah.

"Wouldn't surprise me none," answered Rachel.

Before Hezekiah and Rachel could turn around a week had come and passed. Sunday was tomorrow and she suggested that they go and visit the Hankins and maybe the Mastin family. We need to have a worship service she explained. Hezekiah agreed and planned to get out early on the Lord's Day and travel over to the Hankins and maybe get with the Mastins. Hezekiah would handle the service if none of the others wanted to.

THE PATRIOT, HEZEKIAH WHITT

It was Saturday evening and Hezekiah went out to scout around the fringes of their farm to make sure no Indian sign was about. He came upon a great big black panther working on a big deer. It looked at him with its big green eyes and screamed in protest of his interruption. Hezekiah readied his musket in case the great cat decided to charge him. It went the other way, but did not seem to be too scared of Hezekiah.

Hezekiah was relieved that it moved out of his way. He had heard a panther one of the nights the previous week, but did not tell Rachel. The scream that the big cats make sounds much like a woman screaming and will literally raise the hair on the back of your neck. I will tell her about it he thought. I may have to hunt it down to protect the animals and even Rachel he thought.

Hezekiah went on to explore the area around Cedar Grove, but found no sign of Indians. He shot a young deer for meat and watched over his shoulder while he field dressed it. Upon completing the dressing of the deer, Hezekiah lifted it to his shoulder and proceeded to the cabin about a mile away.

Rachel met him in the front of the cabin and ran to him.

"Husband I heard something, it sounded like a woman screaming, could it be a panther on the prowl?" she asked?

"Did that thing run close to the cabin?" wondered Hezekiah without speaking.
"Yes it very well could be," said Hezekiah.
He let the carcass down and spoke to her about what he saw.

"I ran upon a big black panther, if it hangs around too close I will have to hunt it down," said Hezekiah.

"They are very territorial, we had one stalking our animals and even our children, back in our Ohio town," stated Rachel.

"What happened?" asked Hezekiah?

"It was running all the game away as well as stalking around our village; it killed a dog and one little girl!" exclaimed Rachel.

"What did your people do?" asked Hezekiah?

"The men set traps to no avail, and finally the whole tribe drove the great cat into a trap where our best warriors awaited with guns and bows'" said Rachel.

"This time they killed it. It was huge and black as the night," continued Rachel.

"Well let's not get too alarmed just yet, this cat will most likely stay clear of us," said Hezekiah in a comforting way.

They cut up the deer and salted some of it down, some was cut into strips to make jerky. Rachel took a big roast off the rump and started it to boil. It would cook during the

THE PATRIOT, HEZEKIAH WHITT

night until the fire died down. She would cook it some in the morning before they headed over to the Hankins and Mastins.

It was a quiet night and the Whitts had a restful sleep. Next morning after a little loving Hezekiah got his clothes on and went out to do the normal chores. Rachel was beginning to show pretty good, but it did not slow her down any. She got the roast cooking again and prepared a breakfast of porridge.

Hezekiah came back in and they sat down to eat. After a blessing was asked and the porridge eaten, Hezekiah suggested that they get ready and head over to Baptist Valley to see the Hankins. They put on their better clothes as it was the Lord's Day, June 9, 1782.

Hezekiah looked all about again as he saddled Johnny and Betsy for the ride. He brought the animals up to the cabin.

"Mrs. Whitt, are you about ready?" asked Hezekiah? (Men waited on their women in those days also.)

"Just about," Rachel answered as she opened the door.

Hezekiah could not but notice how lovely his wife was. She had a glow about her as most expectant mothers do, which added to her natural beauty.

"I am the luckiest man in America!" exclaimed Hezekiah.

"Why do you say that?" asked Rachel feeling Hezekiah's eyes moving over her body.

"You are so beautiful and you are all mine!" exclaimed Hezekiah.

"Thank you, but you are silly," answered Rachel.

Hezekiah helped Rachel upon Betsy, got his musket and mounted Johnny for their ride. They went down the little trail out of the cedar grove, followed the branch from the spring and turned right up the valley. It was but a mile or so to the Hankins home. Hezekiah instinctively spied the surroundings and the ground for trouble. It was an enjoyable ride as they rode up to the Hankins cabin.

John opened the door wide and the Whitts could see that he was setting his musket down and leaning it on the wall just inside the cabin.

"Good morning Uncle John," said Hezekiah.

Elizabeth looked out of the cabin beside John and spoke just ahead of John.

"Good morning Whitts" said Elizabeth Hankins.

THE PATRIOT, HEZEKIAH WHITT

"Good morning Hezekiah and Rachel," said John Hankins.
After hugs and questions about the prior week the families sat together for a few minutes on blankets. John was just about like Hezekiah, he had plenty of work to do including the building of furniture.

"Uncle John, we would like to visit the Mastins, would you all like to ride over with us?" asked Hezekiah?

"Well, I reckon we could, do you intend to have a worship service over there?" asked John?

"I brought my Bible, bet Thomas has one anyway," answered Hezekiah.
"Elizabeth, are you for going down Indian Creek this Lords Day?" asked John Hankins?

"Well John I don't see no reason why we can't, we better get ready it is a good hours ride," said Elizabeth.

"I will go and saddle our horses, you put on your purty blue dress," said John.

"I will help you Uncle John, Rachel can visit with Aunt Elizabeth," said Hezekiah.

While John and Hezekiah saddled the horses, Hezekiah asked John if they had seen or heard any sign of the panther.

"We have not, what have you seen and heard?" asked John?

Hezekiah told him about coming up on the big Black Panther in the woods and also hearing it scream during the week, also it screamed near the cabin not long after the encounter in the woods.

"A big panther can be dangerous to man and animal alike, we may have to get rid of him," said John Hankins.

"Don't mention it today, Uncle John, I would like for the ladies to have a peaceful Lord's Day," said Hezekiah.

"I won't say a word in front of the ladies, Hezekiah," answered John Hankins.
"By the way Hezekiah, what is today's date?" asked John.

"It is June 9, 1782," answered Hezekiah without blinking an eye.
In a short time the two couples headed down Indian Creek, the two men were in front and the ladies followed closely behind. The men talked of the weeks work in the short time they had on the waters of the Clinch and the ladies talked mostly about the baby coming in October or November 1782.

The ride passed fast and before they knew it they were coming up on the little hollow that the Mastins claimed. They rode up the trail single file, it was not much more that a path. There ahead was the Mastin's cabin and the children ran in the cabin to tell

THE PATRIOT, HEZEKIAH WHITT

Thomas that they had visitors. Thomas and Agnes came out to greet the Whitts and Hankins.

After a proper welcome the women got together to start dinner and the men gathered out by the corral to talk. Hezekiah said that after dinner he thought they should have a worship service. Thomas Mastin was glad and agreed wholeheartedly. They talked about work that needed to be done and about the panther. They also talked of staying vigilant for Indians. Thomas mentioned that about half a mile on down the creek was where Joseph Ray and his family settled.

"I went over last Wednesday and helped them get some of their cabin laid together," explained Thomas Mastin.

"That was good of you, we all have a plenty to do fore the snow flies," said John Hankins.

"Speaking of that I brought that old cross cut saw with me and it can be borrowed any time a friend needs it, right now Joe Ray has it," said Thomas Mastin.

"That's good news, we all could use it to put up our winter wood," answered Hezekiah.

After a meal of venison stew, wild greens, and a sweet cake of not much more than flower, molasses, and some leaven to give it arise was served with tea for desert.

Thomas asked if Hezekiah would lead in the worship service. Hezekiah seemed to be the spiritual leader, at least in these three families. Hezekiah read several passages of scripture and spoke for about ten minutes. The talk drew questions so all the men took part in one way or another. They worshipped their Lord for about an hour including the singing of hymns that Hezekiah also led them in. After a good prayer where many folks were named by name and lifted to the Lord, all the folks there including the children said, "Amen," aloud.

The Hankins and Whitts got ready to ride up Indian Creek to their homes. The Mastins all hugged the Whitts and Hankins. The Mastin Children were thrilled at the visit of their friends especially Aunt Rachel.

While the men talked earlier they had agreed that they had to send for or send people east to bring the tools, animals for stock, and some expressed that they needed a good dog. They talked about getting some geese or guinea birds. They make a real good alarm system. If someone or something comes around they make a big commotion. They agreed to wait until the spring of 1783 and see how things were going then, because every family had so much work to do.

The Whitts and the Hankins had a real good day. They got back home without any problems and enjoyed a spiritual lift for taking the time to worship God.

The next week came and Rachel did much of the planting while Hezekiah worked on other projects. The crops should do well even though some were planted a little late. The soil was so rich and manageable. Hezekiah talked Rachel out of catching enough fish to put one in each hill near the new little plants peeking from the dark dirt. He told her that a new ground like theirs was rich enough without fertilizing.

Hezekiah was digging a deep hole on the east side of the cabin near the edge of the great cedars. Rachel watched in between planting and working in the field. She began to wonder what he was doing.

It was time for a water break so she got some good cool water from the spring and took it to Hezekiah.

"Thanks sweetheart," said Hezekiah when he looked up to see his beautiful wife and the water.

"Welcome Hezekiah, what are you doing?" asked Rachel?

"Digging a hole," answered Hezekiah.

"Well I can see that, what are ya digging it for?" she asked a bit perturbed.

"I am digging a pit to catch elephants," said Hezekiah trying not to grin.

"Mister Whitt, I may be an Indian woman, but I saw an elephant in the Reverend's picture-book, and I know they ain't no elephants in these woods," answered Rachel.

"It's going to be our new privy, don't you think it's time we quit going to the woods or using that old slop-jar?" asked Hezekiah.

"That will be better, especially in the rain or darkness," she said.

"You will still have to bring a candle in the dark, I will cut us a quarter-moon in the door for light in the day," said Hezekiah.

"Why is it a moon, why not something else," asked Rachel.

"I be dab-burned, I don't know, all I know is that every respectable privy has a moon in the door," answered Hezekiah with a smile on his face.

"How is the planting going, need some help, sweetheart?" asked Hezekiah?

"I am doing fine, you just go on and dig your elephant catching hole," said Rachel laughing.

In these days with just the basics for life and security, the simple little things were precious. A smile, a joke, a prank, and on the serious side the songs sang or prayers prayed were what brought happiness. And of course the love of family and God brought happiness.

Hezekiah had one other job he had to do before cold weather and that was to fix the leaky roof. As soon as he could borrow Thomas Mastin's cross cut saw he would cut a bunch of six to eight inch limbs in lengths of about a foot. He then would split them into slats and put them on the roof, fastening them with wooden pegs. If ever a fiery arrow landed on the roof the slat could be knocked off from underneath with a pole. This was learned all across the frontier and many cabins and lives were saved.

No matter what Hezekiah did Rachel was at his side helping him. The summer was passing fast and Rachel was getting bigger with her baby growing so well. Hezekiah had to slow her down often, for the health of her and the baby's health. Elizabeth had visited her often and was working with her on diet and herbal tea she made from local plants. Also Agnes Mastin had paid a few visits. Rachel had showed Hezekiah many plants in the woods and explained their uses as medicine and health remedies. The Indians had used local plants for years; they accepted them as a gift from the Great Spirit. One plant could be given to wounded warriors, before moving them from the battlefield. This could also be given to a woman during childbirth. Some reports of using this plant was said to alleviate pain all together. Our modern doctors are way behind if this is accurate.

The panther had not been around all summer; they do have a large territory of range. Hezekiah was glad the great cat was someplace else.

The crops were doing good and the folks on the waters of the Clinch have enjoyed really fine produce for some time now. It was the middle of August 1782 and God had blessed his children on the Clinch. The Indians were busy someplace else and the settlers were getting a good start here in Washington County. (Now Tazewell County)

THE PATRIOT, HEZEKIAH WHITT

This cradle is a little nicer than the first ones built in the wilderness; but Hezekiah had one for baby James. It was sanded with creek sand and sealed with bee's wax. It would be used many times.

COLONEL CHARLES DAHNMON WHITT   149

Chapter 18

A Child Is Born

With the busy days of summer and harvest, October was here in Washington County. (Later to be Russell County, then to be Tazewell County.)

Agnes Mastin and Elizabeth Hankins were keeping close check on Rachel Whitt. Her time to deliver was fast approaching. She had not had any big problems, she did retain water and her ankles stayed swollen. She had long passed the morning sickness days, but her weight kept her off balance somewhat. She had some trouble with emotions as most expectant mothers do. Hezekiah was very understanding, yet he had no idea of how to deal with her at times.

The men had met a few times at Fort Witten and the Witten brothers were present now. They had been back east when the Mastin party first arrived around the first of May. The spies had been out, but amazingly no sign was found.

Colonel's Crawford and Williamson had 450 Pennsylvanians and were on the move against the Indians again in the summer of 1782. That is why few Indians were in the frontier of the Clinch Valley.

Hezekiah and Rachel sat around on Sunday October 27, 1782. Hezekiah and Rachel had read some in the book, "Pilgrim's Progress, read some scriptures and had a prayer after their discussion. Rachel was just too far along to ride a horse or walk very far. They enjoyed sitting outside for a little spell but the October air carried a chill. The Mountains in the area were beautiful because of the fall foliage, but the leaves would soon all be on the ground. They knew that the baby could come any day now, but it didn't really sink in to the young couple.

As women through the ages have done, Rachel awakens Hezekiah at about 2:00 AM on October 28, 1782. She patted him a few times and he never moved.

"Hezekiah, Hezekiah, wake up the baby is coming!" exclaimed Rachel.
Hezekiah spring from his bed ran to the fireplace and grabbed his musket.
"My goodness, Hezekiah you aiming to shoot me and get me out of my misery?" asked Rachel?

"Hezekiah looked at her in a dumb way and put his musket back on the pegs over the fire place. He grabbed a couple of logs and placed them on the fire.

"Honey, are you all right?" asked Hezekiah.

"No I ain't, I am having a baby, stated Rachel.

THE PATRIOT, HEZEKIAH WHITT

"Should I run and get Aunt Elizabeth?" asked Hezekiah.

"I reckon so, less you want to be birthing this baby," answered Rachel.
"Sweetheart, I will go fetch her fast as I can, you just stay right there," said Hezekiah.

"Okay, I will stay right here," answered Rachel with a chuckle.

Hezekiah had his buckskins on in a flash and headed to Johnny. He hurriedly saddled the fussy horse and rode down the path out to Baptist Valley. He turned Johnny towards the Hankins home and was there in about twenty five minutes from the start.

"Aunt Elizabeth. Aunt Elizabeth, hollered Hezekiah as he rode up to their cabin. He wanted them to know who it was so he didn't get shot. The door was cracked a little and the light of a single candle shown out.

"Hezekiah, is that you?" asked Elizabeth?

"Yes Ma'am, it is me, Rachel is going to have the baby, answered Hezekiah exactly.

"Well give me a minute, you can help John saddle the horses; I'm sending him after Agnes," stated Elizabeth Hankins.

"That's a good idea, I will," answered Hezekiah. In just a few minutes John Hankins came out and headed for the horses with Hezekiah.

"Howdy Hezekiah, ever wonder why women pick the middle of the night to do their birthing?" asked John?

"No sir, but it sure seems like that is always the way of it," answered Hezekiah.

By the time the two horses are saddled Elizabeth comes out carrying a little cloth sac. John helps her up on her horse and she is ready to ride. Hezekiah and John also mount up and they all head out together. When Elizabeth and Hezekiah make the turn on the path to Cedar Grove, John bids them goodbye and heads down Indian Creek towards the Mastin's place. John carried his musket, but Hezekiah was so involved with the happenings he failed to bring his musket. In a short time Elizabeth and Hezekiah rode up to the door of the cabin. Hezekiah jumped down and helped Aunt Elizabeth down from her horse. She swiftly went into the cabin to be with Rachel. Hezekiah took Johnny and Elizabeth's mount to the corral and unsaddled them. He threw some fodder and corn in the trough and went to the cabin. Rachel was holding back the screams when Hezekiah went in. Elizabeth saw him and told him to go out and watch for Agnes and John, mostly to keep him out of the way.

In no time at all Hezekiah heard the horses in the still morning air. In a minute or two the figures emerged from the darkness. John and Agnes rode up to the cabin door. Hezekiah ran to Agnes and helped her down. In a flash she and her little sack were in the cabin.

Hezekiah had a stick of about eight inches long and about an inch in diameter, whittling on it.

THE PATRIOT, HEZEKIAH WHITT

John asked him, "What are you making?"

"I'm fixing a stick for Rachel to bite on if she needs it during her pain," answered Hezekiah.

"Well, you better get it and some spirits to her, Agnes Mastin brought something in her sack I suspect is for the same thing," said John Hankins.

Hezekiah took the stick into the cabin and got his little brown jug and carried it over to Rachel. She was between pains so he bent down and kissed her. A great frown formed on her face as another contraction seized her body.

"Time for you to get out there with John," said Elizabeth.

Hezekiah sit the stick and jug beside Rachel and turned helplessly to the door.

It was still only about 6:00 AM and barely day light. It already seemed to be a long day as Hezekiah had been up for four hours.

Agnes Mastin, being Indian knew the ways of her kind. She had in her sack, a container of special herbal tea she had prepared for this day. It had several ingredients including one plant that the Indians gave to wounded warriors before moving them from the battlefield.

Aunt Elizabeth was there first so she took charge, but Agnes intervened when she thought it was better. The pains began to come closer and were now about five minutes apart. Agnes would wait for the pain to become almost constant before giving the bitter to Rachel. The tea was powerful, but did not have a long lasting effect. Elizabeth had reservations about some of the Indian ways, but knew Agnes would not give Rachel anything to harm her or the baby.

It was John Hankins job to distract Hezekiah from the commotion in the cabin.

"Let's go a hunting, time we get back you might be a Paw," said John.

"I might ort to stay here, Rachel is having a baby and she might need me," answered Hezekiah.

"Rachel has two fine experienced ladies ministering to her, you would just be a hindrance," answered John.

Hezekiah looked at him showing his helpless feeling.

"Ain't you ever heard the old sailor's saying, it says that you have to be there to lay the keel, but you don't have to be there for the launch," stated John.

"Well I guess we can go for a hunt," said a reluctant Hezekiah.

THE PATRIOT, HEZEKIAH WHITT

"Let's ride our horses over to Greasy Creek. We might get a buffalo, there were several over that'd way last I heard," said John.

"That is way too far, Rachel is having our baby, she might be a needing me," said Hezekiah.

"That is the point, you need to get out of the way and get your mind on other things," answered John.

"Rachel will be needing a buffalo robe to cover up in this winter," answered John.

"I will go hunting out about a mile or so, I reckon, but Greasy Creek is too far," insisted Hezekiah.

They got their gear ready and saddled the horses. Hezekiah ran to the door and cracked it open just as Rachel moaned holding back what would be a scream to most white women.

Agnes saw him at the door and shooed him away.

Hezekiah and John rode back on the hill now called Green Mountain Road, and crossed over slowly to the other side. The Clinch River lay at the bottom of the hill. As they came close to the river, low and behold there stood a great bull buffalo drinking from the waters of the Clinch.

Hezekiah and John could hardly believe their eyes, it was a perfect distraction. They dismounted and began a slow stalk of the great bison. John signaled Hezekiah to shoot when ready. Hezekiah took good aim and squeezed the trigger. The pan flashed, the musket cracked, and the big buffalo stumbled forward two or three steps and collapsed to the ground only a few feet from the water.

"Damn Hezekiah, you got him, I don't believe he will be getting up," said John Hankins.

Hezekiah smiled as he sat back against the hill.

"Guess we should give him a minute," said Hezekiah as he dropped another ball down the barrel and rammed it home; then he put the ram rod back in the guides and then took the powder horn and poured a little powder in the pan for prime.

The two men set silent for about ten minutes waiting for the beast to breathe his last and also make sure no two legged varmints showed up. It was clear the buffalo wasn't getting up, so they got their horses and slowly made their way to the fallen bull buffalo. Hezekiah got to his trophy about two steps ahead of John and pushed on the bull with the barrel of his musket.

"You got him good he is as big as I have seen," said John.

"I have seen them many times, but this is the first one I ever shot," said Hezekiah.

THE PATRIOT, HEZEKIAH WHITT

"Well you sure got a nice'n," said John.

I think there is enough meat here for me, you and some to send to the Mastins, let's get him skinned and cut up," said Hezekiah.

The two men worked feverishly for about two hours. They made sure the hide was removed carefully and cut the meat in to manageable hunks and tied it on the two horses.

There was no room on the horses to ride so they slowly walked the laden animals toward home. Hezekiah had been distracted for a spell, but he began to fret about Rachel. What if something went wrong while I was hunting he asked himself. It would be a good hour getting back and too much time to fret. Hezekiah began to pray that Rachel and his baby would be fine once he and John got back.

Rachel had been having a rough go of it. The baby had not been delivered. She was having trouble having the baby lying in bed.

"I got to get up and squat," exclaimed Rachel.

Agnes agreed, it was the Indian way. Elizabeth was not too keen on the idea, but agreed to help her out on the floor where Agnes had spread a pad. The two women got down on their knees and steadied Rachel while she assumed the squatting position. The last of the bitter tea was given to her and she raised up and down pushing with the almost constant contraction and a little head began to protrude. In another minute or so the little head emerged into this cold dark world. Agnes reached in to guide the little feller and Elizabeth kept a steady hand on Rachel. In just a few more seconds Agnes supported a new little Whitt man-child.

Help her sit down Elizabeth, said Agnes quietly. Agnes quickly tied the cord and cut the baby free. Rachel got back in the squatting position until the after-birth was expelled and Elizabeth washed her up while Agnes washed the little boy. After Rachel was cleaned up the women helped her back in bed and lay the baby at her breast. The little boy went right to work suckling at his mother's breast.

Elizabeth was amazed at the Indian method of child birth. She was as much impressed at the effects of the bitter tea. Rachel had little pain during the actual birth. Rachel relaxed now, looked at her son and smiled at him.

"Well hello little James Whitt," she said quietly.
Just as the women got everything in order, here come Hezekiah and John Hankins with two horses laden with buffalo meat and a big hide.

Hezekiah cracked the door open and peeked into the cabin. He was amazed to see Rachel laying in bed resting quietly with a baby nursing her breast. He also saw Elizabeth and Agnes sitting back smoking their pipes and sipping their tea.

THE PATRIOT, HEZEKIAH WHITT

"Come on in Hezekiah, I think there is someone here you will want to meet," announced Elizabeth.

Hezekiah reverently walked over to Rachel taking in the scene.

Rachel looked up at Hezekiah and said, "Hezekiah meet your son, James Whitt."

"Praise God, he has given us a healthy baby and has taken care of you," said Hezekiah.
"I went ahead and named him James, I know that was your wish," said a triumphant Rachel.

"We are both fine, James is perfect, pick him up and look him over Paw Whitt," added Rachel.

Hezekiah hesitated but picked up the little bundle with the up most care. He gently pulled back the little blanket and peeked at his baby.

"He's a boy, James is a boy," said Hezekiah.

By now John was through the door and he heard the statement. He laughed loudly and said, "I sure hope James is a boy, a little girl would hate that name."

Hezekiah and the ladies also had to laugh.

Hezekiah gently returned him to Rachel's breast and said without thinking, "He's awful little ain't he!"

"He's plenty big fer a new-born," said Elizabeth.
"Where have you been, Hezekiah?" asked Rachel?

"You will not believe it, I killed a buffalo and he is a big bull!" exclaimed Hezekiah.

"Have I been out of it long enough for you to go buffalo hunting?" asked Rachel?

"Honey you ain't been out at all, the buffalo was just on the other side of the ridge, he was right beside of the river," answered Hezekiah.

"We will have us a buffalo robe to cover up in this coming hunger month," said Rachel. (January)

"We sure will, we better get out and tend the meat and let you and little James get some rest," said Hezekiah.

By now the time was 3:00 PM and Rachel had delivered her first born in about 12 hours on October 28, 1782. James Whitt was the first white child born in Baptist Valley.

THE PATRIOT, HEZEKIAH WHITT

John Hankins helped Hezekiah unload his horse, hang the big hide on a wall inside the cabin and get the meat salted down. Hezekiah would start the tanning process as soon as the hide dried out some.

John unloaded some of the meat from his horse for Agnes and Thomas Mastin. He rescued the meat on his horse for the trip back home. John and Elizabeth would ride double on her horse and lead the other. They got ready to leave.

Elizabeth went over and held Rachel's hand and told her goodbye and offered the standard advice for a new Maw and baby. That was stay in bed for a week and let everything get back in place.

"See to it," she said as she looked at Hezekiah.
"I sure will!" answered Hezekiah.
Elizabeth went over and hugged Agnes and thanked her for all that she did.
"Agnes, I have learned new things while helping you birth little James," said Elizabeth.

"I too have learned from you, you are a good friend," answered Agnes.

John came over and bragged on Rachel and little James; Rachel thanked John for being with Hezekiah. The Hankins mounted up and headed down the little path toward their home. Just before going out of sight John turned his horse and waved at Hezekiah and Agnes. Hezekiah and Agnes gave one last wave and went back into the cabin.

"I want to thank you Agnes for all you done, you are staying for the night ain't you?" asked Hezekiah?

"I was glad to help and yes I will tend to Rachel until tomorrow, Thomas will be a coming fer me then," said Agnes.

"Hezekiah, if you will get me some meat, firewood, and a bucket of water I will get it on to cooking," instructed Agnes.

Hezekiah did as she asked then he went over to sit by Rachel and the baby for a spell to soak in all that happened this day. He silently sent forth a prayer to his Lord for all of His loving-kindness and protection.

Hezekiah was walking about two feet above the floor and was so proud of Rachel and little James.

Baby James came at a good time, the winter was just about there and the Whitts were ready as they could be. Hezekiah was a little short on meat, but after harvesting the buffalo that took care of that problem. He had a good roof on the cabin and plenty of firewood stored up. He had a catch in the ground loaded with potatoes and other produce stored from freezing.

This winter they would work on furnishings, make some needed improvements in and out of the cabin. He would do some hunting on nice days to do some scouting for trouble and bring in some game like turkey, geese, and whatever may present itself to Hezekiah.

THE PATRIOT, HEZEKIAH WHITT

There would be plenty to do in the spring, and it would be a time to be extra careful because the Indians could be out killing and plundering again.

Hezekiah didn't just have himself to worry about any more; he had Rachel and his little son, James.

Chapter 19

Trouble On Indian Creek

Early spring had come to the waters of the Clinch and the settlers were anxious to get to work in their fields and make improvements on their farms. Most of the settlers had come from Montgomery County about a year ago and there had not been any Indian attacks or even any sign of Indians. With this much time without any trouble people become complacent.

Word had come through the grapevine that George Rogers Clark had taken over a thousand Kentuckians into Ohio during the late fall. They had burned many villages destroying the Indian's *wegiwas*, (Shawnee name for house.) they burned everything for miles including the dry grass. They had destroyed even the environment needed to support the buffalo, elk, and deer that the Indians needed to survive. About the same time, Colonel Logan from Kentucky County had been busy in another part of Ohio doing the same thing. There were no Indians in any of the villages that were attacked; the Indian's superb spying network gave them time to move out ahead of any white army.

With all of this offensive action going on in the Indian country the Indians had little time to come to the Clinch Valley. The settlers were beginning to believe that the Indians were heading west across the great Mississippi River. Maybe it would be safe here from now on some thought, but Thomas Mastin and Hezekiah Whitt were not among them. Thomas told Hezekiah that it was just a matter of time before someone let their guard down and have to pay the price of death and destruction.

"Hezekiah, don't believe the rumors that the Indian wars are over, be vigilant," said Thomas Mastin.

"Don't worry friend, I will stay alert to guard Rachel and little James," replied Hezekiah.

The settlers had been leaving their muskets in their cabins while working sometimes as far as a quarter of a mile away. They had plowed larger tracts of new ground this spring with hopes of growing a bumper-crop of corn, tobacco, and many other crops. They begin to feel safe and gave into a state of false security.

In the Burke's Garden area of what is now Tazewell County lived Thomas Ingles. He was also a militiaman and served at Point Pleasant against Cornstalk. On April 1783, Black Wolf a Shawnee chief, made a raid upon Burke's Garden and took the wife and children of the Thomas Ingles family hostage.

The Indians hid in the woods waiting and watching. Thomas Ingles and a Negro went out and begin to plow in their field. The Indians went into the house and took the wife, a Negro woman and man slave, and all three children hostage. They gathered all the plunder they could carry and started their long trek back to the Ohio country by way of

THE PATRIOT, HEZEKIAH WHITT

the Tug Fork. The cries of the children attracted Thomas Ingles and he saw his family being carried off. There were a number of Indians so Thomas used his head and did not try to chase them. He and his Negro were not armed. They unhitched the horses and headed for the Holston River settlements across the mountains for help.

They arrived on muster day of the Washington County militia and Captain Thomas Maxwell was drilling the men. As soon as Ingles told him (Maxwell) he took about twenty men and followed Ingles back to his farm. Maxwell had lived in the area for some time and knew the lay of the land. Captain Maxwell also sent two spies ahead to determine which way the Indians were headed.

Joe Hicks and his slave which were the only other settlers living in Burke's Garden, had witnessed the attack and the Negro crossed over to what is now Bland county and arrived back in Burke's Garden, with six men, at about the same time as Captain Maxwell's militia. Captain Maxwell took command of all the men and headed out in heavy pursuit.

Only five days had passed after the capture when Maxwell's spies located the Indians camped in a gap above the Tug Fork. Captain Maxwell came up with a plan. He would take half of the men and circle around the Indians during the night and in the morning they would greet the Indians with an ambush. Ingles and the rest of the men were to drive the Indians to Maxwell.

As they say the best of plans can go astray. Maxwell and his men had a rough night trying to make their way through really rough country and the night was really dark. They did not get in front of the Indians by daylight. The Indians began to get ready for the days journey so Ingles led his men in an attack, thinking Maxwell was ready on the other side. At the first shot, some of the Indians began to tomahawk the prisoners, while others carried on the fight in flight. Thomas Ingles ran for his wife and just as he reached her a warrior gave her a vicious blow with his tomahawk. She fell on top of her baby she was holding. The Indians also tomahawked five year old Mary Ingles and three year old William Ingles. The Negro woman and man escaped into nearby cover. The Indians were making their way down the other side of Tug Mountain as Captain Maxwell and his men almost collided with them. Maxwell was wearing his white officer shirt which made a grand target. Captain Maxwell lost his life that day as did little William Ingles. Mrs. Ingles and little Mary were badly wounded, but would survive. Word of this attack did not reach Baptist Valley until after the next attack on the first Wednesday in May.

In the middle of the week, the first Wednesday in May 1783, a band of seventeen painted Shawnees went visiting to the Joseph Ray farm. They had traveled up the Tug Fork from its mouth at present day Louisa, Kentucky. When the Indians came out on Indian Creek, there was Joseph Ray's farm right on the warrior's path. They caught Joe out without his musket, ran him down and tomahawked him, then they went to the cabin and killed some of the children, they scalped and hacked the bodies so it was hard to identify any of them. Mrs. Ray and a son John were up the creek visiting with other

THE PATRIOT, HEZEKIAH WHITT

neighbors. Another neighbor down Indian Creek, a Samuel Hughes was coming to visit the Rays. It was the wrong time and the wrong place, Samuel lost his hair that morning also. The Indians had also collected eight prisoners on their journey. The Indians main objective was the Russell Fort at Castlewood. When they came up on unready settlers, they took advantage of the situation.

The Indians followed the Clinch River on down toward Castlewood doing mischief at every opportunity. They killed livestock, plundered the cabins and set fire to the white men's buildings.

The Indians were close to the fort when they ran upon a woman too far out and by herself. She had been gathering the lush wild greens of May. Her name was Ann Neece. She screamed while she ran toward the fort, but she was tomahawked. They took her long blonde hair and left her for dead.

Three men working at a gristmill close to the Russell Fort, but were completely unarmed, heard Ann's screams and became alarmed. The Indians had already spied the three white men. The three men were Simon Oxer, Henry Dickenson, and Charles Brickley and the men were in a fearful situation. It became a footrace to the fort; the white men had about two hundred yards of uphill running to reach the fort. The Indians were giving chase, but stopped to fire a volley at the running whites. When the Indians stopped to fire the whites gained some advantage. The Indian's volleys did not find their marks. Several buzzing balls whizzed by the three men, but they reached the safety of the fort. There were only two loaded muskets in the fort, Oxer and Dickenson grabbed them up, took aim and dropped two Indians. The rest of the Indians, having unloaded muskets, grabbed their two fallen comrades and retreated into the woods, not knowing how many frontiersmen were inside the fort.

The discouraged Indians ran upon a slave that was keeping sheep and belonging to Henry Dickenson, he was never seen nor heard from again. All that was found was a few bloodstained sheep scattered on the hill side lying where they fell.

After the Indians left, bloody Ann Neece surprised everyone; she got up and staggered to the fort. No one gave her much hope, but the Lord must have been with her, she got better and lived to raise a family.

Back in Baptist Valley and on Indian Creek the attack had shaken the hearts of the settlers. It also left the sorrowful duty to gather the bodies of the two men and numerous children and give them a proper burial.

Thomas Mastin, the Wittens, the Hankins and many others met at the Crab Orchard Fort to draw up a plan.

Thomas Mastin kept saying, "I told Joe Ray he was too exposed, right there on the creek that is right on the warrior's path when they come here by way of the Tug!"

Fear gripped many of the more light-hearted and some even said it was time to head back east. Major Thomas Mastin had a way with words and soon had their ruffled feathers back in place. He reminded them of the meeting they had last spring over by Rocky Gap. He reminded them that they had all agreed to come on to the Clinch Valley. After fear had subsided somewhat the major led them in a meeting to get better prepared for such happenings. Everyone, including Hezekiah had some second thoughts as to the folly of living on the waters of the Clinch.

They came up with a plan to send out spies again, to have certain places to meet if trouble came and you should never, never, be out without your Brown Betz. It was a good thing in one way, security and safety was stressed once again. Neither man nor woman was to travel out of sight of their cabin without another armed person with them. If they had to, a guard would be posted as others worked the fields.

It was a shock for the Mastins, the Hankins, and the Whitts to hear of the terrible attack. They were all close friends to the Rays. Mrs. Ray and son John moved in with the Mastins for a spell, she would be selling out next year and moving off the warrior's path which ran with Indian Creek.

Hezekiah was asked by Thomas Mastin to follow the Indians to see where they were going and get back to give a warning if they were to come back that way. Hezekiah did not want to leave Rachel and little James, but he knew they would be safer if he knew what the Indians were up to. The Indians were easy to follow; they left death and destruction as they went down the Clinch. It appeared that a prisoner had caused a problem and was swiftly dealt with; he had been hacked and scalped. Hezekiah buried him in a shallow grave on the banks of the Clinch near present day Saint Paul.

Hezekiah followed them all the way to Russell Fort at Castlewood and heard about the happenings there. He was so proud of the three men that held off seventeen Indians and the lady that survived the attack. He followed them on further and found that they had turned toward Pound Gap and would be looking for mischief as they traveled through Kentucky County toward the Ohio. Hezekiah saw that the threat was gone, at least for now, so he followed the beautiful Clinch back upstream to his cedar grove and his little family.

When Hezekiah got back things were settled some and there was a new graveyard on the Ray farm. Hezekiah reported to Major Mastin and a few other men that gathered to hear the report. The men all felt safer knowing that the Indians were heading back to the Ohio country. They felt bad, not being able to warn unsuspecting families in the path of the heathen. The false sense of security was displaced with awareness that life could be very short if they fell back into a complacent state of mind. Now they had two attacks to talk about. Hezekiah learned of the attack in Burke's Garden after he returned.

A little information about Burke's Garden, it was named after James Burke that had settled there several years before. The story says that James Burke was peeling some potatoes for supper one evening and he tossed the peelings out and they took root. Some travelers came by later in the season to see James Burke and noticed the potatoes growing. One man commented that must be Burke's Garden and the name stuck.

THE PATRIOT, HEZEKIAH WHITT

Some say the Indians killed Burke at the door of his cabin; others say he had all he could stand of the Indians and left.

Burke's Garden lies in a giant crater most likely caused by a huge meteorite way back when the Lord created this world. It is a delightful place today.

Something positive to speak of that year, the Treaty of Paris took place in Paris, France in September of 1783. The treaty was signed by Great Britain that officially made the United States free and independent.

The war in the east has been over for a long time, but the Indians continued to show malice to the settlers. There were no big battles, but the deaths added up in a year's time. The spies still went out mostly in the spring. With all the attacks in the spring of 1783, those recorded and many not recorded, kept the settlements in the Baptist Valley and Indian Creek on alert. The men got together that summer and went from farm to farm to work the fields. Sometimes four or five teams of oxen, horses, or mules worked one farm while a guard or two kept watch. They traveled from farm to farm and got their work done this way.

Hezekiah kept busy spying or working farms. They came to Hezekiah's cedar grove and downed more cedars to clear up more new ground. He had a large tract of land planted with corn, tobacco, and all the things they liked to plant.

Hezekiah dragged the cedar logs to the right side of his cabin and stored them off the ground on rocks. He had an idea he would eventually have to build more living space. Little James was growing like a weed, but the three of them lived nicely in the 16'x 16' cabin. Hezekiah and Rachel hoped to have several children in time. Instead of adding to the cabin he had in the back of his mind to build another cabin beside the first. This way there could be a breezeway between them and the cooking heat could be dissipated during the hot part of summer. He still wanted to build Rachel a grand fireplace from cut limestone.

Most people in the region of the Clinch River accepted the few Indians that lived among them. Agnes Mastin, the wife of Thomas Mastin and the four adopted Indian children were of the Mastin family. Rachel Cornstalk Skaggs Whitt was of course the wife of Hezekiah Whitt. There could be more, but I can't account for them.

After the recent attacks upon the waters of the Clinch by the Indians, the attacks brought out hostilities among some of the people. Only one newcomer to Baptist Valley was outspoken against the Indian members of the Mastin and Whitt families. Skag Brown had moved to the area during the winter and many had already thought of him in unsavory ways. He was filthy, used the Lord's name in vain, and positively did not fit in with the upright people of the region.

Word came to Hezekiah that Skag Brown had deliberately attacked Rachel and the Indians of the Mastin family verbally.

"What did Skag say about Rachel?" asked Hezekiah from the informer.

THE PATRIOT, HEZEKIAH WHITT

"I hate to say the bad words I heard," replied the informer.
"Please do!" insisted Hezekiah.

Old Skag said, "we should burn them red niggers living around here with us white folks, we should cut them up in pieces and feed them to the wolfs."

Hezekiah's countenance changed as pressure build up in his heart. He turned red and walked to the pegs holding his musket. He took it down, checked the prime, put on his belt with the musket balls and holding his skinning knife and tomahawk. He threw his leather thong attached to his powder horn around his shoulder and headed out the door. He went straight to Johnny and saddled him up. Even Johnny sensed that Hezekiah was not himself as he never gave the friendly greeting as usual.

Hezekiah brought Johnny to a fast trot and headed down the path of wrath. He was up the valley in no time and came to the filthy shack that housed the unsavory, Skag Brown.

"Skag Brown, get out here and tell me what you said about my wife," screamed Hezekiah.

Johnny was afraid and twisted around wanting to run, but knew better.

The target of Hezekiah's aggression slowly opened the shabby door. He came out carrying his musket, but did not aim it at Hezekiah.

"Well come in Mr. Whitt, you are welcome at my house," said Skag.

"Is it true that you said you wanted to kill my wife and other Christian Indians living among us?" asked Hezekiah in a direct question so Skag could not get it wrong or mix it up.

"Well Mr. Whitt, I said something like that when I was so upset at the Indians for attacking us whites," answered Skag.

By now Hezekiah was face to face with Skag, he drew back his fierce fist and busted Skag in the nose. Skag was lifted off the ground with the fierceness of the blow. Skag lay on the ground with blood streaming from his nose and only partly aware of what happened to him.

Hezekiah put his knee on Skag's chest and spoke as clear as he could in direct words.

"Skag, you are not wanted here, you pack up your trash and get your ass out of Clinch Valley, If I see you in these parts after today I will kill you on the spot, do you understand?" asked Hezekiah.

"I will," said a trembling, bleeding, Skag Brown.

Hezekiah got back upon Johnny feeling much better. Skag Brown sit up holding his bleeding nose and watched Hezekiah walk Johnny back down the valley toward his cedar grove.

THE PATRIOT, HEZEKIAH WHITT

Skag Brown was gone within the hour, he knew he had come. He headed back toward the east a neighbor had reported.

Many neighbors came by to thank Hezekiah for ridding the valley of the unsavory character known as Skag Brown. Some of the folks had been missing items and some of the items were retrieved after looking in the dirty shack that Skag had vacated. The easy going Hezekiah was looked upon with a new respect and no man in the valley wanted to cross him.

Rachel was so worried while he was gone, but very proud of her mighty man of valor. Rachel loved this man more today then even when they were first married.

Baby James was growing and crawling all over the cabin, he was also standing by holding on to chairs and so on. He climbed on his Paw's lap every time he caught Hezekiah still. Sometimes Hezekiah would carry James outside and show him the farm and talk to him like he was a grown man. Little James really loved to visit with Johnny and Hezekiah felt the feelings were mutual.

The Lord provided a bounty in their crops. The rich new ground caused plants to abnormally grow to amazing sizes. Hezekiah did some improvements around the farm when he took the time. He built a corncrib to hold his bounty of maze. He had a roof shed for the horses so he put sides on it to give the horse and mule better shelter. He also made the corral much larger so the animals had more grazing. That pretty much ended the year of 1783 and a cold wintry 1784 was awakening in Baptist Valley.

During the winter, while the threat of Indians was less, several of the folks went to the salt lick below Paintlick Mountain. They did not do well because the salt was sparse and so spread out. They did enjoy seeing the great herds of elk, deer, and a few bison. Also the predators followed the herds and took what they needed.

Thomas Mastin told them that there was a large salt deposit about fifty miles away. It is located in what is today, Smyth County and called by the obvious name of Saltville. Spring was coming so a few men hurried to the Saltville salt licks and acquired enough salt to last for the summer. They got back before the Indians were in the woods again.

The families needed stock and tools from the east. Thomas Mastin agreed to take pack animals and whoever could go to Fort Chiswell and get the things they needed and wanted. Each settler would send a pack animal and money with the list of things they wanted. He wanted to get started and be back by planting time. Some of the larger items would be bought and used as a partnership. Like the big crosscut saw owned by Thomas Mastin, but borrowed by most of the neighbors. The folks needed a good iron turn plow; many needed a good crank sharpening wheel. A good hay-scythe and numerous items fit this category. Each family had a list of live stock they wanted like cattle, hogs and sheep. They also wanted chickens for eggs and meat, geese for cleaning and fertilizing the gardens, and some guinea hens for an early warning system. There were few dogs in the valley so most families wanted a good hunting dog that would also serve as a protector. The number one item wanted was plenty of gunpowder, lead, and a few gunsmith tools. A few muskets were added to the list for the young people now getting big enough to learn the art of shooting.

The women added their wanted items to the list which included candle wax and candle making supplies and tools. They also added things like dress and shirt making material, thread, and buttons. Coffee, tea, and a few spices were added also.

About the end of March 1784 Major Thomas Mastin, his Indian sons, Hezekiah N. Whitt and Thomas Bailey Christian all left for Fort Chiswell, along with nine other men and eight other boys. The boys would go to help with the pack animals and drive the stock back. All together there were about ten men and ten boys on the buying mission.

Tobacco, corn and pelts were packed on the animals to be traded in on some of their items. Each family wrote out a detailed list, sent money and or trade items. The folks on Indian Creek and in Baptist Valley would be looking forward to the pack train getting back.

While the men and boys went back to Fort Chiswell the sap began to run in the trees. Rachel asked Hezekiah if there was a large sugar maple grove near by, she had explained that they would enjoy making syrup and that she knew how to do it. Hezekiah knew about one and the folks got together with boiling pots and were ready for a new adventure. Hezekiah escorted some men and several women to a sugar maple grove that was located down the Clinch near present day Doran. Doran is about six miles down the Clinch from the mouth of Indian Creek. Rachel had them cut the grooves in a "V" shape, in the bark of each tree and put in a peg and hung a bucket to collect the sweet sap. They gathered firewood and boiled the sap into a wonderful maple syrup. Hezekiah and other men continued to watch over the workers and scout about to make sure that no early Indians were about. The maple syrup was a wonderful treat in every house in the valley and on Indian Creek.

About planting time in early May the men came from Fort Chiswell with every animal laden with all kinds of goods and supplies. It was risky getting back this time of year because the Indians would be on the warpath in small groups. Still no Indians had been detected so now the settlers had salt, maple syrup and all manner of goods from the mercantile at Fort Chiswell. Thomas Mastin explained that they had cleaned out the mercantile, but they had left them with a good problem. They would have to restock.

It was wonderful to see all the animals that they drove into the valley. Folks had a start on a herd of cattle, hogs, sheep, chickens and other animals and fowl. Wild meat is good, but a change is always welcome.

A trading post of mercantile was badly needed in the Clinch Valley. Sometime down the road when the area became safer they would have a mercantile, churches and even a tavern.

Mules can be packed with most anything. This rendition is a little more modern.

Chapter 20

Living On Indian Creek

In 1784 Benjamin Harrison is on his final year of being Governor of Virginia. The new little country called the United States of America is looking at ways to grow and expand. Virginia has agreed to and ceded its lands across the Ohio River to the United States for the right to give land grants to the well deserving soldiers and militiamen that won the independence. There would be a large tract of land lying between the Scioto and Miami Rivers in Ohio that will be given to soldiers and sailors that served Virginia. Another tract on the south side of the Ohio River in Kentucky County will be given out to the Virginia fighting men for a job well done. Other lands not already claimed in the Clinch Valley, Holston Valley, and Powell Valley would be used for military grants also. The Government did not have money to give out as military bonuses, but they did claim millions of acres to the west. Other tracts of land in Ohio were made available to other states to give to their fighting men. This was one sure way to get Americans to move and occupy the lands to the west. The Indians were not happy about any of this.

The Indians had sided with the British and when the British were defeated the United States looked on the Indians as defeated and the lands would be taken (stolen) as spoils of war. The settlers in Kentucky County and the other western areas of Virginia are still targets of the Shawnee Indians from the north. Not much has changed on the waters of the Clinch as far as security goes.

One big change around Baptist Valley and on Indian Creek came about when the pack train and droves of livestock came to the settlers. Every farm now had animals and fowl and looked like real farms. The new noises were a welcome sound as cows mooed and the chickens clucked. The grazing animals flourished on the bluegrass of the area.

When breeding time came the folks would take their animals to other neighbors and get them fixed up to have babies. It was strange to hear domesticated animals in this basically wild area of Virginia. Much care had to be taken to protect the tame from the wild. Pens, fences, and cages were constructed to ward off predators.

Little James Whitt was now approaching the "Terrible Two's," and Rachel was not expecting any new little Whitts. Hezekiah said, "it must be because little James is still nursing."

The spies still took turns going up the warrior's path and other areas to check for Indian sign. The Indians were still a threat to isolated farms and small settlements. There would be more bad news of Indian atrocities this year and on into the late 1790's.

Big changes came to Kentucky County during the year of 1784. The Shawnees continued the vicious attacks on the boats coming down the Ohio River. They used their trickery to bring the whites close to the Ohio shore and sometimes the Virginia shore.

THE PATRIOT, HEZEKIAH WHITT

They would use a loyal white captive to come to the edge of the river and scream in distress. Good hearted settlers would come to the rescue and then have to face the fury of the savages. Thousands of white settlers came down the river; hundreds met their fate as the fish dined on their rotting flesh. Also the Indians made quick raids into Kentucky County to do their mischief. They had no mercy on the settlers they attacked and carried off plunder, especially horses.

The settlers kept coming and the little forts became villages and the landscape changed from grasslands and woods to corn and wheat fields. In the once little burgs like Frankfort, Georgetown, Stanford, Danville, Harrodsburg, and Lexington now became big towns. The little log cabins were now being replaced with large stately frame and brick houses.

Folks like Daniel Boone, Simon Kenton, and others that had led the way were claiming large tracts of land. Along with any land rush the lawyers and speculators showed up with their greedy hands out for the spoils from the ignorant.

Kentucky County was so big that it had to be divided into other counties. Fayette and Bourbon Counties were formed out of parts of Kentucky County. There would be much litigation over overlapping land boundaries.

Thank God some good preachers were coming and starting up churches in this fast growing land in the far western parts of Virginia.

In the hunger month (January) of 1785 the chiefs of the Ottawa, Delaware, Wyandot, and Chippewa were summoned to Fort McIntosh on the Ohio River below Fort Pitt. (The Shawnees were not there.) The purpose was to make a lasting treaty with the Americans that now spoke from a position of strength. The Americans spoke and the interpreters explained the white men's words. The Americans basically said that they had defeated the British and that the Indians had sided with the British, thus they were also a defeated people. The Americans explained that there were new boundaries to be set which gave the Indians less land and the settlers more. The Indians sat in disgust, they knew the whites were stealing their lands but were helpless to do anything about it.

Along with civilization come thinking and inventions. Joseph Bramah invented a pump and handle for beer kegs. This was a most needed thing!

Old Ben Franklin came up with a more useful idea, he invented the bifocal spectacle.

Two Frenchmen died in a hot air balloon accident, which marked the first deaths in aviation.

Congress changed the money to be used in this new country from the British currency to the "dollar" and adopted the decimal coinage. Many changes were coming about in the new country called the United States. The Clinch Valley was not as progressive, news, letters, and shipping was very slow to reach the mountains. The Indians were slowing down on the attacks in Kentucky County, but were more prone to attack the isolated folks in what are now West Virginia and the Clinch Valley.

THE PATRIOT, HEZEKIAH WHITT

Hezekiah loved the isolation on the waters of the Clinch. Most all of the settlers in Baptist Valley loved the area and isolation except for the attacks of the Indians from time to time. They all began to think like the Kentuckians, they needed more folks and more of everything that we call civilization.

The patriot leader, Patrick Henry would lead the Commonwealth of Virginia again from November 30, 1784 to November 30, 1785. During this term he made treaties with the southern Indians, helped the patriot veterans secure land to the west and was a great leader even though he was not a highly educated man. Governor Henry stayed abreast of the Indians out in the frontier areas of Virginia by letters from his many militia officers and friends. The area around the Clinch and Holston valleys were mentioned often as the Indians sneaked into the area and done their mischief. It was almost impossible to detect every little band of Shawnee that came for vengeance. The white people were stealing Indian land and had killed so many Indians, so the small raids were the only course the Indians could take to get even.

A typical letter from the time to Governor Henry;

> On May 26, 1785, Major Crockett wrote to Governor Henry of Virginia, the following:
>
> The Indians killed one man on North Fork of the Holston River, the 6th of April last, and wounded a man ten days after, (April 16, 1785) on the head of Clinch, with arrows. There has not been one year since 1774 but the Indians has done more or less damage in this county, (Washington) which covers 80 miles of the frontier of this state.

The man that was wounded with arrows on the head of the Clinch was most likely Richard Pemberton who lived in Baptist Valley about five miles from the little town of Jeffersonville. (Jeffersonville was not established at this time. Jeffersonville is now Tazewell, the seat of Tazewell County.)

On a nice Sabbath morning in April of 1785 Richard Pemberton his wife and two children took a walk to a field a little distance from his farm. The field was worked by the Pemberton family and had a split rail fence around it to keep out the grazing herds of elk and deer. The purpose of this walk was to check the fence and enjoy the beauty of spring in Baptist Valley.

Pemberton carried his trusty musket as always when out like this. As the family finished checking the fence and crops they headed for home. After going a short distance the Pembertons became alarmed to see two devilish painted Indians come bearing down on them and yelling as they came. The two Indians were armed with bows and arrows, tomahawks, and knifes.

Pemberton stayed calm and leveled his musket and aimed at one of the Indians. He pulled the trigger and it misfired. He hurriedly tried to cock the lock again, but it broke.

THE PATRIOT, HEZEKIAH WHITT

The Indians stopped to jump to the side so as not to get shot, and then they let arrows fly at Pemberton. The first arrows did not find their mark, so Pemberton ordered his wife and children to run to a neighbor Johnson's house and he kept himself between them and the Indians. Several men resided at this house and could be of service against the Indians.

The wife and children ran like deer as Richard Pemberton kept cutting the Indians off to shield his family. He would raise his broken musket when the Indians got closer, and they would jump to the side and run back some. Then they would come bounding back to get into range of their bow and arrows. Every time when they stopped they let loose the arrows and some stuck into the chest of Pemberton. The chase continued in a seesaw fashion and Pemberton gained a little ground toward the Johnson farm. The bows the Indians carried were not too powerful from a longer distance so they had to raise the elevation and let the arrows rise high and drop down at Pemberton. He was struck several times but none of the arrows penetrated deep into vital organs. He kept up the defense and the Indians were held at bay with a broken musket. Pemberton suffered much pain, but kept up the running fight. Pemberton got within hearing distance of the Johnson house and could be heard by the men inside.

When the men heard the scream, "Indians," they ran out the back in the opposite direction. Pemberton made it inside the door of the house followed closely by the screaming Indians. His brave wife and children were waiting for him and barred the door just seconds before the Indians arrived.

Pemberton yelled for a musket and the Indians gave a rapid retreat thinking that many men may be in the Johnson house.

Pemberton's wife ministered to his wounds, but could not get all of the flint points out of his chest. He survived and lived many years still with the arrow points in his chest as a reminder of that day.

The men that fled from the Johnson house were counted as cowards and looked down on for years. All of these people were neighbors of Hezekiah and Rachel Whitt. Richard Pemberton was counted among the brave and honored as a loving husband and father for doing his duty.

From reports like these you can picture the dangers that were always present on the waters of the Clinch. Hezekiah was always aware that Indians could attack at any given time at any given day and tried to be ready. The Indians were not prone to winter attacks but it did happen from time to time. The best defense was numbers of armed men. Baptist Valley and Indian Creek areas were getting more and more settlers each summer. Most everyone had a neighbor within a mile of them.

During the summer of 1785 Hezekiah and Rachel build the other cabin next to the first one using the fine cedar logs felled during clearing new ground for crops. They built it about six feet away creating a breeze way between the two cabins. Hezekiah brought the new roof over to the older cabin which formed one common roof. It was basically

THE PATRIOT, HEZEKIAH WHITT

one cabin with two large rooms and one roof. Sitting in the breezeway became a popular thing to do by the Whitts. It was a great place to get out of the heat of the kitchen or just a good place to rest, smoke their pipes, and read from their Bible. On rainy days Hezekiah would sit out there and do repairs, clean the muskets, tan hides and do other rainy day work.

Hezekiah got word late in 1785 that his Paw, the Reverend Richard Whitt gave in to pressure and applied to the Governor for a permit to marry couples in Montgomery County. The Reverend had been a staunch believer that marrying was for the church and not the state. Governor Patrick Henry granted the license in 1785 and the good Reverend married many couples before and after.

Hezekiah also got a long letter telling of all the news back in Montgomery County.

Also Hezekiah had tools now so he cut limestone into blocks and laid up a real nice fireplace and chimney. Rachel was so impressed with the building skills of her beloved Hezekiah. (This fine chimney still stands today.)

Baby James Whitt would soon be three years old and Rachel was still not in a family way. Hezekiah and Rachel both wondered if God was going to give them more children. They continued to love and make love and let nature take its course. This was a wonderful distraction from the fears and stresses of living in Baptist Valley. It was like sour and sweet, the sour was the constant fear that hung in the valley. The sweet was this wonderful land on the waters of the Clinch and of course the family life the Whitts enjoyed.

On January 16, 1786 while the Commonwealth of Virginia's legislature was in session, James Madison made sure that Thomas Jefferson's 1779 "Statute for Religious Freedom," was passed and became the law of the Commonwealth. The Virginians were the first to pass such a law that gave all men the freedom to worship as they pleased. They hoped the example that was set would flow on over to all of the states. That was what this little country was all about. Freedom of Religion was even part of the reasoning that brought on the Revolutionary War. As the news drifted across Virginia into the frontier, the settlers were well pleased to hear such news. It was brought up at most all worship services on the waters of the Clinch and they all thanked God for the passage of this fine statute.

The Shawnees had turned a cold shoulder to Richard Butler and Samuel Holden Parsons whom had come from the Congress to negotiate a treaty at Fort McIntosh. The White Government had hoped to steal the lands of the Shawnee and have peace at the same time.

So on January 31, 1786 a new meeting was set up at Fort Finney to try and get the Shawnees to sign the treaty and avert a war. Fort Finney was near modern day Cincinnati, Ohio the Shawnees brought a belt of black wampum to give to the white treaty makers, which meant war or in modern slang, kiss my behind!

THE PATRIOT, HEZEKIAH WHITT

Butler and Parsons grew angry and threatened the Shawnee Chiefs with an attack as they had much fire power on standby. The white men made it plain to the Indians that they had better sign and cede more land. The American Government had set aside lands for the Shawnees to live on. Of course the whites picked the better lands that the Indians loved the most. To the east the buffalo and elk were becoming scarce and the Indians knew it.

The Shawnee chiefs fearing the American military decided to sign and press Parsons and Butler to promise not to let settlers come into this last land that was theirs. The treaty gave all of southwest Ohio and southern Indiana to the Americans and the Indians could keep the eastern and northern parts of Ohio for their home. Butler and Parsons promised to keep white squatters from settling on the lands set aside for the Indians as the treaty of 1785 had prescribed. (Fort McIntosh Treaty.)

Some of the Shawnee chiefs signed, some would not and would not abide by it. This group of Shawnees reasoned that all lands north of the Ohio River would always be theirs. Those that signed soon moved their villages east or north. Those that would not sign would hang around on the lands that they still claimed.

The white men viewed the treaty at the mouth of the Great Miami River as signed sealed and delivered. (Fort Finney.) The whites would be moving across the big Ohio River and settle on the land that was ceded by the Shawnee in this treaty. The Shawnees were a divided nation and violence would be continued between the Indians and the whites. Some of the Shawnee still claimed Kentucky and western Virginia and would most defiantly be sending raiding parties to kill and plunder. This would include the waters of the Clinch and even the waters of the Holston.

The militia continued to meet in and around Baptist Valley. The men knew that the results of this new treaty at Fort Finney would directly affect them because of the disgruntled Shawnees.

At one time the Shawnees and Cherokees both claimed the waters on the Clinch and basically ignored the whites that came here for the long hunts. Way back in 1768 the Cherokees and the Shawnee had a huge battle over the right to hunt at the saltlick below Paintlick Mountain. There were over one hundred men and women on both sides as they had set up camps to hunt the elk and buffalo. Their hunting camps were less than a mile apart.

At first both groups hunted and let the other tribe be, but the Shawnee were a bit more spirited and detested the Cherokees. The Shawnee hunters caused disruption and soon a battle erupted. The Cherokees had won by a small margin, but after the Shawnees left the Cherokees soon went back south leaving the hunting to the white long hunters.

Both sides lost because of the dead and wounded. A large common grave was dug and all the dead were buried together. All that died were counted as brave and they would get along in the happy hunting grounds. (Indian Heaven.) This mass grave has not been found to this day.

THE PATRIOT, HEZEKIAH WHITT

The Cherokee had even obtained lead and powder from some of the long hunters. This may be one reason the Shawnees still hated the white settlers on the waters of the Clinch.

The settlers would have to be ready for the summer of 1786 and the years to come, what was new on the waters of the Clinch?

Chapter 21

Another Baby Is Coming

Life on the waters of the Clinch was bitter-sweet. It was like the Garden of Eden in many ways yet death and destruction could come at any instance. There had been many attacks on the settlers from the head waters of the Clinch all the way to the Tennessee Country. It was always a hit and run attack. Many of the isolated cabins were burned, hostages taken, livestock killed, and worse many of the settlers from babies to adults were hacked with the tomahawks, scalped, and sometimes used for target practice with many arrows remaining in their bloody bodies. The warriors would try and leave a lasting impression where ever they attacked.

Hezekiah was never directly affected by an attack except for scouting and chasing after a war party that had come into the valley. The Whitt cabin was not directly on the warrior's path and it was partially hidden back in the cedar grove.

Hezekiah and Rachel prayed daily for God's protection and they remained constantly diligent in safety. They would not even venture out of the cabin without taking a good look around the visible area from the door. If any of the animals were acting different or if the birds were silent meant something may be amiss. Hezekiah and Rachel did not have a dog yet, but some of the settlers did. They hoped to get a pup as soon as possible.

Hezekiah and Rachel had gone for four years with out getting in a family way again. Little James was four years old and was becoming quite the little man. One cold morning in the hunger month, (January) after doing chores there was not much to do, Hezekiah got frisky and Rachel responded to the courtship. They put another log on the fire, got little James to take a nap and went back to bed under the buffalo cape. This didn't happen too often, as they usually left these happenings for night time. It was really a special session of lovemaking. It seemed better than their wedding night and lasted until the afternoon when little James wanted to get up and eat. Guess what? Rachel would be having another baby. The baby would be born around the end of September 1787. Rachel was so pleased to be expecting again. She had begun to worry that she may not be able to give Hezekiah any more children. It was part of a woman's self esteem to be able to give her husband children. Rachel had added this request in her recent prayers, that she would have children. Children were cherished on the frontier and they were very important to the family structure. The older children became helpers and even added strength to the family by sheer numbers.

Governor Edmund Randolph was presiding over Virginia now as governor. The eastern areas of the Commonwealth were quiet tame, but here on the waters of the Clinch not much had changed except game was becoming a little scarce. Hezekiah hardly ever saw a buffalo and even the elk herds were declining. You could still go to the waters of Tug

THE PATRIOT, HEZEKIAH WHITT

Fork and find many bear, elk, and a few woods-buffalo also the waters of Louisa River; (Levisa Fork) offered excellent hunting.

Russell County was formed out of Washington County on May 1, 1786. They named it for General William Russell of the region because of his service during the Revolutionary War.

The County Seat was set in Castlewood on the Clinch River thirty to forty miles from Baptist Valley. The new county of Russell contained some 3,000 square miles. The western boundary ran from Cumberland Gap to Clinch Mountain near present day Bluefield. Hezekiah's and Rachel's Cedar Grove was now in the new county of Russell. The new baby would be born in Russell County unless other changes took place. The vast area of the waters on the Clinch was divided frequently and new counties formed as the population continued to grow.

The men in and around Baptist Valley were glad to be in a smaller county. They hoped to be sub-divided more in the future and maybe have their own county with the seat in their own back yard.

"Well we done it again," said Hezekiah to Rachel.

"Done what again?" asked Rachel?

"We went to bed in one county and woke up in another!" exclaimed Hezekiah.

"We now live in the great county of Russell," he added.
"How did you find out?" asked Rachel?

"I saw Thomas Mastin this morning and he told me, a rider came from Castlewood to inform us of the change," said Hezekiah.

"Is that good, Hezekiah?" asked Rachel?

"I reckon so, we go to Castlewood to do county business now, there will be more changing and I want to see us have our own county and seat here in Baptist Valley some day," stated Hezekiah.

"Reckon that will ever happen, husband?" asked Rachel.

"It could happen!" answered Hezekiah.

This new country called the United States has finally got down to the real business as to making it official. The state delegates from each state met in Philadelphia's Pennsylvania State House to consider and vote on the new Constitution. They met on May 25, 1787 and George Washington the Virginian was elected Convention President.

COLONEL CHARLES DAHNMON WHITT

THE PATRIOT, HEZEKIAH WHITT

The Constitution was designed with many checks and balances but most of the states were worried about what could happen. Remember at this point each state was considered its own country and had its own freedoms preserved by its own laws. It was signed on September 17, 1787 but would not be law until nine of the thirteen states ratified it. There was nothing said about getting out if a state wanted to. This whole form of government was a great experiment and had not been tried and tested. Some states reserved the right to secede if they thought it necessary. Much later in the Civil War this was tested, but that will be another story. There was much mistrust by the states of a strong central government because all had suffered under the strong government of Great Britain and its king.

The delegates wanted more of a guarantee of basic freedoms and rights. Someone came up with the idea of amendments to spell it out. They all liked this idea and they started putting this together, I think, the more important first. Amendment I spelled out that the people would have freedom of religion, speech, press, and the right to assemble and petition the government. It went right down the line and they added ten amendments which we call the "Bill of Right."

News like this traveled fast, even to the far reaches of western Virginia. The everyday man held doubts and fears of a strong government, but had faith in the leaders like George Washington.

Thomas Mastin's dog had puppies and Thomas had promised one to Rachel Whitt. Rachel was getting pretty big with her baby coming so she asked Hezekiah to go and pick out a good pup for her. The mother dog was about half hound and half retriever. They did not know the sire, but some thought it may be a wolf. The pups were in good health and almost six weeks old. Some had long hair and some short hair. They were an odd lot, but all should make good dogs, suited to the rigors of the frontier.

While Hezekiah was visiting with the Mastins he discovered that Thomas had made up his mind to move to what is now Sumner County, Tennessee. The area is about half way of the now State of Tennessee and borders what is now Kentucky at Allen and Simpson County. Hezekiah was in shock as this was the first mention of the move.

Thomas Mastin related to Hezekiah that he had itchy feet and yearned to move to the area that he saw in one of his many travels. Also the adopted Indian son called Thomas Bailey Christian wanted to stay at the Mastin farm because he loved the waters of the Clinch. Hezekiah was shocked at all of this abrupt news and could hardly speak.

"I was a wondering if you could look in on my son Thomas Bailey Christian from time to time?" asked Thomas Mastin?

"Sure I will, but when you heading out?" asked Hezekiah?

"Just as soon as your new baby gets here, I promised Agnes to wait till then so she could be with Rachel," answered Thomas.

"Christian is purty much growed up now, ain't he?" asked Hezekiah?

THE PATRIOT, HEZEKIAH WHITT

"He sure is, only problem he will have is with some of these stiff-necked Indian haters, and of course the Indians that may come here on the war-path," replied Thomas Mastin.

"Christian is purty much white in all ways cept his skin is Indian," said Hezekiah.

"He has truly adapted to the white-mans ways and truly loves the Lord," exclaimed Thomas Mastin.

"What does Agnes think about moving?" asked Hezekiah?

"She loves this farm, but she is a pilgrim by spirit," answered Thomas.

"I am so sorry to hear that you are moving, you have been such a good friend as well as a leader for the folks round here," stated Hezekiah.

"I have tried to help and feel like I have friends here, but the Tennessee country is calling me," said Thomas.

"Well, I guess I better get Rachel one of these puppies and head up the creek, we will have to spend some time together before you leave," said Hezekiah.

"I would pick that big one, but the runt seems the smartest," answered Thomas. Hezekiah reached down into the box and got the runt and held him up for a look-over.

"I think Rachel would like this one," said a smiling Hezekiah.

"He may take off a growing, he is smart!" exclaimed Thomas Mastin.

"Thanks friend, I better get back to Rachel, you will be hearing from us soon, I think the baby will be coming soon," said Hezekiah.

"Agnes will be there quick as she hears that Rachel is ready," answered Thomas.

"We are so thankful for Agnes and of course you too, Thomas," said Hezekiah as he climbed on Johnny's back with the little fur-ball pup in his hand.

"What's his name going to be?" asked Thomas?

"Griffith, if he is a boy, Martha if a girl," stated Hezekiah.
Thomas Mastin laughed out loud.
"What is so funny?" asked Hezekiah.

"I meant the pup!" stated Thomas.

"Oh! I don't know, reckon Rachel will do the naming, he's her pup," answered Hezekiah with a smile on his face.

THE PATRIOT, HEZEKIAH WHITT

"See you soon Hezekiah and watch out for your hair," said Thomas as Hezekiah rode up Indian Creek.

Rachel was waiting on the door step to see her new puppy, when Hezekiah rode up. After seeing Rachel waiting he rode Johnny right up to the door and gently handed the fuzzy puppy down to her!

"Oh, he is so beautiful," exclaimed Rachel.

"Cute maybe, but not beautiful," said Hezekiah laughingly.

"Hezekiah, you are just jealous," answercd Rachel.

"I thought I was the only man in your life," answered Hezekiah.

"Nope, I have James, you, and now I have Jesse!" exclaimed Rachel.

"Well I guess you have named him," answered Hezekiah.

"Don't he look like a Jesse to you?" asked Rachel?

"Looks like a pup to me," answered Hezekiah.

"Have you got him a strong box made to protect him from the wild animals that come around at night?" asked Rachel.

"I will get right on it, I forgot to tell you the big news," said Hezekiah.

"What is it, don't make me wait!" said an expectant Rachel.

"Hold your breath, Thomas is taking his family all but Thomas Bailey Christian way to the west to the Tennessee country," said Hezekiah.

"What will I do, I am counting on Agnes to help me deliver the baby?" asked Rachel?

Don't fret on that, Thomas has assured me that he will not move until our baby has safely arrived," said Hezekiah.

"You scared me half to death, I really need her when the time comes!" said Rachel.

"You will have Aunt Elizabeth Hankins like you did with little James," answered Hezekiah.

"I love Aunt Elizabeth, but Agnes was much more help and made me feel so at ease," said Rachel.

"Well don't worry, both of them will be with you when the time comes," answered Hezekiah.

"Look honey, Jesse is licking my fingers, ain't he sweet?" asked Rachel?

"Yes dear, you play with him and I will go and build him a strong box for him to sleep in," said Hezekiah.

Hezekiah kept thinking about the Mastin family and the move they were planning to make. This place is almost heaven with the exception of the Indian threat, Thomas has never stayed in one place for very long, and traveling is in his blood, thought Hezekiah.

"Hezekiah is Thomas Bailey Christian going to stay on the Mastin farm by his self?" shouted Rachel from the step of the cabin.

"He sure is, I promised Thomas to keep check on him," answered Hezekiah in a loud voice.

Hey Hezy, we got to get that recipe for that potion Agnes gave me when little James was born!" exclaimed Rachel.

"We will," answered Hezekiah.

"Let me get my stuff and bring it over to the breezeway, then we can talk," stated Hezekiah.

As Hezekiah gathered materials to build a pup box that would be strong and big enough for Jesse to grow in, Rachel and Jesse played. He was a very alert puppy as some runts are. A healthy runt will mature quicker that the rest of the litter.

Rachel kept calling his name and the pup would wag his tail and lick her fingers. "Jesse knows his name," stated Rachel.

"He is smart, but you just named him," said a doubtful Hezekiah.

"Well he does!" exclaimed Rachel.

Hezekiah mumbled something under his breath as he brought some two inch sticks of various lengths to the breezeway.

"Hezekiah, I know a lot of plants, but I don't know that potion that Agnes gave me when the labor became so strong," stated Rachel.

"I am sure she will share it with us, something that powerful could be dangerous if not used wisely," answered Hezekiah.

"I want to teach all of our children the secrets of the plant world, my people have been using them for thousands of years," said Rachel.

THE PATRIOT, HEZEKIAH WHITT

"God has put everything in his world for our benefit, it is up to us to enjoy everything in moderation," answered Hezekiah.

"Husband, you are so smart, must be the reason I married you!" said Rachel.

"Yes and of course you were "twitter-paited", said Hezekiah with a wide grin on his face.

"Well I know a man that could hardly keep his hands off of me," replied Rachel.
"I love you Rachel," said Hezekiah.
"I know you do and I love you, husband," answered Rachel.

The days of summer were turning into the colorful days of autumn. The leaves of so many trees had already turned to red, yellow and all the shades between on the waters of the Clinch.

The night of September 30, 1787 the weather changed as did the moon. It was unusually cool and the signs of winter were apparent in Baptist Valley, Virginia. Rachel had Hezekiah build up the fire and get out a warm quilt. She also had some changes going on and she told Hezekiah that she felt different somehow.

"It's just the weather change," answered Hezekiah.

"Husband, hold me till I get to sleep," requested Rachel.

Hezekiah held his wife and they drifted off to sleep. They did not sleep too long. Rachel woke up with a sharp pain in her groin area that she recognized instantly as a contraction. It was about 1:30 AM on October 1, 1787.

Hezekiah was awakened when he felt Rachel stiffen up and give out a little whine.
"It's time Hezekiah, better get up and start making ready, the baby is on its way," stated Rachel.

"All right sweetheart, I will get up and light a candle," answered Hezekiah.
Hezekiah got up and fumbled around in a room that was almost in complete darkness. The fire had died down and that was the only source of light. Hezekiah fumbled around getting a candle lit from the fireplace. He put some wood on the fire as the room had a chill in it. He fumbled into his clothes as Rachel tried to hold back a little scream as another contraction seized her body.

"You going to be alright long enough for me to run and get Aunt Elizabeth?" asked a concerned Hezekiah.

"Yes Hezekiah, just hurry and get her, please ask Uncle John to ride for Agnes also," said Rachel.

THE PATRIOT, HEZEKIAH WHITT

Hezekiah leaned over and gave Rachel a quick kiss and lit a lantern. He headed out to saddle Johnny. Hezekiah was heading down the path before he realized that he left without his musket. Too late now he thought, if I run into Indians, I will just have to let Johnny get me to safety. Hezekiah's thoughts returned to getting to John and Elizabeth Hankins' cabin.

Hezekiah was surprised to see a light flicker from the Hankins' cabin. He rode Johnny right up to the door. The door cracked open and a gruff voices ask, "Is that you Hezekiah?"

"Uncle John, it is me," answered Hezekiah.
"Elizabeth is up and almost ready, she said you would be coming tonight," said John Hankins.
John came out with a lantern and headed to the horse stall to saddle his and Elizabeth's horses. Hezekiah followed John to help get the animals saddled.
"How did she know Uncle John?" asked Hezekiah?

"It's a woman thing I reckon, the weather changed and so did the moon, that will do it every time," stated John Hankins.

"You going to the Mastin's?" asked Hezekiah?

"You take care to get Elizabeth to your place and I will go down Indian Creek and fetch Agnes fer you," answered John Hankins.

Hezekiah was well awake now and not as shook up as he was when his first was born.

"I will get Aunt Elizabeth there safely and you be careful Uncle John," said Hezekiah.

"Lord willing I will have Agnes Mastin at you place in about two hours," said John as he rode down Indian Creek.

Hezekiah had both his and Elizabeth's horses saddled and were waiting at the door when Elizabeth came out.

"Morning Hezekiah, John already headed to the Mastins?" she asked all in one breath.

"Morning Aunt Elizabeth, yes John is already riding down the creek," answered Hezekiah.

Hezekiah held the horse sternly and helped Elizabeth get straddle of her horse.

"I ain't got time to ride lady-like," said Elizabeth when she saw the look on Hezekiah's face.
"Yes Ma'am," answered Hezekiah as he threw a leg over Johnny.

THE PATRIOT, HEZEKIAH WHITT

"This is the day that the Lord hath made, let us rejoice and be glad in it," said Aunt Elizabeth Skaggs Hankins.

"Yes it is," answered Hezekiah as he felt a peace and calmness settle over him. "You always know jest what to say, Aunt Elizabeth," said Hezekiah.

"Oh honey, I just follow the Lord and He dishes out His beautiful sayings," answered Elizabeth.

They were at Hezekiah's cedar grove in no time and rode right up to the door of the cabin. Hezekiah jumped down off Johnny and helped Elizabeth down from her mount and she hurried into the cabin. Hezekiah took Johnny and the other horse to the corral and unsaddled both of them. He hurried to the cabin and Elizabeth ordered him to go and fetch a fresh bucket of water and get more firewood in the house.

Rachel was sitting by the fire all bent over engrossed in pain when Elizabeth entered. Rachel sit up as the contraction eased up.

"How you doing missy," asked Elizabeth?

"Purty good, I reckon, the pain comes and goes, well you know about it don't you Aunt Elizabeth?" said Rachel.

"Yes honey, I know about these things, I am going to get your birthing bed ready so you can get back and relax some," said Elizabeth.

"I got clean sheets and rags laid out on the washstand," said Rachel as another contraction hit her.

"Don't worry honey, I will get you fixed up in no-time and this young-un should get here quicker then James did," said Elizabeth.

"Reckon it will, I sure hope so," said Rachel.

"Most likely, the first is usually the slow one," answered Elizabeth while helping Rachel in the bed.

Hezekiah came in with a bucket of fresh limestone water from the spring. He set it down on the table and went back out for more firewood. Once he was back in and shed of the firewood he went to Rachel. He bent down and gave her a kiss just as the strong birthing contraction hit her again. Her face showed pain, but she hardly made a sound.

"Hezekiah, you go and whittle out a biting stick and get some spirits in this house, then you go sit under your breezeway," ordered Elizabeth.

Hezekiah hurried to his chore as that was the only thing he knew to do. He got a nice soft wooded stick and whittled the ends smooth and removed all the bark, then he brought in the little brown jug from the shed. He sat them down on a little table by the bed (The stick was for the birthing mother to bite on in severe pain and spirits were given to take off the edge of pain.) and went out to wait for John and Agnes.

THE PATRIOT, HEZEKIAH WHITT

As Hezekiah sits there he reflected on the happening thus far. Little Jesse, the pup came to Hezekiah with his tail wagging as if sent to relieve the tension of waiting. Hezekiah talked to the pup and his mind went right back to the happening of this day. He realized he had been careless by going out without his musket. John Hankins reminded Hezekiah of this by carrying his musket across his saddle. Hezekiah took a minute to thank God for all of his blessings and ask that He would be with both mother and child. Then he quoted the verse again, "This is the day that the Lord hath made, let us rejoice and be glad in it."

Just about that time Hezekiah heard horses coming. It was about 4:45 AM. This time he had his musket sitting out and leaned against the cabin wall. He figured it was John and Agnes, but he picked up the musket and checked the prime just in case.

John Hankins was in front as they rode up the path and he yelled to Hezekiah just as soon as he saw him holding the musket.

"It's me and Agnes, hold your fire," said John.

"Come on in Uncle John," answered the voice from the breezeway.
Hezekiah went straight to the horse that carried Agnes and helped her down.
"Hello Hezekiah, I got to get in there and see about Rachel," stated Agnes as she headed to the cabin door.
"Morning Agnes, Elizabeth is with her, go right in," answered Hezekiah.

"How she doing?" asked John Hankins?

"All right I reckon, she don't make much noise like some women do," answered Hezekiah.
"Indians are proud people and don't like to show weakness, she learned that from them," said John.

"I told her it was all right to yell out if she wanted to," answered Hezekiah.

"She wouldn't do it, she is a brave woman!" exclaimed John.

"We might as well get these horses took care of," said Hezekiah as he led Agnes' horse to the corral.

"Yep, it's too dark to go a hunting right now," answered John.

"Hunting, we can't go hunting Rachel is having a baby," answered Hezekiah.

"Well, they don't need you, you would just be in the way, don't you remember me taking you buffalo hunting when little James come along?" asked John?

COLONEL CHARLES DAHNMON WHITT   183

THE PATRIOT, HEZEKIAH WHITT

"This-un should come a lot quicker, Aunt Elizabeth said that after the first baby comes the rest don't take as long," answered Hezekiah.

"Well you still need to get them off-en your mind!" answered John.

John followed Hezekiah leading his mount to the corral with his musket in his hand. Hezekiah noticed this and thought it was good that one of them still had their head screwed on.

"Uncle John, you heard of any Indian trouble lately or seen any sign?" asked Hezekiah?

"Not for a few weeks, some come through but must have been too small a party to attack any of us in the valley," answered John.

"Hezekiah you got that little brown jug out here in the shed?" asked Uncle John?
"Nope, I took it in for Rachel," answered Hezekiah.

"Hell, she don't need it, she ain't nervous like us," answered John.

Hezekiah laughed, and then he told Uncle John that he would pick it up the first time he went into the cabin, if Rachel didn't need it.

Inside the cabin, Agnes surveyed the situation and checked Rachel to see if she was dilating.

"Morning Elizabeth, how often are her pains a coming?" asked Agnes?

"Morning Agnes, the best I can tell is about three minutes apart, she ort to be delivering in an hour or so," answered Elizabeth.

"She is getting bigger down there and the baby has moved toward getting birthed," said Agnes.

"You want a cup of tea while we wait?" asked Elizabeth?

"Yes I could use a cup, if you will fix us a cup I will get my potion out and do some mixing," answered Agnes.

Elizabeth went to the door and asked the men to get some more fresh water from the spring; she didn't want to run low right in the middle of things. Hezekiah took the bucket to the spring and filled it from the bountiful spring. He walked over to Rachel and bent down and kissed her. She had little shiny droplets of sweat on her forehead.

"You better go back out fore Agnes gets after you, sweetheart," said Rachel.

"You need that little brown jug?" asked Hezekiah.

"Nope, take it out I ain't going to use it, Agnes will give me the potion dreckley," (directly) answered Rachel.

Hezekiah picked up the jug and carried it outside feeling a little guilty for taking it. After he got outside he handed it to Uncle John and he took a swig and gave it to Hezekiah nodding for him to partake. Hezekiah tilted the jug and took a swallow. They sat there silently for a few minutes and then both got out their pipes filling them methodically and lit up. Jesse the pup was standing vigilant with them! They took turns petting the pup.

By now the eastern sky was lightening up and October 1, 1787 looked to be a great day. Hezekiah and John sat and talked under the roof of the breezeway and watched the making of a new day. Hezekiah was nervous but didn't say much about the happenings going on inside the cabin.

Agnes checked her one more time and said, "Hum!"

Elizabeth looked at her expectantly and Agnes smiled at her.

"I better give her the potion tea now, I can feel a little head down there wanting to get out," said Agnes.

Elizabeth went to the fireplace and retrieved the teapot for Agnes. They set a cup on the table filled with the secrets of nature and poured the hot water in. Agnes mixed it several times and took a half a spoon full to test.

"Hum!" she said, "It is ready."

Rachel let out a little cry fighting against screaming out.

"Here honey, drink this down as quick as you can, that baby will be here soon," said Agnes.

As the pain began to settle into a constant agony; Rachel drinks down the bitter potion. Within two minutes Rachel felt relief and pushed hard hoping to get the baby moving. Elizabeth held on to Rachel's right arm and hand and Rachel pulled and pushed.

"Go right ahead and squeeze all you want," said Elizabeth.

"Wait honey, jest push when you feel the pain again," commanded Agnes.

"Reckon we ort to get her up in the squatting position?" asked Elizabeth?

"Don't think we will have to, what do you think, Rachel?" asked Agnes?
"I hardly feel any pain, but I can feel myself opening up more, I think the baby is coming," said Rachel.

THE PATRIOT, HEZEKIAH WHITT

Agnes got into position to help the new baby into the world. The head popped out with long black hair. Agnes slowly turned the tiny shoulders to help the little feller out. With a gentle pull the infant was out into his new world, and began to cry in protest.

"Look at that long black hair Rachel, you got yourself a little brave," exclaimed Elizabeth.

"I got another little boy?" asked Rachel?

"You sure do and he is dark complected like you, honey," answered Elizabeth. Agnes tied the cord and cut it to free little Griffith Whitt from his mother. She handed the baby to Elizabeth to wash up and get him ready for his Maw. Agnes went about getting the afterbirth and mess gathered up and wrapped in rags so she could get Rachel cleaned up and in a clean bed.

Rachel tried to sit up, but things didn't work right and she became alarmed. Agnes saw it on her face and assured her that the potion was still working. Agnes explained that in another thirty minutes things would work more normally.

Hezekiah smiled as he listened to his baby crying.
"Your young-un has arove, Hezekiah," said Uncle John Hankins.

"They will be coming to give the announcement real soon," said Hezekiah.
"Reckon you were hankering for another boy, but girl babies are so sweet," said John.

"What ever the Lord sends us will be just fine with me and Rachel," answered Hezekiah.
"That is a good way to look at it, that way you wouldn't be disappointed," said John.

"Long as Rachel and the baby come through it good, I will give God the glory," said Hezekiah.
The door of the cabin opened and Hezekiah walked in to see the new baby and his wife. He was waiting for a good report and Agnes gave it to him.

"Mother and Griffith done real good, James looked like you, but Griffy looks like his Maw, said Agnes.

"They need some good rest, so you just take a peek for now," said Elizabeth.

After Hezekiah and Uncle John had a peek they were given a package to take out and bury. It was the effects of birth that needed to be disposed of.

"You dig a deep hole and bury that, so's nothing can dig it up," said Agnes.

As Hezekiah and John went out little James started to cry. He had slept through the whole ordeal, but was hungry and feeling that something was different.

THE PATRIOT, HEZEKIAH WHITT

Aunt Elizabeth picked up James and gave him assurance that all was well. She talked to little James as if he was a grownup.

"Guess what, while you were asleep your Maw found your little brother Griffy, would you like to see him?" asked Elizabeth?

James looked all around and stretched his neck to see the little bundle at his Maw's breast. James was not too impressed!

All was well at the Whitts on the waters of the Clinch. Hezekiah and all concerned had plenty to be thankful for. Hezekiah now had three loved ones to provide for and protect, but he welcomed the duty with love and passion.

Used for smoking and hacking. Made by the British.

Chapter 22

It Is Still A Savage Land

Elizabeth and Agnes have Rachel all comfy and little Griffy was holding on to Rachel's breast. Little James kept walking around the bed saying, "Griffy, Griffy".

Elizabeth had a big brunch started with bacon, fried potatoes, coffee, eggs, and "Cathead Biscuits". After breakfast Elizabeth and John would head back home. Agnes would spend the night and Thomas Mastin would come tomorrow for a visit and escort his wife, Agnes home. It may well be their last visit since the Mastins are moving away shortly.

Rachel was feeling much better, she asked Hezekiah, "Well did you get us another buffalo?"
Hezekiah looked bewildered and answered, "Buffalo, what buffalo?"
"When James was born you brought me a buffalo," she said smiling.
"You got so good at having young-uns, you don't give me time for a hunt," answered Hezekiah with a grin on his face.

"I ain't that good at it yet, maybe you can go for a good hunt a little later on," said Rachel.

Uncle John Hankins was listening and abruptly said, "Me and you, maybe Mastin can go over on the Tug and get a buffalo or a bear."

"Maybe so Uncle John, Mastin ain't going to be here long, I will ask him tomorrow," said Hezekiah.

Hezekiah was past due getting back in the woods. He loved Rachel and the boys dearly, but he also loved being out in the wilds of western Virginia.

Rachel took another, but different toddy to help her rest during the night. Agnes told her it would make her and the baby rest that first night when everything started getting back in place. Rachel had Hezekiah sit with Agnes and carefully write down the formula for both potions, and every detail for gathering the roots and leafs to be used. It was amazing that God had such beneficial plants growing right here on the waters of the Clinch. The Native Americans had used them for thousands of years.

Hezekiah finally got to hold baby Griffy Whitt and he checked him out from head to toe. The little baby was not overly dark, but he would favor the Indians side of the family. He had jet black hair and plenty of it for a newborn. He had those dark buck eyes like his Maw. He was not a fat baby but was quiet long. Hezekiah was proud as punch to have two fine sons and a beautiful wife.

THE PATRIOT, HEZEKIAH WHITT

The night went well and everyone slept peaceably. Hezekiah helped with breakfast and did the morning work that had to be done. He fed the animals and milked the cow. The hens had just about stopped laying for the winter so there were few eggs to gather. Most of the animals were in the pasture and helped themselves to the lush bluegrass. The first frost had not come yet so most of the pasture remained green. The branch meandered through the pasture so the animals drink whenever they got thirsty. The sheep loved their home; they reminded Hezekiah of the Twenty Third Psalm.

Hezekiah took time for a smoke out in the breezeway and waited for his friend, Thomas Mastin to come. Hezekiah had his musket leaned against the cabin just for security, he didn't want to get careless. As Hezekiah sat there he reflected on the day before and prayed a prayer of praise to his Lord for His loving kindness.

Hezekiah played with Jesse the pup while he enjoyed his pipe. It wasn't long before a horse could be heard coming up into the cedar grove. Hezekiah reached and picked up his musket and checked the prime.

"Hezekiah Whitt, this is Thomas coming in," said Thomas Mastin.

"Come on in Thomas'" answered Hezekiah as he sat his musket back against the cabin.

Thomas Mastin was always a striking figure sitting on his fine riding horse. He rode right up to the breezeway to greet his friend Hezekiah.

"Hello friend, is all well with you?" asked Thomas Mastin?

"Hello friend, things are well with me and I hope with you," answered Hezekiah.

"Do you have a larger family today?" asked Thomas?

"I sure do, we got us another fine son, he is strong and healthy, we call him Griffy," bragged Hezekiah.

"Congratulations friend, God is good!" answered Thomas Mastin.

"Thanks Thomas, God is good and so are the Mastins, Agnes worked so hard to take care of Rachel and little Griffy," said Hezekiah.

"We are glad to lend a hand when it is possible, I know you would do the same!" exclaimed Thomas Mastin.

"I sure hate to think about you all are a leavin," said Hezekiah.

"We are pulling out just as soon as we can get things together, we are traveling through Castlewood and get the farm in Christian's name," answered Thomas Mastin.

He will sign the deed whenever he gets over to the courthouse again," added Thomas Mastin.

"We will certainly miss you as neighbors and you as a leader," said Hezekiah.

THE PATRIOT, HEZEKIAH WHITT

"This place is getting purty tame, even the Indians don't come here too much," answered Thomas Mastin.

"One raid a summer is way too many," answered Hezekiah.

"I agree, I am just making talk, Hezekiah," replied Thomas.
0
"You ready to go in and see my new boy?" asked Hezekiah.

"Sure am, you have a good start on young-uns, how many do you want to have?" asked Thomas as they went into the door.

"If he has to have them, it wouldn't be but one more," said Agnes with a wide grin on her pleasant round face.

Rachel smiled and nodded to Thomas Mastin.

"Well Miss Whitt, how you doing, I heard you had a good looking young-un," said Thomas Mastin.

"We sure are proud of little Griffy, Agnes and Elizabeth were such troopers a helping him get here," replied Rachel.

"I treasure Agnes, she is such a blessing to me," answered Thomas.

"I sure wish you all weren't moving, all of you will be missed here in the valley," said Rachel squeezing Agnes' hand.

"You all will be just fine, there is several good folks living in the valley and on Indian Creek," said Thomas Mastin.

"You will be missed, just the same," answered Hezekiah.

Thomas wanting to change the subject said, "Let's see that new baby."

Rachel uncovered him so Hezekiah could pick him up and show him off and little James got as close to Hezekiah as he could. Hezekiah picked up both boys and handed Griffy over to Thomas to hold.

"Ain't very big is he?" Thomas asked before he thought.

"He is plenty big for a new born," inserted Agnes.

"I just ain't used to seeing um this young, I reckon," answered Thomas.
Hezekiah wanted to ask Thomas to go for a hunt, but knew the Mastins wanted to get to Tennessee before the winter hit so he never mentioned it.

After a short visit Thomas took Agnes home to prepare for their journey. Hezekiah and Rachel were by themselves again not counting the babies. Hezekiah sat down and held

THE PATRIOT, HEZEKIAH WHITT

Griffy and gave him a good looking over, of course James was standing by, holding to his Paw's knee.

There may have been babies between James and Griffy and also between Griffy and the next, John Bunyan Whitt, but I have no records of any. Many frontier families lost a baby or two because of the lack of medical knowledge.

Winter was approaching and Hezekiah had his crops in. They had pickled some things, dried some and put some in a catch in the ground.

The Mastins were gone except Thomas Bailey Christian who stayed on at the Indian Creek farm. Hezekiah had been over to check on him a time or two. Hezekiah had asked Christian if he might want to go on a hunt with him and John Hankins. Christian was all for it so a plan was made to go on a hunt over on the Tug Fork for buffalo and bear.

The three men decided to start their hunting trip around the middle of November, 1787. Christian showed up at the Whitt's around 8:00 PM with his gear. He was riding a good saddle horse and had a pack mule in tow. He was wearing his buckskins and wearing moccasins. His long black hair and copper skin truly showed his Indian heritage. Hezekiah gave him a second look as he came up the path into the cedar grove. Christian waved his hand over his head and Hezekiah waved back. Hezekiah never mentioned a word about Thomas Bailey Christian's appearance.

Hezekiah had most everything ready for the hunt and his adrenalin was up. After doing a few last minute things, Hezekiah kissed Rachel and the boys and the two men rode off to meet John Hankins.

John was sitting on the stoop smoking his pipe when he saw the riders coming. From a distance Hezekiah and Christian both appeared to be Indians. John picked up his musket and took another long look as he was expecting his friends. Hezekiah and Christian saw John and gave him a wave.

As Hezekiah and Christian got close John sat his musket down and said, "Damn boys, I thought you'll were Indians!"

"I am an Indian," answered Christian with a smile on his copper skinned face.
"I meant a savage, not a tame one," answered John Hankins.
Thomas Bailey Christian and Hezekiah Whitt both laughed out loud.
"Well fellers, you aim to sit there and carry on all day or are you ready to go a hunting?" asked John?

"We are waiting on you, lets get on to the Tug," said Hezekiah with a crooked grin on his face.

John hollered for Elizabeth and she came to the door to bid them well and hug the grizzled John Hankins. John and Hezekiah both had full beards as did most of the, over the mountain men, in winter. Christian had no beard because Indians have very little facial hair.

THE PATRIOT, HEZEKIAH WHITT

Elizabeth gave John a big hug and said, "You'll be careful and have a good hunt. I pray that you'll will get back with your hair."

John grinned as he mounted his saddle horse and took the reins of his pack animal in his left hand. The three men headed out toward the Tug Fork.

They headed up Greasy Creek and passed through what is now modern day Bandy and Harman. They continued on the warrior path until late in the day. They decided to find a camp so they went up another creek about a half mile and found a rock house to camp under. They went off the trail for safety, even though running into Indians was not likely as to the time of year. As always loud talking and extra noise was subdued out in the wilderness.

The three men did their work in a methodical way. They took care of the animals, unloaded the gear from the animals, gathered fire wood and got ready to cook. The fire would not be a big one and nothing loud was permitted by the three hunters.

After a peaceful evening and night's sleep the three hunters were moving again. By the afternoon they were on the Tug and had seen a lot of big game, but no buffalo yet. They stopped early this day and agreed that one of them should go ahead for a spying mission while the other two tended to the camp. Hezekiah agreed to go ahead a few miles, mostly looking for buffalo, but also to make sure there were not any Indians laying in wait.

Hezekiah rode Johnny about a mile while leaving his pack mule for the others to tend. After about a mile he tied Johnny just off the trail and proceeded on foot in a serious and conscientious manner. Hezekiah was glad to see he had not lost his skill as a scout and woodsman.

After moving on foot for about a mile, Hezekiah was shocked to come up on three Indians busying themselves, butchering a buffalo. Hezekiah stayed concealed in the undergrowth and watched the Indians at work. Every now and then the Indians would stop and look about, one seemed to look straight at Hezekiah, but it just seemed that way to Hezekiah.

Hezekiah watched for about twenty minutes, momentarily scanning the whole area to make sure that there were only three Indians. The three Indians were peaceful looking, not the painted, savage version Hezekiah had faced in the past. There were no other signs of other Indians and they were here to hunt and not on the war path, was the conclusion of Hezekiah. Hezekiah slowly backed out and went back toward his horse. After he was down the trail about an eighth of a mile Hezekiah went into a fast trot, but kept the noisy down. He reached Johnny and mounted up and rode the last mile back to camp.

As Hezekiah rode into camp, John had a fire going and was frying bacon. Hezekiah rode right up to John and said, "Better dampen that fire down some, we have three Indians about two miles down river."

THE PATRIOT, HEZEKIAH WHITT

John pulled off the bigger pieces of wood and threw dirt on them to quench the fire. He kept a real small fire of mostly coals under his pan.

"I will hurry this bacon and put it out," said John.

"Where is Christian?" asked Hezekiah?

"He went back up the trail for a scout and make sure nobody was following us," answered John.
"I don't think the Indians know we are here, they were dressing out a buffalo," said Hezekiah.

"Was they painted up for war?" asked John?

"Nope, they seemed to be here just to hunt, I think they were Shawnee," said Hezekiah.

In a few minutes Christian rode into camp and the two hunters motioned for him to be quite. He rode up quietly to the others and dismounted with an expectant look on his copper face.
"What is it men?" asked Thomas Bailey Christian?

"We got three Indians bout two miles down the creek," answered John.
Christian's countenance changed on his face to concern.
"Are they painted?" he asked?

"Nope, I think they are just hunters, they were cutting up a buffalo," answered Hezekiah.

"What do you think we should do?" asked Christian.

"I think we ort to go and kill them red varmints," answered John.

"Let's think about this a little bit, fore we take off halfcocked," said Hezekiah.
The two men looked at Hezekiah with a little surprise.

"You all heard about the new ordinance from the government, bout us befriending the Indians, or at least letting them be," reminded Hezekiah.

"Only good Indian is a dead-en, I don't mean you Christian and other tame-uns," said John Hankins speaking before thinking.

Christian and Hezekiah frowned at John!

COLONEL CHARLES DAHNMON WHITT 193

THE PATRIOT, HEZEKIAH WHITT

"I think we owe it to the country to try and treat them like men and not attack unless, of course they show hostilities," said Hezekiah.

"Well I don't think we should take no chances with-um," said John.

"How bout we be at their camp at first light and be ready to attack-um, then we can have Christian show his self and try to talk to-um, if they want to fight, then we will drop-um," said Hezekiah

"I like it," John said, "especially the drop-um part."

"How come I got to be the one to show myself?" Asked Christian?

"You look like an Indian, you talk like an Indian, hell you are an Indian," said John. Hezekiah looked at Christian with a crooked grin on his beardy face.
"You just start talking and if they aim to kill you, then me and John will drop them," said Hezekiah.

"They's three of-um, what about the one you don't shoot?" asked Christian?
"Hell, you will have to duck or shoot fast-ern him," answered John with a laugh.

"Just remember the new law and try to do it," said Hezekiah.

"Them fellers in New York that made that law ain't got no Indians after-um," said John.

The Ordinance they talked about was part of Article III of Section 14. Of 1787;

> *The utmost good faith shall always be observed towards the Indians; their lands and property shall never be taken away from them without their consent; and in their property, rights, and liberty they shall never be invaded or disturbed, unless in just and lawful wars authorized by Congress; but laws founded in justice and humanity shall, from time to time, be made, for preventing wrongs being done to them, and for preserving peace and friendship with them. . .*

This would be one of the first tests of this law and no one knew what would happen when such meetings occurred in the wilderness.

The three hunters decided to have a cold camp and alternate on watch during the night. A plan was formed to ride their mounts to within a half of a mile and dismount. They would stalk the Indian camp and be ready at first light to either make friends or kill the Indians. Christian would be the first to show himself and try to talk to the three Indians and the other two would have a bead on the Indians to the left and right of the third one.

The three men were up about an hour and a half before first light. They whispered to each other to finalize the plan and Hezekiah led them in a prayer. One thing he asked God for was that the Indians would greet them in peace.

THE PATRIOT, HEZEKIAH WHITT

The three tied their pack animals in a cleared area in the middle of a thicket. They tidied up the camp so it was not obvious that anyone had been there. They quietly mounted up and walked their horses to a point about a mile and half from camp and about a half mile from the Indians.

They secured their horses just off the trail, but left them saddled in case they would have to mount up in retreat.

The three wasted no time going up the trail to the Indian camp. The eastern sky was already getting light as the three came up on the Indian camp. One Indian was sitting by a tiny fire and two were rolled up in blankets. The three hunters checked their prime and watched for a few minutes while concealed in underbrush. As one of the sleeping braves aroused and sit up, Hezekiah motioned for Christian to stand up and announce to the Indians that he was an Indian. Of course it was to be in the Shawnee tongue.

When Christian stood up and spoke, all three Indians scrambled up to their feet. Two held muskets and one put an arrow in his bow. They faced Christian and asked what he wanted. He told them that he was the son of Elinipsico and the son of the great Cornstalk the Indians were jubilant and said for him to come into their camp.

"I will brothers, but I must tell you I have two white friends with me who come in peace," said Christian.

"Indians have no white friends, what are you trying to do?" asked one of the braves?

"You have nothing to fear from my friends, may they show themselves and come into your camp with me?" asked Christian?

The Indian that seemed to be in charge waved his arm for this to happen. The three Indians were ready for anything as Hezekiah and John slowly rose from concealment. It was a tense moment as the three Indians and the three hunters faced off. Slowly Hezekiah stepped forward toward the three waiting Indians. All held their weapons, but none pointed them at the other. Christian stepped forward slightly ahead of Hezekiah and John followed them to talk to the Indians. Finally the three hunters were face to face with the three warriors and Christian extended his hand to shake. The center Indian grabbed the arm of Christian just below the elbow and greeted him Indian style.

"How I know you Elinipsico's son?" asked the Indian?

"I am Kumskaka, now Christian, my mother is Bailey Standing Deer. I have two brothers, Low Hawk and Shokka Outhowwa, also I have a sister called Mountain Raven." said Thomas Bailey Christian.

"Where have you been for many moons?" asked the Indian still very nervous?

"Me and my brothers and sister were protected by the Cherokee in the Tennessee Country. The Whites attacked during the white man's war and William Skaggs captured us. He was very kind and later Thomas Mastin, the white warrior adopted u." explained Christian..

THE PATRIOT, HEZEKIAH WHITT

The Indians recognized the names and understood the story that Christian had related and become calm.

"Who are these white dogs you travel with?" asked one of the Indians in Shawnee?

"We are not dogs," said Hezekiah in Shawnee surprising the Indians.

John Hankins grizzled up at the tone of Hezekiah, but did not understand the words. Christian spoke comely and introduced Hezekiah Whitt and John Hankins to the three Indians.

Finally the Indians, one at a time extended the right arm of greeting to Hezekiah and John. As they clasped arms the Indians grunted their names. They were "Rock Lizard," "Hungry Bird," and "Moon Gazer".

Rock Lizard seemed to be in charge as they began to talk.

Hezekiah told the three Indians that he was married to Rachel, the daughter of Cornstalk and had two fine sons who were grandsons of the late Chief.

Hezekiah also told them that they came in peace and wanted to befriend the Indians. He told them he could have killed them yesterday while they cut up the buffalo. The Indians were surprised that they had been observed by this white man.

Christian told them that Hezekiah had been an Indian Spy during the war with the Redcoats and was as good as most Indians at tracking and living in the woods.

Rock Lizard raised an eyebrow, but said nothing.
All six men became a little more relaxed as they conversed.

"Want to eat?" asked Rock Lizard?

"Yes, we are hungry, we will eat with our Indian brothers if that is an offer," said Hezekiah.

Hezekiah stood his musket up against a tree as a gesture of peace and started putting wood on the Indian's fire. The Indians did likewise and put down their muskets, but of course all six men carried knives and tomahawks. John Hankins was the last to set his musket down, this was really different for him.

The six men sat cross legged around the fire, the three Indians on one side and the hunters on the other. Rock Lizard motioned to Hungary Bird to cut off some of a buffalo roast and serve the hunters. All ate the meat and some type of corn fritters, and not much was said while they ate. There was still a little cloud of doubt that hung over the six men.

THE PATRIOT, HEZEKIAH WHITT

The three Indians wanted to know what the three were doing in their hunting grounds. Christian answered that they were hunting the same as his red brothers and that this land was free for all now that the treaties had been signed.

Rock Lizard gave a slight frown then said, "This is our land, but you three may hunt here!"

"Thank you," Hezekiah said, "you three may hunt here too!"

Rock Lizard laughed out loud and the ice was broken. All six men laughed and smiled at each other.

Out of the blue John Hankins spoke up, "This is damn good corn bread, how do you make it?"

Rock Lizard laughed and smiled at John. Then Rock Lizard said, "Indian secret!" They all laughed again, but none of the Indians completely trusted the hunters and vice verses!

They talked for about an hour about the times and the past. They talked about hunting, fishing and the dangers each side presented to the other. After awhile the two conflicting sides separated in a much better attitude than when they met. The hunters bid the Indians farewell and went back up the trail toward their horses and the Indians loaded their meat and pelts on their horses and headed down the Tug Fork toward the Ohio River. All six men felt a little better about their counterparts. If three settlers can change and if three Indians can change, there could be a peace on the frontier, but don't hold your breath.

It was midday before Hezekiah, John, and Christian got to their pack animals. Everything was just as they had left it; the mules were loaded and ready to go. John Hankins suggested that they head on down the Tug toward the Indian camp and start scouting for buffalo and bear. Hezekiah and Christian agreed but Hezekiah stressed that they should not push the three Indians so as not to antagonize them.

The three Indians had disappeared from the area and the three hunters went to work with their hunt. They had the good fortune to harvest a buffalo, and the bear they wanted. The bear was fat and ready for his winter sleep which would provide the three men with plenty of bear grease. After cutting the meat and preparing it for the trip back the three men headed back up the head waters of the Tug. The three felt good and thankful for the good hunt and a good meeting with the three Indians. Only time would tell, if a peace would come to the waters of the Clinch.

This new year, 1788, the States began to ratify the new Constitution of the new United States. January 2nd Georgia is the 4th State to sign the document. On January 9th Connecticut is the 5th to sign. February 6th Massachusetts ratifies as the 6th. April 28th Maryland becomes the 7th to ratify. May 23rd South Carolina becomes the 8th. On June

THE PATRIOT, HEZEKIAH WHITT

the 21st New Hampshire becomes the 9th to ratify and the Constitution becomes the law of the land. June 25th Virginia becomes the 10th to ratify with stipulation that they can pull out if it infringes too much on their rights. New York ratified on July 26th to become the 11th. They also had concerns about their State's rights.

On September 13th 1788 New York becomes the first capitol of the United States. Already the States began to look for a place to build a permanent Capitol. On December the 23rd 1788 the State of Maryland voted to cede a 10 mile area of land for the District of Columbia and Virginia would join later to cede land joining this tract that would become the National Capitol called Washington D.C.

The Indians were still committing mischief in the isolated regions of western Virginia. Word would filter through the mountains of these atrocities. I must say that the settlers were as bad when they caught Indians in their area. Some whites would be as brutal as their counter parts.

The summer of 1787 on down the Clinch near present day Scott County the Indians hid around the John Carter farm, waiting for an opportunity to attack. John went out the door and walked about sixty yards to listen for the ringing of his cow and horse bells. He and his family were getting ready to move back to Fort Blackmore so he wanted to gather his stock. He had his crops out and it was chancy to stay on the farm with the Indians on the prowl.

It was the year that the seventeen year locust came out in the area. John wanted to find his stock before the noisy insects began to make their loud music. John was standing and listening when the silence was broken by his wife's scream.

"Oh John" screamed his wife from the open door of the cabin.

John Carter turned to see about 8 or 9 painted warriors busting into the cabin. Two shots were fired toward him, but none hit their mark. John made a hasty decision to run for cover as he was powerless to help his family. John ran at super human speed to the fort as the adrenaline kicked in. A company of men rushed back to the cabin with John, but it was too late. They found the charred remains of the wife and six children as they took poles and raked out the dear souls. They dug graves and buried their remains. One child was missing and assumed to have been carried off by the murdering redskins.

When everything got quiet the sounds of moaning and groaning could be heard from some nearby weeds. John rushed, followed by others to the place to find his little ten year old daughter. She was in peril as she was found with a great gash cut across her belly. John picked her up gently and ran to the Clinch River to wash her wounds, but the little thing died before much could be done.

John carried her to the new family grave yard and with help of his friends he laid her to rest with the rest of the family.

THE PATRIOT, HEZEKIAH WHITT

No one knew when or if the Indians would stop or even when the whites would make a lasting peace with the Indians. It was always an eye for an eye mentality that both sides exhibited.

The following year of the Hezekiah hunt on the Tug a distant neighbor, Henry Harmon and his sons and another man by the name of Draper ventured out to the Tug Fork for a bear hunt. It was November of 1788 that Henry, George, and Mathias Harman and a man named George Draper took pack mules and riding horses and headed to the Tug Fork. They were looking forward to a good hunt that the waters of the Tug always provided. The fear of Indian attack had subsided somewhat because of the lateness of the year. The Shawnees should be back across the Ohio and the Cherokee should be way down in Tennessee Country. The four hunters followed the warrior's path down the Tug toward the Ohio River.

The four men arrived late in the afternoon to the place that they planned to build their camp. Henry and Draper set up the camp while George and Mathias Harmon checked their muskets and headed out to scout around the area and kill a buck for food if they got the chance. Draper got busy hobbling and caring for the animals. He unloaded their burdens and watered them.

In a short time George hurried into camp with the startling news that Indians were nearby. George had found an Indian camp nearby with a fire still burning. He did a quick scout and brought back a pair of Indian leggings to show the older Harman.

Henry scanned the area with his keen eyes in search of anything that wasn't supposed to be there.

"Them red devils could be real close just a watching us right now," he exclaimed.

Henry sat down on the ground and had his son sit and answer questions about the Indian camp. He asked several questions about the camp and was satisfied that there were 5 to 7 Indians.

He stood up and said, "We must pack up and head for home, if we fall in with them we must stand and fight!"

Mathias was called in and the packing of the animals was hurriedly done. Henry noticed that Draper was acting different; he was shaky and breathing in an excited way.

"Damn Draper, you got the "Buck Fever", you ain't gonna be no good in a fight if you don't get a hold of yourself!" exclaimed Henry Harman.

"Don't worry bout me, I will be ready for a fight, I will lead the way and keep a sharp eye as your eyes are not as sharp, Henry," said Draper.

Draper was looking for a way out of the situation and Henry Harman knew it. Draper took the lead with Henry following leading the pack animals while George and Mathias brought up the rear. The party had gone but a short distance when Draper wheeled around and stated that he saw Indians ahead. The three Harmans looked intently in the direction that Draper pointed out, but saw no Indians.

"Damn you Draper, settle down and don't be giving no false reports!" said the senior Harman.

"I swear I saw um," replied Draper.

"Saw um my ass, you got "Buck Fever", calm down!" ordered Henry Harman.

They traveled a little ways further and Draper wheeled his horse again and said, "Indians, over yonder behind that log."

Henry did not believe Draper because a liar is not believed when they tell the truth. Henry's hunting dog ran to the log and shots rang out from the area as smoke filled the air completely hiding the log. This time Draper had spoken the truth!

As the smoke rose the three Harmans dismounted and stood together. Draper rode off with all haste as a scared haint. Draper went a short ways and jumped behind some underbrush to hide. There were seven Indians, four with muskets three with bows. After they had fired the Indians charged toward Henry who backed up to his sons where they stood their ground. The Indians encircled them and the three Harmans formed a triangle of defense. Henry told Mathias not to shoot until he told him to.

"Me and George will shoot and you will be a reserve as a back up!" exclaimed Henry. George and Henry's shot had wounded two of the Indians. George had a limp from childhood and the Indians thought he was wounded so one warrior rushed in to tomahawk him. George raised his long steel barrel and lambasted the Indian on the head knocking him silly. The Indian was on the ground and was rising up to strike again when George leaped over the Indian and tried to find his knife, but failed too. He grabbed the Indians knife and rammed it home and the Indian dropped never to rise again. Mathias also gave the Indian a whack with his tomahawk as he fell.

Two of the Indians, with bows raised, maneuvered around Henry for a shot at his breast. The Harmans all wore their ball pouches on their left side and with the left arm he shielded his breast. He worked frantically to load his Brown Betz and one Indian let loose with an arrow. The arrow hit Henry near the elbow and struck an artery. The blood flowed freely. A second flint arrowhead came in at an angle and lodged against a rib of Henry Harman. Henry finished loading and was raising his musket to fire on the Indians, but his blood got on the prime and spoiled the shot. The effect of raising the musket ran the Indians back while they all held spent muskets.

Mathias who had been almost inactive so far asked for permission to fire.

"Go ahead son, make it count," said Henry to his son.

THE PATRIOT, HEZEKIAH WHITT

Mathias aimed at the Indian that seemed to be the chief who was standing under a tree watching them. The lead ball hit the Indian and the Indian's reflexes caused him to throw his tomahawk high into the tree.

The Indians saw two of their party dead and two badly wounded so they headed out of firing range. Old Henry sat down on the ground because of exhaustion from the loss of blood. Mathias hurriedly tied a tight bandage on the wound and George washed his face with cool water. Henry was refreshed somewhat.

"Here George, how bout filling my pipe and lighting it for me," said Henry.

After taking a puff, Henry exclaimed," We've whooped them boys, go and get the scalps."

Old Draper had hid down the trail and he saw the Indians leave, but could not see the Harmans. He assumed that all of them were dead so he headed back home and reported that all were killed. The settlers got together and on the next morning headed for the Tug to bury the three Harmans. The settlers were shocked and overjoyed at finding them all living and traveling back toward the Clinch.

Before leaving the battle scene, one of the Harman men carved an Indian, a bow, and a gun on the tree to mark the spot, where Mathias dropped the Indian chief.

When would the peace really come to the mountains of Virginia? Hezekiah could only pray and be vigilant!

THE PATRIOT, HEZEKIAH WHITT

The Indians thought that the Great Spirit provided the Buffalo for His red children.

Chapter 23

Rachel's Kindred Come Calling

On February 4th, 1789 the first Electoral College chose George Washington as President and John Adams as Vice President. March 4th the first congress declares the constitution is in effect with 9 Senators and 13 Representatives. March the 11th the city of Washington is being laid out. On April 1st 1789 (Fools Day.) the House of Representatives had their first meeting. April 30th George Washington is inaugurated as the first President of the United States. September 2nd The United States Treasury Department is established by the Congress. September 13th the United States went into debt for the first time by taking a loan from the New York Banks. October 3rd Washington proclaims 1st National Thanksgiving Day. November 8th the first Bourbon Whiskey distilled from corn, Bourbon, County, Virginia. (Now Kentucky) On November the wise old Ben Franklin writes "*Nothing...certain but death and taxes.*"

The year of 1789 would be very productive for Hezekiah and Rachel as far as their crops is concerned. Last year many more of the giant, virgin, cedars were cleared out and crops were reaped from the new grounds in 1789. Hezekiah had built a barn and split so many of the logs for fencing. The cedar logs were easy to work with and the wood was very durable. He had about forty acres fenced in for pasture and about twenty for crops.

They had horses, cattle, sheep, mules, as well as chickens, geese, guinea fowl, hogs in the woods, and one odd looking dog named Jesse.

Jesse had already proven his worth over and over. He helped herd the animals; he could follow a trail, and always stood guard against all kinds of wild creatures that may molest the farm animals. He would stand his ground against the two legged predators also if they came calling. Also Jesse was a fine pet and good friend to the Whitts. Jesse was very tolerant with the boys.

Now that the United States Postal Service was established, mailing and receiving mail would be much improved. Before this a letter or package had to be sent by someone that was going that way or you just had to go and get it yourself. Even though Baptist Valley was on the far eastern end of Russell County they would soon get some type of postal service. Some is better than none and it was a worthwhile service. Hezekiah and Rachel could now get and receive letters from the Reverend Richard Whitt family and other relatives and friends residing to the east in Montgomery County.

Warm weather had come to the waters of the Clinch in early May 1789 and the settlers were plowing and planting while looking over their shoulders for Indians. Hezekiah and Rachel were among these as they planned to reap a harvest in the fall of 1789.

THE PATRIOT, HEZEKIAH WHITT

One morning Hezekiah went out and hitched his mules to the plow and had plowed on some stubborn new ground. He had his musket leaned against a tree, but with the distraction of plowing, he had not been looking around as he should have. The guinea fowl were running around sounding an alarm.

Jesse the dog had ran back to the cabin and was guarding Rachel and the boys while barking. Rachel came and looked out and saw an Indian standing in the edge of the giant cedars across from where Hezekiah was plowing and she was struck with fear. She tried to scream but nothing came out, she settled herself and hollered at Hezekiah. He finally looked in the direction of the cabin and saw her frantically pointing at the Indian. Hezekiah ran the thirty or so yards to grab his musket and turned to face the Indian.

The Indian could have shot Hezekiah while he was busy plowing, but had only watched; now that Hezekiah turned to him, the Indian held his hand high in a gesture of peace.

By now Rachel had her musket trained on the Indian as she watched from the cabin. She was keeping watch over the boys and would guard them with her life if need be. Her thinking was that she would try to cover Hezekiah on his retreat toward the cabin.

Hezekiah raised his arm in peace and lowered the musket to a less menacing posture and began to walk slowly toward the Indian and the Indian did as well. Both parties were watching each other very closely. As the two men met in the open field, Hezekiah recognized the Indian as Rock Lizard, the Indian he had befriended on the hunt.

"Hello, Rock Lizard my friend, glad to see you," said Hezekiah trying to be confident.

"How you, Hes-kiah?" answered Rock Lizard.

"I am fine, let's go to my home and I will introduce you to Rachel, daughter of Cornstalk and my two sons," said Hezekiah.

"I not come alone, I have four braves, I call them out to meet you and Cornstalk daughter," said Rock Lizard.

Hezekiah became alarmed and Rock Lizard noticed.

"Not fear friend Hes-kiah, we not come kill you!" said Rock Lizard.

With a turn towards the giant cedars and raising his arm in a sweeping motion four warriors emerged out of the woods into the field and began walking toward Hezekiah and Rock Lizard. This made Hezekiah and Rachel nervous but they tried to show no

THE PATRIOT, HEZEKIAH WHITT

fear.

Hezekiah studied the four Indians walking toward him and noticed that two were boys of about fifteen and the others were the same Indians he met with Rock Lizard on the hunt over on the Tug Fork last year. None of the Indians wore war paint which was a good sign for Hezekiah.

As the four Indians came within speaking distance Hezekiah spoke saying, "Hello Hungry Bird, and Moon Gazer, welcome to my home."

Both Indians grunted out an acknowledgement with a slight smile on their face.

"And who are these young braves with you?" asked Hezekiah?

"In white man words, this is Running Deer and Bear Walker," said Rock Lizard.

Both boys stood straight and gave their fiercest look at Hezekiah. Rock Lizard chuckled when he saw the boy's posture.

"Our young warriors very brave," said Rock Lizard."

"I see," Hezekiah said, "Let us go to my home and the daughter of Chief Cornstalk will fix us something to eat," said Hezekiah.

The two boys looked at each other in disbelief. Rock Lizard saw this and spoke in Shawnee to them. Hezekiah could only guess that he was explaining to them that Rachel the wife of Hezekiah was truly the daughter of the great Chief Cornstalk.

As the five Indians and Hezekiah walked toward the cabin Rachel lowered her musket; she had come to the realization that the Indians came in peace.

Rock Lizard spoke as they walked, "We been watching you in the dirt field, we could have killed you anytime!"

"I know, I am thankful that you are my friends," replied Hezekiah.

The Indians just wanted him to know that they did truly come in peace and wanted to keep the friendship that was formed on the waters of the Tug Fork.

Rachel opened the door of the cabin and welcomed the Indians in, praying that the Indians meant them no harm.

"I am Rachel, daughter of the great Chief Cornstalk, welcome to our home.   Little six

THE PATRIOT, HEZEKIAH WHITT

years old James Whitt stood strong by his little brother Griffy Whitt who was but two years old.

The Indians looked at the boys.

"These are the grandsons of the great Chief Cornstalk," said Hezekiah as he noticed the Indian's gaze.

"Look brave, but color mostly white on big one," said Rock Lizard.
"Little one look more like Indian," said Moon Gazer.

"Yes, he takes after his Maw more than James, said Hezekiah.

"James, bring Griffy over and meet some of your cousins," said Rachel.
        James and little Griffy walked right up and stuck out their little hands to the Indians. Rock Lizard laughed and then shook hands with both of the little Whitts.

"They brave, must have good Indian blood," said Hungry Bird.

"They have good Indian blood and good white man blood," said Hezekiah.

One of the Indian boys raised an eyebrow, but said nothing.

Rachel went to the fireplace and began to fix dinner for the visitors from over the Ohio River. Gradually both parties began to settle down and really act the part of friends.

Rachel had made corn fritters, fried potatoes, and cooked up some venison in record time. She called them all to dinner. There were only four chairs so the Indians took their plates and sat cross legged all about the cabin. Hezekiah, Rachel, and the boys followed suit and sat with the red men on the floor.

As they were about to dig in, Rachel broke the silence and said,
"Please cousins, may I ask a blessing of our Lord and give thanks for our food?"

The Indians were somewhat surprised, but were silent while Rachel prayed and ended her prayer with, "in Jesus' Name!"

Hungry Bird spoke up saying, "I have heard of the white-man God!"

Rachel saw a chance to witness to the red men about her Lord, Jesus Christ, and asked?
"What did you hear about Jesus?"

"I heard that white man tried to kill their God, but he was not dead, he woke up in three days," stated Hungry Bird.

"Oh no, that's not quiet right, Jesus was killed, plumb dead, then he rose from the dead and was the first to do so. He died for the sinners of the world." stated Rachel.

Hezekiah just sat back and did not interfere with the witnessing of Rachel.

Hungry Bird asked? "How know he was dead?"

To check, the soldiers stuck a spear into Jesus' side and water and blood flowed out and Jesus did not even flinch," stated Rachel.

"Jesus was plumb dead," she said again.

Then she related the story of Lazarus being dead for over four days and his flesh was about to rot and Jesus called him from the grave. The Indians listened intently to Rachel.

"Lazarus rose from the dead and so did Jesus!" exclaimed Rachel.

Then Rachel recited John 3: 16 to the Indians.

"For God so loved the world, that He gave his only begotten Son, that who so ever believeth in Him should not perish, but have everlasting life."

The Indians looked amazed, but none took it to heart. Rachel had sowed the seeds of Jesus' love, the watering and calling would be up to the "Holy Ghost."

After all were full, the Indians pulled out their pipes to smoke, Hezekiah saw this and got his tobacco decanter and passed it around so all could fill their pipes. The Indians smiled as they filled their pipes and lit up. Hezekiah and Rachel filled their pipes last and joined their Indian guests. The Indians tobacco blend was not just tobacco, but also mixed with marijuana, sumac, and other herbs and they called it *Kinnikinnick.* Hezekiah knew this and did not want any of the Indians to have altered minds while visiting within his cabin so he shared his tobacco with them.

The Shawnee brave in most cases were handsome people with carved features and high cheek bones. Their copper red skin made their black hair and white teeth stand out. A few Indians had such dark skin that they resembled the Africans, but had sharper features. Their hair was jet black and straight. They often shaved their heads while leaving a patch of long hair on one side or the other and sometimes wore turkey or eagle feathers in it. Some of the braves kept all of their hair and wore it long. Not many Indians had much facial hair, but a few had a fairly heavy beard.

THE PATRIOT, HEZEKIAH WHITT

Most of the braves wore silver arm bands and used beads to adorn their buckskins. The silver ornaments were always a source of fascination for the white-man. The whites were always trying to find out where the red-men got their silver. The Indians often sent silver hungry white men on wild goose chases in pursuit of the treasured metal.

Sometimes beads had a meaning for this or that, but in all cases decorated their leather attire. Some braves wore earrings or a ring in the nose. They wore breach cloths and leggings resembling chaps. They wore moccasins made of buckskin, sometimes using a heavier skin such as buffalo or elk for the heel. Most had a buckskin shirt for all seasons except for the heat month. All the braves carried a pouch or two to carry the necessities when they were about. Those that carried the white-man's gun of course had to carry lead and powder. They carried some food such as parched corn and jerky.

The warriors always carried buzzard down to poke in a wound to stop bleeding. Some carried pre made flint arrow heads and leather thongs. But all in all they traveled pretty light. Some carried a little bag of herbs and ground up animal bones to ward off evil spirits. The little pouch usually smelled bad.

If they were going to battle they brought war paint, and wore a belt that could carry a knife and tomahawk. In the spring and fall they carried a blanket or skin with hair still attached which gave protection from the elements.

The Indian brave was always in great physical shape and could run for miles or jump in icy water and never show any sign of distress. To complain or cry out was a sure sign of weakness.

The Indians loved a joke as much as their counter parts. They relished in getting a joke on the whites. One example of this was to tell the white men to plant corn in the dark to have a better crop. Then the Indians would sat back and laugh as they watched the whites out in the field planting corn by lantern light.

The five Indians stayed with the Whitts until late in the afternoon. As they prepared to leave Hezekiah reminded them to be careful on their journey.

"Many whites don't trust the Indians and will shoot on sight." said Hezekiah.

"If they do they will regret it," stated Rock Lizard.

"I pray for your protection and that you also will not molest any settlers," said Rachel.

"We pray to our God, *Moneto,* we know he is the Supreme Being; He watches over his red children," said Moon Gazer.

THE PATRIOT, HEZEKIAH WHITT

Rachel smiled as the five Indians left out in single file in a trot back to the cover of the giant cedars.

Hezekiah, Rachel, and the boys all waved to the Indians as the Indians turned for a last look before disappearing into the woodland. All five of the Indians lifted an arm in peace and turned back to their journey.

"I think we have made some progress toward peace, at least with five of our red brothers," stated Hezekiah.

"Maw, will our cousins come back again?" asked James?

"They might honey, will that be alright with you?" asked Rachel?
"I reckon, I like um!" answered little James.

"What did you like about them?" asked Hezekiah?

"They didn't try to cut off my hair!" replied James.

Hezekiah and Rachel chuckled at the wisdom of little James.

"We better get our chores done," Hezekiah said, "We have been visiting all day."

"It was all worth while, we have five new friends that will not be trying to cut off our hair," Rachel said using the words of little James.

Hezekiah laughed as he went outside to get his evening work done. Jesse, his dog, was always with him while he did the chores. Hezekiah would reach down and pet his four legged friend and they would get busy. Jesse would bring in the cows so they could be milked. There were always plenty to do on the little Whitt farm. As the seasons came and went Hezekiah and Rachel would do the things that needed to be done. They taught the children the three "R's" and about the Lord Jesus Christ.

The sheep would be sheared, Rachel would spin the wool, the female animals would be bred, and the babies would arrive. They stayed vigilant as they worked. They loved to visit with other settlers and spin their yarns. They loved to have family fishing days and nut and berry gathering days. They enjoyed the simple things in life as they lived their lives on the beautiful waters of the Clinch.

Hezekiah and Rachel would always reserve a little energy for their night time games. Not much was said in the daylight hours about it, but both looked forward to the special time they shared after the candles were quenched.

THE PATRIOT, HEZEKIAH WHITT

Hezekiah often woke up a bit groggy and he used a favorite saying, "it don't take long to stay all night here!"

"You silly white man," Rachel would say.

News came in a couple of days that Jenny Wiley had been captured and her family had been killed by Indians. Tom Wiley was gone to the mill for the day. Mathias Harmon along with a few settlers had chased after the Indians way down the Tug Fork, but to no avail. Hezekiah could not help but wonder if his five Indian friends had anything to do with it

Chapter 24

Snow

A new year was upon them and the Hunger Month came in cold and blustery. The year of 1790 would be a year of snow. Christmas came and went and on New Year's Day a little skiff of snow covered the ground and the giant cedars were glazed with the beautiful whiteness.

No one thought much about the little snow, but enjoyed the splendor of God's art work. By nightfall a heavy overcast settled over the waters of the Clinch and the temperature was holding at about twenty eight degrees. It was just right for more snow. The snow began to fall and there was a complete "white out."

The stock had gathered in the barn except for the stupid sheep. Hezekiah was not alarmed yet, he would wait until it let up and he would take Jesse to get the sheep. It never let up until the wee hours of the morning. Hezekiah knew the temperature was not so low as to cause much trouble yet so he waited until day light and he got on his winter coat made of wolverine hide with the fur still attached. He got Jesse and headed out to find the sheep. The snow was a good sixteen inches and was still falling, but not as hard. Jesse had to hop and leap through the deep snow as they traveled to the far end of the pasture. It was most enjoyable to be out in the fresh snow, except for the tension caused by the lost sheep. There they were all five of them in one bunch. They had huddled together and were in fine shape except they had no idea how to get home to the barn.

"Go Jesse, fetch the sheep home," commanded Hezekiah.

Jesse looked up at Hezekiah as if to say, "Are you nuts?"

"Go Jesse, get the sheep home!" exclaimed Hezekiah.

Jesse spring into action! He leaped through the snow and went to the far side of the sheep and barked at the sheep. The sheep rose up on their feet and scurried around in their little circle of snow-less ground, but would not budge toward the barn. Jesse jumped at them and barked, but the sheep only scurried more.

Hezekiah was prepared and brought a rope of weaved hide and put it around the neck of the sheep he figured to be the leader. Hezekiah took both feet and shuffled them to clear out a little path toward the barn while pulling the reluctant critter along. It worked; the other sheep saw their leader heading through the snow so they began to follow in single file. Jesse brought up the rear and barked every little bit to do his part. Hezekiah chuckled at the sight, but kept the little train of sheep heading to the barn. The snow was heavy and it tired the strong legs of Hezekiah but it was only about a tenth of a mile

THE PATRIOT, HEZEKIAH WHITT

they had to travel. They reached the shelter of the barn and Hezekiah took the rope off of the sheep and it ran into the barn followed by the little flock. Hezekiah got out some hay for all the hungry farm animals. It was a pleasure to see all of them eating together. Even the chickens joined in and looked so small under the feet of the cows and horses.

Hezekiah went to the cabin after getting an arm load of fire wood. He went back out to get a pail of water from the spring; next he would go and milk the cows. He would be ready for a man sized breakfast after spending so much energy.

Hezekiah gave thanks to God for everything including the beautiful snow. He would have second thoughts about the snow after a few days. The snow was not over by any means. That night it came again. The snow piled up to two feet and the temperature plummeted to around zero by the third day. Still Hezekiah and Rachel were not alarmed. They had plenty of food, fire wood, and hay for the animals. They would just have to wait a few days for a thaw to come. It was a winter wonderland as Hezekiah held the boys at the door to show them the sight. The giant cedars were heavy with the snow and the great billows bent this way and that. Some of the evergreen limbs broke and fell to the ground.

The temperature hovered around zero all week and by the second week it rose up to about twenty-five degrees. It started to snow again. Another foot fell on the already two feet and the temperature dropped again to around zero. The low temperature being so low caused the animals to eat more to stay warm, yet Hezekiah was sure relief would come soon in rising temperatures.

February came and there was still a heavy snow on the ground. There were paths dug through the white stuff to the barn, to the wood shed, to the spring, and to their fine little privy. Hezekiah began to get concerned, would they have enough food, wood to burn, and the flowing spring began to slow down as ice built up around it. How would he keep the animals watered and even the family may suffer.

Hezekiah also knew that the wild creatures were suffering from a lack of food and water by now. When animals become hungry they act in a different way, they lose their fear of man and will come even to a barn for a meal.

Hezekiah and Rachel lit their pipes on a cold morning after eating and talked very seriously about the situation they were getting into with the everlasting snow. The snow had lost its beauty by now and was looked on as a problem.

"Honey, have you ever seen a winter like this?" asked Hezekiah?

"I have seen some big snows in my childhood above the great Ohio, but have never saw one last so long, are we in trouble?" she asked?

"Not yet dear, our Lord will watch out for us," said a confident Hezekiah.

"Hezekiah, get the Bible and read to me from the Psalms, about how God is our protector," requested Rachel.

THE PATRIOT, HEZEKIAH WHITT

"That is a good idea, we need to take a little time and worship and gain confidence," answered Hezekiah.

As Hezekiah went to the mantle above the fireplace, Jesse began a frantic objection and the animals in the barn began to clamor and make a lot of verbal sounds. Instead of picking up the sword of God, Hezekiah picked up his musket, checked the primer and headed toward the door. He opened the door just enough to look out. He was not too surprised to witness a pack of wolfs closing in on Jesse as he guarded the barn full of farm animals.

With quick reflexes, Hezekiah raised his Brown Betz and drew a bead on the lead wolf. Hezekiah squeezed the trigger; the hammer fell and threw a spark in the waiting powder. The powder ignited and sent fire into the loaded barrel. The shot rang out and the wolf was knocked off his feet. As Hezekiah quickly reloaded he peered through the smoke left from the shot and saw the wolves heading for cover.

Through this whole happening Rachel had been silent; she did not want to distract Hezekiah while he was shooting.

"What is it Hezekiah?" asked Rachel?

"Wolves, I have been expecting something like this because of this never ending winter," answered Hezekiah.

Hezekiah opened the door wide and Rachel joined him to look out into the white world. Jesse was at the downed wolf, grabbing at it and barking.

"Good boy, Jesse, now let it be!" yelled Hezekiah.

By now James and little Griffy were holding on to Rachel's legs. Rachel looked down and assured them that all was well, she said, "Your Paw has killed the wolf."

Hezekiah said, "I better get out there and hang that wolf up on the fence as a warning to the wolves, just in case they want to try again."

Hezekiah put on extra layers and headed out to the barn. He met Jesse and gave him some petting and thanked him for being a good watch dog. Then Hezekiah dragged the dead wolf to the fence and tied it up so it could be seen by other wolves. Hezekiah was surprised how little the wolf weighed. The never ending winter was taking a toll on the wild creatures. He would have to watch close because hungry predators lose their fear of man.

Hezekiah went into the barn to calm his animals. When they saw him and he spoke kind words to them they all calmed right down. This made Hezekiah think of the Bible passage where Jesus said, "The sheep know their shepherd."

God reveals everything we need to know from his word, thought Hezekiah as he put out some more food for the stock. He would have to get them more water; it had become a heavy task to water them since the branch from the spring had been frozen. He had the spring covered over and a small pool was kept from freezing so he had to carry two buckets of water at a time to a watering trough inside the barn. The thirsty animals would have it drunk before he could get back with more. This had become a time consuming task, but had to be done. The hay and grain had gone down quickly because of the extended cold weather. Finally Hezekiah and Jesse headed back to the cabin as they heard howls from the woods.

Hezekiah patted Jesse on the head and said, "Don't worry boy, they should stay back now!"

Jesse looked up at his master as if he understood every word.

Jesse went into his little log house and Hezekiah went into the warm cabin. Rachel had water boiling and was making her husband a big cup of tea. Hezekiah checked the primer on his musket and hung it up over the fire place to be ready if the need should arise again.

"Rachel, we need to pray fervently for the Lord to warm up this land, it is March and everything is still froze!" said Hezekiah.

"We shall do that, but you know our sweet Lord knows best, He has some reason for this extended cold," replied Rachel.

Rachel poured Hezekiah a cup of tea while he warmed himself in front of the glowing fire. He sipped at the tea and sat it on the mantle so he could rub his cold legs. Rachel rubbed his arms from shoulders to his hands and then held him in her arms to warm him. Her warm body felt so good to Hezekiah.

"You feel so good to me," said Hezekiah.

"Just don't get too warmed up, the boys are up and about," answered an amused Rachel.

"Now I will get the Bible and read it to you and the boys," said Hezekiah.

"Yes please do that, we need to be fed by the Spirit," answered Rachel.

"You know while I was out, I went into the barn to calm the animals, when I spoke to them and they saw me, they calmed right down," said Hezekiah.

"That is because they know their master," said Rachel.

"Yes, I thought of the good shepherd, Jesus, He said He knows his sheep and the sheep know their shepherd," said Hezekiah.

"I am so glad that we have a loving shepherd looking after us," replied Rachel.

"Me too!" answered Hezekiah as he turned to the 91st Psalm to read about God's protection.

THE PATRIOT, HEZEKIAH WHITT

After reading God's word, the little family including Griffy kneeled down by the fireplace and Hezekiah led them in a long fervent prayer. He started out with praise and gave thanks for all that the Lord had done for them. Then he went to the list of problems they faced and named them all asking Jesus to help. Hezekiah ended his prayer asking the Lord to please send the spring. He asked all of this in the name of Jesus Christ.

The next morning upon arising, the sun was shining. Hezekiah went out to get in water and wood for Rachel. The air felt different, it had a bit of warmness in it and there was a slight breeze coming from the southland.

"Praise your name, thank you sweet Jesus," whispered Hezekiah as he knew his prayer was being answered!

When Hezekiah went to the spring to get water it had already began to thaw around the edges. Hezekiah smiled as he collected a bucket of water for Rachel. When he got back to the cabin and walked in he said, "Praise the Lord Rachel, the sweet Lord has heard our prayer, there is a thaw starting and a southern breeze in the air!"

Rachel jumped up and down with glee as she praised the Lord.
"Thank you Jesus, thank you Jesus," she kept saying.

"Thank you Jesus!" came from the little voice of Griffy Whitt.

"That's right honey, praise the Lord," said Rachel as she hugged the little three year old and James.

The thaw of the spring in 1790 had truly started and the warm winds from the southland brought great change to the waters of the Clinch. This winter would not soon be forgotten, and the Whitts knew without a doubt their prayer was answered quickly and decisively.

"Reckon we could take a trip to see the Whitts and Skaggs on Meadow Creek this summer?" asked Rachel?

"I reckon we might," Hezekiah said, "We need to do some trading anyhow."

"Well let's plan on doing it after we get the crops out," answered Rachel.

"Let's plan it, but with reservation, we don't know what lies ahead in the coming weeks," said Hezekiah.

"Well honey, I didn't mean for certain, only the good Lord knows our future," answered Rachel.

The next few weeks saw a much warmer land in the Clinch Valley. The snow and ice melted slowly at first and then much faster. The waters ran down the creeks causing them to come out of their banks and the Clinch was full to the brim. No great destruction was caused other than mud, slush and some of the stock got their feet wet. Even the limestone spring had a heavy flow and the water was not quiet as clear.

THE PATRIOT, HEZEKIAH WHITT

The Whitts were thankful for the thaw even if it did cause some high waters. Every person and animal alike was pleased that the frozen land was now finally thawing.

Chapter 25

Happenings and A Trip

Some of the happenings in the new little country called the United States were as follows:

President George Washington delivered the very first State of the Union Address on January 8th 1790.

The Supreme Court convenes for the first time in New York City on February 1st 1790.

The first United States Census was authorized on March 1st 1790.

Thomas Jefferson the first Secretary of State reported to President Washington on March 21st 1790. He became official on March 22nd 1790.

One important invention came about on March 27th 1790. The shoe lace was invented. Can you imagine not having shoe strings?

The United States patent system was formed on April 10th 1790.

Rhode Island became the last of the thirteen colonies to ratify the Constitution on May 29th 1790.

The United States copyright law was enacted on May 31st 1790.

The very first book to be copyrighted under the Constitution was. "Philadelphia Spelling Book," on June 9th 1790.

On July 16th 1790, Congress established the District of Columbia from land given by the States of Virginia and Maryland.

The very first patent was granted to Samuel Hopkins for a potash process on July 31st 1790.

The Census of the United States reported on August 1, 1790 was 3,939,214 and Hezekiah, Rachel, James and Griffith Whitt were four of them.

On October 28th 1790, New York State gave up the claim of Vermont for the sum of $30,000.

On December 20th 1790 the first successful United Sates Cotton Mill spun yarn in Pawtucket, Rhode Island, and we Americans have been spinning yarns every since.

The winter of 1789-1790 will not soon be forgotten. Even though the spring is coming on and the folks on the waters of the Clinch can still see the ill-effects of the worst winter they can remember.

THE PATRIOT, HEZEKIAH WHITT

All of the wild animals are thin and down in numbers compared to the last summer. Game birds like grouse and quail are scarce, even the turkey numbers are down.

The predators did very well with the weakened and dying animals during the extended winter weather. Snow was on the ground for a good ten weeks and the food the wild critters needed just couldn't be found.

Hezekiah and Rachel's farm animals thinned down some, but with special care and enough food there should not be any lasting effects from the great winter. If the thaw hadn't come when it did most of the settlers on Indian Creek and Baptist Valley would have lost a lot of stock. You may say it is a coincidence that the thaw came when it did, but the fervent prayers of good men had a lot to do it.

Rachel had her thoughts on making the trip back to Meadow Creek so they could have a nice visit with kindred and friends. Hezekiah didn't show much emotion about the trip, but he could hardly wait to get the crops out so they could start.

Of course the spring would mean working while looking over your shoulder for trouble from the woods. The Shawnee would be coming down into the hills of western Virginia and Kentucky on raids to the isolated and unsuspecting folks which now dotted the landscape.

Hezekiah and Rachel hoped that their friendship with Rock Lizard and his band of warriors would afford them safety. John and Elizabeth Hankins were also counting on this new relationship with the Rock Lizard Shawnees. Rock Lizard and his band had stopped at the Hankins last summer when they traveled to see Rachel and Hezekiah. The visit went surprisingly smooth considering that John had nothing for the Indians and he trusted them as far as he could carry a hundred pound anvil. It was the same with the Indians, but some how a bond was formed. The two factions became friends, sort of!

Thomas Bailey Christian (Indian white man.) came through the winter very well and had come to see Hezekiah and Rachel. He also stopped to see the Hankins which were the Whitt's nearest neighbors. After talking to the Whitts and Hankins, Christian halfway expected Rock Lizard and his warriors to show up at his place sometime this summer. This could create a very dangerous situation.

Thomas Bailey Christian loved being accepted as a white man among the settlers. He also missed his former life as a young Shawnee boy living in the low hills of the Ohio country. Christian was completely accepted by all the folks on Indian Creek and in Baptist Valley. He could attribute that to Thomas Mastin his beloved adopted father. Thomas Mastin had moved his family to the Tennessee country and left the farm to Christian because he loved the waters of the Clinch.

Just as soon as the rich black soil dried enough, Hezekiah had his mules pulling the plow deeply into it. The Robins were back and were following the furrows and eating the worms the plow had thrown out. All the trees had an abundance of baby leaves and the dogwoods had bloomed to end dogwood winter.

THE PATRIOT, HEZEKIAH WHITT

Hezekiah and his little family were in really good spirits. The beautiful spring weather was painting the waters of the Clinch a bright green. The lush bluegrass was getting tall and the grazing animals were taking advantage of its abundance. Hezekiah saw his sheep frolicking about in the green pastures. This reminded Hezekiah of the twenty third psalms. Yes the Lord had truly blessed all of his children on Indian Creek and all of Baptist Valley. Hezekiah could remember vividly the beauty of the waters of the Clinch that brought him to live here.

The Clinch River had been roaring back just after the thaw, but it would soon return to its normal depths. The beautiful river would return to its transparent emerald green and it would beg for Hezekiah to come to his "Honey Hole," to fish once again.

Hezekiah already had it in his head to take Rachel and the boys for a day of fishing just as soon as he had a break in planting. He figured that all work and no play would make the whole Whitt family dull. His "Honey Hole" (A long deep pool that always had fish for the taking.) always paid dividends of Catfish, Bronze Backs (Small Mouth Bass), and big Red Eyes (Rock Bass).

On a nice warm day near the end of May 1790, Hezekiah got up and said, "Rachel get the boys ready for a day of fishing, I'm going out and dig some worms and cut some poles."

Of course James and Griffy heard their Paw and said, "Yeah, yeah, Paw's taking us fishing."

James had become a pretty good fisher boy. He had learned to put on the worm and get the fish off after he lost one or two, Griffy would need help, but he would most likely be lucky as are most Whitt boys as far as fishing goes. James was almost eight and Griffy would be three in September. Rachel seemed to be a natural born fisherwoman. She usually caught more than Hezekiah.

The Whitts got their lunch that Rachel had prepared; they also got their fishing poles and a little pail of nice plump worms and headed out for a day of fishing. They rode two horses with Hezekiah leading, riding double with little Griffy and Rachel followed up riding double with James. Of course Hezekiah carried his musket on a sling across his back.

The day was a great success as far as relaxation was concerned. They all caught some fish, even little Griffy caught a fat Red Eye. They truly enjoyed the day and had fish for supper.

Hezekiah soon had the crops all out and the work caught up. He and the family sheared the sheep and put the wool back in a corner of the attic of the cabin. Little James got the biggest kick out of this and thought the sheep looked so funny.

"Don't laugh at them, you will hurt their feelings," said Rachel with a grin.

Hezekiah grinned at Rachel with that crooked little grin.

THE PATRIOT, HEZEKIAH WHITT

The next day Hezekiah went to see Thomas Bailey Christian and made arrangements with him to come and check on the farm while they were away. The cows had calves now so they would not need to be milked. The animals had access to water and good grazing so there was little for Christian to do. They could only pray and hope that neither wild Indians nor animals would come and molest the farm. It would be hard to take, to come home to find all the stock killed and the buildings burned, so they asked the Lord to bless and protect Cedar Grove Farm while they were away.

Early in the morning of May 31st 1790 the Whitts headed out. They had pack mules loaded with tobacco, pelts, and ginseng to trade. Hezekiah led one mule and carried James on behind him on his mount. Rachel led a mule and carried Griffy in front of her on her mount.

It had been a long time since Hezekiah had traipsed on the trail back to Meadow Creek. As they traveled, many memories came to Hezekiah. He had traveled the mountains and trails many times in earlier years as an Indian spy.

Hezekiah had gone over the rules of travel with Rachel and the boys. Many dangers could await them on the trail. There were mountain outlaws, Indians, and even wild animals to contend with. There were also perils of the land such as slides, slick spots, rivers, and boulders to navigate around or through. Also the mountain rattler may cross their path. In most cases the wild animals would stay at bay, but a mommy bear with cubs or a wounded panther could spell trouble. Even a pack of wolfs may try to get at a mule or horse.

Hezekiah would leave Rachel and the boys to break camp every morning and he would ride ahead a few miles to scout for dangers.

Some of the things Rachel and Hezekiah wanted to trade for were a spinning wheel, spices, coffee and tea.

Hezekiah had heard of a new fruit called tomatoes, he thought it would be great to get some seed and see if they would grow on his farm. The tomato was not trusted for food at first, but animals enjoyed them. They were mostly ornamental plants at first and had originated in South America and had been taken to Europe. The introduction back to North America had been slow because of the mistrust of the big red fruits. Now the tomatoes were being eaten and enjoyed by some.

Hezekiah had it in mind to get plans for a small loom from his father Richard Whitt. If he could get plans and a few pieces of hardware he would build Rachel a loom. She could make rugs and other thing for sale as well as for the family.

The Whitts traveled northeast up the eleven mile valley called Baptist. They would cut across to what is now Tazewell and connect up with the head waters of Bluestone River. Then they would cut off toward Rocky Gap. Hezekiah hoped to accomplish twenty miles per day, but he knew some days they would do well to get ten. He had to be vigilant and with the boys and pack animals they would not break any speed records.

THE PATRIOT, HEZEKIAH WHITT

As they traveled up Baptist Valley they saw folks working their fields in a few places.

Hezekiah remarked, "this land is filling up with people, it use to be so wild and free."

"The more people, the safer it is," answered Rachel.

"I reckon, I just miss the wilderness that is disappearing here in the valley," Hezekiah said.

"Paw, how long will it be fore we eat?" asked James.

"Honey we ate about two hours ago, you are just bored, look around and help us spot trouble and enjoy this grand land that the Lord made for us," said Rachel before Hezekiah could speak.

"That's right, look at the beautiful mountains and hills, you might see a bear or something," said Hezekiah.

This seemed to satisfy James for now.

After three days of travel the Whitts stop again for the night at the foot of the mountain that leads up to Rocky Gap. Hezekiah will find a suitable place to camp and while Rachel and the boys set up camp, Hezekiah will scout all around the area for any signs of trouble.

Hezekiah knows that his little family is vulnerable if they are discovered by a roving war party. The Indians have slacked up a lot, but they are still some coming to the remote areas to do mischief.

Hezekiah always picks a camp off the main trail. To camp on the warrior's path is asking for trouble so he takes the family up a branch or hollow at least a half a mile. He likes to find a mountain meadow if possible that is well hidden by the forest. After the family starts to set up camp Hezekiah goes back down the path to rub out any sign of tracks with a bushy branch. He also scouts around the perimeter to make sure it is a safe place to camp.

If everything looks good, Hezekiah will allow a small fire to cook with and for comfort during the night. The wood most liked is good and dry and slow burning. A wood that gives off little smoke is best.

The family will sleep together under a lean to, made from oiled muslin cloth. (A type of homemade canvas.) The lean to would ward of rain and even dew. Sleeping dry is a must for traveling comfort and health.

During the night both Hezekiah and Rachel kept their muskets handy, Hezekiah would lay his tomahawk and knife in arms reach. If Hezekiah was to see where Indians had come through, he would immediately take the family back a couple of miles for safety.

This trip would sharpen the skills that Hezekiah had learned during his days as an Indian spy.

THE PATRIOT, HEZEKIAH WHITT

Rachel understood the need to be vigilant, but it was a little new for the boys. They were use to the safety of the cabin even though they were taught to look out before going out. They were also taught to watch the edge of the woods for anything different. The boys had never made a trip where they camp out all night in the woods. To the little Whitts, this was a great adventure.

After three days of travel the Whitts came to the foot of the mountain that led up to Rocky Gap. Much of the trail was close to the very edge of the woods. The trees reached across the trail and nature was always trying to reclaim the trail. Much of the trail looked like a great tunnel of trees and wild grapevines. It was the main trail but it was not used that much. Some of the trail had logs and limbs lying across it left over by the great tree-breaking snows of the past winter. If the pilgrims were to run into Indians or mountain outlaws they would have to fend them off or make a run for cover back down the trail.

So each morning before leaving, Hezekiah would lead the family in prayer. He always started with praise to God followed by thanksgiving for God's loving kindness. Then he would ask God to shield them from the snare of the fowler and from the arrows of destruction. Then with confidence the Whitts proceeded on the days travel as they passed through the dangerous areas.

They were at the foot of the mountain so Hezekiah finds a thickly covered hollow and takes the family up it. There was a small branch flowing out of it, which was one of Hezekiah's requirements for a camp. They traveled about a half a mile to a little mountain meadow created by the grazing of deer. The grass was plentiful enough for the mules and horses. A night of eating and resting was important before ascending the mountain in the morning.

To the south side of the field was a natural fort created by boulders and smaller rocks. This is where Hezekiah picked for the camp. It would be a great place to make a stand if they were discovered by any enemy.

After a scout around and going back to the main trail to rub out any sign of their passing he came back to the little camp in the midst of the rocks. Hezekiah was satisfied that it was safe for a little fire to cook with and even keep it through the night for comfort. At night without a fire the woods are pitch black and quite scary.

The boys had gathered good dry wood after a warning from Rachel to watch out for snakes and not to go too far away. Hezekiah helped set up the lean-to and gathered rocks to make a circled fireplace. Rachel had already unloaded the mules and horses and was ready to hobble them for the night.

Hezekiah was satisfied with the camp and felt that all could get rest and have their bellies full for the trip up the mountain in the morning.

After supper was over and bedtime came the family slept good. Hezekiah slept lightly as he listened to the sounds of a wolf, owls communicating, and the lonely sound of a whippoorwill. This was nothing new; these sounds could be heard around the cabin in the cedar grove every night. The only difference was that the family was outside with all of it. Hezekiah remembered these sounds as he had lived off the land and spent many a night in the dark woods doing his duty as an Indian spy.

Next morning at first light, Hezekiah roused up and reached under his blanket to remove a rock that had left an impression on his shoulder during his sleep. After he threw out the rock he laid back and pulled Rachel to him.

"Well woman, it sure don't take too long to stay all night here!" exclaimed Hezekiah!

"You silly white man," answered Rachel as she gave Hezekiah a good morning kiss!

The Whitts were up and getting everything together when Hezekiah spotted a raccoon in the edge of the woods.

"Want some coon for breakfast?" asked Hezekiah?

"Think you can get us one?" asked Rachel?

"Sure," answered Hezekiah indignantly.

Hezekiah picked up his musket, took aim and squeezed the trigger. The raccoon was knocked for a loop. The horses and mules flinched and hopped about with their hobbled feet from the noise of the shot. James and Griffy both jumped up, big eyed!

Hezekiah turned to Rachel and said, "There red woman is your coon go fetch it and clean it!"

"Alright pale face, I fetch coon, you get fire hot," answered Rachel with a crooked little grin!

Hezekiah gave her a big hug and said, "I love you so much!"

Hezekiah reloaded while Rachel went to get the coon, and then he started building up the fire. He sat back for a minute and listened to see if the shot may attract some unwanted guests.

The family enjoyed the creation of God as they traveled through the wooded mountains of Virginia. There were sights and experiences to have each day. They stopped at a mountain stream one day and took time to fish. The family was rewarded with a great meal of Brook Trout. Many animals and birds were seen, but not much different then those at their Cedar Grove. The difference was that they were out amongst the critters and birds. The boys loved it as much as Hezekiah and Rachel.

The trip to Meadow Creek (Now Radford, VA.) was uneventful as far as troubles go. The Whitts enjoyed the outdoor life on the trail, the sights, sounds, and smell of God's world. James and Griffy added to their education while traveling and experiencing nature. James got some of his first lessons on wood lore and even tracking and setting

THE PATRIOT, HEZEKIAH WHITT

snares. Many times a snare was set in the evening and a meal was retrieved in the morning.

It was about the middle of June, 1790 that the Hezekiah Whitt family rode into the little community on Meadow Creek. Richard Thomas Whitt, the now twelve year old brother of Hezekiah, ran to meet them. Richard did not know who they were at first and Hezekiah did not know him, but knew he had to be a Whitt. He had the looks of a Whitt including the crease in his chin.

"Hello young man," said Hezekiah.

"Hello to you sir, where you all a heading'?" asked Richard Thomas Whitt?

"We are heading right here, what is your name?" asked Hezekiah?

"I am Richard Thomas Whitt, my Paw is the Reverend Richard Whitt," answered Richard Thomas Whitt.

"He is my Paw too!" exclaimed Hezekiah.

The boy was taken back at this revelation. Hezekiah smiled at him!

"Ever heard of Hezekiah Whitt?" asked Hezekiah?

"Have I, he is one of the greatest Indian fighters and woodsman I ever heard of," answered Richard.

"Well little brother, I am Hezekiah and I don't know about all of that Indian fighting stuff," answered Hezekiah.

Richard ran to take the reins of Hezekiah's horse while Hezekiah and James dismounted. When Hezekiah sat James down on the ground the younger brother threw his arms around Hezekiah and greeted him with much affection.

Hezekiah gave him a big hug and turned to Rachel to take Griffy so she could dismount.

"Richard Thomas Whitt this is your nephew James, this is your sister-in-law Rachel and the little man is Griffy your other nephew, said Hezekiah.

Richard Thomas gave a little bow and said, "Greeting to you all," in a most formal posture.

Hezekiah turned to Rachel and gave her a crooked little smile.

"Young Richard, you sure have good manners," stated Rachel.

"Well young Richard, where is Paw and Maw?" asked Hezekiah?

THE PATRIOT, HEZEKIAH WHITT

"Paw is down at the mill with Archibald and Maw is in the house," answered Richard Thomas.

"Do they call you Richard or Thomas?" asked Hezekiah.

"Some call me one some the other, but I like to be called "Dick," answered young Richard.

"Well Dick it is, will you put the animals in the corral and we will unpack them in a little while after we go in and see Maw," said Hezekiah.

"Want me to feed and water um?" asked Dick?

"That would be kind of you little brother," answered Hezekiah.

Dick takes the horses and mules to the watering trough and Hezekiah, Rachel, and the boys open the door to the big log house. Mother Susannah and a young woman are working around in the kitchen.

"Maw, is that you?" asked Hezekiah?

"Dear Lord Almighty, is that my son Hezekiah?" asked mother Susannah?

"Yes it is me, Rachel, James and Griffy," answered Hezekiah.
Susannah ran and embraced Hezekiah with tears of joy streaming down her aging face. The young lady was little sister Susannah, who is now sixteen years of age. Young Susannah ran and got in on the family hug as did Rachel and the boys.

Dick took care of the animals and then came running back to the house.

Mother Susannah saw him and said, "Dick, go fetch your Paw and Archibald, don't tell them that we have company, jest say I need them at the house."

"Wouldn't they be fretting if I tell um that?" asked Dick.

"Don't scare um, jest say I need them but they ain't no emergency," said Susannah.

"I will Maw," said Dick as he scampered from the house.

Young Susannah fixed a pot of tea and they had a little visit before Reverend Richard and Archibald hurriedly arrived.

The door was pushed open and Paw Richard came into the room. He saw Hezekiah and Rachel and the boys sitting around with mother Susannah and daughter Susannah.

"My wonderful Lord, look at this, my eyes are so pleased to see this sight, when did you get home?" asked the Reverend.

THE PATRIOT, HEZEKIAH WHITT

Hezekiah stood and the others followed suit. Hezekiah ran to his father and held the aging gentleman tightly.

"Hold it son, you're going to break me in half," said the Reverend.

Hezekiah turned his Paw loose and looked him in the eyes for a long minute. Then he turned to Archibald. He grabbed Archibald and gave him a bear hug.

"Archibald is a full grown and a handsome man!" replied Hezekiah.

"I am twenty now, guess I am pretty well grown," answered Archibald.

"It is strange to see all my little brothers and sisters so grown up," replied Hezckiah.

By now Grand Maw Susannah had her grandchildren, James and Griffy, sitting on the love seat with her. Reverend Richard went over and hugged the boys and sit with Susannah and the boys. Little sister Susannah went to the kitchen and started to prepare a meal for the family. Dick was sent to round up the rest of the family. Robert, Edmund, and Abijah had moved to a little cabin over on the New River, Sister Rachel was married and lived about a mile up Meadow Creek. Elizabeth, and Ruth, was living with James Skaggs since grand maw Rachel Skaggs passed away a few months back.

Hezekiah was shocked and very sad when he heard his Grand Maw Rachel had passed. The Reverend Richard tried to ease the pain by telling them she passed into the Realm of Heaven in peace. Her last words were, "Jesus come, oh come and take me home!" At this a big tear rolled down Hezekiah's face into his beard.

Rachel was yearning to see her adopted father and mother.

"William and Mary Skaggs moved to Green County, way out in Kentucky," explained Susannah in between hugging the boys.

Rachel was disappointed, but at least her adopted parents were alive and well.

The Hezekiah Whitt family stayed a week with his parents and had a really good visit. Hezekiah, Rachel, and his father took his trade goods to the mercantile and made some good trades. Hezekiah's goods were in the best of condition and the merchant was glad to get them.

Rachel picked up several bolts of cloth, needles and spools of thread, a used spinning wheel, quantities of coffee, tea and some spices.

Hezekiah got a good supply of powder and lead. He also bought some store bought boots and hats for the boys. Hezekiah got some stick candy for the boys and some tomato seeds for the farm. He bought a few pieces of hardware to be used in making a loom.

After all the trading was done the Merchant gave Hezekiah $5.00 in silver. Both parties were satisfied.

COLONEL CHARLES DAHNMON WHITT

THE PATRIOT, HEZEKIAH WHITT

Reverend Richard took Hezekiah to a neighbor's home where he knew they owned a loom. The folks were glad to get visitors and allowed Hezekiah to sketch and measure their loom. They even showed Hezekiah how it worked and allowed him to operate it. After tea and a prayer from the Reverend they left for home.

On the trip home Hezekiah learned from his father about the wars raging along the Ohio. It was mostly on the Ohio side of the river. Settlers were moving across the river and it really upset the Native Americans. The Indians had continued raiding deep into Kentucky, attacking isolated cabins, and stealing horses. Simon Kenton and others had chased and even crossed the Ohio River several times. The whites had settled up and down the Ohio River on the Kentucky side. Many brave explorers had traveled the north side of the river. The Americans had established Fort Washington, at the mouth of the Miami River, now called Cincinnati. April 17, 1788 forty-eight men settled at the mouth of the Muskingum River now called Marietta and in 1791 nineteen men settled at what is now Manchester Ohio. This location was near Three Islands in the Ohio River. The islands were used many times to launch attacks on the whites coming down river in boats. Factions, the Whites and the Indians had been ruthless when they attacked each other. Scalping and mutilation was done by both.

Word was out that President Washington was ordering an attack on the Indians from Fort Washington. General St. Clair was trying to gather an army and head up the Miami River and build several forts as they traveled. Chief Blue Jacket of the Shawnees was second in command under Little Turtle of the Miami Tribe; they were going to be ready. They even had spies that even went into Fort Washington and read the notices posted for the soldiers. One such Indian was the young Shawnee Brave called Tecumseh. Tecumseh could read and speak English fluently.

St. Clair would not have enough men and equipment, or the organization to carry war to the well organized Indians. St. Clair and the United States would be defeated in this campaign. The Indians gained confidence by winning battles. Some of this was bound to overflow through the mountains to the waters of the Clinch.

Reverend Richard gave Hezekiah a stern warning to be aware of the angry Indians that may come calling. After a good visit Hezekiah hurried the family back to his cedar grove on the waters of the Clinch. Hezekiah had a farm and family to defend and he had a strong cabin and plenty of powder and lead.

THE PATRIOT, HEZEKIAH WHITT

Frontiersmen had to be ready in an Instant.

Chapter 26

Another Baby Is Born In Cedar Grove

Once back to their farm, they found everything safe and sound. Jesse came running to them and he was real thin. Jesse had lived off the land, but from the looks of him he missed the wonderful scraps from the Whitt table.

Another thing they noticed was new calves, baby lambs and the rooster had been busy. There were three bunches of chicken biddies. The sows in the woods had plenty of pigs. The garden and crops had grown well along with many weeds. Once the weeds are hoed out the crops should present a bounty. The big snows of last winter put a lot of moisture in the rich soil. The Whitts would be busy plumb into cold weather. They had a bunch of wood to cut so that they would have plenty if another hard winter came. They had all of this work to do while being watchful. They realize that screaming, painted Indians could come rushing out of the woods at any given minute. No attacks came to Hezekiah's Cedar Grove, but there continued to be isolated attacks on the waters of the Clinch and in Powell Valley. There was always a threat of attack so the folks had to keep their guard up.

Finally the autumn came and God gave a bounty from the fields. God has blessed the Hezekiah Whitt family. As cold weather came to the waters of the Clinch, the threat of Indian attack diminished.

One cold November night Rachel pulled Hezekiah close to her to warm herself. Rachel got warm and even hot. Guess what there would be another baby in August. Just when the Whitts thought there may be no more young ones, Rachel is in the family way and they both rejoice.

The winter of 1790-91 was nothing like last winter and the folks round about were thankful. It seems that every time there is a mild winter much sickness abounds. All four of the Whitts took a spell of fever and sickness. They doctored with herbs and the old stand by, liquid corn from the little brown jug.

After the sickness left, Hezekiah pulled out his plans for the loom and began to work on it inside the warm cabin. James and even Griffy were right in the middle of things, but Hezekiah never complained, he knew that the boys were learning some good lifelong skills. They kept wood shavings and saw dust on the floor for a few days, but no one complained. One afternoon, Hezekiah had set Rachel down and showed her how to work the new loom. She was a natural.

Rachel stayed busy all winter making clothes, spinning yarn, and working on her new loom.

THE PATRIOT, HEZEKIAH WHITT

As spring came to the waters of the Clinch the land owners got word that they would need to pay taxes to Russell County. Hezekiah would take the family and travel down the Clinch to the county seat in Castlewood and pay their fair share.

Hezekiah tried to quote Benjamin Franklin and got it close, he said, "two things are certain, death and taxes."

"It is a little thing to pay taxes on our wonderful home on the Pellissippi," answered Rachel using the Shawnee word for the Clinch River.

James looked at his Maw with wonderment.

"What is Pel-issy-pee?" asked James?

"It is what I used to call the Clinch River, It was what we Shawnees called it when I was a little girl," answered Rachel.

The trip was taken just as soon as the plowing was done and the crops were out. Hezekiah had planted the tomato seeds in the corner of the garden and was anxious to see what they would do. He had never officially seen a tomato; he had only heard about them and was very curious.

James and Griffy were now nine and four. Hezekiah rode Johnny Rachel rode her horse with Griffy and James rode a mule. Hezekiah led the way with his loaded musket across his saddle. Rachel had never been very far down the Clinch and was looking forward to the trip. Hezekiah was not sure it was a good thing to take Rachel and the boys, after all Rachel was about six months along. He would just have to make it as easy a trip as possible.

James sat up like a little man and kept good control of his mule. Griffy fussed some because he didn't get to ride a mule by himself like Brother James. Griffy had a dark complexion, jet black hair and other Indian features, but James mostly took after the white side of the family.

Hezekiah led them down Indian Creek to the little burg of Indian, (Now called Cedar Bluff.) then they would follow the Clinch River to a wide valley of rich ground. There had been a fort there during the Revolution and was still used in time of trouble. This place is now called Richlands. A hill overlooking the valley was once some kind of Indian village and folks once called it Town Hill. Then the Whitts would follow the river passing Hill Creek and Mud Lick Creek to where Coal Creek enters the Clinch. This place is now called Raven. Raven is the jumping off place to follow the Kentucky Turnpike along Road Ridge. The family would stick to the Clinch and travel past Mill Creek and Long Branch to Daw and set up camp at Swords Creek. The family was tired and needed a nights sleep before heading on to Castlewood.

When they passed Swords Creek, Hezekiah led them off the main trail up a hollow for about a quarter of a mile. He found a place to camp with grazing and a spring. As

Rachel and the boys started camp Hezekiah scouted the area and went back to the trail. (Warriors Path.) He dismounted and took a bushy limb and rubbed out the tracks of their passing.

The family got a good rest and enjoyed their night out in the wilderness; next morning after breakfast they would be traveling again. By noon they reached the confluence of Little River and the Clinch now called Blackford. After a long afternoon's ride they reached the spot that they now call Cleveland. Another great evening and a night of rest the family would be moving on again after eating. That evening Hezekiah and James went out and set some snares and in the morning they had a woods hare and a squirrel for breakfast. Hezekiah took James and sprung the other snares so that some animal would not be caught and die needlessly. The next day of travel would take them to Carbo, Carterton, and finally Castlewood. There would be an inn at Castlewood and the Whitts would sleep in a rope bed with a feather-ticking mattress. When they went to bed Hezekiah said, "Sleep tight and don't let the bed bugs bite."

James thought that was funny and asks what his Paw meant.

Hezekiah explained the saying, "The ropes that hold you up get loose and you sleep in a sag, this ain't very comfortable, and the bed bugs, well that's up to you!"

"Next morning Hezekiah roused up and said, "It sure doesn't take long to stay all night here in Castlewood!"

Rachel and the boys had heard this many times and knew what he meant, but still laughed at the saying.

They would eat their meals that Rachel didn't have to cook and serve up. This would be a real treat for Rachel. The boys thought it was fun to eat at the Inn with several other folks. Hezekiah enjoyed talking with other folks.

The next day Rachel went to the mercantile and Hezekiah went to the Russell County Court House to pay taxes. Rachel bought a few little items and some stick candy for the boys while Hezekiah took care of business and talked to the men at Castlewood. They started for home about 1:00 PM and would ride to Carbo and camp in that area for the night. Two more nights on the trail and they would be back home. They passed a few families on the trail going to Castlewood to pay their taxes. Each time the men would talk for a minute about any dangers they had encountered. There was no Indian sign to report this trip.

The Whitts made it home safely and had a good trip. It had been a little stressful for the pregnant Rachel, but she never once complained.

Some happenings in the United States in 1791:

On February 25th 1791 the first Bank of the United States was chartered.

On March 3rd 1791 the first Internal Revenue act took place. They would tax distilled spirits and carriages. Good luck taxing corn liquor over in the mountains.

THE PATRIOT, HEZEKIAH WHITT

Also on March 3rd 1791 the United States established the U.S. Mint.

On March 4th 1791 Vermont became the 14th State.

On August 2nd 1791, Samuel Briggs and his son patented a nail making machine.

On August 26th 1791 John Fitch was granted a patent for his working steamboat.

On November 3rd 1791, the Shawnee Indians under Blue Jacket and Miami Indians under Little Turtle attacked the United States Army in Ohio under General St. Clair and won overwhelmingly by killing 637 soldiers and militia. The Indians were well organized and the U.S. Army under St. Clair was not. The Army even had a large number of whore's following.

On December 12th 1791 the Bank of the United States is opened for business.

On December 15th 1791 the first United States law school was established at the University of Pennsylvania.

Also on December 15th 1791 the Bill of Rights was ratified after Virginia gave its approval.

On December 17th 1791 the first one way street is born in New York City to help regulate a growing traffic problem.

On a hot night in August 1791 Rachel was awaken with the first pain of labor for her third baby.

"Rouse up honey, the baby is coming, you better go and fetch Elizabeth and Rachel Hankins," instructed Rachel.

Hezekiah jumped up and bumbled around to get some candles lit and find his britches. He got on the easiest things he could find. He put on his buckskin britches, his moccasins, and a thin shirt. Rachel held back a cry from pain that would have made most white women scream. Hezekiah ran over to her and held her hand until the contraction passed and ran out to saddle Johnny.

It was a dark night, but by using Johnny's eyes and his instinct they made their way to their nearest neighbor's house, the Hankins. The Hankins lived about a half a mile away and it was a short trip.

Hezekiah rode up to the cabin door and did not hear a sound.

"John Hankins, it's Hezekiah, I come to fetch Elizabeth to help Rachel," Hezekiah said with a raised voice.

The cabin door flew open as John had been standing there to see who was out side before opening.

THE PATRIOT, HEZEKIAH WHITT

"Hey Hezekiah, Betsy (What John called Elizabeth) is up already, her and Rachel will be ready in a shot. I am coming out and get a horse saddled fer um," said John Hankins.

"Glad you are already up, what time is it any how?" asked Hezekiah?

"I think it is going on 4:00 AM, Betsy got up just a bit ago, she said last night that you would be a coming tonight," said John as he carried a candle lantern toward the barn.

"How did she know?" asked Hezekiah?

"She just added it all up, the moon changed and its Rachel's time I reckon," answered John.

"Who can figure out some of these female things anyhow?" added John.

"You got me John, I can track, plant by the sign, and live off the land, but some of these female things I don't have a clue," said Hezekiah.

By the time John had the horse saddled and led to the cabin Elizabeth and thirteen year old Rachel came out.

"Morning Hezekiah is Rachel getting purty fer along with her pains?" asked Elizabeth?

Morning Miss Hankins, I don't know how far the pains are apart, I think we have time, I hope!" said Hezekiah.

John helped Elizabeth mount up and asked, "Are you sure young Rachel is ready fer this sort of thing?"

"Now John we been over this and Rachel is old enough to learn about birthing," answered Elizabeth.

John didn't say a word, but lifted Rachel up on behind her Maw and they started down the trail towards the Whitt's cabin.

John had handed Hezekiah the candle lantern and he led the ladies.

They did not travel too fast because of the lack of light, but the trip was completed shortly.

Reaching the cabin, Hezekiah jumped down off Johnny and held the Hankins horse. He had to tie them to the hitching post so he could help Rachel down first, then he helped his Aunt Elizabeth down and they scurried into the cabin.

Hezekiah went into check on his beloved and see what he needed to first. Rachel was doing fine so far; she had little droplets of sweat on her from the pain of labor. She smiled at Hezekiah and told him to go and get some water out of the spring and go to kitchen and build up the fire.

Young Rachel Hankins seemed scared, but Rachel told her not to worry, everything would be just fine.

THE PATRIOT, HEZEKIAH WHITT

"Rachel, help me get Miss Whitt out of the bed so we can fix her bed for birthing," said Elizabeth.

They set Rachel in a chair by the bed and prepared the bed by putting down an oil cloth and covered it with an old sheet. They helped Rachel back in bed between pains and covered her up with a thin sheet.

Hezekiah got the water in and a cooking fire going in the kitchen, then he unsaddled the horses and let them out in the pasture. Next Hezekiah brought in his little brown jug and a biting stick for Rachel. He sat with her for a few minutes and let her squeeze his hand during the next couple of contractions.

"Hezekiah you better take the boys over into the new part of your house, Rachel is having these pains purty often," said Elizabeth.

"Alright Aunt Elizabeth, I got the potion stuff on the kitchen table, let me know when to mix it up and get it to you," said Hezekiah.

Hezekiah scooped up the boys in a big blanket and carried them out the door through the breezeway and into the new addition with the kitchen and sitting room. The boys protested some, but Hezekiah assured them that all was fine; he explained that Elizabeth and Rachel Hankins were here to help their Maw find the new baby.

"You want us to help them hunt fer it Paw," said little Griffy.

"Naw, Elizabeth knows where to look and we don't, you can lay on the buffalo skin and rest," said Hezekiah trying to distract the two young boys.

The boys got quiet and soon were in slumber town again. Hezekiah had the water boiled, made some coffee, sat back to have a cup and a smoke from his corncob pipe. After he finished his coffee he looked outside to see if the light of dawn had shown up yet. It was getting light in the southeastern sky and Hezekiah guessed the time to be about 6:00 AM.

He had not heard much from the birthing bed and was a little concerned. He could not wait any longer so he tapped on the door and stuck in his head. Rachel was halfway sitting up with her legs spread wide with her knees elevated. She was partially covered with a sheet but at this point modesty did not mean much. Her chest was exposed and her larger then normal breasts were exposed and covered with the shine of moisture.

Elizabeth was on the receiving end of Rachel and young Rachel was a little more accustomed to being in the situation. Elizabeth come up from examining Rachel and looked at thirteen year old Rachel. The young Rachel turned her head to the door and back to her Maw. Elizabeth turned to the door to see what Rachel was trying to tell her.

Hezekiah, what do you want?" asked Elizabeth?

"Just a checking, do you need the potion yet?" ask Hezekiah slightly embarrassed.

THE PATRIOT, HEZEKIAH WHITT

"Naw not yet, but it ain't gonna be too long, I will have my Rachel come and tell you when it's time," said Elizabeth.

Hezekiah glanced back at his beautiful wife one more time and she sent him a beautiful smile of reassurance. He quietly closed the door and went back into the kitchen feeling much better. After drinking another cup of coffee, Hezekiah heard a light tap on the kitchen door. He went to the door and it was young Rachel Hankins at the door.

"Mister Whitt, Maw sent me to get a basket of clean rags your Rachel has stored in the corner and Maw said to go ahead and fix the potion tea and bring it to the door," said Rachel Hankins.

Hezekiah gave the basket to Rachel and went to work mixing the herbal potion that he had learned from Agnes Mastin at the birth of Griffy. The tea did a wonderful job of taking away the more severe pain in the last part of vaginal birth. Hezekiah worked diligently to make sure the right amount of each ingredient went into the potion, who knows what would happen if he made a bad mistake. Hezekiah had it all mixed up and poured the steaming water over it and stirred it thoroughly.

Hezekiah carried it through the breezeway and tapped on the door. Rachel Hankins opened the door and smiled at Hezekiah and took the hot cup.

"Be careful honey, that is hot and it will have to cool a little fore Rachel can drink it," said Hezekiah.

"Yes Sir, we will get it cool, so she can drink it," answered Rachel.

He gave a glance at his wife before he shut the door. Rachel looked exhausted, thought Hezekiah.

Hezekiah paused in the cool morning air of the breezeway and lifted a prayer for Rachel and the new baby. Then Hezekiah went to sit with James and Griffy and wait for news next door.

About 9:15 Hezekiah's keen ears detected a cry of a newborn coming from next door.

"Listen boys, I believe you have a new sister or brother, said Hezekiah.

"It better be a boy," said James.

"We will take which ever the Lord sent us," answered Hezekiah.

"Well Paw, I hope he sent me another little brother," answered James.

"Wanting to be different, Griffy said, "I want her to be a girl."

Hezekiah laughed and said, "It wouldn't be long now, just pray to the Lord that both Maw and the baby are alright."

THE PATRIOT, HEZEKIAH WHITT

Hezekiah and the boys sit tight and at about 9:30 Rachel Hankins come to get Hezekiah and the boys. Hezekiah led the boys into the slightly dark cabin to meet the new addition and see their Maw. Rachel was sitting up in bed and was holding their newborn baby. Rachel had been all cleaned up and she had a radiant glow about her as she waited to present the new baby to Hezekiah.

James broke the silence, "Maw what kind of baby did you find?"

"The good kind, God sent us another little Whitt boy," said Rachel in a low sweet voice.

"Yeah," said James.

"Shucks," Griffy said, "I wanted a girl one this time."

Elizabeth laughed out loud at this. Hezekiah and Rachel smiled at each other as Hezekiah came close to see his new son.

Looking down on the little boy Hezekiah noticed he had long black hair and a tiny crease in his chin.

"Yes he is a Whitt, Hezekiah said, "what are you going to name him?"

"We talked about naming him Richard after your Paw and I would like to give him the middle name of Nelson so we can keep the Richard's separated," said Rachel.

Hezekiah gently picked up the little boy and looked him over.

"Hello Richard Nelson Whitt, how are you today?" asked Hezekiah.

Next Hezekiah held little Richard down so the boys could get a peek at their new little brother.

Griffy and James both spoke to him and the little Richard Whitt spread his mouth in his first smile since coming into this world.

"Jest look at that precious little thing, he is greeting his brothers with a smile," said Elizabeth.

Rachel smiled and said, I wish you're Grand Maw Susannah and the Reverend could be here to see him," said Rachel.

Young Rachel Hankins was taking this all in and felt good that she had helped bring this new baby into the world. She had matured by years in one night.

It was a tiring day for all concerned, but a wonderful day. God had given Rachel and Hezekiah another healthy son. Hezekiah lifted a prayer to his God and gave thanks and praise for the healthy new son and a good delivery for his wonderful bride.

John Hankins came to check on Elizabeth and Rachel and of course on the status of Rachel Whitt.

Hezekiah was out in the breeze way with the boys. He saw John riding up and both men threw up their hands in greeting. This type of greeting had developed over the years so that both parties would know it was a friend not a foe approaching. After John rode up close, Hezekiah greeted John Hankins warmly and told him about his new little son, Richard Nelson Whitt.

"Wonderful," John said, "You and Rachel now have three sons."

"Yes, the Lord has blessed us, these three boys will be a great help on the farm in a few years," answered Hezekiah.

"Course, a little girl is awfully sweet, you might get one next time," said John.

"Well, if the Lord wants us to have one he will send us one someday, all babies are precious," answered Hezekiah.

"I don't want no girl," exclaimed little James.

"I wanted Maw to find one," little Griffy blurted out.

"Sorry to start a young war!" laughed John Hankins.

"Boys, let's just enjoy little Richard, the Lord sent him to us, we must love and protect him!" explained Hezekiah.

Both boys sat up big eyed in understanding.
"Well Hezekiah, how is your Rachel, did she fare well?" asked John?

"She is a bit tattered, but she did fare well," answered Hezekiah.

"Your Elizabeth is a God-send and young Rachel was a trooper, I owe them so much," continued Hezekiah.

"They's just glad to help, Elizabeth has been planning on helping since she heard Rachel was in the family way," answered John.

"I am jest so thankful for-um," answered Hezekiah.

"Hey Hezekiah, member when little James was born, you was a mess of nerves, I made you go a hunting and you killed that big bull buffalo?" asked John.

"I weren't no mess of nerves, I was just a bit concerned, and yes I remember that day like it was yesterday, that big cape has kept us warm on many a cold night," exclaimed Hezekiah.

"Don't see too many round here no more, you have to go way down the Tug, or down the Louisa River (Levisa now.) to see-um now days," said John.

"That's the only bad part of civilization," answered Hezekiah.
John shook his head sadly in agreement.

THE PATRIOT, HEZEKIAH WHITT

"John, you want to go in and see our new addition?" asked Hezekiah?

"Sure do, is he stocky or kinda lean?" asked John?

Hezekiah tapped on the door out of respect to the women and slowly opened the door of the cabin.

"Come on in; is that John out thar with'ya Hezekiah?" Asked Elizabeth?

"Yes Ma-am, John is with me," Hezekiah said, "come on in John and look for your self."

The proud Hezekiah led John to the side of the bed so he could see Richard Nelson Whitt. John walked up closely to view the new baby. Rachel uncovered the baby with long black hair, a dark complexion and a well built frame for an infant…

"Boy he is stocky, bet he will be a strong man!" exclaimed John Hankins.

"Strong in the Lord, I hope," said Rachel with a smile on her face.

Hezekiah and Rachel had three sons now, one with light, and two with dark complexions. They were all strong and healthy and Rachel gave thanks to God every day for them. She and Hezekiah always ask Jesus to give them protection, during their daily prayers. Hezekiah always read from the "Holy Bible" or from "Pilgrims Progress," in their daily devotions. Young James was beginning to be an accomplished reader and Griffy was learning to read. Rachel had also become a good reader and writer of the English language.

THE PATRIOT, HEZEKIAH WHITT

Lady playing with a "Brandalore" in the late 1700's. Now called a "YO-YO"

Chapter 27

Growing Pains To Civilization

The frontier was getting tamer, but Indian trouble was still a big concern. After the defeat of General St. Clair's Army the Indians in the Ohio country gained confidence and would not negotiate with the fledgling United States.

President Washington and his cabinet had considered the problem with the hostile Indians in the Ohio country. Something must be done, after all how does it look to have a new nation that can't even control the Indian tribes of a few thousand warriors in the Ohio country. The Indians must be taught a lesson. To do this the right General must be found, a new and powerful army must be raised, trained and well supplied.

The great western County of Virginia, called Kentucky, was working for separation from Virginia and working to become the 15th State of the United States. After all Kentucky was a big land and was being settled by many people because it offered free land to the Veterans of the Revolutionary War as a bonus. The United States was basically giving the Indian's land to the Vets. That was enough to make any good Indian become Red-Faced!

The Indians did the only thing they could, mount raiding parties into Kentucky, Virginia, and Pennsylvania. They would hit quick, mostly in small settlements or lone farms. They would come in surprise attacks, taking horses, plunder, killing and mutilating, and sometimes taking hostages. The British in Detroit were keeping the Indians well supplied with guns and whiskey and influencing the Indians to fight the Americans. The British were giving the Indians false hopes and telling them that they would help turn back the Americans across the mountains. They had even set up a trade of money or goods for every scalp they brought in. The British had hopes of taking America back from the Americans sometime down the road.

The settlers on the waters of the Clinch still had to be careful. More folks had moved to the region and Indian raids had lessened some because of it but it was still a wild region.

Talks had been going on out in Kentucky County since December of 1784 about forming a new State. A long struggle had loomed about separation and drafting a constitution. Also while all of this planning was going on the settlers in Kentucky faced a continued threat from marauding Indians from the north side of the Ohio River. The new constitution was based on the Constitution of the United States.

On June the 1st 1792 Kentucky was admitted into the Union of the United States as the 15th star on the flag. Lexington became the temporary capital of the new State. In a tavern constructed of logs, the first legislature met for the first session. By common consent they chose Isaac Shelby to be the first Governor of the Commonwealth of Kentucky. The news flashed through out the United States and also in the Indian

THE PATRIOT, HEZEKIAH WHITT

country. The Indians had called each State a fire. Now they knew that Kentucky was the 15th fire, another part of the United States. Kentucky would deal directly with the Great White Chief Washington and would be a stronger foe.

The folks along the new border between Virginia and Kentucky had mixed feelings. Virginia hated to give up Old Kentucky County and the Kentucky folks were proud to be their own State. Folks on the waters of the Clinch mostly hated to give her up, but now maybe they could get stronger support from Richmond.

Hezekiah would make the trip to Castlewood again to pay their taxes. Even though Rachel and the boys wanted to go with Hezekiah, they decided it might be better if Hezekiah went alone. Hezekiah could make a faster trip and of course the boys could help Rachel maintain the farm. James was now almost ten years old and was a decent shot with the musket and was fair at loading the long, heavy, weapon. Also Rachel could shoot as good as most men. Hezekiah had practiced with Rachel, James and even seven year old Griffy. Griffy was still a little small, but if he could lay the long heavy barrel across something, he could hit a target.

Every year at tax time the men on the head waters of the Clinch would fuss. Hezekiah had become outspoken on the subject and was well know in the region of Baptist Valley and Indian Creek. They all wanted to form their own county and someday about seven or eight years down the road they would get serious about it. First the unrest caused by the Indians would have to cease.

President George Washington would pick a dogged General by the name of Anthony Wayne to deal with the Ohio Indians. Wayne was just what the United States needed to subdue the warring redskins. Anthony had a nickname that many say fit him to a "T", it was "Mad Anthony Wayne." I will tell you more about him later, but for now the Indians from across the Ohio would continue to reach deep into Virginia on their raiding parties, but not as bad as in Kentucky.

Some of the national news of the year of 1792;

Postage was set at from 6 to 12 cents and based on the distance. It was a high cost, but at least you could get a letter to any State in the Union.

Congress, on April 2, 1792 established a *mint* in Philadelphia, PA.

The United States authorizes, on April 2nd 1792, Gold Coins, $10.00 dollar Eagle, $5.00 half Eagle, and $2.50 quarter Eagle. Also the silver dollar, quarter, dime, and half-dime were coined.

On October 13, 1792 the first Old Farmers Almanac is published.

Also on October 13, 1792 Washington laid the corner stone of the Executive Mansion now called *The Whitehouse.*

On

December 5, 1792 President George Washington is re-elected for a second term.

THE PATRIOT, HEZEKIAH WHITT

About a half a days ride on a good riding horse down the Clinch from Hezekiah Whitt's farm lived the David Music family. (Now Honaker) In the summer or fall of 1792 a band of Shawnee Indians meant on doing mischief came up on the Music home and laid under cover to wait for the morning when the unsuspecting settlers would come out to work. Two boys Abraham and Elijah were the first out in the early dawn to gather some fire wood. The Indians jumped out in an attempt to grab the boys, but they ran like the devil, screaming "Injuns". The boys made it in and the door was barred. David had only one musket and it had been damaged. He tried to fire it by sticking a small flame on the pan, but with all the excitement the dang thing would not go off. Before David could get back in the cabin one of the Indian's arrow hit him in the hip and cut an artery and he bled out quickly with the door still ajar. The Indians busted through the door and took Mrs. Music and all the children prisoner. Then they took their time scalping David and then eat all the food that had been prepared. They gathered what plunder they could carry with their bloody hands.

Unknown to the Indians was a neighbor, James Gibbs, which came to borrow a plow from Mr. Music. James Gibbs saw the attack and heard the screams of the Indians and the Music family. James turned and speeded home presumably to get help, but fell dead on his own porch. Most likely James Gibbs had a heart attack.

On the way there the Indians caught a girl out and scalped her alive and left her to die. The girl crawled to a barn and hid. She was found later and survived. Her name was Brumley. She had been out looking to see where her hen hid her nest.

The Indians were ready to travel, so they made the captives march in single file out into a field. One of the cows was grazing there so the Indians killed her and took a big hunk of meat and wrapped it in her hide. This would be their traveling food.

One of the Music boys had bright red hair and the Indians liked him. His brother, they treated badly. They offered him some of the raw meat and he refused it. The Indian grabbed the boy and rubbed his face harshly into the bark of an oak tree, cutting gashes that would leave scars the rest of his life. The boy cried and the Indians saw this as weakness.

The Indians rushed the captives across Big A Mountain toward the Russell Fork of the Big Sandy River. They followed the course to the present day town of Haysi. It was getting to be late evening so they crossed the river where Russell Prater creek enters Russell Fork. There was a small island that offered cover so the Indians decided to camp there. One of the Indians spoke in broken English, "white man no come here." Little did they know that a group of white men were hot on their trail. The frontiersmen came up on the Indian camp during the night and the captain devised a plan. The frontiersmen would quietly encircle the Indians and at dawn when they would be able to shoot all would fire at the Indians and rush in to retrieve Mrs. Music and the children. One nervous white man saw a good shot and pulled the trigger before thinking.

COLONEL CHARLES DAHNMON WHITT   242

THE PATRIOT, HEZEKIAH WHITT

Things happened in a flash, at hearing the shot Mrs. Music and the children made a mad dash towards the sound of the shot. She had the baby in her arms and the children scattered about. One Indian threw his tomahawk at her but it whizzed by her and buried into a tree. Another Indian grabbed a big piece of burning firewood and cast it at her. Other shots came in on the Indians and they dispersed with haste, grabbing only a weapon or a pouch. God had been with the Music family on that morning. Mrs. Music, two sons, a daughter and the baby were all rescued safe. Only injury was the one boy that had his face rubbed on the rough bark of an oak. And of course David Music, the head of the house had been murdered the day before.

One Indian lay dead and one hobbled off with the other Shawnee towards the Ohio. Some years later a skeleton was found under a rock house near Haysi and was thought to be that of the wounded Indian.

Now the whites had a thirty mile trip back to the Clinch Valley. The frontiersmen were very tired after making a forced march across the rugged mountains and decided to camp at the foot of Sandy Ridge by a big spring. Mrs. Music insisted that they cross over the ridge before camping. The men listened to her and did cross over before camping for the night. It was a wise decision, the Indians did return to the very spot and camped on the ground that the whites had planned to camp on. The next morning the Indians gave up the chase and headed back toward their Ohio towns.

Captain Andrew Lewis of the militia got word of the Indian raid and the frontiersmen going out to try a rescue. He got 34 militiamen together and took after the Indians by another direction, not knowing the Music's had been rescued. They came up on a band of Indians at a settler's home, but the house had not been set on fire. The cane was so thick they could not see the Indians until they were within a few yards. The Indians scattered and shots were fired at them. None were killed and the count was never known. The militia recovered nine horses, many weapons and plunder. The Indians had a long trip home without weapons or food. Of course Indians can survive with very little. They would make weapons, and set snares, the only thing they had to do was to stay away from any frontiersmen who would have muskets.

The beautiful Clinch Valley was like Heaven, but could turn in an instant to "Hell on Earth!" It turns out that this attack was carried out on the Musics on the same day little Richard Nelson Whitt was born. When the Whitts got the word they praised the Lord for His protection and loving kindness. There were several attacks down river that summer; Hezekiah could only guess if Rock Lizard and his band had anything to do with them. A half-bred Cherokee by the name of "Benge" had been leading some raids out of the Tennessee country also. He had a following of Shawnee and Cherokee warriors, sometimes even other tribe members would join in on the raids to the Holston, Powell, and Clinch Valleys to steal horses, plunder, and take captives. The black slaves were a favorite for the Indians to capture.

At this time in history the county line between Wythe and Russell ran close to Hezekiah's Cedar Grove. It ran northwest and the folks in the head waters of the Clinch

THE PATRIOT, HEZEKIAH WHITT

mingled with their Wythe County neighbors. Hezekiah lived on the Russell County side of the Clinch.

Major Robert Crockett was in charge of the Wythe County militia. Hezekiah and his neighbors were better acquainted with the Wythe County militia than with the folks down river near Castlewood.

In the fall of 1792 the Indians hit again, this time northwest of the Whitt's home. A large group of Shawnee had slipped into the settlements of Bluestone and the headwaters of the Clinch. The Indians had taken 80 horses and killed some livestock. The Indians did not linger, they had what they came after and were heading back to the Ohio country.

The Indians did most of their stealing during the night and did not travel too far to camp for a rest. The Indians had not been discovered other than some folks had heard noises and started missing horses. A man by the name of Perry was out for a hunt and accidentally came upon the large camp of Indians and horses. He made quick time to Bailey and Wynn's Forts which had a small garrison. The word went out to both sides of the Clinch. By noon two companies of mounted men were raised; one company from Bluestone and the other from the waters of the Clinch. Hezekiah, John Hankins, Thomas Bailey Christian and a number of men from the valley were in the Clinch Company. The forces met at a place that is now called the "Round House". The house was not built until 1840 by Thomas Perry.

Major Crockett moved off with his two companies of men in pursuit of the Indians. The settlers did not take time to get supplies other than their muskets and other weapons. They moved down a trail by Horse Pen Creek where they came to the head of Clear Fork. Next they traveled to the Tug Fork to the mouth of Four Pole Creek. They crossed the ridge that divided the waters of Big Sandy and Guyandotte Rivers. Two men had been sent ahead to a buffalo lick on a creek that flowed into the Guyandotte to scout and if possible to hunt some meat that the men would need. The two men were Gilbert and Lusk and they reached the lick and killed a deer and wounded a big elk that ran off. They followed the elk for awhile, but could never get it.

They returned for the deer and on the game trail near where they left the deer was something new. A stone was hanging from a pawpaw branch right over the trail. Gilbert saw this and stopped in his tracks. He turned to Lusk and gave him a warning that something was up. Without another word shots came in and one hit the hand of Lusk. It knocked the musket he was carrying to the ground and the Indians charged in on the two white men. Gilbert put Lusk behind him and fired a shot at the Indians, they scattered for an instant and Gilbert picked up the Lusk musket and sent another ball at the Indians. This slowed them some again. The two men ran and paused to load when they could. Lusk's hand began to bleed profusely and he became weak.

Gilbert fired another shot at the Indians and tried to push Lusk ahead of him.

THE PATRIOT, HEZEKIAH WHITT

"Go friend, save yourself I think I'm done!" exclaimed Lusk.

"Hell, I can't leave you, I promised your Maw to take care of you," answered the excited Gilbert.

Gilbert should have left his friend, but stayed the course. The Indians overtook them and a flying tomahawk knocked Gilbert down. He raised his musket for the last time and shot the Indian dead. The Indians overpowered Gilbert and hacked him to death and took his scalp. Lusk was luckier, the Indians took him prisoner. They tied up his hand to stop the bleeding and took him with haste down the creek to the Guyandotte River. They followed the river to Island Creek where they set up a camp behind a rocky ridge now called Hog Back. During the night Lusk suffered with his wounded hand. One of the older Indians went out and brought back some roots which he crushed and made a pasty substance and put it on Lusk's hand. This gave him some relief of the pain.

In the morning the Indians separated into two groups. One group took the horses and crossed the river and headed down it. They were planning to follow the river to the Ohio River.

The other Indians pulled out their hidden sunken canoes from the river which they had put there on their trip to this point. They loaded Lusk and some plunder and paddled away down the Guyandotte toward the Ohio River.

Major Crockett did not follow the tracks, but turned west across a ridge to the right fork of Island Creek. The whites camped there which was only about two miles from the Indian camp. Hezekiah and a few other scouts were sent out to check the area. The scouts were back within the hour with news that they were ahead of the Indians by about two miles.

Major Crockett set an ambush for the Indians that would be coming to him. He did not know about the hidden canoes. Hezekiah and another scout were sent back about a half a mile to some high ground so they could watch for the Indians and give warning. The trail wound around the hill about a quarter of a mile from the river so this is where the ambush was set. The Indians traveling by water would never be detected, as they separated in the early morning. The group driving the horses was on the move and Hezekiah signaled the other spy to let the Major know. Hezekiah moved down the hill as the Indians passed and moved in behind them. The trap was sprung and many of the Indians were knocked from their mounts from the great number of shots. The Indians that were not shot road like the wind leaving their bounty of horses behind.

Over on the river in the canoes the Indians heard the shots and paddled harder and were soon around a couple of bends in the Guyandotte.

Most of the horses were recovered and a dozen Indians were killed. None of the whites died except for Gilbert back at the saltlick. One Indian had tried to reverse back up river with a couple of horses toward Hezekiah. Hezekiah raised his musket, took a good aim and squeezed the trigger. The screaming ball found its mark and knocked the Shawnee

THE PATRIOT, HEZEKIAH WHITT

off his horse. He was dead when he hit the ground. The Indians were all scalped, stripped of their moccasins and other usable things and thrown in the river. Hezekiah hated that he had to kill another human being and asked God for his forgiveness.

After all was quiet again the men talked about the battle and all that had happened. The Major was amazed that there were only about twenty Indians in the party. The men had different opinions and it was determined that half of the Indians got away in canoes after the camp was examined.

Lusk was taken up the Ohio River and got away from the Indians near (what is now Gallipolis, Ohio.) and got with some white men near Fort Randolph at Point Pleasant. He got back to Russell County before the first snow.

Lusk went to the family of Gilbert and told them of Gilbert's heroic deed to stay and defend him. His mother could not hold back the tears as Lusk told the story as well as had the mother of Lusk when he told her.

Hezekiah Whitt, John Hankins, and Thomas Bailey Christian got home safely. John Hankins was glad to see Thomas Bailey Christian go against the Shawnee as a white man. (Thomas Bailey Christian was a full blooded Shawnee.) They all praised the Lord for his great protection and loving kindness.

This was the last invasion into what is now Tazewell County, by the dreaded Shawnee. But south of there and in the Ohio country to the northwest there would be more blood shed.

Chapter 28

Four Sons

Over the mountains to the east, the new Government of the United States was off and going. They did not have to deal with marauding Indians or any other enemy at this time. Over the Mountains to the west in western Virginia and in the new State of Kentucky the folks still had to be on alert for the threat of Indians.

President George Washington had been reelected and in March he gave a short 133 word speech on his second inauguration. He and the government did have the west on their minds. He would be working to raise funds and men for a determined army to stop the Indian onslaught once and for all. Whatever he did would not be quick enough as far as the frontiersmen to the west thought.

Some happenings of 1793:

On June 10, 1793 the United States Capital was moved from Philadelphia to Washington City in the District of Columbia… Virginia and Maryland had given this land to the new United States for the Nations Capital and now it was beginning to take shape as masons and carpenters began raising buildings.

On June 20, 1793 a new machine was invented. It would prove to make a big difference between northern and southern thinking. Eli Whitney patents the Cotton Gin. This machine would remove seeds from cotton and free up many hands to plow more, plant more, and harvest more cotton. The machine would create a bigger demand for slaves in the Deep South. Cotton would become a big source of income as it was exported to England and other European countries.

On September 18, 1793 President Washington got his hands a little dirty as he lays the cornerstone of the new Capital building in the new nation named in his honor. (Washington D.C.)

On December 9, 1793 the first daily paper in New York was established by Noah Webster.

The last State to join the Union at this time would be the first State to authorize a State Road. Kentucky would build a State Road from the new capital in Frankfort to the busy area of Cincinnati.

Counties were changing again. The southwest tip of Russell County was given to form Lee County. To the extreme southwest end of Lee County was Cumberland Gap the gateway to Kentucky. Lee County bordered Kentucky and the Tennessee country laid to the south. The south end of Wythe County and the west part of Patrick County were given to form the new county of Grayson. Hezekiah signed a petition with others from the headwaters of the Clinch to form a new county for the first time in 1793. Both

THE PATRIOT, HEZEKIAH WHITT

Russell and Wythe Counties were affected. The State of Virginia never acted on it. Could be too few names or something else taking precedence. Records show that Hezekiah paid property taxes to Russell County again in 1793. The county seat of Russell County would not be moved until 1818. The Russell County court was moved from Castlewood to Lebanon the year of 1818. Lebanon was named from the Holy Bible after the ancient land of cedars that King David mentioned. There were cedar trees all around the area and a big creek named for the cedars. Cedar Creek is a tributary of the Clinch.

During the year of 1793 General Mad Anthony Wayne had organized an army and was moving out of Fort Washington to the north. He was constructing forts as he traveled. This army was different than the St. Clair army in that they were organized and better equipped. The British and 27 tribes of Indians were alarmed at this new American leader that never seemed to sleep. Wayne had tried to establish peace with the Indians by giving them a choice, peace, or death. The Indians did not concur and would fight the Americans, hopefully in a place of their choosing. The Indians were getting organized, but Chief Little Turtle the principal chief of all the tribes that defeated St. Clair bowed out as the commander of this new confederation of Indians. Blue Jacket the white man turned Indian had risen through the ranks of leadership because of his bravery and loyalty to the Indians. A white man would lead the warriors against Mad Anthony Wayne.

With General Wayne building a chain of strength with forts from Cincinnati to Lake Erie the Indians were not raiding as much across the Ohio. Hezekiah and the other folks in the Baptist Valley area and the head waters of the Clinch had a peaceful year in 1793. Raids were conducted on the lower parts of the Clinch. Some of it was from the likes of Chief Benge and his renegades.

The water of the Clinch was a beautiful paradise and wonderful place to live when the murdering red men did not come calling. The area was filling up with settlers and folks were getting together for worship services and social events. They were starting to feel a new sense of freedom. Every summer there would be more cases of the savages attacking to the south near the Tennessee country or in the mountains of what is now West Virginia. This would bring everyone to a better ready state in case it came to them.

Hezekiah and Rachel were having a happy life, but one that we today would call a hard life. The three boys were growing like weeds. James was not going to be a big man and Griffy was about his size already. Richard was showing signs that he would grow to be a big man also. James was very smart and had learned many frontier skills. Hezekiah took James on short hunts now and he was becoming proficient for such a young age. Hezekiah and Rachel would share time with the boys in work and play. They took many fishing trips and other outings to gather berries and nuts. They even collected the sap of the sugar maples to make syrup. They worked together taking care of the farm animals.

THE PATRIOT, HEZEKIAH WHITT

One time James was with Hezekiah while a cow was giving birth to a calf. Hezekiah let James help him pull on the legs of the calf to free it from its mommy. After the calf was freed and both mommy and calf were declared alright by Hezekiah, James asked an interesting question, "Paw, how on earth did that calf get up in Ol Bell?"

Hezekiah was speechless.

"Ask your Maw," Hezekiah finally said.

"How would she know, she ain't even out here with us?" asked James?

"Oh, she will know," said Hezekiah.

Hezekiah and Rachel would explain God to the boys through nature and all the Creator had given them.

"You can see God in all things if you look for him," exclaimed Hezekiah.

The boys being typical had a million questions and they almost always started with, "why."

Sometimes the only answer Hezekiah could come up with was. "Because God made it that way!" or "go ask your Maw."

Hezekiah and Rachel loved each other so much; God just kept blessing them with babies. Sometimes Rachel and Hezekiah could hardly wait until bedtime so they could continue to consummate their marriage. Hezekiah had said where there is love folks continue to consummate every night. Rachel agreed with this idea.

Another baby would be coming in the spring. If it was a girl they would call her Rebecca or Susannah. If the baby was another boy they would name him John Bunyan Whitt after the author of "Pilgrims Progress" that they had read so many times.

The year of 1793 was growing short and Christmas was almost here. Hezekiah, James and Griffy took the ax out into the Cedars where they picked a small one of about four feet tall. They all walked around it and gave it a good inspection. Jesse, the dog, was right in the middle of things. They all agreed that it was the tree they wanted for their Christmas tree. Hezekiah cut most of the way through the trunk and then let James and Griffy take turns with the ax until it fell to the earth. There was a fresh snow on the ground so the boys took turns dragging the tree, Jesse ran along barking at the tree and Hezekiah followed carrying the ax. When they reached the cabin, Richard and Rachel greeted them at the door.

"Oh! What a beautiful tree you all chose for our Christmas tree, ain't it purty Richard?" she asked?

"It's purty," Richard said as he grabbed a hold of it and helped drag it into the cabin.

THE PATRIOT, HEZEKIAH WHITT

Rachel and Hezekiah grinned at each other as Hezekiah fastened a stand to the little cedar. When he stood it up over in a corner all five of the Whitts stood and gazed at their Christmas tree.

"It's a good-un once we get it fancied up with some decorations," said James.

"What are you aiming to put on it?" asked Hezekiah?

"I think we can make a garland of dogwood berries, put on some big pinecones, string some popcorn and make an angel for the top," said Rachel.

"Well we will have to go and gather the berries and pinecones," said Hezekiah.

"We got some dogwoods over in the edge of the woods, Paw," said Griffy.

"We sure do, you know for every berry we pick there will be one less bloom in the spring?" asked Hezekiah?

"Paw, we got plenty of blooms round here, we can spare some for the Christmas tree," said James.

"Alright get a satchel and let's go and get some," said Hezekiah.

This time even Richard went to help pick up pinecones and the red berries from the dogwoods. Jesse ran along with the boys and jumped about playing in the snow.

When Hezekiah and the boys got back with their decorating supplies Rachel had drawn out a beautiful angel on some of Hezekiah's writing paper. She had cut it out and added some rouge to its face and cut out a little piece of blue cloth and made a dress for it.

"How beautiful you made God's Angel," said Hezekiah as he placed her on top of the little cedar Christmas tree.

It was the day before Christmas 1793 and the kitchen smelled so good. Rachel was baking pies and cakes; also a fat turkey was ready to be baked in the limestone oven fashioned to the side of the fire place.

The Whitts expected a few folks to come by next day on Christmas. Thomas Bailey Christian was invited for dinner and other neighbors were bound to stop by for a short visit. The Indians were thought to be keeping warm in their lodges north of the Ohio, so there should be no invited red men.

Under the loving guidance of Rachel the boys popped popcorn and made a garland of the fluffy pops. They also strung up the red dogwood berries to make a nice flash of red against the evergreen cedar. They hung several big pinecones on the little tree. Hezekiah helped the boy's string the decorations and little Richard ate on the extra popped corn.

Hezekiah took some special candles that Rachel had made special just for the family tree and placed them out on the ends of a few branches. The special picked branches were not likely to set a fire to the rest of the tree. They would not light the candles until late in the evening and of course they would not be allowed to burn for long.

After supper on Christmas Eve and the chores done there would be a special family time. Hezekiah and the boys took long sticks and set them on fire in the fire place and lit the candles on their beautiful Christmas tree. The family stood there for a long moment mesmerized. This was a very special time in the Whitt house!

Next Hezekiah would get the family Bible out and everyone would gather around. Hezekiah read some from Matthew, Mark, and the 2nd Chapter of Luke. It all dealt with the birth of God's Son and the reason Jesus came to the world. The boys set quietly as their Paw read and he would answer their questions, if they had some. After the Bible lesson Hezekiah would pray and the family knew it was time to give and get gifts. The boys knew that in the morning to look in their stockings to see if Saint Nick had made a visit.

The boys got some newly woven sweaters and hats from Maw and Paw. Sometimes they got some socks and maybe something special like a quill-pen and ink and some real writing paper to help with their lessons. This year they, all three, got a brand new Silver Quarter. (.25 cents.)

Saint Nick would leave a "Brandalore" in each stocking. A Brandalore was what we moderns call a yo-yo. Hezekiah saw a picture in an old paper of a woman playing with one of the new toys and thought the boys would love them for Christmas. He studied the detailed picture of the spool like toy with a string fastened in the middle. He read that if you rolled up the string then drop the Brandalore it would unwind and wind itself back up with a little wrist action. He worked on them for days all in secret from the boys. He sanded and rubbed in beeswax as he had no paint. The boys all got one in their stocking along with some candy, and a nice apple.

It was a great Christmas for the Whitts. Hezekiah gave Rachel some nice store bought material and sewing goods. Rachel surprised Hezekiah with a new shirt she had made and also a new heavy quilt that would be pleasing on those cold winter nights.

Christmas morning came and the boys could hardly wait to see if Saint Nick had stopped by. Sure enough he had. There was a new fangled toy in their stocking. They had no idea what to do with them.

"Oh, boys I know what they are, I saw them in a paper sometime back, they call them Brandalores," said Hezekiah.

"What do you do with them?" asked Griffy?

"Here, let me have yours and I will show you how they work," explained Hezekiah.

Hezekiah took one of the Brandalores (Yo-Yo) and flipped it down unwinding its string and when it hit bottom it climbed right back up to his hand. The boy's eyes widened at the sight. (Hezekiah had tested them out after he had made them.)

THE PATRIOT, HEZEKIAH WHITT

"Here Paw let me do it said first one then another. Before long the boys had their Brandalores jumping up and down and all were laughing at the sight.

Christian came for dinner about noon and the whole family gathered around the bountiful table for dinner. After a long thankful prayer the food was passed to each person and their plates were filled and all enjoyed an extra special dinner. They had turkey, yeast bread, yams, mashed potatoes, pumpkin, pickled beans and cabbage dug from their catch. Also apple pie and some whipped cream for desert.

After dinner there was much talking and merriment. Christian was usually a quiet man, but he opened up more this day. He talked about his days as a youth living with the Shawnee in Ohio, and then he talked about his adopted father, Thomas Mastin. He finally got around to talking about his new and beautiful lady friend. He had been sparking with Louisa Harman.   Rachel and Hezekiah were a bit surprised that Mathias Harman was allowing her to see Christian that way. After all Mathias was well know for being an Indian hater. Of course Christian was more white than red and had proved his loyalty to the settlers.

Rachel came right out and asked Christian, her nephew, if they had set a date for a wedding yet. He was set back a bit at the abrupt question, but he gave an answer after a long minute.

"Well I ain't ask Mister Harman as yet, but we want to get married in June," explained Thomas Bailey Christian.

"That is wonderful news, let me get us some of my blackberry wine and give you a toast," said Hezekiah.

"Louisa is a sweet girl, she will make you a wonderful wife," said Rachel.

Hezekiah brought out his jug of wine and three of their best cups. He sat down at the table with Christian and Rachel and poured a little of the wine into each cup.

Hezekiah looked right at Christian and asked, "Do you think Ol Mathias will allow it?" "He will have to, me and Louisa are going to get married," answered Thomas.

"Thomas, if you need me to, I can speak to him about it," said Hezekiah.

"I don't think there will be a problem, I have sat in the parlor with them several times and he seems fine with it," said Christian.

"Sittin' and hitchin' are two different things, but let's have that toast," said Hezekiah as he lifted his cup.

Rachel and Christian both lifted their cups and Hezekiah said, "I make this toast to my friend Thomas Bailey Christian and to Louisa Harman, may they become one in marriage and may God bless this union with His great love!"

THE PATRIOT, HEZEKIAH WHITT

"Here, here," Rachel said, "I drink this fine cup of God's bounty and pray for a wonderful life for Christian and Louisa," said Rachel.

A few other folks stopped by for a short visit that day. George Perry and wife, William McGuire and wife, the Hankins, John and Elizabeth and Thomas Perry all visited to name a few. All of them said something about forming a new county in the head waters of the Clinch. After all they had signed a petition and would sign another one in 1794.

It was a week's trip for some folks just to go to the court house. Some folks had to cross as many as four big mountains and navigate through swift mountain streams just to do county business. Hezekiah and Christian were in agreement with all of the locals about this issue.

Rachel was about six months along with her fourth baby. The new little Whitt was expected about the first day of April. This was also mentioned by all the ladies that came by that day.

The boys played with their new Brandalores (Yo-Yo) and this was a source of amusement for all the visitors that day. They all wanted to know when the next addition was due.

William McGuire asked, "Where on earth did you boys get them things?"

"Saint Nick brought them!" all three boys answered in unison.
William laughed out loud and winked at Hezekiah.

As the winter gave way to Spring Rachel's time to deliver was almost there. Elizabeth and Rachel Hankins were ready to assist Rachel once again when the baby decided to come. Hezekiah had the ingredients gathered to make the special potion to relieve Rachel's pain. Many prayers had gone up asking the Lord to be with Rachel and her delivery, also for the baby that would be their forth born.

April 1, 1794, April Fools Day had come and the boys were trying to play April fool tricks on everyone and causing a lot of laughing.

Right after laughing at the boys while she peeled potatoes, right out of the blue, Rachel said, "Hezekiah, go fetch the Hankins, it's time!"

Hezekiah thought she was getting an April fool joke on him and just laughed.

"It is not funny Mister Whitt, I ain't a foolen, go get the ladies, or you will have to deliver this young-un!" exclaimed Rachel!

What really threw Hezekiah off was the time, women never go into labor at noon, it's always about 2 or 3 in the morning, and all the fooling around this morning. Hezekiah jumped to his feet and stood there looking at Rachel as if he didn't know what to do first. The time was about noon!

"Go saddle Johnny and ride to get them," said Rachel.

THE PATRIOT, HEZEKIAH WHITT

"You gonna be alright?" asked Hezekiah?

"Yes, now go," said Rachel as she held to her enlarged belly.

Hezekiah told the boys to get in firewood and go to the spring and get plenty of fresh water and he would be back as quick as possible. Then he ran to the horse pen and saddled Johnny. (Horse.) Jesse (Dog) was right on his heels. He told Jesse to go and watch the house and he rode off to the John Hankins house.

When Hezekiah got to the Hankins no one was in the house. He looked about and saw smoke coming from the barn. Hezekiah spared Johnny and guided him to the barn. He dismounted and opened the door to look in. The Hankins, the whole family, was working their tobacco crop and getting it ready to sell. John and the bigger boys were taking down the hanging tobacco from high in the barn and handing it down to the others to grade and bundle for sale.

Elizabeth looked up and saw Hezekiah.

"Lordy mercy is Rachel ready?" asked an excited Elizabeth.

"Yes she is Can you come now?" asked Hezekiah?

"Yes I can, John come down and help me get ready!" exclaimed Elizabeth.

John came down and greeted Hezekiah and headed out to saddle two horses. Hezekiah followed him to help.

"Rachel you hurry on to the house, I will need you to help me with Mrs. Whitt," said Elizabeth to her daughter.

The boys on the rafters continue to hand down the tobacco. One of the girls put more wood on the fire as it was a cold day. The Hankins children continued to work the tobacco just as if their parents were still with them.

In no time at all Hezekiah and the two Hankins ladies trotted their horses down the hill to the trail back to Cedar Grove. (The name Hezekiah called his home.)

Once to the Whitt house, Hezekiah jumped down from Johnny and helped the ladies down. They hurried into the cabin and Hezekiah took the three horses to the horse pen and unsaddled them. He ran back to the cabin with Jesse leading the way. The time now was about 1:00 PM.

The boys had gathered the fire wood and filled two pitchers of water and had another bucket on stand-by. They moved over to the other part of the cabin where the kitchen and sitting room was. Hezekiah was met at the door by Elizabeth, "You go over with the boys, she is doing fine and I will call you if I need something," she said.

Hezekiah looked in on the boys and was satisfied they were fine, and then he loaded his pipe and went to the fireplace and lit-up. He would just have to calm down and wait. He would have to keep the boys busy so he decided to let them sit with him as he read to them from "Pilgrims Progress"

Hezekiah explained to the boys that a man named John Bunyan wrote the book and if the baby was a boy he would be named John Bunyan Whitt.

The boys liked this idea, a famous name for their little brother.

"Paw what if John Bunyan is a girl?" asked Griffy?

"Well in that case it will be a good idea to name her after a girl, I reckon," answered Hezekiah.
"What name?" asked little Richard?

"Rebecca or Susannah is what your Maw has in mind," explained Hezekiah.

"Well I hope it is John Bunyan Whitt, I want a famous brother," stated James.

Hezekiah laughed out loud and the boy's joined in as laughing is always contagious.

The afternoon drifted away and Hezekiah became a little worried. He went to the door and gave a little knock on the three inch thick cedar door.

Rachel Hankins cracked the door open and spoke gently to Hezekiah, "she's doing fine; I will be a letting you know soon!"

"Thanks, I got to prepare the pain potion just as soon as your Maw thanks it's time!" exclaimed Hezekiah.

"Maw will let you know, I think it will be another hour or more," answered, the 16 year old, Rachel Hankins like she was a pro at being a midwife.

Hezekiah decided to feed the boys and get them started on their chores, so he cut up the potatoes Rachel was working on when she went into labor. Then he mixed up some corn bread and fried the potatoes and fried the corn cakes. He cut up an onion and added it to the frying potatoes and the boy became starved all of a sudden. He cut off a few pieces of salt cured ham and threw it in on the almost done potatoes to warm. He sent James to the springhouse to get some milk and butter and supper was almost ready.

The three boys sat down with their father to eat. Hezekiah lifted a prayer of thanksgiving and a petition for Rachel and the baby. Just after the eating the boys washed the dishes while Hezekiah took a smoke.

THE PATRIOT, HEZEKIAH WHITT

There was a knock on the door from the breezeway between the two parts of the house. Hezekiah hurried to the door and opened it wide. Rachel Hankins was standing there smiling, and she said, "Mister Hezekiah, you can fix that potion now and bring it over, it ain't gonna be too much longer!"

"Thanks Honey, I will have it ready in about two shakes of a dog's tail!" said Hezekiah with a crooked smile.

James, wanting to be funny asked? "Paw, you want me to go and fetch Jesse so's you can shake his tail?"

"Nope, that is just a way of saying I am gonna hurry," replied Hezekiah.

Hezekiah got the secret roots, dried leafs and other ingredients and began the preparation. He crushed it all together measuring carefully and once he was satisfied he poured boiling water into it. He mixed it real good and poured it into a tea cup and headed through the breezeway to his dear wife Rachel.

He didn't even stop at the door but carried the hot cup of Indian pain potion to Elizabeth. Then he bent down and kissed his wife on her perspiring forehead. She gave a quick smile and said, "It wouldn't be long, go back to the boys, I will do just fine."

Hezekiah heard her moan as he went out the door. The boys met him as he came in to that part of the house.

"Did Maw find our new baby yet?" asked Griffy?

"Nope, but I think it wouldn't be too much longer, just say a prayer that the time will be short," instructed Hezekiah.

Elizabeth had Rachel drink the potion and she drunk it quickly because she knew it would give her much needed relief.

At about 7:00 PM Hezekiah and the boys heard the blessed sound of a new born baby crying!
"Paw, Maw done found us a baby!" exclaimed little Richard.
"I think you are right son!" exclaimed Hezekiah as he had a group hug with all three sons.
About 7:20 the sound of a knock was heard on the door. As Hezekiah opened the door Elizabeth asked? "Well Hezekiah, ain't you gonna come over and see your daughter, John Bunyan Whitt?"

"Huh! Daughter, John Bunyan Whitt?" asked Hezekiah?

"April Fool, It be a boy!" exclaimed Elizabeth.

The boys laughed at their Paw, he fell for an April fool joke. Hezekiah headed to see Rachel and the baby and the three boys followed close behind.

COLONEL CHARLES DAHNMON WHITT

THE PATRIOT, HEZEKIAH WHITT

Rachel was a beautiful mother and little John Bunyan Whitt was a beautiful baby with long black hair and a dark complexion.

The First Old Glory!

Chapter 29 The

War In The North

In the spring of 1794 General Mad Anthony Wayne was building up to have war with the Indians and the British too, if they got in the way. He had established a line of communication between his army and Fort Washington down on the Ohio River.

Fort Recovery was built and a trading post nearby was burned. It was run by Peter Loramie whom favored the British and Indians and he had been dealing with the Indians. General Wayne sent him out of the country with the threat of death if he ever came back to the United States to trade with the Indians.

The British were really concerned that General Wayne and his army were in northern Ohio. The British figured that Wayne intended to attack them in Detroit. The British Governor took action in April and sent Military and Indian Agents up the Maumee River. Below the rapids where Indian Agent Alexander McKee had his trading post, The British built a fort. This was clearly a violation of the Britiah-American treaty. The fort was manned and ready to block General Wayne's advance. The British were soon joined by many Indians who came to get free guns, equipment and "Firewater."

General Wayne's army continued to grow. He had 2000 U.S. Troops and 1500 mounted Kentucky volunteers. In April Mike Cassidy rode in with another company of mounted Kentuckians. General Scott came in July with 1600 drafted Kentuckians.

In June Blue Jacket and Alexander Mckee led an attack on Fort Recovery. Men on both sides died but the strong walls of the fort held out the Indians. After two day the Indians took their dead and went back down the Maumee River.

On July 28, 1794 General Wayne was ready and he took his Army up the Auglaize River to the Maumee River toward the British and Indian stronghold. The Indian spies reported back to General Wayne that the Indian towns were being vacated ahead of the onslaught.

At the confluence of the two rivers General Wayne built another fort. It only took eight days to build it. General Wayne inspected the strength of the fort and declared, "I defy the English, Indians, and all the devils in Hell to take it!"

"Call it Fort Defiance!" exclaimed General Scott to General Wayne.

"Damned the British and their red brothers, I will call my new fort, "Defiance," answered General Wayne.

A renegade by the name of Harry May had left the Indians and joined General Wayne. He brought reports to General Wayne. May had the misfortune to fall into the hands of the Indians. The Indians took him to their principal village where seven tribes of Indians were grouped together under the command of the mighty Blue Jacket. There were Shawnee, Senecas, Chippewas, Ottawas, Miamis, Potawatomies, and Delawares.

Poor Harry May was tied to a pole and fifty Indians lined up and shot their muskets simultaneously. He was damaged as if hit by direct cannon fire.

Wayne marched his men on down the Maumee River to a place called Roche de Boeuff. Here he build a small fort to deposit his heavy baggage and called the place Fort Deposit.

On August 20, 1794 Wayne moved his army toward the Indians and stopped four miles short of the British Fort Miami. The place was an ideal place for the Indians to stage an ambush. The whole area had downed trees left over from a severe windstorm. The place was a tangle of fallen timbers.

General Wayne was a very smart commander so he stopped his army short of the ambush. Next he sent in a battalion of mounted troops with instruction to ride up until the Indians fired and immediately retreat so as to draw the Indians out. The plan worked wonderfully and the Indians charged in hot pursuit after the fleeing Americans. The Americans let go on the oncoming Indians and killed more than one hundred with their first shots. A short but hot contest finally turned the Indians back into the tangle of fallen timbers.

General Wayne's army followed the Indians to within site of the British Fort. The battle continued in plain sight of the British. The fort's gates were kept shut and they gave the Indians no assistance. The Indians saw a great betrayal from the British. They wouldn't even let any of the Indians come in the fort for protection.

General Wayne paid no attention to the Red Coats in the fort, but continued to defeat the Indians. Wayne had orders to destroy the fort if he thought it prudent.

After the Indians had fled General Wayne burned all building outside the fort, he ordered all the crops destroyed. Agent McKee's house and trading post were burned to the ground and the British troops in the fort could only groan in disgust at the sight.

General Campbell, The British commander, rushed a note to General Wayne. It basically said that the British and Americans were not at war. General Wayne sent back a clear straight forward letter to General Campbell that the British fort was in the United States and for him to get out.

General Wayne wanted to attack Campbell and his men, but felt better of it. He did not want to diminish a great victory with useless deaths trying to take a strong fort. General Wayne took his men back toward Fort Defiance in a slow march, fanning out in a fifty mile wide sweep on both sides of the Maumee River. They destroyed all the crops and Indian dwellings they came across. Now the winter would become an even greater enemy to the Indians, than Wayne's army had been. The Indians camped at the mouth of Swan Creek and would do well to survive the winter. The British offered little help that winter.

THE PATRIOT, HEZEKIAH WHITT

A strange thing happened that may have changed history. The Indians were going to try and survive with the help of Alexander McKee whom had connections with the British in Detroit. McKee had the ability to bring food and clothes to the starving Indians. But before Mckee could act he had this mishap. Mckee had a pet deer that stayed close to him and even in his lodge. One day Alexander McKee was changing clothes and bent over with his butt exposed to the antlered buck. For no apparent reason the deer charged McKee's hind quarters. It might have been funny, but the deer severed an artery and Alexander McKee bled out.

The Indians took this as a sign from their God, *Moneto!* The deer was overcome with the spirit of Moneto and it was plain that the Indians should ask for peace with the Shemanese at Fort Defiance. Within six weeks seven tribes sent leaders to Fort Greenville asking for peace and help for their starving people. General Wayne accepted the Indians and scheduled a treaty signing at Fort Greenville in the summer of 1795. He had compassion on the Indians and sent some supplies and prisoners were exchanged. Could this be a lasting peace, only time would tell?

News of this victory at Fallen Timbers and the tentative treaty reached with the Indians reached the folks in Russell and Wythe Counties with great joy. Rachel and Hezekiah viewed the news as bittersweet. The Indians would stop raiding Virginia and Kentucky, but a whole era for the Indians has ended. Their will to roam freely over their past hunting grounds has come to an end. The Indians, Rachel's people, are suffering and she feels their pain.

Early in the spring of 1794 a resident of Virginia near Castlewood was aroused by his dogs barking frantically. He took a shot in the dark as a warning to whom or whatever may be out there in the dark. Next morning he was somewhat surprised to find a dead Indian and sign that other Indians had passed near his cabin.

Also in April 1794, Chief Benge and six painted warriors raided the Livingston home on the Holston River. Bob Benge was a half breed that just couldn't quit raiding the western part of Virginia from his home in the Tennessee country. Bob took the name of Captain Benge and proved to be a thorn in the side of the settlers because of his raiding, plundering and savage killings. Captain Benge had six warriors with him and was in search of plunder. His most favorite plunder was the black slaves of the white men. He had made a boast that he would steal every slave in the country west of the Blue Ridge.

Benge carried off two women and one slave from the Livingston's home.. The two grown sons were out working their fields and some of the children escaped. Benge burned the cabin and headed toward a gap in the mountain above Powell Valley. By now Benge felt safe and the word went out from the two Livingston men and a rescue party was sent out. Two men from Lee County got word and ran ahead and watched for the Indians to come their way. It was a very short time when they saw the seven Indians and their captives coming straight toward them. The two men decided to shoot at the first two Indians. They let go on the non suspecting war party and Captain Benge and the next Indian fell dead. The Indians scattered. One of the women was hacked at by her guard but in haste he did not aim his blows too well. She fought off the swinging tomahawk and her hand and arm were cut bad, but she was not killed. The other Indians escaped with only the Negro slave, but some how he escaped and made his way back to the Livingston farm. This proved to be the last Indian raid into Virginia. Mister Hobbs that killed Captain Benge was rewarded with a fancy silver plated musket by the Virginia Legislature. Now Maws and Paws could no longer scare their children into behaving by saying, "Be good or Captain Benge will get you!"

Now the Indians from the north and the Indians from the south were finally squelched. Could peace and civilization truly come to the waters of the Clinch? Yes, it was on the way and some great things would disappear with the influx of more people into the area. The buffalo were practically gone, the elk and bear were getting scarce and the howl of the wolfs would soon be gone. Many of the things that beckoned to the early settlers of the area were going away. A few of the strong hearted explorers would move on toward the west and some would never be heard of again. Most of the folks like the Whitts were ready to settle down to a more peaceful life, after all they had been fighting the British or the Indians most of their lives.

Other happenings that year were that Congress authorized a new United States Flag on January 13, 1794. With the addition of Vermont and Kentucky to the union two stars and two stripes would be added to the flag in May of 1795. Yes, you read that right I said fifteen stars and fifteen stripes.

On March 22, 1794 Congress bans U.S. Vessels from supplying slaves to other countries.

A cold snap hit New England on May 17, 1794 with a killing frost. It killed all the tender plants that had peeked above the ground.

On June 4, 1794 Congress passed a Neutrality Act which banned Americans from serving in the armed forces of other countries.

On June 5, 1794 Thomas Bailey Christian was wed to Louisa Kathryn Harmon. (June was always picked as marrying month because the pioneers found it to be a good month to take a bath.)

Louisa's father, Mathias Harmon laid down the law to Christian once and for all.

"If you ever mistreat my Louisa, I will skin your red ass and send it to the devil," said the out spoken Mathias Harmon. (Christian was a full-blooded Shawnee, raised in the white world.)

"Never fear Sir, I love her deeply and I think I have proven my loyalty to Virginia more than once," answered Thomas Bailey Christian very sternly but honorably.

Mathias never said another cross word to his son-in-law again, because Christian was always a wonderful husband to Louisa.

THE PATRIOT, HEZEKIAH WHITT

The men of the upper Clinch would continue to work to form their own county. Hezekiah was becoming a very prominent man in the area because of his fairness, love of country, Christian beliefs, and education. Most of the early folks in the Clinch Valley had fought for this new nation and had proved their worth. These hardy folks did not and would not allow any unsavory people to settle in their land.

THE PATRIOT, HEZEKIAH WHITT

Chapter 30

There Will Be A New County

The waters of the Clinch became a country of peace as civilization set in. Much of the concern and dread of Indian attack subsided. It became so tame that most farmers never even carried their musket to the fields with them. Children were allowed to run the woods and play out of the sight of their parents. Folks visited their neighbors more often and even had social events such as "Corn Shuckings," "Quiltings," and "Barn Raisings." Many folks met for worship and even dinner on the ground. The men met for political talks and often enjoyed some spirits and smokes together. Forming a new County was always the foremost topic and no one in the area was against it. It would be so nice to have a courthouse near by.

Acquiring more land was something the early settlers always had on their minds. In 1795 overlapping surveys were made of the area by Jesse Evans and Call McGregor. (25,169 acres) They had to note that some settlers had prior claims. Hezekiah was listed with 95 acres, John Hankins had 350 acres, John Vandyke had 250 acres, just to mention a few.

Another thing folks did was to take trips back toward the east to visit kindred and do trading for the things that they could not make or acquire for themselves. It was just a treat to have something "Store Bought," for a change.

The year of 1795 had been different than any year before on the waters of the Clinch. Hezekiah took his whole family with him to Castlewood to pay their taxes. It was a leisure trip with a lot less caution and more enjoyment of the beautiful lands in which they traveled in. So many more people could be seen on the trails and byways. The one thing that the folks had to be cautious about was bandits and outlaws. There are always some evil people in all generations that want to steal and plunder from hard working folks. Hezekiah would not hesitate to shoot if his family was threatened.

James Whitt was thirteen, Griffy Whitt was eight, Richard Whitt was four and John Bunyan Whitt was one. Now on their trips they even took time to fish if they wanted to. The waters of the Clinch always offered up a good catch, unless it was muddy from heavy rains. Back then the rivers didn't stay muddy too long because the lands were thickly covered with all types of plants and virgin timber that quickly sucked up the rains.

Rachel was in the family way again, they expected the next little Whitt in October. Both Hezekiah and Rachel wanted a girl this time if the Lord didn't mind. If the Lord saw fit and gave them a baby girl they would name her Rebecca.

Most of the settlers let their hogs run free in the woods which did cause some problems. One problem was that the hogs became really wild and would attack a person from time

THE PATRIOT, HEZEKIAH WHITT

to time. Another problem was keeping up with who's hog was who's. One example of this took place in the fall of 1795. Hezekiah had his eye on a big boar and intended to harvest him for the family food. Some new arrivals that lived in a little shack over on Middle Creek had not brought any hogs to the area. The man went by Hank and had several children. Hezekiah and James decided to go and get their big hog and as they got into the area they heard a musket shot. Hezekiah reverted back to the Indian spy days and took cover with James. They watched and waited for awhile, but never saw anyone. The Whitts moved cautiously toward the sight that the sound came from. They crept over a little rise to see Ol Hank standing over Hezekiah's prized boar.

"Damn it," Hezekiah said in a low voice, "Hank has killed my hog!"

James looked at his father with amazement as he seldom heard his Paw say such words.

Hezekiah yelled, "Hello there," at Hank and walked toward him. Hank became very nervous, but greeted Hezekiah warmly.

"What's you doing here Hank?" asked Hezekiah?

"I killed me a big hog to feed my young-uns," answered Hank.

"How many children do you have?" asked Hezekiah?

"I got a dozen," Hank sounded proudly.

Hezekiah looked at the man with a little frown on his lips, but said nothing. Then the Lord touched Hezekiah's heart and made him smile.

"Well Hank, you better get this hog cleaned and get it home," said Hezekiah.

Hezekiah took James and headed out to find another hog.

"Paw, weren't that big boar your'n?" asked James.

"He was!" answered Hezekiah.

"Well how's come you didn't take him back from Ol Hank?" asked James?

"I reckon Hank needed him mor'in us, the Lord told me to let it go!" said Hezekiah.

"But he was your'n, Paw," said James.
"The Lord will provide for us, that man has so many mouths to feed and the Lord is providing for them," answered Hezekiah.

THE PATRIOT, HEZEKIAH WHITT

Hezekiah took James over another ridge and saw several hogs rooting in the leaves for acorns and chinkapins. There was a thicket of chinkapin bushes just ahead of the foraging hogs and it was time for the chestnut like husks to open and drop the miniature chestnuts to the ground. A chinkapin is a dwarf chestnut bush with small chestnut like nuts. The name originated from the Algonquian tongue.

"Look down there in that little clearing," said Hezekiah.

Hezekiah quietly handed his musket to James and quietly told him to shoot the big sow in the head. James smiled at his Paw and quietly took the heavy musket.

"Remember to aim little and shoot little, hold your breath, and squeeze the trigger," Hezekiah whispered to his son.

James smiled at Hezekiah as if to say, "I know!"

James took aim and let go on the big sow from a distance of about fifty yards. The lead ball found its mark and took out most of the brain and the sow dropped like a rock. Hezekiah patted James on the shoulder as congratulations. James was as proud as could be.

"Paw, you know you were right, the Lord did provide us a hog," exclaimed James.

In the fall of the year, after the threat of the Indians had diminished, the settlers would take the whole family out to gather the bounty of the woods. They would gather black walnuts, hickory nuts, beechnuts, chinkapins, and chestnuts. The bigger boys would end up with the job of getting the shelling off the black walnuts and their hands became so stained, it took weeks for it to go away. Of course the more they washed with their Maw's lye soap, the quicker it went away.

The girls and boys had a lot of fun cracking the nuts for their Maws. The boys carried the chinkapins around in their pockets for a handy snack. The only thing about chinkapins was that they were time sensitive; if you kept them too long they always ended up wormy. Some kind of insect would lay eggs in the bloom or forming nut and the worms hatched out after a few weeks. Always check your chinkapins for worms before you eat them.

It was a real blessing to be able to go out with the family and not be under strict alertness. Of course the settlers kept some alertness while out. There were always dangers lurking in the wilds of Virginia's mountains in the 1790's.

Happenings in Ohio had a direct bearing on what happened in Kentucky and Virginia. The Greenville treaty had been drawn up and General Wayne made it a strong one. He truly wanted both sides to understand it so neither side could break it through ignorance. It would be clear to all and the twelve tribes would be represented.

Wayne had sent messengers to all the tribes to inform them of the meeting in mid June 1795 at Fort Greenville. General Wayne did not rush the Indian Chiefs; he knew their nature and pride. The council fires were lighted on June 15, 1795 but only the

THE PATRIOT, HEZEKIAH WHITT

Delaware's were there. General Wayne addressed them. William Henry Harrison, other soldiers, and representatives from President Washington were in attendance. The Indian Scouts, Simon Kenton and Isaac Zane were there to observe and give advice if asked.

The next four weeks brought first one tribe then another. General Wayne was patient and everything was gone over word by word. Twelve tribes were there with well over eleven hundred Indians to hear the Mad General Anthony Wayne.

The Indians were told that they would have hunting privileges in all of Ohio, but went on to read the land boundaries that would be set.

The general boundary lines between the lands of the United States and the lands of the said Indian tribes shall begin at the mouth of the Cuyahoga River and run thence up the same to the Portage between that and the Tuscarawas branch of the Muskingum, thence down that branch to the crossing place above Fort Lauren, thence westerly to a fork of that branch of the Great Miami River running into the Ohio, at or near which stood Loramie's Store, and where commenced the portage between the Miami of the Ohio and St. Mary's River, which is a branch of the Miami which runs into Lake Erie (Maumee River): thence sterly course to Fort Recovery, which stands on a branch of the Wabash: thence southerly in a direct line to the Ohio, so as to intersect that river opposite the mouth of the Kentucky or Cuttawa River.

(I have trouble understanding this, I wonder if the Indians, being of a different creed and language truly understood it.)

General Wayne also claimed sixteen different tracts of land to be used as Government reservations inside the Indian Territory. These would be about six miles square. These would be strung out so the United States could build forts.

In the treaty the Indians would cede 25,000 square miles, plus the sixteen tracts of land as reservations. What did the Indians get? Each of the twelve would receive $1,600, plus $825 once a year.

The Indians were not happy and each Chief spoke a lengthy message of protest. The Indians succumbs and signed the treaty by August 3, 1795, as did General Wayne. On August 7, 1795 the treaties were exchanged. Chief Tarhe of the Wyandots was given the document on behalf of all the assembled Indians.

General Wayne bid the Indians farewell and wished them a peaceful life. The twelve tribes departed and that ended the Indian wars, maybe. Not all of the Indians agreed with the treaty and did not honor those that signed away all of their wonderful lands. The gates were thrown open and the whites would rush in.

With all of these happening, the western end of Virginia and the State of Kentucky would have some peace from the rampaging Indians. Folks would be able to socialize and move about without the tension they had felt for years. Now they could think more about government, elections, and have many more gatherings. The folks in the upper sections of Wythe and Russell County continued to petition Virginia to form a new county. Hezekiah had to travel to Castlewood each year to pay his taxes. Some of his neighbors lived in Wythe County and they had to travel across three mountains to pay their tax.

During the year of 1795 two babies were born in the Baptist Valley, Indian Creek area. Thomas Bailey Christian and his wife, Louisa, had a big boy and named him Moses. Hezekiah and Rachel Whitt celebrated the birth of their first girl after having four boys; they named the little darling Rebecca.

The Christian baby and the Whitt baby were both dark complected with black hair. Both babies were half Indian and half white. Both babies were beautiful. Even Grand Paw Mathias Harman was thrilled with his new grandson.

Of course Hezekiah, Rachel, James, Griffy, Richard, and John Bunyan Whitt were all thrilled to have a little girl in the family. The little girl, Rebecca, would be spoiled by all of them. Rachel was especially thrilled with having a daughter after being encircled with five males for so long.

Guess what, Rachel got in the family way again just after Rebecca was born. In 1796 another little girl was born to the Whitts. Rachel named her Susannah after Hezekiah's mother. In just over a year the Whitt family increased by two little girls.

Susannah was fairer with light hair. James and Susannah took after Hezekiah while the others took after Rachel. They were all beautiful to Hezekiah and Rachel.

"My Lord, what has happened to us, Are you sure?" Hezekiah asked Rachel?

"Well it ain't just me, you had a part in it," said Rachel.

On the first day of the year 1797, Rachel gave birth to her last baby. The baby came early in the morning and Rachel was beat. The baby was a man child and Rachel called him Jonas. Jonas was small but strong. Most likely Jonas Whitt was the first baby of the year 1797, at least west of the Blue Ridge. He was light with light hair just like Hezekiah. Jonas would someday be my GG Grandfather.

Thank the Lord, He took over and Rachel went through the change of life early and there would be no more babies. The Whitts were kept busy with four babies ranging from one month to three years old. James and Griffy were becoming a great help with the younger children. They never complained too much, but you could see they would rather be out doing boy things.

More happenings in 1796 and 1797;

The Tennessee country got together like Kentucky and petitioned the United States to become a new State in the Union. On June 1, 1796 Tennessee became the sixteenth State to join the United States.

Hezekiah and Christian talked about this and wondered what Thomas Mastin thought about it, since he lived there. They discussed it and wondered if it would be wild enough for Thomas now that they were an official State.

THE PATRIOT, HEZEKIAH WHITT

"I wish my father, (Thomas Mastin) could see his new grandson," said Thomas Bailey Christian.

"He will be thrilled when he finds out," answered Hezekiah.

The United States started celebrating their birthday and on July 4, 1796 the whole country had a celebration and called it Independence Day. Even the scattered folks in Baptist Valley, Indian Creek, and the folks on the head waters of the Bluestone River had celebrations. Some were small and some included several families. This was the first of a new tradition.

On September 19, 1796, the man that could have been King of the United States gave his farewell address as President of the United States. There would never be another leader like George Washington, who always put the country first.

On November 3, 1796 John Adams was elected the second President of the United States. If only he could be a man like George Washington. John Adams was the Vice President under George Washington. (I guess he was in charge after George Washington left and before John Adams was officially elected.)

Hezekiah paid his land tax to Russell County again in 1796 and 1797. This time he was listed with 100 acres instead of the original 86 acres. (Increase of 14 acres?)

Hezekiah and Rachel made a trip back to Montgomery County, in the fall of 1797, to visit kindred and do some trading. Susannah Whitt, Hezekiah's dear mother, did not meet them.

What they learned on their visit;

Robert Whitt, Hezekiah's older brother, moved his wife Nancy and the children to the Ohio country. They settled near what is now Jackson County. (This happened after the Greenville Treaty.)

Abijah, another older brother, had married Elizabeth Elswick and had two children.
Rachel Whitt, Hezekiah's older sister, had married Abraham Henderson.
Hezekiah's sister Elizabeth had married William Cassidy.
Brother Edmund was single in 1796, but would marry later and settle in Carter County, Kentucky because he would receive a land grant for his service in the Virginia Militia.

Brother Archibald was married and had seven children by 1796. His daughter Susannah was born in 1794 and would grow up to marry Jonas Whitt the son of Hezekiah and Rachel Whitt. Jonas would be born in 1797. They were first cousins.

Hezekiah's little sister Ruth married a distant cousin, Jesse Witt.

Hezekiah's little sister Susannah married Henry Creswell.

The youngest brother, Richard Thomas Whitt, would become a Medical Doctor. He would marry in 1797 and end up in Morgan County, Kentucky.

Hezekiah's dear mother, Susannah passed away on October 4, 1797.

THE PATRIOT, HEZEKIAH WHITT

The Reverend Richard Whitt would not want to live without a wife. He would marry his second wife, Betsy Baxter, in 1798 and not have any children.

In 1797 Hezekiah bought 160 acres from John Fowler, for the price of 65 pounds. (This is about $65.00 dollars. Why they were using the pound instead of the dollar I don't know, unless the frontier was still using some English money. (It was because there were no distribution banks in the western parts of Virginia.)) This property was on Reedy Ridge, one of the ridges that run parallel with Baptist Valley. Hezekiah could start expanding now with bigger crops and he had help as the boys become bigger.

On March 4, 1797 John Adams was inaugurated as the second President of the United States.

On May 10, 1797 the United States launched their first Navy ship made in America and called her the "United States."

On July 8, 1797 the Senator, William Blount of the new State of Tennessee, was expelled by impeachment.

On September 20, 1797, the United States Frigate, Constitution, was launched in Boston. Her nickname would become, "Old Ironsides."

While on their trip in October 1794 Hezekiah learned of his mother's passing, she had just been buried three days before their arrival. Hezekiah was in shock and he wanted to be by himself. He told Rachel that he was going hunting and James wanted to go with him. Rachel knew that Hezekiah needed to be alone so she told James to stay with her this time. Hezekiah went out the door with watery eyes and hiked about a mile to the New River and up it about another mile. He climbed a small ridge that over looked the river and sat down to think. His first feelings were of guilt. He felt guilty because his busy life and the miles of separation had kept him from seeing his mother in her later years and he was not with her when she passed away.

Hezekiah began to pray for understanding and asked God to forgive him and give him peace. Hezekiah began to feel peace and he began to understand that he had done what sons do. He recollected the Bible Story that told that a man should take a wife and cleave to her. He knew his mother was a saint and was now walking in the glorious realms of Heaven with her Lord Jesus Christ. Hezekiah stayed out most of the day and thought over his whole life. His guilt left as he remembered all the things he had done and all the blessings God had given him. It was up in the afternoon when Hezekiah started back to Reverend Richards big log house. He had seemingly seen nothing on his trip out, but now saw so many of the familiar places of his youth. He enjoyed his journey back and was quite different when he got back. He went to his father, Reverend Richard Whitt, to talk with him.

"Son, did you get everything sorted out between you and the Lord about your Maw passing?" asked Richard?

THE PATRIOT, HEZEKIAH WHITT

"Yes Paw I did, the Lord is so wonderful as a comforter," Hezekiah said, "He made me know that Maw was with him and it gave me a real peace!"

"The sweet Lord is always standing by to receive us in his midst, He is the only one we have when it comes to death and understanding," answered Reverend Richard Whitt.

"Paw, I should have come to you right off to console you, but I was overcome," said Hezekiah.

"I understand son, now go visit your family, it's been a time since you saw most of-um," Reverend Richard Whitt said, "I am going to enjoy all of my new grandbabies!

The Hezekiah Whitt family spent about a week in Montgomery County and had many hours of pleasure visiting family and friends. Hezekiah told his family once again about the beauty of the Clinch River and the lands he called home.

Edmund, his brother, was very interested. Edmund wanted to see Kentucky, but thought he would move to Russell County for a while. Edmund got all of his belonging together and traveled to Cedar Grove in Baptist Valley with the Hezekiah Whitt family. The trip back just flew by because of all the stories that were exchanged on the trail. The party traveled slowly because of the babies and Hezekiah's horse Johnny began to show his age. Hezekiah didn't want to push his old friend. Hezekiah planned to retire old Johnny after this trip and get himself a young horse.

The Whitt party got back to Baptist Valley around the first of November. The nights were already getting cold and Rachel sure was glad to get her family home.

Edmund was not married so he had the freedom to go and come as he wanted. He had no family to provide for and just wanted to do some visiting and hunting on the waters of the Clinch.

Edmund Whitt bought a piece of ground and would stay around a few years in the area. Hezekiah and Edmund got to have many visits and helped each other with their farms.

The year of 1798 was a busy one with all of the babies at Cedar Grove. Hezekiah stayed busy outside and did not have as much help from the boys. James and Griffy didn't complain too much about helping their Maw with, Richard, John Bunyan, Rebecca, Susannah, and Jonas. Hezekiah would let James and Griffy help outside when Rachel wasn't using them.

Edmund still had a free spirit and did not get too interested in politics, but did favor a new county mostly in support of big brother, Hezekiah. He often came to eat supper with the Hezekiah Whitt Family as he didn't like to cook. Edmund was not a dedicated Christian at this time, but he did go to worship services with the Whitts to the home prayer meetings and sometimes to the new Methodist Episcopal Church at Pisgah. Pisgah Church was built in 1797. It was real close to Crab Orchard Fort. (Witten Fort.) Reverend Simon Cotteral was the first official Baptist Minister to preach in the Baptist Valley. (Prayer meetings had been held in the settler's homes for years.)

THE PATRIOT, HEZEKIAH WHITT

To get to the point there was a certain young widow by the name of Hanna Lestor Skaggs. Hanna's husband, Jeremiah Skaggs, passed away and left Hanna with two little girls to raise. Hanna lived in the area and was faithful to go to church. The church helped Hanna with food and some heavy labor on her little farm. Well anyway, Edmund had helped on the farm some. He became interested in Hanna and her girls. Edmund was a young man but very experienced in life. He was a veteran of the war against the British and the Indians. He was interested in Hanna, but was not about to jump into anything. It would take some time for Edmund to come around and Hanna felt the same way.

Hezekiah put Johnny out to pasture and did not work him or ride him any more. Johnny didn't like this at first, but Hezekiah still paid attention to his old friend. Hezekiah bought a nice foal from his friend Christian and was starting to train him. He was going to be a big horse, but not like a draft horse. He was growing long and lean. He would be sixteen hands high by the time he was grown. He was black with two white front feet and a blaze of white marked his face. Hezekiah would call him Blaze. When he was working with the young stud, Johnny would be right there trying to instruct the new horse. By golly it worked, Blaze learned manners and much more from the old horse, Johnny. Johnny died in January of 1799. The Whitts were all hurt with the loss of their old friend. Most of the children cried and so did Hezekiah.

So in the year of 1799 Edmund Whitt and Hezekiah went to Castlewood together to pay their tax. By now there was much talk and some actions were taking place to form a new county from the upper portions of Wythe and Russell Counties! The folks in the upper regions of Wythe and Russell began to feel that it was really going to happen.

Good news and bad news will reach those in western Virginia late in the year. The bad news was that the "Father of the Country," passed away on December 14, 1799 at his home on the Potomac River, Mount Vernon.

His body was interned there on December 18, 1799. The Virginia Statesman, Henry Lee III, eulogized the "Father of our Country." He stated that: *"George Washington was "first in war, first in peace and first in the hearts of his countrymen!"*

All Americans were so strongly hurt that their hero was called home by his Heavenly Father.

The good news was that a new county was formed from the upper sections of Russell and Wythe Counties. Tazewell County was created on December 20, 1799. Politics was used to get it done. Virginia Delegate Littleton Waller Tazewell had opposed the formation of the new county. (I don't know the reasons.)

Simon Cotteral, who drew up the bill to form the county used politics to get it passed. Cotteral changed the proposed name to Tazewell in honor of the recently deceased Virginia United States Senator, Henry Tazewell, the father of Littleton Waller Tazewell. How could Littleton Tazewell not vote for the formation of a county named after his beloved father?

THE PATRIOT, HEZEKIAH WHITT

Excitement was high on the waters of the Clinch. How big would Tazewell County be? Where would the new Tazewell County Seat be located and how would they decide the location? Who would be the Tazewell County Officials? When would the new Tazewell County officials meet? Who would Governor James Monroe appoint?

THE PATRIOT, HEZEKIAH WHITT

Top picture: The gear from the water wheel to drive the saw.
Center picture: The power is transformed from the water to the wheel.
Bottom picture: The Frame Saw and the reciprocating blade. This saw could cut a 2 1/2'
tree up to 20' long.
This was the type of mill that Reverend Richard Whitt and his sons built.

Chapter 31

Tazewell County is Formed

"What a Christmas present for the settlers on the head waters of the Clinch and Bluestone Rivers. The children were excited about the coming of Saint Nicholas and the fathers were excited that they were getting their own county. Now the folks in the new Tazewell County would have more say in the local government, not to mention the convenience of a closer county seat.

The new county would be big compared to today's thinking. (3,000 Sq. Miles.) It would take in a lot of area. In 1800 Tazewell County contained all or parts of Bland County, Virginia; Giles County, Virginia; Buchanan County, Virginia; Mercer County West Virginia; McDowell County, West Virginia; Wyoming County, West Virginia; and Logan County, West Virginia. The population in 1800 was 2127.

The boundaries of Tazewell County in 1800 were as follows:

"Beginning on the Kanawha line, and running with the line which divides Montgomery and Wythe Counties, to where said line across the top of Brushy Mountain; thence along the top of the said mountain to its junction with Garden Mountain; thence along the top of said mountain to the Clinch Mountain; then along the top of said mountain to the top of Cove Creek, a branch of the Maiden-spring fork of Clinch River; thence a straight line to Mann's Gap, in Kents Ridge; thence north 45 degrees west, to the line which divides the State of Kentucky from that of Virginia; thence along said line to the Kanawha line, and with said to the place of beginning."

Where and how the location of the county seat of Tazewell would be chosen? The vast area of land that now came under the leadership and control of the county of Tazewell had no county seat. Every one in most every part of the county wanted the new county seat to be in their neighborhood. It boiled down to two areas, one up toward the area that is now West Virginia, the other that is now Tazewell and Richlands. The argument could not be settled so someone suggested that both factions chose a champion and let them fight. The winner would pick the location. This was not too unusual since the whole area was settled by fighting men.

A lot of the folks thought it was barbaric, but that was what the majority wanted. There was much talk and praying about this decision. The two men chosen were big strong hardy men that had made their way through life with their fighting skills. The two factions took their champion and gave them training and served them the best of foods until the day of the fight. The site of the fight was in the upper part of Baptist Valley, now North Tazewell. They decided to have the fight on the first Saturday in May, 1800 and it would start at high noon. Both factions would be there to support their man and cheer him on. The only rule was that nobody besides the two chosen fighters could

THE PATRIOT, HEZEKIAH WHITT

fight. The fighters were to fight fair without weapons and there were no ring set up besides the spectators standing around. The last man standing would be the winner and have the right to choose the site of the new county seat. I am sure some side bets were placed. The crowds watching were ecstatic on that day.

High noon arrived and the two fighters stripped down to their pants; they stood in the midst of some one hundred interested men. The women and children did not come and watch this affair. William McGuire was appointed the referee and would make sure everything was done in a safe and equitable manner.

William stood between the two fighters and told them to fight fair and if one wanted the fight ended he was to just lay on the ground for a count of ten. William stepped out of the way and the two men put their fist up in a defensive manner and the whole crowd began to cheer. First one fighter landed a blow then the other. The fight went for about thirty minutes and William McGuire called a break so the two fighters could get a short rest and drink some water. Also the blood was wiped from their faces. Their faces were both swollen from the vicious blows.

William asked both fighters if one would like to yield and end the fight. The crowd began to scream again and both fighters met for another round. The men fought for almost two hours when the fighter from the area of Baptist Valley gave the other a vicious blow to the nose and down he went, to stay this time. William McGuire went over and counted over the downed man to the count of ten. He grabbed the winners hand and asked, "Where do you want the new county seat?"

While some were helping the fallen fighter up, seats were provided for the two warriors and their faces were washed. They were offered water or corn whiskey. Both chose whiskey and sat beside each other to rest. Both fighters patted each other as a compliment and took in some of the spirits. While this was going on most every man there took a drink of corn whiskey.

William McGuire went to the winner and asked again, "Sir you have won the contest, you get to choose where the new county seat will be, what say ye?"

The winner who looked like he was a loser because of his bruised body spoke up saying, "Mr. Perry and Mr. Ferguson have agreed to give land for a new town. They want to call it Jeffersonville and build a court house there."

William McGuire turned to find William Perry and Samuel Ferguson and asked that they come up to address the people.

"Is this right, you two gentleman offering ground to build a town and courthouse?" Asked William McGuire?

Both gentlemen agreed to give the land, but insisted that they call it Jeffersonville in honor of the Virginia Statesman and newly elected President of the United States, Thomas Jefferson.

COLONEL CHARLES DAHNMON WHITT   275

THE PATRIOT, HEZEKIAH WHITT

"Please tell the folks where this place is," said William McGuire.

"It is on that little ridge just south of us," said the fighter as he stood and pointed toward the tract of land that is now the town of Tazewell.

The whole group of the new Tazewell County Constituency cheered, because they all knew the sight was won fair and square.

Hezekiah, Thomas Christian, John Hankins, and seventeen year old James Whitt had rode there together and were not really for the method picked to choose a county seat, but all were happy with the location.

John Hankins said, "No more a going to Castlewood jest to pay taxes!"

Hezekiah and Thomas both smiled in agreement.

"Paw, will the fighters be all right?" asked James?

"I reckon so, they both have been in some purty bad scraps!" replied Hezekiah.

Hezekiah was now a prominent man in the new county of Tazewell. The Governor was looking for upright, Christian Men that would be fair to the people and do a good job in the local government. Governor James Monroe included Hezekiah in a list of appointed Gentlemen Justices of the Peace. The appointments would be for life.

There were seven justices living in the areas of Russell and Wythe Counties when the formation of Tazewell County came about. David Hanson, Henry Bowen, and David Ward from Russell County: Samuel Walker, William Neal, George Perry, and Robert Wallace from Wythe County. By law these gentlemen became part of the government of Tazewell County. They had authority to organize the new county government before the new justices were appointed. First court in Tazewell was held at the home of Henry Harman Jr. on June 12, 1800. He was compensated $2.00 for it.

During the September term in 1800, John Perry asked for and was voted the permission to build a water grist mill. The justices agreed that they needed a mill near Jeffersonville, but had concerns about the fishes in the Clinch River. There were an abundance of fine fishes in the Clinch and if a dam was built that would stop the migration of the fishes. The justices told John Perry that he had leave to build the mill if he would build a slope in the dam so the fishes could migrate up stream. The mill would be built about a mile below Pisgah.

John Perry knew that Hezekiah Whitt came from a family of mill rights. John contacted Hezekiah for consultation. Hezekiah knew the basic workings of a water grist mill and agreed to help with advice.

The roads in the new county were very poor because of their distance from their former county seats of Wythe and Russell County. Tazewell County wanted more than traces

THE PATRIOT, HEZEKIAH WHITT

with cleared trees. They needed graded roads with crushed stone. This would be the number one problem besides building a court house and jail.

The September term brought nine new appointments for Gentleman Justices' of the peace. Governor James Monroe had sent appointments to these upstanding gentlemen. Justices' were men of high character, sound common sense and very patriotic.

> *"John Perry, Joseph Davidson, Thomas Witten, William George, John Thompson, (Hezekiah Whitt,) Thomas Gillespie, Hezekiah Harman, and John Tollett produced a commission from his Excellency the governor appointing them justices of the peace in and for the County of Tazewell and thereupon they took the necessary oaths of office accordingly."*

The Governor of Virginia at the time was James Monroe.

The November 1800 term brought three more appointed justices. William Hall, James Brown, and James Thompson and they took their oaths. This made a total of nineteen justices' of the peace for Tazewell County. Hezekiah Whitt was marked present at the November, 1800 term.

Hezekiah Whitt paid his land tax to the new county and was listed with two sons over the age of sixteen.

In the July 1801 term of Tazewell County the rates for taverns was set:

Dinner	*.25 cents*
Breakfast and Supper	*.17 cents*
Lodging with clean sheets	*1 Shilling*
Whiskey @ ½ pint	*1 Shilling*
Rum, French Brandy, Wine @ ½ pint	*.25 cents*
Cider, Beer, or Mathalgalum @ quart	*1 Shilling*
Peach or Apple Brandy @ ½ pint	*.25 cents*
Corn, Oats, or Barley by gallon	*1 Shilling*
Stable for Hay or Fodder 12 hours	*.12 ½ cents*
Pastourage 12 hours	*.12 ½ cents*

It was Virginia law at the time for each county to set the rates for taverns and stables. The prices set for Tazewell County were quite fair.

If you are wondering what "Mathalagalum" is, it is made from boiling honey and water and fermenting it. By the way honey bees are not indigenous to this country. The Spanish, French and English brought honey bees to America. The Indians called them "White Man Flies."

In the term of September 1801 contracts for work in the county were awarded.

William Smythe (Smith) to build a jail.	$220.00 dollars.
William Williams to build a court house.	$938.00 dollars
Joseph Moore to lay off lots in Jeffersonville.	$12.00 dollars

THE PATRIOT, HEZEKIAH WHITT

Taverns were important to the people of Tazewell County for meeting places and for lodging on court days. Thomas Perry was the first to open an *"Ordinary."* (Early name for Tavern.) He opened it on December 7, 1800 at his home in Jeffersonville. By April 3, 1802 there were three Ordinaries.

Things had changed so much around Tazewell County since its formation. Hezekiah Whitt was considered a Gentleman and regarded with respect. He began to dress better when he went to Jeffersonville for business. He was still a farmer and a great family man.

In the April 1801 term at the court house Hezekiah Whitt and James Wilson were appointed to view the workmanship of the jail and make a report. They reported that the work was being done agreeable to them.

Rachel and the children were so proud of Hezekiah. They all knew he was a good upstanding man, now the Governor of the Commonwealth and local prominent folks recognized Hezekiah Whitt as such.

Not only did Tazewell County get a new capital, but the United States was beginning to move into her Capitol. On June 4, 1800 John and Mrs. Adams moved into the White House in Washington City. On November 17, 1800 the Capitol was complete enough for the Congress to hold its first session there.

March 4, 1801 Thomas Jefferson becomes first President to be inaugurated in Washington D.C.

March 7, 1801 Massachusetts enacts a law that voters have to be registered.

November 10, 1801 the Commonwealth of Kentucky outlaws dueling and they still ask if you have fought a duel in the Kentucky oaths for office.

On March 16, 1802 the United States Military Academy at West Point, New York was established.

March 1, 1803 the Ohio country became the 17th State in the United States.

April 30, 1803 the United States doubles in size with the Louisiana Purchase from France for the price of $27,000,000. This was a great opportunity and Thomas Jefferson grabbed it. France needed the money for war debts.

On the tax list of Tazewell County in 1803, Hezekiah was listed with 360 acres, 2 white males over 16, and 7 horses. Also his son James Whitt was listed over 16 and no horses.

On March 10, 1803 at the court house a case of William Cecil versus. Timothy Roark was given by consent of both parties; to be heard by Hezekiah Whitt, William George, John I. Trigg, and William Neil. Their judgment shall be the judgment of the court.

Hezekiah began to rely on the children to do much of the farm work since he had added duties at the courthouse in Jeffersonville. The children were all growing up and there was not a slacker in the bunch. Hezekiah and Rachel's children's ages in 1803 were, James 20, Griffy, 16, Richard 12, John Bunyan 9, Rebecca 8, Susannah 7, and Jonas was 6.

Much of the schooling took place through the cold days of winter. Rachel taught the children much, but Hezekiah was the teacher of the three "R's." Both parents took time to teach and to have regular Bible study at night or on long cold winter days. Each child learned to read the Bible.

Hezekiah along with the other farmers in Tazewell County was very self supporting. But being self supporting did not bring in much money. At first the farmers devoted all of their time to growing grain, but there was no market for the excess grain. The farmers began raising horses, cattle, sheep, and hogs. They could feed them the excess grain and through the summer they flourished on the natural blue grass in the cleared pastures.

The folks in Tazewell County began to drive the herds east and south and bring back good profits of gold and silver. Some of the cattle were sent to Europe. Europeans were amazed at the size and quality of the Tazewell County beef. Horses too, were of good quality. They raised both the big draft horses and also the fine riding horses.

Another thing the farmers did was to plant orchards of apple, pear, and peach trees. The climate and soil quality produced bounty crops of fruit.

I said they were self supporting, by this I mean they made linsey-woolsey, jeans, tow-linen, flax seed thread. They made carpets and bed linens and quilts. They or their neighbors made most everything they needed. They made leather products such as saddles, boots, shoes, they did some iron founding and even made baked bricks. (I have a home made nail forged on the Hezekiah Whitt farm and also a brick baked on the same farm, over 200 years ago.)

Everyone was not an expert at everything, but in the numbers of people there were experts at most everything. Special tools were at a shortage, but there was always one that could be borrowed from a neighbor.

The people were good neighbors that did not meddle in others business. This was a way of life that started with the first settlers. The first settlers came to the wilderness to get away from the over bearing rules of the British. They came so they could worship God in the way they thought best. They came through the rough mountains and crossed the swift streams, for chance to obtain land and work it the way they wanted. Basically the whole concept of coming to the wilderness was based on freedom. I said they did not meddle, but all the folks in early Tazewell County were always ready to reach out a helping hand to anyone that needed it.

Hezekiah would perform his first wedding on October 27, 1801. Edmund Price Whitt, the brother of Hezekiah, went to Hezekiah and asked him if he would marry him and Mrs. Hanna Lester Skaggs.

THE PATRIOT, HEZEKIAH WHITT

Hanna was a widow with two daughters, Nancy Skaggs 12 years old, and Martha Patty Skaggs age 10. Hanna was a beautiful lady and had wound Edmund up around her finger.

Edmund was 33 and Hannah was 28 and both needed a mate. Edmund had dodged matrimony several times. Now he was sure that he wanted Hannah.

Rachel and the other ladies got together to plan the wedding. It would be held at the Hezekiah Whitt home and Justice Hezekiah would officiate. Hezekiah borrowed a book from William McGuire that had the written words of Christian Marriage. He got his Bible and looked up a verse or two to read at the wedding. Hezekiah was honored, but nervous about officiating.

Tuesday, October the 27, 1801 rolled around and the wedding party gathered at 10:30 AM in the sitting room. The ladies had decorated the room and hung Hezekiah's Betsy Ross Flag on the wall behind where the Justice would stand. Two pillows with fancy covers were placed on the floor in front of Hezekiah. The bride and groom stood before Hezekiah. Nancy and Martha Skaggs stood beside their mother, and James Whitt stood beside of his uncle Edmund.

Hezekiah had the bride and groom face each other as he we went through the I wills and I dos. Then he had them kneel on the pillows and Hezekiah read the Twenty Third Psalms. James almost laughed out loud when his paw read about the valley of the shadow of death. Most all of them grinned at the passage Hezekiah had picked.

Finally Hezekiah had them stand and pronounced them husband and wife. The couple kissed and was led to the cake that Rachel had made for them. The wine was brought out and many folks made a toast to the new couple that Hezekiah announced them as Mr. & Mrs. Edmund Whitt.

After the wedding party cleared out, he asked what was so funny when he read the Bible passage. Rachel told him that the Twenty Third Psalms was usually read at funerals. You made it sound like marriage was like going through the valley of the shadow of death!

"Oh my! I never thought of that," answered Hezekiah.

"Don't worry Paw, "Griffy said, "You did a wonderful job and now Uncle Edmund is hitched!"
Rachel smiled at her beloved husband.

Nancy and Martha would spend the night with the Hezekiah Whitt family to give the new couple a private wedding night. James and Griffy had a plan for a "Chivalree."

James was noticing Nancy Skaggs as she was a mature 12 years old. Griffy and Martha Polly Skaggs also hit it off. They found sitting at the table playing games of Checkers

THE PATRIOT, HEZEKIAH WHITT

and the new game of Dominos to be real fun! Up to now Griffy only put up with girls and now he was beginning to see a whole other side of the female persuasion.

The girls wanted to join James and Griffy and the other folks in a Chivalree for their Maw and new Paw.

Chapter 32

Antebellum

Edmund took his bride, Hannah, to his cabin that was just but a couple of miles from the Hezekiah Whitt home.

James Whitt was the leader of the chivalree and he was joined by Griffy, Richard, John Bunyan and the Skaggs sisters. Nancy and Martha Polly Skaggs were excited as the boys. They all gathered every noise makers possible from pot and pans to cow bells. They started out about a half an hour before dark, taking a couple of candle lanterns for the trip back.

They reached the Edmund Whitt house just after dark and there were no light showing from the windows. The chivalree was begun by forming a circle around the cabin and being close to every window and door. At a signal from James they all made as much noise as possible.

Candles were lit in the cabin and the dim light shown from the windows. The chivalree was kept up until Edmund and Hannah cracked open the door and waved to the joyous youngsters.

James was joined by all the others in front of the cabin to see the slightly embarrassed honeymooners.

"All right, you all done your duty, now go home and we will see you tomorrow," said Edmund.

The youngsters cheered and began their trip back to Cedar Grove. They made all the noise they could as they walked away with their lanterns lighting their path. James walked with Nancy and Griffy walked with Martha Polly. The children all had a good time and it even thrilled the honeymooners with the interruption.

Hezekiah and Rachel wanted to know all about it when the youngsters got back. Even Rebecca, Susannah, and Jonas were excited even though they didn't get to go. All were tired, but wound up from the days excitement.

Thomas Jefferson wasted no time in sending a party to explore the new Louisiana Purchase. He sent Lewis and Clark and a group of men to explore the new lands. He also ordered them to find passageways to the Pacific Coast. Jefferson had in his mind to claim all of America. On May 14, 1804 Lewis and Clark left Saint Louis to explore the unknown western lands.

Thomas Jefferson was popular and was re-elected on December 5, 1804. Tazewell County voted overwhelming for Jefferson. The folks in the mountains believed

THE PATRIOT, HEZEKIAH WHITT

Jefferson had the same ideas as them and would best serve them as President. Doubling the size of the country didn't hurt any either.

In March 1804, Hezekiah Whitt, Richard Oney, William Oney, and John Hankins view the road across Rich Mountain. Rich Mountain divides Jeffersonville from the Maiden Spring fork of the Clinch. This fork is now called Little River.

In June 1804, Hezekiah Whitt, Henry Bowen, and Thomas Gillespie were asked to view the estate of the deceased Joseph Belshee. Any of the three could do it.

A new or improved road was being built from Hezekiah Whitt's house to the county line. I think this was the Kentucky Turnpike that would be built all the way to the Kentucky line. It would climb Road Ridge out of Raven and then follow the Levisa Fork of the Big Sandy. (Burg of Raven wasn't there in 1804.)

Hezekiah and his entire family went to the John Perry Mill to get their corn ground and while they were waiting they planned a family fishing trip and dinner on the ground. It was a beautiful May day in 1804 and the Whitts got started early. The two Skaggs girls, Nancy and Polly were invited and could not wait to go.

While the corn was milling the Whitts settled on the bank below the dam and began to fish. They were having good luck right down to little Jonas. They were catching Redeye's, Sunfish, Bronze backs, Catfish and having a great time. Rachel even caught a Brook Trout.

Hezekiah put on a small fish for bait on his heavy line. Something grabbed his bait and just about tore the pole from his hands. He jumped up and followed the great fish up and down the Clinch doing everything he could not to loose this monster. It took some thirty minutes of fighting before anyone could see who the victor might be. Finally the big fish began to tire and Hezekiah pulled it close to the bank. All the Whitts were cheering with excitement as Hezekiah pulled it closer to the bank and James got into the water and helped land the monster. It was a good five feet long and its head was a foot wide. They got it way up on the bank and Hezekiah put a rawhide rope through it gill and made sure it would not get away. It was a giant catfish with six inch whiskers. There would be a big fish fry at the Whitts tonight.

Nancy Skaggs praised James for his part in landing the great fish. Many folks stopped to see the monster at the mill and even at the Whitt home that afternoon. Edmund and Hannah came over and helped clean and cook the fish.

Griffy rode Blaze over to the John Hankins home and took them a mess of fish. He told John all about the giant Catfish. By this time the fish had grown to seven feet. John could see by the fish cuts it was a dandy, but doubted it was seven feet long.

Rumors were all over Tazewell County that Hezekiah had landed a giant catfish from below the John Perry Mill. It was sort of like the Griffy tale. The fish just kept growing and by now it was eight feet long. There would be many renditions of the fish tale and Hezekiah had a lot of fun with it.

THE PATRIOT, HEZEKIAH WHITT

Some happenings of 1805 & 1806:

On May 26, 1805, Lewis and Clark see the Rocky Mountains.

On June 5, 1805 it was recorded that a tornado struck in the southern Illinois area. Now this area is part of what is known as "Tornado Alley!"

On November 18, 1805 Lewis and Clark reach the Pacific Ocean. They were the first Americans to cross the continent.

On July 1806 Zebulon Pike began a trip to explore the American Southwest.

On September 23, 1806 Lewis and Clark are back in Saint Louis in the Missouri country.

On November 15, 1806 Zebulon Pike sights a high peak in the Colorado Country and names it "Pikes Peak."

A strip of ground in northwest Russell County wanted to be part of Tazewell County. The folks petitioned the General Assembly of Virginia and on December 20, 1806 it was approved.

This annex took in Jacob Francisco's Mill. The mill was located on a creek that is now called Mill Creek. Mill Creek empties into the Clinch River about half a mile down stream from the present town of Raven. There is a falls about one fourth of a mile up Mill Creek from the Clinch River and this is where the mill was located. I was raised about an eighth of a mile from the falls. I have seen the old mill stones.

The annex also took in the house and property of one Daniel Horton. The new county line ran with Mill Creek and then a straight line to the Kentucky border.

Lumber was plentiful, just for the cutting and milling. Now there was a saw mill on the Clinch and Hezekiah decided to modernize his cabin. If you remember, the cabin was two separate cabins with a breezeway between them and covered with one common roof. Hezekiah would cover all the structure with weatherboard and add some windows; He would add a lower porch and a second floor porch. With all the modern homes being built, the Justice wanted to make his home fit in. Hezekiah would add six columns across the front porch to support the roof and part of the second floor. The whole house would be whitewashed and it was truly a southern mansion, at least for the western part of Virginia. These old homes were part of what they called the antebellum period in the south.

Hezekiah set up a small forge and made molds to pour in iron. The product was nails that resemble horseshoe nails.

Hezekiah also built a brick baking oven to make red brick. He eventually had a fine home that stood for over 200 years. The brick were laid up for underpinning of the front porch, and of course the nails were used wherever they were needed in the building project. All of the Whitt sons took an interest in learning the building trades. Jonas Whitt, but nine years old was always right in the middle of any building works. He

THE PATRIOT, HEZEKIAH WHITT

seemed to have a special trait in building and handling tools. This early learning and his natural abilities would serve him well in later life.

There would be two roads to the Hezekiah Whitt home. One came through his property that crossed what is called Green Mountain and the other was in front of his house that was called the Kentucky Turnpike. Hezekiah's great limestone spring became a popular stopping place for the travelers. They could water their animals and visit with the Whitt family.

Now what did the antebellum period mean? It was taken from the Latin language. *Anti* meant before and *Bellum* meant war. Thus it meant the period from the birth of the United States to the American Civil War. This was mostly a happy time and a time of industrial revolution. It was a time of increased exploration and a time of great increase in the use of slaves in the Deep South. The use of the cotton gin to free up so many hands made it possible to grow much more cotton which had a great market in Europe. The raising and selling of cotton expanded so much that they gave it the name of, "King Cotton."

Education was brought to the front as a great need for the people of a voting democracy. Many of the frontier families were illiterate. It was also a great period of religious increases and revival!

The Antebellum period gave the rich folks time to enjoy the arts and enlightenment. The western counties of Virginia was always a little behind the eastern counties in progress mostly because of their isolation in the mountains. The folks in Tazewell County would not trade their beautiful mountains and streams with any.

By 1806 Edmund and Hannah had two children, Rachel Rebecca and Richard Price Whitt. Archibald and Hannah Lowe Whitt had eleven children by 1806.

The 1806 land tax posting showed that Hezekiah had 85 acres, 260 acres and 44 acres.

There was a lot of overlapping in land claims in these early days. On January 25, 1806 term at Tazewell Courthouse an order was made for Sidney Hanson, Hezekiah Whitt & Rachel, his wife, be bound in a recognizance to appear at the next District Court held at Washington Courthouse to give evidence on behalf of the Commonwealth against John Deskins.

Some happenings of 1807:

On February 19, 1807 the vice president, Aaron Burr was arrested in Alabama country for treason.

On March 25, 1807 British Parliament voted to abolish the slave trade.

On May 22, 1807 Aaron Burr is tried for treason in Richmond, Virginia. He was accused of trying to set up an empire. He was acquitted.

On June 22, 1807 the British boarded the United States Ship, Chesapeake; this would lead up to the war of 1812.

THE PATRIOT, HEZEKIAH WHITT

On August 17, 1807 Robert Fulton steamed up the Hudson River on his new invention, a steamboat. Robert added a steam engine to a boat and this would be a revolution in the use of steam engines. By September 4, 1807 Fulton began operating his steamboat commercially.

All of these happenings gave the folks something to talk about. Jonas was thrilled to hear of steamboats and other inventions.

"Paw, do you think they will ever make a flying machine?" asked Jonas.

"Well son I hear they have some big bags filled up with hot air that will carry a man up into the heavens, but I don't think man will fly like birds," answered Hezekiah.

"I hear that some of them congressmen are described that way," said Rachel.

"Like what?" asked Hezekiah?

"Like big bags filled with hot air," laughed Rachel.

Hezekiah smiled and said, "I guess you might be right about some of-um!"

If you have forgotten that Hezekiah started growing tomatoes a few years back, he has had good luck with them. The myth about the pretty red fruit being poison has been disproved. It seems like they are in every garden in Tazewell County and the folks have become very fond of them.

In the early spring of 1808, When James Whitt was 26 and Griffy Whitt was 21, Hezekiah and Rachel decided to sell them 160 acres each for a modest sum. Both Hezekiah and Rachel had thought it over and decided it would be better to sell the land to them instead of giving it as an out right gift. It would make them feel more responsible.

Hezekiah quoted his father whom he had heard several times say, "Children should not be given everything, it will spoil them and they will get the idea that others owe them a living!"

Hezekiah was not really worried that he would spoil his sons, but thought they would appreciate the land if they paid something for it. The land was on Reedy Ridge and contained 260 acres.

In the Tazewell County deed book #1, pages 378-380, recorded on March 12, 1800.

Indenture made 12th day of March1808 Between Hezekiah Whitt and Rachel his wife, of the County of Tazewell on part and James Whitt on the other part…Hezekiah and Rachel sold James Whitt 130 acres for the sum of five pounds, a track of land deeded to Hezekiah by John Fowler on 12th day of May 1783

COLONEL CHARLES DAHNMON WHITT

THE PATRIOT, HEZEKIAH WHITT

containing 260 acres being on the Upper North Fork of Clinch River on Reedy Ridge. James Whitt's beginning on top of a ride at three white oaks...

Indentured made 12 th day of March 1808 Between Hezekiah Whitt and Rachel his wife of the County of Tazewell on the one part and Griffy Whitt on the other part...Hezekiah Whitt and Rachel his wife have granted, sold 130 acres for 5 pounds a track of land deeded to Hezekiah by John Fowler containing 260 acres being on Upper North Fork of Clinch River on Reedy Ridge Beginning at a buckeye, a Conditional Corner made by said Griffy Whitt and James Whitt...Signed Hezekiah Whitt, Rachel Whitt, and witnessed by James, Charles, and John Vandike.

The only drawback to owning land was there would be land tax to pay each year. On the tax list for Tazewell County in 1809 was listed Hezekiah Whitt 230 acres, Griffy Whitt 130 acres, and James Whitt 130 acres.

James Whitt and Nancy Skaggs were to be wed in June of 1808 and younger brother Griffy had already taken Patty Skaggs to be his wife on March of last year, 1807.

As you remember Nancy and Martha Patty Skaggs are the step daughters of Edmund Price Whitt and daughters of Hanna Lestor Skaggs Whitt. James Whitt was the older brother of Griffy and Nancy Skaggs was the older sister of Patty Skaggs..

So both young men need a spread of land in order to provide for their brides and prospective families.

Griffy and Patty would not waste much time in starting a family. On the 3rd of November 1808 Patty would deliver a son and they would call him Timothy Whitt. James and Nancy would never be blessed with children.

Justice Hezekiah Whitt would be officiating the wedding in June for James and Nancy as he did for Griffy and Patty back in March of 1807.

Hezekiah Whitt did not officiate at his little daughter, Rebecca Whitt's and John Husk Lowe's wedding. He and Rachel would not give permission at first. Rebecca was only thirteen years old when she married James Husk Lowe on December 13, 1807. (This was not too uncommon.)

Hezekiah had another Justice do the marriage, but Rachel and he was there. Rachel said, "there is no need in interfering, a young-un will do what her mind says."

"I hope they are in-love not just twitter patted!" replied Hezekiah.

On December 7, 1808 James Madison was elected the new United States President. George Clinton was elected as vice-president. The great experiment of the American Democracy was working. Another peaceful exchange of power took place in the White House.

Hezekiah and Rachel's son Richard Nelson Whitt is now seventeen years old. He has become the story teller and prankster of the family. His latest tale was about John Hankins hoeing in his garden. Richard said, "John was hoeing in his garden when he came upon a big Timber Rattler. The big snake took John by surprise and struck at him but missed and hit his hoe handle. The big snake slithered off out of the garden and into the nearby under brush. John was quite shaken but noticed that his hoe was getting heavy and even getting bigger. He threw down the hoe and stood there mesmerized at the sight. Before long the hoe handle grew to 30' long and had a diameter of 4'. The giant log took up most of his bean patch. John thought for a few minutes and came up with a splendid idea. He ran to the barn and got the mules all hitched up and a heavy logging chain. John got that big log and the straining mules pulled it to a saw mill. He had the log cut up into some fine boards and got them back home. He worked diligently for a few days and built a nice barn. John was so proud of his barn. He was tired so he didn't move any of his animals into the barn, but went home and slept all night long. He slept like a log!

Next morning John got up and could hardly wait to go and look at his barn again. Wow! To John's great shock the barn shrunk dawn so much the only thing he could use it for was a chicken coop!

Richard told so many tales and was always pulling pranks. He loved to spend time in the wooded hills in the beautiful Tazewell County. He noticed a man going and coming from Widow Smith's house. Richard made it a point to find out what this was all about. The man was a married man and he had been going to the Smith house to be of service to Mrs. Smith, if you know what I mean. The man was a Blankenship and he got a glimpse of Richard nosing around. Blankenship decided to follow Richard out into the woods and put the fear of God into him. Richard was quiet tricky and caught on quickly. He hurried quickly and climbed a steep bluff over the Clinch River. Blankenship was on the bank of the river and he hollered at Richard. Richard was way above the cheating man. Richard answered him.

"I'm up here, what do you want?" asked Richard?

Blankenship looked up on the rocky bluff to see Richard. How in the hell did he get up there he wondered!

"I got something to talk to you about, come on down se we can talk with out yelling," said Blankenship.

"Naw, you come up here I like it up here better," replied Richard.

Blankenship looked down at the ground and whispered, "Damn that Dick!"

Blankenship looked up and said, "Give me a little time and I will join you on your perch."
Richard watched as Blankenship began the climb the steep bluff. Richard knew these hills and woods better than most folks so he knew a quick way down to the river below. Blankenship huffed and puffed all the way to the top and did not see Richard. Blankenship hollered out, "Richard, where are you?"

THE PATRIOT, HEZEKIAH WHITT

By now Richard was standing on the bank of the Clinch River looking up at the top of the Bluff.

"Damn, Dick how did you get down there?" Asked Blankenship?

"I thought you wanted me to come down here," hollered Richard.
Blankenship's countenance fell as he was filled with anger and frustration.

"Dick, you stay right there and I will be right down, hollered Blankenship.

As soon as Richard saw Blankenship start down he hurried back up by his short cut to the summit of the rocky bluff. Blankenship arrived on the river bank and there was no Richard. Blankenship yelled out to Richard, "Where are you Dick?"

Richard answered from high above, "I thought you wanted me to come up here!"

By now Blankenship was steaming but very tired of climbing the steep bluff. He looked down at the ground and thought, "That stupid Devil Dick ain't gonna say anything anyway."

Blankenship didn't say another word as he headed down the river toward home.

Richard was far from stupid, he was as crafty as a fox.

With all the pranks and stories, folks gave Richard Nelson Whitt the nick name of "Devil Dick Whitt." Hezekiah was not too proud of that handle for his son, but knew it was given in a complimentary way!

THE PATRIOT, HEZEKIAH WHITT

Chapter 33

A New Threat To The Fledging Nation

The census was taken in Tazewell County in 1810 and every one wanted to make sure every soul was counted. The higher the number the better they would be represented in the Commonwealth and in Washington D.C. After all of the folks were tallied up the population of the big County of Tazewell was 3007 people. Slaves were counted only as onc half a person on the insistence of the Northern States.

The county had matured quite a bit since it was formed and the folks were basically happy. The roads were a constant problem, but there were now at least roads where there were just bridle trails. As I told you before, the road across Green Mountain came between the Hezekiah Whitt House and his fine limestone spring. In most cases Hezekiah was glad to allow folks a drink for themselves and their stock, but certain folks began to take advantage of the hospitality of the Whitts. Some folks thought the spring belonged to the county or State. There were some drovers, driving sheep and cattle and let them run rough-shod over the Whitt land and even tore down the spring house that Hezekiah had built. There was a little pool outside the spring house to be used for the travelers and their animals.

Hezekiah's patience ran low and he took his musket down off the wall over the fireplace and went to confront the drovers that were causing problems. Hezekiah made it a point that they were trespassing and damaging his property. Some of the feisty drovers had no idea who they were up against so they got belligerent and Hezekiah drew a bead on the leader. Also from the front porch Richard, Jonas, and John Bunyan leveled their muskets at the same time. The drovers were going toward Jeffersonville so they went on without as much as a by-you-leave.

The next day Thomas Witten came riding up to the Hezekiah Whitt house. He was one of the justices of the Court of Tazewell County.

"Hello Hezekiah, what happened here yesterday between you and some folks driving their stock through here?" asked Thomas?

Hezekiah got Thomas a cup of tea and they sat on the porch to discuss the issue. Hezekiah explained the whole problem of folks taking advantage of his hospitality and even wrecking his spring house and leaving manure all over the place. They let their cattle right in the part of my spring where we keep our milk and butter. Hezekiah explained that the sarcastic drovers got his dandruff up and he defended his spring and property.

Thomas suggested that Hezekiah come in tomorrow and clear this up as he was challenged in court for obstruction of a road. Hezekiah said he would head into Jeffersonville just as soon as he ate breakfast the next morning, being April 15, 1910.

THE PATRIOT, HEZEKIAH WHITT

"I will see you then, Hezekiah, I know we can get this thrown out," said Thomas Witten.

"I hope so, I was just defending my property, You know I agreed to let the road come through here, but I didn't agree to put up with a bunch of hoodlums," answered Hezekiah.

"Don't even think on it, I am sure it will be dismissed," replied Thomas.

"I aim to put up a sign, telling folks not to bother my spring house and respect my property," said Hezekiah.

"That will be a good idea," Thomas said as he wheeled his horse around and trotted up the Green Mountain road.

Next morning, the 15th of April 1810, Hezekiah was up and dressed in his court clothes. Rachel had him a nice breakfast fixed and after his second cup of coffee he was ready to ride. John Bunyan had Blaze saddled and tied to a porch column. Hezekiah kissed Rachel and she gave him a good bear hug.

Hezekiah said, "Now don't fret, everything will be fine, but if I ain't back by dark I'm in the fine jail I inspected. It is quiet strong!" laughed Hezekiah.

"Oh get on outta here fore I put you in jail myself," said Rachel with a wide smile.

Hezekiah enjoyed his ride across Green Mountain and forded the Clinch about the place now called Pounding Mill. He admired the beauty of the Clinch and the Mountains in his Tazewell County. He spoke to the Lord with Praise and Thanksgiving as he often did while Blaze carried him about.

Hezekiah met with several of his justice friends and they had a good talk, but none of the drovers had come back to back up their claims against Hezekiah.

They all went over to the Thomas Perry Tavern to have dinner and a drink of spirits. After dinner Hezekiah thanked them for dinner and the dismissal, and headed back to his Cedar Grove.

Once again the rumors of war were reverberating through the mountains and valleys of Ohio, Kentucky, and Virginia. The greatest of all Indian leaders, Tecumseh, had been at work for years. He had traveled to the deep south and out to the west and even to the northeast to sell his idea of deliverance to his Indian Brothers. He had torn down the walls between the tribes and it seemed the oration of the great leader was having a great impact on all Indians. He was gathering many tribes on the Tippecanoe River in the Indiana Territory. His message to all of his Indian Brothers was this. If we gather a great army we can make a peace with the white man through power. We can give the whites a choice, go back across the mountains or we will kill every one of you. The Indians Tribes were responding to Tecumseh. He spoke with authority and made all the Indians yearn for the old days before the encroachment of the whites. Tecumseh was a bit of a psychic and made many predictions. He got so good at it that he would tell his brother, Tenskwatawa who would tell the Indians and he acquired the name of Prophet. Tecumseh predicted a solar eclipse which stunned even the whites. He merrily said that it would get dark at noonday and the birds would go to roost and night animals would come out to forage. William Henry Harrison, the Governor and Commander-in-Chief of the Indiana Territory was quite concerned of the happenings of the Indians. He also wondered at the signs Tecumseh was showing the world.

Tecumseh's great sign for all the Indians to come together would be when he stomped his foot. When he stomped his foot at a time of his prediction the earth would shake and the rivers would run backwards, lakes would drain and new lakes would be formed. Great boulders would roll from the tops of hills and mountains; every Indian and white alike would feel the tremors and know it was a sign. Yes, Tecumseh was predicting a great earthquake in the eastern United States and far to the west where there had never been a recorded earthquake. When Tecumseh does stomp his foot and the earth shakes; even the doubtful Indian Tribes will become believers in the majestic Shawnee Chief.

The biggest mistake Tecumseh made was trusting his brother, Tenskwatawa. Tenskwatawa was ambitious and egotistical. While Tecumseh traveled about to far regions gathering support for his plan, the Prophet took charge and began to feel like he was the true leader. His duty was to keep all the tribes at peace and under no circumstance fight the whites until all the pieces were together. When Tecumseh would leave on one of his organizing trips, Tenskwatawa would parade around in his cape and decorated garb. He was one of three triplet brothers and was always in trouble. He had one eye poked out by an arrow he shot straight up while playing. Yes, it came straight back down and stuck in his eye. He had an ugly scar and usually covered it with a patch. When he wanted to show all of his grim features as a way of intimidation he would pull up the patch and show a wretched frown. Just wait and see this brother will be the undoing of Tecumseh's grand plan.

William Henry Harrison was communicating by messengers and written letters. He knew that if the Indians loaded up in canoes they could move swiftly down the Wabash River to Vincennes and the fort would be over run. Harrison was trying to make peace and buy time. He had respect for the Chief because of all he had heard about him. When he heard that Tecumseh had predicted the solar eclipse he made a statement;

"We will have hell to pay now," stated Governor Harrison.

He said that because of the predictions that many more of the red men would join the confederation of many Indian tribes.

August 12, 1810 Captain Floyd wrote a letter from his garrison about two miles above Vincennes.

Nothing new has transpired since my last letter except that the four hundred Indians have come; they passed this garrison, which is two miles above Vincennes, on Sunday last, in eighty canoes. They were all painted in the most terrific manner. They were stopped at the garrison by me, for a short time. I examined their canoes, and found

THE PATRIOT, HEZEKIAH WHITT

them well prepared for war in case of attack. They were headed by the brother of the Prophet, Tecumseh, who perhaps is one of the finest looking men I ever saw—about six feet high, straight, with large, fine features, and altogether a daring bold looking fellow. The governor's council with them will commence tomorrow morning...

The folks to the east and south waited for whatever bit of news that came their way. The unrest with the Indians and the old problems with the British was causing concern. The only good thing about the possible war was that it would be further away if it came, but they all knew it could fall upon them in time. The Tazewell County Militia was meeting and drilling. James, Griffy, John Bunyan, Richard and even Jonas were getting a taste of military. Hezekiah observed the meetings and probably would be called on to be an Indian Spy again if conditions worsened. He wondered if he would have the stamina and the skills to do this. After all Hezekiah Whitt was pushing fifty. He prayed daily for peace and for the problems of the United States to be solved without bloodshed.

Rachel and other Indians that had made their homes with white families through marriage and had accepted the white men's ways had mixed feelings. They didn't want war and they wished their people would be left alone by the United States. (It all boiled down that the Indians were in the way of the white men's progress.)

The council at Vincennes started out poorly. Tecumseh did not trust Governor Harrison and Harrison did not trust Tecumseh. Harrison had planned to meet near his mansion where there would be chairs and things would be handy, but Tecumseh thought a nice shady area under a grove of trees would be better. He told Harrison to bring chairs for the whites and his people would sit upon the earth. Harrison didn't like it, but the whites carried chairs to the grove and had a seat. All the Indians set cross legged except the Great Chief Tecumseh. Harrison sat in a big armchair and Winamac, the chief of the Potawatomi tribe stood beside Harrison. Winnemac was a foe of Tecumseh and had sided with the whites. He was jealous of the great Shawnee Chief and was there to serve as interpreter.

Tecumseh was a great speaker and he had a lot of stored up words for the whites. Tecumseh spoke boldly and pointed out that the whites were killing many Indians and stealing land from the Indians and still sitting back and saying they wanted peace. Tecumseh pointed to the whites and plainly said that the whites were pushing the Indians to do mischief. You are trying to stop the Indians from uniting, but you whites are united under the seventeen stars. (United States.)

Some of our village chiefs have been selling land to the Americans in which they have no authority. Our braves will deal with these unwise chiefs. The treaty made at Fort Wayne was made through threats of Winnemac; in the future we will deal with chief that sell our land that is not theirs to sell. Tecumseh cast eyes of daggers at Winnemac and he looked at the ground.

Tecumseh began to speak slowly to make a point on each issue. We plan a big council where all the chiefs that sold land to you that had no right will be there and we will decide how to deal with them. Listen to my words, if you do not I will assume that you want me to kill all the chiefs that have sold land to you. I have authority of all the tribes to do so.

Chief Tecumseh rarely showed a personal pride in his position, but he did this day to show that he was a warrior and head chief of the combined Indians.

At the council in a couple of months we will deal with the chiefs and if you (Governor Harrison) do not restore our lands, it is you that cost the chiefs deaths.

All the whites setting with the Governor became alarmed and whispers rose from them. Tecumseh and Harrison both raised a hand and silence fell on the crowd.

We did not come here to get presents, and if you offer we will not take any.

We have the council fires burning at the Huron village, and the guilty chiefs will be brought there to suffer from their bad conduct.

If you do not give us back our lands we can not have peace. You shall not cross further than your present settlement.

Tecumseh sensed that his words were bouncing off the ears of the palefaces. He abruptly slapped his hip and the clap brought back the attention of every one.

How can we trust the white man, Your God, Jesus Christ came to the earth and you killed Him by nailing Him to a cross. You thought you killed Him but he was not plumb dead. I am inspired by the Great Spirit and speak only the truth to you.

Harrison sat still and looked at on Tecumseh with an expressionless face.

You whites have been listening to bad birds. You may send a man to give us good news and if we think you offer presents out of true friendship we will accept them at that time. The Huron village is close to the British and we will visit them. If they offer us presents, we will not accept them after you have shown us your friendship and give us back our land. If the British offer us powder and tomahawks we will take the powder and leave the tomahawks. We want peace with our American Brothers, but you must act in peace and restore our lands and save the chief's lives.

Tecumseh took a seat in front of his warriors. Governor William Henry Harrison stood to address the Indians.

Right off the Governor denied that the Indians were one nation; he declared that when the whites came to America the Indians were spread out and each tribe had certain lands. He gave examples of location where certain tribes made their homes. If the great Spirit had wanted the Indians to be one nation why did He give them so many different tongues? The thoughts of many attending had to realize that this was true for the whites as well, French, English, Spanish, German, and many other languages were among the white race. Nothing was said at this time about one nation of many tongues.

THE PATRIOT, HEZEKIAH WHITT

The Shawnees have come from Florida to the land of the Miami's and dictated to them about the sell of land for the things they need.

Winnemac rose to translate what Harrison said for those that did not know the English language. Tecumseh understood every word and he did something he did not mean to do, He lost his temper and jumped to his feet.

Tecumseh screamed at Harrison about every point. Harrison was surprised and looked behind to see Winnemac priming his pistol in secret.

General Gibson was in the white contingent and understood Tecumseh's words. He sent Lieutenant Jennings back to the fort to bring up the guard.

Every one was on alert as both sides' brandished weapons. The Methodist Minister, Reverend Winans was there that day to observe and when all of this happened he ran to the house and grabbed a musket and stood guard at the door to protect the Harrison family if all hell broke loose. Jennings ran back with all the soldiers at the ready. Only a little hope prevented an all out battle from starting.

Harrison raised his hand to stop the guard and asked Winnemac what Tecumseh had said. He said you are a liar and that you and the seventeen fires had cheated and mistreated the red men.

Harrison stood his ground and told Tecumseh to take his people and leave in safety. The two sides parted company and after a nights rest, Tecumseh realized his temper was wrong. He got his interpreter to go back to Harrison and ask for another meeting, He regretted his uproar and wanted to explain the outburst. He did not mean to threaten the whites and wanted Harrison to know that.

Chapter 34

Tippecanoe

Governor William Henry Harrison agreed to another meeting with Tecumseh, but asked that only a small group of warriors and chiefs be his escort. This time Harrison had every man armed and ready for trouble.

Harrison opened the council by asking Tecumseh if he intended to stop the survey on the waters of the Wabash. Tecumseh had cooled from the day before and would answer directly, but dignified. He told Harrison that he was determined to keep the old boundary as before.

Harrison looked at the other chief hoping they would not agree with Tecumseh. The chiefs all took their time to address the Governor and plainly stated that they agreed with their head chief. They stated that the old boundary should be the one to go by and they would stand with Tecumseh. The chiefs present were heads of the Winnebago, Ottawa, Potawatomi, Kickapoo, and Wyandot tribes.

Harrison stood again and stated that he was glad to know the minds of his red brothers and felt that they were being honest. He turned to Tecumseh and told him that he would write the President a letter and explain your wishes as to the old boundary and your dispute over the lands the seventeen fires bought and paid for. I am sure that the President will not agree that land belongs to all Indians, but only to the tribes we dealt with and have lived on these lands as long as the white man can remember. I know that the President will protect these lands by musket and sword. Tecumseh with his chiefs and warriors left and went back to their camp only a couple miles upriver from Vincennes.

Now the Governor had some things to ponder. The more he thought about all that had transpired the more he felt he should have a private visit with Tecumseh. The next morning Harrison rode alone to the Indian camp and was received politely. He asked if could talk to Tecumseh alone and he agreed by taking the Governor for a short walk away from camp to the Wabash banks. The Governor said a few words of small talk and then asks Tecumseh if he truly meant what he said at the council.

Tecumseh told Harrison that he did not want to have war with the seventeen fires because I have no complaint except the purchase of our lands. I want to preserve the peace between the Indians and the Americans. If you make the President understand this and give us back our lands and only deal with the combined Indian nation I will be on your side even against the British. I know the British incite us to attack the Americans and use us as fighting dogs for their purpose. I would prefer to be friends of the Americans. The British only want to use us to fight their battles. Then Tecumseh turned to face Harrison and stated plainly and firm that if the President took a stand to claim all of the disputed lands he would have to go another way.

Harrison was holding his breath and he let it out in a blow as he began to answer. He told Tecumseh that he would tell the President of all of your propositions. He added that he doubted that the President would change his mind on the matter.

Tecumseh answered that he hoped the Great Spirit would put wisdom in the head of the President to have him give back our lands. Tecumseh continued by telling the Governor that the President is far away and would sat in his big chair drinking wine while you and I fight it out. The President is far out of arrow shot and even out of musket shot. He will not lose his hair but we are the ones that will be hurt. They looked at each other and both men knew that they would have a worthy foe.

William Henry Harrison sent salt up the Wabash to be shared with all the tribes. The Prophet (Tenskwatawa) was in charge because Tecumseh was away gathering support from distant tribes. The Prophet took all of the salt and the boat was back down to Vincennes in 24 hours. This upset Harrison, but also opened his eyes that the hundreds of warriors could descend on them in a very short time. He would take actions by requesting reinforcements and for permission to launch a strike on the unsuspecting Indians if he thought it prudent.

There was several Indians killed by settlers and several families attacked and burned through out the spring. Harrison knew that much of the trouble was caused by the white settlers.

Harrison felt better when the entire Fourth United States Regiment, led by Colonel Ben Boyd, arrived and was made even stronger by 65 volunteers from Kentucky.

Now the Governor could speak from strength so he penned a strong letter to Tecumseh and his brother at Tippecanoe. The letter went straight to the point that the actions of all the tribes gathering together alarmed the whites with a threat of war.

It has come to me from all direction that you plan mischief and even murder, even me he continued. The white people are arming themselves to defend and they will not be surprised by an attack. He asked if the Indians thought they could stand against the seventeen fires or even against the Kentucky fire. He stated that the Indians were brave, but by sheer numbers alone they would be wiped off the face of the earth. He stated that the seventeen fires did not want to hurt the red brothers. He wished them peace and happiness.

We sent a big boat of salt to share with all the tribes, but the Prophet took it all. I am shocked at his actions.

The people of the seventeen fires must be satisfied that you mean them no harm. You are planning to come and parlay with me and I welcome you, but I insist that you bring only a few of your young men. If you come strong in numbers I will not meet with you.

THE PATRIOT, HEZEKIAH WHITT

I still advice you that one or both of you should visit the President of the United States and lay your problems at his feet. If you can show that the whites have done injury to you the President will give you justice. If you do this the seventeen fires and I will see you are not just planning war.

As far as the lands purchase the President will deal with it, I would go to see him. I will give you the means to travel to Washington City.

Please don't harm my messenger as he is a good brave man. Harrison ended the letter and sent it fourth.

Captain Wilson was treated well and fed. Afterward Tecumseh wrote a letter in his own hand. He basically said that the Whites were alarmed needlessly. We both need not pay attention to all the bad stories. I mean you no harm and I hope you mean me no harm. He also said that he would come for a council in 18 days from this day.

We can only hope the Great Spirit will guide our feet. I hope we can wash away all the bad stories. I hope this letter will ease your worry. Let your people know I intend to bring peace and we can settle our problems then. If I can come early I will send a young man to advise you and he signed it and gave it to Captain Wilson.

Back in Tazewell County the people were staying on alert for bad news from Indiana. The Militia was still drilling and improving their defenses. The officers decided to have a shooting match to improve shooting and to see if they had anyone that needed help. They had every man shoot until the best ten were determined. Then they sat up ten 12" round barrel lids with a 1" black dot in the center and placed them 150 yards away on ten different poles. The officer marched the ten men out in front of the targets and gave them an order of left-face. Now all ten men were facing their targets. Ten men were picked to monitor each shooter and retrieve the targets after shooting was finished. Now there were ten men to shoot, ten targets and ten men to do the monitoring. The men took numbers from 1 to 10. Griffy Whitt was one of the ten finalists and placed as number 4 in the line.

The prizes were a silver dollar and a day off from drill for third place. The second place was a five dollar gold coin and two days off from drill. The first price was a whole ten dollar gold piece and three days off from drill and all supplied from a collection of officers and Justices.

Hezekiah Whitt along with many of the county Gentlemen to witness the match and Hezekiah was proud as punch that his Griffy was in the line of finalist.

The shooters were all called to attention and ordered to check their muskets. Then they were ordered to kneel and aim. They were to fire spontaneously on command as in battle. The officer in charge saw that all were ready and called out in a loud voice to fire. The muskets all went of and sounded almost as loud as a five pound cannon. Smoke rose from the black powder as the men looked toward the targets. The order was given to rise and check muskets. All had been fired. Then the ten monitors were released to retrieve the targets. Number one was to bring number 1 target and so fourth. The officer had the ten shooters reload while the monitors ran the one hundred and fifty yards down and back with the targets. Once the monitors were back the officer had each monitor stand by the corresponding shooter.

Three officers started with number 1 and looked at the target. Number one hit the target, but was 4" away from the black dot. They looked at each target and found that number 4 (Griffy) hit the edge of the dot, another man by the name of Brown was about ½" from the dot, and William Sims took out the dot. Griffy Whitt came in second place and this was an honor as he was up against some of the best shooters in Virginia and probably the whole United States. James, John Bunyan. Richard and Jonas presented themselves well as marksmen, but did not make the final ten.

The men really enjoyed the shooting match and did not realize they were doing target practicing. Hezekiah was one of the three to hand out the prizes and was really honored to hand Griffy the five dollar gold piece.

Rumors were flying all over the Western lands of Indiana and Ohio and even back east to Tazewell County, Virginia. The rumors were about the murders of many whites and also many Indians. Most likely it all started with the British instigators.

Governor William Henry Harrison sent word to Tecumseh not to bring many braves with him or he would not meet with him. Tecumseh brought only a fraction of what he brought the last time. He didn't want the settlers to think they were a war party, yet he was a leader of high rank and 270 men and 30 women was few in Tecumseh's eyes. The Chief and his people camped just north of Vincennes at the same place of the last council. Tecumseh took the chiefs and a selected group of warriors, a total of about 180, to the council. Harrison was on edge as he saw all the Indians with Tecumseh as was Tecumseh as he saw so many soldiers, fully armed, marching on the grounds around the mansion.

Governor Harrison started the talks by mentioning all the deaths of white settlers all around the Indiana and Ohio lands. He also talked about the alarm Tecumseh caused by bringing so many warriors with him down the Wabash after promising to only bring a few. Tecumseh begin to grizzle up in anger.

Tecumseh only brought a small group according to his position and rank as the head chief over several tribes. Tecumseh was insulted by Harrison's words and how he had been greeted. William Henry Harrison had no idea as to how close he was to death!

Harrison went right on to the land purchase disputes not noticing that the chief was extra "Red." Harrison stated that he could not talk about the boundary or giving back any land as it was in the hands of the President.

Then he went on about the seizure of salt by the Prophet when it was meant for all of the tribes.

THE PATRIOT, HEZEKIAH WHITT

Tecumseh now answers Harrison in a sarcastic manner as he explains that he was not in the town when it happened. The salt was refused the year before and this angered you, now we take the salt and this also angered you. You are very hard to please stated the chief.

Now the Governor flared up and stopped the meeting until the next day.

Next day about noon the Indians came to try and talk again. Before Harrison could start, Chief White Loon of the Weas Tribe stood and began to reflect and cover every treaty the Indians had ever had with the United States. He showed that the whites had played in deceit and never ever kept the bargain as was explained to the Indians.

The arrogant Harrison stood and quickly changed the subject and completely ignored Chief White Loon and thus handed him an insult. Harrison went on to demand from Tecumseh the two Potawatomi warriors that were supposed to have murdered some white men. Harrison explained that if he handed over the two they would be tried in the white man's court and this would show him the sincerity of the Indians for peace.

Tecumseh went to another subject telling Harrison that he had organized the Indian tribes just as the United States had done and gave them the example. The Indians did not complain of the white men forming the seventeen fires and why would the white men think it strange for the Indians to follow the example.

As for your demand for the two Indians for murder, this is false, the two whites were executed for killing two Wea Indians without an excuse. The white people are supposed to be following their God, Jesus Christ, in forgiving others. It seems you want the Indians to do all of the forgiving.

The council was closed and Tecumseh told Harrison that he was heading way to the south and would be bringing the Creeks, Cherokees, Mobiles and other tribes back with him to live on the lands around Tippecanoe. Tecumseh did not tell it all, he knew Harrison would jump on the chance to do something underhanded while he was gone. Actually Tecumseh would try and be back before winter. He told Harrison not to let more whites move to the north of Vincennes before he got back in the spring.

Harrison looked surprised, but said nothing as Tecumseh explained that in the spring he would go to visit the President and explain their desires. Both parties parted and the Indians went back to Tippecanoe.

Harrison hatched out an idea that while Tecumseh was gone for the winter there may be peace, if not it would be a good time to attack the Indians. Harrison had business calling him to Kentucky and it might be a good time to take care of it. This all took place in July 1811.

Tecumseh hand picked twenty warriors to travel with him to the south. He chose them for their bravery and some had abilities to converse with other tribes. They were ready to go just as soon as Tecumseh finished his talk with his brother Tenskwatawa, the Prophet. He looked into his eyes and made it plain that Harrison may attack or want concessions while he was gone. Do not fight, give concessions if you must. Keep preaching to our people and make everyone happy. If the long knives come, move out and scatter our people until they leave. Then Tecumseh asked three times if he understood. He affirmed he understood every detail. Tecumseh explained to him that once he was back all the pieces would be in place. I will stomp my foot as a signal for all of our red brothers to come. They all will feel the earth move when I stomp my foot. They will come from the far west, the south, and the north. Then I will go to the President and demand our rights and all of our land back or else. Tecumseh rode out with his young men bound for Georgia, Alabama, and the Tennessee country.

Pride and arrogance rose in the heart of Tenskwatawa almost before Tecumseh rode out of sight.

Governor William Harrison sat down and wrote a letter late in July 1811 to Secretary of War Eustis, describing the last meeting and the man, Tecumseh.

> *The implicit obedience and respect which the followers of Tecumse pay him are wonderful. If it were not the vicinity of the United States, he would perhaps be the founder of an empire that would rival in glory Mexico or Peru. No difficulties deter him. For four years he has been in constant motion. You see him today on the Wabash, and in a short time hear of him on the shores of Lake Erie or Michigan, or on the banks of the Mississippi; and wherever he goes he makes an impression favorable to his purpose. He is now upon the last round to put a finishing stroke to his work. I hope, however, before his return that part of the work which he considered complete will be demolished, and even its foundation rooted up.*

I remain, Sir, Your Most Obedient Servant,
William H. Harrison

Tecumseh took bundles of red sticks and gave some to each tribe he visited.

Back before the bundles were large, but now they were getting smaller.

He had gained fame with the Cherokee, Seminoles, Lower Creeks, the Santee's, Catawba's, Choctaws Biloxi's, Chickasaws, Alabama's, and the Mobiles as he gave them a bundle of red sticks. Some tribes wanted a sign now and he always came up with one. The Seminoles doubted him and he told them to go to the sea at a certain point on the Florida coast and they would receive guns and power from a ship. They went and a British ship was waiting for them and gave them what they wanted. They were believers now.

Next Tecumseh headed to the land across the Mississippi to visit the Upper Creeks, Natchez, Caddos, Tawakiois, and Yazoo and more. Those that had doubts of this Shawnee chief he would tell them of the great sign. He told them when he got back to the north and each red stick had been burned watch and listen. He would stomp his foot and their houses would fall. This will be the time to come and join the whole Indian Nation.

Back at Tippecanoe half a dozen warriors, of several tribes, bent on mischief came and ask the Prophet if they could sneak down to Vincennes and steal a horse apiece undetected. All the tribes had learned to work together. Tenskwatawa knew better, but he let them go as if it was his idea.

The Indians returned in a few days with their horses and bragging about the affray. Next day rode in fifteen armed white men whom had followed the horse prints to Tippecanoe. They rode in and spoke to the Prophet demanding the horses be returned.

Tenskwatawa laughed it off as if saying boys will be boys, but the soldiers didn't think it was funny. They took the horses and headed back down the Wabash.

Tenskwatawa went to his *wegiwa* to think about what happened and came out in a short time. He called the people together and told them he had a vision. The vision was for him to send a large group of warriors to intercept the whites and get the horses back. He told them none would be harmed and that the horses were theirs. In a short time about fifty warriors thundered out after the horses the whites had come and stolen.

The warriors came up on the fifteen white men at their night camp and rode right in. They took the six and also the fifteen horses the white men rode. They set the whites to foot and told them to never come back to Tippecanoe.

William Henry Harrison waited for such an excuse as this and Tecumseh was not at home. In three weeks Harrison was leading his 900 man army toward Tippecanoe.

Tenskwatawa worked the Indians into frenzy and they were ready for a fight. Tenskwatawa had told the warriors that the white man's bullets would not strike them. The plan was drawn up that the chiefs of the different tribes would go and talk to the Governor whom now had his army stationed on a nearby hill. The chiefs would make any concession the Governor demanded and leave except for two. The two lingering chiefs were to yank out their pistols and kill William Henry Harrison and this would start the battle.

During the dark night Tenskwatawa danced around as if in a trance and acted as if the Great Spirit had his mind. He came abruptly back to himself and said that half the white soldiers are crazy and the other half are dead. You need only to go in and finish them off with tomahawks.

Tenskwatawa couldn't wait until the daylight. He sent them, at least 1000 painted warriors, to attack the Shemanese. It was around 4:00 AM on November 7, 1811 and Harrison was putting on his boots to call the men to rise. A shot rang out and a soldier shot an Indian that was sneaking up on him. The soldiers had slept with their muskets in their hands and rose quickly. The fires were put out and the battle was on. They fought in darkness as they tried to determine who was friend or foe. Screams, gun blasts disturbed the quiet night. Even the hacking and slamming of war clubs and tomahawks made the eerie sounds of bones crushing.

The Governor jumped on his horse and rode from one place to another directing his men. He rode to the hottest places of the battle and had his hair parted and a ball through the brim of his hat, but no ball hit him anywhere else. His bravery stopped a clear victory by the Indians.

Tenskwatawa stood on a hill, out of range of the battle, danced, chanted, and screamed encouragement to the warriors. He had it in his mind that the warriors were winning a great battle. Some of the Indians ran to Tenskwatawa and told him that the bullets were indeed killing the warriors. He just kept chanting and urged the warriors to fight on. Tenskwatawa screamed louder even then the gunshots and screams of battle. The Indians believed the Great Spirit was protecting them and rushed right into awaiting bayonets. In the gray dawn it became so apparently clear that the Great Spirit was not helping the red warriors. The Indians regained their wisdom and disappeared into the nearby woods.

After the battle 188 bodies laid all about. Only 38 were Indians, yet it was a victory for Harrison and his army. Tenskwatawa had undone many years of work by Tecumseh in only one night. The battle was over and Tecumseh would be enraged to the point of murder when he would hear the news. The news of the victory would spread like wild fire to the east and south. Now what tribe could put confidence in the brothers, Tenskwatawa and Tecumseh?

Kentucky, Ohio, Pennsylvania, and Virginia would be pleased to hear of the great victory.

THE PATRIOT, HEZEKIAH WHITT

Chapter 35

Tecumseh Stomps His Foot

The men at the Tazewell Court House in Jeffersonville talked and retold the stories of the great hero, William Henry Harrison, and how he demolished the Indian Confederation at Tippecanoe. Now if the British would just leave the United States alone.

In the year of 1811 Hezekiah received a letter from his father, Reverend Richard Whitt, which by reading between the lines Hezekiah could see his father was not doing too well. He decided he had better take the trip back to Meadow Creek while he could. The Indians were squelched for a time and Richard may not live too much longer. It was the time of harvest so he decided to leave the family home so he could travel faster and get back before the snows began. Jonas had not seen too much of Montgomery County and asked his father if he might go with him. Hezekiah asked if the Perry Mill could do with out him as he worked there most everyday. Jonas informed Hezekiah that he could get permission to go and he wanted to talk to grand paw Richard about mill building. You can go with me, but your grandfather may not be able to talk much about the mill. He told Jonas that his uncle, Archibald and others may be of some help. He told Jonas that the good Reverend may be really sick, after all he was 86 years old.

Jonas was 15 years old and very handy with horses and at home in the woods. Hezekiah had taught all the boys about tracking and living off the land. He had given them a good education for the mountains of Virginia. Jonas as per most boys was not too happy to sit and learn the three "R's," but he faired well in his schooling. He wanted to be a mill right and carpenter and was handy with tools.

Hezekiah and Jonas headed toward Rocky Gap on November 15, 1811, it was a cold morning, and they both rode fine horses and had a pack mule to carry their gear. They made good time in the brisk air and were not too concerned with bandits and not at all with Indians.

They rose on November 16, 1811 and felt something they had never witnessed before. The earth shook under their feet and alarmed the horses. There were rocks rolling down the hills and the sky was filled with birds that were scared from their perches in the trees and bushes. A herd of deer bolted from the woods and almost ran over the Whitts, while they were trying to calm their horses.

"Paw, what on earth is happening?" asked an alarmed Jonas?

"It has to be an earthquake," said an excited Hezekiah.
"Paw, wasn't that the sign that Tecumseh said he would give, I thought they were all beaten by Harrison," said Jonas.

THE PATRIOT, HEZEKIAH WHITT

"Well son, I just don't pay too much attention to all the tales coming out of Indiana, I doubt this shaking of the earth has anything to do with that Indian," said Hezekiah trying to sound convincing.

"I sure hope it didn't brother anything back around home," said Jonas.

"Me to, we better get on the trail, I doubt it will happen any more," said Hezekiah.

Hezekiah and Jonas made good time and were in Meadow Creek on the big New River in a few days. They talked about the quake and wondered if it was just a local thing around Rocky Gap. Hezekiah and Jonas were greeted so warmly by the Whitts. The Reverend Richard had become so feeble, but still had a good mind. Things were so different to Hezekiah as he thought about the saying, "You cain't go home!"

Archibald's daughter Susannah was staying with the Reverend and Betsy Baxter Whitt and helping the aging couple. Susannah laid eyes on Jonas and his eyes met hers. There was a spark of electricity between the two. Jonas thought Susannah was the prettiest girl he had ever seen. Susannah was very attracted to Jonas. During the time they stayed in Meadow Creek Jonas made it his business to talk with Archibald and others about the mill work and mill building and of course this put him close to the lovely Susannah Whitt.

After a good visit with the Whitts and some of the Skaggs, Hezekiah and Jonas would start back home. The talk of the earthquake came up several times during the visit. The quake was even felt on Meadow Creek and had shaken an oil lamp from a neighbors table and set a fire, but they were home and quickly extinguished it. Another farmer had an old leaning barn fall to the ground. Hezekiah had prayed for God's protection on Rachel and the folks back in Tazewell County so with his great faith he left it to God.

Jonas and Susannah took a little walk in the woods the evening before their departure to say goodbye. They agreed to write and stay in touch and the two embraced and Susannah kissed Jonas passionately on the lips.

"Jonas, please come back to me," Susannah said quietly.

"I will, just as soon as I can, do you think your Paw and my other uncles will train me the work of mill building?" asked Jonas.

"Yes Jonas, I will write you often until you come back to me," said Susannah.

They finally tore lose from each other and the next morning Hezekiah and Jonas headed for Tazewell County. Susannah did not come out and bid Jonas goodbye, she was afraid that her true feelings would come out and she would cry and cling to Jonas. Hezekiah was really glad to visit his father and other family. Reverend Richard would do well to last through the winter.

The quake had hit in Tazewell County, but little damage occurred. It was bad enough for everyone to notice it and some damage was done here and there. As the Whitts rode into Hezekiah's Cedar Grove Rachel and the others ran to greet them. The first thing she said was, "Tecumseh's earthquake happened here, did y'all feel it on the trail?"

"We sure did Maw," blurted out Jonas.

Hezekiah gave him a look that spoke volumes. Jonas knew better than to talk when a question was to his father, but youth and excitement had played a hand.

"Sorry Paw," Jonas said quickly.

Hezekiah nodded approval and began to talk to Rachel after he had kissed and hugged his beloved princess.

Back on Tippecanoe River it was as if a bomb had gone off. The Indians saw that the Prophet had no real power and they scattered. A strong group of the Indians that were loyal to Tecumseh started a new village on Wildcat Creek. In the center of the new town was an ugly little Indian tied to a pole, it was the Prophet, Tenskwatawa.

The old village was pillaged by Harrison's army and burned. They found cases of brand new muskets that had been given by the British. There was nothing left of "Prophet Town".

Cheers went up as a party of Indians entered the town on Wildcat Creek. It was their beloved leader, Tecumseh and his faithful braves. Tecumseh stopped his horse abruptly and dismounted. His hardened eyes had spotted his brother. Tenskwatawa had hoped that Tecumseh would take pity on him, but his hope was dashed as he saw his livid brother walking toward him with a big skinning knife in his hand.

Tecumseh jerked Tenskwatawa's head around by gripping his hair. He laid the sharp blade to his exposed neck and pulled it slightly and drew a trickle of blood that slowly moved down to the base of his neck. Tenskwatawa thought he was dead fore sure! Tecumseh shoved him to the ground and stood to face his friends that had saved a remnant of his Confederation.

Death for the Prophet was too good, in a single day he had destroyed ten years of work. He had caused pain and coming destruction to all Indians as the great plan was all but broken. Tecumseh cast his brother out to be scorned. He was no longer the Prophet, not a brother, not an Indian, not even a man. Tenskwatawa would have neither family nor people; he would die a little each day until the demons of the underworld came for him.

Tecumseh would have to go to plan "B" and he hated it so badly. He would have to join the British against the seventeen fires. Tecumseh believed that many of the brave warriors that had lost hope could be brought back.

Tecumseh was still guided by the Great Spirit. Two signs had been given. The earth shook on December 16, 1811 and the Mississippi River ran backward for a time. The other sign was in the night sky, a great Comet of greenish light had passed through the sky (Remember that Tecumseh's name means panther crossing the sky as a comet did cross the sky the night the great man was born.) and now the tribes were to take the last

THE PATRIOT, HEZEKIAH WHITT

red stick that had been given to almost all the tribes in two thirds of what is now the United States They cut it in to thirty pieces. A piece was burned each morning, now all was gone and the tribes would not have a fire until the great sign came. Indians to the far north, to the south to Florida, to the west beyond the Dakotas sat in the last night with no fire and waited. Of course the northern tribes were wrapped in blankets to ward off the winter cold. (Some of the tribes became know as the red stick people.)

On December 16, 1811 at about 2:30 AM, Tecumseh stomped his foot! The whole eastern half of the land now called the United States shook as if the Great Spirit was venting his anger. Tremors were felt all over America and it is still considered to be the strongest earthquake in history.

Creeks and lakes empted out and formed new paths and lakes, trees fell all over the land, huge boulders rolled down the mountains from Florida to way up in Canada. Reel Foot Lake on the Kentucky-Tennessee border was not a lake until on that faithful day when the earth shook so violently that millions of gallons of water spring up from the earth to form it. It is still there today. The Great Lakes churned with huge waves that came up over the highest banks. It shook as far as Yellowstone to the west. (Anvil Rock in Greenup County, Kentucky is documented as proof of this great sign. It lies at the foot of a hill near Lloyd, Kentucky to this day after rolling off the ridge above it.)

Wild animals and birds were scared from their beds and roosts, cattle in the fields fell to the ground. There was no doubt as to this great sign predicted by the great Chief Tecumseh. The center of the quake was near New Madrid, Missouri and is thought to be an 8 plus on the rector scale. This quake happened where there had never been one recorded before; no scientific explanation could be given. Only that the Great Tecumseh had stomped his foot.

There is no record to the lives lost or property destroyed, but if it happens today the cost may have been one million lives and billions of dollars lost in property. Memphis Tennessee would be leveled. Back in Tazewell County, Virginia many folks were shaken out of their beds and any weak structures hit the ground. Many rock houses in the cliffs of the mountains collapsed and some think that Swift's Silver Mine vanished this way.

The Whitts were up and quiet alarmed. Rachel spoke quietly to Hezekiah, trying not to scare the others in the house.

"It's Tecumseh's sign," she said.

Even Hezekiah knew something super natural was going on, could it be from God or could it be evil power from the devil?

The shaking on December 16, 1811 was only a starter. It lasted two full days and the sky was filled with a thick dust and smoke and even several days later the sun shown through a brown dingy sky.

COLONEL CHARLES DAHNMON WHITT

307

THE PATRIOT, HEZEKIAH WHITT

Many folks got down and prayed for forgiveness as they thought the end times were upon them.

Indians all around knew that the Great Chief Tecumseh was not a liar and he was truly ruled by the Great Spirit. Many of the Indians that had ran away after the Tippecanoe battle now would began to come back to Tecumseh.

The British were thrilled with the new circumstances and that the Indians would truly be their ally. Now with their promise to the Indians that they would help drive the Americans back across the Blue Ridge Mountains, was what the Indians wanted to hear. The Indians would be ready to fight the Shemanese when the British picked up the musket and tomahawk.

Was Tecumseh still stomping his foot? On January 23, 1812 another 7.8 earthquake hit near New Madrid, Missouri and again an 8.2 quake hit on February 7, 1812. Each quake had loosened up the ground, rocks, and trees and the eastern half of what is now the United States was in a jumble. The last quake was the worst and did the most damage. Who could doubt Tecumseh now, after all he had given the prediction months before that the people would feel the earth shake when he stomped his foot.

Back in Tazewell County, Virginia the folks were thinking it must be close to the time that Jesus was coming back to claim His Church. Jesus had give warning as to the signs of His coming in Matthew Chapter 24: Verses 6-7.

> 6. *And you shall hear of wars and rumors of wars: see that ye be not troubled: for all these things must come to pass, but the end is not yet.*
> 7. *For nation shall rise against nation, and kingdom against kingdom: and there shall be famines, and pestilences, and earthquakes, in divers places.*

Hezekiah looked up this passage as it was so much on his mind. He read it to Rachel and some of the children that were around that evening.

"It sure looks like all of this is coming to pass," said Rachel.

"We are having wars and rumors all around the world and it looks like the British and the Indians are going to challenge us again," said Hezekiah.

"Yes it does and we sure have had the earthquakes and pestilences, and there are famines in some places," exclaimed Rachel.

"We have to be ready for the wars and for the coming of our Lord," replied Hezekiah. Then he had a long prayer of praise, thanksgiving, and of repentance.

All we can do is pray, follow the Lord Jesus Christ and be ready to fight our enemies when they come.

Back in the Indiana territory the Indians that had deserted the cause because of the shortcomings of Tenskwatwa were now reconsidering Tecumseh as their leader against the Shemanese. Some thought it prudent to start the fighting where the nearest whites lived. They began to burn cabins, kill white folks and plunder their goods up and down the Wabash plumb to the Mississippi. Once again the settlers were going out prepared by carrying their muskets wherever they went, even out to get wood, water or work in their fields. The attacks spread to the State of Ohio and even some in Kentucky.

William Hull, the Governor of the new Michigan Territory was sending out scouts and getting nothing but bad news. The Indians were building up in big numbers and they all carried the new British Muskets. Hull was in contact with the government in Washington and asking congress to give permission to attack the Indians and British at Fort Malden. He urged the capture of Canada before the forces became too great.

President Madison authorized Hull and gave him the rank of General. He would send regular troops and call up 1,200 Ohio Militia and equip them with supplies and new blue uniforms with red collars. He also would provide a cocked hat with a white plume for each man.

The headquarters were set up at Dayton, Ohio. Governor Meigs came to inspect the troops and meet with General Hull. They decided the best place to meet was in the McCullum's Tavern.

Now the new army of the northwest had 2,500 men and Hull accepted command from Governor Meigs. Hull had experience in soldering as he served with General Anthony Wayne during the Revolution. Hull felt very positive as he looked at his well dressed and well supplied army. Hull was not the man he was forty years ago. Now he was fat and sluggish and not the best man to be the leader. They marched on the first day of June, 1812 and in about six days reached Urbana. More local men joined the army as they marched toward the north.

Word spread like wild fire that the United States had declared war on Great Britain. Every able bodied man was ready to serve if called. President James Madison had been urging Congress for sometime to declare war. It was not just because of the Indians and British in the northwest, but the British had been boarding the American ships. The British had set up blockades to prevent goods to come or go to France and other countries. It was hurting the United States badly.

General Hull took his army toward Detroit and the going got rough because there were no real roads to the north. It took the army over two weeks to breach the Maumee River, only 95 miles distant. The men were exhausted and many of the horses and mules died from exhaustion of pulling wagons through brush and knee deep swamps.

General Hull took control of the United States Ship Cuyahoga and had all the supplies loaded aboard her. He would send it ahead as he marched his army up the river. The General did the unthinkable thing of placing all of his papers and plans for the campaign on board. The Cuyahoga did not go too far before a British gunboat captured her and all of the supplies including Hull's plans. The information was forwarded to British General Isaac Brock.

THE PATRIOT, HEZEKIAH WHITT

Hull was unaware of this and his spies confirmed that Fort Malden was weak because reinforcements had not arrived. Hull commanded his army to move on Detroit, but when he got within about 15 miles he became plagued with the "what ifs". What if the attack cost many lives, what if the American General (Hull) was killed, what if Tecumseh unleashed his Indians on the settlers? Hull became so worried he turned his army back to Detroit, even though all the men were ready for a fight.

Back in Tazewell County the Whitts got word that the Reverend Richard Whitt had died. Hezekiah would take his family for a visit even though the old Patriarch would be long since buried. Edmund Whitt and Hannah Lestor Skaggs Whitt would take Rachel Rebecca Whitt age 9, Richard Price Whitt age 6., and little Abijah age 3 and travel with the Hezekiah party. Even some of the grown children would go on this trip to honor Richard Whitt. Griffy Whitt and wife Martha (Patty) Skaggs Whitt would go and take Timothy Whitt age 4, and Shone Whitt age 2. John Bunyan was not yet married and would also go. Rebecca Whitt Lowe was too much in the family way to travel; her Husband was John Husk Lowe. Little Calvin Lowe would be born in 1812. Susannah Whitt Webb and her husband Joseph Webb had no children as yet so they would also go. Jonas was glad to go for another reason, he would get to see his Susannah again.

Reverend Richard Whitt's grown children that would be there were Robert, Abijah, Rachel, Elizabeth, Ruthy, Susannah, and Richard Thomas Whitt.

The trip was uneventful and that is what they wanted. The men carried their muskets across their saddles just in case the Indians or outlaws attacked. There was a great reunion as kindred came home to Meadow Creek to honor the good Reverend. They had an all night and all day Wake for their beloved Richard. They had a good time and laughed and cried. They all knew that the Old Reverend was walking around with Jesus and would want them to have a good visit as life is so short and they may never be all together again, at least here in this old world. Archibald took over as a leader during this time because he was the son that stayed home and took care of the Reverend during his declining years. After all the visits were over and folks were planning to go back home, Archibald brought out the will of the Reverend Richard Whitt and read it to everyone. He wanted all the folks to know what the Reverend's last will and testament was.

Richard Whitt, Sr. Will

25 April 1807
   Montgomery County, Virginia
   Will Book---? Pages 120-121

In the name of God I, Richard Whitt Senior of the County of Montgomery being in a feeble state of health, but sound of mind do ordain and declare this instrument of Writing to be my last Will and Testament Revoking all others. It is my wish after my death and for that purpose do will and bequeath to my son Archibald Whitt all the tract of Land whereon I now live and that the title shall fully be invested in him with all other claims that I may have to that and any other adjoining said tract to him and to his heirs

COLONEL CHARLES DAHNMON WHITT

THE PATRIOT, HEZEKIAH WHITT

forever. This tract is to be understood to contain the whole of the land that I bought from John Harrison on Meadow Creek supposed to be one hundred acres be it more or less to include the part which I have allotted to my son Richard at the upper end of said tract which son Archibald has bought and a title never was conveyed for it. I do also will to my beloved wife her equal one third of all my personal estate her natural life time the balance to be equally divided between my three daughters, Elizabeth Cassiday, Ruthy Whitt, & Susannah Creswell, and also should there be any part of wives Levasee left at her death also to be equally divided among my three daughters and their heirs forever. And for the good performance of my will and to execute the contents I appoint John Ingles & my son Archibald Whitt to act as executors and it is my request as I can place the fullest confidence in them that they shall act without being bond in security.

*Signed and subscribed to this my hand and seal this 25th day of April 18*Appointed as appraisers of personal property in 1813, were James Charlton, Jacob Peake, and William Sarles. The items including farm stock, produce, farm and household equipment. (log chains, lifter, log slide, drawing chain, 3 horses, which attest to the operation of "Whitt's Mill." A gray mare was listed at $40.00. Bearing proof to the education of the Whitts was writing tablets, books, and 1 pair of spectacles and case.

(By James Whitt in 1983)

There was much talk about the earthquakes and the war with Great Britain. Who knew what this would bring after a time of peace and great growth of the United States. All of the citizens thought that we would beat them again and put the savages down for good.

Jonas and Susannah spent all of their time together and fell even deeper in love. They really hated to part again and both promised themselves to each other. There would be a wedding someday, as Jonas promised to return and learn the mill building trade from his kindred, and take Susannah for his wife.

The Hezekiah party left after having a prayer for traveling mercies and of course praised God for His loving kindness. The trip back was basically fun and the beauty of southwest Virginia was enjoyed by all. Jonas was a little down, but the other Whitts kept making jokes and cheering him up. Hezekiah even explained to him that if it is meant to be, it will happen.

Chapter 36

Wars and Rumors Of War

General Hull had not been informed that the Congress of the United States had declared war on Great Britain. General Hull settled in Detroit and then sent Major Thomas Van Horne with 600 men to escort the mail and meet a supply convoy under a Major William Brush located near the mouth of Raisin River.

Tecumseh and about 70 warriors along with the British Captain James Muir who had but 40 soldiers intercepted them with ambush and the first battle of the War of 1812 took place. Van Horne was soundly defeated and retreated with haste back to Detroit.

Tecumseh had what he needed to win back some of the tribes. He sent swift runners to the tribes with the news. A battle had been fought with the Americans against great odds and the Indians and British won. All of the Americans will be defeated soon and if the tribes want in on victory and plunder they must come at once. They also told them that Tecumseh was commissioned by the British as a General.

General Hull sent word to all the forts in the northwest, Fort Wayne, Fort Dearborn and Chicago, and all the little settlements that they must evacuate. The Indians would be on the warpath in the whole region.

It was too late for Chicago, the settlers and soldiers tried to leave, but the Indians attacked under Chief Blackbird. It was not a battle, but a massacre. William Wells the adopted son of Chief Little Turtle was despised by other Indians because of his siding with the whites. Wells blackened his face as a sign of death before they rode out of the fort and he was killed by Chief Blackbird. Blackbird immediately cut out his heart and ate it as to gain the strength of a strong enemy.

General Brock at Fort Malden, called for Tecumseh to talk of an attack on the American Fort at Detroit. Tecumseh knew the ground of the area and conveyed it to Brock in a drawing of a map. Brock saw an opportunity and proceeded to attack the Americans. General Hull had lost his nerve and all confidence; he gave up the fort without firing a single shot. The American Soldiers could not believe it at first and then felt disgraced.

There was a detachment of 350 men, under Colonels Lewis Cass and Duncan McArthur out on a mission to get supplies but had failed. They returned to Detroit and were stunned to see the Union Jack of the British flying over their fort. There were also Indians running about killing the American supply cattle. The state of the 350 men was not good as they were starved and weak. The Colonels saw no way out except to surrender. They sent in a rider under a white flag.

Tecumseh honored the flag of surrender and prevailed upon the warriors not to harm them. Tecumseh had a code he lived by and demanded it of his warriors. He always

THE PATRIOT, HEZEKIAH WHITT

said, *"Kill the enemy if possible and leave none to be captured, but if prisoners fall into our hands we will treat them humanely."*

The frenzied Warriors did not like it, but they obeyed Tecumseh. They always loved to torture their captives as a spoil of victory. They believed they should cut captives up or burn them and that would teach them a lesson.

The men under General Hull were shocked, outraged and extremely disappointed. The following letter was written by a private in Hull's army.

Detroit

August 19, 1812

My Dear Brother,

I have only time to inform you that our army has surrendered to the British under General Brock on the 16ᵗʰ. We could have whipped hell out of the rascals but General Hull has proved himself a traitor and a coward. On the 12ᵗʰ of July, we crossed the river at this place and encamped on the Sandwich in Canada, with the object driving the red coated devils away from Malden…General Hull was informed that Fort Mackinaw above Detroit had surrendered to the British and Indians, who were rushing down the river in numbers sufficient to crush our people. Old General Hull became panic struck and in spite of the entreaties of his officers and private Soldiers run us back to this place where we were made to submit to the most shameful surrender that ever took place in this world. Our brave Captain Harry James cursed and swore like a pirate and cried like his heart would break.

The War of 1812 started badly for the Americans. Now the numbers of Tecumseh's Army grew and blood was let all over the northwest. The confederation of Indian tribes was growing almost like it was before the floundering Prophet had so damaged it.

Wars were raging in Europe as Napoleon was determined to take all of Europe. Napoleon's latest success was the invasion of Russia. He burned Moscow and destroyed 90% of the homes and more than 1,000 churches. There were wars and rumors of war.

The American warship, Constitution, captured the British warship Guerriere on August 19, 1812. On October 25, 1812 the United States frigate, United States, captured the British vessel Macedonian. It was great that the Americans had some early success on the high seas against the strongest Navy in the world.

On December 2, 1812 the American people reelected James Madison as their president. The people did not want to switch horses in the middle of the stream. It was another time that the American people would have to pull together and run the dreaded red coats from their country.

People in Tazewell County and around the country were mad and concerned with the latest developments.

COLONEL CHARLES DAHNMON WHITT 313

THE PATRIOT, HEZEKIAH WHITT

"We whooped them red coats and Injuns once already, by Gawd we will just havt' to do er again!" was the sentiment of some illiterate, but wise Americans in the hills of Virginia and Kentucky.

Jonas Whitt can hardly stand being away from Susannah Whitt. He started talking about going to Montgomery County and working for Uncle Archibald. He talked about the opportunity he would have to learn more about milling and even building mills. Richard (Devil Dick) Whitt listened to Jonas and it seemed to be a great idea if he went also.

Hezekiah had been listening to Jonas and Richard and thought it was time to intercede.

"Jonas and Richard, if you are serious about going to Meadow Creek, you first must write a letter to Brother Archibald and ask him if he would take you on as an apprentice," said Hezekiah.

"Paw I asked him when we was up there," replied Jonas.

"Well, something like this has to be official you fellows both write a letter and get it cleared by Archibald, fore you hike off over the mountains," said Hezekiah.

"Can't we just put it in one letter Paw?" asked Richard?

"Nope that wouldn't be proper, you both write and then put them in one envelope, cause both of you want a position," replied Hezekiah.

"Well Paw I ain't plumb sure I want at go," replied Richard.

"Well you better decide one way or the tuther, you can't sit betwixt yea and nay, once you go you will have to fulfill your promise to work and learn!" exclaimed Hezekiah.

"I will," said an anxious Jonas, thinking mostly of the dark haired and gray eyed beauty, Susannah Whitt.

"Well boys, did either of you ask your father if you could go?" asked Hezekiah?
"Paw, we are grown men, I am 22 and Jonas is 15," replied Richard.
"Where do you fellers live?" asked Hezekiah?
"Paw you know we live with you and Maw, I figured it was about time for you to throw your baby birds outta the nest," said Jonas.

"You are right about part of it, you do live under my roof and I am still the head of this family, I do deserve your respect," said Hezekiah.

"Paw we do respect you could we please go to Meadow Creek to work for Uncle Archibald if he will have us?" asked Jonas?

"You boys write your letters to Archibald and if he wants you to come, I will not stand in your way, but who knows what this trouble with the British and Indians will bring," replied Hezekiah.

THE PATRIOT, HEZEKIAH WHITT

"Thanks Paw, we will get ready and head out in early spring if that is alright with you, Maw and Uncle Archibald, I aim to write my letter tonight and give it to the post carrier tomorrow," said Jonas.

"Me too!" exclaimed Richard.

"Let me know what Archibald has to say about it and you can plan from there, I was thinking of taking a hunt over on the Louisa River, (Levisa Fork.) And get in some elk, bear, and maybe a buffalo for winter meat," said Hezekiah.

Both of the young men were thrilled about that news.

Hezekiah was proud of all of his children and knew it was time they became men and stand on their own feet. He was proud, but also had concern about them leaving. Hezekiah thought back to his days of youth and remembered that he was in the militia and on campaigns at the age of 17.

The Indians around Detroit could not be controlled; they did many savage things to any white family they could find. The British with Detroit in hand moved south along with the red warriors. They built a fort at French Town at the mouth of the Raisin River. This was to block any American attack from land.

The Americans got their dandruff up like in the old day of the Indian Wars and Revolutionary War. The Kentuckians enlisted in the militia in very large numbers as well as in other parts of the country. Kentucky commissioned William Henry Harrison as a brevet major general to lead the Kentucky Militia against Detroit. Following on the heels of Kentucky the Federal Government commissioned Harrison as brigadier general. Then the federal government turned around and gave the U.S. Army another old soldier command over Harrison. General James Winchester had been retired for 30 years and was about the same caliber as General Hull. Back then as today Washington never learns and make stupid mistakes.

General Winchester was not well received by his army because of his overbearing attitude; he was another fat, stubborn general that had no idea how to lead an army against Tecumseh and the British. General Harrison was placed second in command and old Winchester would not listen to him or any other officer in the command. Harrison averted a widespread desertion by the men. Harrison knew the time would be short that Old Winchester would shoot himself in the foot, so to speak.

The Indians went against Tecumseh's order to wait before attacking Fort Wayne and Fort Harrison. The Indians were jacked up after an easy victory in Detroit. They wanted to take over Ohio and Indiana so they attacked both forts in September 1812.

Fort Wayne was commanded by a drunk, Captain Oscar Rhea, which had 70 solders. He did drink a lot and was not an able leader this day.

Chief Winnemac came up with a crafty idea to get the Officers out of the fort after having them under siege for a week. The Chief and three braves were to openly

THE PATRIOT, HEZEKIAH WHITT

approach the fort with a white flag. The chief and the three braves were to be covered with blankets and each with a hidden pistol. There were hundreds of Indians hidden in the cover of brush around the fort. Winnemac believed if the three junior officers were killed, Captain Rhea would fold and open the gate to save his hide.

As the plan was unfolding, two Shawnees and a white man rode up. It was William Oliver an Indian Spy for Harrison and the Indians were Bright Horn and Johnny Logan, both loyal to the Americans.

Winnemac knew at once that the American Army may be real close so he changed his plans at once and shook hands with Captain Rhea and the other officers. Then Winnemac told Rhea he had changed his mind about talking peace and the four Indians did an about face and headed to the woods.

Heavy musket fire from the woods and the fort took place and the three riders quickly made it into the partially opened fort door. After talking with Captain Rhea the two Shawnees volunteered to go and warn General Harrison that Fort Wayne could fall. As the firing of the muskets subsided and most Indians were holding empty weapons the two Shawnee volunteers rode out of the gate in a mad dash. After they were out of firing range, Johnny Logan waved his arm and shouted a triumphant yell that only an Indian could do. The men in the fort waved and cheered for their two Indian friends. The two brave Indians reached General Harrison quickly.

The attacks from the Indians on the fort continued. Lieutenant Joseph Curtis put Captain Rhea in confinement and took over. Rhea was too drunk to direct anything. Curtis was smart, he had the men load every musket, and some men had three or four muskets ready to fire from the palisade of the fort. Their orders were not to fire until the Indians were in close shooting range. The Indians made a large charge and the massive musket fire from the fort drove them back leaving a good number of dead warriors on the ground.

The Indians had one more trick to try. They staged a false battle just out side of the fort by shooting and making smoke and the screams of warriors could be heard. The farce was to draw the whites out to help the assumed army of General Harrison, but the men behind the walls did not fall for it.

Over at Fort Harrison the Indians began with trickery, but had no success. A band of warriors along with squaws and children came to the fort, which was under the command of Captain Zachary Taylor, with a request of food and showing themselves to be friends. Captain Zachary Taylor was cautious so he lowered some food over the wall. Captain Taylor only had 50 men and some of them were sick.

The Indians stayed close to the fort professing to befriend the whites, but the next day they set fire to a wall and burned a breach into the fort. A large number of Indians fired into the hole in the wall. The fire died out and the Indians made a charge, but a withering fire drove them back. Captain Taylor had a makeshift patch made up from small logs and the breach was filled. The Indians stuck around for about 8 more days and became very frustrated. They left and went to the little settlement of Pigeon Roost and took out their anger on the whites there. They showed no mercy on the 21 men, women, and children. They killed, hacked and scalped even the babies.

The word got back to Kentucky and Virginia that Fort Harrison and Fort Wayne had withstood the attacks and siege of the Indians. This gave the Americans new hope which brought new enlistments into the militia from all of the states.

Hezekiah once again prayed for Virginia and the United States asking God for protection and guidance during this trying time. Rachel loved her people, but felt that they were fighting a lost cause.

"The belligerent British only use the Indians to fight their wars," said Rachel.

"I am afraid you are right there will be much blood spilled and the Indians will not further their cause one iota," replied Hezekiah.

Jonas and Richard wrote their letters to their Uncle Archibald and were waiting for a reply. Jonas got letters from Susannah on a regular basis and this kept the fire of love burning brightly.

In November 1812 Hezekiah decided to take that hunting trip. He had Richard, John Bunyan and Jonas to prepare for a two week trip. Hezekiah was going to take them over on Levisa Fork about 75 to 100 miles from home. They would travel down the Clinch to the base of a ridge (Now Raven) that was becoming known as Kentucky Turnpike. They would travel the ridge and drop off to what they call the Head of the River. (Levisa Fork comes out of the ground there as a big spring) Then they would just follow the Louisa River, (Now called Levisa Fork) to the prime hunting grounds around what they call Pikeville and Prestonsburg. This land was still primitive and bear, deer, and elk were still in abundance. The bears were so thick at one time that reports stated that as many as 10 bears hibernated together in large dens. This was also on the warrior's path, but the Indians had not run the traces for sometime. Hezekiah would have his sons on the alert, who knows, the Indians may make a strike now since war is going on.

Hezekiah and the three sons started out early one morning all riding a saddle horse and leading a pack animal. They had the basic supplies, but would rely on their hunting skills to keep meat in the camp.

After another little talk about traveling in primitive and hazardous grounds Hezekiah led them in prayer. They all hugged Rachel and rode off. James and Griffy would be keeping check on Rachel while they were gone.

Hezekiah wanted to use this trip to bond more deeply with his sons and teach them more about hunting and tracking. He wanted them to learn more about being ready and never be ambushed by the arrows that come from the thickets and woodlands.

As they traveled he would have the sons take a turn at point and even moving ahead as far as a mile to scout out the area ahead. Richard, Bunyan, and Jonas took to it like a duck to water. Hezekiah was really proud of the young men and thought it must be in the blood. He was always good as a scout and the Indian blood from their Maw's heritage didn't hurt any either.

They made it to the hunting grounds without a mishap. They had not seen any Indian sign and began to relax somewhat. They set up a camp and began to scout about for elk and bear. The next day they came in on the downwind side of a herd of elk and took a big bull. Jonas ran across some big bear tracks and the next day they hunted bear. The bears were about ready to go to den for a long winters nap. They found a big den under a rock house and it looked like several bear had been using it.

Hezekiah cautioned his sons about hunting bear.
"We only need one so don't wound any besides the one we settle on," explained Hezekiah.
"Bears can be dangerous can't they Paw!" exclaimed Jonas.

"Sure can, any wounded or cornered critter can be very dangerous," said Hezekiah.

Hezekiah made a plan to get a nice fat bear out of the den, he would place the three other Whitts on watch with their muskets on the ready and he planned to throw stones in the den to rouse out a bear. Plan "B" would be a little more dangerous; He would get a long pole with a fork on the end and would stick it into the den until he felt the soft fur of a bear. Then he would poke it in and twist it into the winter fur of the bruin. His hopes were that the bears would be groggy and just come out and take a look. The dread was that one of the big muscular critters would make a charge to get rid of his tormentors.

Hezekiah had to use plan "B" and it worked wonderfully. A nice big bear come out into the winter air and sniffed the breeze and looked about. He saw Jonas and decided to scare him off. The bruin weaved from side to side and growled a warning then he took about four steps toward Jonas. Hezekiah had side stepped the den opening and had a bead on the bear as did the other sons. The bear used his body language as a warning and moved once again toward Jonas now closing in at about ten yards. Jonas took a real good aim and let go with the old Brown Betz. The bear lurched to the side and blood came from his nose, but he was not done with life. He started for Jonas again and Richard and Griffy unloaded on the bear. Hezekiah was on the ready but did not have to fire. He came within two yards of Jonas' feet and went to bear heaven. If there were other bears in the den they never showed themselves. Hezekiah told the three to reload and to watch and wait for a few minutes. This was always practiced in the wilderness, a shot often brought in warriors if they were about.

No one showed up so the bear was gutted and cut up enough to tie on the pack animals. Back at camp Richard asked his Paw about the wait after the bear was shot.

THE PATRIOT, HEZEKIAH WHITT

"It was for two reasons, one to make sure the life has left a dangerous quarry and the other is a shot in the wilderness alerts the Indians or even outlaws that someone is about. I heard once that Daniel Boone and one of his brothers were hunting somewhere here in Kentucky. Daniel stood on guard after they shot a deer. The brother went to retrieve the deer and in no time two shots rang out. Daniel had to flee to save his life. He went back later and found his brother shot and scalped. Even the deer had been carried off, it is a good idea to always wait," explained Hezekiah.

The four Whitts had a good hunt and all of them sharpened up their wood lore skills. All four became closer to each other and had a good hunt. They brought back an elk and a bear. When they got home Rachel would take over and with the sons help would do more butchering and smoking of the meat. They would render as much grease as possible from the bear as it was a useful commodity.

When the four Whitts got back to Cedar Grove it was already December. Jonas had a letter from Susannah, but there were no mail from Uncle Archibald.

Back in the northwest, Johnny Logan was doubted by the old and numb General Winchester, so to prove his loyalty he took his friends Bright Horn and Otter. After moving down the Maumee River they ran into six Indians led by Winnemac and a British Officer. The Potawatomies were very suspicious of the three Shawnees. Johnny Logan told Winnemac that they had left the Americans and were on their way to join up with Tecumseh. Winnemac disarmed the three and they all began to ride towards the camp of Tecumseh. After awhile Winnemac was convinced that the three Shawnees were truly on their side and gave them their muskets back. It became late and four of the Indians left to scout the area ahead. When they were out of sight Johnny Logan nodded at Bright Horn and Otter. They all shot at the same time and killed Chief Winnemac, Matthew Elliott the British Officer, and the other Potawatomie warrior.

The four other Potawatomies heard the shots and came storming back. Bright Horn took a ball in the shoulder, Johnny Logan killed one as did Otter and the last two retreated. Almost out of musket range the two turned and fired another round. They did not know it but Johnny Logan took a ball in the belly. After Johnny Logan and Otter got back to Fort Winchester, Johnny Logan lingered about three days in gruesome pain, but died happy that he proved his loyalty and honor. Johnny Logan laughed just before he died.

"What is funny?" asked his white friend William Oliver, who had sit with Johnny the past three days.
"It was so funny, how Otter took Winnemac's scalp," he said.
"Why, what did he do?" asked William Oliver?
Johnny Logan, (Spemica Lawba, Shawnee name.) was gone. He became the first Indian to have a military funeral given by the United States Soldiers that respected him so much.

In January of 1813 General Winchester gathered his army and took them from their warm, but boring duty. They were not at all happy until now the General told them

THE PATRIOT, HEZEKIAH WHITT

since Lake Erie was frozen over he would march them across and take Fort Malden by surprise. They marched to the Maumee River rapids and were very cold. They set up a camp and morale was very low. A rider came riding hard to the encampment. The rider was from Frenchtown at the mouth of the Raisin River. He reported that about 300 British and Indians had taken over the town. He was afraid of a massacre and the burning down of the settlement.

General Winchester saw a chance for an easy victory so he sent 600 men to rid the town of their pestilence. He and 250 men would stay there and wait. The men were glad to be going to a town that had houses and hot fires to warm by. They rushed and covered the 30 miles and caught the enemy by surprise. After a quick, but heated battle the British and Indians were evicted.

General Winchester was elated and marched to Frenchtown to join the rest of his army. He never even gave a thought that just 18 miles from Frenchtown was General Proctor's army and many Indians.

Winchester's men were very worn by being out in freezing weather for over two weeks. They were not prepared for any attack, but at 5:00 AM on January 22, 1813 General Proctor along with an army of 2,000 soldiers and Indian warriors paid them a visit. The British and Indians surrounded the Americans and the battle began. Winchester and about 50 men tried to escape, but most of them were killed and scalped. Winchester was taken to Proctor. The army that Winchester left behind was giving the British a good fight so General Proctor ordered Winchester to have his army to quit the fight. The American Army agreed only if Proctor would care for their wounded and protect every man from the savagery of the Indians. General Proctor promised. He took his captives and his victorious army and left the wounded under guard of Indians and one British officer.

Just as soon as Proctor was out of sight the ravaging savages went to work on the 100 worst wounded Americans. They put them all in one house and set it on fire. None could escape and the screams were horrific. They took the ones that could walk and began a march toward Fort Malden. Every time one fell behind he was hacked to death with a tomahawk. Not many of the wounded under the Indians made it to Fort Malden.

Two major battles of the war of 1812 and the British won them both.

At first the American government had not put as much emphasis on the land war in the northwest along the Great Lakes. They were mostly trying to beat the British at sea. With the Indian forces growing stronger behind Tecumseh and even in the south the Indians were taking up the hatchet against the Americans.

Things would begin to turn around as America put more into their fights in the North West.

On April 27, 1813 General Pike of the United States defeated and captured Toronto, but Pike was killed.

COLONEL CHARLES DAHNMON WHITT

THE PATRIOT, HEZEKIAH WHITT

On May 27, 1813 the Americans capture Fort George in Canada.

On June 1, 1813 the saying of "Don't give up the ship," was uttered by Captain John Lawrence of the United States Navy.

On June 24, 1813 the Americans take another defeat at the battle of Beaver Dam.

On July 31, 1813 the British invade Plattsburgh, New York.

On September 7, 1813 the nickname of the United States, ("Uncle Sam") was coined by the newspaper, Troy Post of New York.

Good news, on September 10, 1813 Commodore Oliver Perry defeats the British in the battle of Lake Erie.

On October 5, 1813 the Americans defeat the British at the battle of Thames in Canada.
In the south, on November 3, 1813 General Coffee destroyed the Indian Village at
    Talladega Alabama.
On December 18, 1813 the British take Fort Niagara.
On December 29, 1813 the British burn Buffalo, New York.
As the year of 1813 wound down, the affray has not been settled.
Life in Tazewell County, Virginia has not changed too much in 1812. The men were basically ready if the fighting came to them, but most of the Indians were tied up with the fighting in the northwest or in the deeper south.

THE PATRIOT, HEZEKIAH WHITT

The Elk was a staple of the Indian and the Frontiersman.

Chapter 37

America Endures More War

As the new year of 1814 rolled in, a letter from Archibald Whitt arrived and addressed to Jonas and Richard Whitt. The young men almost fought over it to be the first to read it. After they both read it about three times they were both elated at the news. Uncle Archibald was pleased for his nephews to come and serve an apprenticeship in carpentry and mill building.

Hezekiah gave his blessing to his son to go and work for Archibald in Montgomery County. Jonas was not a big man, but was still growing, Richard was really big for his age and he was still growing. I think Bunya

played football if they lived in the 21st century.

As they were packed and were ready to leave for Meadow Creek the news came that a General Jackson had defeated the Creek Indians in the battle of Horseshoe Bend. Hezekiah was glad that the fierce Creeks were put down so that the United States could get back to growing and becoming more civilized. Rachel was sad and glad, her father Chief Cornstalk was born to a Shawnee woman, but his father was a Creek Indian. All of her children had some Creek, Shawnee, and Cherokee blood flowing in their veins.

Some news came from overseas that would affect the war with Great Britain. The British had defeated France and this would leave Britain with only one foe, the United States. Napoleon would resurface later.

Richard and Jonas say their goodbyes to the whole family as they all gather to see the young men off. Rachel broke down and cried as she hugged her boys. Hezekiah gave them the talk about being vigilant on the trail and trust no man in these trying times. Most likely there would be no Indians, but watch for their sign anyway. Beware of mountain outlaws and even for the dangers of traveling in the wilderness. After he told them all of this he had a prayer for the young men and asked God to give them traveling mercies and help them to follow the Lord Jesus Christ all of their days. Richard and Jonas rode off excited to be on their own. They both sit straight in their saddles and held their muskets across in front of them. As they road up Green Mountain Road toward Jeffersonville they paused and wheeled their horses around and gave one last wave.

The year of 1814 proved the resolve of the American spirit as they began to win more battles against the British and Indians. The leaders such as William Henry Harrison were smart and brave. They were willing to die rather than to give up ground to the British as did the early Generals. The Americans captured Fort Erie, Canada on July 3, 1814. On July 5, 1814 the Americans defeat the British at Chippewa, Ontario, Canada. On July 25, 1814 the Americans defeated the British at Niagara Falls, Lundy's Lane.

THE PATRIOT, HEZEKIAH WHITT

The British have done the unthinkable, on August 24, 1814; they attacked Washington D.C. and burned much of the city. They burned the Library of Congress and destroyed 3,000 books.

On September 11, 1814 the Americans defeat the British at the battle of Plattsburg. Also on that day the United States Navy defeated the British Navy at the battle of Lake Champlain, New York.

On September 14, 1814 our National Anthem was born in the poem written by Francis Scott Key as he watched the British attack on Fort McHenry in Baltimore, Maryland.

Key was a well establish lawyer by 1805 and had even appeared before the Supreme Court many times by 1814. Key was a Christian and had deep roots as to justice and love.

This poem came about when Key was asked to talk to the British about releasing Dr. William Beanes. Dr.Beanes was taken prisoner and put aboard a British ship. Key went to Baltimore and met with Colonel John Skinner who worked to make the prisoner exchanges with the British. Skinner and Key got in a small boat and rowed out to meet the Royal Navy. They were treated well and negotiations went well and the British agreed to release Dr.Beanes, but there was a catch. The Royal Navy was just about to attack and bombard the American Fort McHenry. Key, Skinner, and Beanes, were retained and would watch the show as the exploding shells were released on the fort. The Americans in the fort had two United States Flags and were flying the small one for the 25 hours of almost constant bombardment. Key, Skinner, and Beanes were apprehensive that the fort may fall due to the enormous attack of exploding shells lobbed at the fort.

The British guns were quieted in the early morning of September 14, 1814 and the Americans in Fort McHenry lowered their small flag and raised their enormous flag in defiance. Francis Scott Key was so touched at the site in the dawn's early light that he quickly penned a poem from his impressions. The three Americans were elated as the Royal Navy had not been able to dislodge the Americans in Fort McHenry. He called his poem "Defense of Fort McHenry." Later the poem was renamed the "Star Spangled Banner," and became very popular as a patriotic song. It would become the National Anthem in years later in 1931. The huge flag that waved over Fort McHenry on the morning of September 14, 1814 is now proudly displayed in the Smithsonian's American History Museum in Washington D.C.

"The Star Spangled Banner"

By: Francis Scott Key

> *Oh say, can you see, by the dawn's early light,*
> *What so proudly we hailed at the twilight's last gleaming?*
> *Whose broad stripes and bright stars, thru the perilous fight,*

COLONEL CHARLES DAHNMON WHITT

THE PATRIOT, HEZEKIAH WHITT

O'er the ramparts we watched, were so gallantly streaming?
And the rockets' red glare, the bombs bursting in air,
Gave proof through the night that our flag was still there.
O say, does that Star - Spangled Banner yet wave
O'er the land of the free and the home of the brave?
On the shore dimly seen through the mists of the deep,
Where the foe's haughty host in dread silence reposes,
What is that which the breeze, o'er the towering steep,
As it fitfully blows, half conceals, half discloses?
Now it catches the gleam of the morning's first beam,
In full glory reflected, now shines on the stream:
Tis the Star - Spangled Banner: O, long may it wave
O'er the land of the free and the home of the brave!
And where is that band who so vauntingly swore
That the havoc of war and the battle's confusion
A home and a country should leave us no more?
Their blood has washed out their foul footsteps' pollution.
No refuge could save the hireling and slave
From the terror of flight or the gloom of the grave:
And the Star - Spangled Banner in triumph doth wave
O'er the land of the free and the home of the brave.
O, thus be it ever when freemen shall stand,
Between their loved home and the war's desolation!
Blest with victory and peace, may the heav'n-rescued land
Praise the Power that hath made and preserved us a nation!
Then conquer we must, when our cause. It is just,
And this be our motto: "In God we trust"
And the Star - Spangled Banner in triumph shall wave
O'er the land of the free and the home of the brave!

I need to reflect back to the battle of Thames as this is a turning point in the War of 1812. The Americans under General William Henry Harrison were pushing the British north. Tecumseh tried to shame the British General Proctor to take a stand and defeat the Americans. Proctor was satisfied to go deeper into Canada and take a stand there. Tecumseh and his warriors served as the rear guard as Proctor moved his army up the Thames Valley.

As you know Tecumseh was very mystical and had predicted many occurrences such as a solar eclipse, a comet, and an enormous earthquake besides many other small occasions. He had one more prediction and it was to take place on October 5, 1813 at the battle of the Thames. He got up that morning and told his people that this is a good day to die and then gave them a prediction.

THE PATRIOT, HEZEKIAH WHITT

"Today I will be shot and will die, but I give my war club to my good friend Chaubenee, when he sees me fall, he is to rush to me and touch me with my war club, I will rise up and lead you to a great victory over the Shemanese!" said Tecumseh.

The Indians all sat quietly and listened to their great leader.

"If my most trusted friend, Chaubenee, cannot reach me and give me the touch, you will be defeated. If I and Chaubenee both die I want you to depart from the British and go home and learn to live with the Americans," explained the great Chief Tecumseh.

As the battle started in a rage, the 45 year old Tecumseh was felled with a lead ball from the Americans. Another Indian was seen running to Tecumseh, but a ball struck him and he dropped dead. The Indians saw this and they all dispersed into the shelter of the woodland and headed home.

Richard Mentor Johnson was given the credit of the shot that took Tecumseh down and this glory helped him be elected as vice-president to serve with President Martin Van Buren.

The Americans hated Tecumseh as a dreaded foe and they all wanted a piece of his hide, literally. Only old Simon Kenton was there to point out Tecumseh to the blood thirsty souvenir seekers. Simon had great respect for the Noble Indian Chief. Tecumseh as usual did not wear a lot of decorations and such when in battle as did some chiefs. He basically looked like a normal brave lying on the field of battle. Kenton saw Tecumseh, but pointed out a lesser chief as he knew the Americans would butcher the great chief. It was awful how the Americans acted that day, the poor Indian they thought was Tecumseh was basically skinned; some took bigger parts such as ears and apiece of his scalp of long black hair. Some just took a feather or a piece of clothing. Tecumseh was spared of this disgrace because Simon Kenton did what he did.

Tecumseh is one of the most famous Native Americans in history. Some folks say it is his depiction on the Indian Head Penny. The name has been given to many Americans and all of the Indians had a hole in their heart for many years after Tecumseh died.

Rachel was saddened by his death, but knew it was best for the freedom of America from the British. All of the Indians that lived as whites felt the same; it was Thomas Bailey Christian that brought the word to the Hezekiah Whitt family. After Tecumseh passed on to his happy hunting grounds the British did not have the bite as before.

Hezekiah and his family were saddened about the death of Tecumseh, but also very glad the war did not come to the waters of the Clinch. Maybe now the war could be ended and a lasting peace would fall on the United States and especially Tazewell County, Virginia.

Jonas and Richard were doing well in Montgomery County. Jonas was learning the mysteries of building water powered grist mills, but Richard was learning blacksmithing.

THE PATRIOT, HEZEKIAH WHITT

All of the sons of the late Reverend Richard Whitt were well adapted to using tools and most were proficient in carpentry, mill work, and some knew blacksmithing. Jonas and Richard were quick learners and Archibald was impressed with the quality of their work and they were never slackers.

Jonas was seeing Susannah regularly and they planned to be married as soon as Archibald would give permission and he felt he could support her as she should be.

Richard and Jonas shared a small cabin on the Archibald Whitt property and were self sufficient even though they did share meals at Uncle Archibald's home. Jonas got to spend more time with Susannah even if they were washing dishes or weeding the garden. Every Sunday afternoon after church and dinner were over Jonas and Susannah would steal away and take walks. They truly were in love.

On the 1814 Tazewell County tax list: Hezekiah Whitt 85 acres in Baptist Valley; Griffitt (Griffy) Whitt 130 acres on Reedy Ridge; James Whitt 130 acres on Reedy Ridge.

The British and the Americans both became sick of war and destruction! They came to a negotiated settlement at the Treaty of Ghent and signed on the dotted line to end the war. This was done late in the year of 1814, on the day before Christmas, December 24, 1814.

Both governments were so anxious to end the war that neither side mentioned the causes of neither hostilities, nor even the Indians grievances over land. The cost of this war will never be accurately depicted. The official numbers of killed, wounded, or missing were 8,600 British and 11,300 for the Americans, but these numbers are just a shot in the dark. The Indians that gave their life for freedom and land will never be known, but the greatest Indian that ever lived gave his life, that was Chief Tecumseh. The clear losers were the Native Americans. In the summer of 1815 the United States signed 15 treaties with the tribes, but not one acre was returned to the rightful owners of this great land.

The French speaking Canadians and the English speaking Canadians had learned to work together and Canada became unified against a common foe. They still praise Tecumseh and his army for defending Canada.

The war made heroes in both Canada and the United States. Many veterans of the United States became famous and were elected to the Senate and to the House. Three heroes became President of the United States. William Henry Harrison, Andrew Jackson, and Zachary Taylor all became President.

This news was slow to cross the Atlantic and some fighting continued.

Andrew (Andy) Jackson (Old Hickory) took his army, clad in buck skins and wore coonskin hats, to New Orleans to face the British. This was the last battle of the War of 1812 and was fought after the war was over. The battle was fought on January 8, 1815.

THE PATRIOT, HEZEKIAH WHITT

There was a song about this famous battle that the American frontiersmen won. This song helps people to remember a war that many folks don't know about.

And once again the sentiment of the illiterate, but wise frontiersmen was, "By Gawd, we whopped 'um again!"

The Battle of New Orleans
Written by Jimmy Driftwood
Sung by the late Johnny Horton

© 1991 Sony Music Entertainment Inc.

In 1814 we took a little trip
Along with Colonel Jackson down the mighty Mississippi.
We took a little bacon an' we took a little bean
And we caught the bloody British at the town of New Orleans.
Refrain:
This is the Refrain:
We fired our guns an' the British kept a 'comin'.
There wasn't nigh as many as there was awhile ago.
We fired once more an' they begin to runnin'
Down the Mississippi to the Gulf of Mexico
We looked down the river an' we seed the British comin',
There must a'been a hundred of 'em beatin' on the drum.
They stepped so high an' they made their bugles ring,
We stood beside our cotton bales an' didn't say a thing.
Refrain:
Old Hickory said we could take 'em by surprise.
If we didn't fire our muskets 'til we looked 'em in the eyes.
We held our fire 'til we seed their faces well,
Then we opened up our squirrel guns an' really gave 'em ...well!
Refrain:
Yeah, they ran through the briars an' they ran through the brambles
An' they ran through the bushes where the rabbits couldn't go.
They ran so fast that the hounds couldn't catch 'em
Down the Mississippi to the Gulf of Mexico.
We fired our cannon 'til the barrel melted down,
So we grabbed an alligator an' we fought another round.
We filled his head with cannon balls an' powered his behind,
An' when they touched the powder off, the 'gator lost his mind.
Refrain:

Now in 1815 the country can go back to the antebellum period and grow and enjoy the arts as education takes on a new importance. A man can once again go and work in his fields and harvest the bounties of rich ground, without the fear of being attacked by

COLONEL CHARLES DAHNMON WHITT

Indians. The old conflict of arguments between the north and south will slowly come to light again.

Chapter 38

Era Of Good Feelings

I will give you a look at the sons and daughters of Hezekiah and Rachel in the year of 1815.

James Whitt and Nancy Skaggs Whitt still have an empty nest. They both loved children and were always anxious to help with their nieces and nephews.

Griffy Whitt and Patty Skaggs Whitt have four children by the end of 1815. Timothy Whitt, born November 3, 1808; Shone Whitt born on Christmas Day in 1810; Assena Whitt was born February 19, 1810; Cinthia Whitt was born on December 9, 1815.

Richard Nelson (Devil Dick) Whitt is still playing the field as an available bachelor.

John Bunyan Whitt had married in 1813 to Ana Shackelford, but God called her and her little baby home. It was really hard for Bunyan and the entire family. He remarried to Hannah Sarles on February 11, 1815 and they had no babies yet.

Rebecca Whitt had married James Husk Lowe and has Calvin Lowe that was born in 1812; they also have William D. Lowe that was born in 1815.

Susannah Whitt was married to Joseph Lowe and they did not have any babies yet.

Jonas and Cousin Susannah would love to be married, but this would not happen until October 10, 1816.

Jonas was doing well at learning about mills and he spent much time around Uncle Archibald's home, because the dark haired, gray eyed Susannah lived there.

Richard was learning much about blacksmithing and he looked the part. For some reason most blacksmiths are big men. Richard took after his Maw's side of the family in his appearance; he had black hair, and high cheek bones, but had the Whitt's gray eyes. Most likely Richard would not stay too long in Montgomery County.

Some of the happenings of 1815:

On January 30, 1815, Thomas Jefferson donated 6,500 books to replenish the burned Library of Congress.

On March 3, 1815 the United States declared war on Algiers for piracy.

Napoleon would not behave so the British under Wellington defeated him at the Battle of Waterloo. (A new phrase came from this, "He met his Waterloo!")

On June 30, 1815 the United States under Stephen Decatur ended the attacks from the Algerian Pirates.

On July 9, 1815 the first natural gas well was discovered, we have had gas ever since.

August 16, 1815 the Marines were in Tripoli.

THE PATRIOT, HEZEKIAH WHITT

Also a mention of the Shawnee nephew of Rachel Cornstalk Skaggs Whitt, (Kumskaka) Thomas Bailey Christian. Thomas and his wife Louisa Kathryn Harman Christian had been fruitful and multiplied.

Moses Christian born 1795
James Christian born 1796
Ruth Christian born 1797 (May be a twin)
Mastin Christian born 1797 (May be a twin)
David Christian born 1802
John Christian born 1804
Daniel Christian born 1807
Nancy Jane Christian born 1812
Thomas Skaggs Christian born 1813

Thomas and Hezekiah were neighbors and friends through the years. Hezekiah had promised Thomas Mastin that he would watch over his adopted son, Thomas Bailey Christian. Thomas had basically grown up in the white world and had adapted so well that most folks never considered him to be an Indian.

During this time with peace in the land, many folks began visiting their neighbors and spending their time in Jeffersonville. The ladies met to quilt, put up produce, and helped each other in many ways. The men would meet to raise a barn or help kill a hog or beef. Of course the men would meet to smoke and have some spirits while they talk over the current events.
The ladies began to dress up in the long full dresses on Sundays and special occasions and their resemblance to a "Bell" brought forth the name of "Southern Bells!"

Hezekiah was in Jeffersonville on a regular basis. He was always there on Court Day and spent a lot of time with his friends which were the upper class of the county. I am not saying that the Gentlemen Justices of the Peace were uppity, because they were not. They all knew where they came from and did not forget the hardships of the earlier years.

The Whitts were always eager to hear from their kindred in Montgomery County, especially Richard and Jonas. All of Hezekiah's brothers and sisters were married and had families by now. Archibald had become a prominent man on Meadow Creek near modern day Radford, Virginia.

Hezekiah was more or less a Gentleman Farmer by now, since he did not have as many mouths to feed. He raised only enough grain for the table and to feed his cattle, horses, and other stock. By now most folks were penning up swine to fatten for the winter. Many farmers were raising enough hogs to drive them toward Abington or to the east.

THE PATRIOT, HEZEKIAH WHITT

Horses, cattle, sheep and hogs brought eastern money into Tazewell County.

Paint had made its way across the mountains and the Gentlemen began to paint their houses and even their barns. In the towns, the churches, and court houses and businesses were painted bright white. The frontier towns and buildings took on a new look of the east. A sense of pride was felt by the ladies and gentlemen. Another thing that began to show up was the fine buggies and carriages. A pride in good horses was developed and a few races took place to settle some disputes as to who had the fastest horse. When several horses were tied at the rail in town the gentlemen compared and admired the best looking horses.

Three years after the great earthquake, the strongest ever in American history, the United States Congress passed the first relief act in history. On February 17, 1815 they passed the New Madrid Relief Act.

It was set up to help the land owners in Missouri to exchange the ruined lands for other tracts of government land in Missouri. They placed a limit of 160 to 640 acres no matter how much land they had lost. As in many acts from the government, fraud became rampant in the many land exchanges. Some folks started calling it the Fraud Act. Things would begin to happen that would divide the north from the south. All the states had pulled together to fend off the British and Indians. The thinking in most southern states was that they had rights as a free state. They looked at it as the state comes first and second the Union of the United States.

After a great Christmas Tazewell Country was starting a new year.
Some happenings of 1816:
On March 20, 1816 the Supreme Court of the United States affirmed its right to review state court records.

On April 9, 1816 the Negro's around Philadelphia organized their own church called the African Methodist Episcopal Church.

On April 10, 1816 the second Bank of the United States was chartered.

On May 5, 1816 the American Bible Society was organized in New York.

On June 6, 1816, a ten inch snow fell in New England. It was caused by the eruption of a volcano in Indonesia. They called it a "Year without summer!"

On June 11, 1816 the Gas Light Company was founded in Baltimore, Maryland.
More winter weather in July, Waltham, Massachusetts on July 8, 1816 reported having a frost.

THE PATRIOT, HEZEKIAH WHITT

On July 27, 1816 the United States Army destroyed Fort Apalachicola, a stronghold of the Seminole Indians, because they were harboring runaway slaves.

On October 7, 1816 the first double decked steamboat, Washington, arrived in New Orleans.

On December 4, 1816 James Monroe from Virginia was elected the 5th President of the United States. He defeated Rufus King of the Federalist Party.

On December 11, 1816 Indiana became the 19th state to join the Union.

That is just a few things going on in the year of 1816. The southern states were enjoying the fruits of growing cotton and other exports. Slavery was an important part of the work on the great plantations in the Deep South. The north was becoming more industrialized. Eli Whitney had developed a new system in manufacturing that entailed replacement parts. When a machine broke down, you simply removed the bad part and installed a new one. This really enhanced the growth of manufacturing.

Under the leadership of the noted Kentuckian, Henry Clay, an 1816 tariff was passed to protect American manufacturing. The northerners loved the new tariff, but the southerners disliked it because they had little manufacturing. They had to pay higher prices for their goods from the north. This was another thing that began to divide the north from the south. Henry Clay was a southerner and did not mean to hurt the south.

Tazewell County, Virginia was not as isolated as before with products coming in from the north by way of the east. The folks had given up some of their self reliance as they begin to buy manufactured goods. Some ladies were now buying the antebellum style dresses and the gentlemen of means were buying fine suites and polished boots of fine leather. Many of the gentlemen in the frontier were always on the watch for new and better firearms.

A new pistol came out in 1816 made by Simeon North. It was a single shot flintlock of .54 calibers. It was made mostly for the United States Navy. Some would be converted to percussion in later years.

The marvel of Eli Whitney's idea of interchangeable parts was adapted to gun making about this time.

Another musket came out in 1816 to improve on the old 1812 model. It has a 42" barrel of .69 caliber. This musket would be carried in the Mexican American War and later carried by Confederates as a modified musket in the War of Northern Aggression. It was modified to percussion and used a cap to supply the fire to the powder instead of flintlock. They had not started using rifling in muskets yet so they were still called muskets.

Hezekiah and many other gentlemen quit carrying their long and bulky muskets and carried the smaller concealable pistols. Some of these pistols would be used in the challenge of dueling. It was an honorable way to settle a severe difference of opinion by two gentlemen, especially in the south. Even the future President of the United States, Andrew Jackson, once fought a duel.

For many years there were not many Christian Ministers in the area of Tazewell County. A few ministers mentioned in marriage records from 1815 to the 1830's were David Young, Jonathon Quicksal, Hugh Johnston, Jacob McDaniel, David Payne, William Henkel, John Perry, William McGuire the son of Hezekiah's friend the elder William McGuire, John Sizemore, Samuel Miller and the traveling preacher Brother Robert (Bob) Sheffey.

Churches were built and the good folks in Tazewell County were very faithful to attend and take their children. Hezekiah and his family went to different churches, but were mostly deemed to be Baptist. David Young was a Baptist Preacher that became a friend to the Whitt family.

President James Monroe was elected in 1816. He was a Democratic-Republican from Virginia and ushered in the period called, "Era of Good Feelings." President Monroe was an excellent administrator that bolstered the federal government and made several internal improvements. The Nation was so pleased with him that he ran uncontested in the election of 1820.

Good feelings didn't last as the Missouri Crisis would come and divide the North and South even more. Also he would provoke the Monroe Doctrine later in 1823.

The Era of Good Feeling was felt even in the hills of Tazewell County. The folks were enjoying the post war era of the War of 1812. The prominence of Hezekiah Whitt grew and he was known as an honorable man as were the other lifetime appointed, "Gentlemen Justices of the Peace." The County was growing and the folks enjoyed a time of new relationships with new neighbors and old alike. For many years the settlers had to be so cautious just to work a field or be away from the cabin at all. Now the threat of Indian attack was gone and the British were treating the United States as another nation. Imports and exports once again flowed from the two countries.

Over on Meadow Creek in Montgomery County, Jonas and Susannah were given permission to marry. Archibald had made the couple wait for a long time to make sure that it was to be. Richard (Devil Dick) Whitt would be the best man and he was going to return to Tazewell County. Jonas would stay in Montgomery County because of his connection with Archibald and his family. Archibald was prominent and had a large amount of land and besides Susannah wanted to stay there. You know when a wife wants something she usually gets it. Jonas would always want to move back to Tazewell County, but would make himself satisfied because of the advantages he felt he had on Meadow Creek. Richard had learned to be a blacksmith and Jonas was still learning mill building. He had worked on many, but had never built one on his own.

On October 10, 1816 he was 19 and Susannah was 22. Some folks teased her about marrying a younger man. Some said she was robbing the cradle, but her reply was that she would raise him up to suit herself. It was wonderful for both Jonas and Susannah. They had waited for almost four years since they had first met. They had yearned for each other ever since. They had a wonderful wedding night as they had never gone so far with their sexual exploration. Sure they did a little forbidden feeling the last year but they both did not want to go all the way as both felt that to be a serious sin. They wanted to start out right without sin and not take the chance of having a baby out of wedlock. Now they were married and they could love and have pleasure all they wanted. They were so happy!

In the early spring of 1817 Richard Whitt returned to Tazewell County and had his pack mule loaded with hand tools to use in his new trade as a blacksmith. He had plans to set up a shop and practice blacksmithing in Tazewell County.

Rachel ran to him and greeted him with a big hug and kiss, and then Hezekiah did the same.

"My gracious Richard, you were big when you left, but you are a man's man now," said Rachel.

"You are strong and your muscles are hard as nails," replied Hezekiah as he gripped the strong biceps of Richard.

Richard smiled widely at his beloved parents.

"Ol' son, you are a site for sore eyes, I am so happy to see you and how is your little brother Jonas and his new bride?" asked Rachel?

"I am really glad to see you and Paw too!" replied Richard.

"As for Jonas and Susannah, they are as happy as young-un with a big poke of candy," continued Richard.

"I sure wish we could-ah been there to see-um get hitched," said Rachel.

"It went off without a hitch, uh', I guess there was a hitch," replied Richard.

THE PATRIOT, HEZEKIAH WHITT

"Anyway it all went well and that evening we had fun tormenting them fer about an hour with a grand chivalree" laughed Richard.

"What did you all do?" asked Hezekiah?

"One thing we done was to put a pair of pantaloons on a stick and waved it lik'a flag fer um to see, then we pecked on the windows and doors and made all kinds of noise," answered Richard.

"Were they embarrassed?" asked Rachel?

I think Jonas was embarrassed more-un Susannah," laughed Richard.

"How many took part in tha' chivalree?" asked Hezekiah?

"There was a whole bunch of us, they was probable bout fifty count-un the young-uns," replied Richard.

"We better get your animals took care of, then we can talk while your Maw fixes you some vittles," said Hezekiah.

"Yes honey, I bet you are nearly starved to death, I will rustle you up something, go on and get your animals cared for," said Rachel.

Hezekiah walked to the barn and helped Richard get his animals unpacked and fed.

The pack mule had a heavy load and Hezekiah asked, "What in thunder do you have in this box?" asked Hezekiah?

"Here Paw, let me get that, it is heavy cause it's got all of my blacksmithing tools in it," replied Richard.

"No wonder it so heavy, you are packing a lot of iron here son," replied Hezekiah.

"Paw, I aim to set me up a shop here abouts and serve the area as a blacksmith; I am purty good and think I can make a decent living," said Richard.

"That sounds real good son, but there is a few smiths around, I recon you will get enough work to make it; I bet you could set up right here and take care of Indian Creek and this end of Baptist Valley," replied Hezekiah.

"Sounds good, I guess ol' man Wurts still has his shop in Jeffersonville, don't he Paw?"

asked Richard"

"Yes he does and he seems to stay busy," replied Hezekiah.

"Paw I gotta get me ballast and a few things, but I am bout ready to get me some of Maw's cooking first," said Richard.

Hezekiah was tall and straight and walking beside the big Richard Whitt he looked really small.

Hezekiah and Richard built a good sized building and set up Richard's blacksmith shop. Richard painted a big sign on the wall facing the road and it read, "Whitt's Blacksmithing and Farriering." (Horseshoeing.)

The young Baptist Preacher, David Young called Elder by his position in the Baptist faith was building a new church up the Valley about five miles from Hezekiah's farm. Hezekiah, James, Griffy, Richard, Edmund and other neighbors all donated some cash and muscle to get the little Baptist Church up and finished. John Bunyan worked with some other finish-carpenters and built a pulpit and several pews for the church.

They had a day set for the dedication in which all the folks would bring picnic baskets and after preaching they would all go out and eat together on the ground in the shade of an oak grove. They called it "alls days preaching and eating on the ground."

One of Edmunds youngest got it mixed up and called it, "All days eating and meeting on the ground."

Richard Devil Dick Whitt loved the saying and he used it every chance he got.

Hezekiah was in Jeffersonville a day or two a week dealing with the affairs of Tazewell County. He had a nice black suit, but only wore it on Sunday and special affairs. Hezekiah bought Rachel a new blue Southern Bell dress. It had a six bone hoop slip. She was so beautiful in it even though she was in her upper fifties.

"Lordy Mercy, I could make five dresses and two shirts with all the material in this one dress!" she exclaimed.

"You deserve it and you are so beautiful in in it," replied Hezekiah.

"I use to be sort of purty when I was young, but now I am just an old woman," replied Rachel.

"Nonsense, you are still the most beautiful woman in Tazewell County," exclaimed

THE PATRIOT, HEZEKIAH WHITT

Hezekiah.

"Thank you for saying that, but I am getting old," replied Rachel.

"I am so proud of you, if they ever had a beauty contest I know you would win," said Hezekiah.

"I doubt there will ever be such a thing, you men would rather have a beauty contest for your horses," she laughed.

Hezekiah laughed with Rachel and right out of the blue he asked, "Honey would you fix me and Richard some of your famous corned beef gravy and a few eggs and maybe some fried tators?"

"Well, I reckon I can, we ain't had breakfast for supper in a awhile, you go out to the springhouse and rake off some of that rich cream and bring it in, get some butter too," said Rachel.

It was about 5:00 PM that Richard came in and saw his Maw fixing the gravy and eggs.

"My goodness Maw, you sure are flinging a craven on me, I surely love your corned beef gravy!" exclaimed Richard (Devil Dick) Whitt.

"You fellers are all alike, go and wash your paws and come back and set the table and holler at your Paw," instructed Rachel as she was pouring the gravy into a very large bowl.

If you have never tried corned beef gravy that came down from the Whitts, you must try it. I will not give the Whitts credit for the invention of the recipe, but I know it was in the Whitt family for many years.

(I give permission for you to copy this recipe and genealogy only and nothing else)
Colonel Charles Dahnmon Whitt

Corned Beef Gravy Recipe
Modern version!
1 can of Corned Beef.12 0z.
1 can of canned cream (evaporated milk)12 oz.
2 tablespoons of shortening, (bacon grease is best)
I cast iron skillet # 8 10 ½ inch.
   2/3 cup of floor

THE PATRIOT, HEZEKIAH WHITT

Spray down your skillet with Pam or spread out some shortening and start with medium heat.

Add your shortening and open your can of corned beef and put it in the warm skillet. Cut up with a fork and raise the heat to brown it some. If too dry add a little vegetable oil.

In a large bowl pour in your canned milk and take the empty can and fill it with water and mix the water and milk together.

After the corned beef is hot and brown and well stirred with a fork, add the floor. Continue to stir.

Turn the heat up a little and pour in the milk and water mixture.

Take a large whisk and continue to stir until the gravy is thick and creamy. Be sure to scrap the sides and bottom as you stir.

Use a ladle and pour it over a torn up "Cathead Biscuit" and eat. Be careful, your tongue will go wild and knock your brains out!

Some happening in 1817:

On March 3, 1817 the Mississippi Territory was divided to form Alabama and Mississippi.

On April 15, 1817 the first deaf school was opened in Hartford, Connecticut.

On Independence Day in 1817 the construction was begun on the Erie Canal System.

On August 18, 1817 the papers in New England reported that a great sea serpent was seen off sure of Gloucester, Massachusetts.

On September 22, 1817, John Quincy Adams became the Secretary of State of the United States.

The new steam boats frequented the waters of the Ohio, Mississippi, and other rivers. The boats had been used for work and to carry passengers up until now. On October 1, 1817 the first "Showboat," left the banks of Nashville on the Cumberland River on its maiden voyage.

In November the United States is at war with the Seminole Indians in Florida. On December 10, 1817 Mississippi becomes the 20th state to join the Union of the United States. This was a time of inventions, arts, and learning all bringing good feelings.

Chapter 39

Itchy Feet

On March 18, 1818 Congress approved the first pension plan for government service.

On April 4, 1818 the United States Flag was changed back to 13 stripes and the star count is up to 20. Did you know that the flag carried 15 stripes for awhile?

On April 7, 1818 General Andrew Jackson takes St. Marks, Florida from the Seminole Indians.

In order to form a good relationship with our northern neighbors the Canadians, President Monroe disarms the U.S. Navy on the Great Lakes.

For you baseball fans, on May 11, 1818, Hod Eller, the pitcher for the Cincinnati Reds pitched a no-hitter against the St. Louis Cardinals and won 6 to nothing. Did you know baseball has been around that long?

On May 24, 1818 General Jackson captures Pensacola Florida.

On October 20, 1818 a formal border between Canada and the United States was agreed on and it would follow the 49th parallel. The Oregon country would be controlled jointly by Great Britain and the United States. Good luck with that.

On December 3, 1818 Illinois became the 21st state.

On the day before Christmas 1818, the great Christmas Hymn, "Silent Night," was composed by Franz Joseph Gruber and was first sang on Christmas day 1818.

A letter came to Hezekiah and Rachel late in the year of 1818 from Jonas and Susannah Whitt. They had a great announcement of the birth of their son John Bunyan Whitt. They named him after Jonas' big brother and of course the John Bunyan that had authored the great book, "Pilgrims Progress."

John Bunyan was pleased that Jonas and Susannah had named their son after him. Bunyan liked his name and in the future he would have a son that would also be named John Bunyan Whitt, Jr.

The era of good feelings would not last. As folks moved west and the territories became states a real conflict arose. It was much like a wedge being driven between the north and the south. Missouri was becoming a state and the north wanted it to become a free state, (No slaves.) the south wanted it to be able to choose so the folks moving there could take their slaves.

Another thing that ended the era of good feelings was the depression of 1919. The financial panic was caused by over speculation in western lands. The depression lasted a decade and folks had an era of not so good feelings.

THE PATRIOT, HEZEKIAH WHITT

With so many things happening nationally and in the world, Tazewell County went about mostly unaffected because of their isolation in the mountains. They were mostly self reliant, but were slowly coming into the 19th century. Most folks were happy to have a home, food, and the beauty of the mountains on the waters of the Clinch.

On February 22, 1819 Spain renounces claims to the Oregon Country; this will open the door for the United States to gain complete control a little later.

On March 2, 1819 the Arkansas Territory is organized. Can you read between the lines and see that the United States is moving to take all of America?

Also on March 2, 1819 the first immigration law was passed.

On May 22, 1819 the first steam powered vessel crossed the Atlantic; it was the Savannah and it sailed from Georgia.

On December 14, 1819 Alabama became the 22nd state to join the Union of the United States.

Rachel Rebecca Whitt, daughter of Edmund and Hannah Lestor Whitt, would capture the elusive Richard (Devil Dick) Whitt. They were married on November 12, 1820 and would move to Floyd County, Kentucky near present day Prestonsburg.

The 1820 United States Census was taken and Tazewell County had grown to 3,916. The county had an increase of 909 souls since 1810. On the Census report, Hezekiah was listed as male 45 & up, 1 male 16 to 26, 1 female 45 & up. Also listed were Edmund, James, Elizabeth, and Griffy Whitt. Also the population of the United States was 9,638,453 of which was 1,771,656 blacks about 18 %.

Tazewell County 1820 Personal Property Tax:

Hezekiah Whitt 1 white male over 16 and I horse; Griffy Whitt 1 white male over 16 and 2 horses; Richard Whitt 1 white male 16+ and 1 horse; Edmund Whitt 1 male 16+ and three horses; Elizabeth Whitt 1 white male 16+ and three horses; James Whitt 1 white male+ and 1 horse. I am not sure who this Elizabeth Whitt is.

On March 20, 1820, surveyed for Hez Whitt 120 acres part of a Land Treasury Warrant assigned by Hez Harman assignee of John Cally and part of Warrant No. 5334 for 500 aces dated January 6, 1814;

Beginning at a black oak and cucumber on top of Reedy Ridge, a corner to James Whitt…crossing Cabin branch to a white poplar…Crossing Indian Creek to three spruce pines in an island… crossing said creek to a Dogwood…crossing creek to two beaches.

This would be official on August 22, 1821; Hezekiah would get the land grant for 120 acres On Indian Creek, a branch of the Clinch River…Grants Number 70, page 305; Tazewell County, Virginia.

THE PATRIOT, HEZEKIAH WHITT

On February 6, 1820 there was an organized emigration of Negroes back to Africa from New York to Sierra Leone.

On March 3, 1820 the Missouri Compromise passes, allowing slavery in Missouri.

On March 15, 1820 Maine is admitted as the 23rd state.

On October 20, 1820 the United States bought part of Florida from Spain for $5 million dollars. Spain must have become a little worried with General Jackson and his army moving around Florida.

On December 6, 1820 James Monroe was re-elected President of the United States.

On December 20, 1820 Missouri imposed a $1.00 bachelor tax on all unmarried men between the ages of 21 and 50.

Double good news came from Meadow Creek, Montgomery County. Susannah and Jonas sent a letter to Hezekiah and Rachel reporting the birth of two little girls. They named the twins Rachel and Rhoda. They looked identical and were both a bundle of joy. Susannah was well pleased as she would have help in any arguments against the males in the family. Susannah would have help in the women's work and someone to confide in when the girls got bigger. Jonas had two little sweethearts and praised God for their safe arrival.

Rachel jumped for joy as she read the letter and as soon as Hezekiah learned of its contents he was also well pleased to hear of his two new granddaughters.

"We just have to go back to Meadow Creek and visit our grandbabies, we ain't even seen little Bunyan yet!" exclaimed Rachel.

"Well I reckon we can make a trip, just as soon as we get the planting done," answered Hezekiah.
Rachel grabbed Hezekiah and pulled him close while kissing his lips.
"Woman, you are getting me in a mood," said Hezekiah.
"Well that's alright, we are married and there ain't no young-uns about," replied Rachel.
Hezekiah squeezed Rachel and kissed her passionately.
"Oh Hezekiah, I love you, go lock the door and make me happy," said Rachel in her sexy voice.
Hezekiah went to lock the door while he was thinking of the time, "We ain't made love in the afternoon for a long time," he thought.

Rachel was standing beside the bed with only a blanket around her. Hezekiah dropped his clothes and Rachel opened her blanket and received Hezekiah. This was an Indian way to start a love session and it will bring out the juices of love.

After they made love, they lay for a long time holding on to each other and talked about their long happy marriage.

COLONEL CHARLES DAHNMON WHITT   342

THE PATRIOT, HEZEKIAH WHITT

"I'm gonna get the boys to write us good news more often," said Hezekiah with a crooked little grin.

Rachel slapped Hezekiah on the behind and said, "We don't need no letters to make love!"

"I am going to write the children and tell them we are planning a trip out their way as soon as we get the planting done," said Rachel.

I better get the fields ready, it wouldn't be long to planting time," answered Hezekiah.

"Husband, I sure love you, you always make me so happy!" said Rachel with a wonderful smile on her lips.

It seemed that every one wanted to move to Kentucky and even further to the west. John Bunyan Whitt and Richard Whitt were both hankering to go to Kentucky. Bunyan wanted to settle close to Maytown in Floyd County and Richard wanted to settle on Gimlet Creek just off of Little Sandy River in Carter County, Kentucky.

Spring was coming to Tazewell County and was exceptionally warm for the time of year in 1821. Hezekiah took Rachel to church on Easter Sunday 1821. This particular Sunday it was just about as hot as June. The leafs were not even out, but the birds were mightily twitter-pated; they were all out chirping noisily and carrying straw and other building materials about to build their nests.

Hezekiah helped Rachel up into their fine buggy and they headed up the valley to their little church. As they arrived at the church several other folks were arriving. Everyone had on their best Easter outfits. Many of the ladies were wearing their beautiful southern bell type dresses. Most of the men were wearing nice suits and their heads were covered with nice hats of the time.

Rachel whispered to Hezekiah, "I feel funny being so dressed up!"

"Sweetheart, I love showing you off, you are the most beautiful lady in Virginia and I venture to say in the whole United States," said the admiring Hezekiah.

"Old man, you are plumb crazy, but I sure do love you," answered Rachel.

As the ladies entered the church with their flowing dresses they made a lot of swishing sounds that caused all the men to watch them waltzing into the little church.

The young Elder Young stood at the front of the church with a wide smile on his face as he enjoyed the scene.

It was quiet warm in the church so the deacons opened every window to the fullest and left the door opened that was normally closed.

It was time to start the worship service and Elder Young called on Hezekiah to open the service with a prayer. Hezekiah prayed to the Lord and ask that He join them and asked if He would accept their worship. A few folks were mentioned that needed to be blessed by the Lord and he ended with a thanksgiving and Amen.

THE PATRIOT, HEZEKIAH WHITT

The song leader came to the front and led the congregation in several old hymns. The Old Baptist sings like no other church. The song leader would word a sentence and then the congregation would join in with perfect harmony and sing in unison the sentence that the leader had worded to them. To your ears today the sounds may make you think of natives in darkest Africa. I am not bashing them, they just sing different and have no music in their services. I am sure it was a joyous noise to the Lord Jesus Christ.

Elder Young preached the Easter message about Jesus rising from the grave on that first Easter, but as usual he ended up preaching on the Blessed Hope.

Hezekiah whispered to Rachel, "He always comes to that no matter what the sermon is about!"

"Shhhh" whispered Rachel with a grin for Hezekiah.

The church was fuller than usual because of it being Easter and many folks wanted to show of their Easter outfits.

On the way out Hezekiah overheard a conversation between an older lady and a young boy. The Lady called the boy Johnny and he called her grand maw. The older lady had brought Johnny to church for the first time and grand maw was pleased with Johnny's conduct.

"How did you like church Johnny?" she asked?
"I sure did like it a bunch," little Johnny said.
"What part did you like the best, the singing or the preaching?" grand maw asked?
"Neither one, I liked it when they passed the money around, I got a quarter and three pennies, how much did you get grand maw?" asked little Johnny?

The lady grabbed little Johnny and rushed him toward the family wagon. Her face was as red as a cardinal in heat. Hezekiah had to turn his head to laugh.

After Rachel and Hezekiah said their good byes to all of their friends; Hezekiah helped his beautiful Rachel up into their fine buggy. It took some doing to get all of that dress up and out of the wheels.

"What was so funny, I noticed you about to bust a laughing," said Rachel.
Hezekiah was still laughing as he told Rachel about what he had overheard.
"All that money being passed around!" said Hezekiah while laughing out loud.
"My word, reckon that young-un thought he was supposed to dip into the offering?" asked Rachel?"
"He must-at, he helped himself according to what he told his grand maw." answered Hezekiah.
"Young-uns are so funny and yet they are so innocent," replied Rachel as they headed down the valley toward their Cedar Grove Farm.

THE PATRIOT, HEZEKIAH WHITT

After they got home and Rachel took off her special dress and put on an everyday dress she started to fix dinner. Most of their children arrived to enjoy Easter afternoon with their parents. The daughters and daughters-in-law all went in the kitchen to help Rachel.

John Bunyan Whitt and Richard (Devil Dick) Whitt were both there and after dinner, at the right time they were going to tell Hezekiah and Rachel about their plans to move to Kentucky. Bunyan was going to move to Floyd County near the little settlement of Maytown. He planned to set up a carpenter shop and make his living. Richard was moving much further to Carter County on Gimlet Creek that is tributary to Little Sandy River. His work as a blacksmith was going good, but he had itchy feet and wanted to set up in Kentucky as did so many folks at that time.

Griffy Whitt was thinking about going all the way to Missouri, but would set tight for now, but after he left and with Jonas and Susannah way back in Montgomery County, only James and Nancy would be left. Of course the daughters Rebecca and her husband John Husk Lowe were still close by. Susannah married Joseph Webb and they were on the north end of Tazewell County and would be West Virginia someday.

After a fine Easter dinner of lamb and many other things the folks went into the sitting room and lit their pipes. Hezekiah said we shouldn't have any spirits on the Lord's Day, especially Easter so they drink tea and coffee.

Richard was always out spoken so he started the conversation about his and Bunyan's family moving to Kentucky.

Rachel's beautiful dark eyes welled up with tears of sorrow. Both sons kneeled in front of her and held her to console her.

Hezekiah spoke up, "Rachel, don't you remember when we were young it was so exciting to come to this land flowing with milk and honey?"

"Yes, but these are my babies!" exclaimed Rachel!

"Our sons are all grown up with families of their own and they want some adventure in their lives, every young family is wanting to head west," replied Hezekiah.

"We still have plenty of milk and honey flowing here on the waters of the Clinch," said Rachel.
"I know honey, but they want to go," said Hezekiah.
"I just hate to think of my babies being plumb off into Kentucky," said Rachel.
"Maw we want to stand on our own two feet and we will write often, maybe you and Paw can come for a visit and see the Bluegrass State, said Bunyan.

Rachel finally quit crying as the news slowly sunk in. She wanted to know when and then she revealed that Hezekiah and she were making a trip to Montgomery County to see Jonas, the babies and other kindred.

They all talked about their planned trips and Bunyan said he was going to follow the Kentucky Turnpike and follow the Louisa River (Levisa Fork) to his new home near present day Prestonsburg. Richard said they would follow the Clinch and cross the Powell Valley to Cumberland Gap and then cross Kentucky to the Little Sandy River. Richard and wife Rebecca were more or less following her father Edmund Price Whitt to Kentucky. You know how it is when a wife wants to be close to her family. Edmund was already on his way to Carter County, Kentucky.

John Bunyan and his family sold all they could and loaded their prized positions in their wagon took a cow and a riding horse tied to the back of the wagon. He had two strong mules to pull the wagon. He put Hannah and young John Bunyan up in the wagon and they left Rachel and Hezekiah standing in the yard. Richard and Rebecca who had been having morning sickness and followed the Bunyan family down the Kentucky Turnpike towards the turn off point. That is where Raven is today. Richard would follow the Clinch until he got down to about Castlewood where he would head southwest. He would cross the Powell valley into Lee County and then travel through Cumberland Gap.

John Bunyan would have a tough trip following the Levisa as it was not much more than a bridle trail at that time.

A funny thing happened to Richard and his family, they stopped off in Lee County and it suited them nicely. (This happened after 1827) They ended up staying there for several years. With the confrontation Richard had that second night in Lee County, you would think they would get out as fast as possible, but they didn't. The confrontation was with six men that were out looking for trouble and they saw the big Richard and sized him up. They figured six to one was good odds. They meant to hurt him or run him out of Lee County. Those six men made a big mistake when they picked Richard Devil Dick Whitt.

Richard told them politely that he didn't want any trouble, but the six thugs were bent on roughing up the newcomer. The leader waded in on Richard and the other five joined in. After kicking, gouging, biting, and the six hitting Richard's fist with their noses several times; big Richard Devil Dick Whitt was the last one standing. He helped them up one at a time and they looked like whipped pups.

"Sire, who are you?" one of the men asked?
"My name is Richard Devil Dick Whitt," Richard said.
"The name sure fits," said one of the men.

THE PATRIOT, HEZEKIAH WHITT

My sweet wife is modeling this Southern Bell Dress for me.

Sharon Gail My Southern Bell!

Chapter 40

Hezekiah and Rachel Visit Jonas

Edmund Price Whitt, Hannah his wife and all the children and their children loaded up and left as a small wagon train about a week before John Bunyan and Richard Whitt. The county had new folks moving in and plenty of them moved west to Kentucky and further. All the talk about moving west ignited a fire in many folk's souls and they wanted to move.

I guess Edmund was wondering what happened to his daughter Rebecca and Richard Whitt as they had stopped of in Lee County and decided to stay there. Of course mailing addresses were easy back then. You only had to put the name, town and county and state and the mail would reach the party. I am sure Rebecca wrote a letter to her Maw and Paw.

James and Nancy would be spending more time with Hezekiah and Rachel and helping with any of the heavy work. Hezekiah and Rachel were in great shape for their age, they were 61 in 1821. James was the first born and would eventually be willed the old home place.

Rachel was really looking forward to the trip back to Meadow Creek to see Jonas and his family. She talked about little Bunyan and the twins, Rachel and Rhoda most every day. Hezekiah was anxious to go also. This would get their minds off the other children that had left Tazewell County.

After the planting was done and Hezekiah took care of his civic duties they were ready to head out to Montgomery County. He had James, the Hankins family, and Thomas Bailey Christian to look over the farm while they were gone. Hezekiah packed their possible on a mule, and saddled their fine riding horses and was ready to go. They both wore plain clothes as not to attract bad men and outlaws on the trail. Hezekiah dug out his old buckskins to wear and Rachel wore a pair of linsey-woolsey britches. This helped them to look as if they had no money. Besides that it was more comfortable on the trail. Hezekiah packed a musket on top of the mule for easy access and carried his pistol on him. He also had a skinning knife and his old tomahawk.

"Hezekiah, you expecting an attack from a hundred warriors?" asked Rachel?
"Nope, but I will be ready if there is any mountain outlaws that decide to take us on," he said.
"It don't hurt to be ready I reckon," replied Rachel.
They mounted up and Hezekiah prayed a prayer of thanksgiving and ask Jesus to protect them on their trip and give them traveling mercies. Hezekiah looked at Rachel and she looked at him.

THE PATRIOT, HEZEKIAH WHITT

"We have done everything I know to do, so are you ready to leave, Princess Rachel?" asked Hezekiah.

"Yes you handsome thing, I'm ready," replied Rachel.

The two headed up the road across Green Mountain towards Jeffersonville to start their trip.

As Hezekiah and Rachel rode through Jeffersonville, many folks had to give them a second look. They had not seen the Whitts dressed this way for a real long time. It was common for people to dress down while traveling through the mountains. It was more comfortable as well as adding safety to the travelers. If a person traveled all dressed up that would defiantly make them a target for mountain outlaws.

Rachel was excited to be traveling again and could hardly wait to see Jonas and the new grandbabies. Hezekiah yearned to travel through the beautiful mountains and valleys and to enjoy the creation of the Almighty.

It was not long before they were at the foot of East Mountain. They had passed a couple of travelers heading to Jeffersonville and one man herding his flock to a greener pasture. They saw an eagle fishing in the headwaters of the Blue Stone River. They enjoyed watching some river otters sliding down a steep bank into a pool of the Blue Stone River. They saw a flock of passenger pigeons, but there were no flocks as big as years past.

"The Lord sure made us a beautiful world," commented Hezekiah.

"Yes he did, and He just about out did Himself when he made this part," answered Rachel.

"Let's go ahead and camp here tonight and get a fresh start in the morning, I want the horses to be fresh when we cross over to Rocky Gap," said Hezekiah.

"Suits me!" exclaimed Rachel as she looked around.

Some things that happened in 1821:

On January 17, 1821 Moses Austin brought 300 United States families to settle in Texas with the blessing of Mexico.

On February 24, 1821 Mexico gained her independence from Spain.

On July 17, 1821 Spain cedes the rest of Florida to the United States.

On August 10, 1821 Missouri was admitted as the 24th state.

The Santa Fe Trail is opened and on the 1st of September 1821 colonies were established along it.

On December 17, 1821 Kentucky abolishes debtor's prisons.

During a term of court 1821, Tazewell County recommended three men to the Governor of Virginia, Thomas Man Randolph Jr., as fit persons to serve as Sheriff. The three men were Hezekiah Whitt, John Thompson, and Thomas Witten.

THE PATRIOT, HEZEKIAH WHITT

Back to Hezekiah and Rachel, the next day Hezekiah and Rachel rose early, had breakfast and loaded up and were heading toward Rocky Gap. They shot the gap in the early afternoon and were heading down the other side toward Wytheville. The road was not much more than a bridle path as nature worked relentlessly to reclaim it. Little saplings and weed were in the path and the Mountain Laurel was abundant on each side. It was a perfect place for an ambush which brought Hezekiah to a new awareness. It was places like this that the Indians loved to attack from in years past. Now it was outlaws and bushwhackers you had to watch for.

Hezekiah turned to Rachel and whispered, "Keep a sharp eye out!"

Rachel whispered back, "I am and trying to keep the horses quiet also."

They were most of the way down the mountain when Hezekiah's sharp eyes spotted something shinnies in the edge of the woods ahead. He told Rachel about it in a low voice and pulled out his pistol. He checked the prime on the pistol and handed it to Rachel and retrieved the Old Betz from the pack animal. The prime looked a might weak so he primed it to make sure. Then they slowly moved down the mountain. When they got to within 25 yards of the place Hezekiah stopped and hollered at the figure in the woods.

"Who are you, come out and be recognized!" exclaimed Hezekiah.
The man knew that he had been spotted so he rode out into the open.
"What were you hiding in the shadows for?" asked Hezekiah?
"Sorry to alarm you sir, I had a run in with two fellers yesterday and thought you were them coming back to do me harm," answered the man.

"I saw you and the missies coming way up the mountain so I took to cover jest in case," said the Man.
"Who are you?" asked Hezekiah?
"I am Billy, Billy York," answered the man.
"Billy, what is your business, where do you hale from?" asked Hezekiah?
I live over on Cripple Creek jest south of Wytheville and I am going to Jeffersonville to see George Perry," replied Billy.

"What's wrong with it?" asked Hezekiah?
The man looked dumbfounded at Hezekiah.
"What's wrong with what?" asked Billy?
Without cracking a smile, Hezekiah asked, "The creek, what's wrong with it?"
Billy looked at Hezekiah real serious and said, "There ain't nutton wrong with the creek!"
"You said it was crippled," answered Hezekiah.
Billy laughed out loud and so did Hezekiah and Rachel.
The tension was gone and both parties felt relieved that there was no trouble facing them. They talked about the two men and tried to figure out where they went to and what they were up to. Hezekiah told Billy that George Perry lived in the Abbs Valley

section of Tazewell County. Billy said that the men were ahead of him and that is why he was concerned. Then he told Hezekiah that George Perry had some slaves and he sent a letter about buying a good house woman. I am going to talk to him as my Paw has a good one and is still in her prime.

The number of slaves in Tazewell County in 1820 was 286!

"I didn't need to know your personal business long as it ain't meant to cause me a problem," said Hezekiah.

"Well Sir and Ma'am, I aim to travel on if you-ins don't mind," said Billy.
We don't mind, we will go on down the mountain, be careful Billy," said Hezekiah.
Rachel gave him a wave and said, "God Speed."
Not too far down the trail Hezekiah spotted the spring that he had stopped at so many times while scouting out the Indians.

"Rachel, look there is the spring we always stop at. The first time I stopped at it there was a black snake eating a copperhead; do you remember me telling you that story?" asked Hezekiah?

Hezekiah walked up close to the spring and jumped back.

"I will be damned, there is a blacksnake eating a copperhead!" exclaimed Hezekiah.

"Heze, stop that cussing, it can't be the same snakes, it might be their great great grandchildren," said Rachel.

Hezekiah laughed!

"Well can we get us some water without brothering the wiggly things?" asked Rachel?

"Sure thing, I will get us some water, they can't hardly move no how," replied Hezekiah as he filled the canteens.

After they drink their fill Hezekiah took one horse at a time and let them drink being careful not to let them get spooked.

Hezekiah and Rachel traveled on down the mountain toward Wytheville and never met anyone else this day. After crossing the 3,500 feet mountain both the horses and the Whitts were spent. They camped on a creek that had a clearing of good grass for the horses and mule. From habit, Hezekiah set up their lean to in the edge of the woods with a clear view of the field. They were not expecting any trouble, but it didn't hurt to be prepared.

After supper Hezekiah and Rachel regained their energy and enjoy the evening. They went to bed as the sounds of the evening soothed them to sleep. The creek made music as the water tumbled over the rocks, a whippoorwill called for her mate. Night critters came out and made some rustling in the leaves as they moved about. A distant wolf howled a few times and an owl gave a few hoots. Rachel snuggled up close to her man Hezekiah and they had a good sleep.

THE PATRIOT, HEZEKIAH WHITT

Next morning Hezekiah looked over the clearing at first light. His groggy eyes counted two horses, but didn't see the mule. He set up quickly and looked harder over the whole area. There was the mule over in the creek getting his self a morning drink.

Rachel looked over at Hezekiah and said, "It sure don't take long to stay all night here!"

Hezekiah laughed and both of them got up and went over a few feet deeper in the woods to take their morning pee. They both looked at each other and smiled.

"Not this morning," said Rachel.

"I was just smiling at my princess," said Hezekiah sheepishly.

Hezekiah fixed up a fire for breakfast and Rachel fried some smoked bacon and made some stick bread and she got the coffeepot going Hezekiah un-hobbled the horses and mule and brought them close by so they could be loaded for the journey.

They were once again on the path toward Wytheville and both were in a good spirit. The trip was a good distraction for Rachel so she would not worry about her children moving off.

They went through the valley and would have to cross another mountain before they would reach Wytheville. Walker Mountain lay ahead and it was about 4,000 feet high. It was just another mountain to cross and enjoy the scenery. There were still dangers in traveling, but since the Indian raids had subsided it was safer. They just had to watch for the perils of the path and of course, bad men.

This day was routine and they made it almost to Wytheville before they stopped for the day. This trail they followed is basically where Interstate 77 now runs.

Hezekiah and Rachel enjoyed their time away from everyone, but would be glad to see Wytheville. Hezekiah would compare it with his town, Jeffersonville. They took time to wash off in Stony Fork and caught their supper also. Hezekiah caught two Redeye's and Rachel caught four. Of course she had to rub it in that she had out fished him. Maybe she would make it up to him in the sack. Lovemaking wasn't talked about too much, but it was their favorite recreation.

Next day they rode through Wytheville and stopped at the mercantile and picked up a few things. They talked to the locals and some folks were surprised at the learning and mannerism of the couple dressed in buckskins and linsey-woolsey. Hezekiah had to walk through the courthouse to compare it with his courthouse back in Jeffersonville. They didn't have anything on the Tazewell Court House. It was a little bigger, but much older. No one paid too much attention to Hezekiah and Rachel as they were not dressed as a gentleman and lady, but as lowly folks.

If they had good luck and didn't lolli-gag they could be on Meadow Creek in three more days.

Rachel and Hezekiah were both anxious to see the new grandbabies, Jonas, and Susannah. They would be glad to see all the Whitts and Skaggs that still lived in the area. Little John Bunyan was three and the twins were about a year old. Rachel wanted to see Rachel and Rhoda as they were the first twins in the recently born babies.

Jonas had mastered his trade as a millwright and carpenter. He was making a good living working on mills in the area and building anything anyone needed. He had a knack for building and understanding the mechanics of water powered mills.

Jonas had it in the back of his mind that he would like to move his family to Tazewell County, but for the time Susannah was not sold on the idea and Jonas had more work than he could do.

The last leg of the journey was covered quickly and on the evening of the third day from Wytheville they rode into the settlement on Meadow Creek. (Now Radford, VA.)

Hezekiah and Rachel rode up to the old home place where his brother Archibald now lived. Archibald was home and ran out to greet them. The brothers hugged, and then Archibald hugged Rachel.

Archibald tied up the horses and ushered Hezekiah and Rachel into the house. Hannah (Wife of Archibald.) was thrilled to see Rachel and Hezekiah.

Sixteen year old Milburn (Son of Archibald.) greeted his uncle and aunt and went outside to care for the horses and mule. After a little chit-chat Hannah and daughter Hannah Jane rustled up some supper for the tired travelers.

The talk quickly turned to Rachel's grandbabies.

"Where does Jonas and Susannah live from here?" asked Rachel?

"They live over in my old place, remember it is just about a quarter of a mile from here," replied Archibald.

"I sure will be glad to see-um!" exclaimed Rachel.
"Soon as Milburn gets in, I will send him over to fetch-um, if it ain't too late," said Archibald.
Just then Milburn came in.
"Son, would you hitch up the surrey and go get Jonas and his family, tell them I need them as soon as possible, but let them know I am not ill or anything!" instructed Archibald.

"I sure will," said Milburn with a wide smile on his face.

In record time Milburn was pulling out in the family surrey on route to the Jonas Whitt house.

Just as Hezekiah and Rachel finished supper and were drinking some of Archibald's favorite wine; a horse was heard outside, followed by excited voices.

The door swing open and entered Jonas carrying Rachel, Susannah carrying Rhoda and leading little John Bunyan Whitt.

THE PATRIOT, HEZEKIAH WHITT

"Praise the Lord, here are my babies," said the excited Rachel as she ran to hug them. Hezekiah joined in and there was a group hug.

Archibald, Hannah, Jane, and Milburn stood there taking it all in.

Rachel first hugged little Bunyan and passed him to Hezekiah, then she took both of the twins and sat down. Jonas and Susannah stood there with a big smile on their face.

"I see how we rate," Jonas said, "Maw and Paw just come to see the young-uns!"

"They will get around to us, dreckley!" exclaimed Susannah.

All the Whitts had a good visit and stayed past everyone's bedtime. Milburn got the Jonas Whitt family loaded up and lit the lanterns on the Surrey and headed back to their house.

As the wheels began to roll, Jane hollered out, good night, sleep tight, and don't let the bedbugs bite!"

Jonas and Susannah waved back at her.

The next day they awoke early and the smell of coffee and bacon filled the Archibald home. Hezekiah hugged Rachel and said one of his favorite saying while traveling, "Morning honey, it sure don't take long to stay all night here."

Rachel smiled at him and said, "Get up, you good look-un paleface."

After breakfast was over, Hezekiah and Rachel loaded up and rode over to Jonas and Susannah's home.

Before they left, Hannah invited all of them back over for supper. Archibald would kill mutton and Hannah would cook up a big meal for everyone.

After a good visit with Jonas, Susannah, and the grandbabies, they all went back to the Archibald home for another family visit. Hannah had most of the supper ready; she was just finishing up with a big apple cobbler.

Hannah said, "You all wash your paws and come to the table."

All the hugging took place again; then everyone washed their hands and everyone was seated at the big family table. Archibald prayed a long prayer of thanksgiving and asked for continued protection on the family. After everyone ate their fill and then some, Archibald and Hezekiah went through the Whitt's ritual of their favorite after meal saying.

Archibald started it as an old man that had bad hearing, he said, "Eat some more young feller!"

Hezekiah said, "I have had sufficient!"

Archibald said, "Been a fishing?"

THE PATRIOT, HEZEKIAH WHITT

Hezekiah said, "I had a plenty!"

Archibald said, "Caught twenty?"

Hezekiah said, "I have had enough!"

Archibald said, "And they were tough?"

Everyone laughed at the old Whitt sayings!

The whole family knew it was coming, but laughed loudly as the brothers finished the old Whitt saying. Then Hannah Jane (Daughter of Archibald.) popped up and said the tongue twister, "A red pod of cotton and white cotton pod!"

Little John Floyd Whitt tried it, but had got it all twisted up.

Then Hannah Jane said, "A long, slick, slim, slender, sycamore, sapling!" The Whitts all laughed as different ones tried the sayings.

It was simple little things like this that families did for amusement and joy. Sometimes they would tell the children Bible Stories, such as Jonah and the great fish, how Gideon became a great warrior because the Lord empowered him. They talked about the strength of Sampson and how he was taken down by a woman. Then Archibald said, "We men have been taken down by women since Adam and Eve."

Hezekiah laughed, but Hannah and Rachel didn't find it that funny.

After a week of visiting, Hezekiah said, "we got to get back home, the crops will need attention and court day is coming up soon."

Archibald said, "That is a great honor to be an appointed Gentleman Justice of the Peace by the governor, I am so proud of you big brother."

"I am truly proud of your accomplishments too, and I am grateful to you for helping my boys with their trades as well," said Hezekiah.

After a wonderful visit Hezekiah and Rachel packed the animals and donned their rough traveling clothes and headed toward Tazewell County. It was hard to leave the babies and of course Jonas and Susannah, but they were once again traveling the roads and bridle trails toward home.

The only problem they encountered on the trip home was two young men rode up on them in a big hurry. Hezekiah gave Rachel the pistol and he got the musket in hand before they got to them. After a meeting with them it turned out that the two young men were heading home from North Carolina to see their sick paw. After Hezekiah was satisfied that they were not up to mischief he lowered his musket and wished the men Godspeed!

THE PATRIOT, HEZEKIAH WHITT

When they arrived back to their Cedar Grove home, they found the fields well kept and the stock in good shape. James Whitt, Thomas Bailey Christian, and Moses Hankins (Son of John Hankins and Elizabeth Skaggs Hankins) had all donated some time to help take care of the Hezekiah Whitt farm.

James and Nancy came to visit just as soon as they had learned that paw and maw were home.

Griffy also came to visit as did Rebecca and Susannah. (Daughters of Hezekiah and Rachel.) This took away some of the pain from the moving away of John Bunyan and Richard Whitt. Also Hezekiah's brother, Edmund had moved his family to Carter County, Kentucky.

Hezekiah made love to Rachel that night and assured her that it was a natural thing for the children to move away and find their own way. Rachel still hated that her babies were gone away!

Chapter 41

Where Does The Time Go

On March 30, 1822 east and west Florida was combined to form the Florida Territory.

Charles Graham patented his invention of false teeth on June 9, 1822.

On July 13, 1822 a new little girl was born to Jonas and Susannah Whitt. They named her Emily L. (Emma) Whitt. This great news would gladly be received by Rachel and Hezekiah.

On December 12, 1822 Mexico is recognized as an Independent Nation.

On December 1, 1822 James Plesants was elected as Governor of Virginia. He would serve until December 1, 1825.

Time seems to fly when you are still in the period of good feeling and the isolated folks on the waters of the Clinch were just that.

Life was hard, but wonderful as well in the beautiful mountains of Tazewell County. The folks found time to socialize in church meetings, picnics, and community work. If a family needed help in raising a barn, the community came out and got it done. The women would cook and feed the workers and the men had a good time working together. There were corn shucking's, there were hog killings, and there were all types of fun things in their social life. Barn dances, weddings, and even all night wakes were held where folks sit up all night with the deceased and talk about the good old days.

The men and boys still enjoyed going hunting and fishing, but the days of buffalo were gone and elk were scarce around Jeffersonville. Fishing was still good on the Clinch. Fishing on the mountain streams like Clear Fork, Wolf Creek, Big Tumbling, Little Tumbling and Laurel Creek, produced the spotted Brook Trout and even the big Brown Trout. Even the head waters of Big Tumbling on top of Clinch Mountain called Red Creek supported little native rainbows. You had to sneak up on the creek to catch these gamey little fish.

Time went on as Hezekiah did his duty as a Gentleman Justice of the Peace and kept his farm up. He worked to improve the cattle and horses by selective breeding and most gentlemen had some fine thoroughbreds as well as some fine draft horses.

Hezekiah was recommended for sheriff again in 1822 by the Tazewell County Court. The Gentlemen Justices handled so many functions of the county government. They were of the best of quality in integrity and quite literate and this was the reason they were appointed for life. It seemed that they took turns serving as sheriff.

THE PATRIOT, HEZEKIAH WHITT

Again in May 1823 Hezekiah Whitt, John Thompson, Thomas Gillespie are recommended by the court as fit to serve as sheriff. It looks like Hezekiah may end up as High Sheriff if they keep recommending him.

On January 27, 1823 President James Monroe appoints the first U.S. Ambassadors to South America. The United States is beginning to take on the Idea of Global Citizenship.

On April 22, 1823 roller skates are patented by R. J. Tyers.
The song, "Home Sweet Home" was first sung in London England on May 8, 1823.

On July 9, 1823 John McLean took office as the 9th Postmaster General.

On September 21, 1823, the leader of the Mormons Joseph Smith testified that he saw Moroni. Joseph Smith established the "Church of Latter day Saints." His claim was that God gave him tablets of stone with a new list of laws carved by the hand of God on them. He claimed that the experience was just like the one Moses had with God. Their church also favored polygamy and encouraged the men to have a great many wives.

On September 21, 1944, 121 years later Charles Dahnmon Whitt would be born.

On December 2, 1823 the great declaration of the "Monroe Doctrine" was made by President James Monroe and we still live by this today. The Western Hemisphere would be protected by the United States of America from any European Power.

The State of Georgia became the first to pass a birth registration on December 19, 1823.

On December 23, 1823 the, "Visit from St. Nicholas," was published in Troy, New York by C. Moore. The children could now prove that Old Saint Nicholas did come on Christmas Eve, it was even in the paper. Of course "Old St. Nick always came to the Whitt's homes on the night before Christmas Day.

On June 1824 term of Tazewell County Court once again recommended Hezekiah Whitt, Thomas Gillespie, and John Thompson as fit persons to serve as Sheriff.

Corruption in politics has always been. In the 1824 Presidential election, John Quincy Adams ran against Andrew Jackson, but neither gained enough electoral votes to win the Presidency. Jackson was a hero from the battle of New Orleans and the fight with the Creek Indians to open up Florida. The election went to the House of Representatives. Henry Clay, the speaker of the house supported John Quincy Adams under an assumed deal for the job of Secretary of State. This "corrupt bargain" tainted his term and Adams was impotent as the President.

During this time of the antebellum period all men did not have the right to vote. A man had to own property and pay property taxes and also have literacy qualifications. Many Americans did not agree with this thinking and a force to end this began. Hezekiah thought if a man can fight for his country, he should have a vote.

THE PATRIOT, HEZEKIAH WHITT

Through these years the North and the South grew further apart on many ideas. The North was becoming very industrial and the South depended on their crops such as King Cotton and tobacco for their commercial strength. Also there was a division as to how the Federal Government should be. The North wanted a strong Federal Government and the South still felt that each State was its own country and states rights were important. As you look back from the time of the Civil War you can see these early years were definitely leading up to the Civil War.

On February 4, 1824 rubbers are invented, I mean galoshes, J. W. Goodrich did it.

On March 11, 1824 the U.S. War Department creates the Bureau of Indian Affairs.

April 17, 1824 Russia gives up claim of America south of the 54th degrees 40' N line.

May 26, 1824 Brazil is recognized as a country by the United States.

On July 24, 1824 a newspaper in Harrisburg, Pennsylvania published the first public opinion poll. They said that Andrew Jackson was clearly ahead in his bid to become President of the United States. As in many polls this one was wrong in one respect. Jackson led the popular vote, but the House of Representatives had to decide between four candidates because none had enough Electoral College votes.

On October 21, 1824 Portland Cement was patented by Joseph Aspdid in Yorkshire England. This will be the foundation in construction to this day.

On October 21, 1824 the steam locomotive is introduced. This will have great ramifications!

On November 2, 1824 the first presidential election (popular vote) is published.

By the end of 1824 Hezekiah and Rachel had a passel of grandchildren. They were scattered from Montgomery County, all over the large county of Tazewell, some in Lee County Virginia. Some were in Floyd County Kentucky. Rachel loved babies so much especially her own children and grandchildren. She was the type that spoiled grandbabies and Hezekiah was just about as bad. All the grandchildren loved Rachel and Hezekiah. Letters came regularly from the children that were far away. And the others close by visited often.

Richard (Devil Dick) Whitt and wife Rebecca Whitt have Hannah who is 3, Susannah who is 1, and Edmund Ned will arrive on 14 November 1825. Edmund would be named for Rebecca's father, Edmund Piece Whitt. Yes this was another cousin marry cousin wedding. It was very common in the 18th and 19th century. They live near Cumberland Gap in Lee County, Virginia. Edmund Ned was named for Rebecca's Paw.

John Bunyan has two children, John Bunyan Whitt Jr. by first wife Ana Shackford and baby Hezekiah Whitt by second wife, Hannah Sarles. They live in Floyd County,

THE PATRIOT, HEZEKIAH WHITT

Kentucky near Maytown. John Bunyan would lose his second wife and marry again to Sarah Oney years later.

Jonas Whitt and Susannah Whitt have John Bunyan, the twins Rachel and Rhoda and also Emma. Jonas and Susannah will get their next baby on 10 July 1825 and will call him James Griffith Whitt. They live in Montgomery County near present day Radford. Jonas and Susannah were also cousins. It almost seemed that the Whitts wanted to keep it all in the family or else there were not many options.

Rebecca and husband James Husk Lowe have three children. The children are Calvin Lowe 12, William D. Lowe 9, and another John Bunyan Lowe. The Whitts loved certain names and used them over and over as you can see. The Lowes resided in northern Tazewell County, now McDowell County, West Virginia. They could still come and visit Hezekiah and Rachel often.

Susannah and Joseph Webb have William Webb, Rachel Webb 7, Mary Webb 5, and James Harvey Webb only 2. They live in Tazewell County also.

Griffy and Martha Patty Skaggs Whitt have seven babies by now. Timothy 16, Shone 14, Assena 11, Cinthia 9, Olivia Mary 6, Noah B. 4, and Jeremiah is 2. They still live on Reedy Ridge near Baptist Valley in Tazewell County. They do have some long range plans to move to Missouri. It seems that so many folks have itchy feet as the building of America goes on.

During the summer visits Hezekiah would sneak out some of Rachel's thread and help the children catch "June Bugs." Then Hezekiah would take a five or six feet piece of the thread and tie it on a hind leg of the bugs. Then the June Bugs would fly around and the children had a great time. They called it flying June Bugs. Hezekiah told them not to jerk on the bugs or hurt them. He explained that when they were tired of the fun the bugs should be released as they were creatures of God. The children had a great time and most likely Hezekiah did also.

Another thing they would do in the twilight of the warm summer days was to catch lightening bugs. Hezekiah would get them a clear jar, most of the time it was Rachel's fruit jar. Then Hezekiah would lead the children out and help them catch lightening bugs. Some folks called them fireflies. The bugs would rise from the grass and weeds flashing their lights in an attempt to attract a mate. When the jar had several bugs in it they shone brightly in the darkening evening.

The bigger children played "Red Rover, Red Rover, I dare you to come over." During hog killing times they would get the bladder and blow it up into a fine ball. The children also played Indians and frontiersmen.

Hezekiah and Rachel would pack a dinner in a basket, get the fishing poles and take the children to the Clinch for a day of fishing. Some times they would wade in Indian Creek and catch crawdads to use for bait. They would overturn rocks and grab the crawdad before it flipped it's tail in an attempt to escape. Catching crawdads was just about as

THE PATRIOT, HEZEKIAH WHITT

much as pulling in a big Redeye. Hezekiah would warn the children to watch for snakes and waterdogs, but it did not deter them from getting in the creek. Hezekiah would laugh at the smaller ones as they often stumbled and sit down in the water. Life was good for the children, grandma, and grandpa. Hezekiah was the biggest duck in the puddle while playing with the children; he was the serious dignified gentleman while doing business or serving on the Court of Tazewell County.

On January 19, 1825 Ezra Daggett and his nephew Thomas Kensett patent tin cans to be used to store food in. It will take some time for this to catch on.

The House of Representatives cleared up the election deadlock on February 9, 1825 and elected John Quincy Adams.

Another example of taking the Indians land occurred on February 12, 1825. The Creek Indians signed a treaty and agreed to cede their lands in Georgia to the United States. They agreed to migrate to the west by September 1, 1826. Some white feller discovered gold in northern Georgia.

On February 22, 1825 Russia and Britain agree on a boundary between Alaska and Canada.
The weather went nuts on June 4, 1825 as a hurricane hit New York City.
When was the safety pen patented? June 13, 1825 Walter Hunt did it.
First leg of the Erie Canal is opened. On October 26, 1825 the canal boats began to move to and from the Atlantic Ocean and Lake Erie. This was a great engineering feat. There would be many canals built under the Erie Canal system name. There would be one built from Lake Erie to Portsmouth, Ohio and connect the lake to the Ohio River. A man would be able to ship goods from the Atlantic Ocean to Lake Erie, to the Ohio River, to the Mississippi River, to the Gulf of Mexico in New Orleans and back.

On December 27, 1825 the first railroad using steam powered locomotives was completed in England. This time in history men had time to think and work on inventions and nothing seemed impossible, except maybe a flying machine.

John Tyler became Governor of the Commonwealth of Virginia on December 10, 1825. He would serve until March 4, 1827.

When the Tazewell County Court met in 1825, once again Hezekiah is recommended as a fit person for Sheriff. Hezekiah becomes the High Sheriff of the whole County of Tazewell. Hezekiah's deputies were Thomas George and Samuel P. Davidson. Hezekiah is duly appointed by Governor James Pleasants to serve as High Sheriff of Tazewell County.

Hezekiah would have a demanding job at the age of about 65. He has never slowed down and was still in great physical shape. People worked hard and had little of the problems that we have today like being obese. The only day they sat around was Sunday and they called it the Sabbath. Some of the folks wouldn't even let the children

THE PATRIOT, HEZEKIAH WHITT

play, but Hezekiah and Rachel were sensible people and allowed their children to play after church.

Rachel said, "The good Lord made our children and He put it in them to play."

"I don't mean to rough house in church or anything like that, but they know to be reverent in church," she continued.

"There weren't no better man than the Reverend Richard Whitt and he let us play out after church, we even went a swimming on some of those hot Sabbaths," answered Hezekiah.

Chapter 42

High Sheriff, Hezekiah Whitt

Hezekiah and Rachel talked it over about being the High Sheriff of Tazewell County. Hezekiah knew something about it, but was still a little unsure of such a large responsibility.

Rachel was a little worried about Hezekiah taking on a full time job at 65 years old. Hezekiah was more concerned with being responsible for all the tax money and afraid of making enemies.

John Thompson, the out going sheriff, assured Hezekiah that he would do just fine. He explained that Hezekiah had a good name and that was about 99% of it. People will trust Hezekiah and the only enemies you will make will be the folks trying to dodge taxes or lawbreakers. John explained that he would be around if ever Hezekiah wanted to ask a question. John also told Hezekiah that he would go over everything at the time he took office.

John Thompson gave Hezekiah a thick book of laws pertaining to the duties of the sheriff in the counties of Virginia. The book looked big and complicated.

John Thompson saw concern on Hezekiah's face and assured him that he would do just fine. You can read about Sheriffing, (Doing the duty of the Sheriff.) in the book. The book is about a lot of Virginia Laws, but very little concerns you.

Hezekiah took the book and went home to look it over. He would not be official until July 1826, so he had time to learn, pray, and even back out if he wanted to.

Hezekiah read in the book and his eyes caught a passage about bridges. It says where a bridge is erected; no one shall run a wheeled carriage or wagon across it in a run. The lawful speed would be a gait no faster than a man walking. Hezekiah remembered that some of the Murray boys hit a bridge at break neck speed every time they came to Jeffersonville. He would have to give them a stiff warning the next time he saw them do this.

Hezekiah looked all through the big law book and found some parts referring to the serving of the High Sheriff and deputies in the counties of the Commonwealth.

If any sheriff shall die in his Sheriffalty, (Old word for Sheriffs term.) the Governor, with the advice of council, may, and is hereby empowered and required to commission some other person nominated by the court to be sheriff in his room. (Place)

Hezekiah knew that all the sheriffs served no more than two years, but he was looking for it in the law book. He looked intently at the book and ran across this section that spelled it out.

THE PATRIOT, HEZEKIAH WHITT

Every sheriff so qualified and commissioned shall serve one year, and with his consents may serve two years. If the next sheriff failed to get bonded and qualified, the residing sheriff may continue in service until the next sheriff can get qualified.

Every person appointed to the position of High Sheriff shall be sworn in open court. He must enter into one bond before the Justices of the County Court. The bond is payable to the governor of this Commonwealth with good and sufficient security in the sum of thirty thousand dollars, for the true and faithful collection, accounting for, and paying the taxes imposed by law and arrears of taxes due in his county, which bond every county court is empowered and required to demand, take, and cause to be acknowledged before them, in open court, and recorded, and an attested copy thereof shall be transmitted by the clerk to the auditor of public accounts, which shall be admitted as evidence in any suit, motion, or proceeding founded there on.

Hezekiah kept thinking about the big responsibility he would be taking on. John Thompson had assured him that most of the time the deputies and clerks would handle the work. Hezekiah would just be the overseer. Then he would think about what could happen if he was not really careful. A Sheriff can get into a heap of trouble thought Hezekiah.

Another law forbade that if the sheriff collected taxes without the proper bond, he could and most likely be fined $1.000. Hezekiah noted this law and thought about such a big fine. A man could buy three nice farms with that kind of money.

Hezekiah also saw that some poor folks may get a break on their tax burden. Taxes and fines collected from the very poor shall be charged at the poor rate and the words,

"Poor Rates," shall be written down on the records following the word "Levies."

Hezekiah was thinking that he would have to learn more about this law as God had put so many poor people in Tazewell County.

The law book also mentioned that a sheriff must be a man of honesty, probity, and of good demeanor.

Hezekiah read this and whispered a prayer that the Almighty would help him fit the bill.

As Hezekiah read on he saw that if a sheriff collected taxes without being sworn in by the Gentlemen Justices of the Peace, he would be fined $1,000 payable to the literary fund.

I will not collect any tax or fine until I am bonded and sworn in, thought Hezekiah.

The High Sheriff and his deputies shall give an account on paper to every person paying officer fees, dues, taxes, county levies, or poor tax.

That shouldn't be a problem; me and my deputies can write very well considered Hezekiah.
Hezekiah continued to read and some of it made sense and some was not too clear. Layer talk, thought Hezekiah.

COLONEL CHARLES DAHNMON WHITT

THE PATRIOT, HEZEKIAH WHITT

No writ can be filed against a person not found in his bailiwick, unless the sheriff shall go to the dwelling place and leave an attested writ.

That must mean you nail it too their door thought Hezekiah.

During this time of history the Lord's Day was kept in earnest and Hezekiah was glad to see a section pertaining to the Lord's Day.

It shall be unlawful for any sheriff or any other officer to execute any writ or process any writ upon the Lord's Day, commonly called Sunday. No public duty shall be done on the Lord's Day, voting, militia duty, or any other, except for treason, felony, riot, breach of peace, or a prisoner escape.

Hezekiah was glad to see this information written out in the law book.

Next Hezekiah read about not over charging the public on fees or taxes.

No greater fee than prescribed by law shall be demanded by the sheriff.

This made Hezekiah think back to the tax collectors in the Bible, they often over charged the people and kept the extra money. Lord please, doesn't ever let me get greedy like the tax collectors of old, prayed Hezekiah.

Now Hezekiah read about getting paid for his duty.

Every sheriff shall have and retain upon all monies collected by him in virtue of his office. In cases where no other commission is provided by law, an allowance of five per centum for collecting and paying the same, and no more.

Well that don't sound like much, but the collecting of tax and fines all over the county will add up, thought Hezekiah.

John Thompson has already mentioned this next law to Hezekiah, but it doesn't hurt to read over it.

When a new sheriff is taking charge the leaving sheriff shall deliver the names of any prisoners that may be in the county jail at the time.

More reasonability Hezekiah thought as he read the next.

The High Sheriff will be held responsible for the writs handled by his deputies. Any deputies in arrears for money, tobacco, or other thing received can be charged and brought to court by the sheriff. The High Sheriff may recover of the deputy the amount of the original judgment.

This thing is making my head hurt thought Hezekiah as he closed the big book. He was just getting into a big section that dealt with slaves and owners when he closed it.

Rachel was sitting on the front porch smoking her pipe and reading the Bible when Hezekiah found her.

THE PATRIOT, HEZEKIAH WHITT

"I don't know about all of these laws and rules I got to know," said Hezekiah.

"Why not, all of them laws are based on this big black book called the word of God," replied Rachel.

"Well when you put it like that I can understand better," replied Hezekiah.

"You have been following the Lord Jesus Christ for years, jest keep him in your Sheriffing," answered Rachel.

"I can always depend on you to help with my problems," said Hezekiah.

"You have always been my lover, husband, provider and protector, all within the love of the Lord," exclaimed Rachel.

"You are always so positive, thanks for being my wife," said Hezekiah.

"I think you ought to get you a black suit to wear as Sheriff," said Rachel.

"I was thinking the same thing, John Thompson always wore one," replied Hezekiah.

"It seems that the preachers and sheriffs all wear black suits," said Rachel.

"Well I got to look like a sheriff, but I ain't wearing no stove pipe hat, I aim to get me a black slouch hat," committed Hezekiah.

"What else will you need for your position of Sheriff?" asked Rachel?

"I aim to get me a 44, you know one of the new converted cap and ball revolvers, an I aim to have my deputies do the same thing," said Hezekiah.

"You know best about those kinds of things," replied Rachel.

"Do you think this is going to be a real dangerous job?" asked Rachel with out taking a breath.

"Not really, we have not lost a sheriff yet," said Hezekiah.

"I remember Sheriff David Ward had a close call back a few years ago when he brought in some outlaws, they shot at him, but he or one of his deputies got the upper hand fore it was too late," said Rachel.

"That is why it is good to wear a fire arm out where folks can see it, that makes-um think twice fore they get into mischief," said Hezekiah.

Hezekiah went to William McGuire's Mercantile and placed an order for a store bought suit, hat, and three cap and ball pistols. He also ordered Rachel a pair of white gloves and a big lace fan to carry when she was all dolled up.

THE PATRIOT, HEZEKIAH WHITT

During this time in Tazewell County the men started to wear side burns, moustaches, and trimmed beards. Just look back a little in time from 1826 the men kept their faces shaved clean. I thought this was amusing as time goes on things change and revert back. Gentlemen began to buy shaving brushes and lather bowls. The upper class often had fine lather bowls with their initials printed in gold as a sign of prosperity.

I remember when I got out of the Navy I decided to grow a beard. Beards were taboo at that time (1968) and my brother overheard two old ladies at church talking about me and my beard.

They said, "That new Whitt man in our church has that disgraceful beard and he is from a good family!"

They thought only Hippies wore beards. Of course now, folks wear beards again.

The period of 1826 to the 1860's folks worked on manners and etiquette. The men began bowing, and the ladies began curtseying. Folks began taking baths more than once a year. Most folks washed off from a pitcher and bowl, the equivalent of a sponge bath. Folks stopped making fun of those that took regular baths.

Ladies wore their southern bell dresses with a drawstring girdle that brought out the shapely bodies of the young women. Ladies began going to hairdressers to get their hair fixed. They wore long dangling curls, with hats or with a snood. (A fancy heavy hair net that held the long hair down the back of the neck.)

A man did not touch a ladies waist or any other part of her body. (At least in public.) She called her neck her chest and her chest she called her stomach. Many of the dresses were cut low in the front to expose the tops of their breast. They did not show any part of their legs but said nothing of the bulging boobs.

When dancing the only parts that touched were the elbows. A man did not ask a lady any questions as it was bad manners. Folks really improved in their manners during this time with the exception of chewing tobacco. Gentlemen and ladies both enjoyed the habit of chewing tobacco. Both sexes smoked pipes also. Cigars were just starting to be found in gentlemen's pockets. Chewing tobacco was so prevalent during this time and folks spit everywhere. They spit on the floors and walls. I guess this led to the big spittoons that were introduced out of necessity. It was so funny with the people being so proper and nice that they changed completely when they put their chew in their mouth.

The world has embarked on speed and power in travel and shipping. They now have canals, steamboats, and now on March 4, 1826 the first railroad is chartered as the Granite Railroad, in Quincy, Massachusetts.

The folks in Tazewell County read about these wonderful inventions, but most will not see them in their lifetimes.

THE PATRIOT, HEZEKIAH WHITT

On April Fools Day, 1826 Samuel Mory patented the internal combustion engine. "Now what will folks do with such a tomfool thing?" many said. What would Hezekiah and Rachel think if they could see the cars and trucks speeding down the broad highways?

Exploring the globe was also in progress as the United States warship, Vincennes, became the first military ship to navigate around the world.

Man's quest for fire reached a new goal after using flint and steel or friction to build fire for centuries when John Walker invented the match in England. Now a Man could take one of the little sticks and strike it on a rock and he had instant fire. I am surprised that they didn't call it "Instant Fire." The name match is a mystery.

With advice of past sheriffs and friends Hezekiah knew he would have to exercise strength and sternness as Sheriff of Tazewell, County. Hezekiah would follow the lead of other sheriffs to keep undesirables out of their wonderful county. Folks were coming into the county from the south and east and some were just passing through to the extreme western part of Virginia (Now West Virginia.) or to Kentucky and beyond. Along with the migrating peoples there was bound to be those that had no respect for people, animals, never less the law.

Hezekiah saw a man whipping his single team of mules while they were hooked to a huge wagon with a weight that should have had several teams to pull the great load. Hezekiah lost his patience for a minute and grabbed the whip out of his hands and hit him across the back. The man was taken by surprise and turned to take revenge until he saw the fire in Hezekiah's eyes.

Hezekiah began to dress him down.

"You don't have the sense that God gave your asses, can't you see you have too much burden for them?" shouted Hezekiah?
Before the man could speak, Hezekiah set in again.

"You damned fool you get you some more animals or unload that wagon enough so your mules can pull it; then I want you to get back to where you came from or head on to Kentucky," shouted Hezekiah.

"Some of our folks might not be to smart, but they don't beat their animals, we don't want your kind around here," Hezekiah spoke calmly, but sternly.

The man went to the back of the wagon and began unloading his stuff by the side of the road.

The deputies did most of the collections and clerical work, Hezekiah just made sure it

THE PATRIOT, HEZEKIAH WHITT

was all done properly. Occasionally there was a breach of the law and Hezekiah had to go out and investigate and sometimes place someone under arrest. Public drunkenness, fighting, and family problems were the norm, but ever now and then an outlaw had to be brought in. There was an incident on the Kentucky Turnpike. An outlaw was hiding in the brush just about the place where the road turns up Road Ridge, (Near Raven) The outlaw would watch for prosperous looking folks and strike with surprise. Hezekiah received word about this and took one deputy to set a trap. Hezekiah sent the deputy under cover of night and had him hide in the area. Next morning Hezekiah dressed in his finest attire and carried a little carpet bag to entice an attack. Hezekiah held his cap and ball revolver behind the bag. The plan worked splendidly. Hezekiah rode nonchalantly across a creek (Coal Creek) and up the creek bank. The outlaw came riding up to Hezekiah to do mischief and the deputy shot out of cover with his pistol in hand. The outlaw fired a shot and two lead balls passed through the bandit's body as Hezekiah and his deputy both fired.

They tied the man across his saddle and brought him back to Jeffersonville. As they rode into town it attracted much attention. Hezekiah proceeded to the court house and dismounted. Everyone gathered around to find out what happened. Hezekiah told them what had happened and asks if anyone knew the man. Most folks took a look at the grim faced corpse, but no one knew him. He was buried and Elder David Young said a few words over him and prayed for his family whoever they were.

A Jackson man had been robbed a couple of days before and came forward and clamed a jackknife and twenty five dollars in gold that had been taken by the bad man. There was $99.00 dollars in mixed bills and coins left over. Hezekiah put the money into the treasury for now. Hezekiah posted a notice for any victims of the robbery to come forward.

Bringing in a dead outlaw tied to his horse leaves an impression on everyone. It was a good one for the sheriff and one of warning to anyone thinking of going against the law.

Another thing that happened while Hezckiah Whitt was sheriff a boy became missing. The boy, Johnny Sheffy, was last seen heading towards Lebanon near what is now Claypool Hill. This was limestone country and there was sinkholes and caves about. Hezekiah with his deputies Thomas I. George, Samuel P. Davidson, and about ten other men rode to the area where the boy was last seen. Hezekiah and the other men dismounted and looked for tracks or any other signs of the lad.

The tracks led down over the hill to where they found an opening to a cave. Some of the men following further back found an opening in the earth about 4' X 7' and almost walked their horses into it. There was about a 30 feet drop to the bottom of a great room. This was very alarming as the men thought of what could have happened. No white men had ever reported this cave.

THE PATRIOT, HEZEKIAH WHITT

The men hollered both from the opening in the top and from the entrance down over the hill. They heard the boy answer weakly. Hezekiah and a few of the men entered the cave with some torches they had made and found the boy. He had gone in and fell after twisting his ankle. He just couldn't walk on it. The lad was about 12 years old and not too big. He was carried out and the men met at the hole on top of the hill. Hezekiah ordered that some small trees be cut and a fence of about 4' high be build around the opening. One of the men, Thomas I. George, had been inside with Hezekiah and looked up at the bright light seeping through the hole. The sunbeam looked like you could climb out because of the smoke of the torches meeting the ray of light. He gave the cave the name of "Chimney Cave." (There is now a Holiday Inn Express built over it today.)

"Wonder if anybody ever fell in that hole?" someone asked?

"There is a pile of bones down there, I didn't see no human's though," said another of the men that had been inside.

Hezekiah made sure Johnny Sheffy got back home safely and thanked all of the men for their help.

Back over on Meadow Creek in Montgomery County, James Griffith Whitt, was born to Jonas and Susannah. He was born on July 10, 1825. Hezekiah and Rachel have not seen their two year old grandson nor the little Elizabeth "Betsy" Whitt that has just arrived. Hezekiah is just too busy to take a trip and plans on catching up in June of 1828 after the new sheriff, Thomas Gillespie, takes over.
On February 27, 1827, the first Mardi Gras celebration took place in New Orleans.

On February 28, 1827 the Baltimore & Ohio became the first commercial railroad in the United States.

On April 2, 1827 lead pencils are being manufactured by Joseph Dixon.

On Independence Day 1827, New York abolished slavery; some were still kept by the wealthy, but called servants.

Racc riots took place in Cincinnati, Ohio on August 10, 1827 and one thousand blacks leave for Canada.

On November 15,1827 the United States have taken all the property from the Creek Indians.

On June 31, 1828, Hezekiah finished his duty as High Sheriff of Tazewell County, Virginia. He served his term in a highly distinguished manner and is now even more prominent in Tazewell County. Some folks asked him to run for state government, but Hezekiah declined. He is now 67 and wants to spend time with family and friends.

Hezekiah hears all the news at the Tazewell Court House and he brings it to Rachel.

"Rachel, guess what I heard today at the courthouse?" Asked Hezekiah?

"Ain't no a telling, you hear everything down there," replied Rachel.

"It seems this feller over in England invented these little sticks that when you rub-um on a rock or something rough the end blazes up in instant fire," said Hezekiah.

"I will believe it when I see it, I an't gonna throw away my flint," replied Rachel.

"Honey, it's true, they call-um matches, and some folks are calling them "Lucifer's," replied Hezekiah.

"Whys that, are they hot as hell?" asked Rachel with a smile on her face.

"Where there's fire they gotta be hot, some say it's brimstone on the tip of-um," replied Hezekiah.

"I wouldn't mind to see some of-um!" exclaimed Rachel.
"Me neither, I guess we might get some, someday" answered Hezekiah.

THE PATRIOT, HEZEKIAH WHITT

Chapter 43

Tazewell County Continues To Change

The Tariff of Abominations, this was a nickname for the Tariff of 1828. The southern people held an enormous objection as did the Vice President John C. Calhoun. Calhoun published the "South Carolina Exposition and Protest," which pushed the nation into a crisis. South Carolina voted the tariff null and void in their state. Andrew Jackson threatened South Carolina with military force. Henry Clay proposed the "Compromise Tariff of 1833 which cooled the whole thing. If you look at all the little differences between North and South and add them up you can see a great clash coming.

Andrew Jackson was President. He had become very popular by his military campaigns with the victory of the battle of New Orleans and in Florida against the Seminoles, also against the Creek Indians.

Jackson's Presidency was plagued with the Bank War, the Nullification Crisis, and the Removal of the Native Americans. Jackson was cocky and despised the Indians. He also was connected to a woman that caused much grief. One man had talked about the disgrace of Jackson and his wife Rachel which sparked Jackson into challenging him to a duel. This happened before Jackson became President.

Come to find out the man Jackson challenged was an expert marksmen. On the way to the duel he was followed by a crowd so he demonstrated his skills by shooting Sycamore Balls of the trees as he traveled. Everyone knew that Jackson was a dead man.

Jackson had a plan that worked wonderfully for him. Jackson was a real slender man and the weather was cool so he wore a great coat to the duel. The single shot pistols were checked by each, and both parties stood back to back and on the signal both men walked ten paces and turned around and faced their opposition. Jackson allowed the other man to shoot first and after an apparent miss, Jackson took a good aim and shot the man dead.

Jackson and his entourage mounted up and rode away. Blood began to drip down on Jackson's boot. No one knew he had been hit until then.
Jackson knew the man would shoot for his heart so he turned his slender body sideways in the great coat and took a hit through his side instead of his heart. Many people never knew Jackson had been shot; only his closest friends knew and they all swore to keep it a secret.

People were amazed that Jackson had killed one of the best shooters in the land. Many duels were fought by gentlemen during the antebellum period. It happened in the North some, but mostly in the South. Nine times out of ten it was over a woman.

THE PATRIOT, HEZEKIAH WHITT

Some state oaths still have a section that you have to swear that you never fought a duel. The Commonwealth of Kentucky keeps this in theirs as a tradition.

William Branch Giles became Governor of the Commonwealth of Virginia on March 4, 1827 and served until March 31, 1834. Governor Giles would have Giles County named for him in future years.

The Gentlemen Justices of the Peace played a big part in politics in each county. Many folks would ask Hezekiah which way to vote. He would not tell them who to vote for, but would tell them which man was better qualified for this reason or that.

Noah Webster published the first American dictionary on April 14, 1828.
I guess that is why words were spelled so differently across the nation. Good teachers stressed the correctness of spelling.

In July 1828 construction on the B & O Rail Road was going on and it would be the first passenger rail road. Hezekiah and others read about these things, but doubted they would ever see such a thing, never the less, ride on one.

The elite ladies wore their fine gowns to church, and social gatherings, but only limited it to those days. Most days the middle class wore full dresses with pin on aprons. Hats gave way to bonnets. The fancy gowns were a chore to keep clean. They had to remove the lace and other parts before they could be washed. The gown often had five yards of material in the make up and was hard to wash in a tub. They would hang them out to dry and then have to sew the lace back on. The slicker materials like silk were wanted so that dirt didn't stick as bad. Many bright colors were used for the grand gowns, but red was rare because it signified the wearers as "Ladies of the Evening!" Everyday clothes were made from cotton, wool, or the combination called "Linsey-Woolsey".

Back on Meadow Creek, Montgomery County Virginia, Jonas and Susannah had begun to yearn to move to the waters of the Clinch, now called Tazewell County. Jonas loved his boyhood days and spending time with all of his kindred. He especially loved his Paw and Maw. Jonas talked about it so much that Susannah and the children began to love the mountains and valleys of Tazewell County.

They had stayed in Montgomery County all of this time because of Susannah's kindred and of course Jonas had work there as a Millwright and house builder. He was trying to get money together so he could own a nice farm someday. He hoped it would be on the Clinch in Tazewell County. It had been financial and economical reasons that they still lived in Montgomery County.

On March 4, 1829 Andy Jackson, "Old Hickory" was inaugurated the 7th President. That night at the inaugural ball an unruly mob showed up in protest of the new president. I guess things never change, some group is always upset no matter who the nation chooses as their leaders.

THE PATRIOT, HEZEKIAH WHITT

The State of Ohio was the first to authorize high school and it would be taught at night. This happened on March 4, 1829.

On May 5, 1829 Joseph Smith claimed to be ordained by John the Baptist as a leader of the "Church of Jesus Christ of Latter Day Saints," the Mormons.

On July 23, 1829 William Austan Burt's invention he called the "typographer," was patented. We call it the "typewriter." Now with computers, the typewriter is going extinct.

It was time to think about the Texas part of Mexico. President Andrew Jackson made an offer to purchase Texas from Mexico on August 25, 1829, but the Mexicans refused. This will become a hot topic as the years go by.

On September 28, 1829 the pamphlet, Walkers Appeal about racial and antislavery was published in Boston. Just another Northern Thorn in the flesh of the Southerners.

Also in Boston the first modern hotel was opened on October 16, 1829. They named it the Tremont Hotel. Before this time the Inn's across the country had served the purpose and needs of travelers. Some were plain and some were a bit more fancy for the wealthy traveler, but now the age of Grand Hotels was coming about.

Another canal opened on October 17, 1829. It ran from the Delaware river to the Chesapeake Bay.

The first stone arch railroad bridge is finished and dedicated on the B & O railroad on December 21, 1829.

The folks eagerly waited for anything in print. Sometimes a newspaper would be a year old before it reached Tazewell County. News traveled by word of mouth much faster. Any time herds of sheep, cattle, or horses were driven east or south the herders would bring back news. Also the mail was slow, but it did go through. Any of the state business was rushed to Richmond and vice versa.

Now Hezekiah is no longer serving as High Sheriff and can get back to a simpler life. He is still a member of the Tazewell County Court as a Gentleman Justice of the Peace as he was appointed by the Governor, James Monroe, for his lifetime. He still would go into Jeffersonville a day or two a week. Now he can go back to being a gentleman farmer and do some fishing and hunting. Rachel and all of his grandchildren were glad of this.

Hezekiah and Rachel have the grandchildren spend the night and often take them to church. When it gets to be bedtime, Hezekiah tells them stories and usually sends them to bed with another Old Whitt saying.

"To bed, to bed," said sleepyhead!"

"Oh no!" said Slow!"

THE PATRIOT, HEZEKIAH WHITT

"Put on the pot," said Greedy Gut and we will eat before we go!"

Papaw, I am hungry, or Papaw I want a drink, would always be said! After the entire request was answered they would go with Mama.

The grandchildren would give Grand paw Hezekiah a big bear hug and Rachel would tuck them in with a good night prayer and kiss.

Now the job of counting the people was coming up as 1830 approached.

John Floyd was elected and would take the office of the Governor of the Commonwealth of Virginia on March 4, 1830. I see some folks named their boy babies John Floyd, as did Archibald Whitt who named his youngest son, John Floyd Whitt.

Notice was put up at the Jeffersonville Post Office stating the census was going to be taken. All people must be counted to determine how many congressmen each state is allowed. It also gives local government a look at the population so plans can be made for different services.

The population of Tazewell County in 1830 was 5,749. The County had been divided again to add Logan County, Giles County, and parts of other counties. Hezekiah and Rachel made sure they were counted and the total reflected the two of them. Hezekiah hated that the beloved Tazewell County was being divided, but in the next few years she would be cut on some more. This would actually reduce the work load in Tazewell Court House in Jeffersonville.

The National Census in 1830 was 12,866,020. The deaf, dumb, and blind were listed separately. Also the North trying to overrule the South in Electoral Collage votes and increase their numbers in Congress made the South count a slave as three-fifths of a white. This was added to the list of enragements caused by the North. Hezekiah said, "the North will bring about a great war someday and it will come before we know it."

The first railroad station in the United States opened in Baltimore on January 7, 1830. Trains were new, but they were here to stay. Hezekiah heard that a train could move at speeds up to 25 miles per hour and pull a big load at the same time. That was hard to imagine for 1830.

On January 13, 1830 a great fire burned much of New Orleans and was thought to have been started by rebel slaves.

On January 21, 1830 in Portsmouth Ohio, blacks were gathered up and deported.

On May 18, 1830 Edwin Budding of England invented the lawnmower. Look what he has done to our Saturdays.

D. Hyde patented his invention, the fountain pen, on May 20, 1830. Only the rich would have such a luxury.

Someone wrote the poem, "Mary Had A Little Lamb," on May 24, 1830.

THE PATRIOT, HEZEKIAH WHITT

Our fine ancestors serving in Congress on May 28, 1830 authorized the removal of all Indians from all states to the western prairie. Jackson felt the Indians should be moved in the name of progress. Many folks disagreed.

On July 15, 1830 three Indian tribes signed a treaty agreeing to give up their claim to most of Minnesota, Iowa, and Missouri. The three tribes were the Sioux, Sauk, and Fox. The Sioux wouldn't have to fight the whites again until the whites wanted their lands way west of the Mississippi. The white man was always looking for ways to take more land from the red men.

The Native Americans were forced under the point of musket and bayonet to march to permanent reservations in Oklahoma and Nebraska. Thousands died along the way, it has been called the "Trail Of Tears." The Black Hawk War and another Seminole War was fought because these Indians stood up to the United States again.

Hezekiah and Rachel always felt bad at the mistreatment of the Indians by the United States. Thomas Bailey Christian often discussed this with Aunt Rachel and Hezekiah. Hezekiah liked the politics of Andrew Jackson, but he sure disagreed with the Indian Removal act.

On August 4, 1830 the plans for the city of Chicago were laid out. It was very windy and the folks nicknamed it the "Windy City."

On September 9, 1830 the daring aeronaut flew his hot air balloon from Castle Garden, New York City to Perth Amboy, New Jersey. Who says you can't get a rise with hot air?

The unlucky William Huskisson was the first man to be ran over by a train. It was on September 15, 1830 in England.

Another great invention occurred in 1830. Thomas Hancock invented "Elastic." It was first used in gloves, suspenders, shoes, and stockings. Of course only the rich enjoyed the stretchy stuff in the beginning.

Hezekiah had a great surprise, Rachel and the children all pitched in and ordered him a watch. They ordered it in January of 1830 and it arrived in December just in time for Christmas. Hezekiah had an old watch and it just wouldn't keep correct time. Rachel saw the watch in an old newspaper and all of them started saving.

Rachel finally had the money by January 1830 so she ordered the Agassiz Pocket Watch all the way from Zurich, Switzerland. The cost for this above average watch and gold fob was almost $30.00 and Hezekiah was never to know this. He would probably have sent it back for such extravagance

The watch was given to him on Christmas Day in 1830 by Rachel, and the family that still lived near. The grandchildren took all the credit which made Hezekiah's weathered face smile from ear to ear and his gray eyes sparkled like diamonds. It was a beautiful thing to see.

THE PATRIOT, HEZEKIAH WHITT

The watch was smaller than most pocket watches of the time. The case was hinged and made from 18K yellow gold. It had a jeweled movement which was so accurate it would keep time within five minutes per month. The smaller size made it fit into Hezekiah's vest pocket with ease. The Gold Fob was a great addition to the watch. It had an Irish Green stone at the end encased by gold.

Hezekiah walked around all day pulling the watch out and checking the time. He was proud of it and of his loving family.

After the Christmas Dinner the talk went to John Bunyan's family, Richard, and Jonas. Rachel said that Jonas and Susannah were starting to yearn to come to Tazewell County. Rachel mentioned the latest letters and stated she could read between the lines and Hezekiah agreed.

James and Nancy were there on a regular basis and still had no children. Both of them loved children and were always doing something for their nieces and nephews.

The first book on birth control came out in 1830, but respectable publishers would not advertise it. None the less 25,000 copies sold and I bet most of these went to women.

Jedediah Strong Smith was at home in the wilderness of the west. He was a brave and daring mountain man and he led the first covered wagons to the base of the Rocky Mountains.

Jedediah was the first white man to discover the famous "South Pass." He discovered the "Great Basin." He was the first white man to cross the high Sierras into California. He was also the first white man to travel the coast from southern California to northern Oregon.

Hezekiah read about these feats and reflected back to his days in the wilderness of the waters of the Clinch. He thought it would be wonderful if he was young again and go exploring with Jedediah Smith.

News came that President Jackson fired his whole cabinet. It all came about when Secretary of War, John Eaton married a beautiful Innkeeper's daughter by the name of Peggy O'Neal Timberlake. Tongues wagged all around Washington and the proper ladies would not entertain her. Jackson became inflamed by the senseless gossip and called a special session to discuss the virtue of Mrs., Eaton. President Jackson was still enflamed by the gossip that drove his dear Rachel to her grave. During the meeting all agreed that Mrs. Eaton was a virtuous woman. Then when the minutes were written down, Jackson fired the Cabinet.

After hearing of this, Rachel Whitt asked? "Why can't folks keep their mouths shut, The Bible says that people sin with their tongues?

In James 1:26 it says.

If any man among you seems to be religious, and bridleth not his tongue, but deceiveth his own heart, this man's religion is vain.

COLONEL CHARLES DAHNMON WHITT

THE PATRIOT, HEZEKIAH WHITT

Hezekiah and Rachel both noticed that they were having problems seeing distance and up close. By 1830 over 300 retail eyeglasses stores were opened around the country.

Ben Franklin invented the bifocal spectacles many years ago. He had become frustrated at having to take one pair off and putting on another. It seemed he did this all the time so he decided to put two lens in the same frame. It worked after a short period of getting use to them.

Hezekiah heard about an eye, ears, nose, and throat doctor over in Abingdon. He decided to take Rachel and get them both fitted for a pair of the bifocal spectacles.

They both had trouble reading the Bible or doing close work. They could see, but they had to hold things way out in front and here lately their arms just wasn't long enough. They also had some trouble seeing way off.

They got to Abingdon in Washington County and checked in the local inn. They inquired as to the location of the Eyes, Ears, Nose, and Throat Doctor and received good directions. They went on over and found the doctor and sit down to wait their turn. The doctor brought both of them back.

"What brings you in today?" the doctor asked?

"We can't see like we use to, come to think there is a lot of things we can't do as good," stated Hezekiah.

The doctor spit some tobacco juice into a brass spittoon, and said, "I know what you mean I can fix up your seeing, but some things you will just have to get use to," laughed the doctor.

Hezekiah smiled and said, "Doc, this is my bride Rachel and I am Hezekiah Whitt."

"Glad to meet you folks, I am Doctor Benjamin Frank," replied the doctor.

"Heck, you gotta be good with a name like that, Ol Ben Franklin purty near invented spectacles," answered Hezekiah.

"That's Frank," replied the doctor.
"I know, but it is almost Ben Franklin," replied Hezekiah.
Doctor Frank asked, "Who's first?"
"Rachel, you should go first," said Hezekiah trying to be a gentleman.
"Thanks husband," Rachel said as she sits in a strange looking chair with all kinds of gadgets facing her.

"Now don't be alarmed, my whole examination is painless," said Doctor Frank.

Hezekiah took a little chew of plug tobacco and sit down to watch. After both of them had been checked out, the doctor told them that they would get their new spectacles in a few months. Just put-um on and get use to-um," continued the Doctor. Hezekiah picked out the deluxe gold frames for both Rachel and himself. Thanked the doctor and paid the fee.

THE PATRIOT, HEZEKIAH WHITT

After a night in the Inn the couple headed back to Cedar Grove, the Whitt house.

They basically forgot the order that made it easier to wait for something. Finally in about five months the package arrived in September 1831. They were both anxious to un-wrap the package and get their new spectacles out. The package contained two cases with Doctor Benjamin Frank's name on them. The cases were not marked as to which one belonged to whom. They both took a case and opened it and put on their new gold bifocal spectacles.

Rachel said, "If these are mine they ain't no good!"

"Mine are awful," replied Hezekiah.

"Here let's swap, I bet I got yours and you have mine," said Rachel.

They traded and put them on again.

"Heck, I can see good except for that line a running through-um!" replied Hezekiah.

"Me too, but don't you remember Dr. Frank said we would have to get use to-um? Asked Rachel?
"Yip, look down through the bottom," said Hezekiah as he looked at his watch.
Rachel went over and picked up their Bible and flipped it open and read all good things come from God, and she could see every word sharply.

"Old Ben Franklin was a hero and also a smart man for inventing these things," said Hezekiah.

"Yes, these are a God send," declared Rachel Whitt as she looked all about through her new gold bifocal spectacles.

This is a "Southern Bell Ball" dress, modeled by Sharon Gail Whitt.

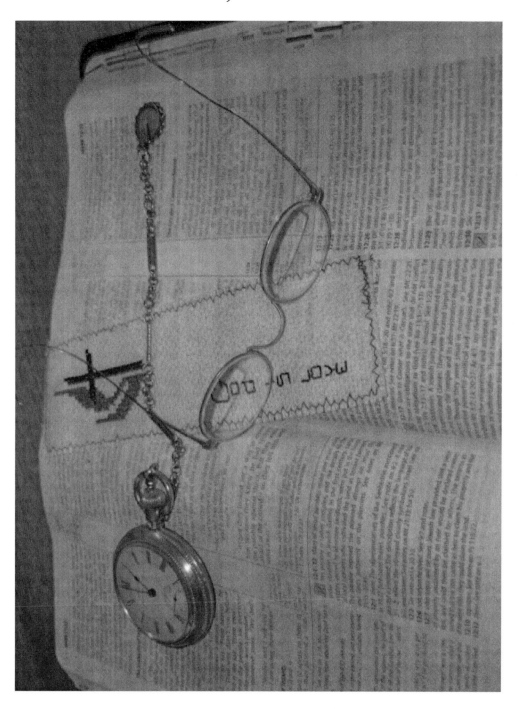

A rendition of Hezekiah's watch and spectacles.

Chapter 44

Hezekiah Buys More Land

An Act of Congress was passed on June 7, 1832 to give the Revolutionary War Pension to those deserving patriots. Hezekiah would help many of the veterans by being a witness that he knew they served. Later Hezekiah would go for his. (Why he waited is a mystery, unless he was too modest.)

On January 2, 1832 the first "curling club was formed in the United States. They called it the Orchard Lake Curling Club. Know what is curling? It is a game similar to shuffleboard, except the players use heavy granite stones and slide them on ice and try to stop on a circle on the ice. This was a game that originated in medieval Scotland. Just like now, many people in the United States in 1832 asked, "What the heck is curling? It is now an Olympic Sport.

On January 6, 1832 some folks got together in Boston and organized the, "New England Anti-Slavery Society. This was another difference between North and South.

Piracy was going on and a United States war ship destroyed a Sumatran village on February 6, 1832. It was for retaliation.

On March 4, 1832 Joseph Smith the self proclaimed leader of the Mormons was taken by some Ohioans and beaten, tarred, and feathered.

On May 21, 1832 the Democrats held their first National Convention in Baltimore, Maryland.

Garret Moll was the first to measure the noise given off by discharging guns. He did this on June 28, 1832. He decided that it was harmful to a person's hearing.

The song, "America," was first sung in Boston on July 4, 1832 on our Nation's Birthday.

On July 10, 1832, President Jackson used his power and vetoed the re-charter of the 2nd National Bank.

On July 13, 1832 the source of the mighty Mississippi River was found by Henry R. Schoolcraft.

On July 14, 1832 opium was exempted from federal duty. Now it is strictly enforced.

On July 25, 1832 the first railroad accident happened at Quincy, Mass. and one man died.

On August 2, 1832, the United States ended the "Black Hawk War" by defeating the

THE PATRIOT, HEZEKIAH WHITT

Sac and Fox Indians. The Illinois Militia of 1,300 men got the credit. The Indians were decimated at the Battle of Bad Ax. Black Hawk, the leader of the Sauk Indians gave himself up on August 27, 1832. The white man marches on!

The first streetcar, pulled by a horse, appeared in New York City on November 14, 1832. The fare was .12 cents and ran on 4th Avenue it ran from Prince to 14th Street. What on earth will man think up next?

On December 5, 1832 "Old Hickory, Andy By G-- Jackson" was reelected to the Presidency.

All of the year of 1832, Charles Darwin journeyed all around the world trying to prove that folks descended from apes and everything happened accidental like. I don't think he proved a thing. I believe that Adam was a handsome man and Eve was a most beautiful woman. Hezekiah and Rachel fussed about such ignorant people that don't know about Jesus Christ.

On December 28, 1832 the Vice President, John Calhoun, resigned because his thinking was just opposite of President Jackson. At this time in history the President and Vice President did not run as running mates. The Vice President was voted on separately.

Hezekiah and Rachel marveled at all the changes that had occurred in their lives. One real old man in Jeffersonville celebrated his 90th birthday and folks asked him many question as to his longevity and one man asked him about all the changes he had seen. "I have seen many changes and I have been a-gin ever one of-um," reported the ninety year old. At my age I understand! (The Author.)

As the year of 1832 closed Hezekiah and Rachel were so thankful for their lives and what the Lord had done for them. They had made it through another year and still were very healthy.

Jonas and Susannah's letters grew stronger with their desire to come to Tazewell, County. They would come to the Promised Land before too many more years pass. Elizabeth "Betsy" Whitt was their last child and it looked like they were done with having babies. (They may have lost a baby or two between Elizabeth 1827 and David Crockett Whitt which will come along on December 13, 1836. There were no records of another birth in this almost nine years.)

Hezekiah was always on the lookout for more land. He had acquired several nice tracts and made sure his children got some of it at a great bargain price. (He would sell it for pennies on the dollar to his sons.)

He had a little farm across Green Mountain on the Clinch that he rented out and was saving it for another Jonas and his family.

Hezekiah and Rachel enjoyed these years as they prosper and still have good health. Hezekiah is in Jeffersonville a couple of days a week and stays abreast of all the news. Rachel is always anxious to see what Hezekiah has heard in town. She always said that the Justices of the Peace were the biggest gossipers around and that her social groups didn't hold a candle to them.

Often Hezekiah would bring an old newspaper home to read and let Rachel study every word of it. The papers were sometimes a year old before he ever got them. They often sit on the upper porch in the evening and spit their tobacco juice over the railing to the front yard. Sometimes they would smoke their pipes and read the Bible or the old book called, "Pilgrims Progress."

They enjoyed their new spectacles and did not know their sight had been so bad. They enjoyed reading anything they could get their hands on. Just as twilight approached Hezekiah would pull out his most admired pocket watch and look at the time. He would always say, "Almost bed time, my bride!"

Hezekiah and Rachel encouraged Jonas to bring his family to Tazewell County. They had a big roomy house across Green Mountain and rented it out. It had 160 acres of ground and a good barn. They would let Jonas and Susannah have it if and when they moved to Tazewell County. Rachel and Hezekiah composed a letter to Jonas and Susannah and made them the offer. Hezekiah also told Jonas of the progressive nature of the new county and that he should be able to get building and milling as well as earn a good living on the farm work.

John Bunyan and Richard had already moved to Kentucky and Griffy and his family were dreaming of moving to Missouri. The girls were married off, but not too far away. James and Nancy were fairly close by, but they had no children. They would be happy it Jonas' family was close so they could help with the children. If they could get Jonas and his family near they all would be happy.

On May 6, 1833 John Deere made his first steel plow. The name is still big in farming machinery today.

On June 27, 1833 Prudence Crandall was arrested in Canterbury, Connecticut for conducting an academy for black females. Prudence was a white woman.

On August 10, 1833 Chicago became an incorporated town of about 200.

On August 23, 1833 the British abolished slavery in her colonies. They freed about 700,000 slaves.

On September 3, 1833 the New York Sun began to publish the first daily newspaper.

On October 2, 1833 The New York Anti-Slavery Society became organized.
A train derailed at Hightstown, New Jersey on November 8, 1833 and 2 people were killed.
On December 3, 1833 Oberlin Collage in Ohio became the first coed College.

THE PATRIOT, HEZEKIAH WHITT

On December 4, 1833 the American Anti-Slavery Society was formed in Philadelphia by Arthur Tappan. As you can see the times are changing and slavery is on its way out, at least in the North.

Hezekiah has come across a farm and he can get it at a good price.

1833 Tazewell County Deed Book 5, page 467 Indenture dated 28 October 1833, John Ratliff & Charlotte his wife, Tazewell to Hezekiah Whitt for $135.50, 245 acres in Tazewell County bearing date 16th day of December 1819 lying and being on Dismal Creek a branch of the Levisa fork of Sandy and bounded as followed beginning at two spruce pine of south side of said creek.../S/ John Ratliff Wits: John Brown, James Whitt, William Brown, Jane Brown proved November Term 1833 Tazewell Court by oath of James Whitt and John Brown.

I am not sure if Hezekiah went to inspect this property before he bought it or not. It is located in a narrow hollow with little flat land. It is in present day Buchanan County and typically there is little flat land. The wood was full of virgin timber at this time and has proven to be a rich county because of the discovery of massive coal deposits. During this time most buyers of land were looking for farm land. Now the land on Dismal Creek was rich, but most of it was on steep hillsides.

I think that maybe John Brown told Hezekiah about the farm and agreed to rent it if Hezekiah would purchase it. I think Hezekiah had a word of mouth contract with John Brown and they shook on the deal. Back in this time of honor very few gentlemen ever went back on a deal after shaking on it. Hezekiah was pleased with the deal. It was always good to have some extra property on hand.

It was a good two days ride on a good horse from Baptist Valley to the mouth of Dismal Creek and Hezekiah would wait until spring of 1834 to go and inspect his new farm and collect the rent. John Brown had told Hezekiah Whitt about the farm and the steep hill sides. Hezekiah remembered the terrain of the area and was not buying a pig in a poke. The price of land had gone up in recent years and 245 acres was a good sized tract for the price of $135.50. It was less than $1.80 per acre and that was a fair price, even for a farm with some steep hills.

In 1833 Hezekiah Whitt was 73 years old and that was old for some folks, but Hezekiah could still ride all day or work all day, but he needed a little more rest than a younger man did. Rachel was the same; she was still agile and could pretty well stay with Hezekiah on his outings.

Around the first of May, 1834 Hezekiah and Rachel put on their traveling clothes, packed a few necessaries and rode off to Dismal Creek to see their farm and collect the rent from John Brown. They traveled the Kentucky Turnpike which followed the Clinch River to what is now the village of Raven. There they climbed the ridge, (Road Ridge) and followed it several miles and went down the other side to the Head of the River area. This was the origin of Levisa Fork of the Big Sandy River. Hezekiah had been in

THE PATRIOT, HEZEKIAH WHITT

this country several times, but not recently so Rachel and he both marveled at the closeness of the hills and the abundant virgin trees.

After a camp on the ridge the Whitts made it to Dismal by the evening of the second day and found the John Brown family just getting ready for supper. The Browns set two more plates and Mrs. Brown had plenty of food fixed. It was simple fare but mighty filling. The Browns were really glad for the visit as they seldom saw visitors.

John paid Hezekiah part of the rent and as per their agreement and would pay the rest after the harvest.

James Whitt was the first born of Hezekiah and Rachel. Hezekiah relied on him and Nancy his wife for many things. You will see that James was on many papers as a witness and always stayed close to his mother and father. James and Nancy would end up with the farm if he out lived his parents.

Jonas and Susannah would eventually come to Tazewell County, but he was the youngest of the family and had been gone for years. Jonas would once again become close to his parents in their latter years.

Also in 1833 Liles Dolsberry applied for his Revolutionary War Pension and Hezekiah was called to be a witness along with Aaron Higginbotham. Both men knew Liles and that he had served his country against the Indians and the British. Hezekiah was slow to apply for his pension. Maybe he thought that his service was given from the heart and he should not be paid for it. He was getting older and a little pension money might be nice. He had to decide what to do.

The hours of the time glass were flowing faster as Hezekiah and Rachel grew older. They had trouble believing that the year of 1834 was upon them.

Hezekiah often said, "the older I get the faster the time goes."

"Yes Hezekiah, I know what you mean, it seems like yesterday that we fell in love, now our hair is white and our bodies are aging," replied Rachel.

"Well, my bride, we can still cut the mustard, I hear that some old men just can't get a rise at our age," replied Hezekiah.

"If you want me to brag on you I will, you have always been a great lover and you still fulfill my greatest desires," said Rachel.

"All of this talking is getting me a bit twitter-pated," said Hezekiah.
"Maybe tonight, you big handsome man," answered Rachel.

"Big," answered Hezekiah with a crooked little grin.

Rachel turned to him and smiled as only she could do.

THE PATRIOT, HEZEKIAH WHITT

On January 5, 1834 the Kiowa Indians recorded this night, as the night the stars fell, there must have been meteor showers in the winter sky.

I guess President Jackson was the first union busting President. On January 29 Jackson ordered out troops to suppress a labor dispute.

Workers were beginning to find out that strength was in numbers and they began to organize. The first labor newspaper "The Man'" was published on February 18, 1834 in New York City.

The railroads were here to stay and in Pennsylvania the first railroad tunnel was completed on March 18, 1834.

The United States Senate Censured President Jackson for taking federal deposits from the Bank of the United States.

Now man can begin to explore under the sea. On June 14, 1834 the hardhat diving suit was patented by Leonard Norcross of Dixfield, Maine.

Every time Hezekiah got a paper he marveled at the new inventions and often said, "Man will never fly in a flying machine, cept maybe big balloons."

In these days wood was smoothed with glass, rocks, sand, and even rough leather, but now a man by the name of Isaac Fischer Jr. from Springfield, Vermont invented sandpaper. His invention was patented on June 14, 1834.

Inventions were being patented in all fields, on June 21, 1834 Cyrus Hall McCormick patented his reaping machine. When Hezekiah saw that in a paper he said, "I doubt I will live to see that in Tazewell County."

On June 30, 1834 Congress created a great Indian territory in what is now Oklahoma. The Indians could live there for a few years until the white man needed more land! On

April 22 1889 congress opened part of the land to whites who rushed to claim a plot. They became to be known as "Oklahoma Sooners."

On July 5, 1834 a provisional government was formed in Oregon Country.

On August 1, 1834 The whole British Empire abolished slavery. They were the ones that started it and brought many to the United States in prior years.

On October 14, 1834 a black man by the name of Henry Blair patented a corn planter. He was the first Negro to patent anything in the United States.

On November 1, 1834 the first published book on poker came out as gambling became popular on the Mississippi Steamboats.

On November 14, 1834 the first known Whiz-Kid, William Thompson, entered the Glasgow University at the age of 10 years old.

On November 25, the famous New York Restaurant, Delmonico's, offered a meal of soup, steak, coffee, and half a pie for the exorbitant price of .12 cents.

COLONEL CHARLES DAHNMON WHITT

THE PATRIOT, HEZEKIAH WHITT

On December 25, 1834 Charles Darwin celebrated Christmas on the ship Beagle at Tres Montes, Chile. I thought he didn't believe in God as his research was to prove that everything was relevant and we all evolved from a simpler organism. Man came from apes and so on. What was he doing celebrating Christmas if there is no God? He was a hypocrite in my mind.(Author)

On January 30, 1835 an unemployed painter from England jumped out of a crowd near the Capital and is the first assassin to shoot at a sitting President. Richard Lawrence yanked out a pistol and tried to shoot Andrew Jackson but his pistol misfired. Jackson also pulled out a pistol and tried to shoot Lawrence, but his gun also misfired. The weather was damp and both men's primer was too moist. Several men around, one being Representative David Crockett rushed the man and subdued him.

On March 3, 1835 the United States Congress authorized a United States Mint in New Orleans, Louisiana.

On May 6, 1835 the first edition of the New York Herald came out at the cost of .01 cents each.
On June 2, 1835 the circus owned by P.T. Barnum began its first United States tour.

On July 8, 1835 the Liberty Bell cracked again.

On August 18, 1835 the last of the Pottawatomie Indians leave Chicago to the palefaces.

On November 2, 1835 the Seminole war begins for the second time at Osceola, Florida. Osceola was the name of the great Seminole Chief.

On November 23 a horseshoe making machine is patented by Henry Burden of Troy, New York. What will the blacksmiths think?

On November 24, 1835 Texas Rangers are formed by the Texas Provisional Government.

On December1, 1835 Hans Christian Anderson published his first fairy tale book.

On a cold day in New York, December 16, 1835, over 600 buildings in New York City burned to the ground.

On December 30, 1835 gold was discovered in northern Georgia, guess what, the Indians were moved out and sent across the Mississippi River. I guess Indians don't need gold. (Author.)

In Tazewell County a Survey was made in June 1835.

Survey made the 5th of June 1835 by virtue of Land Office Treasury Warrant number 7546 there is granted by the Commonwealth of Virginia unto Hezekiah Whitt 98 acres lying in Tazewell county on waters of Dismal Creek, waters of Louisa fork (Levisa) of

THE PATRIOT, HEZEKIAH WHITT

Sandy River and bounded as follows: Beginning at a white oak and sugar tree on a hill side just below his old survey....to a spruce pine on edge of Dry Fork of Dismal.

It seems that land just came to Hezekiah; of course he took a terrible chance when he signed the Patriot Oath and stood against the King of England. They had to stand together or hang separately.

Chapter 45

Jonas Brings His Clan To The Promised Land

David Crockett from Tennessee arrived in Texas with a party of volunteers from Tennessee to defend the new Republic of Texas on January 5, 1836. David Crockett was already known for his exploits against the Indians and a term in the House of Representatives at Washington. He like Andrew Jackson was from Tennessee. David Crockett was outspoken against Jackson's Indian Removal Act, and this got him beat in his next election. David Crockett was very wise, but not so literate. He had no idea, but this little trip to Texas would create his legacy.

On February 3, 1836 the Whig Party held it's first national convention at Albany, New York.

On February 23, 1836 3,000 Mexicans besiege the Alamo under General Santa Anna. The 182 Americans were garrisoned in the old mission church called the Alamo.

On February 24, 1836, the Mexicans attacked. How long could the 182 Americans hold off a 3,000 man army with cannon? Why did they do it? They were buying time for Sam Houston to get his army together.

On February 25, Samuel Colt patented his invention, the first revolving barrel, multi-shot firearm.

On March 2, 1836 the Republic of Texas declares her independence from Mexico.

On March 5, 1836, Samuel Colt starts manufacturing his new 34-caliber "Texas," model pistol. It came too late for the men at the Alamo.

In the early morning of April 6, 1836 Mexico attacked the Alamo and finally after 13 days and by sheer numbers defeats the men of the Alamo. History says that David Crockett was one of the last to die and he went down fighting for the freedom of the Republic of Texas. David Crockett was an instant American Hero and many mothers would name their boy babies after this man.

On March 16, 1836 The Republic of Texas approved their constitution. And on the following day they abolished slavery in their little country.

On April 14, 1836 the territory of Wisconsin was formed by the United States Congress.

On April 21, 1836 the Battle of San Jacinto was fought and the Texans yelled, "Remember the Alamo," and beat the Mexican army to win their official Independence.

On June 15, 1836, Arkansas was admitted to the Union of the United States to become the 25th State.

THE PATRIOT, HEZEKIAH WHITT

On September 5, 1836, Samuel Houston became the first President of the Republic of Texas. He was inaugurated on September 22, 1836. Texas has been the headliner in the newspapers all year.

On December 7, 1836 the United States elected Martin Van Buren as the 8th President.

On the 13th of December 1836 Susannah gave birth to David Crockett Whitt in Montgomery, County Virginia. His proud father was Jonas Whitt. You will hear much more about this fellow who went by, "Crockett." After you finish this book you can continue in the series, "Building America" in the book, "Legacy, The Days Of David Crockett Whitt."

By St. Patrick's Day 1837 Hezekiah had a big garden plowed up at his farm across Green Mountain and planted about one hundred pounds of seed potatoes. He also plowed a bigger field to ready it for corn planting. Yes Hezekiah was making preparations for the return of his son Jonas and his family. The renters had moved out of the nice big house and Hezekiah was going to have it ready for his prodigal son.

Hezekiah and Rachel had been getting letters on a regular basis from Susannah and Jonas. They were also getting ready for the move and the December 13, 1836 birth of David Crockett Whitt did not deter or shake their plans to move. By May of 1836 Susannah was surprised to find out she was expecting another baby; it had been eight years since Elizabeth Betsy was born and she was a little lady by then.

Rachel and all the kindred in Tazewell County were looking forward to the arrival of Jonas, Susannah, and all the children. James and Nancy were especially anxious to see the children and would be a big help with the little ones. Nancy had a love for children and for some reason the Lord never blessed her and James with any babies.

Archibald and all of the Whitts over in Montgomery County hated the idea of Jonas taking their Susannah and grandchildren way off over the mountains to Tazewell County. They were pleased to have them all of these years and would not try to deter them in their wish to move. They prayed that when the time came that God would travel with them and protect them from the hazards of travel.

By late summer 1837 Jonas hoped to be on the trail with his family and with all that they could carry on pack animals or herd over the narrow trails to the promised land of Tazewell County. Jonas remembers the great beauty of the waters of the Clinch, but Susannah and the children had not seen it. Susannah and the children had fallen in love with Tazewell County by the many stories Jonas told with great descriptions.

By Independence Day 1837, Hezekiah and the rest of the Whitts were already in a spirit of excitement at the anticipation of the Jonas Whitt's family arrival. It would be late summer before that day would come, so Hezekiah told everyone to be patient and go about their work and before they knew it Jonas would lead his family into Tazewell County.

THE PATRIOT, HEZEKIAH WHITT

After a stormy night on the trail the Jonas Whitt family arrived in Jeffersonville and stopped at the James Vandyke tavern to eat and find out the best way to get to Hezekiah and Rachel's home.

Jonas with his stock, pack animals, and all the children arrived in Jeffersonville in August 1837. They were ready to eat and find Grand Paw Hezekiah's house.

Jonas, Susannah, 19 year old John Bunyan, (Named for his uncle.) 17 year old twins Rachel and Rhoda, 15 year old Emma, 12 year old James Griffith, (Named for two uncles.) 10 year old Elizabeth Betsy, and seven month old David Crockett Whitt all sat down to eat at the James Vandyke eatery.

James Vandyke sent a little black boy over to the court house to find Justice Hezekiah Whitt.

After a good twenty years from Tazewell County, Jonas was back home and all of his family felt like it was their home. All of the children had seen Grand Paw Hezekiah and would know him when they saw him again.

Rachel was the first to see him!
"Grand Paw," she exclaimed.
All eyes turned toward the door!
A big grin was on the face of Hezekiah Whitt as he looked upon his son and family.

I have taken you on a journey with Hezekiah Whitt from 1760 to 1837 for the rest of the story read another book on Building America, called "Legacy, The Days Of David Crockett Whitt," by Colonel Charles Dahnmon Whitt.

(Published with the Jesse Stuart Foundation in Ashland Kentucky).
http://dahnmonwhittfamily.com

THE PATRIOT, HEZEKIAH WHITT

Dedication for Hezekiah Whitt .He served in the Virginia Militia during the Revolutionary War. A marker stone was placed by the DAR and a brass marker was placed by the SAR. Whitt-Lowe Cemetery, Baptist Valley, Virginia. June 4, 2004 Notice the flash of the prime as the old flintlock muskets discharge in the salute to Hezekiah Whitt.

THE PATRIOT, HEZEKIAH WHITT

The Hezekiah Whitt house in Baptist Valley, Tazewell County, Virginia. It was taken down in 2000 and moved. The 230+ year old 16" Cedar Logs were still in tact. The house was built in three stages. The Limestone chimney is still standing today.

THE PATRIOT, HEZEKIAH WHITT

The Grave of Hezekiah Whitt in the Whitt-Lowe Cemetery, Baptist Valley, VA.
He was a Patriot, Statesman, Militiaman, Indian Spy, Sheriff, and a Gentleman
Justice of the Peace appoint by the Governor of Virginia, for life. 1761-1846

THE PATRIOT, HEZEKIAH WHITT

Descendants of Justice Hezekiah WHITT

1. Justice Hezekiah WHITT (b.1760-South Carolina d.29 Mar 1846 Sunday-Tazewell,C,V,Near Cedar Bluff)
  sp: Rachel SKAGGS(INDIAN MAIDEN CORNSTALK) (b.Abt 1761-Shawnee Nation,Ohio m.1782 d.Abt 1846-)
  ├ 2. James WHITT (b.28 Oct 1782 Monday-Cedar Grove,W,VA. (Now Tazewell) d.19 Sep 1855-Tazewell,County,VA.)
  │   sp: Nancy SKAGGS (b.1789-Washington County,N,C,VA. m.Abt 1808 d.23 Oct 1868-Tazewell,County,VA.)
  ├ 2. Griffith (Griffy) WHITT (b.1787-Cedar Grove,RC,Va. (Now Tazewell) d.23 Aug 1853-Grundy County,Mo.)
      sp: Martha (Patty)) SKAGGS (b.2 Aug 1791-Russell Co. Va. m.21 Mar 1807 d.22 Apr 1855-Grundy,Co.,Mo.)
      ├ 3. Timothy WHITT (b.3 Nov 1808-Ready Ridge,Tazewell County, Virginia d.1862-Pea Ridge,Arkansas)
      │   sp: Nancy HINKLE (b.Abt 1811 m.19 Jan 1832)
      │   ├ 4. William WHITT (b.Abt 1833-Va.)
      │   ├ 4. Grifee WHITT (b.Abt 1835-Va.)
      │   ├ 4. John Marion WHITT (b.Abt 1837-Va.)
      │   │   sp: Lottie CLEVELAND
      │   │   ├ 5. Frank WHITT
      │   │   ├ 5. Lillie WHITT
      │   │   ├ 5. Charles WHITT
      │   │   ├ 5. Lloyd Timothy WHITT
      │   │   └ 5. Clarence WHITT
      │   ├ 4. Lorenzo WHITT (b.Abt 1841-Va.)
      │   ├ 4. James Henry WHITT (b.Abt 1843-Va.)
      │   ├ 4. Noah B. WHITT (b.Abt 1845-Missouri)
      │   └ 4. Jasper WHITT (b.Abt 1849-Missouri)
      ├ 3. Shone WHITT (b.25 Dec 1810-Ready Ridge,Virginia d.Grundy County . Mo.)
      │   sp: William HARRISON (b.15 Mar 1801 m.11 Sep 1827d.Grundy County . Mo.)
      │   ├ 4. Alexander Perry HARRISON (b.1828-Tazewell Co.,Va.)
      │   ├ 4. Griffith HARRISON (b.1835-Tazewell Co.,Va.)
      │   ├ 4. Austin HARRISON (b.1837-Tazewell Co.,Va.)
      │   ├ 4. Martha Jane HARRISON (b.27 Dec 1841)
      │   ├ 4. Thomas HARRISON (b.1844)
      │   ├ 4. Jeremiah Skaggs HARRISON (b.29 Jan 1845-Grundy County,Missouri)
      │   ├ 4. James Crockett HARRISON (b.14 Dec 1849-Grundy County,Missouri)
      │   ├ 4. John HARRISON (b.1849-Grundy County,Missouri)
      │   └ 4. Martha HARRISON (b.Abt 1852)
      ├ 3. Assena WHITT (b.19 Feb 1813-Ready Ridge,Virginia Tazewell County. d.8 Jul 1882-Harrison Co.,Mo.)
      │   sp: John VANDIKE (b.Abt 1810-Tazewell Co.,Va. m.5 Mar 1835 d.1 Sep 1863-Benton Barracks,SL,Mo.)
      │   ├ 4. Martha Jane VANDIKE (b.31 Dec 1835-Virginia d.5 Jan 1905-Harrison Co.,Mo.)
      │   ├ 4. Charles VANDIKE (b.25 Mar 1838)
      │   ├ 4. Mary VANDIKE (b.13 Sep 1842)
      │   ├ 4. Griffee VANDIKE (b.Abt 1843-Mo.)
      │   ├ 4. Israel VANDIKE (b.Abt 1846-Mo.)
      │   ├ 4. John VANDIKE (b.10 Apr 1847-Grundy County,Missouri d.31 Mar 1924-Wray,Yuma County,Colorado)
      │   │   sp: Frances Ellen COLE (m.15 Feb 1872)
      │   │   └ 5. Ellis VANDIKE (b.9 Mar 1881-Harrison County,Missouri d.12 Aug 1946-Wray,YC,Colorado)
      │   │   sp: Ida E. TIFF (m.24 Nov 1908)
      │   │   └ 6. Eva A. VANDIKE
      │   │   sp: Gale ROGERS
      │   │   └ 7. Beverly ROGERS
      │   │   sp: TRACY
      │   ├ 4. William VANDIKE (b.Abt 1852-Mo.)
      │   └ 4. Richard VANDIKE (b.Abt 1865-Mo.)
      ├ 3. Cinthia WHITT (b.9 Dec 1815-Ready Ridge,Virginia d.Aft 1880)
          sp: John Yancy CRESSWELL (m.15 Oct 1837)
          ├ 4. Manerva CRESSWELL (b.Abt 1839-Va.)

THE PATRIOT, HEZEKIAH WHITT

Descendants of Justice Hezekiah WHITT

```
        ├─ 4. Cosby CRESSWELL (b.Abt 1841-Va.)
        ├─ 4. Ballard CRESSWELL (b.Abt 1843-Va.)
        ├─ 4. Louisa CRESSWELL (b.Abt 1845-Mo.)
        ├─ 4. Sophrona CRESSWELL (b.Abt 1847-Mo.)
        ├─ 4. Erastus CRESSWELL (b.Abt 1849-Mo.)
        ├─ 4. Emily CRESSWELL (b.Abt 1852)
        ├─ 4. Patrick H. CRESSWELL (b.Abt 1854-Mo.)
        └─ 4. Griffee CRESSWELL (b.Abt 1856-Mo.)
   ├─ 3. Olivia Mary WHITT (b.24 Aug 1818-Va.)
      sp: Washington DESKINS (m.12 Jun 1839)
        ├─ 4. Mary J. DESKINS (b.Abt 1841-Va.)
        ├─ 4. William DESKINS (b.Abt 1843-Va.)
        ├─ 4. Martha DESKINS (b.Abt 1845-Va.)
        ├─ 4. George DESKINS (b.Abt 1847-Mo.)
        └─ 4. Lilly A. DESKINS (b.Abt 1849)
   ├─ 3. Noah B. WHITT (b.19 Apr 1820-Ready Ridge, Virginia)
      sp: Matilda MCGUIRE (b.Abt 1821-Va. m.30 Jun 1843)
   ├─ 3. Jeremiah WHITT (b.10 Nov 1822-Ready Ridge, Virginia d.1 Aug 1862-Little Rock,Ark.)
      sp: Malinda MCGUIRE
        ├─ 4. Narcissa WHITT (b.Abt 1844-Mo.)
        ├─ 4. Francis D. WHITT (b.Abt 1848)
        ├─ 4. Nepoleon B. WHITT (b.Abt 1848)
        ├─ 4. Martha A. WHITT (b.Abt 1852)
        ├─ 4. Nancy E. WHITT (b.Abt 1854)
        └─ 4. Matilida WHITT (b.Abt 1857)
   ├─ 3. Richard WHITT (b.13 May 1826-Ready Ridge,TC,Virginia d.10 Mar 1867-Pea Ridge,Missouri)
      sp: Catherine SHIRLEY (b.21 Jan 1827-Indiana m.21 Jun 1847 d.Aft 1880-Grundy County,Missouri)
        ├─ 4. Cinderella WHITT (b.27 Oct 1847 d.1848)
        ├─ 4. Hulda Ann WHITT (b.6 Nov 1848)
        ├─ 4. Shirley WHITT (b.25 Apr 1850)
        ├─ 4. Zelda Jane WHITT (b.29 Sep 1852 d.29 Dec 1872)
             sp: William BUSHONG
             sp: William SOUVERN
             sp: John UTTERBACK
        ├─ 4. Luenburg Girge WHITT (b.4 Apr 1854)
        ├─ 4. Christopher Columbus WHITT (b.11 Apr 1856)
        ├─ 4. William Cruso WHITT (b.2 Jun 1858)
        ├─ 4. Noah Sebastian WHITT (b.2 Jun 1860 d.6 Aug 1944)
             sp: Cordelia M. STILL (m.1 Sep 1883 d.4 Apr 1895)
               ├─ 5. Addie D. WHITT (b.1894 d.19 Dec 1901)
               ├─ 5. William Lesley WHITT (b.1889 d.22 Nov 1954)
               ├─ 5. Hubert V. WHITT (b.1893 d.1961)
               ├─ 5. Grover S. WHITT (b.1887 d.1946)
                    sp: Macoe MURPHY (b.1900 d.1988)
                      └─ 6. John Noah WHITT
                           sp: Marcie RICE
             sp: Annie M. RAYBURN (b.26 Dec 1907 m.26 Dec 1907)
        └─ 4. Richard Jeremiah WHITT (b.29 Jun 1862)
             sp: Lucy F. WYNNE
             └─ 5. Claude WHITT
   ├─ 3. Hannah WHITT (b.16 May 1828-Ready Ridge,Tazewell County,Virginia d.13 Sep 1861-Daviess Co.,G,Missouri)
      sp: William WALLACE (b.1825-Ohio,Car Crash m.22 Mar 1845 d.7 Sep 1869-Daviess County,Missouri)
```

THE PATRIOT, HEZEKIAH WHITT

Descendants of Justice Hezekiah WHITT

- 4. Ann E. WALLACE (b.5 Feb 1847-Daviess County,Missouri)
- 4. Caroline WALLACE (b.27 Dec 1849-DAViess Co.,Gallatin,Missouri d.14 Oct 1924)
- 4. SARAH WALLACE (b.1851)
- 4. AMANDA WALLACE (b.1853)
- 4. LYDIA WALLACE (b.11 Sep 1856-DAViess Co.,Gallatin,Missouri d.25 Jul 1932)
- 4. CHARLES HENRY WALLACE (b.1 Dec 1885-DAViess Co.,Gallatin,Missouri)
- 3. John WHITT (b.24 Aug 1833-Ready Ridge,TC,Virginia d.5 Aug 1862-Benton Barracks,Mo.)
  - sp: Lucy Ann MIKELS (b.1835-Indiana m.8 Mar 1855)
  - 4. Mary WHITT (b.1857)
- 3. Jonas WHITT (b.17 Aug 1837-Ready Ridge,Tazewell County,Virginia d.29 Jan 1900-Washburn,Mo.)
  - sp: Frances CRESSWELL
  - sp: Phoebe FIELDS (b.1857-Mo. m.10 Mar 1878 d.1933)
    - 4. John William WHITT (b.11 Dec 1878-Coffey Co.,Ka d.14 Aug 1949-Modesto,Ca.)
      - sp: Mattie Lee COOPER (m.3 Nov 1897)
        - 5. Athea Rachel WHITT (b.20 Jul 1907-Granada Co.,Mo. d.6 Dec 1993-Modesto,Ca.)
          - sp: Charles BEARDEN (m.30 Jan 1926)
        - 5. Sharman Boddy WHITT (b.?)
    - 4. Elnora WHITT (b.15 Jan 1881-Coffey Co.,Ka)
      - sp: William HICKMAN
    - 4. Melvin WHITT (b.20 Aug 1882)
    - 4. Maudie WHITT (b.1884-Washburn,Mo.)
    - 4. Griffie Chambers WHITT (b.5 Mar 1888-Washburn,Mo.)
      - sp: Opal May SMITH
    - 4. Grover Richard WHITT (b.25 Dec 1890-Washburn,Mo.)
    - 4. Nellie Lavina WHITT (b.20 Jan 1897)
      - sp: John Waterman RUMSEY
- 3. Griffith (Griffy) WHITT Jr. (b.16 Aug 1836-Tazewell County,Va d.5 Aug 1862-Mississippi)
- 2. Richard (Devil Dick) Nelson WHITT (b.1791-ROWC,VCG,(Now Tazewell) d.2 Sep 1855-Carter County,KY.)
  - sp: Rachel (Rebecca) WHITT (b.1803-Tazewell County,Va m.12 Nov 1820 d.25 Mar 1884-Carter Co.,Ky.)
  - 3. Hanna A. WHITT (b.28 Dec 1821-Va. d.25 Dec 1900-Elliott Co.,Ky.)
    - sp: Miles MCFARLAND (m.18 Dec 1841)
  - 3. Sussanah (Susan) WHITT (b.1823-VA. d.18 May 1888)
    - sp: James SPARKS (m.13 Apr 1843)
  - 3. Edmund(Ned) WHITT (b.14 Nov 1825-Lee Co.,Va. d.18 Oct 1900-Elliott Co.,Ky.)
    - sp: Mary Jane PERRY RICE ROSE (b.10 Jun 1834-Morgan Co.,Ky. m.4 Oct 1856 d.13 Sep 1916-EC,Ky.)
    - 4. Sabera WHITT (b.23 Mar 1850-Letcher Co.,Ky.)
      - sp: Silas MAGGARD (m.27 Sep 1868)
        - 5. James MAGGARD
        - 5. David MAGGARD
        - 5. Susan MAGGARD
    - 4. Lavenia WHITT (b.31 Jul 1851-Carter Co.,Ky. d.26 Jan 1915)
      - sp: William CARROLL
      - sp: Elihu Allen TABOR (b.1848-Carter Co.,Ky. m.15 Dec 1869)
        - 5. Lillie Jane TABOR (b.1871-Elliott Co.,Ky.)
        - 5. James E. TABOR (b.7 Mar 1874-Elliott Co.,Ky.)
        - 5. Lula Allen TABOR (b.8 Jan 1877)
      - sp: John P. ROSS (m.15 Mar 1883)
    - 4. John James WHITT (b.23 Dec 1852-Carter Co.,Ky. d.25 Dec 1941)
      - sp: Mary GARRISON
      - sp: Nancy Adeline LEEDY (b.7 Feb 1856-Wyth Co.,Va. m.3 Feb 1876 d.23 Jun 1911)
        - 5. Mary A. WHITT (b.1877-Elliott Co.,Ky. d.24 Jun 1878)
        - 5. Sarah Florence WHITT (b.1878-Elliott Co.,Ky. d.1925-Kentucky)

THE PATRIOT, HEZEKIAH WHITT

Descendants of Justice Hezekiah WHITT

```
        ├ 5. Paulina WHITT (b.1882-Elliott Co.,Ky. d.1975-Boyd Co.,Ky.)
        │     sp: Jesse ROSE
        ├ 5. Erin Jane WHITT (b.1888-Elliott Co.,Ky. d.29 Jan 1965-Boyd Co.,Ky.)
        │     sp: James N. ROSE
        └ 5. Geneva Ray WHITT (b.18 May 1901)
  ─ 4. Travis H. WHITT (b.10 May 1854-Carter Co.,Ky. d.15 Nov 1854-Carter Co.,Ky.)
  ── 4. Richard Nelson WHITT (b.12 Nov 1855-Carter Co.,Ky.)
        sp: Mary A. BOGGS (b.Apr 1861-Ky. m.1 Mar 1877)
        ├ 5. Mary E. WHITT (b.1879-Ky.)
        ├ 5. Edwin C. WHITT (b.Feb 1886)
        ├ 5. Richard N. WHITT (b.Jun 1889-Ky.)
        ├ 5. John M. WHITT (b.Mar 1892-Ky.)
        ├ 5. Wyatt D. WHITT (b.Mar 1899-Ky.)
  ─ 4. Sarah R. WHITT (b.18 Dec 1857-Carter Co.,Ky.)
        sp: John DURM (m.31 Mar 1874)
  ─ 4. William Henry WHITT (b.15 Dec 1859-Carter Co.,Ky. d.2 Jan 1915-Menifee Co.,Ky.)
        sp: Catherine DEBORD (b.19 May 1863-Carter Co.,Ky. d.25 Sep 1909-Menifee Co.,Ky.)
        ├ 5. Alfred E. WHITT (b.28 Sep 1883-Elliott Co.,Ky. d.21 May 1945)
        ├ 5. Robert WHITT (b.7 Apr 1885-Elliott Co.,Ky. d.15 Sep 1886)
        ├ 5. Charles WHITT (b.14 Jan 1887-Elliott Co.,Ky. d.13 Oct 1967)
        ├ 5. Sabra WHITT (b.5 Apr 1889-Elliott Co.,Ky. d.9 Dec 1892)
        │     sp: Silas M. MAGGARD
        ├ 5. Lillian Myrtle WHITT (b.24 Jan 1892-Elliott Co.,Ky. d.14 Jun 1956)
        ├ 5. Evelyn WHITT (b.7 Feb 1893-Elliott Co.,Ky.)
        ├ 5. Walter Dee WHITT (b.14 Feb 1895-Elliott Co.,Ky. d.13 Jan 1954)
        ├ 5. Clifford WHITT (b.18 Dec 1897-Elliott Co.,Ky. d.2 Sep 1977)
        └ 5. Elijah Stewart WHITT (b.27 Sep 1902-Elliott Co.,Ky. d.20 Mar 1979)
  ─ 4. Alfred E. WHITT (b.29 Aug 1861-Carter Co.,Ky. d.29 Sep 1862-Carter Co.,Ky.)
  ── 4. Robert Jonas WHITT (b.18 Mar 1863-Ibex,Elliott Co.,Ky. d.12 Jul 1949-Ironton,Ohio)
        sp: Ellen Rose WHITT (b.18 Jan 1868-Elliott Co.,Ky. d.30 Mar 1946-Ironton,Ohio)
        ├ 5. Mary E. WHITT (b.25 May 1886-Ibex,Elliott Co.,Ky. d.4 Dec 1974-Stark Elliot Co.,KY.)
        │     sp: John French THOMPSON (b.14 Dec 1883-Stark,Elliott Co.,KY. m.14 Jan 1911 d.15 Jul 1963-)
        ├ 5. Julia WHITT (b.Abt 1890)
        │     sp: Gabriel H. GABE PARSONS (b.Abt 1882 m.Abt 1908)
        │         ├ 6. Kenneth PARSONS
        │         ├ 6. Claude PARSONS
        │         ├ 6. Christal PARSONS
        │         ├ 6. Mildred PARSONS
        │         ├ 6. Lake PARSONS
        │         └ 6. Ellen PARSONS
        ├ 5. Mae Mertie WHITT (b.23 May 1891-Ibex,Elliott Co.,Ky. d.20 Sep 1918)
        │     sp: Tom PARSONS
        │         ├ 6. Beral PARSON
        │         ├ 6. Theral PARSON
        │         ├ 6. Jewel PARSON
        └ 5. Charles Edward WHITT (b.18 Aug 1896-Ibex,Elliott Co.,Ky. d.18 Feb 1981-Ironton,Ohio)
              sp: Lucy Esther CARROLL (b.19 Aug 1896-Ibex,Elliott Co.,Ky. m.30 Dec 1916 d.8 Jan 1974-)
                  ├ 6. Maggie May WHITT (b.21 Feb 1919-Elliott Co.,Ky. d.19 Feb 1920-Ibex,Elliott Co.,Ky.)
                  ├ 6. Charles WHITT (b.18 Dec 1920-Ibex,Elliott Co.,Ky. d.18 Dec 1920-Ibex,Elliott Co.,Ky.)
                  ├ 6. Mary WHITT (b.23 Oct 1921-Ibex,Elliott Co.,Ky. d.23 Oct 1921-Ibex,Elliott Co.,Ky.)
                  └ 6. Elizabeth Ellen WHITT (b.29 Nov 1922-Ibex,Elliott Co.,Ky. d.23 Jun 2002-BC,Florida)
                        sp: Raymond Edward GODDU (m.24 Nov 1943)
```

THE PATRIOT, HEZEKIAH WHITT

Descendants of Justice Hezekiah WHITT

```
            └── 7. Michael Edward GODDU (b.5 Mar 1946-Lake Forst,IL. d.14 Sep 1996-Myrtle Beach,SC.)
            ── 7. Ellen Marie GODDU
                sp: Chris John ROBINSON
                └── 8. Kevin Alan ROBINSON
            ── 7. David Anthony GODDU
                sp: Margaret M. HANNA
                ── 8. David James GODDU
                ── 8. Lisa Marie GODDU
                sp: Vicky
                sp: Dawn Kay COX (m.1990)
                ── 8. Brent Anthony GODDU
                └── 8. Bl;ake Andrew GODDU
            ── 7. Richard Alan GODDU
                sp: Sheila MCCASLAND (b.26 Oct 1956-Tupperlake,NY. m.6 Oct 1984)
            └── 7. Elizabeth Ann GODDU
        ── 6. Ruby Evelyn WHITT (b.31 Dec 1924-Ibex,Elliott Co.,Ky. d.22 Oct 1997-Ironton,Ohio)
            sp: C.J. BRANNIGAN (m.26 Jun 1943)
            sp: Claude BROOKS (m.22 Oct 1945)
            ── 7. James BROOKS
            sp: MOBLEY
            ── 7. Jason MOBLEY
            sp: Claude BROOKS (m.Abt 1957)
            ── 7. Clinton Dee BROOKS
            sp: FARR (m.Abt 1980)
            sp: William WAITS (m.Abt 1990)
        ── 6. Claude E. B. WHITT (b.29 Jul 1927-Gimlet,Elliott,Co.,Ky. d.26 Jun 1929-Gimlet,Elliott,Co.,Ky.)
        ── 6. James "Lowell" WHITT (b.14 Aug 1929-Gimlet,Elliott Co.,Ky. d.2 Aug 2000-SC,Ohio)
            sp: Elizabeth Sis PIERCE
            ── 7. Keith WHITT
            └── 7. Connie WHITT
        └── 6. Charles "Clinton" WHITT (b.29 Dec 1935-Ibex,Elliott Co.,Ky.)
            sp: Marlene ROSE (b.16 Nov 1938 m.7 Jul 1957 d.Mar 1995-South Point,Ohio)
            ── 7. Georgian WHITT
            ── 7. Kathy WHITT
            └── 7. Eddie WHITT
    ── 5. Jewell WHITT (b.22 May 1903-Ibex,Elliott Co.,Ky. d.19 Oct 1909-Ibex,Elliott Co.,Ky.)
    ── 5. Opel WHITT
        sp: Russell HOLBROOK Sr.
        ── 6. Russell HOLBROOK Jr.
        ── 6. Carl HOLBROOK
        ── 6. Kenny HOLBROOK
        └── 6. Johnny HOLBROOK
    sp: Della LAWSON
    ── 5. Mary Jane Lawson WHITT (d.12 Sep)
    ── 5. Milford Miff Lawson WHITT
        sp: June MCFARLAND
        └── 6. Jean Lawson WHITT
    ── 5. Glen Lawson WHITT (b.18 May 1915-Ibex,Elliott Co.,Ky. d.25 May 1997-Rowan County,Ky.)
        sp: Mary Glear SCAGGS
        ── 6. John Robert Lawson WHITT
        ── 6. Hazel Lawson WHITT
            sp: KNIPP
```

THE PATRIOT, HEZEKIAH WHITT

Descendants of Justice Hezekiah WHITT

```
          — 6. Linda Lou Lawson WHITT
                sp: Randy Edmon WHITLEY
          — 6. Larry Estill Lawson WHITT
       — 5. Faye Lawson WHITT (b.21 Apr 1912)
             sp: Burl HOLBROOK
    — 4. Hiram C. WHITT (b.22 Aug 1865-Carter Co.,Ky. d.4 Mar 1935-Elliott Co.,Ky.)
    — 4. Mary Mildred WHITT (b.13 Apr 1867-Carter Co.,Ky. d.27 Jul 1950-Ashland,Boyd Co.,Ky.)
          sp: William C. HORTON (b.1844 m.24 Dec 1882)
          sp: Elijah HORTON (b.1854)
    — 4. Clifford Columbus WHITT (b.12 Apr 1869-Elliott Co.,Ky.)
          sp: Alice FLANERY (m.28 Dec 1898)
    — 4. Edgar Milford WHITT (b.22 Dec 1871-Elliott Co.,Ky. d.8 Jul 1923)
    — 4. Charles Walter WHITT (b.8 Dec 1873-Elliott Co.,Ky. d.13 Sep 1927)
    — 4. DeWitt Clinton WHITT (b.21 Aug 1875-Elliott Co.,Ky. d.1955)
 — 3. John Bunyan WHITT (b.28 Dec 1827-Va. d.23 Jun 1909-Elliott Co.,Ky.)
       sp: Susan G. MAGGARD (b.Jan 1845-Ky. m.Abt 1871)
    — 4. Rebecca WHITT (b.1872)
    — 4. Laura WHITT (b.30 Mar 1873-Elliott Co.,Ky. d.25 Aug 1892-Carter Co.,Ky.)
    — 4. Edgar Hansford WHITT (b.1875-Elliott Co.,Ky.)
    — 4. David Oscar WHITT (b.Dec 1876)
          sp: Sarah Jane LEADINGHAM
          — 5. Samaria WHITT (d.Died At Birth)
          — 5. John Melvin WHITT (d.Died At Age 4)
          — 5. Lissa Jane WHITT (b.Abt 1917 d.1 Jan 2005)
                sp: LEWIS
    — 4. Gemillia(Gemela) H. WHITT (b.Mar 1879-Elliott Co.,Ky.)
    — 4. James Eddy WHITT (b.Apr 1881)
          sp: Eliza A.  (b.Abt 1888)
          — 5. Roy WHITT (b.Abt 1907)
                sp: Lela MAGGARD (b.Abt 1912)
             — 6. Kenneth WHITT (b.16 May 1930-Elliott Co.,Ky. d.20 Dec 2007-Elliott Co.,Ky.)
                   sp: Malinda Mayme WADDELL (m.Abt 1951 d.23 Dec 2003)
                   — 7. Roy Franklin WHITT
                         sp: Carolyn
                   — 7. Gary Wendell WHITT
                   — 7. Evelyn WHITT
                         sp: Frank MORGAN
                   — 7. Louwanna WHITT
             — 6. James WHITT
                   sp: Ruby
             — 6. Wayne WHITT
                   sp: Eithel
             — 6. Ronnie WHITT
                   sp: Linda
             — 6. Lonnie WHITT
                   sp: Johnda
             — 6. Mary WHITT
                   sp: SKAGGS
             — 6. Rose Mae WHITT
                   sp: Jim ROWE
             — 6. Geneva WHITT
                   sp: Arville DUNCAN
```

THE PATRIOT, HEZEKIAH WHITT

Descendants of Justice Hezekiah WHITT

```
│  │     │        ├─ 6. Betty WHITT
│  │     │        │      sp: Gary DUNCAN
│  │     │        ─ 6. Shirley WHITT
│  │     │               sp: Paul SETTERS
│  │     ─ 5. Myrtle WHITT (b.Abt 1917)
│  │     ─ 5. Mae WHITT (b.Abt 1920)
│  │     ─ 5. Ethel WHITT (b.Abt 1924)
│  │     ├─ 5. Ray WHITT (b.Abt 1928)
│  │     ├┤ 5. Jewel WHITT (b.Abt 1912)
│  │     ├─ 5. Eva WHITT (b.Abt 1916)
│  │     ─ 5. Maisie WHITT (b.Abt 1919)
│  └─ 4. Richie P. WHITT (b.Mar 1883)
├─ 3. Nancy Belle WHITT (b.18 May 1832)
│     sp: John "Jack" KELLY (m.14 Sep 1849)
│     ├─ 4. Hezekiah KELLY (b.Abt 1851-Ky.)
│     ─ 4. James E. KELLY (b.Abt 1853-Ky.)
│     ─ 4. Richard KELLY (b.Abt 1854-Ky.)
│     ┌─ 4. Rebecca KELLY (b.Abt 1857-Ky.)
│     └─ 4. Thomas L. KELLY (b.1860)
│          sp: Louisa SPARKS
├─ 3. Lavisa Lee WHITT (b.28 May 1834-Lee Co.,Va. d.2 Jun 1891-Elliott Co.,Ky.)
│     sp: Henderson ROSEYGRANTS (ROSE) (b.29 Feb 1832-Lawrence County,Ky. m.31 Aug 1852)
│     ─ 4. Fernando Cortez ROSEYGRANTS (ROSE) (b.1852-Carter Co.,Ky.)
│     ─ 4. Perry Belle ROSEYGRANTS (ROSE) (b.17 Apr 1858-Carter Co.,Ky.)
│     ─ 4. Mary Virginia ROSEYGRANTS (ROSE) (b.12 Aug 1860-Carter Co.,Ky.)
│     ┌─ 4. Hannah S. ROSEYGRANTS (ROSE) (b.13 Feb 1863-Carter Co.,Ky.)
│     ├─ 4. Richard W. ROSEYGRANTS (ROSE) (b.1868)
│     ├─ 4. James Henderson ROSEYGRANTS (ROSE) (b.1871-Elliott Co.,Ky.)
│     └─ 4. John J. ROSEYGRANTS (ROSE) (b.28 Apr 1872-Elliott Co.,Ky.)
└─ 3. James G. WHITT (b.11 Nov 1836-Va. d.1 Nov 1906-Elliott Co.,Ky.)
      sp: Rebecca NETHERCUTT (b.Abt 1839-Va. m.?)
      ─ 4. Alice WHITT (b.1862)
           sp: Adie S. SHELTON
      ├─ 4. George E. WHITT (b.1863-Ky.)
      └─ 4. Edgar M. WHITT (b.1865-Elliott Co.,Ky.)
2. John Bunyan WHITT (b.1794-Cedar Grove,Russell County,Va. (Now Tazewell) d.Aug 1867-Floyd Co.,Ky.)
   sp: Ana SHACKELFORD (b.Bf m.Abt 1813)
   ─ 3. John Bunyan WHITT Jr. (b.1819-Floyd Co.,Ky. d.1890-Lawrence Co.,Ky.)
      sp: Louisa Jane ALLEN (m.1840)
      ─ 4. Burgess WHITT
      ─ 4. John Bunyan WHITT III (b.15 Jan 1841-Greenup County,Kentucky d.1 Jul 1912-Boyd Co.,Ky.)
         sp: Surrilda Frances BALL (m.19 Jul 1867 d.15 Jan 1870)
         ─ 5. William Thomas WHITT (b.6 Feb 1869-Keelville,Cherokee,Co. Kansas)
         ─ 5. Samuel V. WHITT (b.1878)
              sp: UNKNOWN
              └─ 6. Samuel S. WHITT (b.18 Jul 1911-Columbus,Franklin Co.,Ohio)
                     sp: Janie E. CHAPMAN (m.6 Feb 1942)
         sp: Julia Ann BALL (m.11 Sep 1873 d.28 Feb 1998)
         ├─ 5. Cynthia Quin WHITT (b.12 Sep 1876 d.1956)
         ├─ 5. Samuel Vanatta WHITT (b.8 Apr 1878 d.25 Jan 1956-Columbus,Franklin Co.,Ohio)
              sp: Sadie Jane MARION (b.9 Sep 1879-Fort Gay,WV (Wayne Co.) m.15 Aug 1901 d.25 Jun 1954-)
              ─ 6. Julia Mildred WHITT (b.17 Feb 1908-Columbus,Franklin Co.,Ohio)
```

THE PATRIOT, HEZEKIAH WHITT

Descendants of Justice Hezekiah WHITT

```
                    sp: Arthur COFFEE
                  ┌─ 6. Samuel S. WHITT (b.18 Jul 1911-Columbus,Franklin Co.,Ohio) ** Printed on Page 7 **
                  └─ 6. Marion Woodson WHITT (b.11 Oct 1913-Columbus,Franklin Co.,Ohio)
                       sp: Vera WOOD (m.1945)
                ┌─ 5. John Rockwell WHITT (b.20 Aug 1881 d.1955-CA.)
                ├─ 5. James Sandy WHITT (b.8 Apr 1884-On A Raft In Big Sandy Flood d.1956-AR)
                ├─ 5. Grover Cleveland WHITT (b.17 Apr 1886)
                ├─ 5. Girl Baby WHITT (b.17 Apr 1886 d.Died At Birth)
                ├─ 5. Elihu (Hugh) WHITT (b.3 Aug 1888 d.1 Feb 1955-Atlanta,Ga.)
                ├─ 5. Stonewall Jackson WHITT (b.12 Feb 1891 d.1957-Cuyahoga Falls,Ohio)
                   sp: Mary Elizabeth "Maggie" DANIEL (m.27 Dec 1899)
             ┌─ 4. James P. WHITT (b.Abt 1844-KY.)
             ├─ 4. Sarah Jane WHITT
                sp: Dr, Lee MARION
                 ┌─ 5. Sadie Jane MARION (b.9 Sep 1879-Fort Gay,WV (Wayne Co.) d.25 Jun 1954-Columbus,FC,Ohio)
                      sp: Samuel Vanatta WHITT (b.8 Apr 1878 m.15 Aug 1901 d.25 Jan 1956-Columbus,FC,Ohio)
                       ┌─ 6. Julia Mildred WHITT (b.17 Feb 1908-Columbus,Franklin Co.,Ohio) ** Printed on Page 7 **
                       ├─ 6. Samuel S. WHITT (b.18 Jul 1911-Columbus,Franklin Co.,Ohio) ** Printed on Page 7 **
                       └─ 6. Marion Woodson WHITT (b.11 Oct 1913-Columbus,Franklin Co.,Ohio) ** Printed on Page 8 **
             ┌─ 4. George W. WHITT
             └─ 4. Hezekiah WHITT
                sp: Mary Jane ALLEN (m.27 Aug 1846)
             ┌─ 4. William WHITT
             ├─ 4. Jack WHITT
             ├─ 4. Jonas WHITT
             ├─ 4. Richard WHITT
             ├─ 4. Perry D. WHITT
             └─ 4. Woodson WHITT
          sp: Hannah SARLES (m.11 Feb 1815)
        ┌─ 3. John Bunyan WHITT Jr. (b.1819-Floyd Co.,Ky. d.1890-Lawrence Co.,Ky.) ** Printed on Page 7 **
        ├─ 3. Hezekiah WHITT (b.1825-Floy Co. Ky.)
           sp: Mary Jane ALLEN
           sp: Sally ONEY
        sp: Sarah ONEY (b.Abt 1790 m.2 Oct 1833)
        ┌─ 3. Elizabeth WHITT (b.1836-Floyd Co.,Ky.)
        ├─ 3. Douglas WHITT (b.1836-Floyd Co.,Ky.)
        └─ 3. Sydney B. WHITT (b.1840-Floyd Co.,Ky.)
     ┌─ 2. Rebecca WHITT (b.1795-Cedar Grove,Russell County,Va.(Now Tazewell))
        sp: James Husk LOWE (m.31 Dec 1807)
        ┌─ 3. Calvin LOWE (b.1812-Va.)
           sp: Lettitia PRUETT (m 7 Oct 1883)
        ├─ 3. William D. LOWE (b.1815)
        ├─ 3. J. "Bunyan" LOWE (b.Abt 1821-Tazewell Co.,Va.)
           sp: Rhoda WHITT (b.Abt 1820-Montgomery Co.,Va. m.2 Jul 1844)
           ┌─ 4. Amos LOWE (b.1844)
           ├─ 4. Anna LOWE (b.1845-Tazewell Co.,Va.)
           ├─ 4. Jonas LOWE (b.1846)
           ├─ 4. James LOWE (b.1847)
           ├─ 4. Rachel LOWE (b.1849-Tazewell Co.,Va.)
           ├─ 4. Martha LOWE (b.1851-Tazewell Co.,Va.)
           └─ 4. John Luther LOWE (b.May 1852-Tazewell Co.,Va. d.Tazewell Co.,Va.)
              sp: Margaret DAY (m.2 Aug 1876)
```

```
├ 5. Isaac Noah LOWE (b.17 May 1876-Buchanan Co.,Va. d May 1953)
│   sp: Samantha Victoria COLE (m.1 Jan 1901 d.Aug 1935)
│   ··· 6. Lovisa Jane LOWE (b.Died As Infant)
│   ─ 6. Moses LOWE
│   ─ 6. Nick LOWE
│   ─ 6. Sylvia Margaret LOWE (b.Died As Infant)
│   ├ 6. John Franklin LOWE (b.3 Sep 1903 d.9 Jun 1974)
│   ├ 6. Jesse LeeRoy LOWE (b.31 Mar 1907 d.18 Aug 1973)
│   ├ 6. Glennah LOWE (b.2 Apr 1906 d.1924)
│   ├ 6. James Blain LOWE (b.31 Oct 1908 d.25 May 1969)
│   ├ 6. Edward Theodore LOWE (b.2 Oct 1912)
│   ├ 6. Cleo Midas LOWE (b.19 Jun 1916)
│   ─ 6. Isaac Daley LOWE (b 17 Mar 1920 d.3 May 1944)
│   ─ 6. Georgie Melissa LOWE (b.15 Jan 1922)
│   ─ 6. Zelda Mae LOWE (b.8 Jul 1925 d.1983)
│       sp: Edward SCHILLING 1st
│       └ 7. Edward SCHILLING 2nd
│           sp: Melanie
│           sp: Crystal CLATTERBUCK
│           ├ 8. Edward SCHILLING 3rd
│           └ 8. Jennifer SCHILLING
│   ├ 6. Eldridge Eugene LOWE (b.7 Nov 1927 d.Mar 1981)
│   sp: Audrey Arminda BOOTH
│   ─ 6. Robert "Rob" Noah LOWE (b 6 Nov 1939 d.2008?)
│   sp: Maria Angela DAVIS (b.1867-Russell Co.,Va. m.Apr 1886 d.10 Feb 1946-Greenbrier WV)
├ 5. Zenia LOWE
├ 5. John LOWE
└ 5. Louemma( Emma) Victoria LOWE (b.Nov 1886 d.10 Jan 1961-Buchanan Co.,Va.)
    sp: Peter Cleveland KEEN (b.Oct 1884 m.6 Feb 1902 d.27 Sep 1935-Buchanan Co.,Va.)
    ─ 6. Lucy Jane KEEN (b.24 Apr 1906-Greenbrier Co.,W V. d.20 Apr 1990-Okeechobee,Fl.)
        sp: Joseph McKinley STREET (b.27 Jan 1908-BC,Va. m.16 Dec 1925 d.18 Oct 1993-)
        ─ 7. Jean Rader STREET (b.14 Nov 1938-Tazewell Co.,Va.)
            sp: Sidney ABSHER (b.Nov 1936 m.Jul 1954 d.Feb 1955)
            sp: Carl Greever Jr. DESKINS (b.Dec 1931 m.18 Apr 1957)
            ─ 8. Celesta Lynn DESKINS (b.28 Jan 1958-Bluefield WVA.)
                sp: Mark SARGENT (b.4 Oct 1955 m.24 Nov 1976)
                ├ 9. Joshua Ben Mark SARGENT (b.21 Sep 1980-Montgomery Co.,Va.)
                ├ 9. Thomas Andrew SARGENT (b.29 Aug 1985-Montgomery Co.,Va.)
                └ 9. Jeanna Lucia Viola SARGENT (b.28 May 1987-Montgomery Co.,Va.)
            ├ 8. Carl Greever III DESKINS (b.25 Mar 1959-Roanoke,Va.)
                sp: Un Suk KIM (b.27 Jun 1955-Korea m Nov 1985)
                ├ 9. Alexander DESKINS ADOPTED (b.16 Jul 1979-Korea)
                └ 9. Jennifer Kim DESKINS (b.24 Mar 1988-Newport News,Va.)
            ├ 8. Elizabeth Jane DESKINS (b.14 Feb 1963-Richmond,Va.)
            sp: Roland HANKINS (b.25 May 1930-Tazewell Co.,Va. m.27 Nov 1992)
        ··· 7. Eula Viola STREET (b.4 Sep 1926-Tazewell Co.,Va.)
            sp: Troy Robert GOLDSMITH (b.Sep 1920-NC m.11 Feb 1950 d.Mar 1972)
        ─ 7. Curtis Carnval STREET (b.16 Jan 1930-Tazewell Co.,Va. d.16 Jul 1957-Tazewell Co.,Va.)
            sp: Mary Annajean HAY (b.12 Feb 1936-Dickenson Co.,Va.)
            └ 8. Rita Jo STREET (b.9 Mar 1953-Tazewell Co.,Va.)
                sp: Ronald Kyle SAGE (b.13 Dec 1948-Smyth Co.,Va.)
                ├ 9. Christina Dawn SAGE (b.15 Feb 1974-Washington Co.,Va.)
```

THE PATRIOT, HEZEKIAH WHITT

Descendants of Justice Hezekiah WHITT

```
                              sp: John Allen POURROY (b.18 Aug 1973-Sagamon Co.,Ill.)
                               —  10. Jacob Allen McKinley POURROY (b.9 Jun 1998-Polk Co.,Fl.)
                          —  9. Joseph Klyle SAGE (b.14 Mar 1985-Polk Co.,Fl.)
                    —  7. Thurman Cleveland (Pete) STREET (b.2 Jun 1933-Buchanan Co.,Va. d.23 Jun 1956-)
                       sp: Joan WHITED (b.31 Dec 1934-Russell Co.,Va. m.2 Jun 1952)
                        └ 8. Joseph Chester STREET (b.17 Mar 1953-Russell Co.,Va.)
                              sp: Fannie Jane COMPTON (b.16 Sep 1954)
                             ├— 9. Joseph Chester Jr. STREET (b.11 Jun 1980-Newport News,Va.)
                             —  9. Cora Jane STREET (b.18 Oct 1883-Newport News,Va.)
           —  4. Susan LOWE (b.1853-Tazewell Co.,Va.)
           —  4. Mary LOWE (b.1853-Tazewell Co.,Va.)
           —  4. Rebecca LOWE (b.1855-Tazewell Co.,Va.)
      —  3. John LOWE (b.1828)
      —  3. Assena LOWE (b.1795)
      —  3. Luther LOWE (b.1810)
      —  3. Susannah LOWE (b.Abt 1813-Va.)
      —  3. James W. LOWE (b.1828-VA d.1897-VA)
           sp: Ruth CHRISTIAN (b.1828)
           ├— 4. Luther LOWE (b.Abt 1855)
           —  4. Franandus LOWE (b.8 Mar 1856)
           —  4. James M. LOWE (b.1861)
           —  4. David Crockett LOWE (b.Sep 1865)
      —  3. Rachel LOWE (b.1827)
      └  3. George Washington LOWE (b.1818)
—  2. Susannah WHITT (b.1796-Cedar Grove,Russell Co.,VA.,( Now Tazewell) d.1865)
     sp: Joseph WEBB (b.Abt 1783-Russell County,VA. m.Abt 1814 d.1841-Tazewell Co.,Va.)
     —  3. William WEBB
     —  3. Rachel WEBB (b.17 May 1817-Russell Co,Va. d.28 Nov 1887-Roane Co.,WV)
          sp: Charles Mathias BOOTHE Sr. (b.24 Feb 1814-Russell Co,Va. m.2 May 1843 d.11 Feb 1874-RC,WV)
          ├— 4. Julian Flavius BOOTHE (b.27 Feb 1844-Russell Co,Va. d.Abt 1925-Roane Co.,WV)
               sp: Mary HIVELY (b.25 Jan 1840-Botetourt Co.,Va. m.13 Nov 1872 d.21 Aug 1914-Roane Co.,WV)
          —  4. Melissa Jane BOOTHE (b.23 Oct 1846-Russell Co,Va. d.22 Jan 1937-Roane Co.,WV)
               sp: David L. CASTO (b.22 Apr 1820-Jackson Co.,WV m.22 Apr 1820 d.15 Jul 1909-Jackson Co.,WV)
               —  5. Laura CASTO (b.25 Sep 1885)
               └  5. Clora CASTO (b.15 Oct 1888)
               —  5. Eva CASTO (b.25 Jul 1895)
          —  4. Joseph Nelson BOOTHE (b.6 Sep 1849-Russell Co,Va. d.1919-Spencer,Roane Co.,WV)
               sp: Rachel CASTO (b.31 Aug 1851-Jackson Co.,WV m.27 Sep 1869 d.10 Oct 1885-Jackson Co.,WV)
               —  5. Nancy BOOTHE (b.15 Jul 1870-Roane Co.,WV d.9 Jan 1917-Roane Co.,WV)
               —  5. Edward BOOTHE (b.25 Sep 1872-Roane Co.,WV d.21 Dec 1920-Charleston,West Virginia)
               —  5. Louisa BOOTHE (b.21 Mar 1874-Jackson Co.,WV d.28 Jun 1957-Roane Co.,WV)
               —  5. Melissa BOOTHE (b.May 1878-Roane Co.,WV d.Aft 1930)
               —  5. Mary Bertha BOOTHE (b.9 Nov 1880-Roane Co.,WV d.1958-Roane Co.,WV)
               —  5. Margaret BOOTHE (b.9 Nov 1880-Roane Co.,WV)
               —  5. Cora B. BOOTHE (b.Jul 1884-Roane Co.,WV d.Aft 1930)
               sp: Mary Lee CURRY (b.1876 d.1920)
          —  4. Susannah BOOTHE (b.16 Jun 1852-Russell Co,Va. d.19 Sep 1919-Roane Co.,WV)
               sp: Zachariah Taylor COBB (b.15 Apr 1850-Roane Co.,WV m.10 Jun 1879 d.4 Jan 1928-Roane Co.,WV)
               —  5. Julian Franklin COBB (b.7 May 1870-Higby,Roane Co.,WV d.24 Apr 1915-Roane County,WV)
               —  5. Melissa Jane COBB (b.15 Oct 1872-Higby,Roane Co.,WV d.29 May 1956-Charleston,West Virginia)
                    sp: Miles Herbert RHODES (b.10 Oct 1855-Jackson County,WV m.2 Oct 1892 d.2 Apr 1950-)
                    —  6. Arlie RHODES (b.16 Jun 1908-Higby,Roane Co.,WV d.15 Jul 2004-Cedar Rapida,Iowa)
```

THE PATRIOT, HEZEKIAH WHITT

Descendants of Justice Hezekiah WHITT

```
                    sp: Helen ANDREWS (b.11 Feb 1906-Kenasha,WI. m.2 Mar 1946 d.14 Aug 1996-B,FL.)
                    — 7. Joyce RHODES (b.19 May 1947)
                       sp: MERTENS
            — 5. Charles Hughett COBB (b.17 Aug 1876-Roane County,WV d.12 Jun 1956-Kanawha Co.,WV)
            — 5. Rachel Minerva COBB (b.2 Feb 1880-Roane County,WV d.2 Aug 1954-Roane County,WV)
            — 5. Susannah Colona COBB (b.17 Oct 1882-Roane County,WV d.Feb 1985)
            — 5. Nelson B. COBB (b.13 Feb 1889-Roane County,WV d.30 Jun 1974-Hurricane,West Va.)
            — 5. William Edward COBB (b.27 Oct 1893-Roane County,WV d.22 Mar 1972)
            — 5. Rosetta COBB (b.24 Jul 1886-Roane County,WV d.12 Oct 1961-Roane County,WV)
      — 4. Charles Mathias BOOTHE Jr. (b.19 Apr 1855-Higby,Roane Co.,WV d.31 Mar 1930-Flat Fork,RC,WV)
          sp: Samantha Estelline CASTO (b.11 Aug 1858-Jackson Co.,WV m.16 Oct 1879 d.24 Feb 1934-)
          — 5. Nettie Lee BOOTH (b.1881-Roane County,WV d.1965-Charleston,WV)
          — 5. Hattie May BOOTH (b.11 Mar 1883-Roane County,WV d.12 May 1958-Clendennon,WV)
          — 5. Walter BOOTH (b.11 Mar 1883-Roane County,WV d.11 Mar 1883-Roane County,WV)
          — 5. Roy Earnest BOOTH (b.6 Jun 1894-Higby,Roane Co.,WV d.27 Jul 1976-Ripley,Jackson Co.,WV)
              sp: Ella Mae ROMINE (b.17 Apr 1898-Roane Co.,WV d.5 Oct 1994-Ripley,Jackson Co.,WV)
              — 6. Mildred Meryle (Merle) BOOTHE (b.1 Nov 1917-Red Nob,Roane Co.,WV)
                  sp: Wilbert "Ty" TOLLEY (b.30 Nov 1916 m.15 Nov 1936 d.10 Feb 1983-Hanoverton,Ohio)
                  — 7. Anna M. TOLLEY (b.8 Feb 1938-Zona,Roane Co.,WV)
                      sp: John E. ROSEBURG (b.Lisbon,Columbiana County,Ohio)
                  — 7. Roy Wilbert TOLLEY (b.11 Dec 1939-Zona,Roane Co.,WV d.18 Feb 2006-H,CC,Ohio)
                  — 7. James (Jim) TOLLEY
                  — 7. Lois Jean TOLLEY
                  — 7. Merle Elizabeth TOLLEY (b.11 Jan 1942-Mecca,Trumbell County,Ohio d.17 Jul 1942-)
              — 6. Vivian Berdiehl BOOTH (b.8 Jul 1919-Higby,Roane Co.,WV)
              — 6. Hobert Edwin BOOTH (b.18 Aug 1921-Roane County,WV d.1 Jun 1998-C,West Virginia)
              — 6. Evangeline BOOTH (b.28 May 1929-Roane County,WV)
              — 6. Jesse Howard BOOTH (b.12 Nov 1940-Roane County,WV d.11 Dec 1940-Roane County,WV)
          — 5. Doctor Howard Dewey BOOTH (b.16 Nov 1899-Roane County,WV d.10 Feb 1939-C,West Virginia)
  — 3. Mary WEBB (b.2 Aug 1819 d.18 Mar 1859-Russell Co,Va.)
      sp: James Jasper BAYS
      — 4. William Webb BAYS (b.1839 d.1916)
          sp: Harriet HEURETZO (b.1845)
      — 4. Rachel BAYS (b.1841 d.1908)
          sp: William Harvey REMINE (b.1820 d.1874)
          sp: George CANADAY
      — 4. Hezekiah Webb BAYS (b.1843 d.1921)
          sp: Frances "Fannie" Virginia HERBERT (b.1850 d.1919)
          — 5. Margret Astore BAYS
          — 5. Mary Herbert BAYS
              sp: BLACKMAN
              — 6. Webb Bays BLACKMAN Sr.
                  sp: UNKNOWN
                  — 7. Webb Bays BLACKMAN Jr.
      — 4. James Harvey BAYS (b.1846 d.1917)
          sp: Mary DYE (b.1853 d.1892)
          — 5. Nancy Virginia BAYS
          sp: Ann GREGORY (b.1856)
      — 4. Mary James "Witty" BAYS (b.1846 d.1861)
      — 4. Silas Jasper BAYS (b.1849 d.1932)
          sp: Armelda FULLEN (b.1854 d.1943)
      — 4. John Casius BAYS (b.1852 d.1923)
```

THE PATRIOT, HEZEKIAH WHITT

Descendants of Justice Hezekiah WHITT

```
              sp: Sarah Gage FINDLEY (b.1862 d.1908)
          — 4. Nancy Virginia "Nannie" BAYS (b.1856 d.1933)
              sp: James Granderson GRACE (b.1851 d.1880)
              sp: Thomas King DYE (b.1856 d.1932)
          └─ 4. Lorenzo Lafayette BAYS (b.1858 d.1916)
              sp: Josephine BAYS (b.1858 d.1945)
      — 3. James Harvey WEBB (b.1822 d.1851)
      — 3. Henry WEBB (b.1829)
          sp: Rebecca KEEN (m.4 Sep 1854)
      — 3. Nancy WEBB (b.Abt 1832-Tazewell Co. Va. d.Bef 1878-Fannin Co. Tx.)
          sp: James Griffith WHITT (b.10 Jul 1825-Montgomery Co. Virginia m.4 Sep 1850 d.8 Jun 1899-,San Patricio)
          — 4. Jonas Griffith WHITT (b.19 Oct 1851-Tazewell,County,VA. d.1935-Fannin Co.,Tx.)
              sp: Phoebe FIELDS (b.1857-Mo. d.1933)
          — 4. David Crockett WHITT (b.18 Mar 1855-Tazewell,County,VA. d.4 Jun 1939-Fannin Co. Tx.)
              sp: Lou Ella MULLINS (m.1883)
          └─ 4. Joseph Wilshire WHITT (b 20 Feb 1857-Tazewell,County,VA. d.21 Mar 1923-Garvin Co.,Ok.)
              sp: Erie Alaska PARKER (b.18 Aug 1868 m.1885 d.8 Aug 1951-Purdy,Garvin Co.,Ok.)
              — 5. Oscar WHITT (b.Died Young-Fannin Co.,Tx.)
              — 5. David Crockett WHITT (b.3 Jan 1886-Savoy,Fannin Co. Tx. d.25 Nov 1963-Duncan,Stephens,Co.,Ok.)
                  sp: Nora May MASONER
                  ├─ 6. Mary WHITT
                  sp: Nora May PRIBBLE
              — 5. Margaret WHITT (b.3 Nov 1888-Savor,Fannin Co.,Tx. d.7 Dec 1940)
              — 5. Reynolds Griffin WHITT (b.18 Sep 1890-Savor,Fannin Co.,Tx. d.5 Mar 1964-Lindsey Garvin Co.,Ok.)
                  sp: Nettie SNIDER (m.13 Jun 1915)
              └─ 5. Grover Cleveland WHITT (b.6 Sep 1892-Savor,Fannin Co.,Tx. d.17 Apr 1964-Marlo Stephens Co. Ok)
                  sp: Maude STATERS (m.22 Aug 1915)
              — 5. William Lee WHITT (b.22 Sep 1894-Savor,Fannin Co.,Tx. d.10 Feb 1988-Maysville,Garvin Co.,Ok.)
                  sp: Sylvia Mazie DENSON (m.26 Oct 1928)
              — 5. Oran Collins WHITT (b.17 Aug 1896-Savor,Fannin Co.,Tx. d.27 Nov 1952)
                  sp: Opal DENSON (m.13 Oct 1927)
              — 5. Jonas Austin (Pete) WHITT (b.2 Nov 1898-Savoy,Fannin Co. Tx. d.21 Aug 1974-DE Queen,SC,Ar.)
                  sp: Hennie May SKAGGS (b.9 Feb 1903-Big Clifty,Grayson Co.,Ky. m.21 Jan 1922 d.1 Jun 1972-)
                  ├─ 6. Healen Ophelia WHITT (b.20 Jan 1923-Foster,Garvin Co.,Ok.)
                      sp: Hebert Royce MELOTT (m.26 May 1951)
                  — 6. Robert Austin (Bob) WHITT (b.1 Nov 1925-Purdy,Garvin Co.,Ok.)
                      sp: Virginia Lee COOK (m.19 Sep 1947)
                  — 6. Edith May WHITT (b.16 Mar 1930-McFarland,Kern Co.,Ca. d.Apr 2005-Texas)
                      sp: Virgil Junior "Nig" TANNEHILL (m.3 Jan 1949)
                  — 6. Eugene WHITT (b.6 Jul 1933-Delano,Kern Co.,Ca. d.20 Apr 1935-Oakland,Alameda Co. Ca.)
                  — 6. Thomas Paul WHITT (b.16 Jul 1936-Earlimart,Kern Co.,Ca.)
                      sp: Lucy Fay LONE (m.8 Nov 1957)
                      sp: Linda Kathryn RHODES (m.29 Apr 1970)
              — 5. Clint Pat WHITT (b.1 Feb 1907-Savor,Fannin Co.,Tx. d.30 Aug 1926)
          — 4. Mildred Susannah WHITT (b.May 1859-Tazewell,County,VA.)
              sp: Dan MELUGIN
              sp: Robert (Bob) HANDCOCK (m.1881)
          — 4. Laura R. WHITT (b.1864 Or 1856-Tenn. Or VA.)
              sp: Jessie HUMAN
          — 4. May C. WHITT (b.1867-Tazewell,County,VA.)
              sp: Christopher Columbus (Lum) WALDRUM
          — 4. Milburn WHITT (b.Abt 1870 d.Bf 1880)
```

THE PATRIOT, HEZEKIAH WHITT

Descendants of Justice Hezekiah WHITT

```
        └─ 4. Louisa WHITT (b.1864)
   ─── 3. Elijah WEBB (b.1835)
        sp: Julia Ann BAYS (b.1823)
        ┌─ 4. Susan WEBB (b.1855)
        ├─ 4. Levisa WEBB (b.1856)
        ─ 4. Luammia WEBB (b.1859)
        ─ 4. Nancy WEBB (b.1862)
        ─ 4. Howard WEBB (b.1864)
        └─ 4. Louisa WEBB (b.1858)
   ┌─ 3. Rebecca WEBB (b.1838-Russell Co.Va.)
        sp: Dr. Alexander BEAVERS (b.25 Mar 1842 m.27 Dec 1865)
        ├─ 4. Joseph William Columbus BEAVERS (b.1867 d.1920)
        ├─ 4. Mollie Rachel BEAVERS (b.1868)
           sp: Joseph KINDRICK (b.1867)
        ─ 4. Cosby S. BEAVERS (b.1872 d.1930)
           sp: Doctor John L. MILLER
        ─ 4. Thomas Jefferson BEAVERS (b.1875 d.1930)
           sp: Minnie  (b.1895 d.1930)
   ─── 3. Doctor Hezekiah Jackson WEBB (b.1825 d.1901)
        sp: Martha KENDRICK (b.1829 d.1890)
        ─ 4. Joseph WEBB (b.1845)
           sp: Mary  (b.1845)
        ─ 4. Mary WEBB (b.1847)
        ─ 4. Margaretta WEBB (b.1850)
        ─ 4. Susan WEBB (b.1853 d.1906)
        ─ 4. Richard WEBB (b.1863)
        sp: Laura A. ROBERTS
   ─── 3. Richard WEBB (b.1826 d.1917)
        sp: Elizabeth "Betsy" DAVIS  (b.1832 m.11 Nov 1850)
        ─ 4. Mary Mollie WEBB (b.1866 d.1950)
           sp: James Buchanan BERRY (b.1857 d.1910)
        ─ 4. Susan WEBB (b.1852 d.1928)
           sp: George MOORE (b.1854)
        ─ 4. Joseph Harry WEBB (b.1856)
           sp: Emily Emma WHITT (b.1857)
        ─ 4. Martha Jane WEBB (b.1859 d.1944)
           sp: William Dickie ADKINS (b.1862)
        ─ 4. Hezekiah Jackson WEBB (b.1861 d.1929)
           sp: Elizabeth BROUGHTON
           sp: Mary Jane THOMPSON
        ─ 4. James Elijah WEBB (b.1868 d.1959)
           sp: Isabelle JORDAN (b.1882 d.1941)
        ─ 4. William H. WEBB (b.1872)
           sp: Martha  (b.1876)
        ─ 4. Adelaide M. Addie WEBB (b.1875)
           sp: William A. AKERS (b.1864 d.1897)
           sp: William H. DAVENPORT
        sp: UNKNOWN
   └─ 3. Harry Harvey WEBB (b.1829 d.1902)
        sp: Rosina KEENE (b.1837 d.1900)
        ─ 4. James Harvey WEBB (b.1860 d.1948)
           sp: Sarah Tinsley SMILEY (b.1865 d.1935)
```

THE PATRIOT, HEZEKIAH WHITT

Descendants of Justice Hezekiah WHITT

```
    ├─ 4. Nancy WEBB (b.1863)
    │      sp: Andrew Jackson ADKINS
    ─  4. William Joseph WEBB (b.1864)
    │      sp: Amy ADKINS
    ├─ 4. Susannah WEBB (b.1867)
    │      sp: Franklin KEENE
    ├─ 4. Richard WEBB (b.1868)
    ├─ 4. Charles W. WEBB (b.1869)
    ─  4. Edward WEBB (b.1875)
└─ 2. Jonas WHITT (b.1 Jan 1797-Cedar Grove,Russell Co.,VA.,( Now Tazewell ) d.2 Jul 1865-T,B,Greenup Co. KY.)
       sp: Susannah WHITT (b.Abt 1794-MC,Virginia m.10 Oct 1816 d.Abt 1839-Tazewell County,VA.)
    ├─ 3. John Bunyan WHITT (b.Abt 1818-Montgomery Co.,Va. d.Aug 1860)
    │      sp: Catherine BEAVERS (b.1819 m.14 Apr 1842)
    │   ├─ 4. Reverent Lucien Jonas (Little Jonas) WHITT (b.Abt 1842-Tazewell County,Va)
    │   ├─ 4. Susan WHITT (b.Abt 1843-Tazewell County,Va)
    │   ├─ 4. Robbin WHITT (b.Abt 1846-Tazewell County,Va)
    │   ─  4. Polly WHITT (b.1850-Tazewell County,Va)
    ─  3. Rachel WHITT (b.Abt 1820-Montgomery Co.,Va.)
    │      sp: Adam BEAVERS (b.1817 m.6 Jan 1841)
    │   ├─ 4. Harriet BEAVERS (b.Abt 1845-Tazewell County,Va)
    │   ├─ 4. Hamiliton Wade BEAVERS (b.Abt 1847-Tazewell County,Va)
    │   │      sp: Nancy C. CROCKETT (m.8 Feb 1882)
    │   │   ├─ 5. Robert C. BEAVERS (b.Dec 1882-Tazewell County,Va)
    │   │   ├─ 5. Elmer L. BEAVERS (b.Aug 1896-Tazewell County,Va)
    │   │   └─ 5. Hamiliton Wade BEAVERS Jr. (b.1909-Tazewell County,Va)
    │   ─  4. David BEAVERS (b.Abt 1849-Tazewell County,Va)
    ─  3. Rhoda WHITT (b.Abt 1820-Montgomery Co.,Va.)
    │      sp: J. "Bunyan" LOWE (b.Abt 1821-Tazewell Co.,Va. m.2 Jul 1844)
    │   ├─ 4. Amos LOWE (b.1844) ** Printed on Page 8 **
    │   ├─ 4. Anna LOWE (b.1845-Tazewell Co.,Va.) ** Printed on Page 8 **
    │   ├─ 4. Jonas LOWE (b.1846) ** Printed on Page 8 **
    │   ├─ 4. James LOWE (b.1847) ** Printed on Page 8 **
    │   ├─ 4. Rachel LOWE (b.1849-Tazewell Co.,Va.) ** Printed on Page 8 **
    │   ─  4. Martha LOWE (b.1851-Tazewell Co.,Va.) ** Printed on Page 8 **
    │   ─  4. John Luther LOWE (b.May 1852-Tazewell Co.,Va. d.Tazewell Co.,Va.) ** Printed on Page 8 **
    │   ─  4. Susan LOWE (b.1853-Tazewell Co.,Va.) ** Printed on Page 10 **
    │   ├─ 4. Mary LOWE (b.1853-Tazewell Co.,Va.) ** Printed on Page 10 **
    │   └─ 4. Rebecca LOWE (b.1855-Tazewell Co.,Va.) ** Printed on Page 10 **
    ─  3. Emily L. (Emma) WHITT (b.13 Jul 1822-Montgomery Co.,Va. d.15 Jun 1895-Greenup Co.,Ky.)
           sp: John Madden STEPHENSON (b.27 May 1820-Tazewell Co.,Va. m.15 Apr 1845 d.29 Dec 1895-)
        ├─ 4. Lilla STEPHENSON (b.Abt 1846-Tazewell County,Va)
        ─  4. Martha STEPHENSON (b.1848-Tazewell Co.,Va.)
        ─  4. Mary STEPHENSON (b.Sep 1849-Tazewell Co.,Va. d.2 Mar 1913-Ky.)
        ├─ 4. Robert STEPHENSON (b.Abt 1853-Tazewell County,Va)
        ─  4. William "Zachariah" STEPHENSON (b.26 Jan 1856-Tazewell County,Va d.2 Apr 1933-Portsmouth Scioto)
               sp: Clara PECK (b.25 Feb 1860-T,B,Greenup Co. Ky. m.28 Dec 1881 d.Aug 1937-Portsmouth,Ohio)
            ─  5. Maurice Lester STEPHENSON (b.4 Mar 1884-Greenup Co.,Kentucky d.26 Jun 1948-Portsmouth Ohi)
                   sp: Lucilla "Lucy" BAILEY (b.Abt 1890-Kentucky m.Abt 1910 d.1954-Cincinnati,Ohio)
                └─ 6. Raymond Lestor STEPHENSON (b.24 Oct 1912-Portsmouth Scioto Co. Ohio d.1 Jan 1967-)
                       sp: Anne Lee TAYLOR (b.18 Jul 1917-L,Sciato Co. Ohio m.1936(div) d.30 Jun 1997-)
                    ├─ 7. Maurice Lestor STEPHENSON (b.23 Mar 1937-Portsmouth Scioto Co. Ohio d.15 Jun 1999-)
                    └─ 7. Sharon Kay STEPHENSON (b.7 Jan 1939-Portsmouth Scioto Co. Ohio)
```

THE PATRIOT, HEZEKIAH WHITT

Descendants of Justice Hezekiah WHITT

sp: Howard Frederick MCCOY Sr. (b.21 Feb 1936-Portsmouth Scioto Co m.19 Mar 1955)
— 8. Howard Frederick MCCOY Jr. (b.1 Nov 1955-Portsmouth Scioto Co. Ohio)
   sp: Debbie Lu HERRMANN (b.19 Oct 1955-Portsmo m.19 Aug 1978 d.7 Mar 2005-)
   — 9. Patrick William MCCOY (b.29 Dec 1982-Sylvaina,Oh.)
      sp: Emily PAPP (b.31 Dec 1982 m.15 Oct 2005)
      — 10. Emma Grace MCCOY (b.8 Aug 2006-Cincinnati,OH)
      — 10. Ashley Elizabeth MCCOY (b.11 Oct 2008-Cincinnati,OH)
   — 9. Kristin Kathleen MCCOY (b.20 Mar 1985)
      sp: Tyler PIERSON (m.unmarried)
      — 10. Nathan William PIERSON (b.18 Jul 2008-Sylvaina,Oh.)
— 8. Kathy Elizabeth MCCOY (b.7 Dec 1956-Portsmouth Scioto Co. Ohio)
   sp: Michael Ray LOVENGUTH (b.7 Dec 1956-Portsmouth Scioto C m.28 Oct 1978)
— 8. Mary Carol MCCOY (b.4 Aug 1965-Portsmouth Scioto Co. Ohio)
— 5. Jesse STEPHENSON (b.Jun 1887-Greenup Co.,Ky.)
   sp: Jesse Clayton WHITT (b.Feb 1877-Greenup Co.,Ky. m.?)
— 6. Elsa WHITT (b.11 Jul 1908-Greenup Co.,Ky. d.2 Oct 1908-Greenup Co.,Ky.)
— 6. Samuel Douglas WHITT (b.18 Jul 1909-Greenup Co. Ky. d.16 May 1989-Greenup Co. Ky.)
— 6. Rodney O. WHITT (b.23 Jan 1912-Greenup Co. Ky. d.24 Feb 1996-Greenup Co. Ky.)
— 6. Donald WHITT (b.Abt 1917-Greenup Co.,Ky.)
— 6. Rolfe Clayton WHITT (b.8 Jul 1918-Greenup Co.,Ky. d.10 Apr 1984-Greenup Co.,Ky.)
   sp: Julia M. (b.7 Mar 1932 m.?)
   — 7. Jesse Clayton WHITT (b.30 Oct 1961-Portsmouth,Ohio)
      sp: Donita CARVER (b.17 Oct 1954)
   — 7. June Marie WHITT (b.19 Feb 1959-Portsmouth Ohio)
      sp: David BURTON
      — 8. Mark BURTON (b.7 Apr 1979-Ashland,Boyd Co.,Ky.)
         sp: Erica NICHOLS (b.29 Sep 1989-Ashland,Boyd Co.,Ky. m.14 Aug 2006)
         — 9. Anastrianna Grace BURTON (b.26 Mar 2007-Ashland,Boyd Co.,Ky.)
         — 9. Persephone Ella BURTON (b.9 Apr 2009-Ashland,Boyd Co.,Ky.)
      — 8. Chad Eric BURTON (b.6 Oct 1985-Ashland,Ky)
         sp: Andria RICE (b.10 May 1990-Ashland,Boyd Co.,Ky. m.30 Aug 2008)
         — 9. Alexis Taylor BURTON (b.16 Jul 2009-Ashland,Boyd Co.,Ky.)
      — 8. Crystal Diane BURTON (b.5 Dec 1983-Ashland,Boyd Co.,Ky.)
   — 7. John WHITT (b.6 Apr 1958-Big White Oak Creek,Greenup Co.,Ky.)
   — 7. Mary Ann WHITT (b.18 Feb 1960-South Shore,KY)
   — 7. Rolfe WHITT Jr. (b.10 Apr 1965-Portsmouth Ohio)
— 6. Alta WHITT (b.4 Dec 1924-Greenup Co.,Ky.)
— 6. Wayne WHITT (b.13 Sep 1926-Big White Oak Creek,Greenup Co.,Ky.)
   sp: Earnestine DOWDY (b.4 Dec 1927-Greenup Co.,Ky.)
   — 7. Stephen WHITT (b.1952)
      sp: UNKNOWN
      — 8. Heather WHITT (b.Abt 1975)
   — 7. Robert (Bob) WHITT (b.1955)
— 6. Audrey WHITT (b.18 Sep 1931-Greenup Co.,Ky.)
— 5. Floyd STEPHENSON (b.1890-Greenup Co.,Ky. d.1915-Greenup Co.,Ky.)
— 5. Maria STEPHENSON
— 4. David STEPHENSON (b.Abt 1858)
— 4. Amanda STEPHENSON (b.Abt 1862)
— 4. Alfred STEPHENSON (b.Abt 1867)
— 4. Nettie G. STEPHENSON (COULD BE GRANDDAUGHTER) (b.7 Jul 1889-Greenup Co.,Ky. d.Jul 1890-)
— 3. James Griffith WHITT (b.10 Jul 1825-Montgomery Co. Virginia d.8 Jun 1899-Ingleside,San Patricio Co. Tx.)
   sp: Nancy WEBB (b.Abt 1832-Tazewell Co. Va. m.4 Sep 1850 d.Bef 1878-Fannin Co. Tx.)

THE PATRIOT, HEZEKIAH WHITT

Descendants of Justice Hezekiah WHITT

```
— 4. Jonas Griffith WHITT (b.19 Oct 1851-Tazewell,County,VA. d.1935-FC,Tx.) ** Printed on Page 12 **
— 4. David Crockett WHITT (b.18 Mar 1855-Tazewell,County,VA. d.4 Jun 1939-) ** Printed on Page 12 **
— 4. Joseph Wilshire WHITT (b.20 Feb 1857-Tazewell,County,VA. d.21 Mar 1923-) ** Printed on Page 12 **
— 4. Mildred Susannah WHITT (b.May 1859-Tazewell,County,VA.) ** Printed on Page 12 **
— 4. Laura R. WHITT (b.1864 Or 1856-Tenn. Or VA.) ** Printed on Page 12 **
— 4. May C. WHITT (b.1867-Tazewell,County,VA.) ** Printed on Page 12 **
— 4. Milburn WHITT (b.Abt 1870 d.Bf 1880) ** Printed on Page 12 **
— 4. Louisa WHITT (b.1864) ** Printed on Page 13 **
  sp: Louisa Ann HUNTER (b.3 Jul 1855-Etna,Mo. m.24 May 1878 d.1941-Savoy,Fannin Co. Texas)
— 4. John Hunter WHITT (b.1879-Savoy,Fannin Co. Tx. d.1891-Savoy,Fannin Co. Tx.)
— 4. Alice M. WHITT (b.Oct 1881-Savoy,Fannin Co. Tx. d.15 Dec 1973)
    sp: Oscar Jack WITHROW (m.(div))
      — 5. Evelynn WITHROW
          sp: Clyde SUBLETT
            — 6. Garren SUBLETT
      — 5. Doyle WITHROW
          sp: Bertha
      — 5. Pearl WITHROW
          sp: Paul PRITCHETT
      — 5. Mayrene WITHROW
          sp: MORROW
      — 5. Anna Bell WITHROW
          sp: J.W. BALDWIN
            — 6. Betty Clark BALDWIN
      — 5. D.B. WITHROW
          sp: Maybelle BLAKEY
            — 6. Jackie WITHROW
            — 6. Patsy WITHROW
                sp: LANDER
— 4. James Edward WHITT (b.Aug 1884-Savoy,Fannin Co. Tx. d.Dallas,Dallis Co. Tx.)
    sp: Lillie BOMPART
— 4. Holly Lee WHITT (b.13 Jan 1889-Savoy,Fannin Co. Tx. d.26 Sep 1982-Los Angeles Co.,Ca.)
    sp: Rena Mytrle (m.31 Dec 1918)
    sp: Norma B. DULIN (m.1927)
— 4. Eva D. WHITT (b.1891-Savoy,Fannin Co. Tx.)
    sp: Oscar BURRIS
— 3. Elizabeth "Betsy" WHITT (b.Abt 1827-Montgomery Co.,Va.)
  sp: Abijah "Bige" BALDWIN (b.1805-Ashe Co.,Nc m.Between 1840 and 1852 d.Bf 1870-TC,Va)
  — 4. James BALDWIN (b.Abt 1853-Va.)
  — 4. Joseph BALDWIN (b.Abt 1855-Va.)
  — 4. Lydia BALDWIN (b.Abt 1857-Va.)
— 3. David Crockett WHITT (b.13 Dec 1836-Montgomery Co. Virginia d.28 Nov 1909-Swords Creek,NRV,R,Co.)
  sp: Arminda ROBINETT (b.9 May 1844-Wyoming County,Va. m.12 May 1859 d.1 May 1923-SCNR,V,Co.)
  — 4. John Floyd WHITT (b.30 May 1861-Tazewell County,Va d.10 Aug 1954-Swords Creek Near Raven,V,Co.)
      sp: Mary M. "Meg" (b.20 Mar 1863-Va. m.Abt 1883 d.20 Feb 1935-Swords Creek Near Raven,V,Co.)
        — 5. William Floyd WHITT (b.Abt 1884-Russell Co.,Va.)
            sp: Dora Ethel DYE (b.Russell Co.,Va.)
              — 6. Hazel M. WHITT (b.Abt 1915 d.Died)
                  sp: COMPENELL
              — 6. Helen Delcie WHITT (b.Abt 1918-Russell Co.,Va. d.18 Mar 2004-Bristol,TN.)
                  sp: Winfred Elmer JUSTICE (b.1915-Tazewell County,Va d.16 Feb 1997-,Tazewell Co. Va.)
                    — 7. Earl JUSTICE
```

THE PATRIOT, HEZEKIAH WHITT

Descendants of Justice Hezekiah WHITT

```
                    sp: Peggy RICHARDSON (b.Raven,VA.)
                 ─ 7. Phyllis JUSTICE (b.Swords Creek Near Raven,Va.Russell,Co.)
                    sp: Gary MILLER
              ─ 7. Joan JUSTICE (b.VA.)
                 sp: Herbie BALL
              ─ 7. Joyce JUSTICE (b.VA.)
                 sp: Tom HARMON
              ─ 7. Carl JUSTICE (b.VA.)
                 sp: Marlys
              ─ 7. Mike JUSTICE (b.VA.)
                 sp: Ann
              └ 7. Larry JUSTICE (b.Va.)
                 sp: Mary
           ─ 6. Olaf L. WHITT (b.Abt 1920)
              sp: Clarence BOYD
           ─ 6. Dorothy Pearl WHITT (b Abt 1922)
              sp: STEVENS
           ─ 6. William F. WHITT (b.Abt 1924 d.22 Jul 1981-Sacremento,California)
              sp: Elizabeth COMPENELL
                 ─ 7. Glynnis WHITT
           ─ 6. George Harold WHITT (b.Abt 1926)
              sp: Maxine SHORT (b.Va.)
           ─ 6. Jack Herbert WHITT (b.Abt 1928-Swords Creek,RC,Va. d.12 Oct 2004-Clearwater Florida)
              sp: Dorris WELLS
                 ─ 7. Scott WHITT
                 ─ 7. Dane WHITT
                 └ 7. Bruce WHITT
           ─ 6. Glen WHITT (d.Died)
           ─ 6. Guy WHITT (d.Died)
           └ 6. Ronald WHITT
              sp: Loretta
        ─ 5. Mary Belle WHITT (b.Abt 1888)
           sp: Grover RAKES
           └ 6. Stella May RAKES (b.4 Dec 1913 d.29 Jan 1936)
              sp: Clearence R. HICKS
        ─ 5. Albert Jesse WHITT (b.24 Jun 1889 d.Aug 1965)
           sp: Ava Elizabeth WHITE (b.1 Nov 1901-SCNR,Va.Russell,Co. d.23 Feb 1925-M,Russell Co. Va.)
           sp: Florance Euna WHITT (b.25 Jan 1902 d.1 Aug 1982)
           ─ 6. Ralph W. WHITT (b.Abt 1923-Va. d.Passed Away)
           ─ 6. Willard R. WHITT (b.Abt 1928-Va.)
              sp: Laura
           ─ 6. Donald J. WHITT (b.8 Sep 1930-SCNR,Va.Russell,Co. d.6 Nov 2004-Mars Hill H. Care,Maine)
              sp: Rowena HOWLETT
              └ 7. Rebecca WHITT
                 sp: Conrad BROWN
                 ─ 8. Amy BROWN
                    sp: Matthew PROCTOR
                    └ 9. Elias PROCTOR
           ─ 6. Thomas WHITT
              sp: Carol
           ─ 6. Dean WHITT (d.Passed Away)
           └ 6. Frank WHITT (b.18 Jan 1928-SCNR,Va.Russell,Co. d.18 Jan 1928-SCNR,Va.Russell,Co.)
```

THE PATRIOT, HEZEKIAH WHITT

Descendants of Justice Hezekiah WHITT

- 5. Jonas C. WHITT (b.Abt 1890)
  - sp: Gladys (b.Abt 1900 m.Abt 1916)
  - 6. Douglas WHITT (b.Abt 1917)
  - 6. Garland WHITT (b.Abt 1919)
  - 6. Frazier WHITT (b.Abt 1923)
- 5. Florence E. WHITT (b.Abt 1892)
- 5. Rosa Arminda WHITT (b.4 Jan 1896 d.17 Jul 1969)
  - sp: William Charlie "WILL" BYRD
  - 6. William Hebert BYRD (b.7 Mar 1929-SCNR,Va.Russell,Co. d.10 Aug 1950-Korea)
  - 6. Mary Magaline BYRD (b.6 Apr 1913-SCNR,Va.Russell,Co. d.19 Sep 1992)
  - 6. John Harvey BYRD
  - 6. Robert Cornus BYRD Sr.
  - 6. Delora Mae BYRD
    - sp: Clarence Mervin ROBINETT (b.3 Jan 1917-Swords Creek Near Raven,Va.Russell,Co.)
    - 7. Rosie Gaynell ROBINETT (b.17 Dec 1946 d.29 Jun 2005)
  - 6. Maude BYRD
  - 6. Grace BYRD
  - 6. Floyd Curtis BYRD (b.13 Jan 1931-Tazewell County,Va)
    - sp: Bonnie Ellen SALYERS (m.1955)
  - 6. Clarence BYRD
  - 6. Emily BYRD
  - 6. Thelma Betty Jane BYRD (b.11 Dec 1935 d.15 Nov 2002)
- 5. Geroge Washington WHITT (b.Abt 1899-Va.)
  - sp: Winnie YATES (b.13 Aug 1897 m.Abt 1922 d.4 Dec 1994)
  - 6. Lucy B. WHITT (b.4 Oct 1922-Swords Creek Near Raven,Va.Russell,Co.)
    - sp: Shanon Montague WEBB (b.11 Aug 1913-Va. d.17 Nov 1996-Mercer Co.,West Va.)
    - 7. Garnet WEBB
      - sp: Martha
    - 7. Gaines Edward WEBB (b.3 Jul 1947-Raven,VA. Tazewell Co. d.3 Jul 2009 Friday-)
      - sp: UNKNOWN
      - 8. Lora Gaye WEBB
        - sp: Tim BLANKENSHIP
      - 8. Tracy Lynn WEBB
    - 7. Brenda WEBB
      - sp: Johnny DAVIS
    - 7. Monica WEBB
      - sp: Ronnie RICHARDSON
  - 6. Waneta B. WHITT (b.Abt 1925)
  - 6. William Buford WHITT (b.Abt 1927)
    - sp: Goldie Marie PECK
    - 7. Connie Marie WHITT
      - sp: Kerry E. MCGLOGHLIN (b.5 Feb 1950-Richlands,Tazewell Co.,Va. m.5 Sep 1969)
      - 8. Kem Edward MCGLOGHLIN (b.25 Jun 1971-Holyoke AF Base,Mass.)
        - sp: Marlene Beth SPARKS (m.30 Nov 1990)
        - 9. Kraig Edward MCGLOGHLIN
        - 9. Logan Conner MCGLOGHLIN
      - 8. Tina Marie MCGLOGHLIN (b.13 May 1973-Holyoke,Mass.)
        - sp: Brian Keith KEEN (b.24 Jan 1972-Richlands,Tazewell Co.,Va. m.15 Jun 1991)
        - 9. Kerry Edward (Twin) KEEN (b.21 Mar 1995-Johnson City,Washington Co.,Tenn.)
        - 9. Keith Robert (Twin) KEEN (b.21 Mar 1995-Johnson City,Washington Co.,Tenn.)
    - 7. Jerry Buford WHITT (b.13 Feb 1961-Swords Creek Near Raven,V,Co. d.28 Feb 1961-)
    - 7. Barbara Sue WHITT

THE PATRIOT, HEZEKIAH WHITT

Descendants of Justice Hezekiah WHITT

```
                    sp: Barry HONAKER
            ┌─ 7. Linda Gay WHITT
            │   sp: Dennis WHITE
            │       ├─ 8. William WHITE
            │       │   sp: Ellen COOPER
            │       │   └─ 9. Thler WHITE
            │       ─ 8. Brian WHITE
            │           sp: Christina ROBINETTE
            │           ─ 9. Brett WHITE
            ├─ 7. Ruth Ann WHITT
            │   sp: Jerry HONAKER
            │       ├─ 8. Stephanie HONAKER
            │       └─ 8. Vickie HONAKER
            ├─ 7. Janice Faye WHITT
            │   sp: Edward GROSS
            │       ─ 8. Amy (twin) GROSS
            │       ┌─ 8. Jamie (twin) GROSS
            │       sp: Elmer COMPTON
            └─ 7. Shiela Maxine WHITT
                sp: Gary DYE
                    ├─ 8. Heather DYE
                    │   sp: Shane JOHNSON
                    │   ─ 9. Jonthan JOHNSON
                    │   ─ 9. Adam JOHNSON
                    └─ 8. Amanda DYE
      ┌─ 6. Hershel L WHITT (b.Abt 1928)
      ├─ 6. George Harold WHITT
      │   sp: Maxine SHORTT
      │   ┌─ 7. William WHITT
      │   │   sp: Sherri MILLER
      │   │   ─ 8. Brett WHITT
      │   │   sp: Donna RASNAKE
      │   ├─ 7. Douglas WHITT
      │   │   sp: Sandy MILLER
      │   │   ├─ 8. Adam WHITT
      │   │   │   sp: Jessica JACKSON
      │   │   │   ├─ 9. Gavin WHITT
      │   │   │   └─ 9. Maggie WHITT
      │   │   ─ 8. Jordan WHITT
      │   └─ 7. Angie WHITT
      │       sp: Jimmie HALE
      │       ─ 8. Brittany HALE
      │       ─ 8. Mathew HALE
      ─ 6. Ralph WHITT
          sp: Eliza OWENS
          ┌─ 7. Ralph WHITT Jr.
          │   sp: Wilma WHITE
          │   └─ 8. Michelle WHITT
          │       sp: Josh HYLTON
          ├─ 7. Larry WHITT
          │   sp: Bonnie ROBINETTE
          │   └─ 8. Ryan WHITT
```

THE PATRIOT, HEZEKIAH WHITT

Descendants of Justice Hezekiah WHITT

```
              └─ sp: Heather FIELDS
                 7. Willard WHITT
                    sp: Laura LOWE
                    ── 8  Freda Gay WHITT
                          sp: Calvin Paul HAYES
                    ── 8. Curtis WHITT
                          sp: Kathy BALDWIN
                          ┈ 9. Heather WHITT
                              sp: Michael STILWELL
                              ── 10. Lauren STILWELL
                              ── 10. Logan STILWELL
                          ── 9. Ashley WHITT
                              sp: Wesley AYERS
                              ├─ 10. Desirea AYERS
                              └─ 10. Sklar AYERS
        ── 4. Jonas Lee WHITT (b.10 Jun 1863 d.1 Aug 1904)
              sp: Mary Virginia ROBINSON (b.20 Mar 1863 m.? d.20 Feb 1935)
              ── 5. George Dewey WHITT (b.1 Jun 1898 d.16 Nov 1962-Steelsburg,Va. Farm)
                    sp: Annie Marylin STEELE (b.8 Mar 1900 m.5 Jan 1921 d.17 Nov 1996)
                    ├─ 6. Kermit Leo WHITT (b.14 Mar 1935)
                    │     sp: Mary Lou JOHNSON (b.21 Mar 1927 m.?)
                    │     ├─ 7. John Bryan WHITT (b.8 Oct 1969)
                    │     │     sp: Tamela Denise COOK (b.20 Jan 1976 m.?)
                    │     │     ── 8. Bryan Austin WHITT (b.3 Dec 2002)
                    │     ── 7. Timothy Leo WHITT (b.8 Aug 1965)
                    │     │     sp: Cynthia Sue SCHRADER (b.20 Sep 1966)
                    │     │     ── 8. Lindsay Michelle WHITT (b.18 Feb 1986)
                    │     │     └─ 8. Derek Troy WHITT (b.4 Oct 1989)
                    │     └─ 7. Sherry Lynn WHITT (b.7 Apr 1967)
                    │           sp: David Mark HARRILL (b.3 Dec 1960 m.?)
                    │           └─ 8. Housan Gene HARRILL (b.2 Aug 1989)
                    ── 6. Arville Phillip WHITT (b.28 Jan 1931)
                    ── 6. Geneva Largey WHITT (b.11 Dec 1928)
                    ── 6. Dortha June WHITT (b.21 Feb 1927)
                    ── 6. Edna Iris WHITT (b.11 Dec 1924)
                    └─ 6. Edith Estelle WHITT (b.13 Feb 1923)
                    ── 6. Margaret Evelyn WHITT (b.21 Sep 1921)
                          sp: UNKNOWN
                          └─ 7. Wayne
              ── 5. Joseph E. WHITT
                    sp: Eulah
              ── 5. James Henry (Jim) WHITT (b.18 Jan 1894-Buchanan Co.,Va. d.4 Sep 1913-RCSC,Va.)
              ── 5. Walter WHITT
                    sp: Elsie
              ── 5. Ada Samantha WHITT (b.4 Aug 1900-Russell,Co.,Va. d.15 Feb 1940-Russell,Co.,Va.)
                    sp: Marvin WADE
        ── 4. Margret E. S. (Maggie) WHITT (b.Abt 1867-Tazewell County,Va)
              sp: Charlie Boston STEELE (b.20 Feb 1863-Tazewell County,Va m.25 Nov 1885)
              ├─ 5. Walter STEELE (b.20 Feb 1891-Tazewell County,Va d.6 Jan 1969)
              │     sp: UNKNOWN
              │     ── 6. Frank STEELE (b.11 Feb 1919 d.12 Aug 1991-Richlands,Tazewell Co.,Va.)
              ── 5. Pearl STEELE (b.2 Jan 1905-Tazewell County,Va d.27 Dec 1981)
```

THE PATRIOT, HEZEKIAH WHITT

Descendants of Justice Hezekiah WHITT

```
— 5. Ethel STEELE
— 5. Fred STEELE (b.9 Apr 1897 d.Jul 1970)
— 4. James Crockett WHITT (b.28 May 1869-Near Cedar Bluff,VA. d.13 Nov 1940-Killed in Coal Mine acciden)
    sp: Maude Grief Ellis Sulan BISHOP (b.24 Jul 1878-Maytown,Ky. m.? d.8 Aug 1959-SCNR,V,Co.)
    — 5. Claudy W. WHITT (b.6 Aug 1896 d.26 Oct 1897)
    — 5. Clarence M. WHITT (b.19 May 1890 d.13 Feb 1901)
    — 5. Florance Euna WHITT (b.25 Jan 1902 d.1 Aug 1982)
        sp: Albert Jesse WHITT (b.24 Jun 1889 d.Aug 1965)
        — 6. Ralph W. WHITT (b.Abt 1923-Va. d.Passed Away) ** Printed on Page 17 **
        — 6. Willard R. WHITT (b.Abt 1928-Va.) ** Printed on Page 17 **
        — 6. Donald J. WHITT (b.8 Sep 1930-SCNR,Va.Russell,Co. d.6 Nov 2004-) ** Printed on Page 17 **
        — 6. Thomas WHITT ** Printed on Page 17 **
        — 6. Dean WHITT (d.Passed Away) ** Printed on Page 17 **
        — 6. Frank WHITT (b.18 Jan 1928-SCNR,Va.Russell,Co. d.18 Jan 1928-) ** Printed on Page 17 **
    — 5. Della Margaret (Mae) WHITT (b.24 May 1905 d.4 Apr 1995)
        sp: Samuel Jackson CHRISTIAN (b.25 Dec 1895 d.28 Feb 1954)
        — 6. Ruby Claire CHRISTIAN (b.22 Jan 1924-Russell Co.,Va.)
            sp: Giles SIMS
            — 7. Linda Clair SIMS
                sp: MURPHY
            — 7. Rodney Palmer SIMS (d.May 1977)
            sp: Frank Alden BREWER (d.Oct 1946)
            — 7. Rodney Dane BREWER (b.25 Aug 1946-Gatesville,Texas.)
                sp: Jennifer Lynn CLEVENGER (m.28 Aug 1965)
                — 8. Leslie Alden BREWER (b.27 Jul 1968-Sebring,FL.)
                    sp: Joann Walker BRITT (b.7 Dec 1999)
                    — 9. Lauri Nichole (Adopted Grandchild) BREWER (b.26 May 1999-Bristol TN.)
                    — 9. Brittney Lynn (Adopted Grandchild) BREWER (b.29 Jan 2001)
                — 8. Cathryn Renee BREWER (ADOPTED) (b.10 Jun 1969-Welch,West Virgina)
                    sp: William Alexander BOATMAN (m.11 Nov 1992)
                    — 9. William Alexander Mackenzie BOATMAN (b.1 Nov 1993)
                    — 9. Victoria Leigh BOATMAN (b.5 Jul 1996)
                — 8. Lori Nichole BREWER (b.14 Oct 1976-Bluefield,WV d.15 Jul 1998-C,VA.)
                — 8. Lauri Nichole AG BREWER (b.26 May 1999-Bristol TN.) ** Printed on Page 21 **
                — 8. Brittney Lynn AG BREWER (b.29 Jan 2001) ** Printed on Page 21 **
            sp: Giles SIMS
        — 6. Harold Edward CHRISTIAN (b.6 Jul 1925 d.16 Nov 1997)
            sp: Nellie LANE
        — 6. James Loyd CHRISTIAN (b.15 Sep 1927 d.19 Nov 1989)
            sp: Audrey KEITH
        — 6. Phyllis Lee CHRISTIAN (b.16 Jan 1933)
            sp: James Floyd GIBSON (b.1932 d.1982)
        — 6. Bobby Dean CHRISTIAN (b.21 Feb 1935)
            sp: Patrica Ann LAMBERT
            — 7. Deanna Lynn CHRISTIAN (b.21 Feb 1959)
                sp: Micheal FAULK (m.?)
                — 8. Christopher Allen FAULK (b.4 Aug 1975)
                    sp: Betty Joy WHITE (m.?)
                    — 9. Christopher Roland FAULK (b.16 Apr 1995)
                    — 9. Melody Ann MCKENZIE (b.9 May 2001)
                sp: Ronald WALTON (m.?)
                — 8. Bobbie Jo WALTON (b.14 Oct 1979)
```

THE PATRIOT, HEZEKIAH WHITT

Descendants of Justice Hezekiah WHITT

```
                    sp: Jason CROSS (m.?)
                      └─ 9. Ashley Nicole CROSS (b.30 Mar 2000)
                  ─ 8. Angela Margaret WALTON (b.13 Aug 1986)
                    sp: Richard RUSSELL
                    sp: William CROSS
                    sp: William BAKER (m.?)
                  ├ 8. Christopher Allen FAULK (b.4 Aug 1975)
                  │   sp: UNKNOWN
                  │   ─ 9. Christopher Roland FAULK (b.16 Apr 1995) ** Printed on Page 21 **
                  │   ─ 9. Melody Ann McKenzie FAULK (b.9 May 2001)
                  ├─ 8. Bobbie Joe BAKER (b.14 Oct 1979)
                  │   sp: CROSS (m.?)
                  │    └─ 9. Ashley Nicole CROSS (b.30 Mar 2000)
                  ─ 8. Angela Margaret BAKER (b.13 Aug 1986)
                    sp: WALTON
              sp: Mary Elizabeth (Dillon) BARRETT
              sp: Mary Elizabeth (Dillon) BARRETT
              sp: Charolyn Elaine LOWE (b.29 Oct 1935)
          ─ 6. Dennis Ray CHRISTIAN (b.23 Dec 1945)
            sp: Nancy SHAFERMAN
    ─ 5. Thomas Albert (Abb) WHITT (b.Nov 1907-MC,Russell Co.,Va. d.9 Sep 1955-Russell,Co.,Va.)
      sp: Alice Gray WHITE (b.12 Feb 1914 d.24 Mar 1970)
      ├ 6. Billie Eugene WHITT (bu.Evarat,Mi.)
      │   sp: Rose Marie SHANNABERRY
      │   ─ 7. James Albert WHITT (b.14 Jan 1960-Deerborn,Mi.)
      │       sp: Betty STEADMAN (bu.Evaet,Mi.)
      │       ├ 8. David STEADMAN (b.Step)
      │       ├ 8. Tammy STESDMAN (b.Step)
      │       ├ 8. Mark STEADMAN (b.Step)
      │       ├ 8. Sherry STEADMAN (b.Step)
      │       └ 8. Daniel STEADMAN (b.Step)
      ─ 6. Doyl Garnett WHITT (b.5 Nov 1934-Virginia)
        sp: Ruth Ann BALES (b.11 Feb 1936 m.4 Nov 1953 d.9 Sep 1984)
        ─ 7. Connie Lynn WHITT (b.8 Sep 1954-Virginia)
          sp: Claude DOTSON (b.8 Apr 1953 m.31 Jan 1974)
          ├ 8. Joshua Alexander DOTSON (b.5 Mar 1982)
          │   sp: Rebecca GRIFFITH (b.9 Jun 1983 m.22 Dec 2003)
          │    └─ 9. Alexia Brooklyn DOTSON (b.28 Aug 2005)
          └ 8. Shannon Marie DOTSON (b.27 Jun 1988)
        ─ 7. Tamara G. WHITT (b.10 Oct 1960)
        ─ 7. Mark Doyle WHITT (b.6 Jul 1968)
        ─ 7. Christy Beth WHITT (b.22 Mar 1972-Virginia)
          sp: Jimmy Keith ABSHER (b.13 Nov 1973 m.6 Jun 1994)
          ├ 8. Ambern Nicole ABSHER (b.18 Dec 1996)
          ├ 8. Kelli Denise ABSHER (b.21 May 1999)
          └ 8. Kristen Danielle ABSHER (b.1 Oct 2001)
        sp: Norma Jean GOODIE (m.12 Oct 1996)
    ─ 5. Anna WHITT (b.11 Feb 1911-SCNR,Va.Russell,Co. d.11 Feb 1911-Swords Creek Near Raven,V,Co.)
├ 4. Mary F. (Mollie) WHITT (b.Abt 1873-Tazewell County,Va)
  sp: Rosco Staten HALL (b.4 Mar 1884-West Virginia d.Aug 1986-Princeton,Mercer Co.,WV)
  ├─ 5. Ocie Kathryn HALL (b.Abt 1909-Mercer Co.,West Va.)
  ├─ 5. Stanley L. HALL (b.1911-Mercer Co.,West Va.)
```

THE PATRIOT, HEZEKIAH WHITT

Descendants of Justice Hezekiah WHITT

— 5. Paul B. HALL (b.1912-Mercer Co.,West Va.)

— 5. Hazel E. HALL (b.1913-Mercer Co.,West Va.)

— 5. Ethel C. HALL (b.1914-Mercer Co.,West Va.)

— 5. Lawrence C. HALL (b.1916-Mercer Co.,West Va.)

— 5. Virginia Ruth HALL (b.1918-Mercer Co.,West Va.)

— 5. Gertude E. HALL (b.Abt 1920)

— 4. William Johnson (Bill) WHITT (b.Oct 1875-Cedar Bluff,TC,VA d.1946-Applichia,VA)

    sp: Addie Louise RICHMOND (b.12 May 1882-Hindman,KY m.7 Mar 1900d.Wythville,VA)

    — 5. Fred H. WHITT (b.10 Mar 1901-Richlands,Tazewell Co. Va. d.20 Apr 1972-Whitesburg,LC,Ky.)

        sp: Osia SUBLETT (b.Abt 1904-West Virginia m.Abt 1923)

      — 6. Virginia Lee(Adopted) WHITT (b.Abt 1923-West Virginia)

      — 6. Ralph GOINGS

    — 5. Effie G. WHITT (b.20 Dec 1903-Raven,Tazewell Co.,Va. d.6 Oct 1904-Raven,Tazewell Co.,Va.)

    — 5. James Crockett WHITT (b.10 Jul 1905-Raven,TC,Va. d.7 Nov 1905-Raven,Tazewell Co.,Va.)

    — 5. William Frank WHITT (b.5 Sep 1907-Blackford,VA d.16 Jun 1944-Sipan Island,iTMI,Central Pacific.)

    — 5. Robert Glen WHITT Sr. (b.15 Aug 1910-East Stone Gap,VA d.30 Sep 1999-Weber City,VA)

        sp: Evelyn Marie LANE (b.14 Nov 1918-Big Stone Gap,Wise Co. m.21 Nov 1940 d.21 Aug 1999-)

      — 6. Robert Glen WHITT Jr. (b.2 Mar 1948-Big Stone Gap,Wise Co.)

          sp: Shirley PERRY (b.12 May 1950 m.20 Dec 1969)

        — 7. Robert Glen (Rob) WHITT III (b.15 Apr 1972-Big Stone Gap,Wise Co.)

            sp: Dodie DENISON

          — 8. Abigail WHITT (b.1999)

          — 8. Robert Glen WHITT III

          sp: Debora WILLIAMS (b.25 Feb 1955 m.10 Jan 1974)

        — 7. Richard Allen WHITT (b.1 Dec 1974)

            sp: Patti WOOD (b.6 Dec 1972-Texas m.12 Jan 1996(div))

          — 8. Alexis Elizabeth WHITT (b.21 Jan 2000-Texas)

            sp: Samantha MASON (b.21 Oct 1972 m.20 Mar 2006)

          — 8. Asher Earnest WHITT (b.8 Oct 2003-Chesterfield Co.,England)

          — 8. James Mason WHITT (b.18 Oct 2007-Ambergate,England)

        — 7. Ryan Leigh WHITT (b.21 Sep 1978-Big Stone Gap,Wise Co.)

            sp: Kevin WHITE (b.27 Mar 1978-Boulder Co. m.Jan 2001)

          — 8. Bradley WHITE (b.5 Feb 2000-Boulder Co.)

          — 8. Ella Marie WHITE (b.8 Jan 2003-Joplin,MO.)

      — 6. William John WHITT (b.16 Sep 1949-Big Stone Gap,Wise Co.)

          sp: Diane DOOLEY (m.1 Jan 1974(div))

        — 7. William John WHITT Jr. (b.4 May 1967)

        — 7. Tracey Briane WHITT (b.22 Jul 1974)

        — 7. Christopher Ware WHITT (b.6 Nov 1982)

          sp: Martha CUNNINGHAM (b.10 Jun 1953 m.17 Jun 1984(div))

        — 7. Julia Michelle WHITT (b.23 Jul 1984)

        — 7. Clifford James WHITT (b.4 Sep 1985)

      — 6. James Richmond WHITT (b.5 Aug 1951)

          sp: Deborah STAPLETON (b.5 Aug 1955 m.2 Aug 1974)

        — 7. Brandy Marie WHITT (b.12 Aug 1978)

    — 5. Isaac Richmond WHITT (b.5 Feb 1913-Applichia,VA d.22 Feb 1915-Appalachia,Va.)

    — 5. Arthur McDowell WHITT Sr. (b.23 May 1916-Appalachia,Va. d.14 Feb 2008-BSG,Wise Co.)

        sp: Winfred Cornelia DIXON

      — 6. Sandra WHITT

        sp: Unknown SMITH

      — 6. Jenny WHITT

        sp: Unknown COLLIER

THE PATRIOT, HEZEKIAH WHITT

Descendants of Justice Hezekiah WHITT

17 May 2010   Relationship Codes: Page 24

```
            — 6. Shirlee Jane WHITT
                 sp: Unknown DYSARE
            └─ 6. Arthur McDowell (Buster) WHITT Jr.
                 sp: DeRhonda BACH
                 ├─ 7. Amesha McDowell WHITT
                 sp: Sherry Lynn SPARKMAN
      └─ 5. Ralph Carter WHITT (b.29 Jul 1918-Appalachia,Va. d.Wythville,VA)
            sp: Mary Evelyn EMMERIT
            — 6. Tamara (Tammy) WHITT
                 sp: Dr. Randy CHITWOOD
                 ├─ 7. Randolph CHITWOOD
                 └─ 7. Ann CHITWOOD
   ┬ 4. Robert Milburn WHITT (b. 22 Jul 1879 Tuesday-Tazewell  County,Va d.18 Jul 1967 Tuesday-Ind.)
     sp: Mollie Alice PUCKETT (b.26 Feb1891 Thursday-Va. m.Abt 1906 d.5 Dec 1965 Sunday-Ind.)
   — 5. Rosania Armind WHITT (b.18 Jan 1907 d.15 Nov 1954)
        sp: Albert PRICE
        ├─ 6. Joe PRICE
        ├─ 6. Fred PRICE
        sp: Jess SCHRADER
        — 6. Betty Lou SCHRADER
        — 6. Norma Jean SCHRADER
        — 6. Shirley SCHRADER
        — 6. Lois SCHRADER
        — 6. Monk SCHRADER
        — 6. Vernon SCHRADER
        └─ 6. Fred SCHRADER
   ┬ 5. Lera Maglina WHITT (b.27 Nov 1908 d.11 Jun 1979-Greencastle Ind.)
     sp: John K. STINSON (b.16 Dec 1908 d.5 Mar 1947-Died In Coal Mine Accident)
     — 6. Harry Glen STINSON (b.10 Sep 1931-Tazewell  County,Va d.11 Jan 2009-Indiana)
          sp: Grace Goldie MESSER (b.24 Dec 1917 d.7 Feb 2002)
     ┬ 6. John David STINSON (b.23 Jan 1933 d.16 Nov 2008-Indianapolis,IN.)
     ├ 6. James Perry STINSON (b.2 Aug 1934)
          sp: Wanda Lee CAUDILL (b.18 Apr 1939)
          ├─ 7. William Perry (Bill) STINSON (b.14 Nov 1960)
               sp: Cheri Lee ROOT (b.23 Nov 1959 m.(div))
               ├─ 8. Cody Leigh STINSON (b.28 Apr 1984)
               ├─ 8. Cheyanne Charity STINSON (b.3 Aug 1987)
               sp: Cynthia Sue (Cindy) JONES  (b.21 Nov 1964)
               └─ 8. Robert Earl STINSON
          ├─ 7. Douglas James (Doug) STINSON (b.1 Jan 1962)
               sp: PRICE SUSAN MARIE (b.12 Apr 1963)
               — 8. Raymond Perry (Raymie) STINSON (b.2 Mar 1994)
               sp: Teresa Gail COVAULT (b.29 Dec 1964)
               — 8. Conner Dale STINSON (b.24 Dec 2004)
          — 7. James Dee (Jamie) STINSON (b.9 May 1963 d.3 May 1982)
          — 7. Lori Leigh STINSON (b.28 May 1964 d.12 Jul 1969)
          ├ 7. Amy Lynn STINSON (b.11 Jul 1970)
          └─ 7. Thomas Edward STINSON (b.21 Sep 1978)
               sp: Amber Renee SEDAM (b.3 Dec 1980)
               ├─ 8. Maddison Elizabeth STINSON (b.25 Sep 2000)
               └─ 8. Gracie Niccole STINSON (b.23 Apr 2003)
     └─ 6. Betty Jean (Jean) STINSON (b.22 Dec 1935)
```

THE PATRIOT, HEZEKIAH WHITT

Descendants of Justice Hezekiah WHITT

```
      sp: Robert Eugene (Bob) ALLEE (b.23 Sep 1934 d.30 Jun 1995)
      ─ 7. Ray Edward ALLEE (b.24 Jan 1960)
          sp: Carolyn Lea (Carol) MEANOR (b.15 Dec 1962 m.(div))
          ─ 8. Sarah Elizabeth ALLEE (b.4 Dec 1982)
              sp: Brian PLUMMER (b.19 Mar 1982)
          ─ 8. Jennifer Lynn ALLEE (b.6 May 1986)
              sp: Albert Leon HEAD) (b.20 Aug 1982)
              ─ 9. Alexia Raylea HEAD) (b.23 May 2006)
              └ 9. Emily Elizabeth HEAD) (b.30 Sep 2009)
          └ 8. Christopher Ray ALLEE (b.20 Oct 1987)
      ─ 7. Michael Anthony (Mike) ALLEE (b.16 Aug 1961)
          sp: Lisa Ann HOUK (b.30 May 1963)
          ─ 8. Ashley Raye ALLEE (b.4 Nov 1982)
              sp: Shane Nathan DEBRULAR (b.29 Mar 1980 m.Not Married)
              ─ 9. Mikayla Ann ALLEE (b.12 May 2003)
              └ 9. Makynzee Lin ALLEE (b.16 Apr 2007)
          ─ 8. Linley Jean ALLEE (b.10 Oct 1988)
          sp: Denise Nancy (Nancy) BRITTON (b.25 May 1954)
      ─ 7. Melissa Kay ALLEE (b.30 Jan 1965)
          sp: John Mark HALL (b.28 May 1963 m.(div))
          ─ 8. Whitney Kay HALL (b.8 Jun 1989)
              sp: UNKNOWN
              ─ 9. Lucas Matthew HALL (b.26 Oct 2009)
          ─ 8. Darcey Rose HALL (b.23 Feb 1995)
          └ 8. Kyle Robert HALL (b.31 Aug 1997)
      └ 7. Dewayne Edmund (Dee) ALLEE (b.31 Mar 1970)
          sp: Kimberly Michell (Kimmie) STEVENSON (b.7 Aug 1979)
          ─ 8. Autumn Renee ALLEE (b.26 Mar 2002)
          ─ 8. Blake Edmund ALLEE (b.18 Nov 2004)
  ─ 6. Hansford Graham "Hank" STINSON (b.4 Nov 1938)
      sp: Phyllis Marlene MCCORMICK (b.7 Mar 1944)
      ─ 7. Larry Marshall STINSON (b.25 Aug 1962)
          sp: Pamela Jo (Pam) TILFORD (b.9 Sep 1965)
          ─ 8. Tara Nichole STINSON (b.6 Oct 1981)
              sp: Timothy Russell VANWANZEELE (b.Nov 1969)
              ─ 9. Allison Jo (Addi) VANWANZEELE (b.21 Aug 2006)
              └ 9. Marley Louise VANWANZEELE (b.1 May 2009)
          sp: Amy Katherine LAVINE (b.15 Dec 1972)
          ─ 8. Sterling Irene STINSON (b.14 Aug 1997)
          ─ 8. Spencer Marlene STINSON (b.1 Nov 2000)
      ─ 7. LaDonna Marlene STINSON (b.17 Aug 1963)
          sp: Marshall Gerald SINGLETON (b.15 Nov 1946)
          ─ 8. Nicholas Ty (Nick) SINGLETON (b.29 Sep 1981)
              sp: Stacy MURRAY
              └ 9. Asher Wesley SINGLETON (b.3 Jul 2009)
          ─ 8. Sierra Marlene SINGLETON (b.5 Jun 1984)
          ─ 8. Skyann Lacy SINGLETON (b.25 Sep 1987)
          sp: Kelly Edger CHESSHIR (b.16 Jan 1957)
      sp: Rhonda Gay COOKSEY (b.11 Oct 1952)
      ─ 7. Angela Gay STINSON (b.13 Nov 1976)
          sp: Aaron Kane MOLINE (b.23 Jul 1978)
          ─ 8. Kennedy Reese MOLINE (b.5 May 2008)
```

THE PATRIOT, HEZEKIAH WHITT

Descendants of Justice Hezekiah WHITT

```
            └─ 7. Jason Graham STINSON (b.30 Aug 1981)
         ├─ 6. Robert Jeremiah STINSON (b.28 Feb 1945)
            sp: Donna Marie HENDRICH (b.26 Sep 1946 d.30 Sep 2003)
            └─ 7. Shane Allen STINSON (b.9 May 1964)
                 sp: Teresa Mae GALLOWAY (b.3 Sep 1966 d.7 Jun 1999)
                 ─ 8. Jeremiah Shane STINSON (b.18 Sep 1985)
                      sp: Jessica Dawn SMITH (b.15 May 1984 m.Not Married)
                      └─ 9. Cowan Shane STINSON (b.24 Aug 2008)
                 ├─ 8. Jessica Marie STINSON (b.15 Aug 1988)
                 sp: Bianca JOHNSON (b.26 Sep 1963)
                 ┆── 8. Blake Gene STINSON (b.21 Aug 1985)
                 └─ 8. Hanse Kai STINSON (b.29 Sep 1986)
                      sp: Natasha Renee LUKE (b.12 May 1989 m.unmarried)
                      ─ 9. Nakaiah Janae STINSON (b.13 Sep 2007)
            └─ 7. Christy Ann STINSON (b.24 Jul 1967)
                 sp: Howard Dewayne (Howie) RAY (b.6 Oct 1966)
                 ├─ 8. Lacy Deanne RAY (b.25 Jul 1987)
                      sp: David Eugene BUMGARDNER (b.14 Nov 1986)
                      ─ 9. Kenly Marie BUMGARDNER (b.3 Jan 2008)
                      ─ 9. Brooklyn Jean BUMGARDNER (b.25 Aug 2009)
                 ─ 8. Darian Elizabeth RAY (b.26 Jun 1993)
                 ├─ 8. (Adopted) Jordan Chebly RAY (b.13 Sep 1993)
                 └─ 8. (adopted) Brittany Nicole RAY (b.22 May 1995)
         sp: Tom COOK
         sp: John K. STINSON
         └─ 6. James Perry STINSON
              sp: UNKNOWN
      ─ 5. Raleigh Graham (Grim) WHITT (b.29 Sep 1910-Tazewell Co. Va. d.2001-Stilesville,Ind.)
         sp: Euva Lorene SPARKS (b.13 Jan 1917-CB,Va.,Tazewell m.30 Sep 1933 d.29 Jun 2007 3:44PM-)
         ├─ 6. Janice N. WHITT (b.18 Jan 1936)
            sp: William Rhudy WRIGHT
         ├─ 6. Alice June WHITT (b.4 Dec 1942-Tazewell County,Va)
            sp: Arthur W. DAILEY
            ─ 7. Kristena Elizabeth DAILEY
                 sp: Pedro
                 └─ 8. Sophie Bryana DAILEY (b.31 May 2007 5:15 PM-Indiania)
            sp: Jacce RUSH
         ├─ 6. Linda WHITT (b.20 Oct 1944)
            sp: Glenn BREMER (d.21 Dec 2007)
            ├── 7. Brian BREMER (d.1988)
            └─ 7. Scott BREMER
                 sp: Becky
                 ├─ 8. Brett BREMER
                 ─ 8. Bailey BREMER
                 ── 8. Bently BREMER
                 ── 8. Bella BREMER
         ├─ 6. Mary WHITT (b.24 Jul 1946)
            sp: Daniel LAWRENCE
            ─ 7. Jarrod LAWRENCE
         ─ 6. Bobbie WHITT
            sp: Ann
            ├─ 7. Debra "DEBBIE" WHITT
```

THE PATRIOT, HEZEKIAH WHITT

Descendants of Justice Hezekiah WHITT

```
                    sp: Rick ZIMMERMAN
                      ─ 8. Tiffany ZIMMERMAN
                      ├ 8. Lisa ZIMMERMAN
                      └ 8. Blake ZIMMERMAN
                   ─ 7. Linda WHITT
                      sp: David MCCARTHY
                        ─ 8. Becky MCCARTHY
                        ─ 8. Katy MCCARTHY
                        └ 8. Sarah MCCARTHY
              ─ 6. Bill WHITT
                 sp: Georgia
                   ├ 7. Tim WHITT
                   ├ 7. Danny WHITT
                   ─ 7. Michael WHITT
                   ─ 7. Patty WHITT
            ─ 6. Richard (Rick) WHITT (b.5 Feb 1952)
               sp: Caroline
            ├ 6. Jackie Ezra WHITT (d.Jun 1987)
            └ 6. Pamela (Pam) WHITT (b.11 Apr 1960 d.Jan 2006)
               sp: ALLTOP
                └ 7. Matthew ALLTOP
        ─ 5. Robert Pascal WHITT (b.9 Jan 1913 d.11 Jun 1914)
        ─ 5. Leatha Martha WHITT (b.27 May 1915-TC,Virginia d.11 Feb 2008-Plainfield,Ind.)
           sp: Otis Andrew STINSON (b.7 Feb 1913 m.20 Aug 1930 d.28 Sep 1972)
           ─ 6. Geraldine F. STINSON (b.1 Aug 1931-JR,Va.Tazewell Co. d.19 Jan 2008-Plainfield,Ind.)
              sp: Kenneth NICHOLS
              ─ 7. Joyce NICHOLS
                 sp: HOWARD
              └ 7. Charlene NICHOLS
                 sp: HUESTON
           ─ 6. Helen STINSON (b.28 Dec 1932-Virginia)
              sp: Eugene SCHRADER
           ├ 6. Robert Daniel STINSON (b.8 Apr 1934-VA.)
              sp: Mary
           ─ 6. Molly STINSON (b.16 Apr 1936)
              sp: Gifford ODOM
           ─ 6. Jerry O. STINSON (b.2 May 1939)
           ─ 6. Jimmie Rogers STINSON (b.29 Aug 1941-Caretta,WV.)
              sp: Patricia Ann HUDSON (b.1943? m.19 May 1962)
              ─ 7. Donna Marie STINSON (b.15 Jun 1965-Creve Coeve,Missouri)
                 sp: Unknown FOUST
                 ├ 8. Shaun L. FOUST (b.1983)
                 sp: Unknown RICHARDSON
                 ├ 8. Mary E. RICHARDSON (b.1986)
                 └ 8. John S. RICHARDSON (b.1989)
              ─ 7. Ira Andrew STINSON (b.22 Sep 1970-Creve Coeve,Missouri)
                 sp: Patricia Lynn HOWARD (b.22 Sep 1970-Creve Coeve,Missouri m.16 Nov 1991)
                 ─ 8. Lelsey Lynn STINSON (b.17 Aug 1993)
                 ─ 8. Ashley Nichole STINSON (b.26 Sep 1997)
              ─ 7. James Patrick STINSON (b.25 Jan 1967-Creve Coeve,Missouri)
                 sp: Leatha D. BOOTH (m.1 Jul 2000)
                 ─ 8. Gabrielle STINSON
```

THE PATRIOT, HEZEKIAH WHITT

Descendants of Justice Hezekiah WHITT

```
                  ├─ 8. Alexandra STINSON
                  └─ 8. Ian J. STINSON
               ─ 7. Karen Denise STINSON (b.28 Jan 1972-Creve Coeve,Missouri)
                  sp: Unknown PORTWOOD
                  ├─ 8. Tayler L. PORTWOOD (b.1993)
                  └─ 8. Ty D. PORTWOOD (b.1999)
            ─ 6. Andy Joe STINSON (b.15 Jun 1944)
               sp: Mary
            ─ 6. Margaret Ann STINSON (b.15 Jan 1950)
               sp: John ANECHIARICO
            ─ 6. Steve STINSON (b.29 May 1952-Greencastle,Ind. d.14 Sep 2007-Cloverdale,Ind.)
      ── 5. James Alderson (Fuzz)(JOSH) WHITT (b.27 Apr 1919-Honaker,Russell Co.,Va. d.19 Dec 1998-)
         sp: Mary Sue HARMAN (b.25 Jan 1922 m 6 Nov 1938 d.10 Jul 1973-Ark.)
         ─ 6. Mollie Alberta WHITT (b.11 Jul 1940 Sunday-Tazewell County,Va d.19 Mar 2006 Sunday-)
            sp: James L. SCOTT  (m.22 Apr 1961)
            ─ 7. Barbara Faye SCOTT  (b.14 Nov 1961 Tuesday)
               sp: Don MCCAMMACK (b.25 Sep 1956 Tuesday)
               ├─ 8. Vicki Lynn MCCAMMACK (b.11 May 1985 Saturday)
               │  sp: HUBER
               ├─ 8. Michelle Rae MCCAMMACK (b.2 Sep 1989 Saturday)
               └─ 8. Christine MCCAMMACK (b.7 Mar 1998 Saturday)
            ── 7. Lora Ann SCOTT  (b.1 Jul 1963 Mon.)
               sp: BAKER
               ├─ 8. Amber BAKER (b.22 Nov 1981 Sunday)
               ├─ 8. Dustin Wayne BAKER (b.9 Aug 1984 Thur.)
               │  sp: Jessica KELSO (b.16 Dec 1983 Fri.)
               │  ─ 9. Alexander BAKER (b.19 Aug 2003 Tue.)
               sp: Brian MARTIN (b.9 Jun 1966 Thur.)
            ─ 7. Karen Louise SCOTT  (b.27 Jun 1965 Sun.)
               sp: JONES
            └─ 7. Jeffrey D.( JD) SCOTT  (b.26 Sep 1969 Fri.)
               sp: Patricia  (b.30 May 1970 Sat.)
               ─ 8. Dylan James SCOTT  (b.12 Jan 2000 Wed.)
               ─ 8. Evan Gene SCOTT  (b.24 Jun 2003 Tue.)
         ── 6. James Garland WHITT (b.28 Mar 1942)
            sp: Peggy Lynn MESSER (b.19 Mar 1944 m.15 Dec 1961)
            ├─ 7. Clifford Wayne WHITT (b.31 Oct 1962)
            │  sp: UNKNOWN
            │  ── 8. Chloe Lynn WHITT (b.9 Apr 1993)
            │  ─ 8. Calub Wayne WHITT (b.21 Feb 1995)
            ├─ 7. Debora Lynn "Debbie" WHITT (b.10 Oct 1964)
            │  sp: WILLIAMS
            │  ├─ 8. Kesha Marie WILLIAMS (b.18 Jul 1982)
            │  │  sp: ROELL
            │  │  ── 9. Jacob Micheal ROELL (b.9 Sep 2002)
            │  │  ── 9. Mackenzie Marie ROELL (b.26 Nov 2003)
            │  │  ─ 9. Matthew James ROELL (b.15 Dec 2005)
            │  │  └─ 9. Graceland Lynn ROELL (b.19 Mar 2008)
            │  ├─ 8. Zachary Micheal WILLIAMS (b.19 Sep 1985)
            │  └─ 8. Jessica Lynn WILLIAMS (b.21 Mar 1987)
            │     sp: UNKNOWN
            │     └─ 9. Jalynn Diane WILLIAMS (b.6 Jun 2007)
```

THE PATRIOT, HEZEKIAH WHITT

Descendants of Justice Hezekiah WHITT

```
        ├─ 7. Angela Lynn WHITT (b.12 Nov 1973)
        │     sp: UNKNOWN
        │     ├─ 8. Christopher Wayne (Alberson) WHITT (b.Mar 1993)
        │     ├─ 8. Bailey Austin (Jones) WHITT (b.20 Apr 1996)
        │     ├─ 8. Bradley Eugene (Jones) WHITT (b.4 Sep 1997)
        │     └─ 8. Dawlson Lee WHITT (b.27 Feb 2003)
        └─ 7. James Matthew WHITT (b.7 Jun 1972 d.8 Jun 1972)
  ├─ 6. Janice Sue WHITT (b.10 Nov 1946-Richlands,Tazewell County,VA.)
  │     sp: Robert KELLY
  │     ├─ 7. Terri Lynn KELLY (b.30 Mar 1969)
  │     │     sp: MCHANEY
  │     │     └─ 8. Nathan Matthew MCHANEY (b.23 Jul 1992)
  │     ├─ 7. Debbie Nicole KELLY (b.21 Oct 1970)
  │     │     sp: MELLO
  │     │     ├─ 8. Joshua James MELLO (b.14 Feb 1988)
  │     │     ├─ 8. Nicholas Brian MELLO (b.21 Feb 1995)
  │     │     ├─ 8. Robert Anthony MELLO (b.19 Apr 1998)
  │     │     └─ 8. Zachary David MELLO (b.31 Jul 2003)
  │     ├─ 7. Nathan Garrick KELLY (b.24 Feb 1973 d.22 May 1990)
  │           sp: Darwyn NELSON
  ├─ 6. Judy Gail WHITT (b.27 Oct 1948-Richlands,VA. Tazewell Co.)
  │     sp: Max MORPHEW (m.3 Nov 1967)
  │     ├─ 7. Max Alan MORPHEW (b.19 Jul 1971 Monday)
  │     │     sp: UNKNOWN
  │     │     └─ 8. Gage Alan Douglas MORPHEW (b.1 Jul 2004 Thursday)
  │     ├─ 7. Troy Lee MORPHEW (b.4 Dec 1973 Tuesday)
  │     │     sp: UNKNOWN
  │     │     └─ 8. Kelly Sue MORPHEW (b.4 Nov 1996 Monday)
  │     └─ 7. Crystal Gail MORPHEW (b.6 Nov 1979 Sunday)
  │           sp: CARTER
  │           ├─ 8. Courtney Marie CARTER (b.9 Dec 1998 Wednesday)
  │           ├─ 8. Madison Nicole Gail CARTER (b.16 Nov 1999 Tuesday)
  │           sp: DELONG
  │           └─ 8. Adhley Renee DELONG (b.15 May 2004 Saturday)
  ├─ 6. Gerald Ray (Twin To Carol Gay) WHITT (b.17 Oct 1950)
  │     sp: UNKNOWN
  │     ├─ 7. Jerry Ray WHITT (b.9 Dec 1973 bu.12 Aug 1997)
  │     ├─ 7. Jimmy Allen WHITT (b.20 Dec 1975)
  │     │     sp: UNKNOWN
  │     │     └─ 8. Elizabeth WHITT (b.6 Nov 1997)
  │     ├─ 7. Elizabeth WHITT
  │     └─ 7. Misty Marie WHITT (b.1 Jul 1978)
  │           sp: Mark CRUMBPACKER
  │           ├─ 8. Kristina Marie CRUMBPACKER (b.17 Dec 1987)
  │           sp: Jeff KNIGHT (m.don't know)
  │           ├─ 8. Faith Rose KNIGHT (b.5 Nov 2002)
  │           └─ 8. Sierra Dawn KNIGHT (b.7 Sep 2003)
  ├─ 6. Carol Gay (Twin To Gerald Ray) WHITT (b.17 Oct 1950 Tuesday-Clinch Valley Clinic,R,VA.)
  │     sp: Edward H. JONES (b.9 Jul 1947-Chisholm,Minnesota m.22 Apr 1983)
  ├─ 6. Raleigh WHITT
─ 5. Wyniferd Francis WHITT (b.1922)
      sp: Edgar E. BRYANT (m.23 May 1938)
```

THE PATRIOT, HEZEKIAH WHITT

Descendants of Justice Hezekiah WHITT

```
    ├─ 6. Freeda BRYANT
    │     sp: Kenneth SPENCER
    ├─ 6. Rita Carol BRYANT
    │     sp: Ted PIERCE
    ├─ 6. Kenneth BRYANT
    │     sp: Phyllis
    └─ 6. Lonnie Ray BRYANT
          sp: UNKNOWN
          └─ 7. Christy BRYANT (b.Abt 1972)
                sp: UNKNOWN
                └─ 8. Jackie (b.Abt 1991)
─ 5. Carol Lue Ellen WHITT (b.23 Jul 1924)
      sp: Frank L. BAXTER (b.20 Apr 1924 m.3 Oct 1946)
      ├─ 6. Brenda Carol BAXTER (b.25 Sep 1948)
      ├─ 6. Larry Elwood BAXTER (b.2 Jun 1950-Cedar Bluff,Tazewell County,Va)
      │     sp: Debbie BOSHERS
      │     ├─ 7. Angela Carol BAXTER
      │     │     sp: B. SLADER
      │     │     └─ 8. Haley Brooke SLADER (b.14 May 1991)
      │     sp: Emma Sue DEAMON
      ├─ 6. Frankie Darrel BAXTER (b.21 Sep 1952)
      │     sp: UNKNOWN
      │     └─ 7. Matthew Franklin BAXTER (b.Abt 1977)
      │           sp: UNKNOWN
      │           ├─ 8. Johathan Franklin BAXTER (b.23 Feb 2007)
      │           └─ 8. Kaitlynn Marie BAXTER (b.6 Sep 2008)
      └─ 6. Sheila May Francis BAXTER (b.17 Mar 1964)
            sp: Plil ALTMEYER
            sp: MIGILANO
            └─ 7. Sara Danielle MIGILANO (b.23 Jul 1986)
─ 5. Alica Rebecca WHITT (b.12 Jul 1926)
      sp: Ralph Edward SPARKS
      ├─ 6. Sandra Ellen SPARKS (b.5 Oct 1946)
      │     sp: Unknown MOORE
      │     ├─ 7. Amanda MOORE
      │     ├─ 7. Nathan MOORE
      │     └─ 7. Molly MOORE
      ├─ 6. Connie Rebecca SPARKS (b.23 Sep 1950)
      │     sp: Unknown MCCUNE
      │     ├─ 7. Cathy MCCUNE
      │     ├─ 7. Terry MCCUNE
      │     ├─ 7. Alex MCCUNE
      │     └─ 7. Michael MCCUNE
      ├─ 6. Ralph Randall SPARKS (b.4 Feb 1954)
      │     sp: Denise APPLE (m.(div))
      │     ├─ 7. Jeremy SPARKS
      │     ├─ 7. LeAnn SPARKS
      │     ├─ 7. Jordan SPARKS
      │     └─ 7. Jessie SPARKS
      ├─ 6. Paula SPARKS (b.27 Aug 1958)
      │     sp: Unknown MEYERS
      │     └─ 7. Cody MEYERS
```

THE PATRIOT, HEZEKIAH WHITT

Descendants of Justice Hezekiah WHITT

```
            ┌─ 6. ALisa Wrenn SPARKS (b.21 Nov 1960)
            │     sp: LEWIS
            │     ┌─ 7. Jonathan LEWIS
            │     ├─ 7. Allie LEWIS
            │     ├─ 7. Anna LEWIS
            │     └─ 7. Samuel LEWIS
            └─ 6. Terry Rejeania SPARKS (b.14 Jan 1964)
                  sp: Unknown KNAUSS
                  ┌─ 7. Emily KNAUSS
                  ├─ 7. Samuel KNAUSS
                  sp: Unknown MCCULLOUGH
                  └─ 7. Tyler MCCULLOUGH
      ─ 5. Thomas Thurman WHITT (b.16 Oct 1928 Tuesday d.1 Apr 1974 Monday-Greencastle,Ind.)
            sp: Alma Jean COOK (b.11 May 1930 Sunday d.2 Oct 1996 Wednesday-Mn.)
            ┌─ 6. Alma Louise WHITT (b.7 Oct 1951 Sunday)
            │     sp: Martin KOSLUCHER
            │     └─ 7. Jayson E. KOSLUCHER (b.1 Oct 1973-Hibbing,MN.)
            │           sp: Robin CARTON (m.1998)
            │           ┌─ 8. Hunter E. KOSLUCHER (b.7 Apr 2001-Neenah,WI.)
            │           ├─ 8. Adien M. KOSLUCHER (b.4 Mar 2005-Neenah,WI.)
            │           └─ 8. Corina Louise KOSLUCHER (b.17 Jun 1977-Hibbing,MN.)
            ├─ 6. Harold Thomas WHITT (b.6 Oct 1952 Monday)
            │     sp: Shirley KOEPKE
            │     ┌─ 7. Jennifer WHITT
            │     ├─ 7. Kristian WHITT
            │     └─ 7. Kinsey WHITT
            ├─ 6. Deloris Ann WHITT (b.3 Apr 1960 Sunday)
            │     sp: HILL
            │     ┌─ 7. Ericka HILL
            │     └─ 7. Lee HILL
            ├─ 6. Leonard Thurman (Tiny) WHITT (b.2 Sep 1966 Friday)
            │     sp: Rhonda Gail RHOADS (b.7 Apr 1974 Sunday)
            │     ┌─ 7. Jackson Thurmon WHITT (b.19 Jan 1997 Sunday)
            │     └─ 7. Thomas Leonard WHITT (b.25 Jun 1999 Friday)
            └─ 6. Marty Allen WHITT (b.24 Sep 1971 Friday-Hibbing,MN.)
                  sp: UNKNOWN
                  ┌─ 7. Ashlynn WHITT
                  ├─ 7. Amber WHITT
                  ├─ 7. Alexandrea WHITT
                  └─ 7. Angelica WHITT
   ─ 5. Isaac H. WHITT Sr. (b.24 May 1931-Tazewell County,Va d.30 Jan 2007-Danville,Ind.)
         sp: Dolly
         ┌─ 6. Juanita WHITT
         ├─ 6. Milburn R. WHITT
         ├─ 6. Elizbeth WHITT
         ├─ 6. Isaac H. WHITT Jr.
         ├─ 6. Paul William WHITT
         ├─ 6. Amanda Grace WHITT (b.Died)
         └─ 6. Leara Jean WHITT
─ 4. Charles Henry WHITT (b.29 Sep 1881-PM,Tazewell Co. VA. d.3 May 1967-Raven,Tazewell County VA.)
      sp: Amanda Elizabeth (Mandy) PUCKETT (b.29 Jan 1887-RC,Va. m.7 May 1902 d.2 Mar 1920-)
      ┌─ 5. William Henry WHITT (b.27 Mar 1906-SCNR,Va.Russell,Co. d.14 Dec 1933-Virginia)
```

THE PATRIOT, HEZEKIAH WHITT

Descendants of Justice Hezekiah WHITT

```
                    sp: Annie M. (b.Abt 1914-Va. m.Abt 1928)
                    ─ 6. Alice F. WHITT (b.Abt 1929)
                    ── 6. Pauline WHITT
                        sp: STILWELL
            ─ 5. Ular Exie WHITT (b.11 Feb 1909-Russell Co,Va. d.25 Sep 1987-Russell Co,Va.)
                    sp: William Jesse "Willie" HESS (b.11 Apr 1903-Russell,Co.,Va. d.25 Jul 1992-L,Russell Co. Va.)
                    ─ 6. Margery Jean HESS (b.11 Nov 1927-River Mountain,Russell Co.,VA.)
                        sp: Jack Whited RAY
                    ─ 6. Onna Exie HESS (b.19 Sep 1930-River Mountain,Russell Co,Va.)
                        sp: Silas MILLER
                    ─ 6. Roseann HESS (b.28 Nov 1941-River Mountain,Russell Co,Va.)
                        sp: Leon Jennings HALE (b.10 Oct 1940-Swords Creek Near Raven,V,Co. m.31 Oct 1959)
                    ─ 6. Daphne HESS (b.22 Aug 1945-River Mountain,Russell Co,Va.)
                        sp: Glen STINSON
                        sp: Caroll SLATE
                    ─ 6. William Harrison HESS (b.Jan 1933-River Mountain,Russell Co,Va.)
                        sp: Betty HONAKER (b.Russell County,VA)
                    ─ 6. Arnold Wayne HESS (b.Apr 1934-River Mountain,RC,Va. d.Apr 1995-Honaker,Russell Co.,Va.)
                        sp: Betty Lou BELCHER (b.Russell County,VA)
                    ─ 6. Charles Ellis HESS (b.1 Apr 1935-River Mountain,Russell Co,Va.)
                        sp: Lucy Ann TURNER
            ── 5. Pearlie May WHITT (b.17 Jun 1911-Swords Creek Near Raven,V,Co. d.Died-Florida)
                    sp: Charles H. JONES (b.Abt 1906 d.21 Oct 1972)
                    ─ 6. Daniel C. JONES
                    ── 6. Robert H. JONES
        ─ 5. Marvin Bertran WHITT (b.5 Sep 1913 Friday-MG,SC,RC,Near Raven, VA. d.3 March 2008 Monday-)
                sp: Edith Lyle (Phipps) FLEMING (b.9 Sep 1919-Trammel,Va. m.14 Sep 1935 d.8 Mar 1999-)
                ─ 6. Colonel Jerry Bertram WHITT (b.17 Feb 1937 Wednesday-Raven,Tazewell County VA.)
                    sp: Etta Sue GILLESPIE (b.20 Jun 1940-Gaylax,Virginia m.2 Jul 1960)
                    ─ 7. Melony WHITT (b.18 Jan 1963-Galax,Va.)
                        sp: Michael HAUN (b.3 Oct 1962 m.28 May 1993)
                    ─ 7. Hollis Lyn WHITT (b.13 Nov 1972-Kokomo,Ind.)
                ── 6. Colonel Larry Paxton WHITT CPA (b.1939 Wednesday-Raven,Tazewell County VA.)
                    sp: Joan GREER (b.1937-St. Charles,Lee County,Virginia m.1957)
                    ─ 7. Rhonda Joann WHITT (b.1960-Galax,Va.)
                        sp: Jason Van (Jake) PITTMAN
                        ── 8. Jacob Paxton PITTMAN (b.2002-Mobile,Al.)
                    ─ 7. Marvin Larry WHITT (b.1965-Oak Ridge,Tenn.)
                        sp: Geneva MULLINS (b.1967-Floyd Co. Ky. m.1988)
                        ─ 8. Tyler Duvall WHITT (b.1993-Ky.)
                        ── 8. Cassie Marie WHITT (b.1993-Ky.)
                    ─ 7. Kenneth Russell WHITT (b.1967-Oliver Springs,Tenn. d.1967-Oliver Springs,Tenn.)
                    ── 7. Teresa Carmen WHITT (b.1968-Oak Ridge,Tenn.)
                        sp: Sean Michael (McCready) JARRELL (b.1969 m.2003)
                        ── 8. Sean Ryan WHITT-JARRELL (b.2006-Charleston,West Virginia)
                ─ 6. Joseph Edward WHITT (b.20 Nov 1940 Wednesday-Richlands,Tazewell Co.,VA. d.6 Mar 1941-)
                    sp: UNKNOWN
                ── 6. Colonel Charles Dahnmon WHITT Sr. (b.21 Sep 1944 Thursday-R,,Tazewell County d.Not Yet-)
                    sp: Sharon Gail COGAN (b.9 Jul 1947 Wednesday-A,KY. Boyd County m.Friday 11 Jan 1974)
                    ─ 7. Matthew Christopher WHITT (b.25 Feb 1975 9:17AM-TMHSC,WV.)
                    sp: Judy Ann LAWSON (b.1 Dec 1946-Raven,Tazewell Co.,VA. m.24 Jul 1965(div))
                    ─ 7. Charles Dahnmon Jr. WHITT (b.18 Oct 1966-Portsmouth Naval Hosp. Portsmouth,VA.)
```

THE PATRIOT, HEZEKIAH WHITT

Descendants of Justice Hezekiah WHITT

        sp: Sarah Ford HITE (b.7 Feb 1966 m.22 Apr 1995)

        sp: Carol Marie WARD (b.26 May 1968 m.6 Jun 1985(div))

        └─ 8. Dennee' Lavonne WHITT (b.13 Jul 1986-Ashland,Boyd Co.,Ky.)

            sp: Colonel Woodson (Tre) SIZEMORE III BBA (m.6 Jun 2009 Saturday)

        ─ 8. Derek Tyler WHITT (b.20 Apr 1990-Ashland,Boyd Co.,Ky.)

      ── 7. Jeffrey Kent WHITT (b.29 Aug 1970-Kettering Hosp. Dayton,Ohio)

        sp: Susan BUTCHER (m.23 Nov 1995)

        └─ 8. Jeffrey Claude WHITT (b.20 Sep 1996-Ashland,Boyd Co.,KY.)

        ─ 8. Joshua Michael WHITT (b.17 Jun 1998-Ashland,Boyd Co.,KY.)

─ 5. Charles Robert WHITT (b.13 Aug 1915-Russell County Swords d.16 May 1999-New Hope,AC,Va.)

sp: Liller Lee SIMMONS (b.16 Apr 1903-Raven,Tazewell Co.,Va. m.2 Sep 1920 d.24 Mar 1984-)

─ 5. Edward Franklin WHITT (b.22 May 1922-R,Tazewell County Va. d.6 May 1956-,Wolfe Creek Boat D)

─ 5. Billy James WHITT (b.1 Sep 1926-R,Tazewell County Va. d.21 Dec 1985-R,Tazewell County Va.)

  sp: Leah OSBOURN

  ─ 6. Deloris Ann (PENNYWINKLE) WHITT (b.16 Nov 1949)

    sp: Jerry Douglas SHORTT (b.3 Apr 1947 m.1967 d.11 Jun 1980)

    ─ 7. Sherry Lee SHORTT (b.14 Dec 1966)

      sp: UNKNOWN

      └─ 8. Christopher Scott SHORTT (b.3 Jan 1983)

      ─ 8. Tiffany Leann Addison SHORTT (b.5 May 1988)

    ─ 7. Marie Shontel SHORTT (b.22 Dec 1967)

      sp: Jesse Dean HESS Jr. (b.28 Jul 1966 m.6 Oct 1984)

      ─ 8. April Dawn HESS (b.25 Apr 1985)

      ─ 8. Nathaniel Dean HESS (b.24 Jul 1987)

      └─ 8. Sarah Nichole HESS (b.2 Oct 1988)

    ── 7. Jerry Douglas SHORTT II (b.9 Feb 1971)

      sp: Debbie JOHNSON (m.1989)

      ─ 8. Courtney Danielle SHORTT (b.17 Mar 1990)

      ── 8. Emily Christine SHORTT (b.17 Jun 1991)

      ─ 8. Cody Daniel SHORTT (b.12 Jun 1992)

      sp: Patricia CHRISTIAN

      ─ 8. Jerry Douglas SHORTT III (b.17 Jul 1993)

      ─ 8. Kimberly Dawn SHORTT (b.9 May 1994)

      sp: Amy SMITH

      └─ 8. Isabella Lauren SHORTT (b.11 Dec 2002)

    sp: Gary D. BLANKENSHIP (m.2 Oct 1987)

  ─ 6. Leon WHITT

  ─ 6. Jeanie WHITT

    sp: HAMILITON

  ─ 6. Susie WHITT

  └─ 6. Keith WHITT

─ 5. David Eugene WHITT (b.11 Sep 1929-Raven,Tazewell County Va.)

  sp: Myrtle Lee BROWN (d.28 Nov 2000)

  ─ 6. Mike WHITT (b.14 Sep 1952)

  ─ 6. Mitzi WHITT (b.12 Dec 1953)

  sp: Betty UNKNOWN

─ 5. Ellis Ralph WHITT (b.16 Apr 1933-R,Tazewell County Va. d.19 Aug 1995-R,Tazewell County Va.)

  sp: UNKNOWN

  ─ 6. Eddie WHITT

  ── 6. Cloyd (Linda) WHITT

    sp: LESTER

─ 5. Madge Lois WHITT (b.4 Jun 1935-Raven,Tazewell County Va. d.8 Jun 2004-Baltimore,Md.)

THE PATRIOT, HEZEKIAH WHITT

Descendants of Justice Hezekiah WHITT

```
                   sp: Warren MABE
                   └─ 6. Barbara MABE
                        sp: Thomas BUSCH
                        ├─ 7. Aaron BUSCH
                        ── 7. Katie BUSCH
                        └─ 7. Justin BUSCH
   ── 3. Henrietta (Hannah) WHITT (b.Abt 1838-Tazewell County,Va d.Abt 1861-Lewis Co.,Ky.)
        sp: Alfred THOMPSON (b.24 May 1819-Kentucky m.12 Jun 1850 d.27 May 1897-Kentucky)
        ├─ 4. Mathew THOMPSON (b.Abt 1852-Kentucky)
        ├─ 4. Alfred THOMPSON (b.1854-Lewis Co.,Ky. d.26 Sep 1855-Lewis Co.,Ky.)
        ├─ 4. Mildred THOMPSON (b.Abt 1857-Kentucky)
        └─ 4. William THOMPSON (b.1861-Lewis Co.,Ky.)
   sp: Mildred (Millie) TRUITT (b.20 Mar 1824-Truittville,GC,Ky. m.8 Feb 1848 d.1907-Greenup Co.,Ky.)
   ── 3. William Randolph WHITT (b.21 Dec 1851-Greenup,Co. Ky. d.Abt 1913-Greenup Co.,Ky.)
        sp: Mary Elizabeth THOMPSON (b.Abt 1854-Greenup Co.,Ky. m.20 Jan 1875 d.1938-Greenup Co.,Ky.)
        ── 4. Jesse Clayton WHITT (b.Feb 1877-Greenup Co.,Ky.)
             sp: Jesse STEPHENSON (b.Jun 1887-Greenup Co.,Ky. m.?)
             ── 5. Elsa WHITT (b.11 Jul 1908-Greenup Co.,Ky. d.2 Oct 1908-GC,Ky.) ** Printed on Page 15 **
             ├─ 5. Samuel Douglas WHITT (b.18 Jul 1909-Greenup Co. Ky. d.16 May 1989-) ** Printed on Page 15 **
             ├─ 5. Rodney O. WHITT (b.23 Jan 1912-Greenup Co. Ky. d.24 Feb 1996-) ** Printed on Page 15 **
             ├─ 5. Donald WHITT (b.Abt 1917-Greenup Co.,Ky.) ** Printed on Page 15 **
             ├─ 5. Rolfe Clayton WHITT (b.8 Jul 1918-Greenup Co.,Ky. d.10 Apr 1984-) ** Printed on Page 15 **
             ├─ 5. Alta WHITT (b.4 Dec 1924-Greenup Co.,Ky.) ** Printed on Page 15 **
             ├─ 5. Wayne WHITT (b.13 Sep 1926-Big White Oak Creek,Greenup Co.,Ky.) ** Printed on Page 15 **
             └─ 5. Audrey WHITT (b.18 Sep 1931-Greenup Co.,Ky.) ** Printed on Page 15 **
        ── 4. James A. WHITT (b.Abt 1880-Greenup Co.,Ky. bu.Whitt Cemetary,Big White Oak,Greenup Co.,Ky.)
             sp: Julia
        ├─ 4. Samuel T. WHITT (b.1885-Greenup Co.,Ky. d.1960)
        └─ 4. Mildred O. (Mollie) WHITT (b.22 Dec 1882-Greenup Co.,Ky. d.Feb 1884-Greenup Co.,Ky.)
   ── 3. Jesse Monroe WHITT (b.18 Jul 1855-Greenup,Co. Ky. d.1910)
        sp: Julia Ann FELTY
   └─ 3. Alfred Jackson WHITT (b.27 Apr 1858-Truittsville,B,Greenup Co. Ky. d.18 Mar 1918-Carter Co.,Ky.)
        sp: Serilda LOGAN (b.15 Dec 1867-Greenup Co.,Ky. m.6 May 1883 d.10 Jan 1934-Carter Co.,Ky.)
        ├─ 4. Baby WHITT (b.24 Feb 1885-Carter Co.,Ky. d.24 Feb 1885-Carter Co.,Ky.)
        ├─ 4. William (Willie) WHITT (b.19 Mar 1886-Carter Co.,Ky. d.25 Aug 1921-Carter Co.,Ky.)
        ├─ 4. Jonas (Jonah) WHITT (b.20 May 1888-Carter Co.,Ky. d.26 Dec 1954)
             sp: Sible  (b.Abt 1900-Ky.)
             ── 5. Carl WHITT (b.Abt 1919)
             ── 5. Earl WHITT (b.Abt 1919)
        ── 4. Baby WHITT (b.23 Sep 1890-Carter Co.,Ky. d.23 Sep 1890-Carter Co.,Ky.)
        ├─ 4. James W. WHITT (b.26 Sep 1891-Carter Co.,Ky. d.27 Mar 1978)
        ├─ 4. Millie WHITT (b.10 Jun 1894 d.15 May 1917)
             sp: Green HIGNITE (b.Abt 1888 m.29 Aug 1910)
             ├─ 5. Russell HIGNITE (b.20 May 1912)
             └─ 5. Eeroy HIGNITE (b.30 Nov 1913)
        ── 4. Nancy WHITT (b.13 Sep 1896-Carter Co.,Ky. d.1 Apr 1984-Grayson Carter Co.,Ky.)
             sp: Boston (Boss) MCGLONE (b.25 Feb 1891 d.11 Nov 1941)
        ── 4. Alfred, "Alf" WHITT (b.13 Feb 1899-Carter Co.,Ky. d.Jul 1967-Ashland,Boyd Co.,Ky.)
             sp: Flossie HIGNITE (b.11 Oct 1902-Carter Co.,Ky. m.? d.9 Feb 1982-Ashland,Boyd Co.,Ky.)
             ── 5. Jack WHITT
             ── 5. Dorothea WHITT
                  sp: Elmo HAMILTON
```

THE PATRIOT, HEZEKIAH WHITT

Descendants of Justice Hezekiah WHITT

17 May 2010   Relationship Codes:

```
        └─ 5. Robert Eugene WHITT (b.7 Jul 1928-Carter Co.,Ky. d.8 Jan 1991-Houston,Tx.)
               sp: Glo STIDHAM
    ├─ 4. Fathie WHITT (b.3 Sep 1901 d.15 Aug 1903)
    ├─ 4. Baby WHITT (b.20 Mar 1904-Carter Co.,Ky. d.20 Mar 1904-Carter Co.,Ky.)
    ├─ 4. Gurwin WHITT (b.9 Aug 1905-Carter Co.,Ky. d.16 Dec 1906-Carter Co.,Ky.)
    ─ 4. Agnes Marie WHITT (b.28 Feb 1908-Carter Co.,Ky. d.27 Mar 1987)
          sp: Johnson COLLIER
          ├─ 5. Paul COLLIER (b.17 Apr 1940-Carter Co.,Ky. d.26 May 2003-Portsmouth Scioto Co. Ohio)
          └─ 5. Gladys COLLIER
                sp: NEWMAN
          ├─ 5. Helen COLLIER
                sp: WHITT
          ─ 5. Lois COLLIER
                sp: LEAL
          ─ 5. Betty COLLIER
                sp: HARDING
          └─ 5. Phyllis COLLIER
                sp: FRAZEE
    ─ 4. Zona WHITT (b.8 Aug 1913-Carter Co.,Ky. d.29 Sep 1993-Carter Co.,Ky.)
```

THE PATRIOT, HEZEKIAH WHITT

Colonel Charles Dahnmon Whitt Author Of:
"Legacy, The Days Of David Crockett Whitt"
"The Patriot, Hezekiah Whitt"
"Dahnmon's Little Stories"
Whitt a native of Tazewell County, Virginia moved to Kentucky in 1970 to carry out his trade as a Sheet Metal Worker with Local 24, Southern Ohio. Although he is now retired, he has always had an interest in genealogy and was always a real history buff for regional and civil war history; however, he didn't pursue his interest until he started researching his ancestry on-line in 1999.

While tracing his family's heritage, Whitt was soon introduced to his great-grandfather David Crockett Whitt. Yes, the discoveries that he had made during his fascinating search led him to create "Legacy, The Days of David Crockett Whitt," a work of historical fiction with his great-grandfather serving as the skeleton for this account of life in an earlier, and harder time 1836-1900 Legacy follows Whitt's great-grandfather "Crockett," through the early settler days in Virginia and Kentucky from 1836 thru 1909, his formative years in Greenup County Kentucky and the time that he spent in a Civil War prison. Whitt has now written another book, "The Patriot, Hezekiah Whitt," which deals with the years of 1760 -1846. Hezekiah Whitt was a founding father of Tazewell County, Virginia. He was a Militiaman, Indian Spy, Sheriff, and a lifelong Gentlemen Justice of the Peace appointed by the Governor of Virginia. Hezekiah Whitt is Whitt's GGG Grandfather. This book abounds with Indian stories.

In "Legacy, The Days Of David Crockett Whitt" and "The Patriot, Hezekiah Whitt" you will soon discover when acquainting yourself with these particular titles is that Whitt encompasses his faith and shows these pioneer families relying on their faith as well to get through trying times.

Charles is able to use the prefix "Colonel" in his pen-name because he is a Kentucky Colonel.

Colonel Whitt also has written a smaller fun book called, "Dahnmon,s Little Stories," which is a collection of short stories and poems. Price is $10.00 for it.

To purchase these books go to http://dahnmonwhittfamily.com or for a signed book, write to Post Office Box 831, Flatwoods, KY. 41139. Price for these researched hardback books is $30. Plus $6 when shipping. Published and sold by Jesse Stuart Foundation in Ashland, Kentucky. My Phone # 606 836 7997 E-Mail c-dahnmon@roadrunner.com

COLONEL CHARLES DAHNMON WHITT

Acknowledgements

http://dahnmonwhittfamily.com
http://www.angelfire.com/co3/Skaggs/whitt.html
www.brainyhistory.com
http://www.sparknotes.com/history/american/precivilwar/terms.html
http://www.visittazewellcounty.org/history.html
http://www.waymarking.com/waymarks/WM46W5
http://www.rootsweb.ancestry.com
http://www.history.com/this-day-in-history.do?action=Article=51316
http://www.stephenjaygould.org/ctrl/jefferson_vsrf.html
http://www.prariegosts.com/cornstalk.html
http://www.genforum.genealogy.com/whitt/messages/871.htlm
http://www.nps.goc/archive/fome/tguide/Lesson9a.html
http://www.warof1812.ca/summary.html
http://www.louisana101.com/battle.html
http://genforum.genealogy.com/christian/
Slaves in Tazewell County, VA. By: S. Paul Perry
The Holy Bible, King James Version
Russell County, VA. Court House
Greenup County, KY. Court House
Tazewell County, VA. Court House
The Book, "The Frontiersman" By: Allan Eckert
The Tazewell County Historic Society
The Montgomery County, VA. Court House
The Library of Virginia on line.
The Russell County, Virginia web site on line.
National Register of Historic Places
Presidential History on line.
The wikipedia free encyclopedia on line.
The research of Beverly Tracy on Hezekiah Whitt.
Montgomery County, Virginia on line.
Sheriffs of Tazewell County, Va. By Deputy Brian Hieatt
Digest of the Laws of Virginia, Volume 1
History of Tazewell County By: William Cecil Pendleton
Information on Captain James Campbell, by Lance Carter
Information on Jonas and Hezekiah Whitt given by Jesse & June Whitt
The work of the Tazewell County, Virginia DAR & SAR
All of the Chief Cornstalk connections to Thomas Bailey Christian and Rachel
Cornstalk Skaggs Whitt come from published messages of J. Red Wolf on the Christian
Family Genealogy Forum.

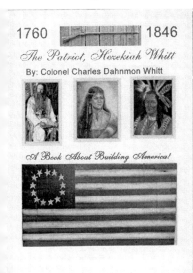

1760 — 1846

The Patriot, Hezekiah Whitt

By: Colonel Charles Dahnmon Whitt

A Book About Building America!

The Building Of America Series

"The Patriot, Hezekiah Whitt"

This is a story about a great man, A Patriot to the free State of Virginia; Hezekiah Whitt lived from 1761 to 1846. We will go to many places and have many adventures.

Hezekiah Whitt will find a beautiful land while scouting for Indians. This place is in present day Tazewell County, Virginia on the "Waters of the Clinch." It would become his beloved home for many years.

I will be as accurate as possible, but I will use my thoughts to fill in the missing links. This will be historic, as well as fictional. I will try to keep names, places, and dates as accurate as possible.

Hezekiah was a rebel to the King of England, but a Patriot to his home country, the Free State of Virginia and the new United States of America. Will you travel with Hezekiah as he goes on campaigns against the Indians, Tories, and scouts out the Indians and defends his liberties against the King of England?

You will meet Hezekiah's family and be with the Whitts as they make a life on the "Waters of the Clinch."

Indian stories abound as Hezekiah becomes a prominent man in the new County of Tazewell.

Indiana, Illinois, Ohio, Kentucky, Tennessee, Missouri, Virginia, what is now West Virginia and Canada are all mentioned in this collection.

This Narrative is a Preamble to the book, "Legacy, The Days of David Crockett Whitt.". These two books are a series on "The Building of America."

INDIAN STORIES ABOUND!

Go to http://dahnmonwhittfamily.com for more information on "Legacy, The Days Of David Crockett Whitt." Al so see and order at: www.jsfbooks.com

This Narrative is based on the life of Hezekiah Whitt, his Indian wife Rachel Cornstalk Skaggs Whitt

This is a large 7 X 10 hardback!

For a personal Signed Copy of "The Patriot, Hezekiah Whitt", "Legacy The Days Of David Crockett Whitt," or "Dahnmon's Little Stories" send check to Colonel Charles Dahnmon Whitt, P.O. Box 831, Flatwoods, KY. 41139. The price for the two large books is $30.00 each plus $6.00 for Priority shipping and handling. The Price for "Dahnmon's Little Stories" is $10.00 plus $4.00 for shipping if required. I wish you the best and enjoy my work!

COLONEL CHARLES DAHNMON WHITT

E-Mail for questions.   C-dahnmon@roadrunner.com

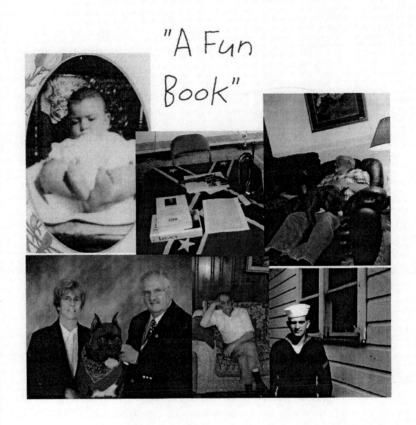

LaVergne, TN USA
09 March 2011
219375LV00004B/5/P